A History of
MOUNT SION

Tunbridge Wells

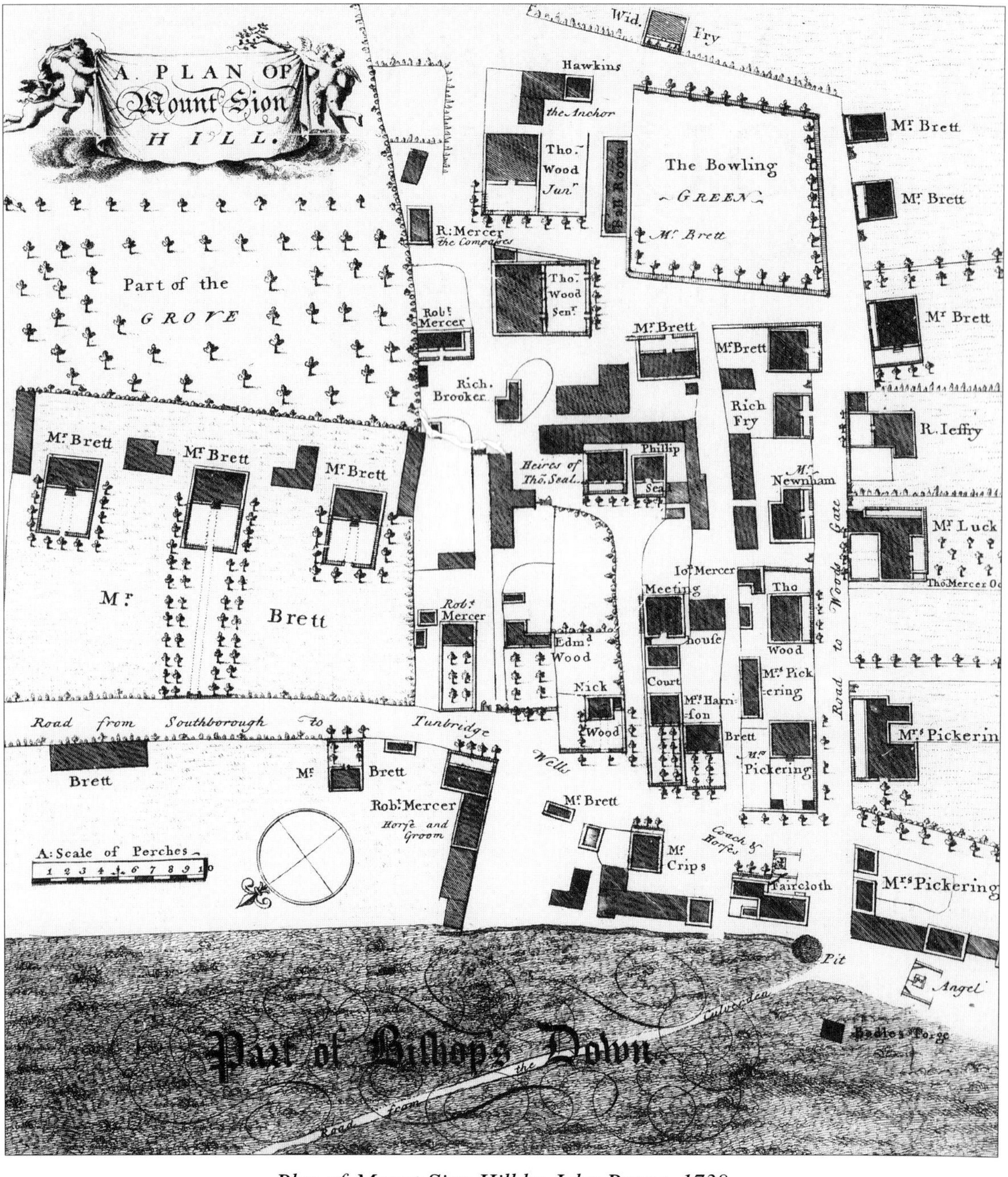

Plan of Mount Sion Hill by John Bowra, 1738

A History of MOUNT SION

Tunbridge Wells

Roger Farthing

Phillimore

2003

Published by
PHILLIMORE & CO. LTD
Shopwyke Manor Barn, Chichester, West Sussex, England

ISBN 1 86077 263 3

Printed and bound in Great Britain by
THE CROMWELL PRESS
Trowbridge, Wiltshire

To the residents of Mount Sion
past, present and future

MOUNT SION

of this First Edition 500 copies
have been printed

This copy is No. ..108..

Contents

List of Subscribers

James Akehurst
Rev. John W. Banner
Barrie Bassett
Ian C. Beavis
Peter Lynn Bellman
Martin Bennett
Wyn and David Bennett
Nick Bensted-Smith
Brian and Adrienne Blake
Lyn Bowman
Denzil and Anne Bradburn
Nicolas van den Branden
Maureen Brewer
Andrew Bridge, Crescent Lodge
Michael Bridge
Mrs June Bridgeman
Antony D. Brown and Miss Claire Lockie
Ian and Judy Burn
George Burnett
Beryl Bush (formerly Constable)
Centre for Kentish Studies, Maidstone
Dr Christopher Chalklin
Ann and John Champneys
Paul Childs
Jane Clark
Paul E. Clark
Paul Geoffrey Copsey
Geoffrey and Brenda Copus
Matthew Copus
John and Sheila Cunningham
Andrew I. Dale
Tony and Nita Davis
Timothy J.M. Day
Sarah Dean
Jeff Delves
Jane C. Dickson
Miss Geraldine Doe
Michael Donovan-Roughsedge and Judy Blott
Roy Douglas
Avril Ebbage
Bruce Farthing
Geoffrey A. Farthing
John Farthing
Julia Farthing
Peter Farthing and Helen Almond
David and Jane Fenwick
John and Marjorie Field
John and Anne Forster
Debbie Freeman
Robin Montier John Freeman
J.G.C.M. Fuller
John Fuller
Valerie and Peter Galbraith
John V. Goodfellow
J. and M. Goulden
R.J. Goulden
Mr C.R. and Mrs I. Graham-Leigh
The Grove Tavern
Ben van Grutten
David Gurdon
Erica Haines
Sally, Doug, Meg and Sam Hamilton
Meredith Happold
Pat Harbour
Rachael Hardcastle
Duncan W. Harrington, L.H.G., F.S.A.
Mrs Lorna Head
Maurice J. Hills
Mike and Sheila Hinton
Guy Hitchings
R.J. Hoad
Jeanne Holloway
Joe Hyam
Don Jeffrey
Hedley B. Jones
D.G. Joyce
Anthony King
B.V. and B.J. Kingsley Smith
Michael Larsen
Max Lewis
Paula Long
Nicholas de Lotbinière
Melanie Mabey
Mark and Juliet Makinson
Mrs Audrey Martine
Peter James McKenna
Lady Marianne Meadow
P. Miller
Sandy Miller
John and Kate Minnis
Christopher Mortley
Michael and Carol Munro
Ian Myers
J.M. Niblett
Maureen Owen
Neil Page
Antony Paine
Michael Paine
A. du Gard Pasley
Lucy and Jeremy Raj
Beverley, Lady Reeves
Richard A. Rogers
Mr and Mrs Francis Salway
Miss Alice Laura Sanderson
Katie Scott and Bob MacSorley
Pamela and Peter Scott
Bryan Senior
Marianne Sheldrick
Mrs I.M. Shepherd
Sheila Brodrick Skinner
Arthur and Mary Skone
Laurence and Christine Smith
Richard Storkey
Anthony D.F. Streeten
Professor Flavia Swann
Susan and Dieter Teubler
Robin Toop
Dr Gareth Tuckwell
Ann Tully
Colin Tully
Tunbridge Wells Library
Tunbridge Wells Museum and Art Gallery
Ali and Angus Turner
John Turner
Gill Twells
Shirley E. Underwood
Lt. Col. and Mrs R.M.A. Wade, Ashenhurst's Great House
Sheila Weekes
Carolyn Lesley Wharton
Dr Philip Whitbourn, O.B.E.
Philip Winter
Richard and Fiona Woodfield

Acknowledgements

The generous assistance I have received over a period of more than fifteen years is too extensive to acknowledge in detail but the following repositories – and in particular their ever-helpful staff – deserve mention: the Tunbridge Wells Museum and Art Gallery, the Tunbridge Wells Reference Library and the Tonbridge Reference Library; the Centre for Kentish Studies and the Kent Archaeological Society Library in Maidstone, and the East Sussex Record Office, Lewes; the British Library, the British Museum, the Public Record Office, the Family Records Centre, London, and its predecessor institutions, the old Somerset House wills repository, Lambeth Palace Library, the Guildhall Library, Dr Williams's Library, English Heritage, the Royal Colleges of Physicians and Surgeons and the Worshipful Society of Apothecaries of London. My thanks also to the Australian connections of the Delves family – Lyn Bowman and Robin Macauley – not forgetting Meredith Happold who was responsible for breaking the logjam; Margaret Blatcher; Maureen Brewer of O'Kill connections; Andrew Bridge; the late Tsapy and Mrs Britneff; Geoff Butler; Richard Constable's descendants Mrs Bush and her sister; Ian and Judy Burn formerly of Richmond Villa; Christopher Chalklin for his pioneering work and continuing assistance; the late Arthur Chatterton, Delves descendant and family historian, of Indiana; the Charity Commission; Vera Coomber; Geoffrey Copus for expert advice; Courier Newspapers; Cripps, Harries, Hall; John Cunningham; Andrew Dale for Bayesian interest and expertise; Claude Delves; Jeffery Delves; the late Richard Delves; Roy Douglas; Avril Ebbage; John and Anne Forster; the Girls' Public Day School Trust; John and Richard Goulden; Haig Homes; Patrick Harbour; Keith Hetherington; Jeanne Holloway; Sabrina Izzard; Ted and Mrs Mepham; Mr and Mrs Metcalfe; Miles Garage; Rosemary Nicholson; Mike Queree; Lady Beverley Reeves; John Reynolds; Sheila Skinner, descendant of Richard Cumberland; Christopher Stacey; Philip Stephens; the late Kathleen Strange and Robin M.J. Freeman of the same family; Thomson, Snell and Passmore; Toc H; the late Margaret Townsend; Tunbridge Wells Borough Council; Devon and Gill Twells; Tony and Jill Wade; Warren Webber of New Zealand; Whitbread; and, last but not least, my wife Sylvia for unfailing encouragement, forbearance and support.

For permission to use illustrations grateful acknowledgement is due as follows: Buxton Homes for that on page 369; Lyn Bowman for those on pages 313 and 314; the British Library for those on pages 5, 63, 70, 85, 87, 89, 105, 108, 120, 126, 158, 159, 177, 178, 188, 202, 225, 258, 261, 263, 282, 332, 349, 356, 371, 372, 385 and 393; the British Museum for page 381; the Centre for Kentish Studies for pages 42, 71, 72, 78, 80, 104, 128, 138, 139,179, 183, 190, 206, 221, 229, 271,304, 319, 326, 335, 338, 341, 364, 395 and 397; Courier Newspapers for pages 30, 116, 367 and 383; Paul Crowther for pages 239 and 241; Claude Delves for pages 315, 316 and 317; Dr Williams's Library for page 350; English Heritage NMR for pages 286 and 419; Enterprise Inns for pages 106 and 121; Anne and John Forster for page 377; the Girls' Public Day School Trust for page 233; Keith Hetherington for page 75; Jeanne Holloway for pages 114 and 115; Sabrina Izzard for pages 388 and 411; the late Beatrice Johnson for pages 223 and 333; Brenda and George Kingsley-Smith for page 94; the Kent Archaeological Society for pages 16, 155 and 262; Ted Mepham for page 267; Mr and Mrs Metcalfe for page 378; the National Portrait Gallery for page 1; the Ordnance Survey for pages 24, 166, 198, 210, 244, 260, 272, 278 and 359; the Parish of Holy Trinity with Christ Church for pages 71, 128, 179, 190, 206, 221, 229, 271, 304, 319, 326, 341, 364, 395 and 397; the Public Record Office for page 36; Rochester Diocese for pages 72, 104 and 183; the Royal Archives, Windsor for page 404; Simmons Aerofilms for page 288; Dr Anthony Streeten for pages 391 and 392; Tonbridge Parish for pages 78 and 80; the Tonbridge Reference Library for pages 156, 274, 301 and 352; Tunbridge Wells Borough Council for pages 197 and 280; the Tunbridge Wells Museum and Art Gallery for pages 53, 92, 101, 110, 118, 122, 130, 146, 171, 175, 204, 208, 209, 214, 215, 232, 236, 242, 243, 255, 264, 281, 292, 302, 322, 329, 347, 386,389, 398, 400, 401 and 417; the Tunbridge Wells Reference Library for pages 26, 98,161, 170, 174, 220, 296, 306, 318, 363, 380 and 387; Devon Twells for pages 309, 390 and 392; Gill Twells for pages 222 and 356; the University of Birmingham for page 375 and others who, despite every effort, have not so far been traced.

Cover: Sion Crescent also known as Queen Anne's Mansion about 1900 – from a colour postcard by the Photocrom Co Ltd London and a painting by Francis – see Chapters 13 and 15.

Preface

The plan of this book is to begin with a few chapters on the first leases of 1684 which led to the settlement of Mount Sion and the court case of 1708 which provides much of the early information and then to cover the ground roughly from north to south, with a diversion to the east, following the plots allocated in the first leases. A chapter on my use of the Poor Rate record interrupts the flow at chapter eight and the final chapter hopes to end on a high note with an account of the Webber Riots of 1864. The area covered is not much different from that mapped by John Bowra in his Plan of Mount Sion Hill – see the frontispiece. The period occasionally strays into the 20th century and to the present day but my emphasis has been on unravelling the less accessible earlier centuries.

The reason for the book is I suppose simply that I have lived on Mount Sion for over forty years and want to make public what I have discovered so that others will not have to do it all again; besides which I hope it will be of interest to those who live in the Mount Sion 'village' and even to some who do not. Members who have attended my talks to the Royal Tunbridge Wells Civic Society over the years seem to have enjoyed them and I must acknowledge my debt to the Society for the encouragement it has given and confess that a lot of my matter is based on these talks.

I am very conscious of the gaps that remain: the newspapers I have not consulted, the Poor Rate disbursements I have not examined, the Poll Books I have ignored, the Town Hall archives I have not seen, the later censuses I have never got round to and the general neglect of anything later than 1900 for not being really historical enough. But a halt has to be called somewhere and enough is too much already.

I have departed from convention by providing a Commentary instead of the usual annoying numbered notes. I hope this will prove convenient. If you want a reference or a query springs to mind while reading just turn to the relevant page number in the Commentary and you should find what you want. A full bibliography and most importantly index are provided.

Illustrations are integrated into the text and not separately listed. If you want to find an illustration or see whether one exists I suggest you try the Table of Contents or the Index.

Chapter 1

Introduction

The story of Mount Sion starts in 1684. This is the 1066 of Mount Sion history as I have told members of the Royal Tunbridge Wells Civic Society often enough. Before 1684 the hill was there for sure and on the hill stood a tall clump of trees. It was all part of a barren heath called Inhams Heath and the clump of trees was Inhams Bush. Inhams Heath was part of the hunting chase of South Frith and belonged to the Manor of South Frith which Queen Elizabeth, out of the goodness of her heart, had given to Frances Walsingham after beheading her second husband. Frances was the daughter of Francis, the Queen's minister, and the second husband was the Earl of Essex. The first had been Sir Philip Sidney and the third was to be the Earl of Clanricarde who built a mansion at Somerhill near Tonbridge at the north-western apex of the triangle which was South Frith Manor (north-east was Pembury while Inhams Heath was the southernmost tip). The Clanricardes had a son, Ulick de Burgh, who fought for the King in the Civil War while his wife and only child, Margaret, lived in Paris and it was in Paris that Margaret met her husband Lord Muskerry. His skull and brains spattered the unfortunate Duke of York during a naval clash with the Dutch in 1665 and Margaret married Viscount Purbeck who died abroad in a duel in 1684. It seems probable that his widow then realised that the southernmost corner of her manor with its heath and its bush of trees was ripe for development.

Ulick de Burgh – Marquess of Clanricarde and Earl of St Albans

Things had been happening since the early 1600s – and only half a mile or so from Inhams Bush. Each summer more and more well-heeled visitors had come from London and elsewhere to drink the water of a spring at the bottom of the hill, staying in outlying villages or even pitching tents and marquees on the waste of the adjoining Manor of Rusthall. In 1629 it had been Queen Henrietta Maria to convalesce after the death of her first-born and the waters had proved so successful that the conception of Charles II followed swiftly – at least the dates are consistent! And then in 1663 after the Restoration Queen Katharine came hoping for the same result and brought the whole Court and even the King himself in her train – not to mention the royal 'Tents, Toils and Pavilions' about which contemporary manuscripts at the British Museum give some details … or Nell Gwyn and other ladies who may or may not have come to entertain the Court. All this can hardly have escaped the notice of the Lady of South Frith. Indeed she was in the thick of it. Her mansion at Tonbridge became an aristocratic lodging house and, although the ball itself may not have taken place there, she cannot escape the nickname 'Princess of Babylon' which her mistaken fancy dress earned her – at least if we are to believe the Comte de Grammont; and in 1676, perhaps to make amends, she donated the land on which the Chapel of King Charles the Martyr was then built to service the souls of the water drinkers – or, if we are to believe John Fuller, to keep them from the rain and provide a community meeting place.

The local people also noticed what was going on. Money, money, money it screamed at them and they wanted their share. So every summer when the first visitors arrived – and it was usually those who hoped to benefit from the chalybeate water who came first – stalls were erected near the spring and the 'fresh-faced country girls' were on hand to sell everyday meat and vegetables from the locality and fish from Hastings and wheatear delicacies from the Downs and fancy souvenirs from wherever. Pipe and Coffee Houses (not to mention Pissing and Bog Houses on the banks of the River Grom) catered for the further requirements of the ladies and gentlemen. The reason underlying all this activity was of course the curing of illness and the improvement of health; but having arrived at this out of the world place the good people had to find ways of passing the time. So they drank coffee and smoked pipes and paraded up and down and gossiped and gambled and danced and went for little excursions; but when the sun went down they retired to their lodgings in Rusthall or Southborough or Somerhill House if they were in with the Princess of Babylon.

There were no lodging houses near the spring because it was located on the waste of the Manor of Rusthall and the freeholders of the manor had rights of grazing which they were unwilling to waive or sell because most of them also controlled the lodging houses in the neighbouring villages. This impasse was not broken, and then only partially, until the Manor changed hands. Since about 1660 it had belonged to the Muskerrys and therefore, after her gallant husband's death at sea, Lady Muskerry owned the contiguous manors of South Frith and Rusthall.

In 1682 she sold Rusthall, but not South Frith. The new owner was Thomas Neale, Master of the Royal Mint, who persuaded the freeholders, in return for a payment of 10 shillings each a year, to allow building near the spring – but still no lodging houses.

By this time a rival to Rusthall and Southborough had appeared on the horizon in the shape of new houses constructed along the ridge above the Common – very soon to be named Mount Ephraim. It was in these circumstances that Viscountess Purbeck, the former Lady Muskerry, saw the opportunities dormant in the heath and bush of Inhams. As the Manor Steward, Thomas Weller, was to tell the Court of Chancery in 1708, the land was 'Heathie and verry barren but the same lay in Tunbridge neare unto Tonbridge Wells very convenient to build upon'.

The chalybeate spring lay by chance very near the meeting point of three manors and parishes and the counties of Kent and Sussex; and possibilities of development were different in each manor. To the south was Abergavenny land and, although the Earl (Marquess later) was the first to pave the spring area and rail it around and later built houses on his land just to the south of the Spring, he was strangely reluctant to build further up the hill on his Sussex land – in fact it was to be three centuries before any such building took place. To the west rose the common land of Rusthall Manor in Kent over which the freeholders had their grazing rights and so the only possibility of development was to the north-east in South Frith Manor, also in Kent. Further afield some building had already taken place, as already mentioned, on the future Mount Ephraim just over the border into Speldhurst Manor. The situation for the Purbecks was anyway plain as a pikestaff, and poles and pales were what Thomas Weller proceeded to set out amongst the bracken and gorse of Inhams Heath.

Between 1684 and 1696 he arranged, on behalf of the manor, to give out leases worth £189 17s. 6d. per annum in 33 separate transactions, with a few individuals taking two or more leases. Not much information is given about the land in the document which records these leases. We are told the date, the name of the lessee, the period of the lease (almost always 50 years) and a description such as 'two pieces or parcels of land'. Occasionally an acreage is given and where this happens the price per acre per annum seems to be about 10 shillings, indicating that some 100 acres in all were involved – although I think this is an under-estimate. You can multiply by anything from 200 to 300 to get a present-day value – so the total annual rental coming into the Purbeck coffers might be up to £50,000 in today's money. The first leases (nine of them) were dated 4 November 1684. About one-third of the total was completed in November that year. Another third were completed by October 1687. The leases cover the whole Mount Sion area but extend northward as far as the Grosvenor Road and Calverley Estate areas which fall outside the boundaries of this history. Within the Mount Sion area it is possible – but mainly from the study of later developments – to piece together how the land was split up and who got what.

The land for which local men and Londoners, yeomen, tradesmen and gentlemen, scrambled in a gold-rush atmosphere must have looked somewhat like the Common at some stage; but the difference was that Bishops Down Common was used for grazing sheep whereas there were no such rights on the South Frith land. Sheep used to keep down the trees on the Common but since the sheep went the trees have grown – at least until the wind came and blew them over in 1987! But on South Frith land there seem to have been well-defined areas of heath and woodland, perhaps due to the nature of the soil or underlying rock. Symonson's map of 1596 – ten years before the discovery of the spring – shows the area: Waterdown Forest, the old name for Broadwater Forest, covered a huge area, taking in the whole of Eridge Park and beyond; but to the north it stretched as far as the boundaries of Mount Sion; Wybourne's Woodlands, in the direction of Hawkenbury, occupied approximately the Camden Park area; and Waghorne's Forest must have lain close by to the east or north.

The earliest leases speak of Inhams Heath or rough ground called Inhams. Certain features are mentioned here and there: a dyke and bank, a hedge and bank, an oak, birches, furze, a greenway; a piece of land formerly a wheat gratten and a parcel of land heretofore a hemp plot. The area was originally disturbed no doubt only by the occasional hunting party; but it is difficult to believe that the discovery of the Wells and the annual influx of visitors provoked no human interference on the adjoining hillside over a period of 80 years. A wheat gratten is a field of old stubble and the hemp plot also suggests sporadic cultivation. A ditch and bank might be natural but a hedge and bank surely point to human hands. There is, however, no evidence of any building except near the Chapel; nor were there any roads crossing the heath.

A glance at Symonson shows that the only road seems to be the one to Rye, which is the present A21 as far as Flimwell; but John Seller's later map of Kent of 1680, in addition to the faint label 'South Frith Wood', does at least mark Tunbridge Wells and Tunbridge Wells Chapel – and it shows a road to Southborough and one to Woodsgate; but the Woodsgate one seems to join the Southborough one some way north of the Chapel – in fact much as the present Pembury Road does. On the other hand the road to Pembury which starts up Mount Sion proceeds in a series of right angles – as some of us know only too well ... Mount Sion – Claremont Road – Grove Hill Road – Prospect Road and so into the Pembury Road. This means it had to take account of existing land holdings.

How then did Thomas Weller, with or without the assistance of the Lady of the Manor, decide to divide this barren heath for development? The main objective was to squeeze the maximum advantage from the proximity of the site to the all-important 'Wells'. For this reason smaller plots for the erection of lodging houses were allocated near the 'Wells' and a greater acreage in the 'hinterland' was given with each building plot, for the grazing of horses and livestock and the making of hay. It seems likely that the two major roads, Mount Sion and the High Street, were part of the development plan; certainly the High Street was called at the time the 'new way to Southborough'. In order then to give as many houses as possible a frontage onto one of the roads, it was necessary to plan narrow strips fronting the roads. This could of course work only one way where the roads met at right angles. John Bowra's Plan of Mount Sion Hill dated 1738 will help.

Bowra plan 1738

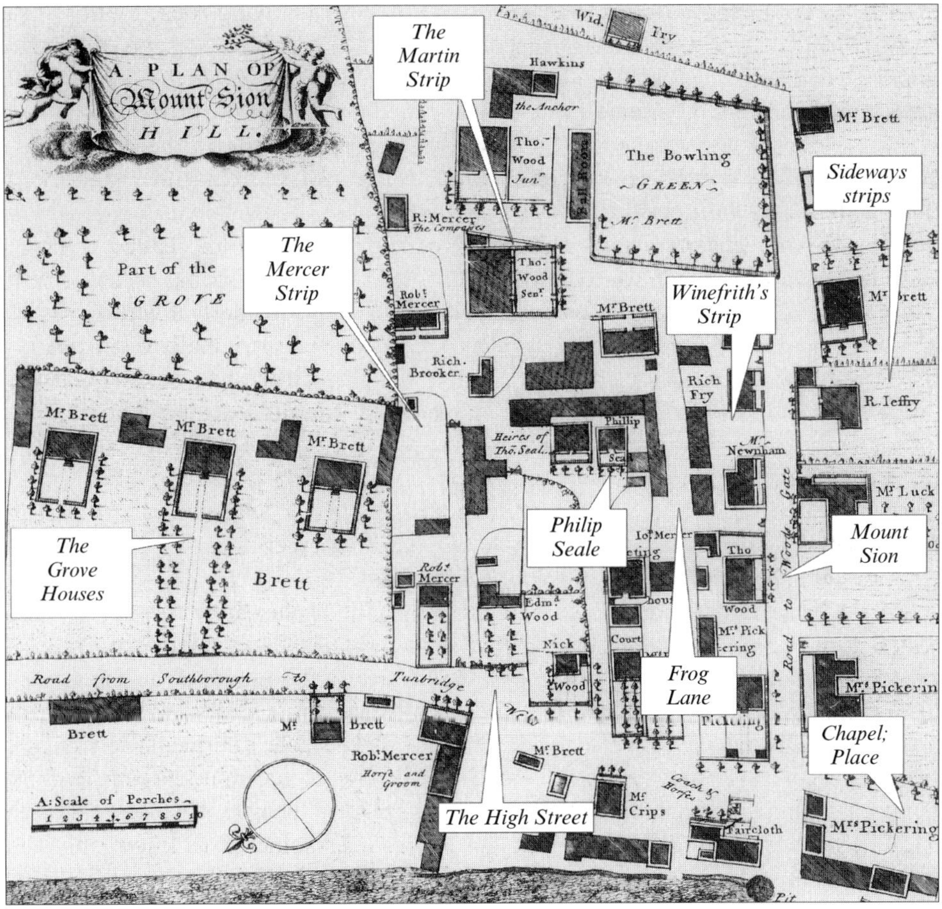

The frontage to the High Street was evidently judged the more important and this led to an arrangement of strips leading uphill. On the southern side of Mount Sion the strips could go sideways; and so they did, extending as far as Cumberland Walk. There were, however, two places where the strips could not go all the way to the top of the hill. The first was below the Grove. Although the Grove was not formally handed over until 1703 there was obviously no question from the beginning of cutting down the trees and building. The block between the Grove and the High Street therefore became the somewhat more rectangular site of the three Grove Houses – where South Grove and Christ Church and Grove Avenues now are. The second place was where the Bowling Green dictated a square shape at the top of Mount Sion Road; or where at any rate it put in an appearance, showing up as the 'Bowling Alley' in the Poor Rate record as early as 1690 – and even earlier in the partition Plan of 1686 about which more below. Finally, there was the Chapel Place block whose boundaries still exist in the shape of the London Road, Cumberland Walk, Cumberland Gardens and Mount Sion.

The Bowra plan above and the labels (or 'call-outs') which I have added illustrate the way Mount Sion was divided for leasing and help explain the arrangement of this book. Chapters 2 to 5 are devoted to the earliest, late 17th-century, period in the story of Mount Sion and, being based on the Buckingham-Weller-Brett court cases, deal at some length with the details of these cases and their eventual outcome some half century later, showing among much else why the name 'Brett' figures so prominently on the plan above. From this point onward, with one interruption in Chapter 8 to consider the Poor Rate record, chapters deal either singly or in groups with the lease plots illustrated above, starting with the Grove and the Grove Houses and moving from left to right or north to south (the compass rose at the bottom of the plan will show the exact alignment) until 'Winefrith's Strip' on Mount Sion is reached. Then the houses round the Bowling Green are considered together with a few off the map at the top before the journey is completed down the other side of Mount Sion finishing with Chapel Place and, leaving the most dramatic to the last, the Webber Riots in which Chapel Place played a part.

Let us consider the lease plots in a little more detail. I am not entirely sure about the Grove Houses but I think that this site, between the Grove and the High Street, was leased to Thomas Neale on 10 February 1685. He was the Lord of Rusthall Manor and chief developer of the Pantiles. His lease included, I think, all the land between the Grove and Grove Hill Road right down to the High Street corner. Next to Neale's land and the Grove came a long, narrow strip which in today's terms lies between Warwick Road and the back gardens of south Grove at its lower end and between Little Mount Sion and the Grove at its upper end; and includes the Compasses and Belgrove. It was first leased to William Fulman, with other land, on 4 November 1684 in one of the very first leases and then taken over by John Mercer – hence the label 'Mercer Strip'.

Alongside this strip of land came a wider one running between Warwick Road and Little Mount Sion at the bottom and extending on the same lines right up to where Miles Garage now is. This strip, also in one of the first leases, went on 4 November 1684 to Edward Martin who, according to Colonel Waring, was the principal joiner and carpenter for the construction of the Chapel. The label 'Martins Strip' points to the top end of the strip but it extends right down to the High Street. Next came a broader strip of land running between Little Mount Sion and Mount Sion road but extending upwards only as far as the Bowling

Green square – in today's terms, to the back of the Toc H site. This strip and the Bowling Green block also were leased to Richard Constable and Robert Brooke, again on 4 November 1684; but in 1686 a partition was agreed giving Constable alone the Bowling Green block (for more see the next chapter page 15) and in 1702 the northern part of the remaining strip was sold to Philip Seale and the southern part to Winefrith Brooke leaving the narrow Frog Lane strip in between – hence the labels 'Philip Seale', 'Frog Lane' and 'Winefrith's Strip'. Winefrith was the widow of Robert Brooke who was an ironmonger from Maidstone whose relationship with Richard Constable I do not know. Constable was a mercer from Groombridge and had leased the Manor of Rusthall from Lady Muskerry for 17 years from 1672 but gave up the lease in 1982 so that she could sell to Thomas Neale.

On the southern side of Mount Sion road and at the bottom of the hill was the Chapel Place block. The greater part of this was leased, with buildings on it, to John Brett on 4 February 1690. This lease was much later than the others because (I'm guessing but it seems fairly obvious) this used to be John Wybourne's and he died about 1689. Above this came, still on the southern side of Mount Sion, the site of Jerningham House which ran back sideways between Cumberland Gardens and Cumberland Yard as far as Cumberland Walk. This piece of land was leased on 10 December 1689 to Edward Allen who, like Richard Constable, was a mercer but came from Rotherfield. He had a shop on the Pantiles on which it is recorded that he paid £9 rent in 1699 and which he bequeathed to his daughter Barbara who was married to William Durrant – a name which survived on the Pantiles for a very long time. Another daughter, Anne, married the Mr Luck whose name appears on the Bowra plan as owner of Jerningham House.

Then there was a strip of land on the other side of Cumberland Yard on which now stands number 22, Mount Sion, formerly the Eye and Ear Hospital which has now reverted to its good old name of Fairlawn House and to its old residential use if in slightly different form from that of a lodging house. Anyway, the 'Fairlawn House' strip, going back as far as Cumberland Walk, was leased, again on 10 December 1689, to one Henry Adams about whom I have no information; but he was succeeded by Thomas Scoones whose grandson was the first of the lawyer Scoones who became Thomson, Snell and Passmore over the centuries. The three houses further up the hill to the east, bordering the Bowling Green and marked, 'Mr Brett' were built on a plot originally leased to Richard Constable, presumably in 1684. Round the corner on the top of the hill are more houses whose story will be dealt with in their place, ending with Belle Vue House in Claremont Road which I have included mainly for the sake of the interesting source material which goes with it.

All this leasing of land for building on a barren heath involved a certain amount of measuring and marking out and prior planning; and some evidence of this is to be found in the Chancery case of which more will be said presently. For instance, an eight-acre parcel of Inhams was:

> bound as the same is marked out to other part of the same Heath and to a Ditch and a Bank there towards the north to the forest of Waterdowne towards the west to other part of the said Heath appointed for a way and other part thereof demised to the said Edward Martin towards the east and south as the same is now measured marked and Dotted out.

(Lawyers never use punctuation, you remember!)

Such phrases as 'except certaine ways to be there laid out' or 'through which A convenient way was to goo' or (as in the above quotation) 'appointed for a way' all suggest the planning of roads. Quite what the operation of 'dotting out' involved I am not sure; but it seems quite certain that Thomas Weller and his minions must have spent hours and days tramping the hillsides. Of course, it would have been very helpful if he had left us a scale map showing his development plan; but all we have is words – as in the long quotation which I just gave you – and it is like piecing together a jig-saw puzzle of a snowstorm. In fact I was only able to work out as much as I did in the light of subsequent developments, although one plan from 1686, the Brooke/Constable Partition Plan (see the next chapter, page 16) did come to light at a later date to confirm (fortunately!) my initial surmises.

Martins Lower House – rear view (now nos 59-61 High Street)

This then was the first stage in the history of Mount Sion. Within a year or two the timber frames of houses began to rise, scattered over the hillside, to be clad with planks or hung with tiles. There was no attempt at grandeur. The houses had to be as large as possible to accommodate visitors at the peak of the season but they were built by local men using local methods and craftsmen. Edward Martin was indeed both craftsman and leaseholder and had a personal hand, I am sure, in building, on the High Street frontage of his strip, the two houses which became known as Martin's Upper and Lower Houses, of which the latter survives as the rear part of Nos 59-61 High Street (notice the tile-hanging in the photograph taken in 1990). Martin, however, hived off to others the development of his land at the top of the hill; and, generally speaking, this is what happened everywhere. Another interesting thing is that with one exception, which will be dealt with later, the basic arrangement of the plots leased out between 1684 and 1690 has not changed to this day: the plots have simply been divided into ever smaller portions and more and more houses have been created. The source for much of this information is the Chancery case of 1708. Lady Muskerry's son John (who liked to call himself the Earl of Buckingham) quarrelled with Thomas Weller and took him to court. If they had not quarrelled, we should never have known all this.

Chapter 2

The First Leases

On 4 November 1684 Sir Thomas Meeres and the Right Honourable Margaret Viscountess Purbeck made nine 50-year leases of South Frith land. Two went to joint lessees, the rest to individuals with ordinary names and no titles like John Horsmer or William Fulman, all male except one. This was the beginning of Mount Sion. Sir Thomas Meeres was 'one of His Majesty's Commissioners for executing the Office of the Lord High Admiral of England', according to a deed of 1682, and was one of a line of mortgagees to whom Lord Muskerry and others following him had had recourse since 1664 and was obviously needed to confirm the leases. His partner was Viscountess Purbeck, former Lady Muskerry (probably widowed by then), and together she and the knight went on to conclude a total of 32 leases up to the year 1691.

The information we have about these leases is fairly sparse. It is contained in the schedule to a 1702 conveyance which comes later in the story and gives the name of the lessee, the term, usually 50 years, the annual rent and a very brief description of the property. 'Four parcels of land, two pieces of land or several parcels' are typical examples; but occasionally more is needed, like 'a messuage and several parcels of land' or 'a shop and a small piece of ground'. The rent varies from £14 (£27 in one special case) to £1 with a total of £163 7s. 6d. and an average of £5 and a fraction – or excluding the special case £4 7s. 6d. approximately. Occasionally an acreage is given and where this happens the price per acre per annum seems to be about 10 shillings, indicating that some 100 acres in all were involved. However, later documentation shows that a part only of all leases accounted for about 105 acres and the grand total must therefore have been rather more than one hundred. The first leases, as mentioned on page 3, were dated 4 November 1684 and about one third of all were completed that November and another third by October 1687.

The area concerned excluded the Manor of Rusthall (the Common and the Pantiles mainly), Mount Ephraim and beyond to the north and west and any land across the border into Sussex – in church terms the parishes of Speldhurst and Frant. It also excluded areas to the east documented as belonging to John Wyborne Esquire or as part of Waterdown Forest – the Camden Estate and Hawkenbury formerly known as Tuttys Village. All these places lay outside the Manor of South Frith. What was included, however, represents most of the central built area of the town of Tunbridge Wells: Mount Sion, the High Street, Mount Pleasant, Grosvenor Road and anything east of this line as far as the Pembury Road. The Manor of South Frith contained about 5,000 acres and branched out from its southern apex at the Church of King Charles the Martyr to follow roughly the lines of the Pembury Road in one direction and the London Road through Southborough to Quarry Hill in the other. Southborough was the *southern* borough of the exceptionally large Parish of Tonbridge.

The interesting line of houses fronting the Common from Thackerays House at the top to Vale Royal and beyond at the bottom marks not only the boundary between the parishes of Tonbridge and Speldhurst but also that between the manors of South Frith and Rusthall and demonstrates how building was not allowed on the Rusthall or Common side but was on the other – from 1684 anyhow and incidentally, to my mind, this proves that Thackerays cannot date from as early as 1660 as is often suggested. The 32 leases must be assumed therefore to range from Mount Sion northwards to the top of the town at the Grosvenor Road junction with Mount Ephraim, and perhaps in an easterly direction also. The documents commonly describe land as part of Inhams Heath or Calverleys Plain but a glance at Bowra's general map of 1738 suggests that most development, apart from that on Mount Sion, took place along the London Road frontage with scattered building at the bottom of Mount Pleasant, more at the junction with Church Road (formerly Jordans Lane) and again at the top of Grosvenor Road.

The names of the lessees might be hoped to be significant but in practice only to those in the know. Names relevant to Mount Sion will crop up *ad nauseam* as we proceed; historians of other parts of the town might well find names of interest but I can only see two or three. On 10 December 1689 William Baynes leased several pieces of land for 50 years at £2 per annum. He ran (maybe founded) the brewery which appears on the Bowra map as Kings Brew-house on the Central Station site at the bottom of Mount Pleasant. The name John Jeffery was certainly important as owner of the big house on the corner of Jordans Lane (now Church Road) and the London Road, and in 1691 a Thomas Jeffery leased a small piece of land for 50 years at 20 shillings a year; but I doubt if John and Thomas are connected. Then there is Mathew Calverley. On 10 November 1686 he leased five acres for 50 years at £2 10s. 0d. He and his brother John can be found on the Bowra general map on either side of 'Ye George' at the top of the London Road and there is some evidence that they later owned land elsewhere; but to my mind this does not mean that Calverleys Plain took its name from them as has often been assumed to be self-evident. For one thing Mathew was described in the record of his 'Fleet' marriage as a carpenter and, honourable as this trade may be, it does not suggest the sort of status which would give a name to a large geographical feature. For another thing the name was in common use to describe this feature at about the same time as Mathew Calverley took his lease, indicating surely that the name Calverleys Plain originated long before Mathew came on the scene. The names on the list that ring a Mount Sion bell are Weller, Brooke, Constable, Martin, Neale, Fulman, Adams and Allen. Weller, Brooke, Constable and Neale were all involved in the Chancery case of 1708 which is the subject of chapters 3 and 4; Martin and Fulman are named as occupiers of adjoining lands;

while Adams and Allen are significant in connection with Jerningham and Fairlawn Houses about which more in chapters 24 and 25.

The scene amongst the hitherto untroubled scrub and gorse of the barren heath of Inhams can be imagined. The documents which open a window on these scenes are not the original leases but the Chancery documents which came some twenty years later and refer back to the original leases. The internal evidence suggests that the wording is mainly taken from the originals with some additions to bring things up to date. For instance, part of the land leased to Brooke and Constable on 4 November 1684 is described as: 'one other piece or parcel of land or heath likewise part of the same heath called Inhams containing by estimation 8 acres in Tonbridge aforesaid and bound as the same is marked out to other part of the same heath and to a ditch and a bank there towards the north to the forest of Waterdown towards the west to other part of the said heath appointed for a way and other part thereof demised unto the said Edward Martin towards the east and south as the same is now measured marked and dotted out'. If part of the heath is planned as a road ('appointed for a way') and the whole plot is measured, marked and (whatever this means) 'dotted out', then obviously no development has taken place and the words must date from 1684. On the other hand part of the land leased to Thomas Neale on 10 February 1686 is described as 'heath ground part of the said lands called Inhams ... through which a way now goeth'; and at other times the building of houses is referred to as in this passage: 'And also one piece or parcel of land formerly a wheat gratten upon which several messuages houses and other buildings are erected and being part of lands called Inhams in Tunbridge aforesaid containing by estimation four acres'.

A wheat gratten is a field of old stubble and tantalising glimpses of the heath as it used to be are afforded here and there throughout the dry legalese of the documents. Cultivation of a sort is again suggested by the reference to a 'hemp plot' to the south of the site of the *Angel Inn* – was this for rope making, I wonder, or another sort of medicinal use to rival the chalybeate water? The ground is often rough; there are ancient banks, ditches, dykes, hedges and a bank planted with birches. A boundary is marked by a fence 'straight by an oak' and mention is made of a parcel of wood called Inhams Bush – later to be called the Grove. Into this barren heath came, in the summer or autumn of 1684 I suppose, a gang of surveyors and workmen supervised by Thomas Weller, on horseback no doubt, and proceeded to measure, mark and dot out the shape of Mount Sion to come. A 'new way from Southborough to the Wells' (the future High Street) was a priority; two pieces of land were intersected by it 'straight cross' to a breadth of three rods (16 yards and a half) and another new way went up the hill from the Common called Bishops Down to where the Bowling Green was to be and continued in the direction of Pembury. Service roads for the houses to come were provided elsewhere. The question is, when did building commence?

Common sense suggests the minimum of delay; but a source of information exists which indicates the time scale – the Poor Rate. This was a tax based on property values which arose from the Elizabethan Poor Laws and was used for the relief of the poor. The earliest records, however, that I have found for Tonbridge Parish start in 1670; for Speldhurst the situation is much worse, 1810 being the earliest date. The Poor Rate record will be considered more fully in chapter 8 but the evidence it provides for the start of building on Mount Sion and elsewhere in the parish is convincing. Out of 26 entries dating from 1687 or earlier seven were for 1687, eight for 1686, three for 1685, two for 1684, one for 1683, one for 1676 and three for 1670. The record only began in 1670 and the ratepayers for that year had no doubt been paying for years before; besides they are special cases. John Wybourne will be discussed in more detail in chapter 3 but he is known to have rented land from the Manor and erected some buildings which got in the way of the Chapel construction around 1676. Thomas Weller was, of course, steward to the manor and I suppose he took advantage of his position to lease some land long before the events of 1684. Finally, Thomas Potter is a mystery. He was probably a farmer who gave his name to 'Potters Green' featured on the Barrow map of 1808 and about whom one of Aretas Akers' children wrote the story of 'Potters Ghost' centuries later – see chapter 23 – but I do not really know. I cannot explain the entry for 1676: the first ratepayer was a John Pawke and entries continue until 1771 for a property called Pawks or later Pococks but where and what it was I do not know – possibly a farm. If anyone knows, please tell me. The entry for 1683 is in the name of Sir Thomas Meeres and he was in a privileged position as principal mortgagee of the Manor lands; and anyway the property in question was a farm named Hawkes Farm and probably miles from any lodging house developments. As for the two 1684 entries, both names John Horsmer and John Weller are found on the list of leases dated November 1684 and why the one should have been charged rates in June and the other in January 1684 I cannot explain. Obviously rates were not collected until houses were up and running. They were calculated on rental values and an empty site or half-completed house was not considered to have any rental value. Anyway that is the way it seems to have worked. Rates were collected half yearly. From this evidence I conclude that building work began in the spring following the November leases, was largely completed in that year and the first visitors were welcomed by the luckiest or most enterprising lodging house keepers in the early summer of 1686. Many more followed, not only in 1687; in 1688 and 89 there were 13, in 1690 and '91 there were six and a further 10 to the end of the century. To summarise then and assuming my interpretation to be correct, a total of 53 new houses appeared in that part of South Frith land which is now Tunbridge Wells in the 15 years between 1684 and 1699 – surely a surprising phenomenon. How much of this however was in the Mount Sion area?

It is time to confront the question, where does Mount Sion begin and end!? I take it to be the area bounded by Cumberland Walk on one side and by the Grove on the other and by the High Street at the bottom and Mount Sion after the right-angle bend at the top. However, I insist on a certain fuzziness at the edges. For instance, the houses on the top side of Mount Sion – Cecil Court (Marlborough

House), the cottages at Nos 34-38, Percy House (Grove Lodge) and even Belle Vue House – are to be included but the houses on the lower side of the High Street are excluded. The old Grove Houses below the Grove generally count as 'in' but the London Road is 'out' except for the *Angel Inn* (*Kentish Royal Hotel*) which with Chapel Place is largely relevant to the Mount Sion story. The Grove itself from its Inhams Bush beginnings onwards is also relevant although preserved from development. Within this area, as elsewhere in the budding town, the timber frames of houses began to arise. The rough layout of the area had been determined by Thomas Weller and his minions but the siting and design of individual houses was surely left to respective leaseholders. There was no attempt at grandeur, that sort of money not being around on the one hand and on the other the emphasis being on seeing the cash come in as soon as possible. The only builders available were local ones accustomed to making farmhouses and to traditional methods – timber frames and tile-hanging or weatherboarding on the upper storeys with perhaps some brick or even stone lower down. A good example of a farmhouse which might have been the template for a lodging house is Downingbury Farmhouse at Pembury. A characteristic found there and on some Tunbridge Wells houses is the low double roof, avoiding, according to my theory, too much weight on the timber frame beneath. The prime example to be seen on Mount Sion today is no 15, Sion House. The imperative was the capacity to accommodate as many visitors as possible during the summer water-drinking season. What houses then, fitting this description, might have been seen on Mount Sion after this first building frenzy?

The very first phase appears to have seen houses fronting the 'new way from the Wells to Southborough' – that is the present High Street, later known as 'Foot of Mount Sion'. There was a house on the corner of the High Street and Mount Sion, where the Natwest bank used to be and the Pizza place now is. This was known as Whites and then Boltons and was demolished in 1849 to make way for Sion Terrace, nos 3-7. It may, therefore, have been built by or for Edward White who first paid rates in December 1687; but the Poor Rate record is not entirely clear. More likely perhaps is Robert Brooke whose first rate payment is dated 27 May 1686. Further up the road Edward Martin, the Chapel carpenter, built his 'Upper House' which was demolished in the 19th century. It stood back from the corner of what are now the High Street and Warwick Road and rates were first paid in May 1686. It was named later Warwick House and gave its name to the road. His second or 'Lower' house which still exists behind the shop frontage of nos 59-61 High Street seems to have come some seven years later. On the other side of 'Warwick' road was another large house later named Camden House and also demolished in the 19th century on which William Fulman possibly paid rates as early as July 1685. All these houses, including two whose Poor Rate record I cannot identify (York House which is the only real survivor and one on the site of the *Dragon Inn* and the Coffee House) seem to have been built with an eye on the view westward over the Common from higher ground on the opposite side of the 'new way'. Next after 'Camden House' came a large front garden or field at the top of which with their backs to the Grove were built the three 'Grove Houses': South Grove House, North Grove House and Middle (or 'the Great') Grove House in the middle! 'Mr Young' first paid rates in December 1687 for a field and then in the second half of 1689 for 'a field and three new houses' and I do not think there is any doubt that these were the three Grove Houses. Mr Young, however, does not figure in the list of South Frith leases and it is almost certain that he took over the land from Thomas Neale.

Thomas Neale was the master of the Royal Mint and general entrepreneur who bought the Manor of Rusthall in 1682 and got things going on the Pantiles. He has been described as one of the more extraordinary and most influential figures of late Stuart England, and one of the least chronicled. He was known as 'Golden Neale' as a result of his somewhat unconventional marriage to Lady Gould which Samuel Pepys records in his diary for 20 June 1664 as follows: '... the rich widow, my lady Gould, is married to one Neale, after he had received a box on the eare by her brother ... at the door, but made him draw, and wounded him ... She called Neale up to her and sent for a priest, married presently and went to bed. Her brother sent to the Court and had a serjeant sent for Neale; but Neale sent for him up to be seen in bed, and she owned him for her husband and so all is past.' On 10 February 1685/6 he leased several parcels of land for 50 years at £18 per annum and among them are two pieces described in somewhat obscure terms in the record of the 1708 Chancery case as bounding to land leased to William Fulman and to Bishops Down (the Common) with a way to Inhams Bush somewhere nearby and a way three rods wide running across them – see above page 12. I think this describes the site of the three Grove Houses together with more land continuing across the High Street as far as the Common (London Road). Neale sold the Manor of Rusthall in 1689 or 1690 and maybe it was this event which led to an assignment of the lease to Mr Young and the construction of the Grove Houses – but this is speculation. Neale died anyway in 1699.

As mentioned already a broad strip of land running uphill from the corner of Mount Sion and the High Street as far as the Bowling Green block was jointly leased by Robert Brooke and Richard Constable on 4 November 1684 but then partitioned by them two years later; and we are fortunate that a keen-eyed antiquarian saw a deed in the hands of a Bromley bookseller on 14 November 1936 and took the trouble to see it preserved in the Kent Archaeological Society Library and doubly fortunate that a rough chart was attached and copied. This is part of the documentation of the 1686 partition and provides a unique graphic confirmation of a few of the verbal descriptions which are so difficult to interpret on their own. The chart is reproduced on the next page and a comparison with the Bowra plan on page 5 of chapter 1 will show how close the correlation is. The scale of the original chart has yet to be established but it is fascinating to speculate whether John Bowra was familiar with the work of the earlier surveyor and who he was. The orientation, of course, is different; the chart needs to be turned 90 degrees anti-clockwise to coincide with Bowra.

A short text accompanies the chart and describes the land leased to Brooke and Constable in 1684 while the chart shows how the land was apportioned in 1686, giving the date 20 September, where the Chancery record can do no better

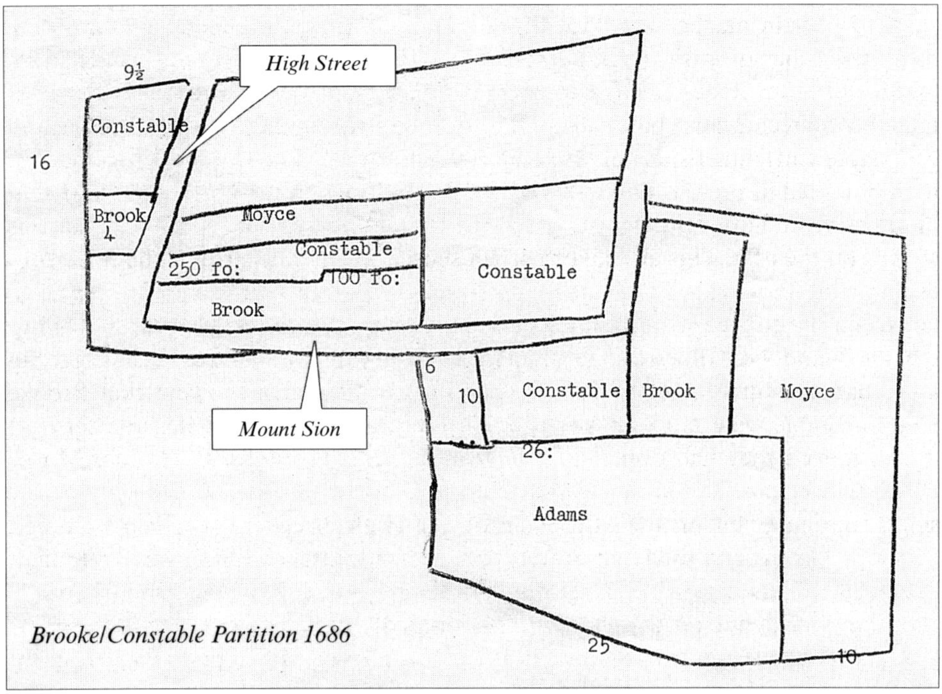

Brooke/Constable Partition 1686

than report 'in or about the month of December'! The Chancery description, however, repeats the 1686 deed almost word for word, confirming that the 1708 record refers back to the 1680s and '90s originals which of course went missing long ago. The deed clearly indicates a north-south line running up Mount Sion with north at the bottom and east and west accordingly. The true compass points can be seen on the Bowra plan. Using the deed's faulty compass then, the large unnamed plot to the east must be the plot measuring eight by 40 rods leased to Edward Martin and covering the area from Little Mount Sion to Warwick Road from the High Street up to the top of Mount Sion together with the adjoining strip bounded by The Grove. The plots named on the chart cover all the land leased in this transaction to Brooke and Constable in 1684. The deed specifies four: (1) part of Inhams Heath 11 rods wide by 23 rods long on the east and 27 rods long on the west 'against a way there to be made'; (2) another part 13 rods wide and 20 rods long part of which is 'fenced in for a bowling green' and lies to the south of (1); (3) another part of Inhams containing eight acres bounded by a ditch and bank towards the north, by Waterdowne Forest towards the west and by an intended way and land leased to Edward Martin towards the east and south 'as the same is new measured marked and dowled out'; and (4) another piece three rods wide by 16 long bounding to Bishops Down towards the north and to an intended way towards the south. Can we identify these plots?

Plots (1) and (2) are said to contain 3 acres 1 rood and to be bounded by land appointed for a way on three sides – north, west and south and by land leased to Edward Martin on the east. Plot (2) contains the Bowling Green and cannot be other than the squarish block marked Constable; while Plot (1) lies to the south of Plot (2) and, if our assumptions on compass points are correct, this means it must be the rectangular block divided into three strips marked Moyce, Brooke and Constable with dimensions of 250 and 100 feet shown. The two plots together are then bounded in present-day terms by the High Street on the north and by Mount Sion before and after the right-angle at the top on the west and south and Martins strip is on the east. This all makes perfect sense. The middle strip of the three subdivisions of Plot (1) is Frog Lane. The lower part of Little Mount Sion seems to be within the Moyce strip. Plot (3) must then be all the named plots up the hill to the south and west (does this not appear to be about two to three times bigger in area than the three acres of Plots (1) and (2) combined?); showing that Brooke and Constable were not only partitioning their land but also subleasing some of it – as indeed they had done with the strip of Plot (1) sub-let to Thomas Moyce which will be considered in greater detail in chapter 13. Plot (4) can only be the small triangular bit on the other side of the High Street between the Common (Bishops Down) and the High Street (part of heath intended for a way), although the width of three rods given differs considerably from what the chart shows.

The dimensions on the chart are undoubtedly rods, poles or perches (i.e. 5½ yards) except the figures 250 and 100 which are feet – 'fo' is perhaps a misprint or misreading? Luckily these figures precisely occur in the right context in the Chancery record: 'one piece or parcel of ground whereon divers messuages houses stables and other buildings are erected and was heretofore a parcel of certain heath ground called Inhams in Tonbridge aforesaid near Tunbridge Wells and bounding towards the north to a new way there laid out and leading from the Wells to Southburrough and to a new way leading to the Bowling Green towards the west to other lands intended to have been sold to the said Richard Constable towards the east and south and doth contain in length from north to south 350 feet or thereabouts and in breadth at the north end 80 feet and continuing of the same breadth in length 250 feet and at the south end containing in breadth 92 feet and so continueth of the same breadth in length 100 feet to the upper end thereof'. This describes part of the land sold to Robert Brooke's widow, Winefrith, in 1702. Unluckily the dimensions given in rods do not altogether tie up with those in feet. Plot (1) is said to measure 27 rods on the west (Mount Sion) side and 27 rods works out at 445½ feet as compared with the 350 quoted in feet. If we take the other side of the strip, said to be 23 rods, we get 379½ feet – a bit nearer the mark; but I am afraid we shall have to content ourselves with the qualification 'or thereabouts'. I do not think anyway that there can be any doubt about the piece of land in question. I am sitting in it at this moment and feel it in my bones! The

Ordnance Survey 1/500 Map measures 10 inches from the High Street corner to the boundary of no 25 Mount Sion which multiplied by 500 results in 416 feet 8 inches – say 350 feet or thereabouts!

Plot (4) is a bit of a puzzle but, since it is outside my area, I shall not concern myself. Plot (3) however is clearly my concern and has its puzzling features. The northern boundary (where are a bank and ditch), judged from its position, must be the boundary between the sites of Fairlawn and Eden House; whereas the list of leases shows that Henry Adams leased land on 10 December 1689 which from other evidence was the site of Fairlawn House – see chapter 24. It seems therefore that Adams (assuming it is the same man!) was sub-leasing a large area of land alongside the house he built in about 1690 and this land later became the site of Eden House with its extensive meadow behind. Chapter 20 deals with Eden House. Another puzzling thing is the small area marked with the numbers 6 and 10; this seems to have been separated from the area behind by a dotted line later ruled over. To the west is said to be Waterdown Forest which covered a huge area but here presumably refers to land down the hill on the other side of what is now Cumberland Walk which was the limit of South Frith Manor land. The Grom stream, a little further on, marking the Kent and Sussex boundary, might have been thought to define the manor boundary but in fact the Earl of Abergavenny owned a strip of land on the Kent side of the stream. In the other two directions, south and east, lay land demised to Edward Martin or 'intended for a way' – I have no information about this but, in any case, all the land partitioned by Brooke and Constable, except two strips sold by the Earl of Buckingham in 1702, fell into the lap of John Brett in 1715 as we shall see in chapter 4. This included the field or fields marked 'Moyce' (with a narrow strip for access from the road) and the plot marked Constable on the other side of the road from the Bowling Green on which Forest Prospect (Ivy Chimneys) and Brunswick House were built – see chapters 20 and 21. Down the hill from the Fairlawn House plot, leased to Henry Adams in 1689, came another lot leased on the same day – 10 December 1689 – to Edward Allen; but all this and the leasing of Chapel Place has already been considered at the end of chapter 1.

In the Little Mount Sion area meanwhile some renegotiation was going on. Philip Seale was not one of the original lessees but he built two lodging houses on one of which he started paying rates in May 1689 and on the other in April 1694. These were sited partly on the land sub-leased by Brooke and Constable to Thomas Moyce and partly on the adjoining two cricket-pitch-wide strip let to Edward Martin. The present lower length of Little Mount Sion was a service road between the two sites and on the evidence of the chart was allotted to the Moyce strip. Philip Seale must already have had an arrangement with Moyce but when the opportunity came up in 1702 le leaped in and bought the land from the Earl of Buckingham. He then took a slice of Martin land to build his second house and diverted the course of Little Mount Sion – but this story is told more fully in chapter 13.

Chapter 3

The Whimsical Landlord

Around 1690 much was happening up the Mount Sion hillside. Let's start right at the top of Edward Martin's strip. He had built his two houses, Upper and Lower, at the bottom of his eight-rod strip and I imagine thought that was enough personal involvement. So he let someone else sublease a plot at the top end. That someone was Nicholas Wood, a fellmonger and glove maker; and he built a typical large lodging house which later took the name Burlington House; but the land he rented extended almost half way down the hill as far as what is now the *Grove Tavern* and this introduces one of the stories, anecdotes, myths or legends of Mount Sion. How did Mount Sion acquire its name? Well, Benge Burr who published the first history of the town in 1766 and Jasper Sprange who published his first guide in 1780 both have a story about an alehouse on Mount Sion. Benge Burr's story runs: 'One of the first houses built upon this hill was an alehouse, to which the whimsical landlord, whose name was Mathews, affixed the sign of Mount-Sion, from whence the name of the hill is derived.' Sprange's story (see left) is identical except that he names the landlord 'Jordan'. Now the Poor Rate for the *Grove Tavern* can be traced back as far as a certain Jo Jordan in May 1689 and contains, from 1728 to 1749, the name 'Mathews' also. I therefore conclude that there is at least some truth in the story but it does not of course tell us why the landlord chose the name 'Mount Sion' nor whether this happened after the name had already become current or whether the whimsical man was the originator. There is no contemporary evidence on the 'Naming of the Mounts' (Ephraim, Pleasant and Sion) but the generally accepted

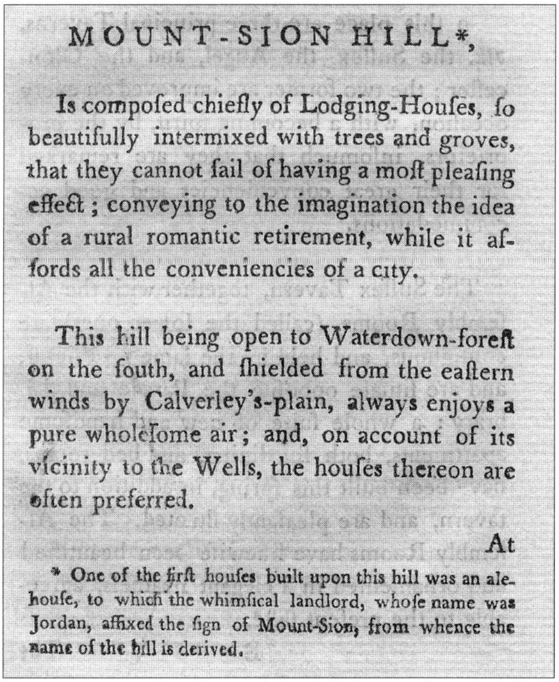

MOUNT-SION HILL*,

Is compoſed chiefly of Lodging-Houſes, ſo beautifully intermixed with trees and groves, that they cannot fail of having a moſt pleaſing effect; conveying to the imagination the idea of a rural romantic retirement, while it affords all the conveniencies of a city.

This hill being open to Waterdown-foreſt on the ſouth, and ſhielded from the eaſtern winds by Calverley's-plain, always enjoys a pure wholeſome air; and, on account of its vicinity to the Wells, the houſes thereon are often preferred.

At

* One of the firſt houſes built upon this hill was an alehouſe, to which the whimſical landlord, whoſe name was Jordan, affixed the ſign of Mount-Sion, from whence the name of the hill is derived.

Extract from Sprange Guide *1780*

theory assigns it to the Civil War period and the biblical inspiration of Puritan soldiers. If this is true then Jordan the landlord was following a tradition of some forty years, predating the development of the 'Mounts'. It would indeed be remarkable if the landlord had invented the name some five years only after the leasing out of the barren heath of Inhams.

Around 1689 and 1690 a notable blossoming occurred at the top of the hill. Rates began to be paid in November 1690 by Mr Ashenhurst or Mr Reynolds 'for a new house and Bowling Alley'. Who Reynolds was I do not know but Thomas Ashenhurst was not exactly a newcomer to the Tunbridge Wells scene. According to Christopher Chalklin, he built many of the shops which were erected after the fire on the Pantiles in 1687. They included the Royal Oak Lottery, the hazard or playroom, seven shops on the Upper Walk and ten butchers' shops in the row opposite ... and about 1700 Ashenhurst was by far the largest tenant on the Walks, paying £115 out of a total rental of £350. I suspect therefore that Mr Ashenhurst was chiefly behind this new venture, although it has to be said that the idea of a bowling green was obviously there from the very beginning as the site was fenced in for the purpose by late 1686, as the Partition Plan text tells us. At the same time a number of houses sprang up round the Bowling Green or site of the Bowling Green: firstly, the house now called Ivy Chimneys but for a long time called Forest Prospect; secondly, its neighbour the old Brunswick House; thirdly, Mansfield house, no 29 Mount Sion; and fourthly, Murray House demolished not so long ago. Eden House might be thought to have been one of them but was not built until about 1734. There is, however, the question of the new house that went with the Bowling Alley in 1690. I think this must refer to the building shown on the Bowra plan as the 'Ballroom'. As will be discussed in much more detail in chapter 10, Ashenhurst built his 'Great House' (Berkeley Place) around 1699 and then had two houses, one of which I think must have been the ballroom which was therefore a lodging house as well as ballroom. Behind the ballroom to the north-east was Nicholas Wood's Burlington House and alongside it, where Miles' workshop now is, a pub called the *Blue Anchor* appeared whose landlord Hawkins was married to one of Nicholas Wood's daughters. The other pub, the *Compasses*, between Burlington House and the Grove, was in Mercer territory and probably opened about 1700. Across the road, which led to Pembury, completing the circle round the Bowling Green, a house appears on the Bowra plan labelled 'Wid Fry' but this was not built until about 1710.

The Widow Fry does, however, appear as the first rate payer in 1694 for one more house which completes the 17th-century picture of Mount Sion: nos 23-25, the house now dubiously named after Nash the Master of Ceremonies of half a century later. Caxton House just below, nos 19-21, was not to be built, however, for another thirty years. Visitors to the Wells were to remark on the rustic nature of the housing, scattered haphazard among trees, orchards and gardens; but how much gardening had been done by the end of the century and how much of the barren heath still remained is a matter of speculation – possibly more heath than might be thought. For a 1780s view see the extract from Sprange reproduced above. We must imagine, therefore, this semi-tamed wilderness dominated by the tall trees of the Grove with the brand-new sparkling Bowling Green alongside it at the top of the hill, encircled by its necklace of new houses, and its turf, described by Count Grammont (see chapter 19) as 'more soft and smooth than the finest carpet in the world' ... but it may have taken a few more years for it to reach this level of perfection! Halfway down the hill we find Philip Seale's two houses and several large houses on either side of Mount Sion Road and then a line of houses along the High Street looking down towards the Common. And everywhere during the summer season a bustle of people and coaches and horses. For we must not forget the horses ... and the accommodation which they required. Besides the lodging houses there must have been as many if not more blocks of stables and coach houses – and certainly Frog Lane, whether spalled then or more probably not, served as the back service road for the big houses on Mount Sion.

One place, however, on the extreme edge of our fuzzy boundary was already well established by the end of the 17th century: the Chapel of King Charles the Martyr which was first opened in 1676. Around it there had been some development perhaps from an even earlier date associated with John Wyborne as mentioned on page 13 of the previous chapter. He may well have been around from 1660 if he is indeed the subject of one of the first petitions received by the restored House of Lords in 1660. It came from 'inhabitants of Bidborough, Southborne [*sic*] and Rusthall in Kent, and other places thereabouts'. 'The wells called Tunbridge Wells,' it stated, 'have been much frequented for fifty years and upwards by many of the nobility, gentry, and others who have found much benefit by drinking the waters, and the petitioners, and many hundreds of poor people have gained a livelihood thereby, and it hath always been free for the poor women to dip and give the waters without restraint, and great charge was bestowed by noble persons to set a marble cistern in the well, and to pave it and rail it round'; but John Wybarne, a saddler, 'for by ends to himself hath lately digged up the cistern and paving stones and carried them away, and hath cut down some of the birches set in a walk there for shadow by those who frequented the wells, and doth threaten to cut down the rest and dig the rails about the wells, and fill them up unless he may have the ordering and disposing of the water, though the same stand in the highway at the end of a common.' Their Lordships referred the case to the justices to sort out the facts, but ordered that 'the Wells be put into the same order as they were formerly, for a public good.' Whether the cantankerous saddler was the same man as the South Frith tenant is not proven, but I suspect he was.

The subscription boards which can still be seen hanging by the staircases to the Chapel galleries testify to the presence of John Wybourne at the time of building. There are actually four entries on the subscription board in the south gallery which refer to John Wibourn and the exact wording, so far as I can read it, runs as follows:

(1)	Paid John Wibourn for his shedd etc. standing on the ground where the Church was to be built –	£4/-/-
(2)	Paid a bricklayer [on twice?] for making a dreyn for Wibourn's water that would otherwise have annoyed the work –	£5/3/-
(3)	Paid John Wibourn at several times for several jobbs for removing his sewer from the chapel ground and the ground upon which the chapel is extended and for his consent to extend it and set the pallisadoes on his ground and removing his house of office that was offensive to the passage and ceiling under the ante-gallery –	£13/2/-
(4)	Paid John Wibourn for his service and attendance as sexton –	£1/10/-

This shows beyond doubt that the shed if nothing else was there before the Chapel; but I am sure there was rather more than that. Since the story of Mount Sion is to some extent tangled with that of Wybourne's Brewhouse a little more attention needs to be paid to Wybourne's activities.

To summarise the evidence, we find, from the Chancery case, that John Wybourne seems to have had, at one time or another, somewhere near the site of the Chapel, a shed, several messuages or tenements formerly one, a house of office, a dwelling house, a barn, a brewhouse, a building later used as a shop and the tenements which he seems to have insisted must remain under the ante-gallery of the church. The 'house of office' seems to have been part of these tenements but it got in the way of the 'passage and ceiling' under the ante-gallery and had to be removed for that reason. My interpretation is that it got in the way rather than that it was offensive because of the smell – although smell I am sure there must have been. What can be said about all these buildings? Where were they and what happened to them? Well, I'm really only guessing but this is what I think.

At least we can be certain where the shed was because it had to be pulled down to make way for the original chapel building; and the house of office was part of the tenements under the ante-gallery. I am inclined to think that the 'several messuages or tenements formerly one messuage tenement or house situate … near … Tunbridge Wells Chapel …' (see later) and the 'tenements under the ante-gallery' are one and the same. If so, the whole lot was located in a rough area behind the present altar and including perhaps the path and steps leading past the old boys' school or present 'Gracelands' restaurant. A bit more about this later on. The building which became a shop was I guess in the Hall's Bookshop area. The barn might have been anywhere but the brewhouse was the immediate cause of the dispute between the Earl of Buckingham and his steward which led to the Chancery case. Did the site of the former brewhouse include the land on which the *Angel Inn* was built in 1690? That was the essence of the quarrel. The *Angel* of course later became the *Kentish Royal* which was demolished in 1878 and replaced by the present Kentish Mansions – see chapter 26. Wybourne's Brewhouse must have been somewhere around that area then. We are left only with the dwelling house. Near the beginning of Thomas Weller's 'Several Answers' in the Chancery case occurs the passage '... about the year of our Lord 1689 ... the said Viscountess had contracted to lett unto John Brett of St Clement Dane Apothecary a dwelling house then built upon part of the same Inhams by one John Wyborne...' This suggests to me that John Wybourne built it after the Chapel was built. Anyway, I'm pretty sure that it was the boarding house which later came to be called Chapel House – and a substantial building it was too. You can see it on Kip's engraving – on the first page of chapter 26 which goes into the topic in more detail.

Shortly after the building of the Chapel therefore, in the latter 1670s, we may imagine the Mount Sion hillside as bare and barren as ever except for the tall crown of Inhams Bush and perhaps a field of wheat and a plot of hemp on the lower slopes – and at the bottom the brand new chapel, smaller than now and without its later cupola, but surrounded by an untidy clutch of rustic buildings – the tenements under the ante-gallery scarcely visible, a shop and a brewhouse. Around 1680 new lodging houses were being constructed on the Mount Ephraim ridge above the common; in 1682 Mr 'Golden' Neale became Lord of the Manor of Rusthall; at some stage, later rather than sooner I think, John Wybourne started building his lodging house at the back of the Chapel and then in 1684 Thomas Weller with his minions marking out the barren heath heralded the biggest change of all, the first 50-year leases of November that year. John Wybourne is not recorded as one of these lessees but he obviously had some arrangement with the landowner. One of the early lessees was Thomas Neale who took a lease for 50 years on 10 February 1685/6 of four largish plots of land totalling 24 acres plus a small slip measuring two rods by eight rods. Then about 1689 John Wybourne died and his holding in the Chapel Place area was apparently transferred to John Brett by a lease for 46 years dated 4 February 1689/90. The odd thing was that Neale's two by eight rod slip was in the Chapel Place area and might have been thought to be part of Wybourne's holding in 1686.

For a description (a map or plan would of course have been helpful!) of the two by eight rod slip and of the land leased to Brett we can go to the Chancery case of 1708 which carefully listed all the South Frith land which had been leased but not sold at the time. The slip of land first: 'one other small piece or slip of land likewise part of the same Inhams and being in breadth Thirty Two feet and in length eight rodds and bounding to the Bishops Down towards the north to another way and a bridge there lately [made?] towards the east to a parcel of land heretofore a hemp plot towards the south and to a shed or building there late built by John Wybourne now standing and used for a shop towards the west'. The 32-foot dimension is elsewhere given as 33 feet or two rods and this makes better sense since two rods is 33 feet ... and incidentally 66 feet is 22 yards is one cricket pitch which is useful for measurement by eye. If you now go down to the London Road at the bottom of Mount Sion, stand at the corner looking towards the

Chapel and lay out two imaginary cricket pitches you will find you have the site of the *Angel Inn* or *Royal Kentish Hotel*. Better still, look at a large scale Ordnance Survey map and you will find that a rectangle of 132 by 33 feet overlays the hotel site very neatly, as I have tried to illustrate on the map below. I have worked out the dimensions on a scale copy of the map and transferred them by eye to the non-scale version above. The long dimension fit is remarkably close; the short one not so close because, I guess, of changes to the rear of the hotel over the centuries. Does the description fit? If we take the top of the map to be north (north-west would be more accurate), then the Common of Bishops Down is certainly in that direction – so far so good. The other boundaries are more problematic but I interpret them to mean that to the south is unused land (heretofore a hemp plot) which could indicate the future site of Bedford Place/Walmer House; to the west

Ordnance Survey 1866 1/500. NOT TO SCALE

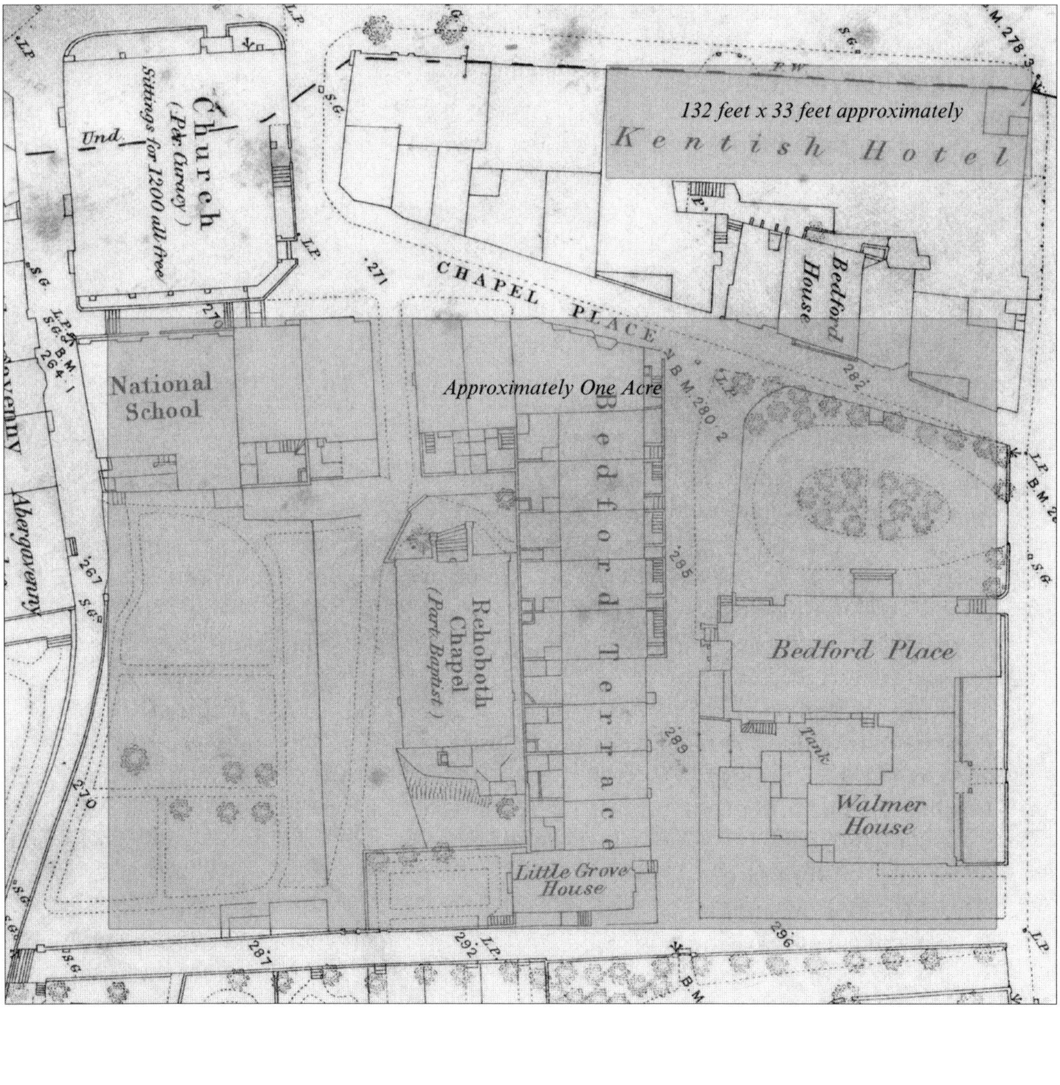

is a shed used by John Wybourne as a shop (in the Hall's Bookshop area); while to the east is the bottom of Mount Sion and surprisingly a bridge lately made. We know that there was a bridge over the Grom Stream near the Chapel but a bridge over Mount Sion or the London Road is something new. On the other hand the Barrow map of 1808 does show a stream running from the lake in the Calverley Grounds, down Vale Road (hence the name) and joining the Grom presumably somewhere near the Chapel; and it may at this early period have needed bridging near the bottom of Mount Sion. Taking then the map and the description into account, I am reasonably happy that I have located Thomas Neale's two by eight rod slip. There is another description from a document of 1710 which does not alter the situation much but should be noted. 'All that small slip or parcel of land containing in length 8 rodds and in breadth 33 feet heretofore parcel of the Inhams demised to Thomas Neale Esquire together with divers other lands at the rent of 18 pounds per annum and whereas tenements stables and buildings are since erected by the said Thomas Weller and the assigns of the said Thomas Neale and all the building and yard garden and backsides thereunto belonging and all the ground on the backside of the said buildings unto a new way there late laid out which said small slip or parcel of ground doth bound to Bishops Down towards the north to the said new way towards the south to a way or lane where a shed formerly stood towards the west and to a new way there late laid out towards the east.' This does not change the situation much: the bridge has disappeared and to the south is not the hemp plot but what I have called the Chapel Place 'street' which of course continues as the 'New way from the Wells to Southborough' or High Street; and Wybourne's shed has become a lane.

What about the land leased to John Brett in 1689/90? There is very little to help us here except the description and mention of an area of one acre. This again is from the Chancery case of 1708: 'severall messuages [or?] tenements formerly one messuage tenement or house situate and being in the parish of Tonbridge in Kent near the Chappel there called Tunbridge Wells Chappel And also the piece or parcell of ground in Tonbridge aforesaid whereon the said messuage or house was [situated?] and being containing by estimation [one?] acre or thereabouts and the barne standing thereon which said messuage or house and the said piece or parcell of ground whereon the same was situate are standing and being between the said chapel and the way leading from the said chapel to the Bowling Green there [on the?] other part on the north and certain lands or ground heretofore in the tenure or reputed to be tenure of Sir Thomas Fitch on the south or south east and the lands of the Lord Bergavenny on the west and the way leading from the Bowling Green to the Common there on the east or north east and also all that [piece of ground?] whereon the Wyburns Brewhouse formerly stood situate lying and being in Tonbridge aforesaid between the said way leading from the said chapel to the Bowling Green on the south or south west and the Common there in part and a house or stable in the tenure of [Mr?] Neale in other part and [Mr?] Wellers stable there in on the part on the part [sic] of the north and [Mr Reeves?]

house and yard on the west or south west and the said way leading from the said Bowling Green to the Common there on the east or north east'.

There are two plots here: the one-acre piece and the site of Wybourne's former brewhouse. Let's start with the one-acre piece. On the Ordnance Survey map on page 24 I have indicated an area of roughly one acre (by my calculation) and located it speculatively within the general Chapel Place area. It is described as the site of a house (sub-divided subsequently) near the Chapel and of a barn. It is between the Chapel and the road or path to the north which leads from the Chapel to the Bowling Green. I take this to be what I call the 'street' of Chapel Place – see below for a 19th-century view. To reach the Bowling Green you would of course have to go to the end of the 'street' and then turn right up the hill. To the south would have been the grounds of Jerningham House which might have had something to do with Sir Thomas Fitch but if so I do not know what. Abergavenny land would naturally lie to the 'west' and on the east would be Mount Sion which could be described as leading from the Bowling Green to the Common at the bottom of the hill. If all this very speculative interpretation is accepted the remaining problem is to establish where Wybourne's Brewhouse formerly stood.

If we look again at the map on page 24 there is evidently only one place left unaccounted for: the area between the two by eight rod strip and the Chapel. Does this fit the description? Well, the 'street' of Chapel Place is certainly on the south or south-west but on the other (north) side are, by my interpretation of the wording, partly the Common (which makes sense), partly Mr Neale's house or stable and partly Mr Weller's stable This suggests that the short London Road frontage as far as the two by eight rod slip is partly vacant (fronting the Common) and partly occupied by the buildings of Neale and Weller and the brewhouse must therefore have been behind these buildings – all very cramped but not impossible. Mr Reeves must be the barber Edmund Reeves whom we meet again on page 35 but I have no other

Chapel Place 'street' in about 1866

information about him; a house on the west or south-west, however, must have been on the other side of the 'street' roughly where the Delves' butcher's shop used to be and the florist recently was. Finally Mount Sion itself (the way from the Bowling Green to the Common) is said to be on the east or north-east. So it is – but some distance away. All in all this is rather speculative and unsatisfactory. I have tried to be specific and definite; but may be wrong. There is in any case a new complication to be faced – the Neale and Weller stables!

The story can be told in the words of Thomas Weller in his answers to the Earl's Chancery complaint: 'And the said Viscountess did sometimes by herselfe make contracts with severall persons to lett them parts of the said land to build upon and in particular she did contract with Thomas Neale Esquire to demise unto him part of the said land called Inhams to build upon (Viz) one parcell then lately a wheat gratten containing by estimation 4 acres and one other parcell adjoining to the same containing likewise by estimation 4 acres Except certaine ways to be there laid out And also one other piece or parcell of rough ground containing by estimation 12 acres and also one other piece containing by estimation 4 acres through which a convenient way was to goo And also one other small slip or piece of land likewise part of the same Inhams being in breadth 33 foot and in length 8 rodds bounding to Bishopps Downe And the said Viscountess did acquaint this defendant with such contract and directed him to cause a lease to be made thereof accordingly and in pursuance of such directions this defendant did by advice of the Counsell of the said Viscountess cause a lease to be drawn accordingly and the same was engrossed and executed by the said Viscountess and the said Sir Thomas Meeres joined with her in the same lease to the said Thomas Neale to hold from Michaelmas in the year 1685 for 50 years at the yearly rent of 18 pounds and under certain covenants by them agreed upon and in the said lease expressed And the said Thomas Neale did some time after goo about to build upon some part of the said premises where [when?] demised as aforesaid and did proferr to lett the defendant one halfe part of the said slip to build upon and this defendant being willing to encourage the building upon the said land believing the same would be to the great advancement of the value thereof and to the advantage of the said Viscountess did take a lease of one halfe part of the same slip or piece of land of the said Thomas Neale to hold for the residue of the terme which the said Thomas Neale had thereon And this defendant did build a stable and other buildings upon some part thereof and did expend very considerable sums of money in building and improving thereof and did enjoy the same peaceably for severall years'.

We are not told when this building on the two by eight rod slip took place but 1686 or '87 would be a fair guess. When John Brett was given his lease in February 1689/90 therefore the buildings were already in place and the description of the site of Wybourne's brewhouse would take account of this fact; so that Neale's house or stable and Weller's stable abutting on the north are in all probability located on the two by eight rod slip. This could mean that the site of Wybourne's brewhouse lay partly between the two by eight rod slip and the Chapel Place 'street' and extended possibly as far as Mount Sion in that direction and in the other direction as far as the Chapel including a frontage on the London Road. This would satisfy the wording 'abutting to the north partly on the Common and partly on Neale's house or stable and partly on Weller's stable'. Mr Reeve's house could then perhaps be allowed space where Hall's Bookshop and the estate agents office (old Lloyds Bank) now are. A further advantage of this interpretation is that it places the eastern abuttal on Mount Sion where the description says it should be.

Let us see if this interpretation is consistent with the next stages in the story. Some time evidently before February 1689/90 Thomas Weller was instructed by the Countess to draw up a lease to John Brett, apothecary of St Clement Dane, from her and Sir Thomas Meeres and he accordingly made a draft and sent it to Martin Folks, Counsel for the lessors. Thomas Weller then learned, how we are not told, that John Brett had got a lease engrossd and sealed and he was shown this document by John Brett; but it did not accord with Thomas Weller's draft and the two by eight rod slip of land was included. John Brett said (all innocent, you may suppose) that the lease had been made by Martin Folks. When Weller approached Folks he was told that the lease had been drawn by Folks' clerk in accordance with a draft brought by Brett who said it had been made by Weller. Folks then showed the draft to Weller who (of course) discovered that the handwriting was not his and the slip of land was inserted. (Did Thomas Weller write out his own legal documents?) Curiously, Thomas Weller does not seem to have taken the matter any further. We must bear in mind that this sequence of events is as reported by Thomas Weller himself; and also perhaps that communications were not quite as quick and easy as they are today. No picking up the telephone or sending an email! You had to saddle up your horse and ride, in whatever weather, for hours to reach London or one hour at least from Tonbridge to the Wells. It should also be remembered that we are dealing with testimony given in 1708 about events of some twenty years before.

Sometime after, according to Thomas Weller,

> some workmen of the said Brett went about to build upon the said slip of land and said they were imployed by the said Brett soe to doe and that they intended to build upon the wall of this defendants stable then there built by this defendant which he this defendant forbad then to doe And he this defendant was afterwards informed that some person had erected some buildings upon some part of that part of the said slip which was letten to this defendant by the said Mr Neale and that the said Mr Brett had contracted with the said Neale for the residue of the said slip of land which was demised to this defendant And some of the workmen of the said Brett telling this defendant that in case any part of the said building were erected upon that part of the said slip which this defendant had a lease of that the said Mr Brett would give this defendant satisfaction for it and that it being some distance from this defendants stable there it could not be much prejudiciall to this defendant and using many words to persuade this defendant that the said erected building was not erected to interrupt this defendant in the enjoyment of what the said Mr Neale had

> letten to him and this defendant hoping that the said Brett would satisfy this defendant for what injury he had done this defendant did not interrupt the said Brett in the erecting the said building.

A case perhaps of Thomas Weller opting for the easy life?

As noted above, Thomas Weller had sub-leased half the slip of land which was leased to Thomas Neale and had built a stable on his half; but at some stage (see the paragraph above), presumably when he sold the Manor in 1689 or '90, Thomas Neale seems to have come to some arrangement with John Brett regarding the other half – or both halves. It is worth pointing out that John Brett, although by profession a mere apothecary, had good connections and was a London man with an address in Essex Street off the Strand. His father was a Colonel and his sister had in 1663 married Dr Hugh Chamberlen of the family of obstetricians who had invented the 'Chamberlen forceps' – a family secret kept so strictly that in the 18th century the thing had to be re-invented and the original box of tricks was only discovered in 1813 hidden under the floorboards of the old family home in Essex! In 1688 Dr Hugh was supposed to be attending the labour of James II's queen, Mary of Modena, – but the wretched woman started too soon and the doctor was away on another call at Chatham – and so he was not able to say whether the baby boy had arrived in the usual way or had been smuggled into the room in a warming-pan! There were of course scores of other people milling around but that did not prevent the rumour spreading – much to the delight of the anti-Catholics and WillemanMary and all that. So if John Brett's brother-in-law had been where he should have been on 10 June 1688, who knows? We might have had a Stuart on the throne today! I ask you, gentle reader, what more in the way of historical notoriety does Mount Sion want? The moral of this tale is that I reckon John Brett and Thomas Neale could well have talked to each other on level terms and perhaps they did. Incidentally, I note from an appendix to John Fuller's splendid *New History of the Church of King Charles the Martyr* that Dr Hugh was a Fellow of the Royal Society and subscribed towards the building of the Chapel between 1676 and 1684. I suppose this means he actually came to the Wells – and I wonder whether he brought his brother-in-law with him or indeed whether his brother-in -law was not already well known round the chalybeate spring.

What John Brett was up to was building the *Angel Inn*. The 46-year lease to John Brett of the Chapel Place block, John Wybourne's old stamping ground, was completed despite its dubious origins and bore the date 4 February 1689/90. Brett was to pay £26 for the first five years and £27 per annum thereafter by equal portions at Midsummer and Christmas. No time seems to have been wasted in building the new inn and in 1691 Poor Rate began to be paid by 'Mr Pottinger for Mr Bretts new house' and from 1692 to 1694 payment was recorded from 'Mr Brett for the Angell'. Who Pottinger was I do not know; perhaps the first landlord? There are a couple of passages in the Chancery record dealing with the construction of the *Angel*. One passage was quoted above, about Brett forbidding workmen to build on the wall of his stable. The other suffers from the condition of the document held at the Public Records Office. Tears, creases and interlinings, not to mention the generally dirty state of the parchment, made a complete transcription impossible for me. Others, more expert, might have better luck. The Earl of Buckingham is concluding his 'Complaint' by asking the court to resolve a number of specific questions, one of which is whether Thomas Weller 'did not make the workman Henry Heath or any other to take the foundation of the Angell [illegible.........] ground of Wyburns Brewhouse adjoining to his stable and remove the same six foot [further?] from the said Bretts ground declaring that he would have a [safe?] way between them and [illegible.........] the workmane removed it as it now stands and to whom the said way doth belong'. What seems to have happened is that Henry Heath and his mates intended or even started to build a wall butted against a wall of Weller's stable. Whether this was a brick wall we are not told. Anyhow Thomas Weller did bestir himself sufficiently to insist ('declaring that he would have a safe way between them') that a gap of six feet should be left between the two buildings, so that the question remained to whom the six-foot gap belonged. The question that concerns us is where this interface fits on the map – and where if anywhere Wybourne's brewhouse fits in. I am assuming of course that the *Angel Inn* was built on the two by eight rod slip and that Weller's stable would have been built on one end or other of the site, not the middle. The map on page 24 shows the semicircular entrance porch at the Chapel end of the *Kentish Hotel* and this is where the main part of the hotel always was, so that Weller's stable was presumably at the Mount Sion end and the original *Angel Inn* did not extend that far. Nineteenth-century photographic evidence tends to confirm this. The photograph below, taken during the time of landlord J. Braby from 1872 to 1874 (see chapter

Royal Kentish Hotel 1872-74

26) shows, of course, the refurbished hotel; but the lower building labelled 'Hot and Cold Baths' might conceivably be where Weller's stable used to be.

The reference to Wybourne's brewhouse is obscure owing to gaps in the Chancery document and further doubt is thrown by this passage from Thomas Weller's answer: 'And this defendant doth further say that if the brewhouse mentioned in the Complainants said bill were in or att any other place than the said slip demised to Thomas Neale and not in the same slip this defendant doth not clayme anything in the same but if the same be within the said slip and be letten to the said Brett together with other lands then the same was inserted by the said Brett without the knowledge of this defendant and contrary to the draught thereof made'. In other words there seems to have been some doubt whether the brewhouse site and the two by eight slip might not have overlapped. Further uncertainty is revealed in the Earl of Buckingham's complaint: ' … Thomas Weller pretended that your Orator John Earl of Buckingham for forty pounds which he never received had conveyed to some person the said piece of ground whereon Wyburns Brewhouse formerly stood but that he could not find the counterpart of the conveyance and that part of the said piece of ground was comprehended in the said lease to Neale as part of the said parcel of 33 foot and 8 rodds therein mentioned and that the said Neale had lett part of the said 33 foot and 8 rodds to the said Thomas …' That is to say, if I understand correctly, that part of the brewhouse site was contained in the two by eight rod slip – meaning that the three parcels were not entirely distinct from each other. This, however, is Thomas Weller's story according to the Earl. A few words later the Earl goes on to say that 'in truth the said piece of ground whereon Wyburns Brewhouse formerly stood …' but unfortunately a tear in the document prevents us knowing the truth – although the next word after the tear seems to be 'Brett' and the text continues 'whose rent of 27 pounds per annum and also all the said rent of 18 pounds per annum your Orator hath constantly received …' and the obvious supposition is that truly the brewhouse site was part of Brett's lease and therefore not contained wholly or partially in Neale's two by eight rod slip. The Earl goes on to say that Thomas Weller was never in possession of the said piece of ground 'but hath for about twenty years suffered the said Brett quietly to enjoy the same'. Thomas Weller, of course, foresaw this line of attack and countered it, as we have seen, by saying that he had not wanted to make a fuss and trusted that he would be recompensed in the end. Elsewhere, towards the end of his answer, Thomas Weller says that 'Mr Bretts workmen did intend to build upon or very near unto the wall of this defendant's stable which this defendant did forbid them to doe but by what words this defendant doth not remember it being near twenty years since and saith that he believeth the ground by this defendant hired of Mr Neale doth extend further than the stable by him built and into the house there built by Mr Brett and hopes he may be at liberty to recover his right thereunto'. All this, however, is running ahead of the story and for the moment, as the last years of the 17th century pass by, we can leave John Brett and Thomas Weller in quiet enjoyment side by side at the bottom of the hill of their respective *Angel Inn* and stable.

Chapter 4

From Insolvency to Foreclosure

In or around the first year of the 18th century the Viscountess Purbeck, the former Lady Muskerry nicknamed the 'Princess of Babylon', died. She had found a little gold mine in the far corner of her South Frith Manor but it does not seem to have done her finances a lot of good. Perhaps her latest husband was to blame. He was Beau Feilding, her third and worst, who went on to distinguish himself by a bigamous marriage to the Merry Monarch's old mistress, the Duchess of Cleveland. Lady Purbeck left one son by her second marriage and he inherited her estate, mortgages and all. He liked to call himself John Earl of Buckingham, but he was not really entitled because of an illegitimacy in his father's pedigree so that he is often called the *soi-disant* Earl of Buckingham. I shall accord him the title for the sake of convenience and, as we have seen already, he used it throughout the Chancery Court proceedings. Unfortunately, title or not, he seems to have inspired little confidence in his financial backers.

About 1700 he acquainted his Steward, Thomas Weller, 'that the mortgagees to whom the said estate was engaged for great sums of money were very pressing for their money and had gotten or intended to get a decree to bar him the said Earl of his equity of redemption of the same and to sell the estate'. The Earl of Buckingham, therefore, decided to sell the whole estate and pay off the mortgages and told his steward to have everything surveyed and valued. The estate was then offered for sale as a whole and negotiations were held with several prospective buyers but agreement could not be reached. The Earl of Buckingham then told Thomas Weller that he would sell in parcels 'and the mortgagees being pressing for their money' the steward was directed 'to enquire for chapmen and propose the selling it in several parcels and to treat with such persons as will become purchasers about the same'. The principal mortgagee was still apparently Sir Thomas Meeres but who any others were is not revealed.

I surmise that Sir Thomas Meeres and any other mortgagees there may have been did not altogether trust the Earl of Buckingham because, instead of straightforwardly allowing him to hand over the purchase money as land was sold, a trust was set up as an intermediary, the sort of arrangement often used in cases of insolvency. Anyway, on 16 May 1701 and again on 20 November 1702 the whole estate was conveyed by Indentures Quinquapartite to Thomas Weller, Thomas Lake and George Weller in trust for the earl. The five parties to the deed of 1702 were (1) the Earl of Buckingham (2) Sir Thomas Meeres (3) Thomas Hatcher Esq. (4) Thomas Lake Esq., Thomas and George Weller and (5) Daniel Tilden and Edward Overy. Thomas Hatcher was I think acting on behalf of Sir Thomas Meeres; Thomas Lake was a lawyer of the Middle Temple; George was probably the son of Thomas Weller; Daniel Tilden was a City of London merchant and Edward Overy was dead by 1708. Tilden and Overy were, by a peculiar arrangement of the time which need not concern us now, guardians of terms of 500 years set in mortgage deeds. The three trustees were to sell so much of the estate as would be sufficient to pay all debts and convey what was left back to the Earl of Buckingham.

Most of the estate was sold during the next few years but there is no separate record. The purchasers were mainly the leaseholders themselves who could scarcely believe their luck in obtaining valuable freeholds at what were very likely bargain prices. We do know, however, something about four transactions: sales to Philip Seale and Winefrith Brooke; the Grove Trust Deed; and the Chapel Trust Deed. Reference was made above (page 15 and elsewhere) to the lease made to Robert Brooke and Richard Constable which in 1686 was partitioned. Both these men would have – indeed were probably in the middle of negotiations – bought out their leases but they died around 1700 and part of the land was sold to Brooke's widow, Winefrith, and part to the sitting sub-tenant in Little Mount Sion, the plumber Philip Seale. Both these conveyances bear the same date – 28 November 1702. It can be guessed that most of the conveyances took place about this time, The Grove and Chapel Trusts were another matter. The Chapel Trust formalised an arrangement of more than twenty years standing. The Countess had around 1676 given the site of the Chapel apparently without any documentary confirmation but the great and the good who decided these matters felt no need for it at the time. When, however, the whole of the South Frith Manor was in a state of flux and disintegration someone probably thought that loose ends should be tied and persuaded the Earl of Buckingham to do the right thing by the memory of his mother. Hence the formation of the Trust, the appointment of Trustees from among the local aristocracy and gentry and the confirming deed, a good colour copy of which hangs in the Chapel. The deed is dated 15 February 1703 and there has been some confusion over the correct interpretation of this date. As mentioned above, this is a clear case of a date before 25 March being allocated to the (according to our present way of thinking) previous year. The date is 15 February 1703/4. The Grove Trust might also be called the formalisation of a long-standing arrangement but this was even less formal than the Chapel one. The tall clump of trees called Inhams Bush might well have been leased out by the Countess in the 1680s like all the other plots on Mount Sion but the fact is that for whatever reason it was not. Perhaps the axemen were daunted by the number and size of the trees; but my guess is that it was regarded as an attraction from the start and as the houses sprung up and the visitors came and wandered around before or after their daily drink at the spring they came to love the Grove and it would have been sacrilege to cut it down. In his desperation for money the Earl might have been tempted by the value of the timber but the strength of local opinion was such that, instead, he has bathed in the gratitude of centuries for his charitable gift. The Trust Deed is dated unambiguously 20 April 1703 and the Trustees, not so exalted as for the Chapel, comprised Thomas Weller's brother Henry of Frant whom we shall meet presently, together with John Dyke esquire also of Frant, Robert Baker esquire of Rotherfield and gentleman Nicholas Fowle the younger of Wadhurst. Chapter 6 deals with the Grove in more detail.

According to Thomas Weller's story, when all possible sales had been completed, he and the Earl got together and ' upon computing the same did find it did not amount to soe much money as would pay of all the mortgages and incumbrances'. Then the Earl 'did proferr to this defendant and he this defendant did contract to purchase of the said Earl the fee of the said slip of land so let to the said Mr Neale as aforesaid and part thereof let by him to this defendant for the remainder of the said lease of 50 years being of the breadth of 33 foot and in length 8 rods and bounding to Bishops Down upon which slip of land several buildings and stables were then erected and also the said buildings and stables with the yards gardens and appurtenances thereunto belonging with such reasonable ways and passages thereunto as were then used and enjoyed therewith And this defendant did agree to give the said Earl for the purchase thereof 80 pounds'. They also agreed that a small part of Thomas Neale's rent should go to the new owner. Thomas Weller then says that he was advised (but by whom or why he does not say) that the conveyance should be made to a friend; and his brother Henry was chosen because Henry could include his brother's slip of land in a larger transaction he had to conclude with the Earl. Henry, according to his brother, paid a total of 'twelve hundred and three pounds which was all paid by the directions of the said Earl unto Sir Thomas Meeres towards discharging his mortgage upon the premises'. All the conveyances were made, says Thomas, by consent of the Earl and by advice of his counsel – a statement later disputed hotly by the Earl, as we shall see.

Things now chugged along quietly but in January 1706/07 the Earl of Buckingham acquainted Thomas Weller 'by letter' that he had 'bought a purchase' and wanted £600. How it is possible to buy anything other than a purchase bewilders me but the Court of Chancery was given no particulars and my curiosity remains unsatisfied. £600 in 1707 was worth about £100,000 today – some sum, some purchase! Where could the improvident Earl lay his hands on this much? Well, it had not escaped his notice that a small proportion of his South Frith land had not been sold; the freehold still belonged to him and could be mortgaged. The land in question consisted of the Chapel Place block and other land which had been leased to John Brett for 46 years in 1690, the considerable amount leased to Brooke and Constable less the parts of it sold in 1702 to Winefrith Brooke and Philip Seale and land leased to Thomas Neale which had been 'assigned' to Mr Young (I assume after Neale had sold the Manor of Rusthall in 1689 or '90). There were also a number of smaller pieces which remained unsold in 1707 and are listed in the court record. The Earl of Buckingham told his steward that he had agreed a loan from someone 'at or about London' and directed him to make a draft of a mortgage accordingly, which he did, inserting the Brett, Neale and Constable leases but excluding any land which was already sold – meaning of course the two by eight rod slip as well as the Brooke and Seale sales. Weller showed the draft to the earl who told him to go and see the mortgagees' counsel, Mr Thornhill, in London and show him some 'writeings' to prove title to the premises.

Mr Thornhill perused the documents and then asked for them to be left in his hands but Weller was unwilling to do this 'without the consent of the purchasers they being committed to him by the said Earl and several other persons purchasers under the same to the value of more than 20,000 pounds'. Weller offered to wait on him longer or another time so that 'he might have what tyme he pleased to peruse the same but not to part with them' out of his custody. Mr Thornhill then seemed to be 'much displeased and in a passion' and refused to discourse further about it. This story is part of Thomas Weller's testimony and, although he does not say so, I assume he took the writings home with him. He then goes on to say that sometime afterwards he was shown some papers 'tending to a conveyance of certain lands by way of mortgage' and, finding that the papers contained lands already sold, he refused to consent to the mortgage. He was in a position to refuse, it must be remembered, as one of three trustees to whom the Earl's whole estate had been conveyed in 1702 in trust for the purchasers and the Earl. Weller's refusal meant, of course, that the Earl was thwarted in getting the money for his purchase and he did not like it. In August or September 1707 John Brett and Edmund Reeves, a barber who had built a house somewhere near the Chapel (see page 26 above), came to see Thomas Weller, at the Earl's instigation I guess, and told him that the Earl had borrowed from Henry Marsh and 'sealed a mortgage' and Brett and Reeves wanted Weller to join in the mortgage. They received the expected answer: the steward was quite willing but not if lands were included which had already been sold.

In the end it seems that the mortgage deed dated 26/27 June 1707 was fully prepared but, still lacking the signatures and seals of the three trustees, could not be put into effect. The Earl now, supported I am sure by Brett and Marsh, decided to sue and 'exhibited a bill in the High Court of Chancery' – see the next page. The Earl's 'Complaint' to the Right Honourable William Lord Cowper Baron of Wingham High Chancellor of Great Britain is dated 26 January 1707/08. Depositions from the defendants were then taken, assuming my interpretation of regnal years is correct, in April 1708 in Tonbridge by three Commissioners '*Hec responsum captum fuit apud Tonbridge in Comitate Kent decimo nono die Aprilis anno regni domina nostra Anne Regina Brittaniae septimo Coram Comitationes Geo Hooper Jo Brett Riplingham'* (This answer was taken at Tonbridge in the County of Kent on the 19th day of April in the seventh year of the reign of our Sovereign Lady Anne Queen of Britain Before the Commissioners George Hooper John Brett Riplingham).

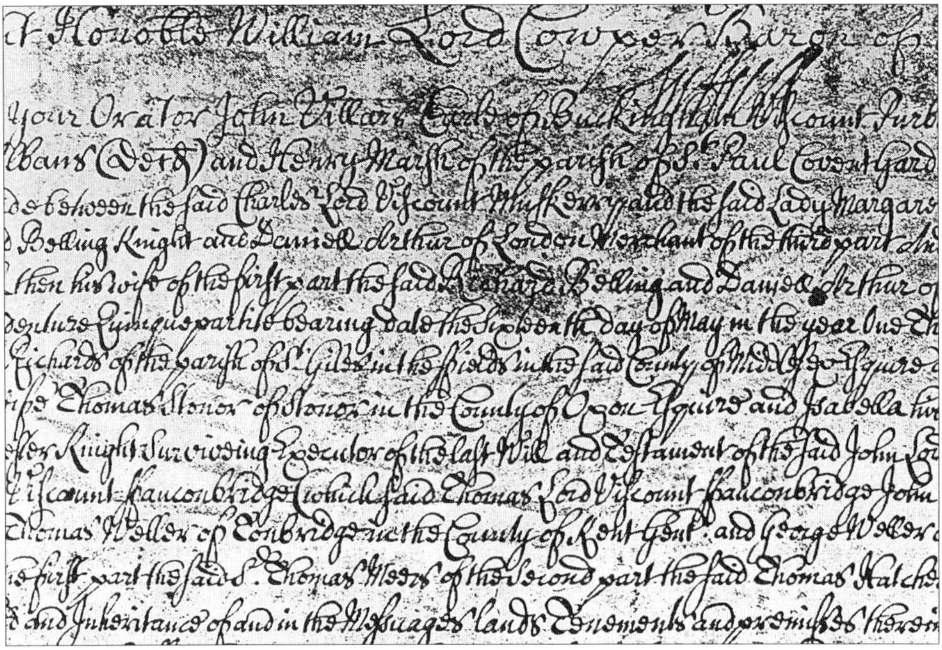
...t Honoble William Lord Cowper Baron of
your Orator John Villars Earle of Buckingham Viscount Purb...
...Barns (Dorset) and Henry Marsh of the parish of St Paul Covent Gard...
...de between the said Charles Lord Viscount Muskerry and the said Lady Margare...
...Bolling Knight and Daniel Arthur of London Merchant of the third part An...
...then his wife of the first part the said Richard Bolling and Daniel Arthur o...
...denture Quinquepartite bearing date the Sixteenth day of May in the year One Th...
Richards of the parish of St Giles in the Fields in the said County of Middlesex Esquire...
...ire Thomas Stonor of Stonor in the County of Oxon Esquire and Isabella his...
...ster Knight Surviving Executor of the last Will and Testament of the said John Lo...
Viscount Fauconbridge (which said Thomas Lord Viscount Fauconbridge John...
Thomas Weller of Tonbridge in the County of Kent Gent and George Weller...
...e first part the said Sr Thomas Stonor of the Second part the said Thomas Halche...
...and Inheritance of and in the Messuages lands Tenements and premisses thereo...

A Detail from the Opening of the Case 'Earl of Buckimgham v Thomas Weller' 1708 illustrating the style of handwriting

George Hooper was, like Thomas Weller himself, a member of the legal profession in Tonbridge. John Riplingham was, I think, a Tunbridge Wells writing master and scrivener and John Brett was, well, a party to the dispute, I should have thought, and therefore quite unsuitable. I suspect he had friends in high places. Be that as it may, the Commissioners took answers from Thomas Weller separately, then from the other two trustees Thomas Lake, the Middle Temple lawyer, and George Weller and from Daniel Tilden the trustee for the terms of 500 years (the second one, Overy, being dead) and finally from Henry Weller into whose name the 'slip of land' had been conveyed.

The case came on for hearing before the Lord High Chancellor on 1 May 1708 and essentially concerned the obstacles to completion of the mortgage with Henry Marsh. The trustees maintained quite rightly that they had no right to mortgage land already sold. Some of the land in question like the parts of the Constable lease sold to Winefrith, the widow of the leaseholder, and to Philip Seale, the sitting sub-tenant, was not in dispute. Other pieces (for instance six acres of woodland near Summerhill Park bounding to land sold to Mr Deakins and other pieces of land listed towards the end of Thomas Weller's answer) could be investigated and uncertainties resolved; but the sticking point was the two by eight rod slip of land half of which Thomas Weller had certainly sub-leased from Thomas Neale and the whole of which he said he had purchased from the Earl of Buckingham for £80 and put into his brother Henry's name. Weller admitted that 'when the said Earl did desire to see the counterpart of the indenture whereby the said slip was sold this defendant could not at that present find the same it being not in town but this defendant did afterwards when the said Earl was at Tunbridge Wells about September last procure Henry Weller the purchaser to show the said indenture under the hand and seal of the said Earl and the other persons who joined in sale thereof and the said Earl did peruse the same and said he was well satisfied therewith and that he would repay the money which he had borrowed of the other complainant and said there should be no further trouble therein'.

I must admit that I found Thomas Weller's story convincing. I have no doubt that he was capable of using his position as Manor Steward and as trustee to slant transactions in his favour on occasions – and did do so. When the dust had settled the Weller family emerged as owners of quite nice slices of land. In fact he acknowledged in evidence that he had 'at several times purchased of the said Earl several parcels of the said estate and the contracts for the same were made by the Earl himself and upon full information of the true value thereof and all paid for at the full value some 30 years purchase or more and most above and none under 20 years purchase and the said Earl was fully satisfied the purchase money for the same and had a true account of the contents of the same and hath had or may have counterparts of the conveyances thereof when he pleaseth paying for transcribing'. The Earl on the other hand was not fully satisfied that he had received true value. In his complaint he says that 'since the said sales and conveyances were made your said Orator hath discovered that the said Thomas Weller in his own and other persons names in trust for him did purchase several parts of the premises for much lower prices than the same were worth and inserted in such conveyances what parcels and words he thought fit he knowing and living near the premises and having an attorney for your said Orator and the deeds evidences and writings relating thereunto in his custody'. At the time and 'long before and ever since' Thomas Weller had been steward and manager of the estate and all this 'plainly shows his fraud and abuse on your said Orator'. Thomas himself talks of having lived 'at Tunbridge Town in Kent for more than fifty years' and been employed by the Earl and by the Lady Purbeck his mother. He was the old family man of law and as such was trusted and left to work on his own. On the other hand the *soi-disant* Earl had only just left Eton and reached his majority. There was a considerable age gap and cultural disparity. Weller was a middle-class professional used to dealing with local gentry and tradesmen; the Earl considered himself an aristocrat deserving the life-style of that privileged class. Weller would shortly retire to the village of Eridge Green; the Earl saw his life before him.

Having laboriously copied out the evidence and read and re-read it, my sympathies lay with Thomas Weller. I tended to believe his story that Lady Muskerry's counsel, Martin Folks, had used a draft lease which John Brett had brought to him, saying that it had been made by Thomas Weller. However, when Thomas got a sight of it, he found that the handwriting was not his own and that the disputed 'slip' had been inserted. I was particularly impressed by his account of the meeting in London with Henry Marsh's counsel, Thornhill, who tried to persuade Thomas to leave all the important deeds with him overnight and flew into a terrible rage when Thomas would not oblige. Moreover, it later emerged, when John Brett died, that Mr Thornhill's general clerk was sufficiently intimate with John Brett to be numbered among the 18 or so friends and relatives who received 20-shilling mourning rings – and who Henry Marsh was will emerge in a minute. My sympathies and suspicions however seem to be misplaced. The Lord High Chancellor decided in favour of the Earl of Buckingham and Henry Marsh and the slip of land had to be handed over to Henry Marsh.

Evidently the conveyance of the slip of land which Thomas Weller had been unable to find initially really did exist and was produced for the case. It was dated 28 November 1702 and appears to be a genuine conveyance from the Earl of Buckingham and the three trustees to Henry Weller of 'All that small slip or parcel of land containing in length 8 rodds and in breadth 33 feet heretofore parcell of the Inhams demised to Thomas Neale Esquire together with divers other lands at the rent of 18 pounds per annum and whereas tenements stables and buildings are since erected by the said Thomas Weller and the assigns of the said Thomas Neale and all the building and yard garden and backsides thereunto belonging and all the ground on the backside of the said buildings unto a new way there late laid out which said small slip or parcel of ground doth bound to Bishops Down towards the north to the said new way towards the south to a way or lane where a shed formerly stood towards the west and to a new way there late laid out towards the east.' However the Court noted that the 'conveyance to Henry Weller was only in trust for the use of Thomas Weller' and decided that 'the said small slip or parcel of ground was so as aforesaid bargained sold released and confirmed to the said Henry Weller by mistake and without any consideration really and bona fide paid for the same' and 'His Lordship did order and decree … that the said Thomas Weller and Henry Weller should convey the inheritance of the said slip of ground to the said Henry Marsh … subject to a redemption by the said Earl according to the said mortgage … but without prejudice to the lease made to Thomas Neale'. And so, 'in obedience to the said decree' they did, by an Indenture Tripartite dated 30 November 1710 between the Earl of Buckingham, Thomas Weller and Henry Weller and Henry Marsh of St Paul Covent Garden Middlesex laceman but there was an endorsement to the deed, incidentally signed sealed and delivered in the presence of Judah Hislop (Mr Thornhill's general clerk referred to above) and dated 9 January 1710 (i.e. 1711 New Style) which reveals John Brett acting as agent for the Earl of Buckingham. 'John Brett Agent for the within named Earl of Buckingham and Henry Marsh did declare that nothing in this Indenture contained was intended or could be construed to affect or concern Mr Neale's Lease of the slip …'. Had John Brett superseded Thomas Weller? What was he playing at? We shall see.

The Earl of Buckingham was now free to take up his loan from Henry Marsh and enjoy his purchase – and more; but there is an anomaly here which I cannot explain. The Chancery record shows that the Earl borrowed, on further charges, sums of £160, £132, £120, £188 and £188 again but the dates of these loans were respectively 29 December 1707, 2 July and 29 September 1708, 25 June 1709 and 27 June 1710. I can only suppose that the lender was certain that the Chancery judgement would be in his favour – not a very satisfactory explanation but the best I can offer. Whatever the explanation, anyway, the fact is that the Earl of Buckingham and the Lady Frances his wife (he had married his mistress Heneage by 1713 or earlier) became more and more indebted and do not seem to have made any effort to repay the interest let alone the principal. I have the impression that they never had any intention of repaying and were simply out to squeeze as much cash out of the situation as possible before Nemesis arrived – which it did in 1712. 'John Brett and James Scott exhibited their said bill in the said Court of Chancery against the said Earl of Buckingham to have satisfaction and to foreclose the Equity of Redemption of the said premises (amongst other things) which cause came to hearing on the 8th December in the 11th year of the reign of the late Queen Anne when amongst other things an account was decreed and that the said Earl should be foreclosed if he did not pay what should be reported due by the said Master Medlicott.' 1712/13 was the 11th year of Anne's reign.

But wait a minute! What about Henry Marsh? He should be exhibiting his bill against the Earl of Buckingham – not John Brett and James Scott. Scott was a London grocer; what part he was playing I do not know and he does not matter but John Brett does – here comes the twist in the tale. All along Henry Marsh the laceman of Covent Garden was merely acting as a front man for John Brett who provided the money. They had made a secret agreement in October 1710 which now came to light, making over all the mortgaged premises to John Brett. As the Court record has it: ' And whereas the money secured by the said last recited indenture was the proper money of the said John Brett and the name of the said Henry Marsh was in all the said indentures used in trust for the said John Brett and so declared by Indentures of Lease and Release bearing date the 15th and 16th October 1710 ... whereby the said Henry Marsh did grant all the said mortgaged premises unto the said John Brett his heirs and assigns.' I wonder when the Earl first learned that the man who had been acting as his agent was in fact his enemy. There was, however, by now not much he could do about it.

The Chancery Master reported that on 29 November 1714 £2102 19s. 8d. would be due on the South Frith mortgage and £276 11s. 2½d. on some other mortgage and 'by subsequent orders of the said Court the said Earl doth stand foreclosed of the Equity of Redemption of all the said mortgaged premises'. By a final settlement dated 12/13 August 1715 John Brett purchased all the mortgaged estate in return for what was owing plus the sum of £50. This is why (anticipating the story for a moment) the 1738 Bowra map and plan of Mount Sion are plastered with the name Mr Brett – not to mention Mrs Pickering his widow-to-be, for poor Mr Brett or cunning Mr Brett did not live long to enjoy his triumph.

Chapter 5

The Brett Aftermath

John Brett died on 13 November 1719 and the register of St Peter and St Paul at Tonbridge recorded the burial of 'Brett Mr John of the Wells' on the 23rd. I have not found his birth or baptism but I do know that his sister Dorothy married (you may remember) Dr Chamberlain of the forceps in 1663 and if we assume that she married in her 20s and that brother and sister were born within a few years of each other then John was well into his 70s when he died. His will reveals most of what little we know about him. One thing that was bothering him was children – or the lack of them. Now that he had all this property he wanted to leave it to his own children. His wife's name was Margaret and she was presumably younger because when he made his will in 1719 he was still hoping that she might be 'ensient or with child at my decease' and he made provision for his acquisitions to be passed on to such child 'whether Male or Female'. Let us hope that they both enjoyed the process for result there was none. Margaret was named sole executrix in the will and she wasted no time – in fact she pretty well broke the record for obtaining probate. On 16 November she hired a coach from Edward Jarrett at a cost of £2 15s. 0d. and journeyed to London. 'First things first' was her motto. The old man can always be buried later.

The will was made on 22 June only four months before John Brett's death – and incidentally witnessed by one Henry Marsh. Among his bequests was one of £20 to his brother-in-law Dr Hugh Chamberlaine and £50 to Captain Chamberlaine his nephew. Another nephew, John Brett, was named as his heir. This John Brett was a Doctor of Physic and had five children of whom the eldest, another John Brett of course, was at Charterhouse. The deceased John Brett gave gold mourning rings of the value of 20 shillings to no fewer than 18 friends and relatives amongst whom was the general clerk of Robert Thornhill who I assume was the subsequently knighted lawyer who lost his temper with Thomas Weller. Brett was generous with cash legacies, including one of £1,000 to his loving wife and £100 each to the children of Dr John Brett – and these were pretty large sums in those days; but he actually created a problem because he did not leave enough cash to fund the bequests. The £1,000 with interest was to be paid within two years 'out of my personal estate and if that shall not be sufficient out of my Real Estate' – prescient words. Apart from his land and houses in Tunbridge Wells, he had leases on two houses in London, one in Essex Street which is a turning off the Strand near the church of St Clement Danes; and the other in Petty France, a street well known nowadays in connection with passports. St Clement Danes was his parish and Essex Street was no doubt his London business premises. He left his wife the remainder of the lease on Essex Street and all the furniture and contents of the Petty France house. Essex Street incidentally was also where Dr Hugh Chamberlen lived – was Dorothy the girl next door, I wonder?

Back to our John Brett and his will. His widow was named sole executrix and she received the absolute gift of the 'New House lately finished and furnished by me near Tunbridge Wells ... now in my possession and the Stables and appurtenances with all the Goods and furniture therein and the tenement in the occupation of Jane Haley all lying near Tunbridge Wells'. 'Near Tunbridge Wells' does not mean near the (present) town but ' near the spring ('The Wells')'. I wish I knew for certain where this house was. There is some slight evidence to suggest that it was called the 'Lanthorn House' and was situated at the top of Mount Pleasant and preceded the Decimus Burton terraces which themselves were knocked down for the present Town Hall. Other persons named in the will are Mrs Adams 'my sister' (probably means sister of brother-in-law); Dawson Brett and his daughter Mary and son Dawson (must be a cousin, certainly not a brother); Mrs Constable (widow of Richard Constable, I wonder?); William Bruncker, general clerk to Robert Thornhill (as already mentioned on page 38); and rather mysteriously a certain Judah Heslopp who is left a legacy of ten pounds 'clear of all taxes and impositions whatsoever for and during the term of his natural life towards his better support and maintanance'. £10 does not seem a lot but it probably equals over £1,000 today.

John Brett was at great pains and testamentary length to ensure that his lands and houses remained intact, giving a life interest only to his nephew, then to his nephew's eldest son, then his second, third and fourth sons, then to Nathaniel Brett and his sons, then Chamberlain Brett and his sons, then his nephew's two daughters Elizabeth and Dorothy as tenants in common and their children and only finally, all else failing, the heirs and assigns of the nephew. All this was subject to the contingency (fairly remote by this time I should have thought) that his wife should be enceinte, in which case half of all his legacies was to go to such 'afterborn' child, whether male or female, together with all and singular his messuages, lands, tenements, rents and hereditaments for ever. He wished to be buried in some dry ground in the country, his funeral expenses were not to exceed £50 and he gave to the poor of the parish of St Clement Danes 50 shillings and to the poor of Tunbridge Wells and Speldhurst five pounds each.

John Brett had become in 1715 the proud possessor of the Grove field and houses, the Bowling Green and its houses, the Chapel Place block with the *Angel Inn* and some smaller pieces on Mount Sion together with several more in other parts of the town – in all, over one hundred acres of prime Tunbridge Wells land and houses; and for four years I suppose he enjoyed his new prestige. There was plenty to do looking after the property. In 1718 he was busy selling some land (later known as the Jack Woods spring and quarry – down the end of the Camden Road). The rather splendid looking 'bond' on the next page, with his signature and seal at the bottom, was one of the sale documents. His widow would complete this transaction after his death. An insight into events going on around this time can be gleaned from the record of a court case in 1752 which we shall come to in a short while.

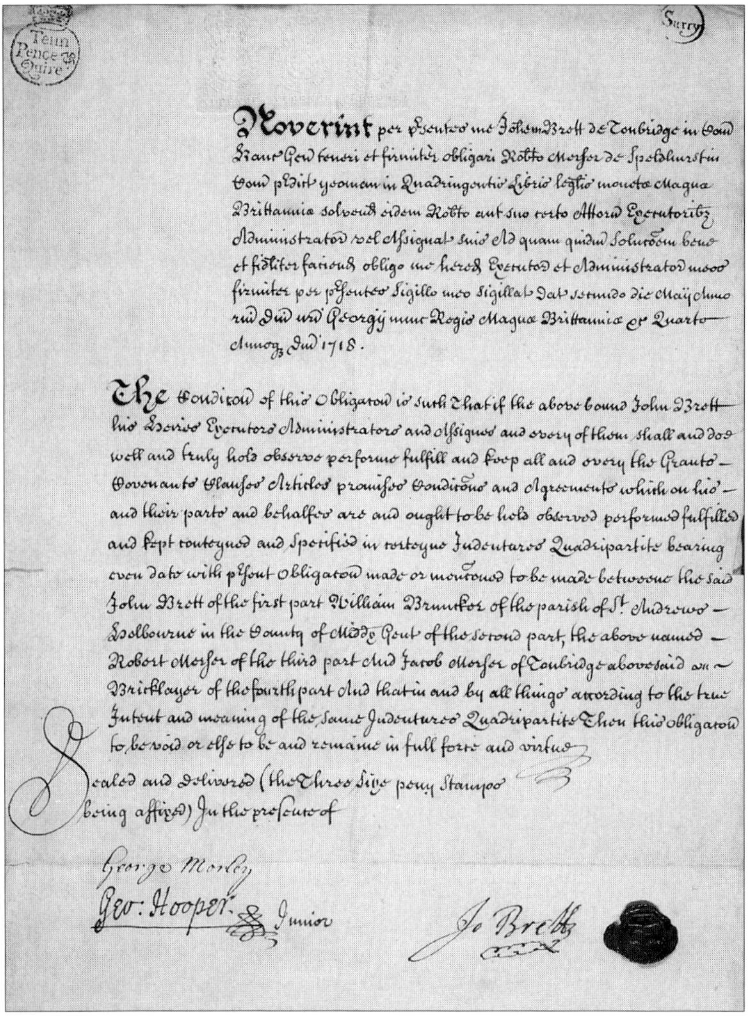
Teun Pence Quire

Surry

Noverint per presentes me Johem Brett de Tonbridge in Com Kant Gen teneri et firmiter obligari Robto Mercer de Speldhurst in Com pdict yeoman in Quadringentis Libris legalis monete Magne Brittannie solvend eidem Robto aut suo certo Attorn Executoribz Administrator vel Assignat suis Ad quam quidm Solucoem bene et fideliter faciend obligo me heredes Executor et Administrator meos firmiter per presentes Sigillo meo sigillat Dat secundo die Maij Anno rni Dni nri Georgij nunc Regis Magne Brittannie &c Quarto Annoqz Dni 1718.

The Condicon of this Obligacon is such That if the above bound John Brett his Heires Executors Administrators and Assignes and every of them shall and doe well and truly hold observe performe fulfill and keep all and every the Grants Covenants Clauses Articles promises Condicons and Agreements which on his and their parts and behalfes are and ought to be held observed performed fulfilled and kept conteyned and Specified in certeyne Indentures Quadripartite bearing even date with presant Obligacon made or menconed to be made betweene the said John Brett of the first part William Bruncker of the parish of St. Andrews Holbourne in the County of Midd Gent of the second part, the above named Robert Mercer of the third part And Jacob Mercer of Tonbridge abovesaid an Bricklayer of the fourth part And that in and by all things according to the true Intent and meaning of the same Indentures Quadripartite Then this obligacon to be void or else to be and remaine in full force and virtue

Sealed and delivered (the Three Sixe peny Stampes being affixed) In the presence of

George Morley
Geo: Hooper Junior

Jo Brett

Bond dated 2 May 1718 between John Brett, William Bruncker, Robert Mercer and Jacob Mercer

There are a few anomalies. For instance, a schedule of expenses met by his widow starts with an entry dated 4 November 1719 recording the payment of 5s. for coach hire from Westminster to the Commons and back again and another 5s. for expenses at the tavern. I presume John Brett was staying in London at the time. The next entry is dated 20 November for expenses 'on a journey after the funeral' although the register of the church says he was buried on the 23rd of the month. On 26 December Mr Heslop is paid the first quarterly instalment of his legacy; but he was not to enjoy it long, since an entry for 18 May 1721 records a payment of £15 'to Lady Day he dying the May following'. On 29 December an unnamed Mister is paid £4 for proving the will but on 30 January Edward Jarrett receives £2 15s. 0d. for coach hire from Tunbridge Wells and back again to prove the will – despite the clear record on the Public Record Office copy of the will that it was proved on 16 November. On 30 February Mr Cripps is paid 15s. for the Lord of the Manor on account of Mr Brett's death. It would seem that Brett had no livestock or a best beast would surely have been taken as a heriot. Maurice Conyers, the said Lord, was to feature in subsequent entries but for his own reasons.

On the same day that due payment was made on account of Brett's death 12s. 6d. was paid for a 'journey to London when served with [a writ] at the suit of Conyers' followed by 2s. for coach hire to Conyers – so he was living in London? In July 1725 as much as £23 9s. 2½d. was paid in law charges to Conyers and £1 17s. 2d. for three journeys to London 'on that affair' and payment to Mr Jodrell for his advice 'if proper to join with tenants in suit against Conyers'. All this of course is to do with the well-known dispute which culminated in the Rusthall Manor Act of 1739. A further £24 7s. 2d. was paid on a 'bill in Conyers cause' and finally £2 2s. 0d. was paid to Counsel for advice and several attendances 'in getting Mr Conyers demand for £50 per annum for 5 years for the Coffee house at Tunbridge Wells and getting him to accept of the net rent received to avoid another law suit'. The major part of Brett's possessions was of course in South Frith Manor but evidently, like everyone who was anyone, he had a finger in the Pantiles pie. He received rent at the rate of £25 per annum for the 'Flat House' whose location is commemorated in today's 'Flat House Passage' near Bath Square. He must, therefore, have been a tenant of the Manor of Rusthall. On the other hand he was paying the Manor something like £50 a year for a Coffee House; where this was situated I do not know. One way or another anyway he was (and so his widow was) concerned with the Pantiles and the Manor of Rusthall.

John Brett's 'personal estate' at the time of his death consisted of £6 6s. 0d. cash in the house, £420 left from the sale of an estate in Suffolk during his lifetime, rents due from the Flat House in Tunbridge Wells and 'Mr Jodrell's house in Essex Street, London', and £37 for 'hops sold and for old materials from the house at Rust Hall after it fell down'. Presumably this was part of the 'farm called Rusthall' which featured in a list of the 'Rents and Profits of the Real Estate' i.e. the freehold possessions. This included also Mrs Berkeley's house at Bromley, the houses of Mr Goodall, Mr White and Mr Bennett at Tunbridge Wells and Ground Rent for Constable's leases. Mr Goodall's was one of the Grove Houses below the Grove, Mr White's (see chapter 17) was probably a house at the bottom of Mount Sion where the Pizza House now is and Mr Bennett I cannot be sure of. The ground rent is a bit of a puzzle. I suppose 'Constable's leases' is short-hand for land which had originally been on lease to Richard Constable such as the Bowling Green at the top of Mount Sion with the houses around it. The ground rent mentioned came to only £13 per annum. There was besides much more land and property which came into Brett hands in 1715 and I do not understand why this income did not figure in the rents and profits of the real estate. The explanation may be found in the rather confused situation at the time. What with her husband's death and chasing around getting probate of the will and attempting to pay off his debts and legacies as well as being the person on the spot left to manage his property, Margaret evidently felt the need for help and in 1724, in London, she married a widower named Robert Pickering. He was a clergyman, apparently from the London area, but does not seem to have had a parish. Together they were faced with legacies totalling £1,660 of which £1,000 was due to Margaret herself and unpaid obligations amounting to almost another £1,000. Remember that this represents at least 100 times more in today's money – much more in my opinion. There was not enough cash in the piggy bank but money from rents kept coming in – some of it from property which rightly belonged to John Brett's nephew and heir, Dr John Brett. Maybe, however, he was receiving those rents which, as mentioned as a puzzle above, seemed to be missing.

The list of outstanding debts stretches to over a hundred items. There were tradesmen and craftsmen to be paid: Rouse the turner, William Dodson for paving, Thomas Martin for five chaldron of coals, Paynter for making bricks and tiles, Embury for clearing laths, Thomas Turley for sawing timber, Robert Bass for hedging and ditching, Mr Chapman for fowls and butter, William Budgen for meat, bills from Knight the plumber, William Ashdowne the shopkeeper and Edward Chapman the carpenter for a day's work, George Beale for hop poles, William Jeffery for shoeing horses, Susanna Ashdown a tailor, Edward Giles a butcher at Bromley, Edward Weaver for hair, Thomas Roberts for boards bought by Mr Brett's order and his bill for joiner's work, Goodman Knight for a day's work, William Groombridge for iron work, Thomas Stacey for fences, Thomas Buert the smith in Petty France, Hollinghurst for mason's work done in Essex Street, John Hull for carriage of goods to the Wells, Mr Sims the glazier his bill, Mr Hockett the oilman his bill, Mr Arnett the plumber in Petty France, Mr [Santer] a bill for paper hangings, Mr Pullen a bill for dying, Mr Andrews the sash frame maker his bill, Mr Ashdown for Cripps the mason his bill, Mr Paxton for 200 of deals bought by Mr Brett, paid Cripps by Mr Brett's order paid to the well digger, Colebrand for paper, Mr Watson the grocer his bill, Thomas Chitterden a bill for timber, John Boorne for carrying deals bought of Mr Paxton, Peat Latter the butcher, Edward Hilder the smith, Mr Luck the postmaster in full of his bill, Simon Wise for turning banisters (a presage of Tunbridge Ware to come?), William Baker for nails and iron work, William Fleet for malt, Elmes for painting and glazing, John Smith in full for his bill for malt, Hollamby the carrier, Mr Cripps for building the chimney at the Coffee House and repairs (tenants on the Walks had to pay their own repairs?), Parnett [Bennett?] for work done and carrying water and Bromley carpenters' and bricklayers' work. There were public obligations: three quarters water rent due at Xmas, a year's scavenger to Xmas, paid in full for the watch due at Xmas, half a year's land tax for Mr Hales House due at Michaelmas 1719, three quarters' ground rent for ditto, paid Latter for the King's taxes due at Xmas at Tunbridge Wells, paid the Poor Tax due at Xmas at Tunbridge

Wells, paid window and lamp lights to Xmas Petty France, paid hop duty for 1719, paid Mr Wood a bill and for Highways due 1719 and paid Richard Fry for Tithe. Then there were more personal family matters: paid Mrs Pickering a bill due for millinery work, paid Ann Berkeley a bill for money laid out for Mr Brett, paid Gardner for a dog collar [bt of – bought by?] Mr Brett, paid a note under Mr Brett's hand to Hammond, Mr Burgess a bill for coach hire journey in Mr Brett's lifetime, Mrs Ann Dudd mantua maker for work done in Mr Brett's lifetime, Mr Brightmore for shoes for Mr Brett, paid Simon Bennett left to pay by Mr Brett, paid Mr Brown a bill for John Brett due in Mr Brett's lifetime, Mr [Meigan] the tailor for making stays for Mrs Brett and Betty Brett (niece Elizabeth no doubt) in Mr Brett's lifetime, James Sancroft for linen sold to Mr Brett, paid Mrs Carter a bill for what her father laid out for Mr Brett, paid [Innocent?] by the hands of Mrs Watkins by promise from Mr Brett towards putting out Mr Berkeley's boy (as apprentice perhaps?), paid a carrier's bill due from Mr Brett for bringing up Jackey Brett (no doubt the great nephew and future Reverend John Brett – but was he brought up to London from Tunbridge Wells or vice versa?). Then there were more obscure financial and miscellaneous items: paid measuring the buildings and expenses, paid Thomas Heley a year's interest for a bond of £100, Dr Hervey a year's rent due at Christmas 1719, Mrs Watkins her bond and what was left to pay for lodging, Thomas Heley in part of his bond, John Priplingham his bill (probably Riplingham the scrivener), paid Constable two years 'ints' (interest?), Thomas Heley's bond principal and interest, paid Mr Constable's bond and interest and Grace Baker a note of Mr Brett and her interest and wages. Finally come health matters: Edward Rose a bill for physic, doctor's advice for Mr Brett and paid doctor for physic and horse hire in his sickness. All this paints a picture of goings-on not only at the Wells but also in Bromley, Essex Street and Petty France.

The measurement of buildings included above was probably connected with the next stage in the story. In early 1727 Doctor John Brett entered a bill against Robert Pickering and his wife Margaret 'that they might account with him for the Testator's estate and deliver up all deeds and writings'. The nephew and heir had lost patience and wanted his inheritance sorted out. Robert and Margaret made answer and soon after exhibited their Cross Bill against Dr John Brett and the petitioners John Brett the elder (the son of Dr Brett) and his sister, Elizabeth Brett, and also against the defendants Nathaniel and Dorothy Brett (infant brother and sister of Elizabeth). The Cross Bill asked that so much of the estate should be sold as would be sufficient to pay all debts and legacies – which at present was not the case. The case came to be heard on 21 May in the second year of George II (1729) and it was decreed that it should be referred to Mr Bennett to take accounts and so on but before he wrote his report Robert Pickering died intestate. The case lapsed and more deaths followed. Dr John Brett died on 8 March 1740/41 having made a will and appointed John Brett the elder and his sister Elizabeth Brett executors; and on 25 March 1743 Margaret Pickering died having appointed John Mallory and William Ashdowne executors. They revived the case with a Bill of Revivor in Hilary term 1744 against John Brett the elder and Elizabeth Brett and also John Brett the recently born son and heir of John the elder. The case was complicated by an allegation from the Bretts that Margaret Pickering had bought for herself a mortgage and conveyance and other property in Tunbridge Wells using her late husband's money and that this should be considered part of his estate. Mallory and Ashdowne pointed out that Margaret had 'advanced several large sums of her own' to pay off debts and legacies and these should be taken into account and they denied that she had made improper purchases.

The case was heard before the Master of the Rolls on 12 August 1747 and was again referred for a report. John Bennett Esquire having died at some stage his replacement Henry Montague reported five years later (these things take time!) on 24 July 1752 and the schedules to his report provide much of the fascinating information we have seen. Master Montague found that the Pickerings received from the personal estate and from rents and profits (Schedule I) £2,100 5s. 1d. but they spent £1,404 15s. 9d. on funeral expenses, payment of debts etc (Schedule II) leaving £695 9s. 4d. due from them. However Schedule III lists more outstanding debts all of which were paid by the Pickerings and amounted to £926 15s. 2d.; and the pecuniary legacies (allowing for the death as an infant of Chamberlain Brett) came to £1,560 of which Margaret Pickering had paid £235 leaving a balance of £1,325 including the widow's £1,000. Interest on this had been paid only since the death of Dr Brett in 1740/1 and the interest before then was computed with the agreement of all parties as: 'From 13 November 1719 to 13 November 1730 @ 5% and from 13 November 1730 to 8 March 1740/41 (10 years 3 months 23 days – proving incidentally that 'Old/New Style dating matters!) @ 4%' which works out at £962 10s. 4d. – although I have not checked this myself! If the £695 9s. 4d. due from the Pickerings were deducted, £267 1s. 0d. should have been paid by the Bretts. However

> a considerable part of the said testator's real estate consisting of several dwelling houses and other buildings situate at or near Tunbridge Wells and elsewhere in Kent, by the evidence which has been lain [*sic*] before me, I do find that although the said Dr John Brett was only Tenant for Life of the said Testator's real estate yet the same being by the said Testator's will settled and entailed on his the said Dr Brett's own family and children he did expend and lay out several large sums of money not only on the repairing but also in the rebuilding some of the said houses and other buildings by means whereof the said estate was much improved and the rents thereof considerably advanced the expense of which said buildings and repairs amounted to considerably more than the said sum of £267/1/0.

The Master taking all things together judged that accounts were even. He assumed that the legacies to Dr Hugh Chamberlain (the obstetrician, you remember) and Mrs Elizabeth Witherden had been paid 'no claim or demand having been made for so many years'. In conclusion part of the estate was sold on Thursday 10 May, with the agreement of John Brett Clerk, to William Davids of Castle Yard London gentleman for £1,670. Costs of £77 0s. 6d. moderated to £69 7s.

10d. and of £88 11s. 4d. reduced to £75 3s. 10d. and of £63 13s. 4d. reduced to £42 13s. 2d. were allotted to the plaintiffs, the defendants and to Nathaniel and Dorothy Brett respectively. Finally the Master stated that no evidence had been laid before him as to the alleged purchases made by Margaret Pickering 'All which I humbly certify and submit to the judgement of this Honourable Court' – and the report was confirmed with the agreement of all parties on 24 July 1752.

This legal saga has taken us rather far ahead of the main story; but forms a necessary background. The Brett family from this time onward ceases to have much to do with Mount Sion. Dr John Brett had died in 1740 and his son (Jacky who was, you remember, 'brought up' to or from London) went into the Church rather than follow the medical leanings of his father and grandfather and set a trend which was followed by at least two more generations. However he seems to have lived in Tunbridge Wells presumably without parochial responsibilities – at any rate when the Lanthorn House was sold after his death in 1784 the conveyance clearly stated that he had lived there – another reason for supposing that this was the house that was bequeathed to widow Margaret in 1719. From his will, proved in September 1784, it appears that towards the end he went to live in East Grinstead with his married daughter, Dorothy, wife of Thomas Wakeham, but the will makes clear that he was 'late of Tunbridge Wells'.

Apart from his daughter he had a clever son who went to Tonbridge School. Those of you who are familiar with these junketings will be pleased to hear that he was selected to recite Vergil's 5th Eclogue on Skinners' Day, 1761. He then went to Queens' College, Cambridge, and was made a fellow of the college in 1766, a year after his graduation and ordination. In 1777 he married the niece of the Reverend Eden Howard of Suffolk and became rector of Grimston in Norfolk – a living incidentally in the gift of Queens' College. A marriage settlement provided that most of the remaining Brett properties in Tunbridge Wells should be conveyed to trustees charged with £2,000, to which the bride's uncle added a balancing £2,000. The income would provide for the couple until the husband died when the property would be sold and the proceeds invested. When his father died the Rev. Brett evidently had no great attachment to Tunbridge Wells and, finding that property values had increased, he was able to sell the Grove Houses and their adjoining 14 acres to George Fry for £2,500, hand over £2,000 to his trustees and keep £500 for himself.

In 1787 he sold the Lanthorn House to Robert Burges of Hall Place, Leigh. It was occupied for some years – as can be seen on the Barrow map of 1808 – by the rector of Speldhurst, the Rev. Gordon. Then in 1822 Robert Burges's widow sold the house to Thomas Beeching the banker who sold it to John Ward and on 23 February 1825 the materials of the old house were on offer in the *Maidstone Journal*. This seems virtually to have ended the Brett connection with Tunbridge Wells. The various houses round the Bowling Green and elsewhere had been sold in the 18th century, the Grove Houses went later in the century, the 'tenements under the ante-gallery' had been sold to the Chapel in 1810 and in 1840 the Tithe map showed a single meadow owned by the Rev. William Brett. I still do not know who he was.

Chapter 6

The Grove Houses

Having set the general scene – the first leases, the 1702 sell-off, the Chancery case, the 1715 foreclosure and the Brett aftermath – I now propose to deal with sections of Mount Sion one by one, starting with the Grove and the three Grove Houses below it and working in a southerly or south-westerly direction towards Cumberland Walk. The Grove and its houses have already been mentioned at least a dozen times but I think the best place to start is a more detailed consideration of the Grove Trust Deed. The copy I have comes from the Abergavenny collection in the East Sussex Record Office at Lewes. This is itself a 19th-century copy, handwritten naturally, using some legal abbreviations and paraphrases, and including a declaration dated 1818 by which the Earl of Abergavenny, the Marquis Camden, George Henry Nevill and Sir John Filmer acknowledge that they hold £500 of Bank of England 3 per cent annuities in trust for the preservation of the Grove.

The original deed takes the form of a conveyance, by the Lease and Release procedure common at the time, dated 19 and 20 April 1703. The owners of the land, the Earl of Buckingham and his trustees our old friends Lake, Weller and Weller, convey it to the four Grove trustees whose names have already appeared on page 34 above: two esquires, John Dyke of Frant and Robert Baker of Rotherfield; and two gentlemen, Nicholas Fowle the younger of Wadhurst and Henry Weller of Frant who was implicated in the Chancery case of 1708 as you may remember. About Dyke, Baker and Fowle or why they might have been chosen I have no information. Interestingly a number of the neighbouring house owners are joined in the conveyance as parties of the third part. These were obviously men who had bought their properties from the Earl and his trustees in the great sell-off of 1702 and who had an interest in seeing the Grove maintained as an amenity for their visitors – and themselves and their families, I suppose. A consideration of their names and the references to them in the deed will give an insight into the state of affairs in 1703.

Nick Wood first of all: he is named as a glover but he was also a fellmonger and will feature largely in a later chapter. His house was later called Burlington and was near the entrance to the Grove from Upper Mount Sion and one stipulation in the deed is that 'there should be one Coachway into the said Grove out of the said Highway there above mentioned near the dwelling house of Nicholas Wood where a gate then was or then late was'. There still is a gate of a sort presumably in the very same spot. The front of the house was not far from where the present Fish and Chip shop is in Little Mount Sion. John Mercer named as a yeoman of Speldhurst will figure as owner of the *Compasses* in the next chapter. The deed mentions and permits 'one Common Footway' into the Grove 'through the ground of Mr Mercer as was then used'. I guess this refers to the little passage alongside the *Compasses* rather than Belgrove since Belgrove House was not built until later. The other parties of the third part had houses slightly more distant: widow Winifrith Brooke had property up the northerly side of Mount Sion; Philip Seal, glazier, had his two precious lodging houses looking down Little Mount Sion which he had bought only a few months before; Edward Allen, mercer of Rotherfield, owned the house to be christened Jerningham more than a hundred years later; William Baynes or Banes the brewer owned Sion House on Mount Sion from 1719 for a year or two (see chapter 17) but he may be unconnected with the William Baynes carpenter mentioned in the Trust Deed; and finally Thomas Scoones, gentleman, owned Fairlawn House on Mount Sion; but of particular interest is the covenant contained in his conveyance which indicates that preservation of the Grove was a consideration even before the date of the Grove Trust Deed. To quote: 'And it is further covenanted ... between all the said parties ... That the Grove standing and being near unto the above bargained premises formerly called Inhams Bush and now called the Grove alias Mount Sion Grove adjoining to the land of Mr Younge shall be preserved for a Grove for the use of the Inhabitants and lodgers of the premises above bargained with others to walk and the trees there growing preserved for shade and not any of them to be cutt downe nor any buildings to be there erected.' This conveyance is dated 27/28 November 1702: the Grove Trust Deed 19/20 April 1703.

There are more names to be found elsewhere in the deed. Firstly there is a list of those who had bought land; this repeats the names from Wood to Baynes but adds Richard and John Waghorne. Where their land was located I do not know. Waghornes Forest is mentioned as an area distinct from Inhams Heath and it must have been somewhere to the east or south-east but whether it had any connection with Richard and John Waghorne I do not know. The bounds of the Grove are given as follows: to the north 'lands theretofore demised to Thomas Neale Esq'; towards the east 'land theretofore demised to Edward Allen & Winifrith Brook'; towards the south and west 'land theretofore demised to William Fullman and then Jno Mercer'. Points of the compass are still being used as if north were what we should probably nowadays call west i.e. down the hill towards the High Street. The lands demised to Thomas Neale undoubtedly therefore signify the Grove Houses and their grounds between the Grove and the High Street. Lands let to Mr Young are referred to later on and there can be no doubt that when Neale died in 1699 his lease was assigned to Mr Young about whom I have no information. To the west lay (still lies!) the *Compasses* and the wording clearly implies that John Mercer succeeded William Fullman. To the south of course would be Buckingham Road and all those houses developed on the Grecian Villa site – all outside my definition of 'Mount Sion'. The land demised to Edward Allen and Winifrith Brook to the east is a puzzle. This would appear to indicate land between the Grove and Grove Hill Road; but I have no information about this and it is outside my area. It would anyway have to be land additional to the Mount Sion and Jerningham properties we know about.

It is worth repeating that the four acres of land were conveyed, in the words of the deed, 'Upon Trust and confidence always and to the intent and purpose that the said Wood called the Grove alias Mount Sion Grove & the trees there growing or to grow should not be cut down nor the said Grove or Trees converted to any private use but should be continually preserved for a Grove & Shade & Walks for the use of all the Inhabitants of the several houses built or to be built or which should be built on the said several purchases or any other the land late parcel of the said lands called Inhams or of the said Park or Forest of Southfrith and for their Lodgers servants & Family to come go & walk in & upon the said Grove at their Will and Pleasure'. This is all clear enough and delightfully worded too.

However the four acres of the Grove were not the only land still belonging to the Manor of South Frith for which provision is made in the Grove Trust Deed. The document continues with a 'further recital' saying that 'there were several ways there newly laid out by the owners of said Land .... for common Highways for all people to travel go lead drive carry and recarry from Tonbridge Wells towards Southborough & towards Woodsgate & so then used and the Ground and Soil of the said Ways was not demised letten or sold to any person or persons'. In other words the Manor of South Frith had laid out roads not just within the Grove but also in the whole area and the land on which they were built had not been leased or sold to anyone. It appears therefore that the High Street, Mount Sion, Mount Pleasant, Grove Hill Road and every other road which was in the South Frith Manor area in April 1703 was handed to the Trustees of the Grove on trust that they 'should always remain as Common Highways for all people to come go lead drive carry & recarry in by over & through the same at their will & pleasure for ever' and in particular that 'they should not be stopped inclosed or straitened' (made narrower). What was legally conveyed into the possession of the Trustees was: 'All the said Grove ... . containing by estimation 4 acres were there more or less And all ways waters trees . ... advantages and appurtenances to the same belonging or appertaining And also the said several Highways newly laid out for Common highways & not before demised or sold to any other person'. I do not think anyone ever made any connection between the Grove Trustees and the local roads during the next near two centuries; but then in 1890 the Grove was transferred to the Corporation as part of the Tunbridge Wells Improvement Act and I do think that the two serving Trustees and their solicitors Thomas Walker and Frank Stone and Mayor Stone-Wigg and his Town Clerk W.C. Cripps should have read the 1703 deed more carefully. The agreement dated 27 March 1890 conveys (First Schedule) the piece of land containing four acres two roods and seven perches called the Grove – and nothing more. The roads are therefore left in limbo except that Section 146 of the Act (Third Schedule Second Clause) says that all 'rights privileges trusts duties and obligations' of the Trustees under the 1703 deed shall cease absolutely and vest in the Corporation – which in the absence of specific provision must I suppose cover the roads. The Grove itself is to be held by the Borough 'upon the trusts and to and for the intents and purposes' of the 1703 deed (Clause 2 of the Agreement). Does this, I wonder, extend to the constraints imposed on the original trustees in regard to stopping enclosing or 'straitening' the roads?

To return to the Trust Deed of 1703, roads and paths within the Grove itself are carefully specified. There should be, in the words of the deed, 'one Coachway into the said Grove out of the said Highway there above mentioned near the dwelling house of Nicholas Wood where a gate then was or then late was and one other Coachway where a way was laid out on the north side of the said Grove between the lands let to Mr Young & the lands of Mrs Brook & that gates be there kept up to prevent same from being used as Common Highways And that one Common Footway [thereinto] through the ground of Mr Mercer as was then used And that one other private Footway with a gate thereto be permitted for the use of Mr Young & the Occupiers & the Inhabitants & Lodgers of the Houses there built or to be built & that no other way or ways be permitted thereunto'. This can be related to the situation today. The main coachway is the broad path from the Claremont Road gate ('near the dwelling house of Nicholas Wood') leading out to Sunderland and Grove Hill Roads. The one other coachway on the north (i.e. north-west) is the path that is now often used to go to the garden rubbish site. It starts I suppose at the top of South Grove which would have been the land let to Mr Young and runs between that place and the lands of Mrs Brooke. All we know about her lands is that they were to the east which indicates Sunderland and Grove Hill Roads again where the two 'coachways' join. The northern one, of course, now continues to the Birdcage Walk archway and then circles round to the Claremont Road gate; but all this could have been later development. Gates are to be provided to prevent the two coachways from becoming 'common highways'. One gate and bollards elsewhere serve this purpose today. Apart from the two coachways, only two footways are to be permitted: one, already mentioned, leads into the Grove alongside the *Compasses*; the other is for the use of Mr Young and the occupiers of the Grove Houses ('the houses there built or to be built') and is to be a private footway with a gate. I take this to point to the stepped and gated entrance from Grove Avenue. No other ways are to be allowed, says the deed optimistically; but time and later building (e.g. Belgrove House) have eroded this stipulation – but not so much as might have been.

The Trustees are enjoined to 'use such lawful ways and means for the preservation of said Grove & ways & to prevent and remedy all trespasses incroachments & nuisances which should or might be committed therein as should be thought fit or advised'; but this action should be taken 'at the request costs & charges of the said Inhabitants or such of them as should require the same'. The Trustees moreover are to be indemnified 'by said Inhabitants or such of them as should require such ways & means to be used from all charges and damages which might happen to them thereby'. Whether these provisions were ever invoked, I have no information. Probably not, if the final provision is any indication, because the Trustees and the Inhabitants failed miserably to provide for the succession. When, said the deed, 'there should be only two Trustees living then surviving Trustees being thereunto required by the then Inhabitants of said Houses or the major part of them & at their costs and charges should convey over their Estate in the premises above said to new trustees for the purposes above named'. What happened in the event we shall see later.

One point seems very clear. From the very beginning there was general agreement that Inhams Bush or the Grove should not be built upon and this agreement was enshrined in the Grove Trust Deed. As the deed says: 'it was agreed between said Earl and said several purchasers that said Grove should not be sold or converted to any private use but same and trees there growing or thereafter to grow should be preserved and not cut down nor destroyed but preserved for a Grove Shade and Walk for all the Inhabitants of the several Houses built or which should be built on said several purchased premises & other the land late parcel of the said Park or Forest of Southfrith and for their respective Lodgers Servants and Family to come go and walk in and upon the said Grove at their wills and pleasures'. Whether this agreement was sincerely endorsed on the Earl of Buckingham's part I have my doubts; but the weight of influence from the purchasers of the houses round and about prevailed and the present-day inhabitants of the 'village' and the children on the swings and down the slides have reason to be thankful, if not only or principally to the charitable Earl.

The *Compasses* and other houses on that side of the Grove will be the subject of the next chapter. The opposite side, between the Grove and Grove Hill Road, is outside the area I have defined as Mount Sion but anyway seems to have been undeveloped until the 19th century when first of all a house was built called Meadow Hill (see more on page 60 below) which explains its location and the name of the road which replaced it – and the Sunderland Road terraces followed later. The Bowra map shows nothing at all and the Barrow map of 1808 shows only a small building labelled North Row on the very corner of Grove Hill Road (called the Turnpike Road to Woodsgate) and the High Street. On the upper side of the Grove was a field on which in 1824 Dr Mayo built the house which later became Grecian Villa and succumbed to developers on the death of Madame Caballero in 1877. On the lower side of the Grove were the three Grove Houses. They had been there since the very beginning and deserve a more detailed consideration. The land on which they were built was part of that leased to Thomas Neale for £18 per annum on 10 February 1685/86 but Neale evidently took little personal interest since Poor Rate was paid by Mr Young first in December 1687 'for a field' and then in the second half of 1689 'for a field & 3 new houses'. Mr Young continued as rate payer until 1700 when a Mrs (or Mr?) Fox took over 'for a field and 3 other houses' until at least 1714. I do not think the word 'other' here is significant – I am sure that the same three houses are indicated.

As will be discussed more fully in the next chapter but one, there is a gap in the Poor Rate record from 1714 to 1728; but in this particular case it can be partially filled because Kip's engraving of 1719 shows the three Grove Houses and in the field in front is the label 'Mr Goodals' – see his splendid contemporary view on the next page. Mr Goodall in fact appears as ratepayer in 1728, on the other side of the gap, to be succeeded in 1732 by Mrs Goodall. In 1733 and '34 it is Mrs Goodall or Mr Elliott, suggesting that the rate collectors were not sure what was going on

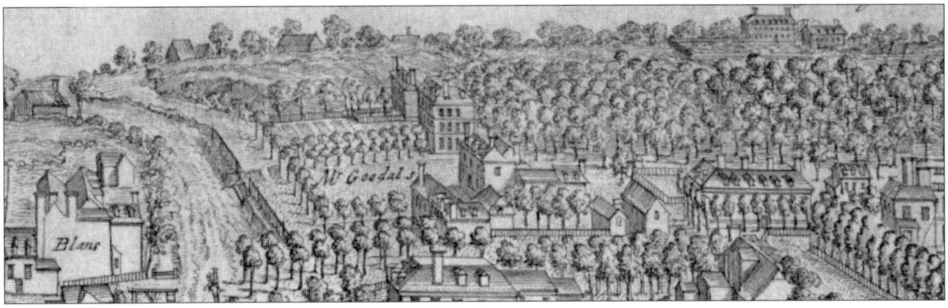

Kip's engraving 1719

and finally in 1735 Mr Elliott takes over on his own. From 1738 to 1744 he is credited with two fields and three houses as also is Edmund Wood who continues until 1749 when Mr Brett appears for the first time. The first Mr Brett had of course been the freeholder of the land from 1715, as we saw at the end of chapter 4, and this is why the name 'Mr Brett' is prominently attached to the three houses and the field in front on the Bowra map of 1738; by this time, however, it is the nephew 'Dr' Brett who is the owner. The Poor Rate collector was concerned only with the occupiers of houses and land, so that when he notes a payment of £12 from 'Mr Brett for ye Grove house and field' in 1750 it presumably means that Mr Brett has become the occupier or, more probably, is personally managing the lodging house – and it is just one house, no longer the three together. The next entry says simply ' Mr Brett for the Great House' indicating that the one house is the Middle Grove House. I have no knock-down proof that the Middle was the Great but I am sure it was. On Bowra all three look about the same size but the middle one has the impressive double avenue going down to the High Street which shows also on Kip's engraving where the middle house does look slightly the biggest. It shows also on this engraving which seems to date from the mid-19th century when it was

The Middle Grove House about 1860

a school (do I see children at play and on a swing?). The house certainly looks impressively large. 'Mr Brett for the Great House' continues from 1751 to 1766 when there is a change to'George Fry for the Great House & field' from 1767 to 1785. The Brett family history outlined at the end of the last chapter sheds some light on these entries. In 1777 the clever young reverend married and went to live in Suffolk. The marriage settlement of 8 November that year handed all the Brett Tunbridge Wells properties to trustees including 'those three messuages on the west side of the Grove and 12 acres of mead or pasture adjoining on the south and middle with land now or late occupied by George Fry and north occupied by ________ Watson'. This rather incoherent description (my notes may be the culprit!) means, I think, that Watson occupied the North Grove House and George Fry the South Grove House and there were 12 acres of meadow besides. Twelve acres is three times the area of the Grove and could account for all the vacant land shown on both the Bowra and Barrow maps on the Grove Hill and upper sides of the Grove. Anyhow, father Brett died in 1784 and the next year his son sold the three houses on the west side of the Grove and 12 acres of land and a two-acre 'close described to be situated near Mount Sion' – but whose exact location I do not know. The price was £2,500 and the Rev Brett handed £2,000 to his marriage settlement trustees and kept £500 which no doubt came in handy for household expenses. The deed says that the marriage was duly solemnized and several children are now living! The purchaser was none other than George Fry who, as the Poor Rate record tells us, had been in occupation since 1767 – but not of all three houses. Edward Watson (now we know his first name) had been paying rates for 'part of Bretts' (the North House I believe) from 1767 also and continued so to do until 1787 when John Fry took over until the record ceases in 1797 (see the next chapter). George was the eldest son of Richard Fry and was a butcher like his father whom we shall meet later residing on Mount Sion. George died intestate in 1791 and most of the real estate passed to his younger brother John who is recorded paying rates from 1793 'for the Great House and field late Geo Frys'.

1782 meanwhile was a landmark year in the history of the Grove. Sprange's *Guide* for 1786 prints in full the Trust Deeds of both the Chapel and Grove and explains: 'The foregoing account of the Grove and Chapel was transmitted to the editor by Beversham Filmer Esq. to whom the inhabitants of Tunbridge Wells are much indebted for the pains he has taken. The account was accompanied with the following polite note.

> The King's Road, near Bedford Row,
> March 5, 1782.
>
> Mr Sprange
>
> After having received benefits by drinking the waters, and likewise many civilities from the inhabitants, it will give me pleasure if I can be of any service to the place; and therefore according to my promise I here send you an authentic account of the original foundation of the Chapel and Grove there.

Mr Filmer, surely a lawyer himself, had discovered 'by the strictest enquiry' that the four original trustees were by this time all long since dead and had not appointed new trustees. By consulting parish registers he found that Robert Baker of Rotherfield had outlived the others, being buried in Mayfield in 1721. Therefore 'it was necessary to find out who are his heirs at law, and this Grove being in the county of Kent, where the custom of Gavelkind prevails, was the more difficult to discover; but after the most diligent enquiry, it appears that the said Robert Baker, and his two brothers, dying without issue, Robert's two sisters, Dorothea and Elizabeth, became his co-heirs. Dorothea married Andrew Kenrick of Chester, Esq. and her grandson, Richard Kenrick, at Nantclywd, near Ruthin, in Denbyshire, Esq. now living is her heir at law. Elizabeth married Mr Robert Bicknell, of Clifford's Inn, and her five great grandsons, now living, are her heirs at law.' The assiduity and perseverance of Mr Filmer were rewarded by a deed dated 26 and 27 July 1782 whereby the heirs of Robert Baker conveyed the Grove, on the original trusts, to Sir Richard Heron and Martin Yorke of Tunbridge Wells, George Children of Tonbridge and Beversham Filmer of the King's Road.

Before this deed was even done someone had been busy in the Grove, probably the assiduous Mr Filmer, and it was reported that on 10 December 1781 the Grove contained 'two hundred oaks, some of them very large, containing about four or five loads of timber in a tree, ten large beech trees, about sixty small trees of lime and sycamore, two fir and two yew trees.' In the winter of 1782, 26 decayed oak trees were felled by order of the new trustees, and sold for £150 part of which was spent in making good the fence belonging to the Grove and painting it, putting up new benches, laying out the walk in the middle of the Grove, repairing and ornamenting the ride round it and planting young trees. The remainder of the £150 was invested on 27 January 1784 in the purchase of £150 three per cent Consolidated Bank Annuities. As mentioned at the beginning of this chapter, this amount had increased by 1818 to £500 in the same stock. Four new trustees had been appointed in 1809 and it is noticeable that one is named Filmer (Sir John Filmer Bart) – surely some connection with the praiseworthy Beversham Filmer, one of those he replaced. In 1794 more felling took place and John Fry was in some way involved. An advertisement appeared in the Maidstone Journal on 28 October 1794: 'Timber to be sold by auction – by E. Strange – By order of the Trustees to the Grove in Mount Sion Tunbridge Wells on Wednesday 5th November next between 12 and 1 on the premises in 3 lots – Thirty-one Oak Trees – may be viewed at any time – further particulars John Fry Tunbridge Wells.'

There is an exasperating paucity of information about the people who came and stayed in the houses on Mount Sion which form such a large part of this history. One who can be accurately placed is Lord North who, after losing America and doubling the national debt, came to stay at the North Grove House. He bore a striking resemblance to the king, George III, and like him became blind. The *Maidstone Journal* on 17 July 1787 reported: 'Lord North – once the great minister of the great country – who saw and foresaw everything – the Sampson of England – is now, like Sampson, led about the Pantiles at Tunbridge – with the only consolation that he is so led by the affectionate hand of a dutiful daughter.' A theory aired in the *Maidstone Journal* was that the sand commonly used for blotting ink had affected his eyes. Richard Cumberland one day walked across the Grove to visit him and he took Cumberland's arm and asked to be conducted to the spring. 'I have a general recollection of the way,' said Lord North, 'and if you will make me understand the posts upon the footpath and the steps about the Chapel, I shall remember them in future.' 'I could not lead blind Gloster to the cliff,' added Cumberland. 'I executed my affecting trust and brought him back to his family: the ministering and mild daughter of Teiresias received her father from my hands.' North died in 1792.

Cumberland's landlord at the house not far away on the old bowling green site was the same John Fry who inherited a share in the Grove Houses. He was also the master of the *Sussex Tavern* on the Pantiles until 1793 when a notice in the *Maidstone Journal* reported that he had let it to J. Smith, his Head Waiter for many years, and he thanked the Nobility and Gentry for their favours over the last twenty years and solicited the same for Mr Smith. A year earlier the re-paving of the Pantiles had been completed 'through the perseverance of Mr Fry of the Sussex Tavern and the liberal subscription of the inhabitants at an expense of near a thousand pounds'. He died about 1803 and his will, dated 30 September 1801, gives an indication how the property was distributed. First, let's look at a sketch family tree. This has reverberations in the story of Mount Sion elsewhere.

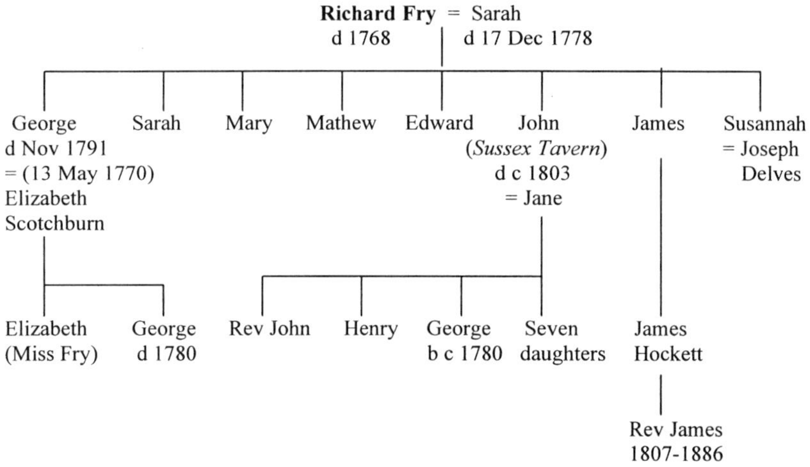

Richard was a butcher and owned and probably lived in the house in whose back quarters I now reside. It is clearly labelled 'Rich Fry' on the Bowra plan. Butchers seemed to prosper at this time; anyway there was money from somewhere to enable the eldest son George, also a butcher, to expend £2,500, as we have seen, on the purchase from the Rev. Brett of the Grove Houses and field. His son, another George of course, died young in 1780, leaving an only child Elizabeth. Meanwhile younger brother John had been hard at it producing three sons and seven daughters. When George senior died in 1791 without leaving a will it seems that Elizabeth and John got a half share each in the Great Grove House and field and the widow Elizabeth had the South Grove House which must have been the family home and had passed by 1808 to 'Miss Fry' the daughter. We have seen already that John Fry took over as ratepayer on the North Grove House from Edward Watson in 1787 and his will confirms that he was the freehold owner of a messuage 'called Lord North's House'. This, with an adjoining meadow, was left to his sons John and Henry together with his half share in the Great House and two houses on Mount Sion. They also were bequeathed the house occupied by Mr Cumberland after their mother's death. Son George was left a farm in Rotherfield and other land including the Grove Field containing five acres. Furniture in the Great and North Grove Houses was not to be touched, being needed no doubt for their use as lodging houses. John and Henry were entrusted to provide from the houses bequeathed to them an income of £100 per annum for their mother and to split any surplus eight ways – one share to George and one share each to the seven girls except that the shares of Lydia, Amelia, Caroline and Matilda were to go to their mother to look after them until they reached 21 or married. The elder girls were named Sarah, Mary and Jane.

A little further information on developments around the turn of the century can be gleaned from the lists of Lodging Houses at the back of *Sprange Guides*. In 1780 and 1786 Watson had the North (called 'Further') Grove House and George Fry the other two (called Middle and Hither). In 1797 and 1801 John Fry had the North, the Middle was unattributed and Mrs George Fry had the 'First'. In 1808 and 1811 only the unnamed 'First' Grove House is listed as a lodging house and in 1817 all three are listed: John Fry, North; Sir W. Bellingham, Great; and Miss Fry, First. The Barrow map of 1808, however, provides more information and a surprise. Barrow uses shading to distinguish lodging and other houses and the North and South houses appear as lodgings: the First Grove House under the name, as expected, of Miss Fry; and the North Grove House under the name of the Dowager Lady Deering. The Middle House is shaded black to indicate private use and is labelled 'Mr Pigou's'. I have no information about the connections of Lady Dering with Tunbridge Wells but the Derings of course were a well-known East Kent family. Frederick Pigou in 1758 and Fred Pigou junior in 1763 were present at the King Charles vestry; Mr Frederick Pigou became in 1765 trustee for £100 of South Sea stock in place of Mr Thomas Godfrey who was thanked on his retirement; and in 1775 it was noted that Mr Pigou had £30 for the Chapel School which he had left with Mr George Fry. Charles Edward Pigou was at one time High Sheriff of Sussex and a churchwarden at Frant in 1803-4 – beyond these scattered facts I can find nothing about the Pigou who occupied the Middle Grove House in 1808. The surprise of the Barrow map, however, is that a new building has appeared abutting the south-western wall of the Middle House, shaded black as a private house and labelled 'Miss Fry's'. This is now the only vestige of the Grove Houses remaining and is known as Grove Villa. How long before 1808 it was built I have no information but I might guess that Miss Fry wanted the income from the family home but could not conveniently live in it at the same time and therefore did what other lodging house keepers had been known to do: live in the grounds and leave the main house free.

There is a dearth of information from 1817 to 1840 but *Pigot's* (not Pigou!) *Directory* of 1827 has a list of Nobility, Gentry and Clergy which puts the Rev. Martin Benson at the 'First Grove House', Miss Fry at the 'Little Grove House' and Lady Poole at the Great Grove House. There is no doubt about the Great House but who Lady Poole was I do not know. Martin Benson was the incumbent at King Charles the Martyr and Miss Fry was surely maiden Elizabeth as before but which were their houses? My guess is that the clergyman was in South Grove House and Miss Fry, as on Barrow's map, in Grove Villa; but there was another Little Grove House on Cumberland Gardens – a fairly remote possibility. In the 1832 Pigot it is all change: Robert Willis Blencowe Esq. is at the Middle Grove; Lady Brisbane at the First Grove; and Mrs Mary Monk at Little Grove. Miss Fry has gone elsewhere or to her final rest but in her place Mr James Fry and Mrs Susannah Fry are listed but not located. James could be her uncle or perhaps her cousin James Hockett; Susannah is presumably a widow but of whom? As for the North Grove House, the *Maidstone Journal* announced on 23 December 1834 an auction of its contents, the freehold residence having been disposed of by private contract, indicating the end of Fry family interest. It is incidentally of some interest to notice, from the furniture on offer, the extent of accommodation in this typical 18th-century lodging house: 12 bedrooms with at least one 'capital full sized four-post bedstead with mahogany and japanned pillars' and chintz and dimity furnishings; single and double chests of drawers, dressing glasses, 'biddets', washhand stands and chairs; dining room and drawing room furniture with 12 chairs for each, dining tables, couches and rosewood loo and card tables; not to mention the excellent kitchen requisites and the China table, dessert, tea and breakfast services, cut glass and tumblers – no mention, of course, of sanitary requisites!

Nine months later, on 15 September 1835, the *Maidstone Journal* reveals a surprising turn of events.

> It is with the greatest pleasure we have this week to announce that on Wednesday last, the ceremony of laying the first stone of the new church to be erected in the private grounds of the North Grove Estate, took place amidst the congratulations of an assembled multitude, amongst whom we noticed the Rev. — Heasman, of Clifton, and many of the resident and neighbouring gentry and inhabitants. A bottle was deposited in the stone, containing a parchment inscription, as well as several coins of the present reign. The inscription was as follows – 'The foundation stone of this building, called 'Christ Church' was laid jointly by William Haydon, Esq and George Walker, Esq, September the 9th, 1835.' The names of the five trustees were also inserted, as well as those of the minister and the architect, Mr. Robert P. Browne, of Greenwich. The building is to be capable of accommodating 1800 persons, and above half are to be free seats. The style of architecture is to be Anglo Norman, and the design is generally greatly admired. The prayers were delivered in a most impressive manner by the Rev. William Bailey.

Between these two announcements lies a curious tale which has yet to be unravelled. The Rev. Thomas Ward Franklyn, a wealthy Anglican vicar, is said according to the latest Christ Church history, to have seen a part-completed theatre lying derelict, its developer having been convicted, apparently for breaching building regulations, and deported to Tasmania. He bought the incomplete building in 1835 and 'with the aid of the architect Robert Palmer Brown of Greenwich, made himself a church for £8,500.' It is hard to imagine that all this happened between December 1834 and September the next year; but it is just possible that the 'theatre' was already building in the garden before the auction sale or even before the sale of the residence. Some hint of what was going on might, however, have been expected. What would possess anyone to start a theatre in this part of the town when the established theatre on the Pantiles could no longer attract audiences? And who was this man? And would anyone even in those days have been deported for jerry-building – for building regulations surely did not exist? The Tunbridge Wells Improvement Act dates only from 1835; before that local government was loosely shared between the magistrates, the various parish vestries and the Manorial Court of Southborough. Yet the present vicar is said to have read a historical document stating that the original builder 'having broken most building regulations, was sent to Tasmania for his misdemeanours'. Where is this document? I wrote and asked the Rev. Banner but his answer on this specific point was less than specific. I quote: 'Over the years a number of people have sent newspaper extracts (I might add photocopies) of articles written, the evidence of which was held in Kent County Archives. I cannot elaborate further.' Be that as it may, the foundation stone of the new church was laid in 1835 and it opened for worship eventually in May 1841. The 'owner' and prospective vicar wrote to the *Sussex Agricultural Express* in October 1840 after that newspaper had complained at lack of information. 'You may inform your readers', wrote the reverend owner, 'that the great delay that has occurred in the opening of the newly-erected church at Tunbridge Wells has arisen from certain difficulties lying in the way of its consecration. The November meeting of her Majesty's Commissioners for building churches will decide whether the church is to be consecrated immediately or at some future uncertain period. In the event of the consecration not taking place, application will be made to the Lord Bishop of the Diocese for his sanction to the opening of the church by Episcopal license with as little delay as possible.' In the event the church was opened only under the licence of the Bishop of Rochester. Exactly what were the concerns over consecration it would be interesting to know.

Anglo-Norman was chosen as the style of the building – whether by the architect or owner or both is unclear. In practice this meant an impressive heavy porch and square tower fronting a great barn of a space which was said at first to hold 1,800 worshippers; but this figure in the end seems to have been reduced to 900 partly because a plan for side galleries was abandoned. The shape of the building can be accurately seen on the Tithe map (see page 71) which also tells us the owners and occupiers of all the Grove Houses in 1840. Christ Church itself was owned by the 'Trustees of the New Church' but the North Grove House was owned and occupied by one Richard Corke who had nothing to do with the church as far as I know – which is a problem since it seems obvious that the Rev. Franklin must have bought the house when he bought the 'theatre' in its garden and, on later evidence, he did own the house – see below. The (Great) Grove House is not only occupied but owned by Esquire Blencowe, head of one of Aretas Akers' 'contiguous families' – see chapter 23. Lady Brisbane is still living at the (South) Grove House which is owned by James Hockett Fry and he is living next door at Grove Villa which he also owns. Evidently he has taken over, by inheritance I suppose, from Miss Fry. In summary then, the old Brett inheritance which was bought by George Fry in 1777 has been whittled down to just the South Grove House and the more recent addition, Grove Villa. The North had been owned by John and Henry Fry and the Middle by them jointly with Miss Fry and both must have been sold, perhaps more than once, before 1840; but the only information I have is that of the auction in 1834. On two other sides of the Grove, although strictly outside my fuzzy borders, there were developments in the first half of the 19th century which are worth a brief notice. On the Grove Hill Road side land was bought and (as mentioned on page 52 above) a large house erected by John Levett Yeats who is sometimes referred to as a doctor, although he does not appear as such in the 1847 Bagshaw directory. He owned and occupied 'Meadow Hill House, Stable, Garden and Pleasure Ground' and two meadows, one on each side. When and from whom he bought the land I do not know. In 1881 the house was occupied by Theodora Countess of Cottenham, the six-year-old Earl of Cottenham and his young brother and the baby Lady Mary Pepys Cottenham, not to mention a governess, butler, housekeeper and five female servants. On the upper side of the Grove, as also mentioned earlier, a house was built by Dr Thomas Mayo in 1824 and sold in 1834 to Madame Caballero who called it 'Grecian Villa'. Another construction of about this time was the double archway which now leads out of the Grove at its eastern corner. This has been variously explained but surely formed part of the Grove Hill Gardens development into which the pathway leads and which has a matching archway at its Grove Hill Road entrance.

Today none of the original three Grove Houses remains; but the later addition Grove Villa is still there. What then happened to the original three? They are still visible on the Ordnance Survey map surveyed in 1866 although the North House has changed its name to 'The Parsonage' indicating its link with Christ Church. The Middle Grove House, if we are to believe later advertisements, became a school in 1845, as illustrated in the splendid print on page 53 above. In 1851 it was called the Grove School, the headmaster was 33-year-old William Earle and there were 64 pupils. In 1861 it was the Classical School and the headmaster was Jams J. Hart, aged 38, who seems to have continued until the early 1880s when a new principal, William Webber (no connection with the notorious Dr Webber), advertised in the *Gazette* on 6 January 1882 that he had been headmaster of a grammar school for upwards of 20 years and that the house and school were large and in a state of thorough repair with excellent sanitary arrangements. The school continued, under various names – Collegiate School, Grove House School and The Tunbridge Wells School Grove House – until 1902 when William Webber no longer appeared in lists of residents' names. Then Grove House disappears from the directories and in 1905 there is the first mention of 'Grove Avenue, from South Grove'. By 1906 there were a half-dozen houses in Grove Avenue and the next year just one in Christchurch

Avenue. Evidently, therefore, the old Great or Middle Grove House was demolished about 1903 and the construction of today's terrace houses on the site followed. About the details of this transformation I have no information. It should be noted that the High Street frontage of the garden had already been built on by 1866, as shown on the Ordnance Survey map, when it was called Grove Terrace and housed the Brackett's Estate Agency, then as now, and also, but not now, the Tunbridge Wells branch of the London and County Bank under its manager Edward Marchant Hunter, husband of one of Ann Friend's grand-daughters – see chapter 12.

This was in fact the last of the three original Grove Houses to go. The first was South Grove House which was still the home of that scion of the Fry family, the Rev. James, in 1874; but he was then 67 years old and decided on a new life in the West Country. The High Street frontage of the South Grove House garden had already been built up as shops, like its neighbour, and named South Grove Terrace; by the 1880s the house itself had been demolished and replaced by the terrace of 1-12 South Grove, leaving Grove Villa on the other side of the road as a memento of what had been. The story of the North Grove House is, of course, linked with that of Christ Church. Despite the evidence of the Tithe Award the house had been used, as indicated above, as the vicarage or 'parsonage', by the Rev. Ridgeway who was incumbent from 1857 to 1871. He was succeeded by Rev. Thomas E. Franklin, a nephew of the founder and first vicar, who, according to the church history by Spiers, lived at 16 Calverley Park and 'generously gave the site of the old vicarage over the tunnel, which was valued at £1,100 and also a donation of £200 towards the building fund for a new vicarage'. The phrase 'over the tunnel' perhaps provides a clue. The Rev. Franklin was evidently a man of means and preferred a house in Calverley Park to the old North Grove House which had suffered a tunnel built underneath when the railway was extended from Tunbridge Wells to Hastings in 1845. Reading between the lines, I guess that he was responsible for the order to demolish the old house soon after his arrival in 1871. The history merely says: 'the old Vicarage behind the Church had been pulled down'. In 1851 incidentally the house had been occupied by a railway contractor's clerk and a school consisting of his wife and three other teachers and 18 pupils. The point is obviously however that the house was the personal property of the Rev. Franklin, presumably by inheritance from his uncle – despite the Tithe Award! The church elders considered building on the donated land but eventually decided against and 67 Claremont Road, a rather grand house built on the site of Aretas Akers' old Belle Vue House (see chapter 23), was purchased as vicarage for the new incumbent. In 1932 it was sold, being too large for the purpose, and 22 Claremont Gardens was rented before a final move was made to the present vicarage not far away at 63 Claremont Road. The site of North Grove House has never been built on to this day; but part of the garden going down to the High Street alongside the church was used in 1899 for a Parish Hall, an unassuming building which nevertheless served many useful functions, not least that of Polling Station, now transferred to the Rev. John Banner's 'Modern Miracle', which saw the old church and hall demolished and replaced in 1997 by a multi-functional Church Centre – a far cry from the three 17th-century Grove Houses which used to dominate the 'new way from the Wells to Southborough'.

Chapter 7

The Mercer Strip

This is the narrow strip of land labelled 'Mercer Strip' on the Bowra plan in chapter 1, page 5. It adjoins the Grove at the top and runs straight down to the High Street taking in the new town houses on the northern side of Warwick Road; but not the older ones on the other side of the road nor the *Grove Tavern* or the back of Berkeley Place or the terrace houses running up to Miles' Garage. It excludes also the houses of South Grove which, as we saw in the previous chapter, were built on the site of the South Grove House. The main buildings included are those flanking Belgrove including Belgrove House, the *Compasses* and the later buildings in the plot above the *Compasses*. This piece or parcel of Inhams Heath was, as already indicated, leased with other land in one of Lady Purbeck's first transactions to William Fullman on 4 November 1684 at £2 15s. 0d. per annum. Who Fullman was I have no information but anyway he did not last long. As the Grove Trust deed suggests and the Poor Rate record confirms, this lease was taken over by John Mercer. The Poor Rate sequence starts with William Fulman in July 1685 and by December has become 'Wm Fulman and John Mercer'; and in 1687 Fullman dropped out and, with some interruptions, John Mercer continued paying rates until 1714 when the entries for two half-years read: 'John Mercer or Cutt Bland' and 'Mr Bland for John Mercer or occ' – after which comes the usual gap until 1728. During this period, of course, and before 1703 John Mercer must, like all those others who became parties to the Trust Deed, have purchased his freehold.

The idea of leasing strips of land going up from the 'New Way from the Wells to Southborough' (the High Street) was to build a lodging house at the bottom and so we should expect to find a house in this position; and if we glance at Bowra's plan on the next page there it is, marked Robt Mercer with a nice double row of trees in the front garden. Robert was one of three sons of John Mercer whose will, in which he described himself as a yeoman of Speldhurst parish, was made in 1730 and proved in 1733. The eldest son Thomas had already been settled with property which is therefore not specified; Robert the next is bequeathed a 25-acre farm at Etherton Hill in Speldhurst together with the *Compasses* and a small house nearby occupied by John Willington; the third son Edward was under age in 1730, since the executors were instructed to put him out to a trade of his choosing and to provide for him during his apprenticeship. He was to receive, after his mother's lifetime, a house on Mount Sion Hill occupied by Cuthbert Bland. At the Centre for Kentish Studies in Maidstone there is a copy of the will which has been annotated, presumably by a later solicitor. On the outside is pencilled: 'Miss Baker to keep in respect of title to Camden House'; and on the inside, against the bequest to Edward, is the note: 'Miss Baker's idea is that this is Philpotts'.

A little local knowledge helps to explain these annotations. In the first place, as we shall see in chapter 15, Edward Mercer chose to be a plumber and glazier; and married Priscilla Seale whose father was a plumber and glazier. Whether he attracted Priscilla because he had already chosen her father's trade or whether he chose his apprenticeship with an eye on the girl who can say? Be that as it may, the marriage proved childless and when Edward eventually died in 1790 he left all his property to his sister who was the widow of Edmond Baker the bookseller and had one spinster daughter – who is the Miss Baker of the solicitor's annotations. What is more, the Barrow and Tithe maps show that the same house was in 1808 labelled 'Mr J Delves (late Philpots)' and in 1840 was called Camden House. So this is clearly the house, marked 'Robt Mercer' on the Bowra map, which stands on the northern corner of the High Street and what later became Warwick Road – which took its name from Warwick House on the other corner.

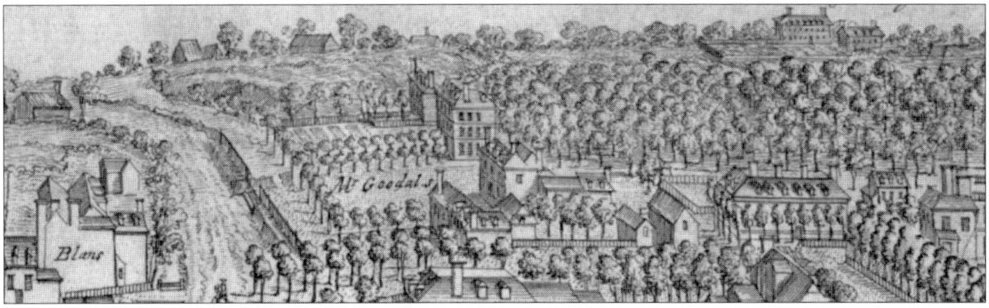

Kip's engraving 1719

As a warning against assumptions, look again at the detail from Kip's engraving which we saw in chapter 5, get in your time machine and take a walk up the High Street. On the right you come to the three Grove Houses lying well back from the road labelled 'Mr Goodals'; but just before this is a building with a tall chimney (by the 's' of Goodals). This must be Camden House and opposite it on the left is a largish block of buildings marked 'Blans'. Now do you remember that Cutt Bland and Mr Bland appeared in the Poor Rate record and that Edward Mercer was to inherit a house occupied by Cuthbert Bland? Surely 'Blans' and 'Blands' must be the same thing? Three independent sources reinforcing one another cannot be a coincidence. The trouble is that the 'Blans' building is on the wrong side of the High Street and seems to correspond with the building called 'Horse and Groom' on Bowra. The only way out is to postulate that Cuthbert Bland had an interest in buildings on both sides of the High Street – maybe not both at the same time. Here it is on the Bowra plan.

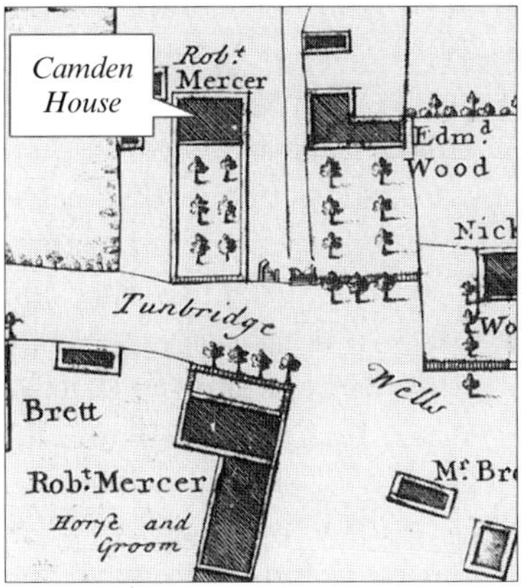

Bowra plan 1738

Back to John Mercer's will. Edward (to recap) was to have the house at the bottom of the hill (Philpots or Camden House) and Robert a farm and the *Compasses* and a small house nearby occupied by John Willington. The exact wording is the 'little messuage or tenement thereto adjoining [i.e. adjoining the *Compasses*] with the garden and appurtenances ... now occupied by John Willington situate ... at or near Inhams Bush commonly called Mount Sion Grove'. Alongside this bequest on the Maidstone copy of the will is another pencilled annotation: 'This is the cottage next Miss Fry's Gateway leading into the Grove from Mount Sion'. Now, we know that Miss Fry was mistress of the South Grove House – so I can only think that the reference is to the tiny house shown on Bowra beside the south-west (bottom right) corner of the Grove – a bit far to be 'adjoining' the *Compasses* but that seems to be what the solicitor's note is suggesting. The *Compasses* is not actually named as such in John Mercer's will: it is described as the 'messuage or tenement with the barn outbuildings garden and appurtenances ... now occupied by Widow Mathews'. Another building not named in John Mercer's will, as the sharper reader will have noticed, is the very substantial building marked 'Robt Mercer' a little way below the *Compasses*. Why does John Mercer say nothing about this important property in his will? Well, it took me a long time to tumble to it but the answer is very simple. It wasn't there in 1730 but it was in 1738! And it must be this house – Belgrove House.

Belgrove House

There is a Poor Rate sequence which tends to confirm this theory. It starts in 1737 with 'William Verrall for a new house' and in 1759 changes to 'Mr William Gratton for Verralls'. And here Robert Mercer's will fits in nicely. It is dated 1759 and it mentions 'My messuage Tenement or Lodging House with the Shops Edifices Buildings Closes Yards Backsides Garden Ground and Appurtenances … situate … on Mount Sion … and now in the occupation of William Gratton'. The Poor Rate record shows that William Gratton continued in occupation until 1765 when the Rev. Mr Johnston took over until 1776 – he was the Minister at the Chapel in Little Mount Sion and we shall meet him and his numerous progeny in chapter 14.

John Mercer's will left the *Compasses* to his son Robert subject to an annuity of £7 which was to be paid, out of the income of the *Compasses* and the Willington cottage, to his daughter Anne Mercer for her maintenance and livelihood for life. This annuity is re-affirmed in the will of Robert Mercer, providing additional confirmation that the messuage occupied by the Widow Mathews and the *Compasses* are one and the same. Robert gave the 25-acre farm in Speldhurst to his son Thomas; the 'new' house occupied by William Gratton to his daughter Jane; and the *Compasses* and the little cottage to daughter Mary, the two girls being jointly responsible for paying Aunt Anne's annuity. Things, however, did not turn out quite as planned. Mary died after her father but under the age of 21 and unmarried. Her interest in the *Compasses*, therefore, passed to her brother Thomas but he in turn died, a bachelor and intestate. This left only one child, daughter Jane, who inherited everything. She had married in 1772 a man who is quite significant in Tunbridge Wells history – Jasper Sprange, the bookseller and publisher of the Sprange guides. These were the first of a series of guide books to Tunbridge Wells which run through Colbran, Clifford and Pelton to the present-day; but, being the earliest in date, are perhaps the most useful in the historical information they contain. The first *Sprange Guide* appeared in 1780 and the last in 1817. Here is the title page from one published in 1780.

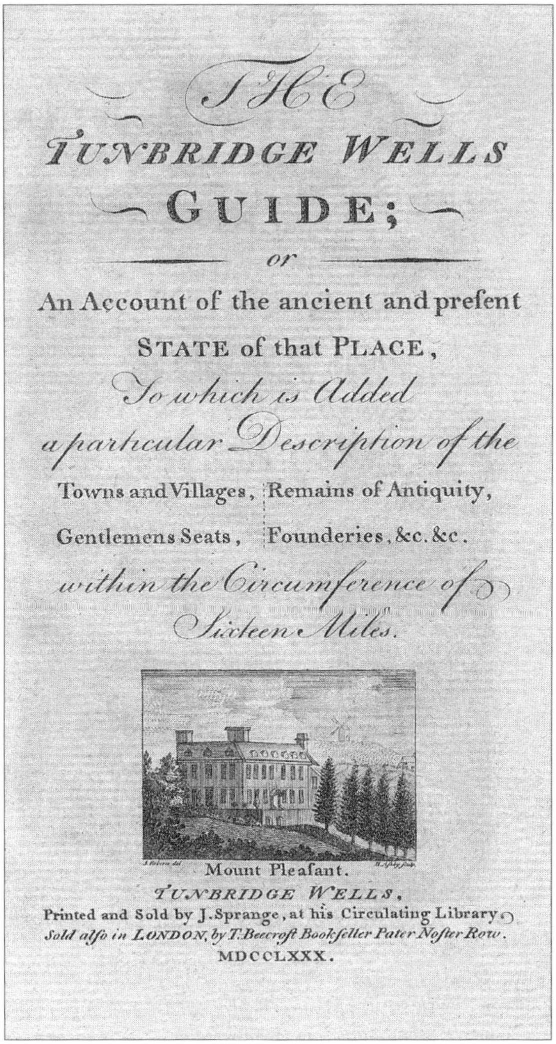
THE
TUNBRIDGE WELLS
GUIDE;
or
An Account of the ancient and prefent
STATE of that PLACE,
To which is Added
a particular Description of the
Towns and Villages, Remains of Antiquity,
Gentlemens Seats, Founderies, &c. &c.
within the Circumference of
Sixteen Miles.

Mount Pleafant.
TUNBRIDGE WELLS,
Printed and Sold by J.Sprange, at his Circulating Library;
Sold alfo in LONDON, by T.Beecroft Bookfeller Pater Nofter Row.
MDCCLXXX.

Sprange Guide *1780 – title page*

One of the most valuable features of the *Sprange Guides* is the list of lodging houses which form a kind of appendix towards the end of each edition. No doubt the list was eagerly scanned by prospective visitors and helped in the choice of suitable accommodation; but what Jasper did not perhaps foresee was how useful his lists would be to historians of two hundred years in the future. Here is an example, from the 1780 guide, showing the Bedlam-house (fifth from bottom of page 4) which will feature in chapter 26. The column headings P, C and S stand

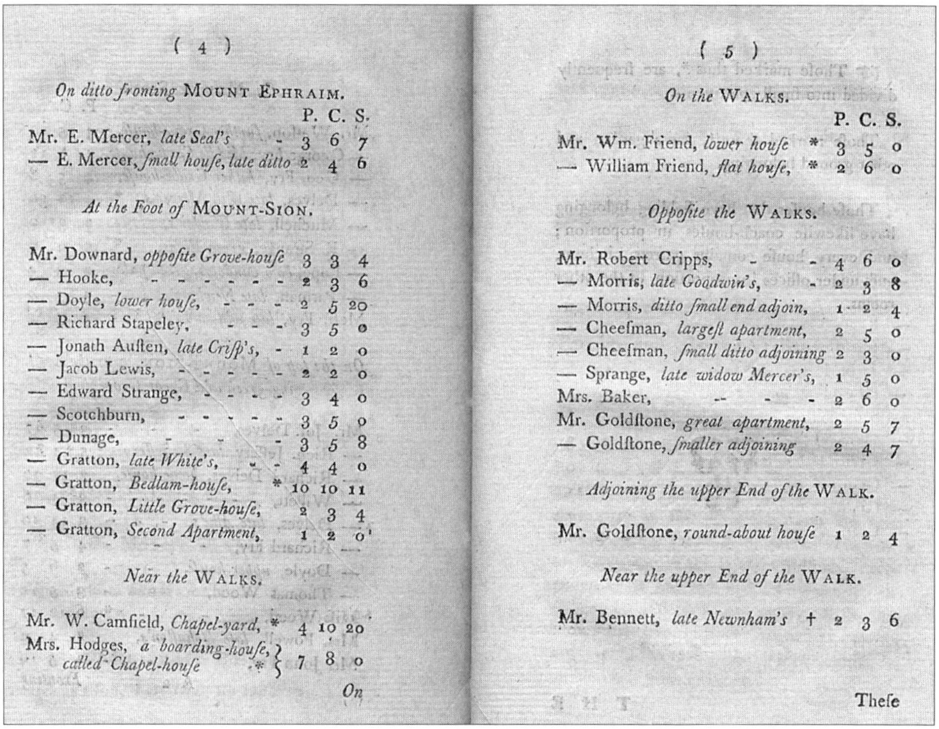

(4)

On ditto fronting MOUNT EPHRAIM.

	P.	C.	S.
Mr. E. Mercer, *late Seal's* -	3	6	7
— E. Mercer, *ſmall houſe, late ditto*	2	4	6

At the Foot of MOUNT-SION.

	P.	C.	S.
Mr. Downard, *oppoſite Grove-houſe*	3	3	4
— Hooke, - - - - - - -	2	3	6
— Doyle, *lower houſe,* - - -	2	5	20
— Richard Stapeley, - - -	3	5	0
— Jonath Auſten, *late Criſp's,* -	1	2	0
— Jacob Lewis, - - - - -	2	2	0
— Edward Strange, - - - -	3	4	0
— Scotchburn, - - - - - -	3	5	0
— Dunage, - - -	3	5	8
— Gratton, *late White's,* - -	4	4	0
— Gratton, *Bedlam-houſe,* *	10	10	11
— Gratton, *Little Grove-houſe,*	2	3	4
— Gratton, *Second Apartment,*	1	2	0

Near the WALKS.

	P.	C.	S.
Mr. W. Camfield, *Chapel-yard,* *	4	10	20
Mrs. Hodges, *a boarding-houſe, called Chapel-houſe* *	7	8	0

On

(5)

On the WALKS.

	P.	C.	S.
Mr. Wm. Friend, *lower houſe* *	3	5	0
— William Friend, *flat houſe,* *	2	6	0

Oppoſite the WALKS.

	P.	C.	S.
Mr. Robert Cripps, - -	4	6	0
— Morris, *late Goodwin's,* -	2	3	8
— Morris, *ditto ſmall end adjoin,*	1	2	4
— Cheeſman, *largeſt apartment,*	2	5	0
— Cheeſman, *ſmall ditto adjoining*	2	3	0
— Sprange, *late widow Mercer's,*	1	5	0
Mrs. Baker, - - -	2	6	0
Mr. Goldſtone, *great apartment,*	2	5	7
— Goldſtone, *ſmaller adjoining*	2	4	7

Adjoining the upper End of the WALK.

	P.	C.	S.
Mr. Goldſtone, *round-about houſe*	1	2	4

Near the upper End of the WALK.

	P.	C.	S.
Mr. Bennett, *late Newnham's* †	2	3	6

Theſe

Sprange Guide *1780 – Lodging Houses pp.4 & 5*

for parlours, chambers and stables. Sprange also reproduces engravings of local scenes, such as on the next page 'A View of Mount Sion Hill Tunbridge Wells from the Common', dated November 1780. You can make out, starting from the right, Mount Sion Road, Frog Lane, narrow and shaded, Little Mount Sion curving to the left, the Grove massive in the background and three Grove Houses in front. More difficult are the three houses we are presently concerned with – the *Compasses*, Belgrove House and the one at the bottom later called Camden House. There is a large house at the bottom of Little Mount Sion, on the left, which must be Rosebury House which is now Silks, and next to, and slightly behind it, must be Warwick House. So the building next on the left again must be Camden House. If you now look behind Camden House, up the hill, you can see what must be Belgrove House and then, nestling in the trees of the Grove, the *Compasses*, and

Mount Sion Hill from the Common 1780

maybe the little hut to the left of Camden House is the Willington Cottage, but it looks too far down the hill.

On 28 February 1774 the *Sussex Weekly Advertiser* carried a report that the Postmaster-general had appointed 'Mr Jasper Sprange, bookseller at Tunbridge Wells, to succeed the late Mr Edmund Baker, as post-master for Tunbridge'; and the next issue announced 'that the bookselling, stationary [*sic*], binding, and perfumery branches, lately carried on by Mr Edmund Baker, is now intended to be carried on in partnership between his widow and Jasper Sprange'. Jasper was the son of a Goudhurst yeoman who had become apprentice to Edmund Baker in 1761, had stayed on after completion of his apprenticeship and had married the niece of his master's wife – and she, as we have seen, inherited her father's entire estate on the deaths of her brother and sister. On 17 March 1776, in consideration of Jane's love and affection for her husband, the *Compasses* and other property were conveyed to Richard Delves in trust for Jasper and his heirs for ever. Why Richard Delves (see chapter 21) should have been chosen as trustee I do not know. Perhaps it was because he was a member of the family, having married Dorothea Mercer in 1752 – but where Dory fitted in I am not sure. Richard Delves incidentally was called a gunpowder-maker in this document which is one of the Whitbread deeds of the *Compasses*. Anyway, no sooner had the wicked Jasper (are not all Jaspers villains?) got his hands on the property than he mortgaged the *Compasses* for £400. It has been suggested that he needed the money for a new venture – into printing. At all events he started printing in 1777 – books, playbills, posters, auction notices and so on; and, as we have seen, he produced his first Tunbridge Wells *Guide* only three years later. We know something about his output because he kept a record by pasting copies into large scrapbooks. Arthur Brackett, whose father

William had purchased the old Sprange printing business, described these scrap-books in his *Tunbridge Wells through the Centuries*, published in 1928, saying that they contained printed specimens from 1779.

In 1781 and 1784 Jasper took out further mortgages and then in 1790 he went bankrupt. It has been suggested that he was so obsessed with tinkering about with successive reprintings and editions of his *Tunbridge Wells Guide* that he neglected his finances. The wicked Jasper soon bounced back thanks to his wife's inheritance. On 15 June 1790 the following notice appeared in the *Maidstone Journal*:

> To be sold by auction by Messrs Skinner and Cheesman at the New Inn Tunbridge Wells on Tuesday 20th July next between the hours of three and six in the afternoon the following Freehold estates, belonging to Mr Jasper Sprange, bookseller, by the direction of his assignees:
>
> Lot 1 A Messuage, Tenement or Public House called the Compasses and Horse Shoe, with a Yard and Garden, containing about a quarter of an acre, with two stables containing together seven stalls and also two coach houses, situate on Mount Sion Hill and now in the occupation of Richard Jeffery, at the yearly rent of £20.
>
> Lot 2 A Messuage, Tenement or Lodging House, Garden and Appurtenances on Mount Sion Hill (situate near Lot 1) and also a small Tenement adjoining in the Occupation of Mrs Mary Powell ... at the yearly rent of £15.

Mrs Powell is recognisable as the ratepayer who succeeded the Rev. Johnston, so Lot 2 must be Belgrove House. Lot 3 was another small house on Mount Sion and Lots 4 and 5 made up the Speldhurst farm which would have belonged to Jane's brother Thomas if he had not died early. I wonder how Jane felt seeing the hammer fall on the whole Mercer family inheritance which had come to her. At least it was not total ruin because in November her husband was granted a bankruptcy certificate and was in business again – which he carried on, bringing out new editions of the *Guide* every few years, until 1817 when his sister's son, John Clifford, took over and Jasper died in 1823.

The *Compasses* was knocked down at £440 to a John Deards esquire who immediately resold to Thomas Wood. The Wood family will be dealt with in chapter 12. Thomas, described in the Abstract of Title by the way as a jeweller, lived in Burlington House just across the road from the *Compasses*. Thomas may have thought it a good idea to purchase his local when it came on the market. Having done so, he mortgaged it on the spot to a tallowchandler from Tonbridge and it was still mortgaged when he died in 1808. As we shall see when dealing with Ashenhurst's Great House in chapter 10, Thomas Wood had no children and his property passed to his three sisters, Sarah and Mary Wood and Ann Friend. Sarah and Mary, however, died in 1811 and 1818. In 1815 the mortgage was taken over from the Tonbridge tallowchandler at an increased rate of interest of five per cent by William Hodges who happened to be the pub's own landlord. This mortgage was only redeemed in 1833 after the death of Ann Friend who bequeathed to her unmarried daughter Jane her 'messuage tenement and public house called the

Compasses ... with the coachhouse stables buildings yards gardens and appurtenances as the same are now occupied by William Hodges ...' The executors, Thomas Fry the Sion Crescent schoolmaster and gentleman William Jewhurst of Tonbridge, sold Berkeley Place and other property but redeemed the *Compasses* mortgage to the tune of £500 12s. 6d. Jane Friend was thus in a position in 1845 to cash in her inheritance 'in fee free from incumbrances' for the sum of £1,200. The purchaser was a Tunbridge Wells brewer named William Henry Lidbetter who immediately raised £1,600 on the security of the *Compasses* and one pub in Speldhurst and another in Ashurst; and then sold all three in 1853 to Newnham and Kelsey of Tunbridge Wells. The subsequent ownership of the *Compasses* within the brewing industry is of no great relevance to the history of Mount Sion; but more details may be found in Hetherington and Griffith's *Old Pubs of Tunbridge Wells and District*.

There was, however, one final change of ownership which is relevant. This concerns the irregular square of land between the *Compasses* and Claremont Road on which the houses at one time called Oak Villa, West Grove and Frankville (now 47 Little Mount Sion and 62/70 Claremont Road) were later built. This square of land was sold by Newnham and Kelsey in 1854, a year after its acquisition, to Henry Chapman, gentleman, and Henry Creasey, butcher, both of Tunbridge Wells, for £375. An agreement dated 7 March 1889 was made between Edward and Henry Kelsey and George Marchant of Warwick House or Oak Villa concerning the construction of windows overlooking the *Compasses* yard and some infringement of the boundary. Warwick House, see page 63 above, was the house which gave its name to Warwick Road. *Kelly's Directory* for 1886 lists George Marchant as a plumber at Warwick House; but I think, in fact, that the house on the High Street had been demolished by 1880 and therefore Marchant must have transferred the name to what later became Oak Villa – but this is somewhat speculative.

My information on ownership of the *Compasses* has come mainly from the deeds held by Whitbreads; but, of course, they do not tell us anything about the other properties which went under the hammer in 1790 – Belgrove House and Camden House in particular. Let's consider first Camden House, also known as Philpots. You will remember that this house, facing the High Street, at the bottom and on the right (looking downhill) of what is now Warwick Road, was left by John Mercer to his youngest son Edward in 1730 and therefore has a different history from that of the *Compasses*; and you may remember that Miss Baker and her solicitor were worrying about the title around 1800. This is all consistent with what we know since Edward Mercer, having no children, left his property to his sister and Miss Baker was the sister's daughter. At this point, however, there is a bit of a gap. The next reliable source of information is the Tithe map of 1840 which tells us that the owner is Mr John Stileman Bostock. He may have bought the house from the executors of Miss Baker who died in 1829; but the occupier in 1840 is Miss Sydall about whom some details can be had from the 1841 census.

She is described as a 55-year-old schoolmistress and seems to be running a school with a staff/pupil ratio of one to one since she has two pupils aged 10 and 13 on her books as well as a 35-year-old female teacher. Whether coincidentally or not, the owner of the adjoining Warwick House is given as Ann Sydall.

Exactly when Camden House was demolished I am not sure. It seems to be there on the Ordnance Survey map surveyed in 1866, nestling obscurely behind a solid row of High Street shops. *Mathieson's Directory* of 1867/8 does not name it, however, showing only the shops under the name Camden Place, nos 1-4, which are also to be found in the 1851 census together with Camden Cottages, nos 1, 2 and 3. Perhaps this was the beginning of the terrace of cottages which eventually replaced Camden House on the north side of Warwick Road. These were demolished very recently to make way for a modern terrace of town houses. Belgrove House is perhaps of greater interest than Camden House because it is still there. The house is marked on Barrow's map of 1808 as other than a lodging house, which means that no details are provided of ownership or occupancy. Here is an enlargement from the rather small-scale map. The main house and all the frontage to Little Mount Sion seem to be there with some of the adjoining cottages; but

Barrow map 1808

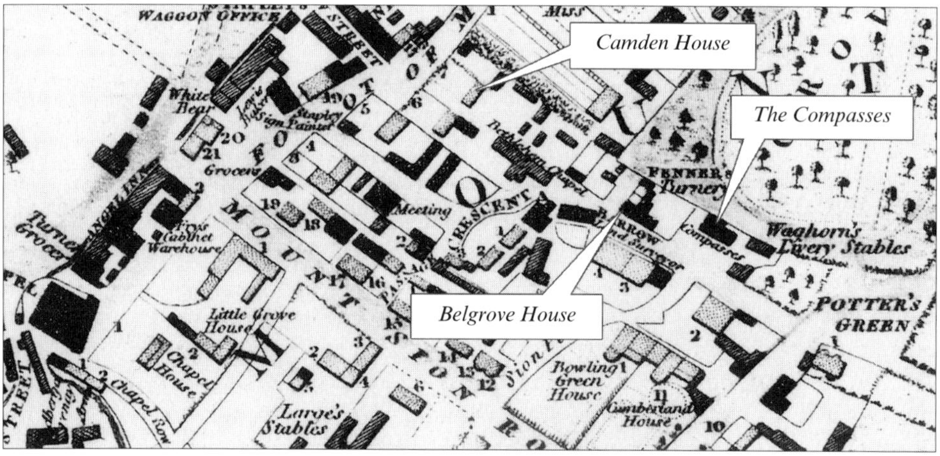

what is intriguing is the label 'Fenner's Turnery' at the Grove end. It is also frustrating because I have never been able to find out any more about what was surely a Tunbridge Ware workshop – Fenner being an important name in the industry. The only slight clue I have come across is in the deeds of Miles Garage which tell us that an old stable at the *Blue Anchor Inn* was used as a turner's shop in 1790 and might possibly have transferred to Belgrove; but this story will be dealt with in detail in chapter 12. As far as Fenner's Turnery in Belgrove is concerned, it cannot have lasted long. The next piece of evidence is the Tithe map of 1840. The next page shows a detail. The colouring of the map at Maidstone is a bit faint although perfectly clear when seen in the original. The piece we are interested in is numbered 3795 and the corresponding entry in the Tithe Award reads: 'Belgrove House and Garden, 6 Houses and Courts, Owner – Sarah Hodges, Occupier – Hodges and others'. As you can see, the property includes not only Belgrove House itself but also the adjoining cottages and the one near the *Compasses* now called Grove Cottage. How this adds up to six houses is not very clear. What is clear is that the Belgrove Cottages were in existence in 1840 and that in all probability Fenner's Turnery had been demolished to make way.

Tithe map 1840

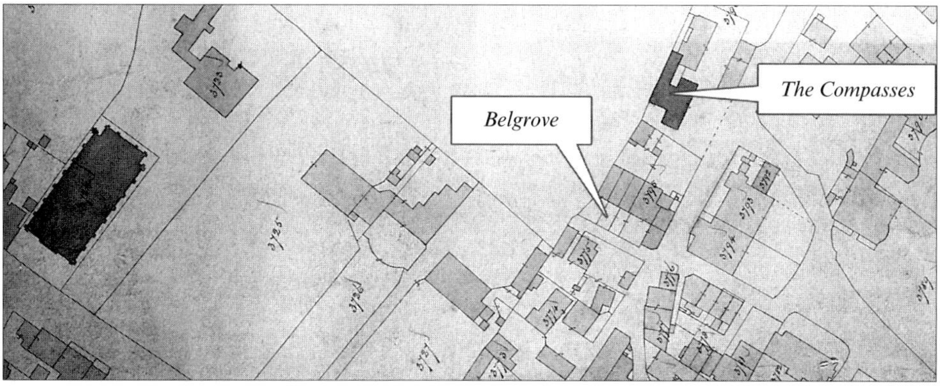

Sarah Hodges was the mother of William Hodges whose name cropped up, you remember, as landlord of the *Compasses* at the time of Ann Friend's will in 1831 – and as the man who took over the mortgage of his own pub in 1815. I know about the mother because I have a copy of William Hodges' will supplied by one of his descendants who made some enquiries at the Reference Library and later contacted me. She did not know about his connection with the *Compasses* but was interested in the family business in Corn, Hay and Coal in Hodges Yard which is now Cumberland Yard. Actually there were two William Hodges, father and son, both of whom were 'occupiers' of the *Compasses* according to the Whitbread deeds; but the mother, Sarah, was evidently the wife of the elder. Anyway, the will which is dated 1854 refers to William's 'right title and interest expectant on the death of my dear mother Sarah Hodges of in and to all those several messuages or dwelling houses hereditaments and premises called or known as Grove Place situate and being on Mount Sion'. He bequeaths the property to trustees for the benefit of his daughter, married to John Martyr Luck, and their children. How the Hodges family came to acquire the Belgrove property I have no information – perhaps at the 1790 auction.

Having explored the ownership history of the Mercer strip it is time to look at the occupants. There is nothing more to add to what has already emerged about the occupancy of Camden House and Belgrove but about the landlords of the *Compasses* more information is available. The first one we can be sure of – and probably the first one ever – is Thomas Mathews. The Tonbridge parish register records the burial of 'Thomas Mathews of the Compasses Mount Sion' on

16 October 1718 and an inventory of his goods taken after his death for probate purposes has fortunately survived – see below with a transcription alongside. It was drawn up by William Baines who ran the brewery on the site of the Central Station and Philip Seale of Little Mount Sion. William Baines had to sign with his mark; so I assume the scraggly handwriting is that of Philip Seale.

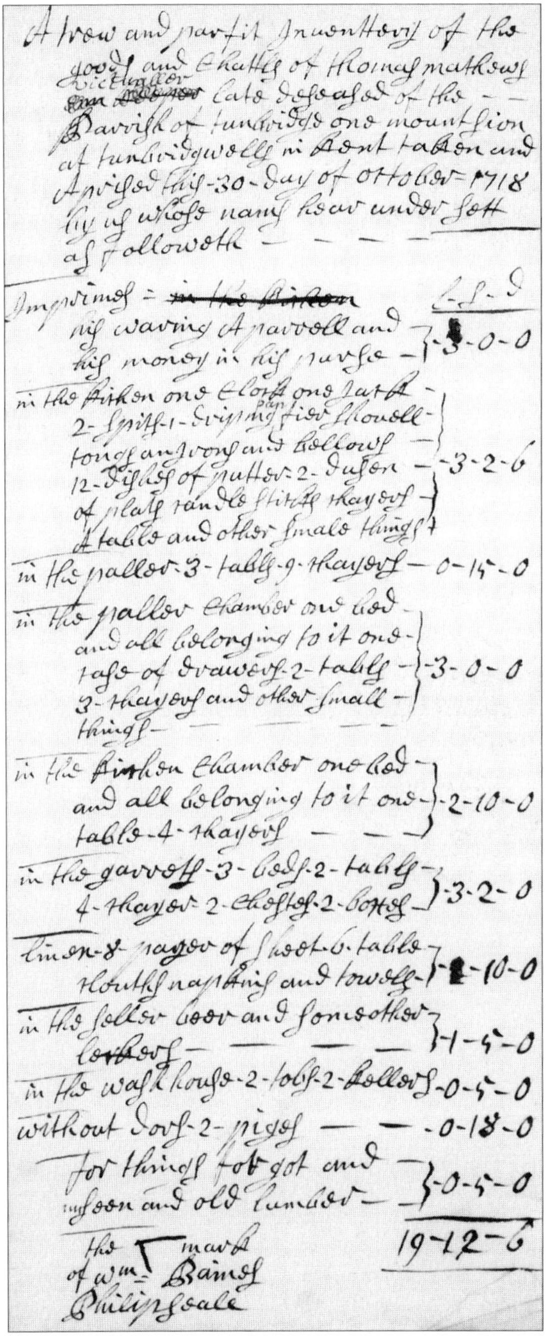

A trew and parfit Inventtory of the
goods and Chattels of Thomas mathews
Victtaller late deseased of the – –
Parrish of tunbridge one mount sion
at tunbridgwells in Kent taken and
Aprised this 30 day of ottober 1718
by us whose names hear under sett
as followeth – – – –
Imprimis = ~~in the kitchen~~ £-s-d
his waring Aparrell and
his money in his purse – 3-0-0
in the kitchen one Clock one Jack
2 spitts 1 dripping pan fier shovell
tongs andirons and bellows
12 dishes of putter 2 dusen
of plats candle sticks chayers
A table and other smale things – 3-2-6
in the parlor 3 tables 9 chayers – 0-15-0
in the parlor chamber one bed
and all belonging to it one
case of drawers 2 tables
3 chayers and other small
things – 3-0-0
in the kitchen Chamber one bed
and all belonging to it one
table 4 chayers – 2-10-0
in the garrett 3 beds 2 tables
4 chayer 2 chests 2 boxes – 3-2-0
linen 8 payer of sheet 6 table
clouths napkins and towells – 1-10-0
in the seller beer and some other
liquers – 1-5-0
in the wash house 2 tubs 2 rollers – 0-5-0
without dors 2 pigs – 0-18-0
for things forgot and
unseen and old lumber – 0-5-0
19-12-6
the mark of wm Baines
Philip Seale

A true and perfect inventory of the goods and chattels of Thomas Mathews victualler late deceased of the Parish of Tunbridge on Mount Sion at Tunbridge Wells in Kent taken and appraised this 30 day of October 1718 by us whose names hereunder set as followeth - - - -

Imprimis his wearing apparel and his money in his purse – £3-0-0

In the kitchen one clock one jack 2 spits 1 dripping pan fire shovel tongs andirons and bellows 12 dishes of pewter 2 dozen of plates candle sticks chairs a table and other small things – £3-2-6

In the parlour 3 tables 9 chairs – £0-15-0

In the parlour chamber one bed and all belonging to it one case of drawers 2 tables 3 chairs and other small things – £3-0-0

In the kitchen chamber one bed and all belonging to it one table 4 chairs – £2-10-0

In the garret 3 beds 2 tables 4 chair 2 chests 2 boxes – £3-2-0

Linen 8 pair of sheets 6 tablecloths napkins and towels – £1-10-0

In the cellar beer and some other liquors – £1-5-0

In the wash house 2 tubs 2 rollers – £0-5-0

Without doors 2 pigs – £0-18-0

For things forgot and unseen and old lumber – £0-5-0

Total – £19-12-6

At first sight this seems so meagre as to be impossible to reconcile with the *Compasses* of today. If, however, the whole of the front building (which a glance at the Tithe map above shows was there already in 1840) is taken away in imagination it begins to make sense. What remains is the little old building at the back which is shown in this photograph. This building had two rooms on the ground floor, the kitchen and the parlour, two corresponding bedrooms on the first floor and a garret above. Underneath was the cellar and alongside the washhouse – and somewhere outside were the pigs.

The Compasses *– side view at back*

Can we go any further back in time? This is where the Poor Rate record ought to come in useful; but unfortunately, as will be discussed in the next chapter, there is a gap in the record from 1714 to 1728. Anne Mathews, widow of Thomas, appears in 1728 and thereafter there is a good sequence until 1797 but the link back to 1714 is tentative. It is based on position on the 'collector's route'. The Widow Mathews is listed between 'Mr Bland for Riders' and William Baines' brewhouse. On the 1714 side of the gap exactly the same position is occupied by 'Mr (Thomas) Penny or tenant for a new house'. This listing continues back to 1702 and then stops. For the years 1702 to 1704 this entry is followed immediately by 'Mr Penny for a Barne and Coachhouse'.

Back to the *Compasses*! We've 'done' the owners; let's take a quick look at the landlords, publicans or 'mine hosts' over the years. The earliest we can be sure of is Thomas Mathews whose probate inventory we saw at the beginning; but there is a bit of a puzzle about him. Records of 'Licensees' Recognizances' exist at Maidstone and there are complete tables for the local district for the years 1715 and 1718; but the *Compasses* appears in neither. Thomas Mathews, however, does – as 'victualler' at the *Carpenters Arms* where in 1715 William Mercer and Robert Friend stood surety for him. Did the name change – there is a certain association perhaps between Carpenters and Compasses? But if so it must have taken place between the date of the recognizances on 21 August 1718 and the burial of Thomas on 16 October. Be that as it may, the widow Anne took over bravely from Thomas until 1757 although there is an interlude from 1745 to 1749 when Charles Beadle appears in the Poor Rate record 'for Widow Mathews'. The Licensees' Recognizances show Ann Bodle at the *Compasses* in 1746 and again in 1752 at the *Compasses* and *Horseshoe*. Ann Bodle was perhaps the wife of Charles Beadle; her will dated 1753 reveals that she was the sister of Christopher Cripps who took over as landlord in 1758. She left money to her brother, who was a cooper, and to Richard Newnham, a Speldhurst brewer, in trust for the benefit of her daughter Ann until she reached the age of 21. The will was witnessed by Thomas Wood junior (perhaps he who was to buy the *Compasses* in 1790) and by William Verrall (occupier of Belgrove House until 1755). A further illustration of the interlocking relationships in the small world of 18th-century Mount Sion is the fact that the wife of Robert Mercer (described as an innkeeper of Speldhurst Parish) was Jane, daughter of Richard Newnham the Elder – see chapter 18.

Here is the Poor Rate record for the Compasses during the 18th century:

1702-04	Thomas Penny or Tenant for a new house
	Mr Penny for a Barne & Coachhouse
1705-14	Thomas Penny or tenant for a new house
1728-42	Wid Mathews
1743-44	Wid Mathews or occ
1745-49	Cha Beadle or occ for Wid Mathews
1750-57	Wid Mathews
1758-61	Chris Crippes for Wid Mathews
1762-64	Chris Crippes for late Mathew's
1765-70	Robt Cripps for late Mathews
1771-74	Robt Cripps for Mathewss
1775	Robt Cripps or occ for Mathewss
1776-78	Robt Cripps for Mathewss
1779-80	Pack Thos for late Cripps's
1781-82	Pack Thos or Widow for late Cripps's
1783-89	Pack Widow for late Cripps's
1790-91	Jeffery __________ for late Wo Pack's before Cripps'
1792-97	Jeffery Richd for late Wo Pack's

You will see that the Cripps family (was Robert the son of Christopher?) followed widow Mathews for a long time, to be replaced by Thomas Pack and his widow. You might assume that the change to Jeffery in 1790 had something to do with the auction sale of that year (which incidentally shows that the missing Christian name was Richard); but there was another compelling reason which I shall come to later.

There is a slight conflict of evidence for the years 1795 and 1796. One of the posters from Jasper Sprange's scrapbooks (reproduced in chapter 22) announces an auction to be held on 22 September 1795 at 'Mr Stephens, The Horseshoe and Compasses, Mount Sion'; and there is additional evidence for Mr Stephens in

November 1796 which I shall come to later. Maybe the conflict can be resolved by assuming that Stephens was a sub-tenant of Richard Jeffery. On 22 January 1805 the *Maidstone Journal* announced an auction sale which may or may not refer to the *Compasses*. To be sold, on the premises at Tunbridge Wells, by T. Cheesman on 25th instant was 'the lease of a good accustomed PUBLIC HOUSE known by the name of Nicholas Jeffery late deceased 20 years of which were unexpired at midsummer day last with the advantage of a well attended Weekly Corn Market'. Well, I am sure that the pub was not called 'Nicholas Jeffery late deceased'! So I assume that the printer missed out a line; but this means unfortunately that we have to guess where the pub was. Further particulars were to be had from Joseph Delves of Mount Sion – which suggests this locality as does also the fact that Lot 3 was a Hay Stack standing near Chalk Hall and Lot 4 was the lease of a two-acre meadow also situated near Chalk Hall 'together with a capital Bay Mare, a quantity of sheep, two hogs, a Dung Cart and a Light Cart'. I think it *must* be the *Compasses* – in which case I assume that Richard Jeffery was succeeded by Nicholas who then died causing the lease to fall in. I guess that it was then taken on by William Hodges but of course there may have been an intervening landlord. It is interesting that there was a weekly corn market – and well attended! I wonder whether it may not have given William Hodges the idea of starting up his corn business in Cumberland Yard?

The Whitbread deeds tell us that the pub was in the occupation of William Hodges in 1845, then of his son William and then of Thomas Baker; and Baker appears as occupier in the Tithe Award and also heads the list of landlords which the co-author of *Old Pubs of Tunbridge Wells and District* has kindly supplied – as follows:

1839-50	Thomas Baker
1852	J Jarvis
1855	C Pantry
1857-59	Benjamin Cooper
1867	C Waghorne
1874	H Clifford
1878-92	W.G.Hobbs
1893-1903	J Wells
1904-15	C.H.French
1916	Mrs French

Or should we say the Widow French? Anyway I think we can stop there with a last example of the good old custom of the widow carrying on behind the bar!

W.G.Hobbs: Compasses *landlord 1878-1892*

In conclusion here are a few stories I have found about the *Compasses*. The earliest comes from the Tonbridge Parish Overseers' Accounts, where the following entry occurs on the 14 February 1730:

> Paid Christopher Turner for a Coffin for a Travelling man that died at the Compasses and for Carriage......£0-7-2.

On 4 November 1796 John, Earl of Darnley, Lord of the Manor of Southborough, held a Court Leet – where is not recorded but the *Hand and Sceptre* by the cricket green seems a likely spot. The Manor of Southborough seems to have taken over the public order functions of the moribund manor of South Frith in the Tunbridge Wells area. Joseph Delves and Charles Cripps were on the Jury; John Callow was the Street Driver responsible for putting stray cattle in the pound; and James Nye, the Tunbridge Ware maker, was the Ale Conner who is supposed to have used the stickiness of beer-soaked trousers to check the strength of the brew. Be that as it may, the Jury on this occasion complained that 'a certain Sewer at the Back of a Public-House called the Horse Shoe and Compasses on Mount Sion Hill in the occupation of Thomas Stevens within the jurisdiction of this Court Leet overflows in and upon the Footpath leading through the Grove on Mount Sion aforesaid being a common Highway leading through the said Grove to Pembury to the great Annoyance of his Majesty's Subjects passing the said Highway and that the said Thomas Stevens do remove or repair the said Nuisance within Six Weeks from this Day or that he be amerced 13s and 4d'. This is the second mention of Stevens (Stephens?) referred to above.

The Jury also commanded Thomas Wood, on the same penalty, to remove the dunghill which he had made 'opposite the Grove Gate at the Head of the Garden of the aforesaid Thomas Stevens near the King's Highway'. This was, I assume, on the piece of land belonging to the *Compasses* which was sold separately in 1854. Thomas Wood, being the owner of the *Compasses*, seems to have felt free to make use of the *Compasses* land in preference to his own garden on the other side of Little Mount Sion.

The same piece of land was the scene for the following story which appeared in the *Maidstone Journal* of 9 March 1830: 'On Saturday morning last the body of a man was found in a garden pond adjoining the premises of Mr Hodges, Compasses Inn, Mount Sion, which was soon recognised to be a person named Samuel Jenner, many years in the employ of Mr Edward Elliott, blacksmith of this place'. The inquest jury sitting 'on the body' at the *Compasses* the following week, before J.N. Dudlow Esquire, the coroner, returned the unexceptionable verdict 'Found Drowned'. A small triangular piece of water is in fact to be seen on the Tithe map in the corner of the square of land nearest to the Grove Gate.

Finally here is the compelling reason I promised just now why the widow Pack was unable to carry on – and I have kept this to the last out of chronological order. On 4 December 1787, in only the second year of its publication, the *Maidstone Journal* reported as follows –and the 'heroine' (if that is the right word) of the story must be the Widow Pack we met earlier although the newspaper spells the name 'Peck'. 'A few days ago while one Fenner, a turner, and Philpot, a carpenter, were drinking together at the sign of the Three Compasses, at Tunbridge Wells, a quarrel arose between them, which proceeded to blows. During the battle, which was severely contested for some time, the fright had so great an effect on Mrs Peck, the landlady, that she expired, though the most immediate and necessary means were applied for her recovery. But what is more, on the news of her death being carried to a Mr Field, at Mount Ephraim, about half a mile distant, and a relation of the deceased, the shock was so great, that he died while the melancholy story was relating to him'. With this shocking story we conclude our look at the 'Mercer Strip' and digress, for one chapter only, to the question of the Poor Rate.

CHAPTER 8

The Poor Rate

This chapter is a diversion from the main story and should be skipped by those not so interested in historical sources. At the Centre for Kentish Studies in County Hall, Maidstone, are six substantial volumes in which generations of local men recorded the collection and disbursement of the Poor Rate for the Parish of Tonbridge. Here is one of the volumes – the archival reference is CKS P371 12/1-6.

A Poor Rate volume

Tonbridge Parish was extensive and was sub-divided into four: Tonbridge Town, Hildenborough, Southborough East and Southborough West. Tunbridge Wells, in so far as it existed at the beginning of the period, was partly in the East and West Southborough sub-divisions. It was also partly in the Parish of Speldhurst and this included the Kent part of the Pantiles. It would be very interesting if equivalent records could be found for the Pantiles but unfortunately the earliest I have discovered begin in 1810. Equally interesting would be a record showing, as I suspect it would, that Mount Ephraim House dates from no earlier than about 1680 and could not therefore have housed Charles and Katharine in 1663 – but this is crying for the moon. Of course, the Hearth Tax records of 1663 ought to come in useful but I defy anybody to pin-point an individual house in these documents. All this is by the way. As far as Tonbridge Parish is concerned the sub-division covering Tunbridge Wells is Southborough East. Even then the properties number hundreds and they are identified only by the names of the occupiers and ratepayers. How might it be possible to narrow the search to manageable proportions? Here comes a stroke of luck for a Tunbridge Wells, not to mention a Mount Sion, historian – the Bowra map of 1738. This shows the names of most individual house owners. This is not always helpful because it was the occupier who paid the rates. Fine if he was owner-occupier but in the case of Mr Brett in particular the label on the map hides the name of the ratepayer. Nevertheless a sufficient number of names remain which rang a quavering bell in the head of a Mount Sion tyro and very occasionally a hint of a location appears: for instance, 'Mr Betts or Occupier for a New house & bowling Greene' or 'Mrs Pickering for the Angell or Occupier'. In the hope, unsubstantiated at the time, that the rate collector would have grouped houses according to their location I guessed where the Mount Sion entries were written and took a spread of one hundred houses to cover the limits on either side. By luck or judgement it turned out well.

The six volumes cover a period of a century and a quarter, from 1670 to 1806 but house details cease in 1797. Why the change occurred I do not know. Perhaps it had to do with the disturbed condition of the country at the time. Perhaps the vestry officer in charge went off to fight the French or was press-ganged on a visit to the Bishop in Rochester or simply handed over to a new broom who did not like unwieldy tomes. Records obviously continued but in assorted notebooks and have not survived in a continuous series. The information anyway ceases to have quite the same historical value and by 1840, with the Tithe map followed by the decennial censuses and the later Town Directories, is available in other forms. At the other end of the time scale, I am not sure why the first date is 1670. What is called the 'Old Poor Law' under which property rates were collected by parishes began in 1597 or 1601. Anyway, I have noted a couple of dozen names in 1670 and then again in 1676 out of which only John Wybarne rings much of a bell. There follows then another interval of years until 1683 when the whole thing begins to take off – although why 1683 when the first leases were only concluded in November 1684 I cannot work out. Remember that it is Tonbridge Parish we are talking about: the Pantiles and Mount Ephraim were Speldhurst Parish responsibilities. Annual records then follow into the new century and 1704 when there is a gap of three years. From 1708 to 1714 the series is continuous but then, as I have said before, there comes a longer and much more lamentable gap until 1728 – why, I have no idea. From 1728 until 1797 there are no more gaps but there was an important change in procedure in 1758.

Until 1758 the order of entries in the book evidently followed the collector's route as he went round his patch whether on foot or on horseback, much as the census enumerator was to do in the next century. In 1758, however, for whatever reason, the Overseer of the Poor, if he it was, decided to change to an alphabetical system. This means that adjacent entries in the book may be widely separated geographically and vice versa; which would have made interpretation of the evidence very difficult if the other system had not been running for half a century already.

The other important aid to interpretation is the fact that when a change of occupancy occurred the collector often referred back to the previous occupier or to an old name of long standing. Here below, for instance, is an extract from the 1728 record:

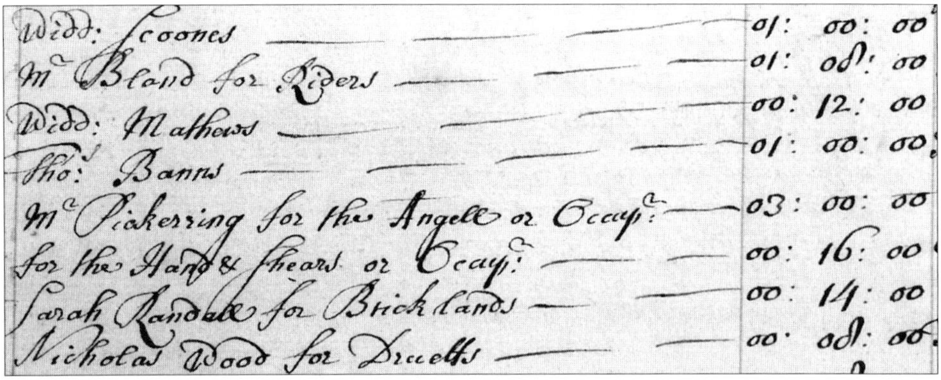

Widd: Coones	01: 00: 00
Mr Bland for Riders	01: 08: 00
Widd: Mathews	00: 12: 00
Tho: Banns	01: 00: 00
Mr Pickering for the Angell or Occup:	03: 00: 00
for the Hand & Sheares or Occup:	00: 16: 00
Sarah Randall for Bricklands	00: 14: 00
Nicholas Wood for Druetts	00: 08: 06

Poor Rate record 1728

Notice 'Mr Bland for Riders', 'Sarah Randall for Bricklands' and 'Nicholas Wood for Druetts'. 'Riders' I shall come to in a minute and 'Druetts' I am afraid means nothing to me; but I do happen to know, from the deeds of Sion House down the road, that Mr Brickland, a cook, was the occupier in 1710 of the house in whose rear quarters I now reside and so, when Sarah Randall moved in, the collector referred to the house by the name of the previous occupier; and I have added confirmation from the Poor Rate record itself that Mr Brickland paid rates from 1698 to 1712 and that the ratepayer at the time of the Bowra plan was Richard Fry whose name appears in the right place on the map. In fact, the house was referred to as 'Bricklands' from the year the cook departed right up to 1761. It must be realised that, although the houses on the ground fortunately stay solidly where they are from one year to the next, the list of ratepayers starts afresh each year. It is therefore vital, if any sense is to be made at all, to identify the house behind the name – and houses did not have names. They were called after the occupier or owner, unless, as in the extract, they were an inn like the *Angell* or the *Hand & Shears* or unless the house was an exception to the rule like 'Green Pales'. This is an example I am fond of quoting because it alone seems to represent a firm anchor for the whole flimsy structure of my Poor Rate record. Among the sequences which I established initially (or hoped to have established) was this one:

1686-1692	Mr Powell
1693-1695	Mr Robert Brooke for Mr Powells
1696-1698	Mr William Brooke for Mr Powells
1699-1704	Mrs Brooke for Mr Powells
1708-1713	Mr Culling for Powells
1714	Thomas Wood for Mr Powells

1728-1758	Thomas Wood for Sarah Hows
1759-1761	Widow of Tho Wood for Sarah Hows
1762-1771	Widow Wood for Sar Hows
1772-1778	Wood John for the Green Pales
1779-1797	Strange Edward for the Green Pales

Now anyone who had undertaken a preliminary read-through of Tunbridge Wells history in the Library knew that 15 Mount Sion used to be called Green Pales and was run as a lodging house by Edward Strange. There was a privately printed family history in the Reference Library, not to mention a present-day survivor of the Strange family in the town to remind him. Then the Bowra plan tells us that the owner of a house in the right location in 1738 was 'Tho Wood'. So I was sure I was on the right track. What I did not know was where Sarah How fitted in or Culling or Brooke or Powell – until I was lent the deeds of Sion House. This will be considered in greater detail in chapter 16; but for the moment it is enough to note that Sarah How about whom I had no inkling turned out to be a friend or companion of widow Winifrith Brooke who herself took a second husband, Thomas Cullen or Culling; and she bequeathed the house to Sarah How. That accounts for everyone except Mr Powell about whom I am still in the dark. It can be seen, therefore, that confirmation of my Poor Rate findings comes from other sources – and so far I have found no contradictions, although there are a number of problems.

I selected my spread of one hundred houses from the latest of the pre-alphabetical lists, that of 1758, hoping it would be the most reliable, and wrote their descriptions down one side of a very large squared sheet. I then worked backwards in time, year by year, ticking those entries which remained the same as the year following and writing in new names of ratepayers and descriptions of houses where they occurred. This took me back to 1728 although there were some problems particularly where properties had been sub-divided. I then had to jump the gap back to 1714 which proved very difficult at times. If the 'for Bricklands' type of designation survived across the gap I was lucky but otherwise the place of the entry in the sequence was an important clue. Another clue, which I have not mentioned before, is the amount of money collected. The calculation was the same as that which continued for centuries until destroyed by Mrs Thatcher in quite recent times. A 'poundage' was set as a proportion of the rental value of the house: two shillings in the pound for example, so that a house valued at £36 per annum would be charged £3 12s. 0d. Since most houses at the time were rented there was little difficulty in assessing rental values – in most cases it was the actual rent paid. Collection was made, then as now, twice a year. The extract above shows the amounts collected down the right-hand side, in pounds, shillings and pence of course. I did not normally note the amounts on my large sheet. Perhaps I should have done but the task was fairly mammoth as it was! I did, however, note most of the amounts for 1728 and 1714 and discovered that the later amounts were very often exactly twice the earlier ones; or more exactly, the 1728 charges were doubled for houses that I judged, estimated or guessed were the same houses in 1714! I took this as proof that my guesses were correct. Rocket science it was not – but it does seem to have stood the test of time.

It was useful on occasions to be able to consider the actual amounts of money paid in rates but what I found most helpful were references back to previous designations. I have all together about sixty index cards (see below) of varying degrees of reliability. I shall refer to them constantly as I have done already. I should like to see them all published so that they could be used by other historians – or shown to be mistaken or amended or identified where I have been unable to do it myself. I did suggest to the Kent Archaeological Society that they should publish them for the general good but they decided not. I think it would overburden this book to include them all and anyway many of them deal with other parts of the town such as the London Road or the Grosvenor or Calverley areas, within Tonbridge Parish of course, but not in the Mount Sion area.

From 1759 onwards I was faced with a similar problem which would have been almost insurmountable if I had not, as I mentioned above, had half a century and more's worth of experience behind me. I now abandoned my (by now) two large sheets of squared paper and started a card index on which I entered the information I had already up to 1758 and then continued from year to year as best I could, hoping to assign each alphabetical entry to the right index card. This is what the 'Bricklands' card looks like. You will see that the entries after 1758 are in pencil – I thought I might have to alter them! The 'Nash' at the top refers to the present name of 25 Mount Sion.

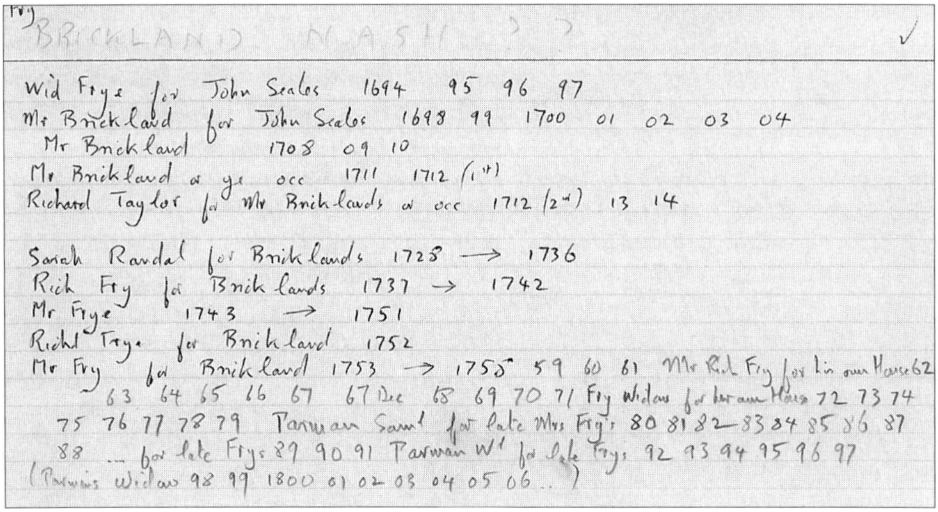
Fry BRICKLAND NASH ? ?
Wid Frye for John Seales 1694 95 96 97
Mr Brickland for John Seales 1698 99 1700 01 02 03 04
Mr Brickland 1708 09 10
Mr Brickland or ye occ 1711 1712 (1st)
Richard Taylor for Mr Bricklands or occ 1712 (2nd) 13 14
Sarah Randal for Bricklands 1728 → 1736
Rich Fry for Bricklands 1737 → 1742
Mr Frye 1743 → 1751
Richd Frye for Brickland 1752
Mr Fry for Brickland 1753 → 1755 59 60 61 Mr Rich Fry for his own House 62 63 64 65 66 67 67 Dec 68 69 70 71 Fry Widow for her own House 72 73 74 75 76 77 78 79 Parman Saml for late Mrs Fry's 80 81 82–83 84 85 86 87 88 ... for late Frys 89 90 91 Parman Wd for late Frys 92 93 94 95 96 97 (Parman's Widow 98 99 1800 01 02 03 04 05 06 ..)

My Poor Rate Index Cards – an example

As an illustration of some of the difficulties encountered here is an example dealt with briefly in the previous chapter on 'The Mercer Strip'. The property in question is the one on the upper, northern corner of Warwick Road and the High Street – labelled 'Robert Mercer' on the Bowra plan, 'Mr. J. Delves, late Philpots' on the Barrow map (1808) and 'Camden House & Pleasure Ground' in the Tithe Award. Two Poor Rate sequences are involved. Here is one:

1690-1693	Jonathan Elmes for Riders
1694(1st half)	Rider
1694(2nd half)	Wm Hodge (Hartridge?)
1695(1st half)	Wm Hartridge or the tenant for Mr Riders
1695(2nd half)	Hy Heath
1696	Hy Heath or Tenant for Jo Riders
1697-1698	Widow Rottenbridge or occ of Riders
1699-1700	Mr Rider for his house
1701-1702	Mr Rider for a new house
1703	Mr Bland or Mr Rider for a new house
1704-1714	Mr Bland for Mr Riders new house
1728	Mr Bland for Riders
1729-1734	Mr Bland
1735-1737	Mr Bland or occ
1738-1749	Simon Wise for Mr Blands
1750	Simon Wise or Mathew Ball for Blands
1751-1760	Matt Ball
1761-1783	Richd Hook (probable link)
1784-1788	Philpott Richd for late Richd Hooks
1789-1792	Delves Joseph for late Richd Philpotts before Hooks
1793-1797	Delves Joseph for late Philpotts

You will see that the name 'Riders' is in every year up to 1728 and fortunately spans the gap from 1714. Even if it had not done, some comfort might have been derived from the payments recorded: in 1714 it was 14 shillings and in 1728 it was double, £1 8s. 0d., which is proof in my rocket science. The downside is that, for one thing, I know nothing about Mr Rider and for another there seems to be a question whether the change from 'his house' to 'a new house' between 1700 and 1701 has any significance. However, there is no doubt about the name 'Bland' which remains anchored to the house from 1703 right through to 1750 and in 1719 the name 'Blans' shows up on Kip's engraving on the lower side of the High Street. When we come to the introduction of the alphabetical system in 1759 the name 'Matt Ball' carries through to 1760; but then comes a problem which I have acknowledged by the bracketed 'probable link'. There is no linkage by name between Matt Ball in 1760 and Richard Hook in 1761. In such cases the only hope is to look through all the entries recording the same payment and eliminate all the known entries. If one entry is then left looking for a home, there is some presumption that the problem has been solved. Here a payment of £4 10s. 0d. is recorded by Matt Ball in 1760 and the same amount (somewhat higher it may be noted than half a century earlier) by Richard Hook in 1761. In this particular example the later appearance of the name Philpott provides some confirmation based on external evidence. I should stress, however, that when I made the link between Ball and Hook it was without foreknowledge of the later entries, because I recorded each year separately as a whole, before moving on to the next year.

As noted above, the Barrow map of 1808 seems to link the final stage of this sequence firmly to Camden House on the Tithe map; but even if we accept the somewhat flimsy argument so far, another difficulty emerges. We know from the *Compasses* deeds that the property belonged originally to John Mercer but the Poor Rate sequence leads back unfortunately not to John Mercer and William Fulman but to Jonathan Elmes and Mr Rider; while on the other hand there is a second sequence which does start with Fulman and Mercer. This sequence runs as follows:

1685 (1st half)	William Fulman
1685 (2nd half)-1686	Wm Fulman & John Mercer
1687-1689 (1st half)	John Mercer
1689 (2nd half)-1691(1st half)	Wid Fry for John Mercers
1691 (2nd half)-1693(1st half)	Wid Fry for Wid Mercers
1693 (2nd half)	Thos Eldridge for John Mercers
1694-1712	John Mercer
1713	John Mercer or occ
1714 (1st half)	John Mercer or Catt Bland
1714 (2nd half)	Mr Bland for John Mercers or occ
1728-1729	Nicholas Wood
1730-1734	Nicholas Wood for Riders
1735-1749	Alex Ashdown for Riders

At this point the sequence sub-divides. 'John Mugridge for part of Riders' carries on from 1750 to 1758, becoming 'Occupr for part of Riders' in 1759 and 1760 and then disappearing from the record. The other sub-division continues:

1750-1751	Thos Dival for pt Dos [= Dittos i.e. Riders]
1752-1753	Thos Dival for pt Dos a Forreigner [!]
1754-1771	late (Thos) Dival or occ for pt Dos

This sub-division then disappears also and there is no reference back or 'hanging' entry of the same rateable value. This seems quite inexplicable if the property in question was on the upper (or eastern) side of the High Street; but by the same token equally plausible if it was on the lower (western) side, for there is evidence both from the Poor Rate record and from Sprange's Guides that between 1780 and 1786 Robert Skinner began the development of New Street, the present Castle Street. The completed development and the 'New Inn' can be seen on Barrow's map of 1808 (see the next page), all labelled 'Mr Skinner', although the little numbers are sometimes difficult to pick out.

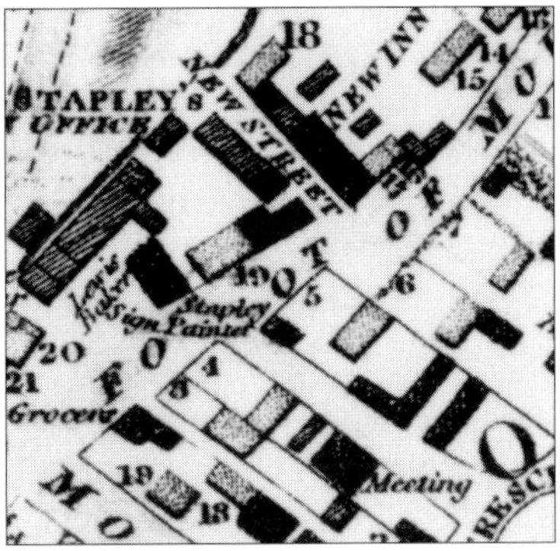

Barrow map 1808

14 : Merrivale
15 : Do
16 : First New Street house
17 : Great New Street House
18 : Corner New Street House

} Mr Skinner

I guess, therefore, that the property called 'Riders' in the Poor Rate record and prominently labelled 'Blans' on Kip's engraving was demolished to make way for Skinner's 'new street' and that this accounts for the disappearance of 'Riders' from the Poor Rate record. What seems to have happened is that I have got the two post-1714 sequences the wrong way round: the one starting William Fulman should finish Joseph Delves; and the one starting Jonathan Elmes should finish with the disappearance of John Mugridge and Thomas Dival for 'part of Riders'. There is some plausibility in this theory since the mistake occurs during the unfortunate gap between 1714 and 1728. There is also one striking anomaly. 'Mr Bland for Riders' should not appear in the 'Philpotts' sequence in 1728 after the gap; and, moreover, the linkage which I first made between 1714 and 1728 was in both cases based on clearly defined positions on the 'collector's route'. In the end, however, some way there must be of reconciling what the Poor Rate collectors wrote in their books and what seems to have happened 'on the ground'. Both are evidence!

After 1797 I have found notebooks recording Poor Rate payments for the years 1799, 1800, 1802, 1807-10, 1816, 1817, 1820, 1831, 1833 and 1834; and there may be others which I have not found. All these are filed at CKS under Tonbridge Parish P371/11 and 12. On some I have made selected notes only. For the reasons already stated I do not attach so much value to them as to the large volume records but they may come in useful in particular instances. There is, however, one substantial portion of the large volumes which I have omitted from my notes. That is the expenditure side of the business. The whole idea, of course, was to collect money for the relief of the poor, so how was the money spent? Well, the volumes record this also. The trouble is that no record that Goodman Smith was given twopence on account of his bad leg or Widow Merry sixpence for the support of her child tells us anything about the history of Mount Sion. A thesis on poverty in the parish of Tonbridge would find plenty of material but could not locate its examples. One anecdote which can be assigned to Mount Sion (the travelling man who died at the *Compasses*) I have already quoted in the previous chapter; but for the most part I have to stick to the story of houses and land which my source material dictates together with what little personal detail the legal evidence allows to escape through the crevices. If only a few Mount Sion residents had left diaries or letters behind; but then they were all a middling sort of people and the scribblings of the great and good alone are thought worth preserving.

Chapter 9

Edward Martin

'Whereas the Right Honourable Margaret Viscountess Purbeck and Sir Thomas Meeres knight by their indenture bearing date the fourth day of November anno domini 1684 did demise and feefarm let unto Edward Martin of Tunbridge ... Kent joiner One piece or parcel of land containing in breadth 8 rods and in length 40 rods as the same was then marked and bounded out being part of a certain piece of heathie ground called the Inhams in Tunbridge aforesaid (bounding as in the same indenture is expressed)... .'

This is only the preamble to a later deed but it does bear witness to the creation of the next 'strip' in our survey of Mount Sion. Chapter 6 dealt with the Grove and chapter 7 with the adjacent Mercer strip. Next comes Edward Martin's strip and we see evidence of it every time we walk up the High Street. It was eight rods wide at the bottom and forty rods long up the hill. As discussed before, four rods make one chain or length of a cricket pitch and, if you care to measure it out, the distance between Little Mount Sion and Warwick Road is two cricket pitch lengths. Then, if you dare to cross the road and cast your eyes at the upper floors of the building opposite, above the present-day accretion of shop fronts, you will be looking at Martins Lower House. A better view is from the back, as illustrated in chapter 1, page 8.

The length of Martin's strip up the hill is more difficult to pace out not only because of its greater length but also because later developments have got in the way of the straight line it might once have been; but it can be done on a map of suitable scale and you can see how ten cricket pitches or 220 yards takes you to Miles' Garage and the upper stretch of Mount Sion Road. The wall of the parking lot where cars wait before and after receiving the attentions of Miles' mechanics in fact marks accurately today the boundary set in the 17th century between Edward Martin's and the adjoining lease plot. On the next page is the Bowra plan with Martin's strip shaded grey and you will see that the garage was then an inn called *The Anchor* or more commonly *The Blue Anchor* presided over by Mr Hawkins. This chapter will deal with the two houses at the bottom of the strip while three further chapters will be needed to cope with the top of the strip.

One of the workmen who built the Chapel of King Charles the Martyr was a carpenter called Edward Martin and I think we can assume he is one and the same as the joiner who took an early lease from Lady Purbeck and Sir Thomas Meeres on 4 November 1684. The schedule says several pieces for 50 years at £5 per annum and the deed already quoted says: 'And also 6 acres of land by estimation other part of the same heathie ground called Inhams bounding as otherwise mentioned together with a reasonable way and passage to come go and carry and carry out of and from the same piece of ground unto the common called Bishops Down (except as in the same indenture is excepted).' I am not sure where this extra six acres was exactly but it was obviously near the Common. At the bottom of the strip on the Bowra plan you will see two houses labelled Edmd Wood and Nich Wood and thereby hangs much of the beginning of this tale. These two houses were originally called Martins Upper and Lower Houses and presumably built by Edward Martin, the lessee of the land. He may very well of course have done the carpentry himself and completed the house on a cooperative basis with the help of other trades like John Waghorne the bricklayer who also worked on the building of the Chapel – and perhaps Philip Seale the plumber and glazier whom we shall meet in chapter 13.

We can be sure about Martins two houses because of Nicholas Wood's will. This was made on 25 June 1724 and proved in March the next year. He leaves to his son Nicholas 'the house and garden ground and courtyard belonging to it as

Bowra 1738 showing Martin's strip

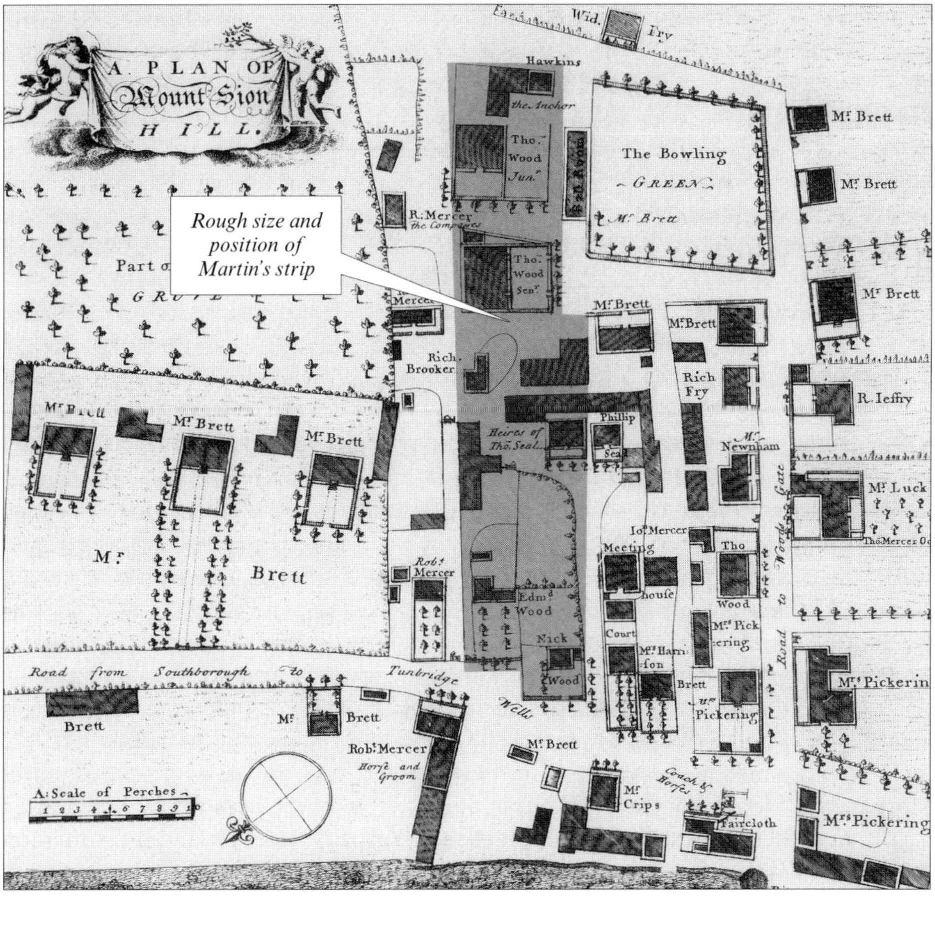

it is now fenced in with the use of the brewhouse known by the name of martyns lower house'; and to his son Edmund 'all that messuage and ground belonging to it, the brewhouse and watter to serve both houses as it hath youse to do with the old slautter house in the possession of Peat Latter formerly called martyns upper house …' – and a dozen or so years later the names of the two sons on the Bowra plan confirm the locations of the two houses. This seems straightforward enough. Martin built two lodging houses on his leased site and at some stage Nicholas Wood bought them and willed them to his sons; but Thomas Ashenhurst and other complications blur the simple picture. The document from which I quoted at the beginning of this chapter is dated 10 July 1701 and seems to be a long story of mortgages passing from hand to hand but ending with a £1,000 loan to Thomas Ashenhurst by one Leonard Bartholomew of the City of Rochester. Then on 26 August 1702 Edward Martin, joiner, made his mark on his will by which he, uninformatively, left all his messuages, tenements, lands, leases, money, goods and chattels to his wife Elizabeth charging her with the care of their three daughters Mary, Sarah and Elizabeth until they came of age 18 or married. When he died I have no information but the will was proved on 16 August 1708. Long before this, however, I guess his Mount Sion strip had passed into the hands of Nicholas Wood. Why not Thomas Ashenhurst? I can only speculate that he had defaulted or passed the charge to Nicholas Wood. We know, from the Trust Deed of the Grove, that by April 1703 Nicholas had become one of the bordering owners and we know from his will, although he does not put a date to it, that he 'purchased of John Earl of Buckingham a ground rent of seven pounds and fifteen shillings a year free from all taxes as appears by an endorsement on the backside of Martyns lease to be paid by Mr Ashenhurst landlords & whereas the ground I purchased of him belonging to my dwelling house is liable to pay a ground rent of five pounds a year by leases payable to Edward Martyn or his assigns during the term of the first leases .....' The upshot (although I wish I could be more certain of the details) was that by the end of his life Nicholas was master of the whole strip from the Martin houses at the bottom to his own house and the *Blue Anchor* at the top; but some parts of the property may have been subject to the 50-year lease not expiring until 1734. This does not seem to have been a problem for other purchasers from the insolvent Earl in or around 1702 but one clause in the old fellmonger's will instructs trustees to pay his son Nicholas 'one and twenty pounds a year during the term of Martyn's lease which will expire and end at Michaelmas one thousand seven hundred and thirty four …' This amount is to be paid 'towards support of his family' by instalments of 35 shillings on the first Monday of each month; but 'when the bequeathed house is taken into possession' those in possession of 'my dwelling house' or receiving rent from it are to pay 20 shillings only per month to son Nicholas or his children if he dies before they come of age 21.

One small slice of the Martin's strip had, however, been sold previously. This was the piece Philip Seale needed to build his second house alongside his first, as has already been mentioned and will be discussed in greater detail in chapter 13. With this exception, then, let us consider the buildings on this important strip; and start at the bottom of the hill first with Martins Upper House which later took the name Warwick House. The Poor Rate record is a little confusing. I have two cards one of which starts 'Edward Martin or his tenant for his own house – May 1686' and continues '... for his new house' in 1686 (2nd half) and April and December 1687; but then alternates between 'own house' and 'new house' until 1692 when 'and for 2 new houses' appears in the second half and goes back to 'for his new house' from 1693 to 1703. In 1704 a new and unexplained name, Robert Arram, appears briefly 'for Martins new house' to be followed after a gap by Mr Ashenhurst and then Madame Catherine Ashenhurst from 1708 to 1710 – we shall meet 'Madame Catherine' in the next chapter. Finally the name Latter appears in 1711, first of all the Widow Latter until 1714 and then after the usual gap to 1728 Peat Latter all the way to 1743. This fortunately ties in with the will of Nicholas Wood who gave to his son Edmund, you may recall, the former Martins Upper House 'in the possession of Peat Latter'. The confusing Poor Rate sequence just noted refers with any luck to the Upper House. Another will throws a small light: Mary Latter of Mount Sion, widow, made her will in September 1716 and it was proved in November. 'Considering my daughter Mary Latter and Peat Latter my son are unprovided for and have been much at home and very helpful to me in my Business I give and bequeath to them ... All the Rest of my goods chattels household stuff and furniture and personal estate ... share and share alike ...' What her business was we do not know – perhaps that of a butcher, but it was an old slaughter house that was mentioned in Nicholas Wood's will. This continues, interestingly, by elaborating on the description of Martins Upper House as follows: '... with the new stable and ground up to the old [birch] leaving a sufficient passage by the meeting house into the way that comes from Calverleys plain'. 'Meeting house' suggests the Presbyterian Chapel in Little Mount Sion but this cannot be; the Presbyterian Chapel had indeed just been opened in 1720 but the location is wrong. I think this meeting house must be the Bethlehem Chapel marked on the Barrow map of 1808 – see below. The 'way that comes from Calverleys plain' must then be what is now the upper part of Little Mount Sion, from the *Grove Tavern* past the *Compasses* into Claremont Road – and thence eventually to Pembury passing by Calverleys Plain on the way. Remember that for a long time the main route to London was via Pembury; the turnpike through Southborough not being opened until 1765. Now prepare for a long story.

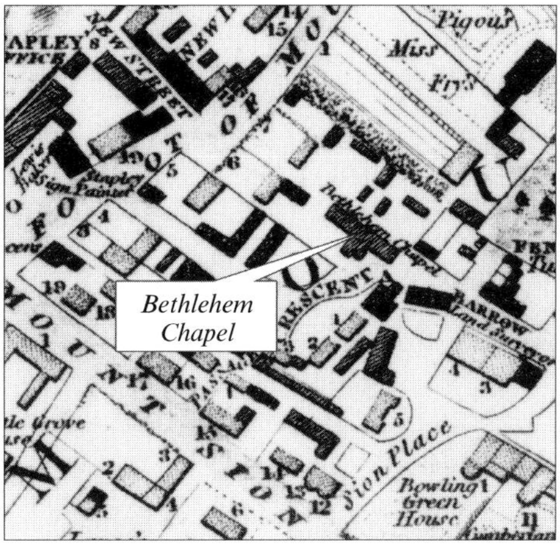

Barrow map 1808

First we take a leap forward in time. On 2 June 1812 the *Maidstone Journal* advertised the sale by auction of 'All that desirable Messuage or Tenement known by the name of Bethlehem Chapel'. The fate of this property will be discussed below and a full transcript of the notice given; but this brief quote will be sufficient to back up the rather unilluminating marking on Barrow's map (see detail on previous page). Now there is a collection of deeds at Maidstone, dated 1742, 1775 and 1806, which deals with the affairs of Edmund Wood. Two deeds of 1742 convey a 'new erected house, coach house and stables', together with a four-acre field, to William Budgen, a butcher of Frant, as trustee in contemplation of the marriage of Edmund Wood, a brazier, with Mary Elliott, widow of William Elliott, formerly a Tunbridge Wells pastry-cook. My theory is that the 'new erected' house was Grove Lodge, otherwise known as Percy House, on the other side of the road from Miles' Garage; and that Edmund built or bought it after his father's death. The field adjoins the Grove and may have been the site of the future Grecian Villa. Anyway, the house and field are to be held for the benefit of Edmund during his life, of Mary for her life (in lieu of dower), of any children of the marriage or, if there are none, of Ann, Mary's daughter by her previous marriage, and of Ann's children if any. The 1775 deed is the 'lease' part only of a 'Lease and Release' transaction conveying property from Sarah Wood, widow, to Henry Goldstone of Speldhurst, yeoman (father of Sarah Wood) and William Mitchell, a coal merchant of Hanover Square, London. The property consists of the 'new erected' house formerly occupied by Edmund, 'the late deceased husband of Sarah Wood' together with a third part of Martins Upper House and its coach house and stables – and a four-acre field which is not the one mentioned in the 1742 deeds but one bequeathed by Nicholas Wood's will. This was 'known by the name of the Great House Field' because (to quote the will) it was 'the field belonging to the Great House'. The Great House was Ashenhursts Great House and had been bequeathed to Thomas Wood but the field was left to brother Edmund. Later developments show that it was the land sometimes mapped as 'Prospect Hill' lying between Camden Park, Prospect Road, Cambridge Street and Camden Hill on which Oakfield Court was built. Since Edmund was given the whole of Martins House and of the Great House Field and since he bequeathed all his real estate to his widow, it is unclear why she had at her disposal only a third share in each; but some family arrangement must be presumed since the other two shares seem to have belonged to brothers William and Thomas. The 1806 deed is again the 'lease' part only of a conveyance to Thomas Delves by Mrs Henrietta Sidney and her son Marlow (a brazier like Edmund Wood), the son and heir of Henry Sidney, also a brazier, of Grove Lodge and an eight-stall stable with hayloft and room over, formerly belonging to Martins Upper House (since called Doyle's Lower House). Grove Lodge is called in the deed 'The Little Grove House', otherwise Doyle's Upper House, otherwise Goldstone's Bow Window House and is said to have been occupied by Edmund Wood, then Richard Waghorne, then Sarah Fenner and 'now' Andrew Fenner. Sarah Fenner (see chapter 12) was the grand-daughter of Nicholas Wood and Andrew was her son. Some of these names are reflected in *Sprange's Guides*: 1780 – Doyle, Upper House; 1797 – Mr Goldstone, Upper House, now Fenner's; 1808 – Mr T Delves (2 parlours, 5 chambers, 5 garrets, 1 coach house, stabling for 5 horses).

This rather random rag-bag of facts might have remained a mystery had not Mr Knocker made his collection of deeds which are now to be found at Maidstone. Among them is a bulky Abstract of Title of fearsome complexity dealing with 'the title of Miss Charlotte Lushington to a certain field' – whose identity may be guessed. The complexity is due in good measure to the fact that for a period the property is divided into three shares each of which has its own independent, but interrelated, history. The shares belonged to the three sons of Nicholas Wood, William, Thomas and Edmund and the story which emerges is the following. Edmund Wood (who must have been previously married since his son, confusingly called Nicholas of course, is mentioned in the 1724 will and must have died young) married the pastry-cook's widow in 1742. There do not seem to have been any children of this marriage and Mary died before her husband, who married again at what must have been a fairly advanced age. His new bride was Sarah, the daughter of Henry Goldstone who was steward to Elizabeth Shorey, Lady of the Manor of Rusthall. Edmund lived for only five years after his marriage and his widow remarried almost immediately. The 1775 deed, of which only the 'lease' part survives, is in fact another marriage settlement and Henry Goldstone and William Mitchell are the trustees for Sarah and her new husband, Francis Doyle who was a butcher living, like William Mitchell, in Hanover Square. In 1776 Francis purchased the other two shares in Martin's Upper House (which then became Doyle's *Lower* House, Grove Lodge being the new *Upper* House) and in the Great House Field and immediately mortgaged them for £400, adding a further £200 in 1777. This was perhaps symptomatic of the state of his business; the fact is anyway that in 1784 he was declared bankrupt and in 1786 his assignees auctioned his property. Father-in-law Goldstone came to the rescue (I assume that was his motive) and made a successful bid for Grove Lodge and his daughter's share of Martin's Upper (Doyle's Lower) House and the Great House Field. There were no acceptable bids for the two mortgaged shares but eventually an agreement was negotiated that Goldstone should have all the shares on redeeming the mortgages, principal and interest. Grove Lodge now became Goldstone's Upper (or Bow Window) House. What became of Francis the bankrupt is not recorded but he was still around in 1788 when, in conjunction with the assignees under the bankruptcy, he sold to Henry his life interest in 'the messuage or tenement third part land hereditaments and premises' for £50 8s. 0d.; thus enabling (I assume) Goldstone to take out on the following day a mortgage with Francis Jones, one of the two assignees, redeemable on payment of £1,403 13s. 9d. The whole thing must have been a worry to poor Henry. There were at least four mortgagees in the case. Sarah, in 1791, predeceased her father. The King's Bench became involved. In 1797 there was another auction of which the sale notice has survived amongst the Sprange printed material held by the Tunbridge Wells Museum (see the photocopy on the next page). Lot I was the Great House Field, Lot II was Grove Lodge, Lot IV was Martin's Upper House named in the sale notice as 'Dorril's Lower House' which is an obvious corruption of 'Doyle's Lower House'; while Lot III was a 'large Brick'd 12 Stall STABLE, with a Hay Loft, and a large Room over the same, which may be easily improved and converted into other uses'. For once (from the Abstract of Title) the result of the auction is known. Henry Sidney, for £563, bought Grove Lodge plus Lot III and Martin's Upper House with its coach house but without the extra stabling was sold to Thomas (or William?) Pratt for £600. The Court of Chancery came on the scene. The auction proceeds were used in part settlement of affairs. An indenture 'Nonapartite' of 1798 points to the complicated stage that had been reached. It was not enough. Goldstone still owed £125. The Great House Field (by this time known as 'Goldstone's Field') had not been sold at the auction but had become security – until 13 July 1800 when, at an auction held at the *Angel Inn*, Tunbridge Wells, – after poor Henry had finally succumbed – it was purchased by Thomas Barber for £380. In 1819 it was sold to William Lushington, owner of the adjoining estate later to become Calverley Park, and on his death came, in 1823, to his daughter Charlotte. She, in 1829, negotiated a right of way (the present Camden Hill) along the edge of her field whereby the Marquess Camden was able to gain access to his future Camden Park development. In 1843 Charlotte sold the field to Charles Cripps, adding substantially to his holding in that part of the town.

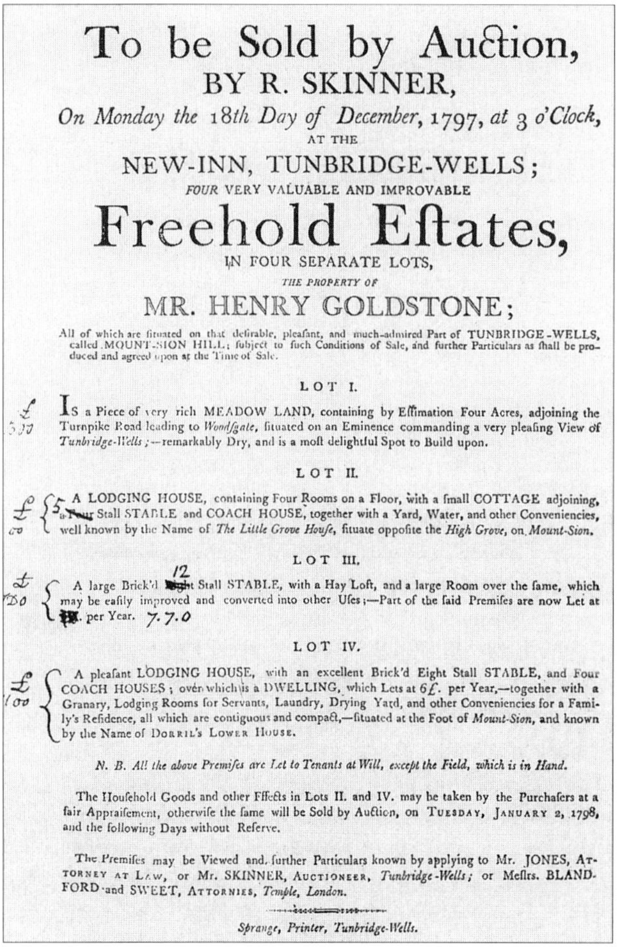
To be Sold by Auction,

BY R. SKINNER,

On Monday the 18th Day of December, 1797, at 3 o'Clock,

AT THE

NEW-INN, TUNBRIDGE-WELLS;

FOUR VERY VALUABLE AND IMPROVABLE

Freehold Estates,

IN FOUR SEPARATE LOTS,

THE PROPERTY OF

MR. HENRY GOLDSTONE;

All of which are situated on that desirable, pleasant, and much-admired Part of TUNBRIDGE-WELLS, called MOUNT-SION HILL; subject to such Conditions of Sale, and further Particulars as shall be produced and agreed upon at the Time of Sale.

LOT I.

IS a Piece of very rich MEADOW LAND, containing by Estimation Four Acres, adjoining the Turnpike Road leading to *Woodsgate*, situated on an Eminence commanding a very pleasing View of *Tunbridge-Wells*;—remarkably Dry, and is a most delightful Spot to Build upon.

LOT II.

A LODGING HOUSE, containing Four Rooms on a Floor, with a small COTTAGE adjoining, a Four Stall STABLE and COACH HOUSE, together with a Yard, Water, and other Conveniencies, well known by the Name of *The Little Grove House*, situate opposite the *High Grove*, on *Mount-Sion*.

LOT III.

A large Brick'd Eight Stall STABLE, with a Hay Loft, and a large Room over the same, which may be easily improved and converted into other Uses;—Part of the said Premises are now Let at [illegible]. per Year.

LOT IV.

A pleasant LODGING HOUSE, with an excellent Brick'd Eight Stall STABLE, and Four COACH HOUSES; over which is a DWELLING, which Lets at 6£. per Year,—together with a Granary, Lodging Rooms for Servants, Laundry, Drying Yard, and other Conveniencies for a Family's Residence, all which are contiguous and compact,—situated at the Foot of *Mount-Sion*, and known by the Name of DORRIL'S LOWER HOUSE.

N. B. All the above Premises are Let to Tenants at Will, except the Field, which is in Hand.

The Household Goods and other Effects in Lots II. and IV. may be taken by the Purchasers at a fair Appraisement, otherwise the same will be Sold by Auction, on TUESDAY, JANUARY 2, 1798, and the following Days without Reserve.

The Premises may be Viewed and further Particulars known by applying to Mr. JONES, ATTORNEY AT LAW, or Mr. SKINNER, AUCTIONEER, *Tunbridge-Wells*; or Messrs. BLANDFORD and SWEET, ATTORNIES, *Temple, London*.

Sprange, Printer, Tunbridge-Wells.

Goldstone Sale Notice 1797

Martins Upper House and Grove Lodge both have adequate provision for coaches and horses, so I suppose that the 'large bricked 12 stall stable' (Lot III) must be a separate item and indeed must be the eight-stall stable with hayloft and room over, formerly belonging to Martins Upper House, purchased by Thomas Delves in 1806. The photocopy shows how the printed 'eight' on the sale notice has been overwritten '12'. Where was this building? It must have been within the grounds of the Upper House and there is no escaping the conclusion that it is the largish rectangular building with a central projection marked on both the Bowra and Barrow maps; but on Bowra it is shown as stabling and on Barrow as 'Bethlehem Chapel'. The trouble is the mention of 'meeting house' in 1724 in Nicholas Wood's will and my theory that the meeting house must be the future 'Bethlehem Chapel'. Could it have been a 'meeting house' in 1724, a stable from 1738 perhaps through to 1806, then a Chapel in 1808 and a mere five or six years later have been on offer for alternative uses in 1812? The only way out seems to be to assume that the 1724 reference was to the Presbyterian Chapel in Little Mount Sion; but that involves a degree of topographical contortion which I refuse to contemplate. At any rate there is no doubt what happened in 1812 and then in 1813. On 2 June 1812, as already mentioned above, the *Maidstone Journal* carried the following advertisement:

> FREEHOLD ESTATE TUNBRIDGE WELLS KENT TO BE SOLD BY AUCTION BY FRY AND CHEESMAN at the Market-house, Tunbridge Wells on MONDAY, JUNE 13, at Four o'Clock in the Afternoon …
>
> All that Desirable MESSUAGE or TENEMENT known by the name of BETHLEHEM CHAPEL, and a DWELLING HOUSE adjoining, situated on that delightful and healthy Situation MOUNT SION, consisting of a CHAPEL, 35 feet in length and 17 in width, with a Gallery 12 feet in depth; also a Vestry Room adjoining the same, and a commodious entrance thereto, capable of great improvement.
>
> The DWELLING HOUSE consists on the basement of a wash-house, 17 feet by 12; a kitchen, 12 by 11 with suitable [closets?]; a coal vault, capable of containing 3 chauldrons of coal which, at a small expense, might be enlarged so as to contain 13 chauldrons – On the ground floor is a front parlour, 12 feet 6 inches by [10?] feet; a bedroom, 8 feet by 10; a shop, 11 feet by 9; and a back paved yard, with proper conveniences – On the one [part?] floor is a bedroom, 11 feet by 11, fitted up with wardrobe, closets etc – The whole of these Premises have been in part newly erected within 3 years and are in good repair. The Conditions of Sale will be produced at the time and place of Sale. Excellent Water may be obtained by a Well in any part of the Premises, at a depth of 39 [38?] feet. For Particulars inquire of Mr Montier, Surveyor, Tunbridge Wells, who will show the Premises; or of Mr J White, North-street, Brighton, who will produce the Title Deeds.

The whole story of this building is a bit of a mystery but the advertisement (not to mention Barrow) prove that there was a chapel there but what denomination can claim it? It seems rather remote from the Bohemian theologian, Jan Hus and the 14th-century Bethlehem Chapel in Prague; but there can be no mystery about its next use. It was taken by the girls of King Charles School in 1813 and used by them until they moved to Murray House in 1858 (see chapter 16). The deeds of 37 Little Mount Sion provide ample confirmation. By a Lease and Release conveyance dated 16/17 April 1813 George Savage White, William Pollington and James White sold to John Lloyd and Thomas Pinckard Bingham property described as follows:

> All that large brick built eight stall stable with the hay loft and room over the same and the coach houses lately erected partly converted into a chapel …

> hitherto belonging … to a messuage or tenement there formerly called Martins upper house late called Doyles lower house abutting a yard belonging to Miss Baker and in the occupation of Thomas Downard and others towards the north-east to a stable and building of John Smith towards the north-west to a road or way leading from the Presbyterian Meeting to … Calverley Plain towards the south-east, south and south-west … formerly in the occupation of Thomas Pratt then late of James Farley and his undertanants and then of George Savage White or his assigns.

Who the vendors, White, Pollignton and White were and how they acquired the property I have no information; but there can be no doubt that the large eight-stall stable is Lot III of the 1795 auction (with the eight overwritten 12).

The Rev. Martin Benson, incumbent of King Charles the Martyr at the time, was a party to the 1813 conveyance which was made in trust for the use of a Charity School. Further confirmation comes in a Committee Book at the Centre for Kentish Studies in the front of which is an 'Extract (made by D.J. Robertson Esq.) from the Trust Deed belonging to the Female National School on Mount Sion dated 1813'. To quote: '… it is hereby declared and agreed between the said John Lloyd and Thomas Pinckard Bingham that they … shall … at all times hereafter permit the said Chapel Ground tenement and hereditament to be used … as a Charity School for the education of poor children in the principles of the Church of England … under the … superintendence of the Clergyman, a minister for the time being of the Chapel of Tunbridge Wells aforesaid …'. There can be no doubt about the location: the plan below was attached to the conveyance of 14 January 1859 when the Girls' School trustees sold the premises in order to move to Murray House. There is an anomaly concerning ownership however. The Tithe Award describes the building as 'Charity School Cottages, Stabling and Yard' owned by Ann Lydall (Sydall?) who was also owner and occupier of Warwick House. How she came to combine ownership of Martins Upper House (Warwick House) and its stabling, which seemed to have been separated by the auction of 1797 (see above), I do not know. For once the Tithe record must be in error; the 37 Little Mount Sion deeds put the matter beyond doubt. The Tithe map seems quite unaware of the situation shown in the plan on the left. It shows a large plot (No 3769) including two buildings, one abutting Warwick House and the other being a continuation of the 'school' down the hill. I think one at least of these two buildings was a 'Charity School Cottage'. Why, by the way, the name 'Charity

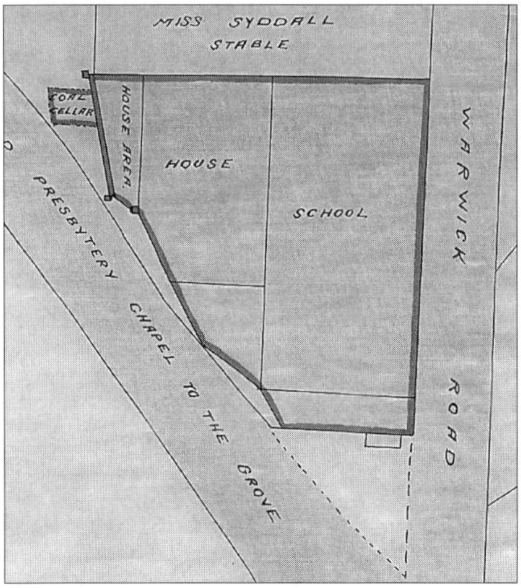

Plan attached to conveyance dated 14 January 1859

School' when the map ignores the school? The Tithe Award says that Plot 3769 is occupied by 'Chapman and Others' and here is another puzzle. The Chapmans were teachers. A letter to the *Tunbridge Wells Gazette* in December 1858 bestows the praise of a 'constant visitor to Tunbridge Wells' on Mr Chapman, 'that excellent master' of the oldest boys' school and on the girls' school 'as efficiently conducted by Mrs Chapman'. I guess this means that the Chapmans were in charge of the King Charles boys and girls at separate premises. The 1851 census shows them, John and Elizabeth, living at the 'National School Cottage' while Elizabeth Clifford, another teacher, was living at Warwick Cottage which must have been one of the Charity School Cottages mentioned above. Indeed a house occupied by a Clifford and situated at the back of the main house is mentioned in a later deed. The puzzle, however, is the 'National School Cottage'. It seems obvious that this must be the house adjoining the school shown in the legal plan; but this did not belong to Ann Lydall and the Chapmans could not have been her tenants

Be all that as it may, the Murray House School records (for more on which see chapter 16) say that £330 from the sale of the 'old school' went towards the purchase of Murray House; but the 37 Little Mount Sion deeds show that the purchaser on 14 January 1859 was one Thomas Dyer, a Tunbridge Wells plumber and glazier who the next day borrowed £150 on mortgage from widow Mary Startin of Frant. I suspect he was acting on behalf of the Christ Church Boys' School. Spiers' *History of Christ Church* (see chapter 6) says: 'There is no record as to when the Christ Church Boys' School was opened. The building was mostly of wood, and situated at the corner of Warwick Lane and Little Mount Sion'. The opening was evidently in or around 1859. The Christ Church School for Girls and Infants had been opened in Vale Road in June 1857. The 'Charity Boys' School' is marked on the Ordnance Survey map surveyed in 1866 and it appears in the 1861 census as 'Christ Church Boys School' inhabited by schoolmaster John Baskerfield. The 1871 census shows the 'District Boys School' without listing any occupant and then in December 1875 Spiers tells us that the school was closed and pulled down; and the boys, numbering 30, were all transferred to King Charles School. The Little Mount Sion deeds reveal that Thomas Dyer sold the property on 11 September 1877 to gentleman Thomas Guilford of Tunbridge Wells, confirming perhaps my suspicion that Dyer had been acting for the school. The 1881 census lists the occupants of what must be the present-day buildings which may therefore be dated to 1878-1880. 39 Little Mount Sion is occupied by widow Laodicia Eversfield, 47, beer retailer, grocer etc; no.37 by boot maker John Singer with lodgers James and Jesty Levene, gymnastic artists; no.35 by David R. Hoper, greengrocer, previously at the *Grove Tavern* (see chapter 11); while no.33 was uninhabited. Warwick House itself seems to have been demolished about the same time as the old school-chapel-stables building. Perhaps it was all part of a combined development project, responsibility for which may perhaps lie at the door of Thomas Guilford.

The Poor Rate record for Martins Upper House confirms the old deeds. Edmond Wood was succeeded as ratepayer by 'Dorrill' or Doyle in 1777 and he by Henry Goldstone from 1790 to 1797. Then it was sold, as we saw, at the auction of 1797 to Thomas Pratt for £600. By the time of Barrow's map in 1808 it is Mr Smith's and a scattered Poor Rate entry for 1802 confirms this change with 'John Smith for late Pratts'. The next Poor Rate entry available is for 1833 and, as does that for the next year also, shows 'Miss Sydall' paying for Warwick House (and incidentally this seems to be the first documented use of that name for Martins Upper House) and a number of other properties: Camden House (next door), Mount Sion Coach House, Buildings and Yard, Camden Mews and three cottages. Miss Sydall is presumably a misreading for the 'Ann Lydall' of the more reliable Tithe Award a few years later when Warwick House was owned and occupied by Ann Lydall and Miss Lydall was the occupier of Camden House – see page 69 above. The 37 Little Mount Sion deeds tell us a little more about Miss Lydall or Sydall but not how she acquired the property. Her full name was Ann Rhodes Lydall and she made a will on 26 December 1857 leaving her real and personal estate to spinster Frances Duly; she died on 16 July 1860 and her will was proved on 22 August. What Duly's relationship was with Ann Lydall we do not know but the spinster in turn made a will on 2 March 1869 instructing trustees, after making some provision for a niece Frances, wife of Thomas Futcher, to sell her estate (known as Warwick House with the adjoining cottages, coach houses, stabling, yards and gardens). Duly died on 21 June 1875 and on 15 December the estate was sold to Thomas Guilford for £4,000.

I assume Warwick House functioned as a lodging house during the early part of the 19th century. On the 1866 map it is still there with its front garden opening onto the High Street and is listed in *Mathieson's 1867/8 Directory* occupied by 'Miss Duly' who figures in the 1861 and 1871 censuses as Frances Duly, fundholder aged 71 in 1871, so I guess that the last stage in the house's life was as a private residence. By 1881, however, neither Miss Duly nor Warwick House appear and by 1889 shops have appeared between the Gazette office at 59 High Street and Warwick Road and both sides of Warwick Road, nos 1-13 on the north and 2-16 on the south are inhabited – and the south side is still with us today. For the north side see page 69 above. Thomas Guilford died in 1880 and left equal shares of his estate to four children in a will the ramifications of which troubled the Chancery courts well into the 20th century; but whose records show that Guilford had acquired the freehold of nos 49, 51 and 53 High Street (built on the site of Warwick House), nos 33, 35, 37 and 39 Little Mount Sion, and nos 2, 4, 6, 8, 10, 12, 14 and 16 Warwick Road; not to mention the leasehold of nos 52, 54, 56 and 58 on the other side of the High Street. It seems a fair guess, therefore, that Gentleman Guilford was responsible for the redevelopment, which is still with us today, of the entire site of Edward Martin's Upper House. Thomas Guilford incidentally makes an appearance in chapter 21 as purchaser in April 1874 of Marlborough Villa, where I think he lived.

Let us now turn our attention to Martins Lower House, next door but further down the hill with less of a front garden – and whose rear parts are still standing (see the photograph on page 8 above). It was not subject to the same alarums and excursions as its Upper neighbour. The Poor Rate record begins in 1693 and continues until 1704 with 'Edward Martin for Henry Savages'. So Martin built this house some seven years after his other and perhaps in association with Henry Savage – whoever he was. The Ashenhursts, Thomas and Catharine, and the Latters then appear but this may be a muddle with the Upper House, or the two may be combined temporarily. In 1735, however, Nich Wood shows up definitely all the way to 1766 to be followed by Robert Jeffery ('for late Nich Wood') until 1777 when Richard Stapley ('for late Woods') completes the sequence to 1797.

The building we are considering is now nos 59-61 High Street and is a dress shop called 'Silks' but before that, in the memory of many of us, it was Goulden & Curry, booksellers, stationers and hi-fi specialists, a business which went back to John Colbran in the 19th century. Before John Goulden decided to sell he showed me some notes made by his father which suggested that the title went back to 1765 and so, when the sale was eventually completed, I was given the opportunity to see the deeds and had high hopes that they would throw light on the 18th-century story of the house – alas no! The suggestion of 1765 for the title root is borne out by the Poor Rate indication that Nicholas Wood died about then and the ownership changed; but the earliest deeds were 19th-century. At least however a link with the Poor Rate story was to be found in the name Stapley. Richard Stapley who was paying the rates in 1797 had a son Michael who bought some land from his father in 1813 and built a row of cottages going up the hill as far as what is now the Little Mount Sion car park – nos 1 to 11 Little Mount Sion. Richard Stapley died in 1820 and the house, by then named Rosebury House, was sold to George Trice. In 1841 George's widow sold the house to John Colbran for £1,000. The Tithe Award shows Harriet Trice as owner and occupier of Roseberry House and Pleasure Ground. The Stapley family recently achieved an unexpected prominence in the town through the short-lived renaming of the pub in Church Road which used to be called the *Clarence*. The *Charles Stapley*, however, soon gave way to the even less pub-like *Biscuit Factory*. What the Stapley link was I do not know. The Stapley family appears in the earliest *Sprange Guide* (1780) in the persons of Charles and Richard. I am only guessing that they were related and I have no evidence of their presence in the town before Richard started paying the Poor Rate in 1777 – there are no locally proved wills. One of the Goulden deeds tells us that Richard was a yeoman from Rotherfield and perhaps this is where the family originated, diversifying its agricultural interests in nearby Tunbridge Wells. Anyhow, in 1780 Charles Stapley had two lodging houses, one on Mount Ephraim and the other on the London Road (perhaps that is the pub building?), while Richard had a lodging house at the 'Foot of Mount Sion' which must have been Rosebury House. In 1797 and 1801 Charles had three houses on the London Road, one occupied, as a matter of incidental interest, by the Dowager Lady Monson who features in the Jerningham Letters (see chapter 25); and Richard had Rosebury House, called his 'upper house', and a 'lower house' which I think was located at the bottom of Castle Street (New Street at the time) and was connected with the carrier business, some details of which are given in the notice taken from Sprange's 1808 Guide reproduced below. The warehouse mentioned therein was probably the old Glassington Theatre in Castle Street (see the Robert Stapley Estate papers). Barrow's map shows 'Stapley's

Wagon office' prominently in this sort of position; and also confirms the location of 'Mr Stapley' at Rosebury House which, according to Sprange, had three parlours, five chambers, four garrets, two coach houses and stabling for six horses. The Goulden deeds tell us that Richard Stapley died in February 1820 and that he had two sons, Richard and Michael. Richard was a wheelwright and I think he took over the carrier's business while Michael who was an upholsterer busied himself around Little Mount Sion. Although I have no information on the purchase, it is evident that Richard Stapley the Elder owned Rosebury House since he relates in his will, made in 1813, how 'some years ago' he sold a slip of freehold ground at the foot of Mount Sion to his son Michael for £31 10s. 0d. and Michael erected a messuage and other buildings which a plan in the deeds shows to have been

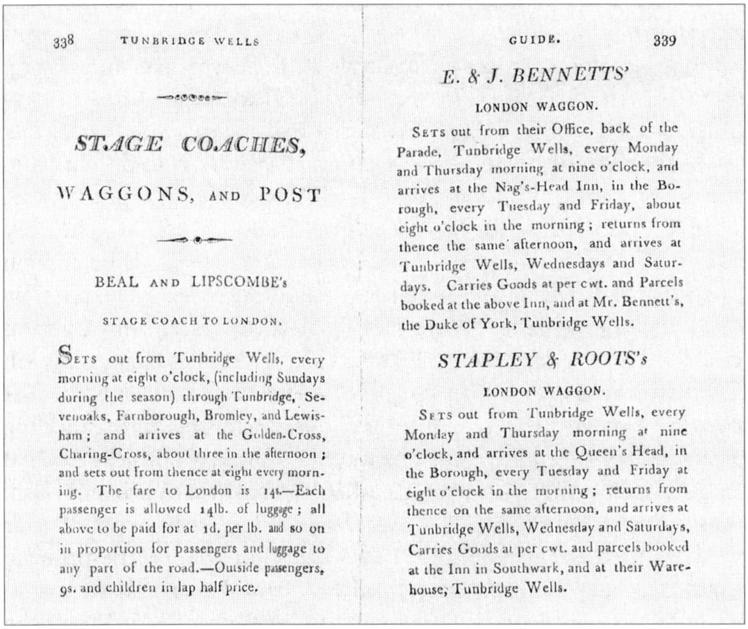
338 TUNBRIDGE WELLS GUIDE. 339

STAGE COACHES,

WAGGONS, AND POST

BEAL AND LIPSCOMBE's

STAGE COACH TO LONDON.

SETS out from Tunbridge Wells, every morning at eight o'clock, (including Sundays during the season) through Tunbridge, Sevenoaks, Farnborough, Bromley, and Lewisham; and arrives at the Golden-Cross, Charing-Cross, about three in the afternoon; and sets out from thence at eight every morning. The fare to London is 14s.—Each passenger is allowed 14lb. of luggage; all above to be paid for at 1d. per lb. and so on in proportion for passengers and luggage to any part of the road.—Outside passengers, 9s. and children in lap half price.

E. & J. BENNETTS'

LONDON WAGGON.

SETS out from their Office, back of the Parade, Tunbridge Wells, every Monday and Thursday morning at nine o'clock, and arrives at the Nag's-Head Inn, in the Borough, every Tuesday and Friday, about eight o'clock in the morning; returns from thence the same afternoon, and arrives at Tunbridge Wells, Wednesdays and Saturdays. Carries Goods at per cwt. and Parcels booked at the above Inn, and at Mr. Bennett's, the Duke of York, Tunbridge Wells.

STAPLEY & ROOTS's

LONDON WAGGON.

SETS out from Tunbridge Wells, every Monday and Thursday morning at nine o'clock, and arrives at the Queen's Head, in the Borough, every Tuesday and Friday at eight o'clock in the morning; returns from thence on the same afternoon, and arrives at Tunbridge Wells, Wednesday and Saturdays, Carries Goods at per cwt. and parcels booked at the Inn in Southwark, and at their Warehouse, Tunbridge Wells.

Sprange Guide *1808*

(together with other buildings erected on an adjoining plot later purchased for £68 10s. 0d.) a complete range of buildings extending from the bottom of the hill to the limit of the Rosebury House garden (from nos 1 to 11, Little Mount Sion, in today's terms). The corner shop which was Goulden's music department and was given a Civic Society award when it was the 'Glass Slipper' (now Thurlwell's) was therefore built by Michael Stapley, probably as a result of the £31 sale 'some years' before 1813. The 1808 map shows a building on this corner, hatched as for stabling, but seemingly labelled 'Stapley Sign Painter'. Rosebury House and its garden, reduced in area by the narrow strip fronting Little Mount Sion, did not remain in Stapley hands. By December 1821, and possibly as a result of Richard the Elder's death in 1820, it had passed to George Trice. At least the plan endorsed on the Goulden deed dated 1821 shows 'George Trice's Boundary fence' and anyway it is Harriett Trice who is named as owner by the Tithe Award. There is a problem here because the Goulden deeds show plainly that the house was sold for £1,000 in 1841 by 'Sarah Trice Tunbridge Wells widow and relict of George Trice Tunbridge Wells ostler'. Who was Harriett then? Did the widow have a second name or was the Tithe Award mistaken? The purchaser anyway was John Colbran who had already published his first *Tunbridge Wells Guide* in 1840 and who was to establish the first real newspaper in the town, the *Tunbridge Wells Gazette* (first published in 1855), and the bookseller's and stationer's business which became known as the Royal Library and later as Goulden and Curry. A month after Colbran bought Rosebury House he split it down the middle with Gardner, a nearby chemist, creating some flying freehold problems for later generations in the process; and they each built shops in the front garden, leaving, however, a wide passage in between which contained the original steps leading up to the old house, as can be seen on the Ordnance Survey map some 20 or 30 years later. Remnants of this arrangement are still to be seen today in the front office at no.57 High Street. Gardner's shop became Edward Dunkley's in October 1876 and later the Dunkley and Rogers that some of us remember. As for John Colbran, he seems to have set about regaining those bits of Little Mount Sion frontage which Richard Stapley had sold to his son; and adding to it the houses which had been built on Philip Seale's old garden (see chapter 13), so that when he died in about 1890 a grand auction sale was held by Bracketts at which the whole of the north side of lower Little Mount Sion was on offer in eight lots, with the only exception of nos 5, 7 and 9. At some stage, possibly in the 1850s before he began producing the *Tunbridge Wells Gazette*, John Colbran built a printing works behind the present nos 9 and 11, Little Mount Sion, to which he had direct access from the back of Rosebury House via the courtyard which is now at the back of the newly renovated nos 5 and 7. The printing works building is now an office. Previously Colbran's printing had been done in a building called Lewis Place on the other side of the London Road at the bottom of Mount Sion. In order to build his new printing works Colbran had to demolish a row of four cottages occupying the site of the present no.11 and the front part of the printing works. These cottages had been built by Richard Stapley the Elder and were sold at auction in April 1848, Colbran being the successful bidder at £135. When the present no.11 was built I have no information but it was obviously after 1848.

A summary now follows of the development of the north side of lower Little Mount Sion during the 19th century, based on the maps of 1808 (Barrow), 1839 (*Colbran Guide*), 1840 (Tithe) and 1866 (Ordnance Survey), using present-day numbering for purposes of identification and working uphill at each stage. The north side only is relevant to this chapter since it is within the 'Martin strip' the subject initiated in the chapter – but it does stray into the territory of Philip Seale, subject of chapter 13. In 1808, as already noted, there was something – a stable or Stapley's sign-writing shop – at the bottom; there was then an L-shaped terrace (neither lodging houses nor stables) starting at about the position of no.5, turning at right-angles at no.11 and continuing to the boundary of Rosebury House grounds (as far as the back gardens of Warwick Road today). This latter part of the terrace was probably formed by the four cottages built by Richard Stapley and it may well be that he built the part fronting Little Mount Sion also. Above this point, in Philip Seale's old garden, there were as yet no buildings. By 1821, as evidenced by the plan accompanying the Goulden deed of December that year, a range of buildings from the shop at the bottom as far as no.3 had been completed. The shop had living accommodation above and behind and no.1 was shown as a wash-house with a yard behind; and no 3 was a warehouse and workshop. The present nos 5 and 7 (recently refurbished ornaments to the 'Chelsea of Tunbridge Wells' – in estate agentese!) were built some years before 1833 as is testified by the following interesting description in a mortgage deed of 1 May 1833:

> All that ... cottage with the yard and premises thereto belonging as the same were sometime since in the occupation of Thomas Bissenden ... situate ... on Mount Sion near to a certain Chapel there called the Presbyterian Chapel and bounding towards the south to a road leading to the Crescent ... and which ... cottage was sometime since pulled down by ... Michael Taylor Stapley and a messuage in two tenements or cottages created on the site thereof, more particularly set forth ... by the plan on the back of the second skin of this present Indenture ... and now in the several occupations of Serjeant Rourke and James Hunt ...

The plan shows what are undoubtedly the present nos 5 and 7, bounded across the passage below by 'Mr Stapley's Warehouse' and above by 'Clarkes Cottage'; to the back by 'Mr George Trice' and to the front by the Chapel and Wilment Lodge on the other side of the road. No.9 therefore existed at this time in the form of 'Clarkes Cottage' but no.11 did not – at least only as part of the row of cottages built by Richard Stapley. Finally, by 1828, another row of (presumably) cottages had appeared at the bottom of Philip Seale's garden, parallel with the four just mentioned. In 1840 the situation is much clearer with Tithe and census information available. The shop house and nos 1 to 7 inclusive are described in the Tithe Award as '3 houses, shop etc.', owned by Charles Stapley and occupied by 'Self and others'. Charles is not mentioned in the Goulden deeds: he was not son of Michael but maybe he was a brother or nephew. Michael had died between 1834 and the year of Queen Victoria's accession, leaving two sons, Henry and Martin, and their half-brother William Wilment and no fewer than six daughters. It is interesting to note that one of these daughters, Sarah, married 'Jabez Scholes, gentleman, of Calverley Road,' who was clerk to the Chapel in Little Mount Sion; while Mrs M. Stapley was Treasurer of the Female British School. Evidently the Stapleys were non-conformists and this may explain their interest in Little Mount Sion. No.9 is shown by the Tithe Award as 'House, Workshop and Yard', owned by Mary Clark (hence 'Clarkes Cottage') and occupied by Jackson. The row of four cottages just above is owned by David Osborne (who bought them from the Stapleys?) and occupied by Hewlett and others; while the newer row of cottages just above is owned by Thomas (another mystery) Stapley and occupied by Carrick and others. There is a limited tie-up with the census and other information here. The census lists Stapley's Cottages nos 1 to 9 and no.1 is occupied by Anna Clark, a 35-year-old widow living with her son of 14, Edward. No.7 is occupied by James Hunt (mentioned in the 1833 mortgage); and no.9 by William Carrick (mentioned in the Tithe Award), a 50-year-old tailor and his family. A possible explanation is that the nine Stapley cottages were made up of no 9 (Clarkes Cottage), nos 5 and 7 (the new pair built by Michael Stapley), the four at no.11 built by Richard Stapley and two new ones above. Finally, between 1839 and the time of the Tithe Award, a house has been built in the middle of Philip Seale's garden and is recorded as 'House and garden' owned and occupied by Richard Standen. The census names the house as Crescent Cottage which is confusing because, as will be discussed in chapter 15, Crescent Cottage was also the name given to part of Sion Crescent after 1850 – and in 1851 in fact Richard Standen's new house has changed its name to Bromley Cottage. Richard Standen was a 40-year-old carpenter and living with him, in addition to his wife and two daughters and two servants, was Sarah Mercer, aged 75. Could she have been his mother-in-law, explaining perhaps his acquisition of part of Philip Seale's garden? In 1851 nos 5 and 7 seem to be called Bassetts House Nos 1 and 2; no.9 is still called Clarks House although no Clark lives there; and after Clarks House and before Richard Standen's Bromley Cottage the enumerator has listed nos 1 to 5 Roseberry Cottages and noted, interestingly, 'Two cottages building'. It was about this time that John Colbran would have been demolishing the row of four cottages at no.11 and building his printing works; so that it is difficult to be sure exactly what the situation was in 1851. By 1861, however, the developments are complete, which can be seen on the Ordnance Survey map and which were still in place (with one small change) at the time of the Colbran auction in 1890 and indeed persisted until the 1950s or '60s. Richard Standen's free-standing house has been extended or replaced entirely to form a terrace called Rosebury Place, one of whose garden entrances can be seen by the little leaning tree in the photograph on the right taken by David Johnson in September 1934.

Little Mount Sion, September 1934

These houses were numbered 25 to 31 Little Mount Sion. Below them, hard up against the Warwick House boundary, was a row of three tiny cottages numbered 13 to 15, Little Mount Sion. Between these and the road, and facing the new printing works and the new no.11, appears on the Ordnance Survey a row of three cottages which seem to be called, in 1861, Roseberry Terrace Nos 1, 2 and 3 with no.4 being the new no.11, Little Mount Sion. In 1871 the buildings seem to be the same but the Roseberry Cottages and Terrace are all called Rosebury Cottages, Nos 1 to 6, and the new no.11 is labelled simply 'Little Mount Sion', but is inhabited, as it was ten years before, by the master bootmaker Richard Cushman and his family. By 1881 the terrace of three cottages facing the printing works has gone, to be replaced by a large pair of semi-detached houses which is the building with the prominent chimney on the right-hand side of Johnson's photograph. These houses, numbered 19 and 21, were shown on the map illustrating the 1890 auction and on more recent Ordnance Survey maps ... until the day not so long ago when all the houses (some million pounds' worth of 'Chelsea style' housing in today's values) occupying the site of the garden which Philip Seale bought from the Earl of Buckingham in 1702 were demolished for the car park which still graces the street scene. The sign hanging, as far as I can tell, from the old no.19 in Johnson's photograph reads 'Worsfold Practical Chimney Sweep Phone 2133'. By 1890 all these properties, except nos 5, 7 and 9, belonged to John Colbran. The corner shop at the bottom (63 High Street) and nos 1 and 3 Little Mount Sion descended by inheritance to Michael Stapley's son Henry who, dying in 1866, left one sixth each to his five surviving sisters and to his half-brother William Wilment, who by this time was a wine merchant living in Cheltenham. The siblings and their spouses came to a family arrangement in 1870 which resulted in the sale of the properties to John Colbran in 1874 for £1,300. Nos 1 and 3 were described in 1890 as houses and had living rooms and sculleries on the ground floor with bedrooms over; but the plan accompanying the deed of 1821 shows them in use as wash house, warehouse and workshop and that of 1874 as storeroom, 'bake offices and oven'; and in 1833, as mentioned above, 'Mr Stapley's warehouse' came below no.5. The 1861 census shows, between Hope Cottage (the new name for Clarks Cottage, no.9) and '1 Little Mount Sion Lodging house', a 'Marine Store Shop' where lived George Tompkin, a railway porter and 28-year-old Ann, his wife, who was a 'dealer in Marine stores'. What were 'marine stores'? I cannot imagine the good citizens of 1861 Tunbridge Wells buying gear for their yachts berthed at the Brighton marina; but it occurs to me that there may be some connection with the curiously named Marine House and Marine Cottage on Cumberland Walk, owned and occupied in 1841 by Jane Cripps (see chapter 25). Be that as it may, nos 5 and 7 seem to have continued in Stapley hands until at least 1877 after which I have no information except that John Colbran did not get his hands on them. In an interesting link with other parts of the Mount Sion story, Michael Stapley mortgaged nos 5 and 7 in 1833 to Thomas Fry, the schoolmaster, and William Jewhurst, the executors of Ann Friend (see chapter 10). Ann left money to be invested for her daughters Eliza (Mrs Plees of Sion House) and Jane (who inherited the *Compasses*); and the executors invested £475 in a mortgage on nos 5 and 7. In 1877 this mortgage was transferred to William Gordon Plees (Eliza's husband) and Edward Marchant Hunter (Eliza's son-in-law) who were jointly executors of Mrs Hodgson (see chapter 12). No.9 was owned, as we have seen above, by Mary Clark in 1840 and continued no doubt to have a separate history about which I have no information. By 1861 Clarks Cottage had become Hope Cottage, as shown on the Ordnance Survey map – a name which continued until 1881 at least, whether named after an eponymous owner or an abstraction I know not. No 11, built on the site of the four cottages bought by John Colbran from David Osborne's executors in 1848, was described in 1890 as 'substantially built of White Brick with Slated Roof' and containing a living room, scullery and WC on the ground floor and three bedrooms over. Since the present building has three storeys and the bricks do not look white and its shape does not quite match that shown on the Ordnance Survey map, I guess it is not the same building. John Colbran bought the sites of nos 13 to 17 and 19-21 in 1850, the first from Benjamin Slight who was the Meeting House minister (but how he comes into the picture is unclear) and the second (probably with existing houses) from Thomas Stapley. The Stapley family, so prominent at the beginning of the century, had been slowly disappearing from the scene. The name no longer appears in 1808 at Mount Ephraim or on the London Road, although 'Mr Stapley' is running one lodging house on Mount Pleasant in that year and in 1817 M.Stapley has Oldenburgh House (just above Thackeray's). There was another branch of the family whose connection, if any, I have not been able to establish which owned most of the south side of Castle Street; but the male line failed and the property (including Picton House on the corner of Castle Street and the High Street and the old Glassington Theatre building) was sold off. Another Stapley whose relationship I do not know was Thomas who was a butcher and became bankrupt in 1811. A John Stapley was leasing Crescent Lodge (see chapter 17) in 1817 and a lingering scion of the family remained there until the turn of the century in the romantic shape of Rose Stapley, teacher of the mandolin and guitar. In 1854 John Colbran collected the final piece of his jigsaw when he bought Richard and Elizabeth Standen's house and garden. The date suggests that he was responsible for the demolition or extension, whichever it was, of this house which was complete by 1861. The 1890 Conditions of Sale contain two items of information about this Plot 8 which are worth recording. Firstly, to quote: 'This property was originally conveyed subject to the right of the owner of a certain stable, situate at Mount Sion, of passing and repassing to and from a well or spring of water on the property ... and taking water therefrom by the way or path only then used and accustomed, leading from Mount Sion Crescent in a direct line through the middle of the garden ... to the said well. It is believed that this right has not been exercised for many years and that the well is closed ...' I guess these references take us back to 1721 and the marriage of Thomas Seale and Priscilla Wagon and the division of the garden into two – for more on which see chapter 13. The 'stable situate at Mount Sion' was, I suppose, the one at the north-east end of the newly-weds' house. The second item of information in the Conditions of Sale is curious. 'A Dust-bin has been excavated underground beneath a portion of the yard or garden ... which ... has been used in connection with the Cottages' numbered 13, 15 and 17. I do not begin to understand this – sounds like a private underground landfill, but what do you do when it is full? Be that as it may, we have now completed consideration of the lower part of Martin's strip – the Upper and Lower Houses (Warwick and Rosebury Houses as they became) and their gardens; and it is time to turn our attention to Berkeley Place, otherwise Ashenhursts Great House.

Chapter 10

Ashenhursts Great House

This was probably the lodging house to which Thomas Wilson referred in his diary for 1736: '…. Woods and brothers upon the top of Mount Sion near the Bowling Green. A very handsome house.' He did not name the house and it was a long time before I established for sure which house was the 'Ashenhursts Great House' that featured (with its Great House Field) in Nicholas Wood's will. He left a ten-page will 'with some intarlining with my own handwrighting to explain the meaning' – and not a little idiosyncratic spelling. Here is the passage where he bequeaths the house.

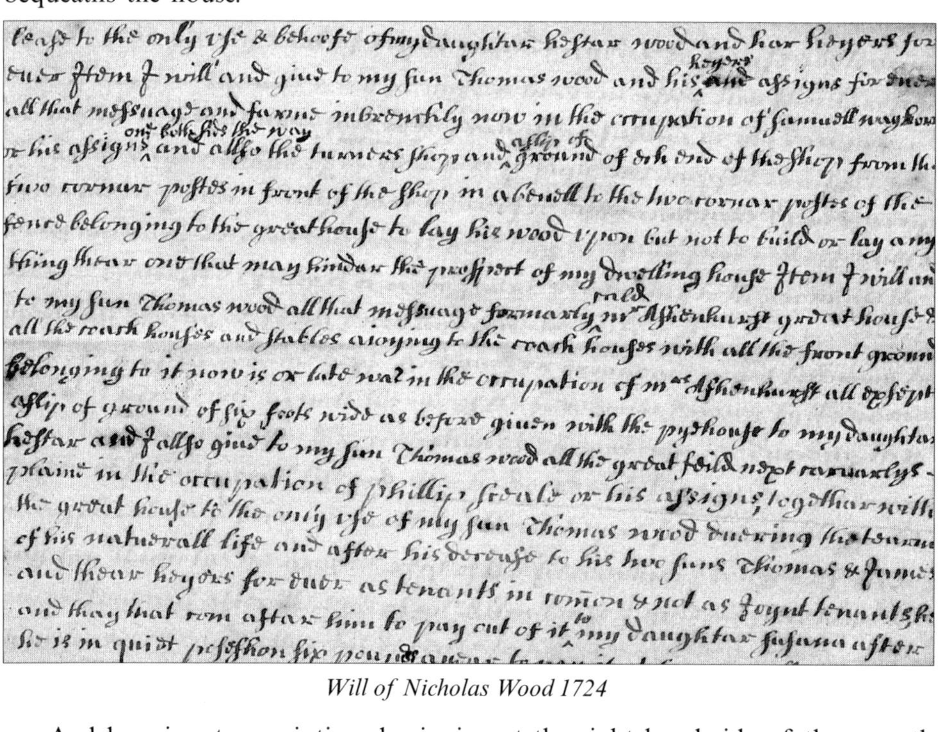

Will of Nicholas Wood 1724

And here is a transcription, beginning at the right hand side of the seventh line down with the word 'Item':

> … I will … to my son Thomas Wood all that messuage formerly called Mr Ashenhursts Great House and all the coach houses and stables adjoining to the coach houses with all the front ground belonging to it now is or late was in the occupation of Mrs Ashenhurst all except a slip of ground of six feet wide as before given with the pyehouse to my daughter Hestor and I also give

> to my son Thomas Wood all the great field next Calverleys Plaine in the occupation of Phillip Seale or his assigns, together with the great house to the only use of my son Thomas Wood during the term of his naturall life and after his decease to his two sons Thomas and James and their heirs for ever as tenants in common not as joynt tenants …

The problem was to disentangle which of several sons and daughters were to have which properties and to identify the properties. There were four sons and three daughters. The eldest son William was to have the house Nicholas lived in; Thomas was to have Ashenhursts Great House; Nicholas junior was to have Martin's Lower House; Edmund was to have Martin's Upper House; Hester was to have the Pyehouse; Susanna the *Blue Anchor*; and Elizabeth who was married got an annuity of £8 and the repayment of £20 lent to her husband Mr Gibbon. Where were all these places? The year was 1724, so a glance at the Bowra plan of 1738 on page 87 should help. How many Woods can we see? Well, the previous chapter dealt in detail with Martins Upper and Lower Houses and Nicholas and Edmund Wood are labelled on the plan. The Pyehouse is marked Rich Brooker and will be considered later; and the *Blue Anchor* is of course marked 'Hawkins the Anchor'. We are now left with the dwelling house of Nicholas senior and Ashenhursts; but oh dear! There are three Woods on the plan, Thomas junior, Thomas senior and plain Thomas. Plain Thomas is shown at the house we know as Sion House and which used to be called Green Pales. This Poor Rate record was used as an example in chapter 8 and was one piece of evidence available from early on, confirming that this house was called 'Green Pales' not Ashenhursts and indeed seemed to have nothing to do with any Ashenhurst. William, the eldest son, was to have his father's dwelling house but only on condition that he follow the trade of fellmonger and glover; but it is his nephew Thomas who is shown on the Bowra plan at this house. So the two Thomases, father and son, have the two big lodging houses at the top of the hill – but which one is Ashenhursts? I suppose the fact that the father had been left Ashenhursts Great House (see the will above) might have given a hint; but it was not until some time later when I was investigating the *Compasses* and the *Grove Tavern* that I found the

Bowra plan 1738

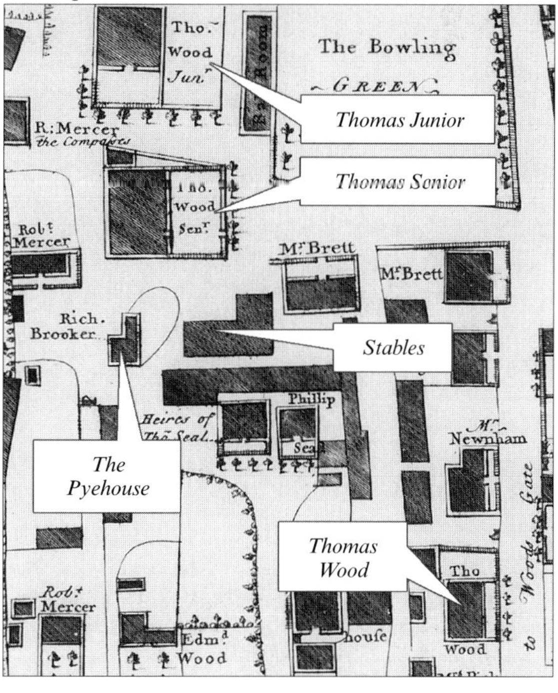

knock-down proof. Since both pubs belonged to Whitbreads I asked if they had any deeds. Yes, they did. In their archives office at Maidstone I found among the deeds of the *Grove Tavern* a large parchment document dated 30 January 1833. Ann Friend's executors were carrying out the provisions of her will. She was Nicholas the fellmonger's great-granddaughter. She died in 1831 and told her executors to sell her Berkeley Place; but as well as the main building there were the stables and coach houses. Let's have another look at Bowra. He tells us elsewhere that 'the Houses have Double Lines and the Stables etc Single Lines round their Plans'. Berkeley Place can be seen with a double line round it but where are its stables? Well, the nearest ones are obviously just down the hill and part of the stable yard was on offer in 1833. The conveyance document now forms part of the deeds of the *Grove Tavern.* To be sold was 'All that piece or parcel of Building Ground situated near Mount Sion ...being part and parcel of the Stable yard and ground belonging **to a certain Messuage Tenement or Lodging House formerly called Mrs Ashenhurst's Great House but some years since converted into two houses and called Berkeley Place**'...The bold type is mine. You can imagine I was quite pleased when I read that. I might even have said 'Eureka'. What better proof could there be?

Here is a detail to provide visual proof – in case you need convincing!

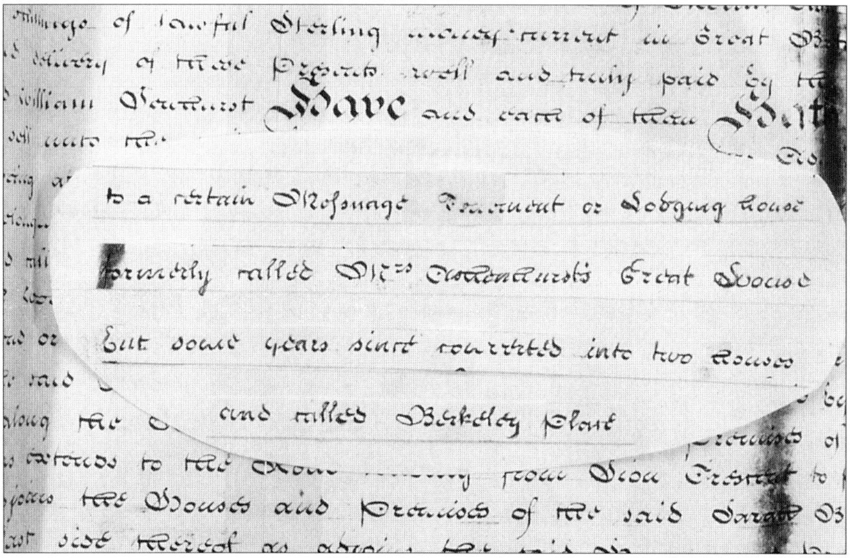

Detail and insert from conveyance dated 30 January 1833

I propose to deal first with this house and its Ashenhurst ramifications which will take the rest of this chapter and then to go on to the *Grove Tavern* and old Nich's dwelling house in the next two chapters. Thomas Ashenhurst then was a gentleman from Lambeth which is not to say that he was courteous, considerate and honest. His treatment of his sister suggests otherwise. It does mean that on the social scale he was below an esquire but above a yeoman or tradesman. He evidently had money because, after the Pantiles fire of 1687, he built seven shops on the Upper Walk, ten butchers' shops in the row opposite and the Royal Oak Lottery – and 'about 1700 was by far the largest tenant on the Walks, paying £115 out of a total rental of £349 4s. 6d.' (see Chalklin's unpublished paper). He also had interests on Mount Sion, as we know, and the mortgage deed of 1701 mentioned in the previous chapter may well have been the first in a sequence of events which led Thomas to sue his sister in 1708. In about 1703 Thomas came in an urgent hurry to his 17-year-old sister Katharine and persuaded her to sign a 'Bill of Sale' of all his goods and chattels and a seven-year lease of a house on the Pantiles called the 'Flat House'. The transaction was carried out 'in such haste that time would not then permit' them 'to come to any just or settled accompt' nor 'to take Counterparts of any deed or writeing then and there signed or executed'. Katharine later denied knowing that the purpose behind these extraordinary proceedings was 'to prevent an execution being served upon his goods and chattels'. Was Leonard Bartholomew of Rochester chasing him or had he been gambling on the Walks? Katharine did apprehend that her brother 'was very willing and in haste to have the .... Bill of Sale and Lease made and executed' which was much to her satisfaction but 'what particular reason moved and induced' him 'to require so much haste and dispatch' she 'conceives is best known to himself'.

Well, it's pretty obvious that what we have here is a trick not entirely unknown in our own civilised times whereby the beleaguered businessman transfers the million-pound mansion to a relative to keep it from the clutches of creditors. One golden rule of family relations is never to do business with relatives – but everything might have been well, I suppose, if Thomas had gone to his sister the next year and asked for his property back; but he got her to work for him, looking after his lodging houses, for the next four years or so and, I imagine, she must have felt that she deserved a bit more by way of compensation than he had offered. So she would not play; and so he took her to court – which of course is how we know all this. Christopher Chalklin found the documents during his trawl of Chancery Lane when he was working on his dissertation back in the 1960s.

I do not know how old Thomas was but I am sure he must have been considerably older than his sister. Their father, Randolph, had died in 1688 when Katharine was only three; and she had been looked after by her grandmother, Mary Ashenhurst, and then by an aunt. For one year she had been 'placed with Mr Lane a Dancing Master'. So I don't suppose the brother and sister were very close. Anyway, according to the record he 'ordered and instructed' her to manage 'the two great houses at Mount Sion and also … Jordans house there' – and this she did, with some success, from 1 May 1704 until February 1708; and as part of her defence against her brother she produced detailed accounts of income and expenditure. These will be discussed in some detail later. Katharine had to look after 'the two great houses at Mount Sion and also … Jordans house there', together with, for the 1704 season only, a house called Speldhurst House which I cannot identify but whose name suggests a site within the Speldhurst Parish bounds, perhaps on the Pantiles or Mount Ephraim. Jordans House and the Pyehouse and the *Grove Tavern* are one and the same and will be considered in a minute; one of the two great houses is obviously Ashenhursts but where, then, was the other?

The answer seems to be the Bowling Green House. There are two arguments for, and one against. The Poor Rate record shows that Thomas Ashenhurst paid rates from 1690 until 1710 for 'a new house and Bowling Alley' (see chapter 19 for the full sequence) in addition to the separate record for Ashenhursts Great House which begins in 1699 as follows:

1699-1712	Mr Thomas Ashenhurst – for another new house
1713	Mr Thompson for a new house
1714	Mrs Thompson for a new house
1728-1732	Mrs Walton
1733-1741	Thomas Wood
1742-1748	Thomas Wood Junior
1749-1757	Mr John Wood Junior
1758-????	Mr Thomas Wood Junior (merging with other Wood property?)

The first 'pro' argument, then, is that the new house with the Bowling Alley must be the Bowling Green House since there is a separate sequence for Ashenhursts

Bowra general map 1738 – detail

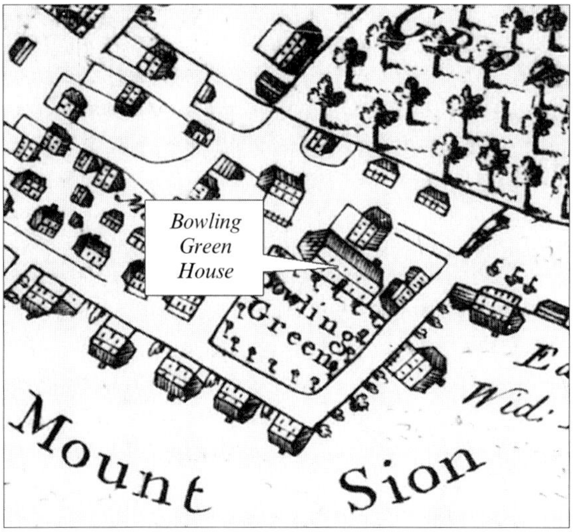

Great House. The second argument is that Katharine Ashenhurst records in her accounts a payment of ground rent to Mr Constable and the Bowling Green House was not built on Edward Martin's strip but on the plot originally leased to Richard Constable and Robert Brooke and then taken by Constable alone in the partition of 1686 (see chapter 19). The argument against is that Bowra's Mount Sion Plan shows the Bowling Green House as nothing but a 'Ballroom' which conveys a picture of a glorified sports pavilion. On the other hand Bowra's general map shows something more like an ordinary house, as you can see in this blown-up detail. Bowra shows the houses in a kind of three-dimensional perspective as if laid on their backs and the Bowling Green House looks a large building of at least two storeys.

For most of Queen Anne's reign then the Ashenhursts ruled over the two great houses and the Bowling Green – but all was not well. Thomas seems to have survived the attacks of his creditors and in 1708 he complained to the Court of

Chancery. We only have Katharine's side of the story but it seems that Thomas wanted his furniture back and the lease on the Flat House and the profits from his Mount Sion houses; while his sister was saying that she had been given the furniture and the lease – she had the papers to prove it – and as for the profits what about her 'trouble and time in letting and looking after the said houses for the years' 1704 to 1708? Unfortunately we do not know what the judge thought nor what became of Katharine. She seems to have been a woman of character who, under the style Madam Katharine Ashenhurst, appears on her own account in the Poor Rate record from 1709 to 1714 (at Martins Upper and Lower Houses and at the Bow Window House – see chapter 19). She was still under thirty. Did she marry? Was she perhaps the Mrs Walton whose name comes next in the Bow Window sequence? What is known is that in 1713 or 14 her brother died. He gave all and singular his messuages and lands to a widow, Elizabeth Thompson of Speldhurst, but his will lays stress on the repayment of his debts to the widow, giving the impression that his financial position was still dodgy. Nevertheless Mrs Thompson's name appears as ratepayer for Ashenhursts Great House in 1713 and 1714 and for the Bowling Green House in 1713 and then no more.

In considering Katharine Ashenhurst's accounts we must bear in mind that they refer to the two 'great houses' together; and it is impossible to be certain that a particular individual stayed in Ashenhursts Great House – it might have been the Bowling Green House. The accounts cover the seasons of 1704 to 1707 and they form an appendix to Katharine Ashenhurst's defence against her brother's complaints in the Chancery Court. The accounts deal simply in Income and Expenditure, so let's start with the income side, the main interest in which is the names of the visitors who provided the income. Perhaps the most newsworthy was Francis Dashwood, father of the notorious second baronet of the same name and the Hellfire Club. There is, in fact, a very close connection between the Dashwoods and Tunbridge Wells. Francis senior and his elder brother Samuel were Lords of the Manor of Rusthall between 1690 and 1720. They seem to have been buccaneering entrepreneurs of the late 17th century, principally involved in the silk trade; but quite what they were up to in Tunbridge Wells no one knows. I guess they saw some commercial advantage in mixing with all the great and the good who flocked to the Wells in the season. There was no fixed 'Manor House' of Rusthall and so it is no surprise to find them using the lodging houses. Samuel was knighted in 1684 and became Lord Mayor of London in 1702. Sir Samuel is recorded in the Ashenhurst accounts as staying for four weeks in 1704. Exact dates are not provided but we do know that he paid £5 for lodging, £1 10s. 0d. for the kitchen and no less than £15 for stabling. His younger brother Francis stayed for four nights only in 1706, paying £2 each for lodging and stabling. He was M.P. for Winchelsea in 1708 and again in 1710. Katharine Ashenhurst calls him Sir Francis although he was not created baronet until June 1707. Does this mean that the accounts are not strictly contemporaneous but were made up by Katharine after the event in order to support her legal case or did she amend the title later as a matter of courtesy?

What other notables are to be found in the Ashenhurst accounts? Nobody very exciting – but briefly there were: Sir Charles Cotterell – he came for six weeks in 1704 – he had been knighted in 1687 and was Commissioner of the Privy Seal in 1697. Another visitor was 'My Lord Villars' who came for a week with Mr Lambeth in 1704. He died the following year, his chief claim to fame being apparently the fact that his wife, the Duchess of Cleveland, had a bastard child, known as 'Goodman Cleveland', by the actor Cardmell Goodman. Lord Huntley, 1st Duke of Gordon, spent £1 on four nights' lodging in 1705 and two guineas on the stables – he was a Catholic royalist who had opposed King William. Elizabeth, Lady Onslow, was a daughter of Sir Henry Tulse, Lord Mayor of London, and had three sons and 'unquantified' daughters by Baron Onslow, Speaker of the House of Commons from 1708 to 1710 – perhaps she brought some of her daughters to Mount Sion when she stayed for five weeks in 1707. And then there was the Duchess of Bolton. This wasn't Polly Peachum, of course; she came somewhat later. This was the wife of the 2nd Duke whom Jonathan Swift called a 'great booby'. The Duchess stayed for seven weeks in 1705 and ran up a bill of £42 10s. 0d. – three times the average rate.

Berkeley Place by D.J. Johnson – 28 March 1934

Not all the visitors were titled, of course; but it is difficult to identify the Messrs Dockwra, Cholmondeley and Mackarty, let alone the Smiths and Woods. A few generalisations can be made. Over the four years the two houses received a total of 69 guests of whom six returned a second year and four a third. The average length of stay was four weeks, the record going to Mr Roberts with 12 weeks in 1707, following five weeks in 1705 and eight in 1706. The average number of guests per week for the season was fewer than four. This seems ridiculous but there must have been fluctuations and a peak period. Again, they show a single name per entry, be it Mr or Mrs, My Lord or My Lady; but it is inconceivable that when the Duchess of Bolton ran up her bill for £42 over seven weeks in 1705 she was not accompanied by a retinue – and not of servants alone. In fact the single name surely represents a family more often than not.

The number of rooms in Berkeley Place is known from Sprange's guides. He does not list the Bowling Green House, probably because by 1780 it was no longer in use as a lodging house; but Berkeley Place (as it had now become) had six parlours, 12 chambers and 17 stables in 1780. In 1786 it had become 'two houses adjoining' each with half the accommodation. In later years a more detailed breakdown is given: each half has four sitting rooms, five chambers, five garrets, six stables and two coach houses. Anyway, there was ample accommodation for the apparent number of visitors. The average bill for lodgings was £1 15s. 0d. per week. Not all guests used the stables or the kitchen but the average bill for the stables, calculated over all guests, was 18s.-6d. and for the kitchen five shillings only. Although the 'Great Dineing Room' made occasional contributions to income, it was the custom, as noted by Celia Fiennes not long before this in 1697, for the gentry to buy their own food at the Market on the Walks. It gave the ladies something to do and the gentlemen a chance to admire the fresh-faced country lasses. A charge was then made for use of the kitchen by the visitors' servants. The kitchen contributed eight per cent of income, the stables 30 percent, lodgings 57 per cent; and the remaining five per cent came mainly from Jordans House and the dining room. Let's now turn to the expenditure side of the accounts which has its own entertainment value.

8.5 per cent of expenditure went on wages; 14.5 per cent on household and miscellaneous items; 33 per cent on the stables; 20 per cent on taxes and repairs; and 24 per cent on ground rent. Ground rent was paid, as noted before, to Mr Constable and must have been for the Bowling Green House. After rent and taxes the biggest item of expenditure was the Stables but nearly all this was for beans, oats, hay and straw and these costs were more than recovered in visitors' bills. The wages item covers the wages of the ostler and the household staff – Sarah, Frank, Anne Board, Mary, Billy and the cook. The most curious category is that of household and miscellaneous expenses: heating (wood, faggots and charcoal); lighting (candles and candlesticks); cleaning (hair brooms, birch brooms, brushes, mops, scouring sand and double tubs of soap), not to mention the cleaning of the well and the emptying of the 'house of office'! The last is an interesting revelation of the method of sewage disposal in vogue – but it has to be said that this operation is recorded only in 1704 and 1707 – and I cannot believe that there was capacity for three years. Can you imagine? Despite the cleaning of the well, about 30s. a year was also spent on water. Other items were to pay the chimney-sweep, for cleaning the clock, for silvering two looking glasses, for 'the watch', for the High Ways, for three new 'umbrellos' and for the 'Eraine bands' – could this be a group of Irish fiddlers?

The Ashenhurst accounts can be summarised as follows:

Ashenhurst Lodging House Accounts

Year	**1704**	**1705**	**1706**	**1707**	**Average**
Income	£231 0s. 6d.	£213 4s. 6d.	£179 12s. 0d.	£218 3s. 0d.	£208 5s. 0d.
Expenditure	£133 0s. 4d.	£157 19s. 1d.	£133 11s. 4½d.	£154 12s. 10d.	£144 15s. 11d.
Profit	£98 0s. 2d.	£55 5s. 5d.	£37 0s. 7½d.	£63 10s. 2d.	£63 9s. 1d.

The average profit as a percentage of income works out at 30 per cent, give or take, which seems all right – but what about the absolute amounts? Back to the old problem – what is it worth today? If we assume a multiplier of 100, that would mean that our two lodging houses – patronised, remember, by duchesses and other aristocracy – made a profit equivalent to just £6,000 a year which surely makes the effort hardly worthwhile. Let's try another way. The accounts tell us how much was paid in wages. The cook was paid £2 a year in 1706 and £2 5s. 0d. in 1707; the ostler £2 4s. 0d. in 1705, £2 10s. 0d. in 1706 and £2 12s. 0d. in 1707. These amounts are not out of line with wages fixed by the Hertfordshire Quarter Sessions in the late 17th century. Let us suppose, for the sake of argument and simplicity, that such persons might nowadays earn £10,000 a year. We then have a multiplier of between 4 and 5,000! Say 4,000 to be on the conservative side. The profits now look a bit healthier: about a quarter of a million. That's more like it, surely! There is, of course, not much consensus on this question – but opinions would be welcome. There is another point. In their great detail, the accounts give a convincing impression of objectivity; but there was no auditor around and the context of their conservation must not be forgotten. They were produced – and certainly tidied up for the court's benefit – as part of Katharine's defence; and she may have had an interest in understating her profits.

The Poor Rate record for Ashenhursts Great House (see page 108 above) is enigmatic. After Thomas Ashenhurst comes Mr[s?] Thompson in 1712 – explained of course by the death of Thomas – see above. She continues until the gap in 1714 to be followed in 1728 by Mrs Walton who I feel sure is the married Katharine Ashenhurst. Then comes Thomas Wood from 1733 to 1741 followed by more Woods – Thomas junior to 1748, John to 1757 and then Thomas junior again at which point the record seems to split or become confused with other Wood property. The family succession looks straightforward enough. Thomas senior inherited in 1724, his son Thomas inherited in turn in 1758 and he bequeathed Burlington House to Thomas III but left Ashenhursts and other bits and pieces to his three daughters 'share and share alike'. He died in 1774 but it was not until 1781 that the surviving trustee of this will, Philip Benge, actually conveyed the property. The division of the house into two halves seems to have followed swiftly. At any rate it occurred between the 1780 and 1786 editions of *Sprange's Guide* which continues to list Miss Wood and Miss Wood until 1811 when an attempt was made to give each half its own name: 'Clifton House' (anything to do with the present Clifton Place I wonder?) and 'Newark House'. It is to this period surely that we must date the present façade. I am sure the building is basically timber-framed, although the bit of timber which was exposed around 1990 and shown in my book as Plate 35 does not necessarily prove the point; but the façade presents a different picture and a puzzle. Why do not the brick courses line up in the middle? Here I have a theory. When the two spinster sisters were given their half-houses in the 1780s one of them decided to modernise her half; but the other sister did not agree – until she saw the result. She then decided to follow suit but the bricklayers were unable to match up the courses! Well, if you have a better theory!

What about the share of the third and I think youngest daughter Ann? I wonder whether she got the cottage at the end? Indeed I wonder when and why it was built. There is a hint of a rudimentary cottage on the Bowra plan but it lines up with the back of the main house not the front. I feel sure therefore that Woods Cottage, or Christmas Cottage as it is now called, (on the right of Johnson's photograph on page 110) was built between 1738 and 1808 when the Barrow map shows it clearly as an 'other house', not a lodging house. It would not quite have equated with a half share in the main house but might have been supplemented with a field or two – academic anyhow because Miss Sarah Wood died in 1811 and Miss Mary in 1818 and Ann came into the lot; and when she died in 1831 she was able to give one property to each of three daughters and still have Ashenhursts to spare. So she gave to her executors, on trust for sale, 'all those my three houses called the Berkeley Places adjoining together and situate on Mount Sion' with their outbuildings, grounds and appurtenances – and I am sure it was she who introduced the name 'Berkeley' and with a lack of significance equal to that with which 'Burlington House' had been named a few years earlier (prove me wrong if you can). By the time of the Tithe map the sales had been completed and the eastern half was owned and occupied by Thomas Benjamin Seamer and the western by Judith Waghorn; the cottage, however, perhaps by sale or perhaps by arrangement with the executors, was owned by Ann's daughter Mary Ann Hodgson. In 1840 it was empty but in 1861 Mary Ann is living there with her niece, Eliza Plees.

The later history of Berkeley Place can be briefly told. It continued in much the same usage for most of the century. *Colbran's Guide* of 1847 carried an advertisement. Mrs Jane Packham respectfully announces that 'she has taken that airy and commodious Lodging House, known as No 2, Berkeley Place, Mount Sion, near the Grove, which she lets in apartments, and trusts, by studying the comforts of her Lodgers, to merit a preference'. Business was not confined to the summer season. The *Tunbridge Wells Gazette* of 6 January 1860, for instance, lists Mrs Finley, Mr Offley, the Rev. Palmer and Miss Tomlinson as visitors at 1 and 2, Berkeley Place. In the 1880s John Brown appears on the scene … more about him in a minute. In 1893 the Misses Barnes are running a ladies' school and in 1907 Mr Carrick a boys' school. In the early 1930s a conversion into flats seems to have been effected. In 1961, following the fashion of the times, furnished 'Family Leave Flats' are on offer and in recent times half the house was run as a guest house for the 'active elderly'.

John Brown's Dairy 1870

Here is a photograph of Woods Cottage taken from an unusual angle and in unexpected circumstances. It is, of course, the building with the weather-boarded side and the half-hipped roof. The photograph forms part of an advertisement in a booklet produced by the *Advertiser* for the Festival of Britain in 1951 which is captioned: '1870. The start of the daily round from our original dairy on Mount Sion, Tunbridge Wells.' The text reads: 'John Brown's Dairies were founded in 1870 from humble beginnings, milk being delivered by roundsmen in bowler hats, carrying the old yoke and pails, or by horse-drawn carts (as shown in the old photograph reproduced above) ...' John Brown was born in Hitchin, Hertfordshire, in 1845, the eldest of a family of ten. After four years' schooling and a period of work in the locality he found himself without a job at the age of twenty. Being, like Napoleon, short of stature but long in energy and enterprise he decided that he was made to be a jockey and walked 28 miles to Newmarket. The trainers, however, failed to see his potential and he was forced to eat turnips from a field and put his shirt on a night's lodging rather than a horse. Shortly after this he moved to Tunbridge Wells and found work for one pound a week, including food and clothes. He was able to save most of his wages and in 1870 invested £100 in a dairy business, married and raised a family of four in a four-roomed cottage. Brown's Dairies prospered until in 1898 he sold out for a substantial sum and became a co-director of the Opera House which opened its doors in 1901. He then, for the next thirty years, directed his energy into a bakery business, the Neville Bakery Company, with shops in Neville Street, the High Street and elsewhere. He represented the South Ward on the Town Council from 1905 to 1918. He died at the age of 88 and much of this story is culled from the obituary which appeared in the *Courier* on 12 January 1934. The dairy business in which John Brown invested his hard-won savings in 1870 must have been the 'milk-walk' which he operated with William Heather according to David Johnson from the

John Brown's Dairy – Berkeley Road

back of Sion House – see chapter 17 page 248. Although there are some inconsistencies in these early stories, it is clear that the Brown family was in Wood's Cottage and No 2, Berkeley Place at the end of the century. In 1886 *Pelton's Directory* lists John Brown, dairyman, at 1, Berkeley Place (22, Berkeley Road), and in September 1888 'Mr Brown, Mount Sion', as owner, submitted an application to build 3 bedrooms, 2 WCs, a shop, dairy and scullery in Berkeley Road and Little Mount Sion. The result can be seen above. The empty site with the spreading tree behind the cottage has been taken for a new dairy building – which still exists, almost unchanged, but now in office use. The architect was W. Hopper of Standen Street and the builders were Messrs Waite and Roots of Mount Sion. The block plan shows Mr Brown as the occupier (and therefore probably owner) not only of No 22 Berkeley Road (Wood's Cottage) but also No 2 Berkeley Place, which is the adjoining, eastern half of the main house. In 1881, however, on the evidence of the census, Brown and his family seem to have been living in the cottage only. At some stage both the cottage and No 2 Berkeley Place were certainly purchased but when and whether separately or together I do not know. The address shown in the 1881 census is 22 Little Mount Sion but I am certain that this means 22 Berkeley Road: the property being on the corner of the two roads accounts for the confusion. The position of the entry in the enumerator's return, between Murray House and Berkeley Place, and the fact that the true 22 Little Mount Sion occurs elsewhere in its proper place, put this beyond doubt.

Now the census shows that Mrs Rose Brown, aged 27 at the time, had been born in Eastbourne and that the eldest child, Alice, was born in Haywards Heath and was nine years old in April 1881; while Kate aged seven, Mabel aged four and little John aged one month were all born in Tunbridge Wells. All this, and the fact that I have not spotted the Browns in the 1871 census, casts some doubt on the obituary account of John Brown's working in Tunbridge Wells for some years before 1870. I suppose, however, that Rose might have gone to Haywards Heath (perhaps to her mother's?) for the birth of her first child. She must have been a rose of sixteen or seventeen when she married and only eighteen when Alice was born. There is no evidence to show exactly when the family moved into Wood's Cottage, although the caption of the old photograph might suggest a connection with the cottage in the early 1870s. Anyhow, there seems little doubt that this is the four-roomed cottage to which the *Advertiser*'s reporter referred. Living with the family in 1881 was Alice Griffiths, a 'general servant' aged 33, described as sister, presumably of Rose and born like her in Eastbourne.

Agricultural Show Committee 1886 – John Brown is standing front right.

The 'milk-walk' evidently expanded and, according to the obituary, John Brown was able, after 12 years, to purchase a larger business together with a farm. It seems in fact to have been less than twelve years because the 1881 census describes John Brown as a dairyman employing four men with six acres of land (they were in Langton, says his granddaughter). More land was acquired subsequently including the 'Little Farm' in the Farmcombe Road area, mention of which crops up in chapter 22; and a farm at Ramslye. At some time, probably after the building of the new dairy in 1888, the family moved into more spacious quarters in the adjoining half of Berkeley Place; and during the last decade of the century the little conglomeration of three premises on the corner of Berkeley Road and Little Mount Sion was the headquarters of the business. Milk was prepared (its purity 'ensured and guaranteed by constant analytical research') in the new dairy building and put into churns for delivery while book-keepers slaved away in the basement of the old lodging house and staff were accommodated here and there. The Brown family continued to live in Berkeley Place for some years but in time the business outgrew the premises. The story of its transfer to St John's Road belongs elsewhere, however. The name and ownership may have changed now but the St John's building is still a dairy and the orange floats which chug around the town are a daily reminder of John Brown and his humble beginnings on Mount Sion.

Closely associated with Ashenhursts Great House was what Katharine Ashenhurst called Jordans House and which I am sure is one and the same with the 'pyehouse' which Nicholas Wood bequeathed to his daughter Hester. This takes us back to the start of this chapter, for if it had not been for Whitbread's archives we should not have been able to identify Ashenhursts Great House and the archives were only relevant because the *Grove Tavern* grew out of Jordans House and the pyehouse was part of the Ashenhurst enclave. Nicholas Wood was very specific about a six-foot-wide slip of land which he gave to Hester in addition to the 'pyehouse now in the occupation of John Mathews with the stables adjoining to it'; and he was careful to take it away from the bequest of the main house to Thomas (see the excerpt at the beginning of this chapter) with the words 'all except a slip of ground of six feet wide as before given with the pyehouse to my daughter Hester'. It follows logically that the main house or its grounds were immediately adjacent to the 'pyehouse'. There is more evidence. The Poor rate record runs as follows:

1689 (May)	Jo Jordan
1689 (2nd)-1691	Jordan
1692-1703	Ralph Jordan
1704, 1708-1710	Mr Ashenhurst or occ of Ralph Jordans
1711-1714	Mrs Ashenhurst or occ of Ralph Jordans
1728-1745	John Mathews
1746-1749	John Mathews or occ
1750	John Mathews or occ for Richard Brooker
1751-1779	Richard Brooker
1780-1781	Reynolds John for late Brookers
1782	Mepham _______ for his house late Reynolds
1783-1795	Mepham Jeremiah
1796-1797	Mepham Jeremiah for late Meeting House

The later entries will come in useful in the next chapter; but note these earlier points: firstly, the Ashenhurst regime starts in 1704 after that of the Jordans, making it quite natural that the name Jordan House should be used – Katharine's accounts include income from 'Mrs Jordans House' (1704 £2), 'Jordans House' (1706 £2) and 'The House called Jordan's House' (1707 £2); secondly, John Mathews is stated in Nicholas Wood's will to be in occupation of the pyehouse in 1724; and thirdly, we know from another source that Hester who inherited the pyehouse from her father married Richard Brooker. The source is the will of her brother Edmund (of Martins Upper House) who left an annuity of 52 shillings to his sister Hester 'wife of Richard Brooker' when he died about 1774. Furthermore 'Rich Brooker' is prominently marked on the Bowra plan in roughly the position of the *Grove Tavern*. The evidence in summary is overwhelming. Jo Jordan (or John Mathews) was no doubt the 'whimsical landlord' of Sprange's (or Benge Burr's) anecdote (see chapter 3); Jordans House became Nicholas Wood's pyehouse and developed eventually into the *Grove Tavern*. When it obtained this title and the details of its history will be the subject of the next chapter.

Chapter 11

The Grove Tavern

This chapter is about the *Grove Tavern*, photographed here by David Johnson in about 1930 with landlord Henry Okell Dadswell standing in the doorway in his waistcoat and shirtsleeves; and about the *Bugler's Arms* which was a few doors away down Little Mount Sion. Both these pubs were within the bounds of 'Martin's strip'; the *Grove Tavern* is particularly associated with Ashenhurst's Great House

The Grove Tavern *about 1930*

and the *Bugler's Arms* adjoins the subject of the next chapter, Philip Seale's houses. Before we get started take another look at the landlord in the photograph. His name was Henry Okell Dadswell and the 'Okell' should ring a bell with anyone slightly versed in Tunbridge Wells history. The correct spelling is 'Okill' and William Okill was the legendary clerk to the King Charles Chapel who had a lodging house on Mount Sion and used to announce the psalm 'Mount Sion is a pleasant place' when he had rooms to let. I thought this was one of those old tales with no basis in fact; but much to my surprise a lady in the audience of one of my Civic Society talks told me that the *Grove Tavern* landlord was her father and her family was descended from the legendary clerk – in fact he was her four-times-grandfather! For more on this story see chapter 15 page 189. Even more curiously her father had selected the *Grove Tavern* from a number of options in complete ignorance of the fact that it was almost on the site of old William Okill's famous lodging house.

There will be more to say about the landlords later but let's go back now to the origins of the *Grove Tavern.* We saw at the end of the previous chapter that a six-foot-wide slip was to be taken from the Great House grounds and added to the 'pyehouse' and noted the implication that the two must be adjacent. It has to be realised that the Great House premises of the time included a large area of stabling 'downhill' to the north-west. This can be seen clearly on Bowra and Barrow. The absence of a double line on Bowra indicates stables and coach houses and diagonal shading on Barrow carries the same meaning. The strip of land along the building on the south side must have been between the pyehouse and the stabling and must surely have been intended simply to provide the pyehouse with rear access and somewhere to hang out the washing. The squashed hemisphere marked on Bowra (see the next page) does not look exactly like a six-foot strip but maybe that is what Hester and Richard actually enclosed for their garden. John Bowra seems to have measured up the buildings on Mount Sion pretty accurately but was not so reliable on the relationship between the buildings. Nevertheless, the building marked 'Rich Brooker', on a scaled up Bowra plan, falls very close to the site of the present *Grove Tavern* and the shape and size correspond quite well if only the alignment is turned about thirty degrees in an anti-clockwise direction. The hemisphere then loses its eccentric shape and appears as on the Barrow map. This is all rather speculative but, as a matter of present fact, the passage between the *Grove Tavern* and no 17 Berkeley Road is not far off six feet wide. There is a bit of a problem about the land on the other side of the six-foot strip. Hester was given the pyehouse 'with the stables adjoining to it' and the six-foot strip in addition. Now, if the stables ground included the six-foot strip there was no need to specify it in two places in the will; on the other hand there seems nowhere else to place adjoining stables, since the house bounded roads on two sides and Seale property on the third and anyway Bowra shows no stables except those between the Richard Brooker property and Murray House to the south-west (marked Mr Brett). The passage in the will is in any case a little difficult to decipher: '... the pyehouse ... now in the occupation of John Mathews with the stables adjoining to it with a strip of ground six feet wide all the length of the building on the south side *& hed where the [stables?] are* (after the end of Martyn lease) ... to the only use and behoof ... ' The italicised portion is written rather illegibly between the lines. 'Hed' might mean 'hedge' but this does not help much. At least there is confirmation that the strip is on the south side – assuming Nicholas has his compass points more or less right. Regardless of all this there is solid evidence that at a later date some stable ground belonged to the Great House. The detail from the Bowra plan of Mount Sion Hill on the next page may help.

The deeds of the *Grove Tavern* where the vital evidence on the identity of Ashenhursts Great House was found start with a conveyance dated 30/31 January 1833 from the executors of Ann Friend to Mrs Sarah Bonham. A detail from the conveyance is illustrated in the previous chapter followed by a transcription. The piece of land under conveyance was described as 'Building Ground situated near Mount Sion ... being part and parcel of the Stable yard and Ground belonging to a certain Messuage Tenement or Lodging House formerly called Mrs Ashenhurst's Great House ...' and continues: '... formerly occupied by Mrs Ashenhurst afterwards in the tenure or occupation of Thomas Wood or his Undertenants since of Sarah Wood Mary Wood and Ann Friend ... and late of Ann Friend'. Mrs Ashenhurst, by the way, I take to refer to Katharine Ashenhurst, the Mrs rather than Miss being used honorifically as was customary for unmarried ladies of a certain status. The description continues with detailed measurements and refers to an accompanying plan (reproduced on the next page) which is quite revealing:

Bowra plan of Mount Sion 1738

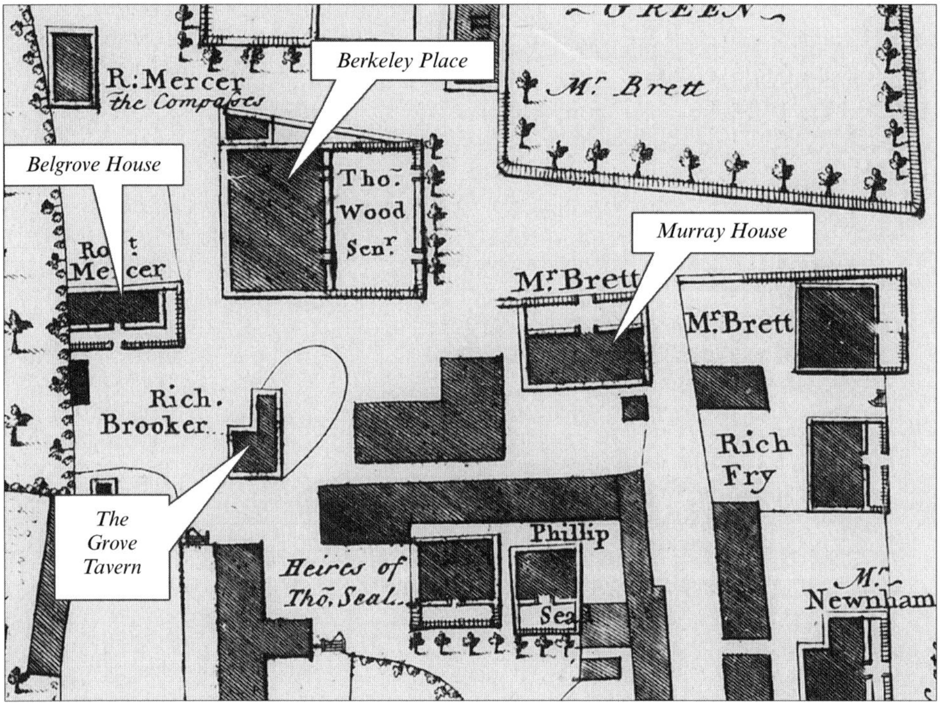

It shows that the purchaser, Mrs Bonham, already owned the *Bugler's Arms* property, now no 32, Little Mount Sion, and that the *Grove Tavern* premises were part of 'Mr Thompson's Estate'. The piece of land bought by Mrs Bonham in 1833 was of irregular shape but can easily be identified on modern maps because it covers the sites of the present no.30 Little Mount Sion and nos 15 and 17 Berkeley Road and their back gardens. The irregularity is due to the fact that the site occupied by nos 32 and 34 Little Mount Sion (34 is the *Grove Tavern*) is excluded. The land adjoining on the south-west side (81 feet in length) is labelled 'Stables Yard and Premises sold to John Taylor' and is referred to in the conveyance as 'other part of the said Stable Yard and the Stables there lately sold by the said Thomas Fry and William Jewhurst to John Taylor'. Fry and Jewhurst were the executors carrying out Ann Friend's instructions to dispose of Berkeley Place. John Taylor was, I suppose, the butcher who occupied Belgrove House from at least 1841 to 1871. It follows from the evidence of this deed that the cottages, nos 11-17 Berkeley Road, sometimes described by optimistic estate agents as 18th-century, must have been built between 1833 and the date of the Tithe map around 1840. Nos 11 and 13 are sited on the land sold to John Taylor; nos 15 and 17 on that bought by Mrs Bonham. Of greater interest is the conclusion that Mrs Bonham's and Mr Thompson's pre-1833 premises, obviously excised from land occupying the corner of Little Mount Sion and Berkeley Road, must represent the site of the 'pyehouse' of Nicholas Wood's will. Therefore Bowra's alignment must be wrong. It is likely on this evidence that the bricks and mortar of the present *Grove Tavern* and the house next door date back to the early 18th century or even to 1689 when Jo Jordan made his first rate payment. For what it is worth nos 30 to 34 Little Mount Sion are all listed buildings and ascribed to the 18th-century, presumably on architectural criteria; an ascription which would carry more weight if there were not, as has just been shown, solid documentary evidence that no 30, like the cottages in Berkeley Road, must have been built between 1833 and around 1840. None of this, however, detracts from the *Grove Tavern*'s claim to be the original Mount Sion alehouse and the earliest pub on the hill.

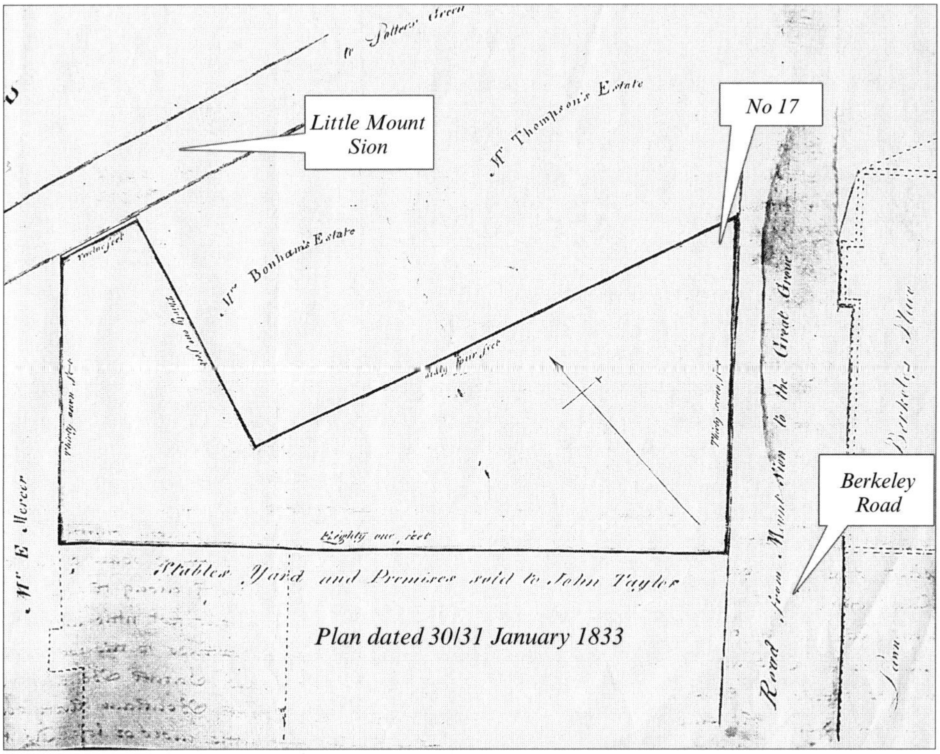

On the other hand, unlike the *Compasses* of chapter 7, the *Grove Tavern* does not seem to have a continuous history as a public house. If I am right, it started life as the whimsical Jo Jordan's alehouse but became a small lodging house in the time of Katharine Ashenhurst and then the pyehouse of Nicholas Wood's will. I suppose a pyehouse was a sort of eating house, but have not yet come across a historical explanation of the term. John Mathews, on the evidence of Benge Burr, ran the place as an alehouse and, on the evidence of Nicholas Wood, as a pie house; and Richard Brooker may well have carried on the tradition. Indeed, the three functions of ale, pie and lodging house could easily have been combined. By 1795, however, it was divided into four tenements including a lodging house and two shops. The evidence is the auction sale notice below, one of those in the Sprange collection at the Tunbridge Wells Museum. The shops might have sold ale or pies but the sale notice is silent on the subject. The same property had been offered for sale a month earlier, on 11 March, as the second of two lots of which the first was William Fry's lodging house (see chapter 22). Presumably the March sale failed and was repeated in April. The descriptions are almost identical except that the one says that the estate 'now is let on lease to Mr J Mepham and his Under-Tenants, eight years unexpired Michaelmas Day last, the premises are in exceeding good repair and are to be kept up as such, by the Tenant during the remainder of the lease'. Whether the second auction was any more successful than

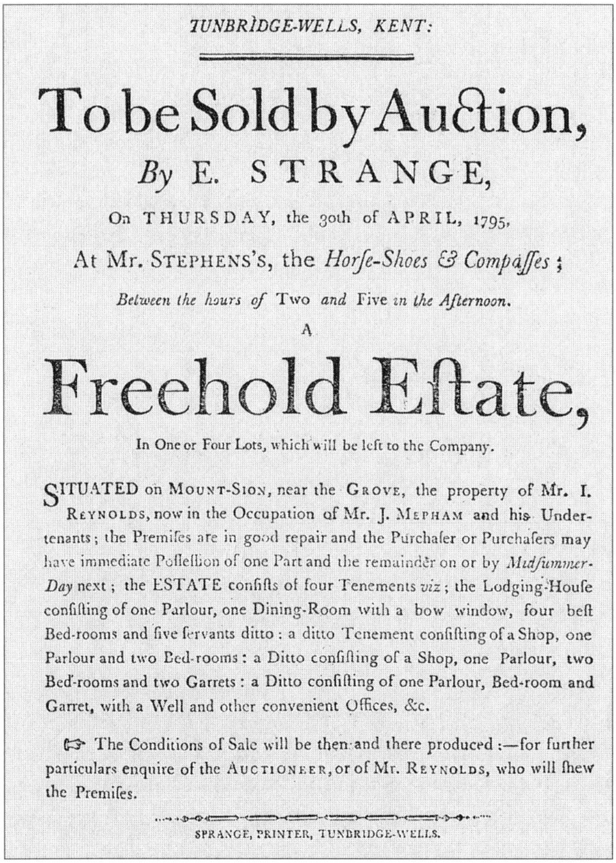

TUNBRIDGE-WELLS, KENT:

To be Sold by Auction,

By E. STRANGE,

On THURSDAY, the 30th of APRIL, 1795,

At Mr. STEPHENS'S, the *Horſe-Shoes & Compaſſes*;

Between the hours of Two *and* Five *in the Afternoon.*

A

Freehold Eſtate,

In One or Four Lots, which will be left to the Company.

SITUATED on MOUNT-SION, near the GROVE, the property of Mr. I. REYNOLDS, now in the Occupation of Mr. J. MEPHAM and his Under-tenants; the Premiſes are in good repair and the Purchaſer or Purchaſers may have immediate Poſſeſſion of one Part and the remainder on or by *Midſummer-Day* next; the ESTATE conſiſts of four Tenements *viz*; the Lodging-Houſe conſiſting of one Parlour, one Dining-Room with a bow window, four beſt Bed-rooms and five ſervants ditto: a ditto Tenement conſiſting of a Shop, one Parlour and two Bed-rooms: a Ditto conſiſting of a Shop, one Parlour, two Bed-rooms and two Garrets: a Ditto conſiſting of one Parlour, Bed-room and Garret, with a Well and other convenient Offices, &c.

☞ The Conditions of Sale will be then and there produced:—for further particulars enquire of the AUCTIONEER, or of Mr. REYNOLDS, who will ſhew the Premiſes.

SPRANGE, PRINTER, TUNBRIDGE-WELLS.

Sprange poster 1795

the first I do not know, but by 1821 two of the tenements were owned by John Bonham about whom there is more on page 127; and the Mrs Bonham of the 1833 plan above was presumably his widow. What proof is there that the property to be sold in 1795 was the *Grove Tavern* building? Apart from the 1833 plan the proof lies in the coincidence of names with the Poor Rate record which was set out at the end of the previous chapter culminating as follows:

1751-1779	Richard Brooker
1780-1781	Reynolds John for late Brookers
1782	Mepham _______ for his house late Reynolds
1783-1795	Mepham Jeremiah
1796-1797	Mepham Jeremiah for late Meeting House

J. Mepham of the sale notice must surely be Jeremiah while the 'I' before Reynolds is probably a 'J' for John as the two letters were often used interchangeably – although the printer might have been consistent in the same sentence!

A second deed in the Whitbread collection is dated 30/31 July 1834 and talks of 'four formerly five messuages tenements or dwelling houses all contiguous together and under one roof'. This makes clear that a single building is involved which may seem surprising in the light of the 1795 sale notice with its four tenements, shops and lodging houses and all. The next news of the building is the Barrow map of 1808 which indicates by shading that the whole building is one of the 'other houses', neither lodging house nor coach house and stables; and it is clearly labelled 'Barrow Land Surveyor'. It is difficult to believe that he used all four (or five) parts of the building for himself or his business but there is no doubt that this was Barrow the mapmaker. On 31 July 1810 he inserted the following advertisement in the *Maidstone Journal*:

T. T. BARROW

Land Surveyor, and House and Land Agent,
TUNBRIDGE WELLS,

Begs leave respectfully to return his most sincere thanks to the Nobility, Gentry and the Public in general, for the very liberal encouragement he has experienced, particularly in their reception of his PLAN OF TUNBRIDGE WELLS; and at the same time he wishes to inform them, that he has removed from Mount Sion to the LONDON ROAD, where he hopes to receive a continuation of their favours.

Estates surveyed with accuracy and elegance, Maps copied in a superior style. The Plan of Tunbridge Wells, lately published, price Seven Shillings, is Sold at his Office; by HATCHARD, Piccadilly, London; and at the Libraries, at Tonbridge and the Wells.

Later the same year, in October, he is advertising for business from his General Estate Agency Office in the London Road. Where precisely this was I do not know but he had definitely left Little Mount Sion and it is unclear who were the owners and occupiers of the building there until the 1820s and '30s when the Whitbread deeds begin to fill in the picture.

The 1833 plan printed above shows Mrs Bonham's and Mr Thompson's estates having roughly equal halves of the building and the 1834 deed gives Sarah Bonham the two 'messuages' at the western end. On the Tithe map, however, the building is divided into four and Thompson has only the easternmost quarter (the present *Grove Tavern* front bar) while Sarah Bonham has the other three portions; and in 1867 her son Benjamin sold 'three messuages … adjoining each other' to Henry Chapman. On the evidence of the Whitbread deeds, however, there appear to have been two messuages at the *Grove Tavern* end and it is difficult to reconcile this with the Bonhams' three messuages. Perhaps Mrs Bonham bought one of Francis Thompson's portions before 1840 but this theory does not remove all contradictions. The main fact of interest, as far as the *Grove Tavern* is concerned, is that a certain Edward Sanders acquired an interest of some sort in part of the property, firstly as early 1809 and secondly in 1836 and that both parts were in the ownership of his descendants from at least 1871 until 28 February 1894 when a deed entitled 'Conveyance of the Grove Tavern Mount Sion' records the sale to the Wateringbury brewer Augustus Leney for £800 of 'All those two messuages or tenements (now used as a Beerhouse) situate at Mount Sion and late occupied by Philip Farmer and now by ______ Downes and which were formerly described as: '*First* All that messuage … at the east end and part of four formerly five messuages all contiguous and under one roof … conveyed to Edward Sanders … 27th and 28th January 1809 *Second* All that messuage … adjacent to the premises last before mentioned and previously belonging to and in the occupation of Francis Thompson … Indenture of Assignment to the said Edward Sanders dated 20th August 1836'. The first description presumably refers to the easternmost quarter of the building (the 'front bar') and the second description to the adjoining quarter, both parts now forming the *Grove Tavern* and numbered 34 Little Mount Sion. The vendor in 1894 was Mrs Mary Elizabeth Taylor Marley of 'Felton', Sutton, Surrey, the wife of Albert Marley the younger and she was, as appears from an Abstract of Title in the Whitbread collection, the granddaughter of Edward Sanders and his wife Catharine. They had one son, Godfrey, and two daughters, Ellen Francis and Mary Elizabeth. Mary married Edward Russell and in 1883 was living at Lintonville, Woodbury Park, Tunbridge Wells; and it was her daughter who rejoiced in the three first names Mary Elizabeth Taylor and married twice, firstly one Filder and secondly Albert Marley.

Whatever the precise facts about the ownership of the *Grove Tavern*, the landlords came and went. Jo Jordan and John Mathews seem certainly to have been the first, whimsical or not. Whether Richard Brooker was an active landlord or not is difficult to tell – I suspect quite unfairly that he married for his wife's inheritance and relaxed thereafter! John Reynolds seems to have had interests in other property and in any case paid rates for two years only. The next on the list is Jeremiah Mepham. When I first wrote to Whitbreads I predicted that this name might crop up in the deeds and was pleased when it did. He does not sound like a jovial landlord but I suppose the Bible is to blame for that; but the sale notice of 1795 suggests that no part of the building was used as a pub and in the next two years Jeremiah is paying rates for the 'late Meeting House'. This is all rather puzzling. We know about the Presbyterian Meeting House lower down Little Mount Sion and we know about the Bethlehem Chapel opposite; but neither of these seems to fit the bill. Perhaps Jeremiah was a part-time preacher (that name again!) and turned part of his house into a meeting place like Mrs Murrell at 63 Mount Sion a century later. If so, I am afraid he was not saved from bankruptcy. On 10 February 1807 a Notice of Creditors appeared in the *Maidstone Journal*: 'the creditors of Jeremiah Mepham of Tunbridge Wells who have executed the Trust Deed may receive a Dividend of his Estate and Effects, of SEVEN SHILLINGS in the pound upon their respective Debts, on Fridays, between 9 in the forenoon and 4 in the afternoon, at the Office of Mr Stone, solicitor, Tunbridge Wells'.

Maybe Mepham moved out more or less at this moment. Certainly by 1808, and no doubt earlier since maps cannot be surveyed and published simultaneously, T.T.Barrow, the land surveyor, on the evidence of his own map, was in occupation apparently of the whole building. He was never more than a tenant, however, and it is difficult to know how much of the building he used and what other activities were going on at the same time. In any case Barrow did not stay long and in the meanwhile, as detailed above, Edward Sanders had acquired part of the building in 1809 and the other in 1836. By 1840, however, the Tithe map and Award show that Francis Thompson was both owner and occupier of the end portion and a reference in the 1867 conveyance to Henry Chapman (see below) makes clear that he was using the premises as a beer house. It is also clear from the 1833 plan (page 121 above) that Thompson's estate owned the place in that year. What is puzzling is that Francis Thompson appears nowhere in the Mount Sion area in the 1841 census and generally there is a surprising lack of information about him. In 1841 the *Grove Tavern* seems to have been unoccupied – for more on the census evidence see below – which might explain why Thompson's name does not appear. In 1851 Saunders House No 2 features in the census and an adjoining house, probably Saunders No 1, is unoccupied. No 2 is occupied by Charles Walter, aged 51, who is a stableman and a widower. Living with him are three young sons, two older unmarried daughters and a 10-month-old grandson. In the 1861 census there is an unnamed Beer Shop in the position where the *Grove Tavern* might be expected and it is occupied by Mary Walters who describes herself as 28, widowed and a beer shop keeper. This could be the widow of Charles, one of the 'young sons' who was 17 in 1851 – if the 's' on the end of the name is ignored. Was his father a part-time beer shop keeper as well as a stableman? By 1871, thankfully, the need for speculation is over and the *Grove Tavern* is actually named in the census. The occupier is David R. Hoper, aged 31, a greengrocer and beer retailer. His wife, Harriet, is 26 but has already presented her husband with six children, from nine-year-old Alice to the latest nameless, unregistered girl of 10 days. Richard Hoper, presumably the same man, appears as a Little Mount Sion beer retailer in *Mathieson's Directory* of 1867/8 and also heads Keith Hetherington's list of *Grove*

Tavern landlords. The next name on the list is William Farmer who is to be found in the 1881 census also as a greengrocer and beer house keeper, at 17, Little Mount Sion (see below for an explanation of the numbering). Hetherington's list continues:

P. Farmer	1892	W. Parsons	1910-1911
J. Downs	1893-1899	Henry Okell Dadswell	1912-1963
E. Hewett	1899-1907	T. Gabriel	1918?
W. Jeffrey	1908-1909	Patrick Burke	1963-1985

Philip Farmer and Downs are mentioned as occupiers in the 1894 conveyance. Dadswell, the longest serving of all, has already been discussed at the beginning of this chapter – perhaps Gabriel took over briefly from him during the war? David Richard Hoper, according to Hetherington, died only in December 1927 at the age of 89, giving his year of birth as 1838. According to this source, Hoper subsequently opened a small greengrocery business just below the *Tavern* in 1877 and was the last surviving tradesman of his era when he died. The 1881 census suggests that this business was at No 35 on the opposite side of Little Mount Sion. Harriet, by the way, does not seem to have survived more than one additional birth and the future octogenarian has a new wife, Sarah, 11 years his junior.

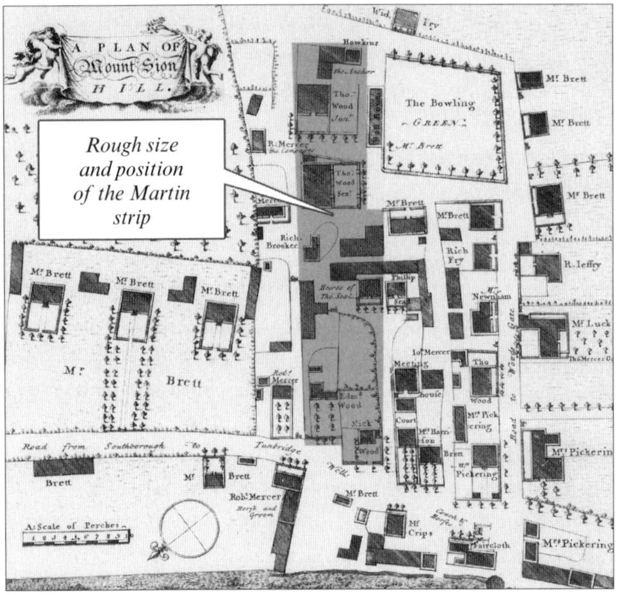

Bowra plan 1738

Having looked at the early history of the *Grove Tavern* and at its landlords, it is time to consider the later period when the story becomes somewhat tangled with that of the *Bugler's Arms*. The reader may be forgiven for forgetting that in accordance with our general plan we are still in the 'Martin Strip' of eight by 40 rods first considered in chapter 9 where the strip was shown on page 87, shaded grey – see the smaller duplicate on the left. As we know, it includes the two Martin Houses at the bottom of the hill, Burlington House and the *Blue Anchor* at the top and in the middle Berkeley Place and the pyehouse or *Grove Tavern* marked Rich Brooker; but encroaching on the strip is the house labelled 'heirs of Tho Seal'. This will be the subject of the next chapter but one. Between the *Grove Tavern* and the Seal house came the *Bugler's Arms* which was the western (or southern?) portion of the messuages 'contiguous under one roof' and today is numbered 32 Little Mount Sion. For the sake of consistency this place has to be considered within the Martin strip.

We have already seen, in connection with the plan illustrated on page 121 of this chapter, that Mrs Bonham bought the irregularly shaped piece of land which adjoined her part of the 'messuages contiguous all under one roof'. This was in 1833. Then by a 'Release in Fee' dated 30/31 July 1834 the executors of the will of John Bonham joined with his two surviving sons, Thomas and Benjamin, to sell the sons' reversionary interest to their mother for £140, so that she should have full control. One of the executors, as a matter of passing interest, was John Baker Stapley, cabinetmaker of Tunbridge Wells, whose name appears as Robert Foreman's trustee in the deeds of Howard Lodge (see chapter 25). He was, I assume, one of those reliable people whose services are in demand for this sort of thing. Anyhow, John Bonham was a British wine merchant of Tunbridge Wells. There is a little advertisement in the Sprange poster collection at the Museum for 'Stone (successor to Mr Bonham) No 1, New Street, Tunbridge Wells, Dealer in British Wines'. I imagine this was the same Mr Bonham. The poster probably dates from 1797. New Street is the original name for Castle Street. Did John Bonham move from there to Little Mount Sion? Be that as it may, he made his will on 20 January 1821 and owned the freehold of the Little Mount Sion property at the time. He died in 1825 and left his real and personal estate to his executors to be converted into money and the capital invested for the benefit of his widow during her life and then divided among his three sons, of whom however John (presumably the eldest) died in 1830 unmarried and intestate. I am not sure that the executors were entitled to sell to the widow but it seems a common sense move since the house was evidently not only her home but also as a lodging house provided an income and an occupation. The description of the property in this 1834 deed concludes with some details of the cellar which may explain not only why the wine merchant bought the place but also why there is a blocked up 'secret' passage in the basement of the present no 32, Little Mount Sion: 'And also all that Cellar thereto belonging and used as a Wine Cellar being part of and situated under the south side of the messuage or tenement adjoining the messuages or tenements hereby conveyed ... on the east side thereof ...'. This seems to mean that the cellar was under the back part of the *Grove Tavern* part of the building; so that it now belongs to the *Grove Tavern* but used to belong to No.32, hence the through passage.

Sarah Bonham was still alive (see later) in 1851 but she and her son Thomas must have died before 13 July 1867 when the surviving son, Benjamin, sold out to Henry Chapman. Benjamin Bonham was a 'Land Engineer' with the curious address of 408½ Oxford Street and Henry Chapman was (by now) a gentleman; the price was £450. What is interesting is that the property in 1867 consisted of three messuages tenements or cottages. The full description is worth recording:

> ... three messuages tenements or cottages adjoining each other ... formerly in the tenure or occupation of Jeremiah Mepham afterwards of John Bonham then of Sarah Bonham widow and since then and now in the occupation of Thos Gilbert senior _______Beecher and others as tenants of the said Benjamin Bonham and the same ... premises do abut ... on the north-east or front thereof upon the public highway leading from Little Mount Sion passing Sion Crescent

> to the Great Grove and Claremont Road on the south-east side thereof upon premises formerly of Mr Thompson now of __________ and used as a Beerhouse on the south-west side thereof upon premises now or late of Henry Cheesman Grocer and and on the north-west side thereof upon premises called Sion Crescent ... Together with the passage or pathway leading to the back of the said premises hereby conveyed and lying between the premises of Mr Henry Cheesman and the premises late of Mr Thompson ... and used as a Beerhouse ...

Cheesman was (or had been) the owner of the present no.17 Berkeley Road and the passage represents in my opinion the six-foot strip of Nicholas Wood's will discussed above. Anyway, the description identifies the premises and their surroundings very clearly. The Tithe map (see below) appears to identify the 'three messuages' quite clearly. It shows Sarah Bonham as owner (and occupier with

Tithe map 1840

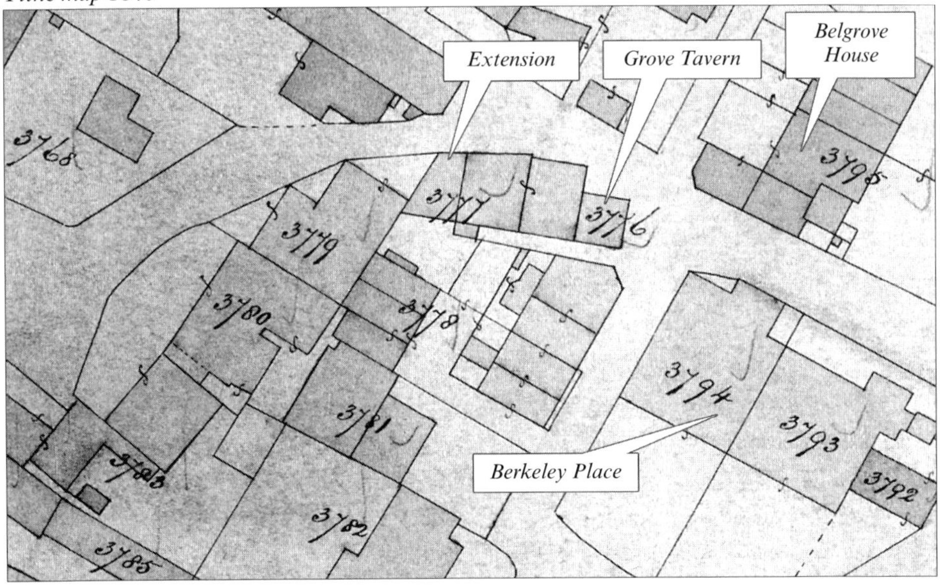

others) of 'Cottages and Yards' (No 3777); but her property seems to include half of the eastern or *Grove Tavern* end of the building. The *Grove Tavern* is number 3776 owned and occupied by Francis Thompson. At the other end of the building (under the figures 37 on the map) is what was obviously a new extension built on the ground bought by Sarah in 1833 and is the present no 30 Little Mount Sion, with the sharply sloping roof and the bay window on the first floor – see Johnson's photograph on page 130. No 3778 is listed in the Tithe Award as 'House, 6 Cottages and Yard' owned by Henry Cheesman, the grocer mentioned above, and occupied by him and others; and the house is no 17, Berkeley Road and the cottages include nos 11-15 together with three cottages behind, now gone.

The 'three messuages' shown on the Tithe map were therefore those sold to Henry Chapman in 1867; but by 1890 both parts of the *Grove Tavern* end of the building had come back into one ownership and were sold to Augustus Leney in

1894. The other two parts of the original building (now no.32) had somehow been acquired by William Charles Cripps the Elder, father of the better-known solicitor and town clerk, and bequeathed to his widow Catharine Charlotte. All this is known from one of the Whitbread deeds dated 24 June 1890; but there is an additional source of information in the shape of a Sale Notice dated 5 May 1882 which helps to fill in the picture. W.C. Cripps made his will in 1879 but, as he did not specify his real estate, it is not certain that he owned the Little Mount Sion property until 1882. Some time, therefore, between July 1867 and February 1882 Henry Chapman disposed of the property either to W.C. Cripps or to an earlier purchaser. On 22 February 1882 W.C. Cripps died and on 5 May the same year his executors offered for sale nos 34, 36 and 38 Little Mount Sion, which were the present nos 30 and 32. No.34 was described as a dwelling house and shop; no.36 as also a dwelling house (with 13 rooms and 'numerous closets'); and no.38 as the first-class Free Beerhouse known as the *Bugler's Arms*. The auction was to be held at the *Camden Hotel*, Tunbridge Wells, (next to the old Town Hall on the corner of Camden and Calverley Roads) under Mr George Langridge but it must have been unsuccessful because eight years later the widow, acting as trustee in a family arrangement, sold what were described as the land and premises known as the *Bugler's Arms* but which, from the accompanying plan, were clearly the nos 36 and 38 of the 1882 Sale Notice. Why the solicitors (W.C. Cripps of course!) could not have made things even clearer by using the street numbering which was in use at the time, I cannot think. The plan shows the premises from back to front equally but I feel sure that this partition, taken from the Ordnance Survey, is too neat for the realities of the beer house and boarding house functions of the old building. The passageway behind (Nicholas Wood's six-foot slip?) was included in the sale but with a right of way reserved to the back of the newer building (now no.30) which was not included in the sale and therefore must have been sold separately at a later date.

The purchaser in 1890 was Alicia Simpson whose simple description as a widow of Lamberhurst conceals the fact that she owned or had a large interest in a brewery business called Smith & Co (Lamberhurst) Limited. In 1896 she mortgaged the *Bugler's Arms*, together with the *Royal Oak* at Pembury, but died in 1898 and the mortgage was redeemed in 1900 by her executors. At some stage Philip Alan Simpson, who I suppose was Alicia's son, bought the business, brewery and pubs, for £89,500 but it did not flourish and went into voluntary liquidation two days after Christmas 1921. One of the consequent transactions was the sale of the 'Old Bugler's Cottage' to Frederick Leney & Sons Limited. According to Hetherington's *Old Pubs of Tunbridge Wells*, the *Bugler's Arms* lost its licence in 1914 and according to David Johnson Mr Pree started his horological business in the old pub from 1913. Either way it seems natural that the place should have been known as the 'Old Bugler's'. The origin of the pub name itself is explained by David Johnson in comments he wrote on the photograph on the next page – one of those he copied and included in his albums: 'Photograph by Mr Spencer. Building on left *Grove Tavern*. (Building) next (on left) with small shop-front was at one time a beer-house kept by Mr Love, the bugler of the Volunteers, and known as *The Buglers Arms*. Afterwards used as a watch & clock repair shop by H. Pree from 1913. Oct 1934 occupied by Petit for Boot Repairing. Projecting Bay Windows removed about 1926.' The last remark solves a puzzle because if you go and look at the place today there is only a single-storey bay on the first-floor level and simply no space for the second-floor window because the roof above slopes steeply to within a few feet of the top right-hand corner of the window. There are still some problems, however. Johnson labelled the photograph 'Little Mount Sion' with his own name and the date *c*.1930 but he usually puts a precise date on the photograph itself, not on the mount; and of course, if the bay windows had been removed in 1926, he could not have photographed them four years later. As will be seen again in chapter 16, photographs by Mr Spencer were probably of an earlier date. There is one other small piece of evidence concerning the bay windows. The Sprange poster of 1795 (see page 122 above) says that the lodging house portion of the original building (long before no.30 was built) had a dining room with a bow window.

The Grove Tavern *and Little Mount Sion* c.*1900?*

By the end of the century street numbers had settled down to their present state and the description in the conveyance to Frederick Leney ran as follows: 'the freehold property known as the Old Bugler's Cottage and numbered 32 Little Mount Sion comprising a shop, two back parlours', a living room, 11 bedrooms, basement, kitchen etc., all let to Mr H. Pree on a yearly tenancy at £28 p.a. When refurbishment of these premises was in progress very recently there was much excited rumour about the surprising number of little cubicle-like rooms and the discovery of items of female corsetry and the all-too-familiar conclusion was confidently drawn. Bear in mind, however, that Sprange's poster of 1795 gives the lodging house four best bedrooms and five servants' ditto and lists 17 bedrooms in the whole building; and that the 1882 Sale Notice speaks of 13 rooms with numerous closets. Bear in mind also, what will be discussed more fully below, the number of families revealed by the censuses to be squeezed into Little Mount Sion in general. No doubt the area sported a brothel or two, particularly in the earlier period before the population became more settled and the visitors more bourgeois; but if the local legends are to be believed the hill was wholly given over to houses of ill-fame and honeycombed with secret tunnels. Perhaps there was some connection between the two things – though why the clients of a Mount Sion Madame should have had to rise genie-like from below the floor with bent backs and mud in their wigs I fail to understand. One story concerns Caxton House (see chapter 18). It was remarked by a prospective purchaser in the 1950s that there were two front doors, a spacious 'salon' on the first floor and lots of little rooms. All of which quite ignores the fact that the house was designed as a lodging house, was originally one house before being split into two by Richard Delves – hence the two (before and after?!) doors – and was later joined into one house again – hence the two doors leading into the same hall.

According once more to Keith Hetherington, the *Bugler's Arms* started as a public house about 1850. The first census to use the name is that of 1871, although the enumerator added it as an after-thought to his designation which was 'beer shop'. The occupiers were Stephen Evans, carpenter, and his wife Ruth, laundress, with their baby son and two lodgers. In the 1881 census Henry Thompsett, his wife, two small sons and three lodgers are to be found at 38 Little Mount Sion and Hetherington (private communication) gives H. Thompsett as the first known landlord of the *Bugler's Arms* in 1881. His list continues:

A Bishop	1882	H Bradley	1896-1904
C Farmer	1892 (should be 82?)	Gadd	1905-1906
W Tucker	1886	George Campany	1907-1908
E Dunham	1890	Robert James Vigor	1909-1912
C White	1891-1895	Charles Hobday	1913-1914

No mention, of course, of the felicitously named Mr Love the bugler and reputedly original landlord. For the following report from the local paper in January 1898 I am indebted also to Keith Hetherington: 'For wilfully damaging a door at 'the Buglers Arms' Mount Sion J. Bassett was sent to prison for seven days as he had no money to pay the fine. Mr Henry Bradford [Bradley?] the landlord said Bassett had lodged for several nights at the premises but on the evening of the damage he had been refused entry.' This certainly confirms that the place was being used as a boarding house as well as a pub.

It is evident, and not only from this story, that beer retailing was only a short-lived and minor episode in the history of Bonhams House, for that seems as good a name as any. It was so called in the census from 1851 to 1871 and the name surely lingered on the common tongue much longer; and it was in Bonham ownership as early as the 1820s. Basically it was a lodging house, but not for the summer visitors to the Wells, rather for the more transient, of the local population. Not everyone was so transient however. One family stayed in the house for 40 years and its history illustrates that of the house. In 1841 the name was Grove Cottage and John Denton was a 28-year-old labourer with a new wife,

Elizabeth, aged 22, and a new six-month-old baby named William. In 1851 the name was Bonhams House No 2 and the family had increased to four, baby John aged one month having just joined William, Samuel (aged seven) and Emma (aged two). In 1861 John described himself as a jobbing gardener and his wife used the diminutive form Betty. William and Samuel had left home but Emma, little John and Elizabeth, the latest addition, were still at 'Bonhams house No 2 Lodging House'. By the time of the next census Elizabeth or Betty was a widow, working as a charwoman, her husband having survived long enough to father a final daughter, Jane, aged nine in 1871. Elizabeth the younger was working already as a nursemaid, while John was a labourer, as his father had been, and Emma had left home, now described simply as Bonhams House. By 1881 finally the widow, now aged 63 and still working as a charwoman, is the only one left at 36 Little Mount Sion, in what had been the Denton family home for forty years or more.

In 1841 Sarah Bonham, aged 60 and described like her late husband, as a British Wine Merchant, was living at Grove Cottage with no fewer than 45 lodgers, made up of households which in turn consisted of 20 adults and 25 children whose ages ranged from four months to 15 years. If this was the part of the building described as the lodging house in 1795 then, allowing Sarah a room to herself, there was one bedroom per household – and there were two households of eight persons each! However I cannot be certain that more of the building was not included in 'Grove Cottage'. In 1851 Sarah Bonham was living at Bonhams House No 1 with her widowed sister Ann Burns, three years younger than herself; they were born in Pembury and described themselves as 'Proprietors of Houses'. In Bonhams House No 2 there were six households, consisting of 18 adults and the four children belonging to John Denton's family. Bonhams House No 3 existed also and contained one family of six. In 1861 Sarah and her sister had dropped from the scene although the Bonham name lingered on. At Bonham House (presumably the old No 1 where Sarah and Ann had lived) there was a greengrocer's shop occupied by a family of seven; Bonham House No 2 Lodging House contained a mere four households – eight adults and 10 children including three of John Denton's; and the old No 3 house had presumably become Bonham Cottage which was occupied by a foreman joiner and his wife. In 1871 the population had gone down further still. The building was still divided into three parts – Bonham Cottage, the Bugler's Arms beer shop and Bonham House. One family lived in the cottage; a family and two lodgers in the Beer Shop; and in the lodging house section called Bonham House were eight persons including Widow Denton and three children and an old lady of private means living as lodger with a young gas stoker, his wife and baby daughter – the total number in the three houses coming to no more than seventeen. In 1881 house numbers had come into use and the population in nos 34-38 Little Mount Sion had gone up a little: 29 people in all with one family each in nos 34 and 38 and four families in no.36, including the solitary Widow Denton.

Some additional information abouit the situation in 1882 can be obtained from the Sale Notice of that year mentioned above. The dwelling house and shop numbered 34 (now 30) was occupied by Mrs Fiddle, a weekly tenant, at 7s.6d. per week, although the 1881 census gives the occupier as one Harold Wickins, a 21-year-old bread baker. No.36 was the lodging house with 13 rooms and the numerous closets and had 'for many years, been in the occupation of Mr Bridge and others, as Weekly Tenants, at Rentals amounting to £24 1s. per annum'. Mr Bridger was the gas stoker of 1871 who had, however, become a general labourer by 1881. It seems likely from all this that the Denton family home had been occupied on a weekly basis for all of forty years. I am not sure what the moral is for the preseent-day but it might be worth thinking about. No.38 is described in the Sale Notice as follows: 'the FIRST-CLASS FREE BEERHOUSE known as the 'BUGLER'S ARMS' let to Messrs. Kenward & Court, Brewers, at £32 per Annum. This House which is now doing a Large Trade, is in the occupation of Mr Charles Farmer, as Under-tenant to Messrs. Kenward & Court.' The Conditions of Sale attached to this Sale Notice incidentally show that the title was to commence with indentures of lease and release dated 30/31 January 1833 for part of the property and 30/31 July for the remainder. Now these were the deeds, already discussed, which form the first two in the Whitbread collection at Maidstone – Whitbreads therefore have all the deeds which were available in 1882.

From the evidence produced so far and from the censuses themselves it is now possible to have a stab at identifying the different portions of the *Grove Tavern/Bugler's Arms* building and their varying descriptions over the years 1841 to 1881. It will be best to try to follow the five enumerators as they trudge up and down the dirty little lanes of Fanny Burney's Tunbridge Wells and on the way some facts of interest not only to this chapter but to previous and future ones may emerge. In 1841 the enumerator's route goes from Belle Vue in Claremont Road, past Grove Lodge, Burlington House, Navarino Cottage (which I cannot identify but which must be somewhere on this section of the route) and the *Compasses* (not named but the publican's name, Thomas Baker, appears) to Belgrove House. It then branches off to Berkeley Cottages (the present nos 11-17 Berkeley Road) and from there back to Grove Place, which on Ordnance Survey evidence means the present Belgrove Cottages. After Grove Place one uninhabited dwelling is recorded before the enumerator proceeds down Little Mount Sion to Grove Cottage (Sarah Bonham's property) and Sion Crescent. On these assumptions I guess that the uninhabited dwelling was the *Grove Tavern* end of the building. What is not clear, however, is how much of the building was called Grove Cottage – with its eight households and Sarah Bonham. The Tithe map (see page 128 above) shows clearly that Mrs Bonham owned half the present *Grove Tavern*, no.34, leaving only the shallower, eastern end (the present front bar) to Francis Thompson who, however, is nowhere to be found in the Little Mount Sion area of the census. Furthermore the Tithe map shows that by this time the building ground purchased in 1833 had been utilised for the present no.30. Does, therefore, the designation 'Grove Cottage' of 1841 cover the whole extent from the present no.30 to the western half of no.34? There seems no way of resolving this problem.

Moving forward to 1851, the enumerator is found to be going up Little Mount Sion this time, from the *Jolly Sailor* below the Presbyterian Chapel to Sackville Cottage, which used to stand behind the present Frog Cottage, and Sion Crescent – the main topic of chapters 14 and 15. After Sion Crescent came Crescent Cottage and a cottage adjoining which together I take to be the old Sion Crescent Academy part of the building and these are followed by Bonhams House Nos 1, 2 and 3. No.1, occupied by Sarah Bonham and her sister, I take to be the then recently erected no.30, while 2 and 3 could together form the main lodging house or, alternatively, Bonham House No.3 could be the adjoining part of the present no 34. The Ordnance Survey map shows the present no.32 split into two parts, which might tend to support the first alternative. What is more, Bonham House No.3 is followed (still in 1851) by one uninhabited dwelling and then by Saunders House No.2. Now Edward Sanders (different spelling but the same man, I assume) is known from the Whitbread deeds (see page 124) to have owned or had an interest in the *Grove Tavern* end of the building from 1836 or earlier. I should guess, therefore, that the uninhabited dwelling would be Saunders House No 1 and that therefore Bonham House Nos 2 and 3 were confined to the limits of the present no.32.

The 1861 enumerator seems to have pursued a zig-zag course, starting up the right-hand side of Little Mount Sion past the *Jolly Sailor* again and Sackville Cottage to Sion Crescent; but then dodging across the road and starting up the other side before repeating the process with Warwick Road. Emerging from the top of Warwick Road he then encounters the nameless beer shop kept by Widow Mary Walters, followed by the Bonham House Greengrocer's shop, Bonham House No.2 (the lodging house) and Bonham Cottage. He then skips over the road again to the Christ Church Boys' School which is unmistakably marked on the Ordnance Survey map in the position now occupied by Nos 37/39 Little Mount Sion. Once more he crosses the road and goes round the corner now occupied by the *Grove Tavern* into Berkeley Road for what was then called Grove Terrace nos 4, 3, 2 and 1 in that order and, following the same order, is the present nos 17 to 11 Berkeley Road. He then goes to Cheesmans Cottages which are now demolished but must have been the three shown on the Tithe map and the Ordnance Survey behind nos 11 to 17. In no.1 lived William Streeter who was 94 years old and described himself as an almsman and an agricultural labourer born in Rotherfield. With him were his daughter, Elizabeth Mackney, and her husband, both in their late 60s. After Cheesmans Cottages the enumerator naturally went to the Murray House Girls' School Soup Kitchen next door and then (refreshed perhaps) on to Berkeley Place and Burlington House before coming back down the other side of Upper Little Mount Sion past Oak Villa and the *Compasses* to Belgrove House and Grove Place (the present Belgrove Cottages). He then visits the Grove Houses (see chapter 6) and finally and surprisingly returns to Berkeley Place to notice the baker's shop at the rear. I cannot help thinking that the 1861 enumerator was a flibbertigibbet whose meanderings cannot be relied upon for any meaningful sequence. For what it is worth I think that the beer shop of Widow Walters refers to the *Grove Tavern*, the greengrocer's shop to the present no.30 and Bonham House No.2 together with Bonham Cottage to the present no.32. On the other hand the Cottage might be no 30 and the greengrocer's shop part of no.32, since the 1871 enumerator seems to have been a more consistent chap and he followed the sequence Sackville Cottage, Sion Crescent, Bonham Cottage, *Bugler's Arms*, Bonham House, *Grove Tavern* and (round the corner) Grove Terrace. On this theory the Bugler's Arms beer shop replaced the greengrocer's shop of 1861 and was part of the present no 32. There is, of course, considerable support for this interpretation in Spencer's photograph (page 130 above) and Johnson's comments on it. He identifies the building next on the left after the *Grove Tavern* – the building with the small shop front – as the *Bugler's Arms*; and this is clearly part of the present no.32 – indeed traces of the shop front still remain. What is more, it reverted to shop use after the demise of the *Bugler's Arms*, showing how easily the greengrocer's could have become the beer shop. The shop, therefore, was necessarily in the front of the building on the ground floor and the lodging house would have made use of the back rooms and upper floors. The 1871 enumerator next followed the same route as the 1861 man, past Murray House and Burlington House and came down past the *Compasses* to the Belgrove House area; but he then took in the baker's at the back of Berkeley Place and, more logically, the Warwick Road area before proceeding down the other side of Little Mount Sion. At the bottom he had to cross over to the *Jolly Sailor* and the cottages below it known as Montgomery Place; but this is because he started by going up Frog Lane from the High Street – altogether a better organised chap in 1871, I reckon.

By 1881 street numbering has come in and ought to make identification of places easier! It can be assumed, I suppose, that a sequence of numbers implies a corresponding sequence on the ground; but there are still some anomalies. In particular the 1880s numbering does not correspond exactly with present-day numbers. The 1881 enumerator follows once more a different route from his predecessors. Having gone down the Christ Church or upper side of the High Street, he turns up the left-hand side of Mount Sion proper, with a diversion to the now demolished cottage at the back of Sion House and no.1 Murray Road, takes in all the houses newly erected on the old Bowling Green site, turns down Little Mount Sion by the newly built aerated water manufactory (now Miles Garage) and, passing Burlington House (still standing at the time) on his left, enters Berkeley Road by its top branch and proceeds to Murray House via the new red brick terrace known then as Bowling Green Terrace but now numbered simply nos 2 to 16 Berkeley Road. From Murray House he goes to Berkeley Place, confusingly putting John Brown at No 22, Little Mount Sion, and including the baker at no 3 Berkeley Place, and then crosses to 13 and 15, 11 and 9 Little Mount Sion – which must all add up the present nos 17 to 11 Berkeley Road. Next he goes to the Warwick Road area where new houses seem to have been built on both sides of the road and where, somewhere, 17 houses are in process of construction. Eventually he returns to Little Mount Sion at no.39 which could well be the present building of the same number but would then have been the newly erected replacement for the Christ Church Boys' School. After this he proceeds logically down the odd-numbered side of Little Mount Sion, past Hope Cottage (no.9) and the now newly renovated nos 7 and 5 to no 1 at the bottom and then crosses over to climb back up the even-numbered side. However, before reaching the 'Standard' (former *Jolly Sailor*) at no.14, he jumps to Crescent Lodge and nos 4 and 5 Murray Road and comes back to Little Mount Sion at no 16. Nos 18 to 32 take in Sackville Cottage and the whole of Sion Crescent. At the end of the Crescent he jumps to Belgrove House, no longer inhabited by the long-established butcher, John Taylor, before reaching nos 34, 36 and 38 Little Mount Sion. No 38 is the *Bugler's Arms* and 36 the home of Widow Denton on her own. The *Grove Tavern* (landlord William Farmer) might have been expected to take the next number, 40 Little Mount Sion but no! It is no 17, Little Mount Sion, obviously taking this number as a continuation of the Berkeley Road sequence 9 to 15, which as already noted is ascribed to Little Mount Sion regardless of the fact that the numbers 9, 11, 13, 15 and 17 have already been used going down the right-hand side of Little Mount Sion as far as Hope Cottage! This anomaly is easily corrected anyway by changing the road name, so that the *Grove Tavern* becomes no 17 Berkeley Road; on present numbering, of course, it would be no.19.

Continuing on his way, the 1881 enumerator goes to Grove Place and no.43 Little Mount Sion where is to be found the butcher, William Oliver; evidently it was between 1871 and 1881 that Belgrove House and the butcher's premises became separated. From here he jumps, unaccountably (perhaps because he missed them by jumping to Murray Road on the way up), to nos 12 and 14 Little Mount Sion, no.14 being the old *Jolly Sailor* now in the charge of Thomas Neale and called the Standard, but still a crowded boarding house. Next he comes to nos 10 to 22 Claremont Road which I cannot identify but which might have some connection with the present Nos 62 to 70 near the entrance to the Grove. After passing the *Compasses* he then goes way across the Grove itself to a vanished big house called Meadow Hill (see page 52) where lived Theodora, Countess of Cottenham, her six-year-old son the Earl and Lady Pepys her sister-in-law; and finally comes to the end of his labours at 37 Cumberland Terrace, now 37 Mount Sion. I can only think that Mr 1881's last pages are a rag-bag of places he missed the first time round – up to that point he seemed fairly well organised. The upshot of all this accompaniment of enumerators round the back streets of Mount Sion Hill is that the various names of Bonham House or the *Bugler's Arms* or whatever are fairly well established in general, if not in every particular; and the general picture of the old building, with its various sub-divisions all 'contiguous under one roof' has not been disturbed by the evidence of the censuses.

On the facing page, to conclude this chapter on the oldest pub on Mount Sion, is a photograph of the *Grove Tavern* taken in April 1994. The lower building, on the other side of the street, is no.39 Little Mount Sion, the end of the terrace which was built on the site of the Christ Church Boys' School as recounted on page 95. At the time of the photograph it was occupied by Garbos, the hairdressers, but is now the offices of the *Index* magazine.

The Grove Tavern *in 1994*

Chapter 12

Burlington and Blue Anchor

This is the story of Nicholas Wood the fellmonger and his family and the house which was his pride and joy.

Burlington House in about 1840

Here it is sketched by one of the Akers girls in about 1840. This must be the south-facing side. Nicholas started paying rates in May 1689 and for over a century it was known as Nicholas Woods or Thomas Woods but then assumed the name Burlington House – there is indeed, to witness the fact, a plaque bearing the name salvaged from the old house and now adorning the front of no.20 Berkeley Road (see left); and the road name 'Burlington Terrace' can be seen above that of Berkeley Road at the corner of that road and Little Mount Sion.

Burlington House plaque

More information on the house can be obtained from the Ordnance Survey map surveyed in 1866 and from the Sale Particulars of 1873. The sketch shows a large house with a basement and three storeys above. It is not clear whether the upper storeys were clad with tiles or weather-boarding, but my guess is tiles; and that if you look at Sion House, Mount Sion, on the side that overlooks the garden of Crescent Lodge and imagine a slightly larger house, you will have a fair idea of what Burlington House used to look like. The roof appears to be of the same double-pitched type. The house faced west towards Berkeley Place (Ashenhursts Great House) with views of the Common in the distance and was approached by a semi-circular 'carriage-sweep'. The main garden which, according to the Sale Particulars, was 'well planted with fruit and other trees' was on the south side, bounded by the back walls of Cumberland and Bowling Green Houses (formerly the 'pavilion') and including buttresses holding up Cumberland House. On the north or Little Mount Sion side, somewhere near the front door of the present no.44, was a well 'of capital spring water'. A wall separated the garden from the back of the *Blue Anchor* but left a way through to Mount Sion between Cumberland House and the *Blue Anchor*. A slightly projecting wing on the south side of the house was windowless but there were windows on every floor above the basement. The garden seemed to consist mainly of lawn with a few trees on the Berkeley Road side. There were six bedrooms and a box room on the top floor and six bedrooms and a drawing room and closet on the first floor. The ground floor boasted a 22 ft by 15 ft drawing room, a 15 ft square dining room, a 14 ft by (into recess) 22 ft breakfast room, a 14 ft square library, a 33 ft by 8 ft hall, a housekeeper's room and a small back room and WC; while in the basement were the kitchen, wash-house, scullery, laundry and wine, beer and coal cellars, not forgetting an outside WC. Sprange's *Guides* (1797-1808), for comparison's sake, list three parlours, six chambers, five garrets, one coach house and stabling for five horses. The chambers and garrets seem to correspond quite well with the six bedrooms on each of the first and second floors, while three parlours leave a

Bedroom in Burlington House

single room only unaccounted for on the ground floor. Evidently, if the house was full of visitors, the family had to squeeze up or move out. The sketch of the house comes from the Akers' family papers (of which more in chapter 23) and is perhaps the work of one of the grandchildren, Isabella maybe, of Jane Akers who lived in Burlington House and died there on 2 May 1842, possibly in the room the sketch of which on the previous page comes from the same source.

The acquisition of Martin's strip by Nicholas Wood was considered in some detail in the previous chapter but what of the man? He was a fellmonger and I shall come back to that in a minute; but he was also a bit of a character – you can hear him talking from his will. It is, I am sure, his own handwriting and his own choice of language. He wants to go on orchestrating his affairs from the grave. Maybe we are all like that – cannot imagine it all going on without us. But old Nich was particularly keen that his lodging house and his fellmongering should keep going. 'Whereas', he says, 'I have of late expended and laid out in building and making a new addition to the house I now live in and furnished it to make it complete for a lodging house at Mount Syon near the Wells at Tunbridge and have been at a considerable charge …' and he proceeds to burden his trustees, one friend and one kinsman, with an impossibly complicated scheme whereby each of his sons and even grandsons, in order of seniority, should be offered the lodging house providing he kept the whole business, lodging house, fellmongering, gloving and all, in its existing state for ever and promised to pay the trustees a penalty of £500 if he failed.

He was proud of his house 'My said dwelling house,' he says elsewhere in the will, 'as it now standeth and is well furnished together makes one compleat lodging house from time to time and at all times hereafter for ever shall stand and be kept redy furnished with the same or as good housall goods fitt for lodging persons of quallity and that my son William or any from and after him in order successively for the time being shall not presume to sell or dispose of take or diminish the same goods or furniture but shall keep constantly the same and every part thereof in the said dwelling house to be used there and not elsewhere and upon the decay wearing or lost of the said goods shall replenish and make good the same …' To make sure his wishes are carried out Nicholas tells his trustees to keep always by them a true copy of his will and an inventory of the dwelling house contents and to meet every five years to inspect them. He wants also to carry on a legal squabble from the grave. 'Whereas', he says, 'I have been of late put to unnecessary charge to defend my right in a slip of ground on part of which I have built a new stable and coachhouses against a confetharacy who had combined together to force or fright me out of my right' – he tells his four sons to continue the fight and share the costs equally between them. Do we, dare I say, detect here a hint that old Nich was perhaps a teeny bit difficult to get on with? Perish the thought – I'm sure he was always in the right! I have no information on Nich's family background. Was his father a fellmonger and his father before him? I have no idea. Like many other old Mount Sionites he came from nowhere, seized the opportunity presented by the influx of rich visitors and the offer of land from Lady Muskerry and flourished. Anyway he made a success of his trade and his lodging house and he was proud of it all … and why not? … and the meat trade, of which he was part, seems to have been profitable – as we shall see elsewhere.

What precisely did fellmongers do? If you think this is an ancient medieval trade that disappeared long ago, you are quite wrong. The Skinners' Company in London, the Company of Fellmongers of Richmond, Yorkshire, the British School of Leather Technology at Nene College, Northampton and the United Kingdom Fellmongers Association in Bradford are there to tell otherwise. One thing is clear: fellmongers still exist. Not only does the process continue (which stands to reason) but the operators still call themselves fellmongers and there are a dozen or so companies working in the UK. What is not yet so clear is exactly what they did in the 18th century. I shall come back to that later. For the moment it is enough to know that fellmongers took skins, particularly those of sheep and lambs, removed the wool and sold the wool to wool-processors and the skins to tanners. The other thing that Nicholas did was to make and sell gloves. This seems to have been a very common association; but it meant that the fellmonger had to be a tanner also – at least sufficiently to provide soft sheepskin leather for gloves. Anyway, Nicholas had a glove shop on the Pantiles. He left to his son Nicholas the front part of his shop at the Wells 'for so long as he sells gloves in it'… more directions from the grave! One of the passages from the Pantiles to the London Road is called Woods Passage and the shop next to it on the south was marked Wood in 1739. Whether Nicholas chose the site of his house with a view to his fellmongering requirements is a matter for speculation; but I think the process took place a few hundred yards away down the hill in what is now Madeira Park and the cottages which still stand at Nos 34/38 Mount Sion were probably built for the workers in the 18th century – for a photograph see chapter 22 page 330. Alongside the end cottage is a lane, Clifton Place, which is now a dead-end but used to lead to a house which was called Knocklofty; and just before Knocklofty you turned at right angles into a track leading to the 'Fellmonger's Yard'. This whole story of the 'Fellmonger Cottages' and the 'Fellmonger's Yard' is dealt with in more detail at the end of Chapter 22 starting at page 325.

What happened as a result of Nicholas Wood's will? He left his messuage 'with the brewhouse coach houses workhouses and stables and all other the edifices and buildings garden orchard and four several pieces of land belonging to it to the outmost extent of all the land belonging to my dwelling house …' to his kinsman Edward Sharp and to Richard Fry of Mitchells, both yeomen of Speldhurst, as trustees. For their pains his 'two trusty friends' were to receive one guinea each for a mourning ring and ten shillings for each inspection of the dwelling house which they (and their heirs for ever) were to make once every five years, keeping always by them a true copy of the will and an inventory of the house contents and ensuring that the occupant of the day made good all losses and damage. The eldest son William 'if he think fitt to follow the implyment of a fellmonger and glover' was to give the trustees a bond of £500 conditional on his leaving everything in good and tenant-like repair; he would then be permitted to receive all the income from the property for 20 years. At the end of this period he was to 'resine up all the premises into the hands of the two trustees or theire heirs' and they were to go, on the same conditions, to the son of the next son in seniority and then to his eldest son and so on; but if there were no son or if he was not willing to be a fellmonger then the premises were to go to the eldest son of the next son by seniority or the next or the son of William or or any son of sons 'as are instructed to keep forward the implyment as aforesaid sucksessive one after another as they shall be in seniority of age or priority of bearth always to prefer the older before the younger if he will follow the implyment and give security to perform all the conditions as aforesaid that is to uphold and keep all the buildings fences and furniture in good and tenant-like repair and to make good all loss and wear of all the goods and as it doth decay to replenish and lay in as good in the rooms …' If there were no male heirs then the trusty trustees were to convey everything to all his granddaughters share and share alike. So what happened to old Nich's plans for eternal fellmongering? A family tree will help:

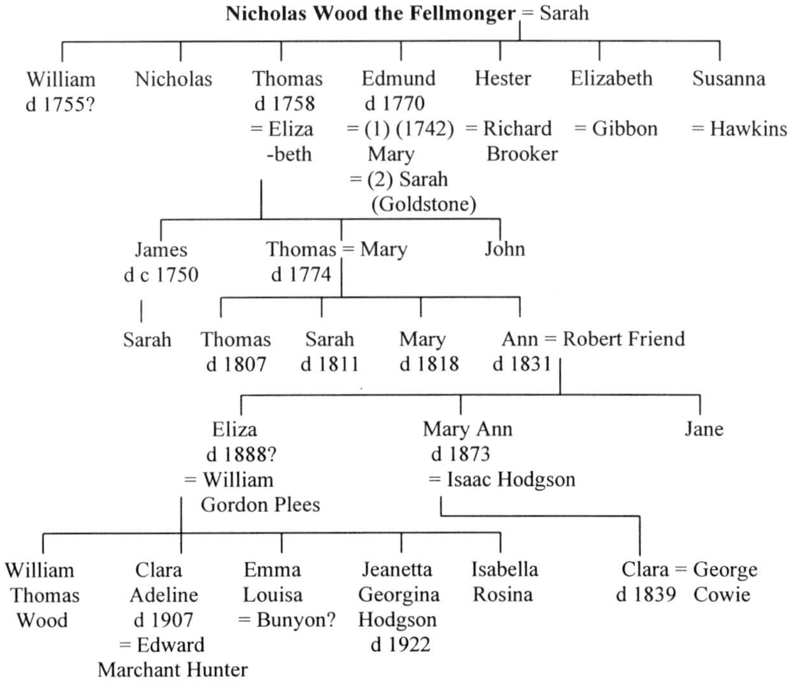

William, the eldest son, seems on the Poor Rate evidence to have taken over the house on the death of his father and to have continued until 1739. This is not quite the 20-year term envisaged by the will but perhaps he came to an arrangement with his successor. When he died in or around 1755 he was living in Hampton,

Middlesex, and described himself as a gentleman. I wonder whether he ever sullied his hands with fellmongering. He conveniently left all his real estate to his nephew Thomas junior who succeeded him in accordance with the will and appears on the Bowra plan in 1738. He continued to pay rates until the time of his death almost forty years later when he was followed by the third Thomas. None of the Thomases called themselves fellmongers. They did not fancy it although I do not suppose they would have dared to tell the old man so. Thomas senior was a hollow turner which might have connected him with Tunbridge Ware; his son called himself simply 'turner'; and his grandson was described in a 1776 deed as a watchmaker and in his will as a goldsmith. What happened to the fellmongering business is unknown; but in 1784 John Peerless appears as ratepayer for the Fellmonger's Yard and his family was still using the facilities fifty years later. In 1807 Thomas the third died but childless and the estate (consisting of Sion House, Berkeley Place and Burlington House) was left to his widow for life and then to his three sisters, share and share alike. Sarah and Mary were unmarried and Berkeley Place was evidently split so that each could have a half; but they both died early and the whole house, therefore, came on the death of widow Mary in 1821, along with the rest of the estate, to the third sister, Ann, who was married to the brewer Robert Friend. She had three daughters of whom Jane is the unmarried one who inherited the *Compasses* in 1831 (see page 69 above). The only one to produce a succeeding generation was Eliza who inherited Sion House (see chapter 17) but was living in Bristol. Burlington House came eventually to the third daughter but indirectly since Ann Friend conveyed it to Mary Ann's husband Isaac Hodgson in 1827 and Mary Ann inherited from him. The house had been let since about 1815 to Jane Akers who, as mentioned, died there in 1842. The year before, the census enumerator had noted a household of seven: the lady herself and a companion of similar age together with five servants of whom one was an old lady of 80. I think the number of servants suggests that some lodging house business was still going on. In 1811 the tenancy had been taken over by Richard Delves (see chapter 20) and, whether by coincidence or not, the name 'Burlington House' is recorded for the first time; but this tenancy lasted no longer than five years or so. This is the period when the old system of calling houses by their owner's or occupier's name was giving way to the assumption of often grandiloquent names.

After his mother's death on 2 May 1842 Aretas Akers had to deal with the lease on her house and two letters in his letter book throw a contemporary light on the scene. On 20 September 1842 he writes to a ______ McGuire Esquire: 'By desire of my brother Mr James Akers I write to let you know that you may have Burlington House in this place from 1st Oct to 1st Apl next for forty guineas. My agents for letting it are Messrs Delves & Jull of this Town, to who I beg to refer you for any further information'. Lack of further references suggests that nothing came of this initiative; and anyhow on 5 May 1843 (the lease having presumably expired in April) he sends to Mrs Hodgson a letter which is revealing of both his and her temperaments:

Whatever doubts you may entertain about the sufficiency of your inventory of Burlington House with which you say the furniture with some trifling exceptions corresponds I am quite satisfied from the Inventories I hold that not only is all yr property there but some few things which my Mother's representatives might claim. But I do not insist on any such consideration.

But you claim 59 panes to be repaired by me. After six and twenty years tenure at a rent vastly beyond the value of the house, I offer to put you in possession nearly a month before the time and you claim to be paid fr 59 pans of glass.

How many must have been cracked or broken when the house was first hired? And who is liable for such as are broken by passers by, by hail or other such accident? Is it possible that you can hold me liable for all?

If you do I can only say that before agreeing to any such claim I shall carefully ascertain whether I am legally liable.

But I propose to you, as a brief and simple way of concluding all transactions between us in this matter, that you should consider what sum you can fairly demand for dilapidations of this or any kind and let me know: when if the amount is at all moderate I shall be rather disposed to consent to the payment than to engage in any dispute.

I beg the favour of an early answer.

In 1851 Burlington House had been taken over by the Knights and the final, scholastic stage in its history had begun. Philip Knight, aged 44, described himself as a proprietor of houses, born in Foulness. His wife Mary, two years younger, was born in Tunbridge Wells but their 14-year-old daughter Eliza was born in Clapham. Mary Knight was described as a schoolmistress and boarding house keeper and to prove it there were 24 scholars, two teachers and three visitors filling the nooks and crannies of Burlington House. *Colbran's Guide* of 1850 called Mrs Kinght's establishment a Seminary; but it did not last long and by January 1860 had been replaced by Mrs Allen's Ladies School. The 1861 census provides a few details. Harriett Allen, born in Yorkshire, was a widow of 46 and she had eight pupils ranging in age from eight to the 23-year-old Marie Gaubert, born in France but a British subject. She also accommodated visitors: in 1861 there was a lady of 30 from Hamburg and, in May, a Mr and Mrs Thompson were sharing the house with the young ladies.

In 1861 incidentally the owner of Burlington House was living (as noted on page 113 above) in 'Woods Cottage' (now Christmas Cottage) just across the road from Burlington House. Mrs Hodgson made her will (witnessed by Thomas Delves and William Stone, the solicitor) in 1843 and never changed it. Her one child, Clara, had died in 1839 and she left everything, with the exception of a few minor bequests, to her sister Eliza Plees and her niece Emma. Eliza was to have furniture and pictures; Emma her piano, wearing apparel, plate, china and jewels. She appointed as trustees her sister's husband, William Gordon Plees, who was a schoolmaster in Bristol, and Edward Marchant Hunter, a local resident and bank employee who seems later to have married Clara Adeline Plees, the niece who was staying with Mrs Hodgson at Woods Cottage in 1861. They were to realise all the real estate. £200 was to go to Emma and the remainder was to provide an income for her sister for life and then be divided between her sister's five children. Under the terms of the will therefore the 'Burlington House Estate' and the 'Fellmonger Estate' were put up for auction at the *Royal Sussex Hotel* on 27 June 1873. The Burlington House Estate comprised three lots: the house and garden proper; the *Blue Anchor* building and stabling; and the vacant plot on the corner of Mount Sion and Little Mount Sion. The Sale Particulars stated that the house 'is now used as a school and in the occupation of Mr Bassett, as a yearly tenant at the very inadequate rent of £50 per annum'. Details from the Sale Particulars have already been used to describe the house on page 139 above.

It seems likely that the sitting tenant was the successful bidder at the auction; anyhow on 21 August 1878 the following announcement appeared in the *Kent & Sussex Courier*:

Burlington House Mount Sion Tunbridge Wells
Highly Important Freehold Investment
Messrs James Richardson & Son

Have been directed by Mr Bassett to sell by auction at the Royal Sussex Hotel on Friday 30th August the above-named Family Residence suitable either for a first-class Lodging or Boarding House, or an extensive Building Speculation.

The times were clearly ripe for the building speculation. The example had been set by the demolition of Cumberland and Bowling Green Houses a year or so earlier (see chapter 19). What is not clear is whether this offer comprised the three lots of the 1873 auction or only the main house and garden. The wording suggests the latter but if so it is a curious coincidence that C.E. Ansell waited until 9 November 1878 to submit his application for a 'Dwelling House and Aerated Water Manufactory' on the corner plot which formed Lot 3 in 1873. Whatever the date of purchase Ansell named himself as owner and W. Mason of 26 Calverley Street as the architect. The builder had not yet been engaged but the result of his labours can be seen, very little changed, in the present Miles Garage. The mineral water business, at first as Ansell and Company and then under the name Grove Spa Mineral Water Company and different management, continued until about 1905 (see Hetherington and Tucker). In 1909 Edward George Miles, fly proprietor, is listed by *Pelton's Directory* at Grove Spa House, whither he had moved, so his grandson told me, from the Royal Oak Stables – the present Tyre Centre opposite the *Royal Oak* pub in Prospect Road. Since then the building, numbered 69 Mount Sion and 48 Little Mount Sion, has continued in the ownership of the Miles family, the horse carriage business becoming by a natural transition a garage for the repair of horseless carriages.

The purchaser of the main Burlington House in 1878 appears to have been a Robert Brown who described himself as both owner and builder in an application dated 26 September 1883 and gives his address as Beulah Road in an 1882 application. It is tempting to link him with John Brown the dairyman but John's grand-daughter is positive that she would have known if Robert the builder had been a relative. The architect for this development was H. Willard of 37 Western Road and then 35 Calverley Street. The plan proposed 10 villas and five cottages all of which were duly erected. The 10 villas survive as nos 20-28 Berkeley Road and, round the corner, nos 38-46 Litle Mount Sion. No.38 which was designed as a house and shop on the corner has since been split to accommodate the fish and chip shop as well as what used to be a general store; but otherwise Robert Brown's villas have survived intact. The five cottages on the other hand were demolished in the 1950s or '60s. They were known during their comparatively brief life as Burlington Cottages and were intended definitely for the working-class tenant. The end wall of the row can be seen on the left of Johnson's photograph below. Robert Brown was certainly cramming his site. It was the Miles garage company which demolished the cottages to provide parking space, after they had acquired the *Blue Anchor* site for a workshop; and it is to the story of the *Blue Anchor* that we now turn to complete this chapter.

David Johnson took the photograph below in 1931 and he had quite a lot to say about it. I guess this is because he was on the spot at the time the *Blue Anchor* was demolished – and he lived just a few yards down the street. 'In process of demolition at the present time. October 23rd 1933,' he commented; and 'The stem of ivy above the arrow measured 10 inches in diameter'. Obviously he was impressed by the ivy and its implications of antiquity. He continues:

> Mr Frank Hobbs the owner of the property in 1934 sent me this note. It recalled the fact that stables existed in my boyhood which I had never previously

The Blue Anchor building demolished about 1933

> associated with the Blue Anchor property. It also gives the Blue Anchor an earlier date than 1724. ... This property was dealt with in 1724 on the death of the owner, so that it must have been in existence a considerable time before that date.

The *Kent and Sussex Courier* of October 1933 had a short article dealing with it under the heading 'Link with Beau Nash' as follows:

> Another link with the days of Beau Nash will be broken by the forthcoming demolition of one of the oldest houses in Tunbridge Wells, 65 Mount Sion, which was formerly a Coaching Hostelry. It is over 200 years old, and has been condemned by the Corporation. When Tunbridge Wells was at the height of its fame as a fashionable resort, Mount Sion was one of the principal thoroughfares and the Blue Anchor as it was called was a stopping place for changing horses on the London-Hastings route. The old oak floors and beams are still to be seen, but the open fireplaces were removed many years ago. With the branches of a patriarch among ivy trees covering most of it, it is difficult to imagine the time when the little old house was alive with waiters and ostlers, with coachmen stamping their feet outside and passengers descending from their seats to drink mulled wine before its blazing fires. The last occupant was Miss C Strange whose family lived there for 130 years.

When Mr Hobbs, the owner in the 1930s, said that the property 'was dealt with in 1724 on the death of the owner' he must surely have been referring to old title deeds in his possession. Oh Mr Hobbs, whatever did you do with them?! The death in 1724 must be that of Nicholas Wood, the fellmonger – but how would Hobbs have known about it except from title deeds? Let us then go back to Nicholas Wood's will and the early story of the *Blue Anchor*. Nicholas bequeathed to his daughter Susanna 'the yearly rent of the blew anker and stable belonging to it with the liberty to take watter and lay wood as hath been yousall for tenants that lived there so to do' during her life and then to her heirs or those entitled under the will to receive the rents of his dwelling house. Curiously enough, the name that appears against the 'Anchor' (*Blue Anchor*) on the Bowra plan is Hawkins and Susanna Wood married Mr Hawkins sometime after her father's death. It looks as if Hawkins married the maiden of property just as Richard Brooker had married into the pyehouse down the hill. Of course I cannot be sure that the Hawkins on Bowra is the Hawkins who married Susannah – I do not know the first name of either – but it seems a racing certainty. I know Susanna married a Hawkins because one party to a deed dated 20 March 1805 kindly lent by Miles Garage was John Ellames Fenner who was the eldest son of Sarah Fenner who was the only daughter and heir of the body of Susannah Hawkins who was one of the daughters and a devisee named in the last will and testament of Nicholas Wood ... fellmonger ... deceased. It is curious also that the name Hawkins appears in the Poor Rate record but not until 1758. The Burlington House Poor Rate sequence bifurcates in 1728, after the gap, and the following appears alongside the main house sequence:

1728-1736	And for the Little House
1737-1740	Do for a little House

1741-1748	Do for a Smaller House
1749-1750	Do for a Smaller House or occ
1751-1755	Pete Blakey or occ
1756	Occr of ye Blue Anchor late Blakey
1757	Occr of ye Blue Anchor
1758-1759	Mr Hawkins for the Blue Anchor
1760-1764	Thos Pack for the Blue Anchor
1675-1766	Hawkins for the Blue Anchor
1767-1774	Wm Hawkins for the Blue Anchor
1775-1778	Wm Hawkins or occ for the Blue Anchor
1779-1791	Webb widow for late Blue Anchor
1792-1797	Wilmshurst Nathl for late Wid Webbs

It seems quite clear that the 'little' or 'smaller' house is the *Blue Anchor*; and reasonable to suppose that it was built between 1714 and 1728, although it might have been built earlier and subsumed under 'Nicholas Wood' for rating purposes until 1714-28. It seems odd that Bowra in 1738 shows Hawkins at the Anchor while the Poor Rate record names no names until 'Pete Blakey' in 1751; and 'Mr Hawkins' does not appear until 1758. Can this be the same as Bowra's Hawkins? Or does the introduction of the first name William in 1767 denote a new generation? It seems unlikely, but not impossible, that one man should have been concerned with the running of the inn for forty years or more. On balance a two-generation hypothesis is more tenable. In any case the hostelry business seems to have died with William Hawkins, since it was the 'late Blue Anchor' that the Widow Webb occupied. For the last three years she was recorded in the Poor Rate book as 'poor' and presumably excused payment for that reason. I know nothing about her or the next tenant, Nathaniel Wilmshurst; and the only other evidence until 1870 is to be found in Licensees' Recognizances.

Alehouse keepers, or victuallers, were licensed by magistrates from the 16th century and records are to be found at the Centre for Kentish Studies, Maidstone. If you are lucky, and if you succeed in keeping open a recalcitrant, noisy roll of parchment for long enough to decipher a faded fragment, you will find the name of the victualler, the 'sign' and location of the inn and the names of those standing surety for its orderly management. For the Tonbridge area there survive, by good fortune, comprehensive tables for the years 1715 and 1718. Neither lists the *Blue Anchor*, although there is a 'Blew Anchor' in Tonbridge Town. I have made searches at selected intervals during the years up to 1752 and have found five mentions of the *Blue Anchor* (of Tonbridge Parish, not town): in 1734 and 1736 (Tho Fells, victualler); in 1743 (Tho Fells of Edenbridge); in 1746 (Daniel Latter); and in 1752 (Wm Hawkins at 'ye Old Blue Anchor'). That seems to tie *William* Hawkins down to an earlier date than the Poor Rate record. Fells and Latter are new names in connection with the *Blue Anchor*; but it is interesting to note that Peter Blakey was landlord of the *Crown & Anchor* in 1752, one of his guarantors being William Fry, and that he himself stood surety for Ann Bodle at *the Compasses & Horseshoes* in the same year and for Marlow at the *Angel.*

The broad outline of the history of the *Blue Anchor* seems quite clear. The fact that it is not listed in 1715 or 1718 does not necessarily mean that it did not then exist; it may have done under a different name but it seems most likely that it began life between 1718 and 1724 when it was named in Nicholas Wood's will. It then functioned as a public house until about 1778 when it became a private house until its demolition in 1933. It may be that the demise of the *Blue Anchor* was caused by the opening of the turnpike road from Tonbridge to Tunbridge Wells by the Maidstone and Tonbridge Turnpike Trust in 1765. Before then the route passed through Pembury. In fact the turnpike from Sevenoaks to Tunbridge Wells, via Woodsgate, was in 1709 the very first Kent turnpike. The opening of the shorter route through Southborough might well have contributed to the end of the *Blue Anchor* as an inn. Since the final destination of visitors was 'The Wells', an obvious route formerly was along Prospect and Claremont Roads (not so called at the time, I imagine) and down Mount Sion, passing the *Blue Anchor* on the way. Even today a sign 'To the Wells' can be seen incised in a stone wall at the Bayhall Road cross-roads. The picturesque account quoted above of blazing log fires and ostlers and stamping coachmen at the old *Blue Anchor* may be put down to journalistic licence but perhaps some of it really happened.

One newsworthy thing for which there is clear evidence is the Tunbridge Ware connection. Susannah Hawkins née Wood had one child Sarah who married a blacksmith named John Fenner and they had three sons: John Ellames, Andrew and William. As far as I can understand the long and repetitive document of three skins referred to above and dated 20 March 1805, the blacksmith and his wife on 1 March 1790 gave each son a third share in the property and in 1805, when both parents had died, one son, William, bought out the shares of his brothers for £100 each. There are some complications concerning an annuity of £6 which I think is the rent of the *Blue Anchor* which Nicholas bequeathed to Susannah in his will; the actual freehold of the property; and the position of Thomas Wood as inheritor of the 'dwelling house'. The upshot, however, seems quite clear. In the end William Fenner took all. What he took was described variously in 1790 as 'ALL THAT Messuage or Tenement wherein Jane Webb then dwelt with the Turner's Shop near thereto in the occupation of the said James Nye...' and in 1805 as the messuage or tenement 'wherein the said Jane Webb formerly dwelt with the Buildings thereunto belonging formerly a Stable but now converted into a Turner's Shop and as such lately used by the said James Nye and all other the Buildings grounds and Appurtenances thereto belonging which said Messuage or tenement was formerly called the Blue Anchor'. Everything here is mutually confirmatory: the Poor Rate record; the Widow Webb; Jane Webb; the Blue Anchor; and the family connection What is newsworthy however is the fact that there was a Turner's Shop converted from an old *Blue Anchor* stable and that it was occupied in 1790 (but perhaps not in 1805) by James Nye, a name well known in connection with Tunbridge Ware. Furthermore all three Fenner sons seem to have been in the trade, William as a cabinetmaker and the other two as turners. Of course there may have been other men with the same names but the coincidences are very suggestive.

According to Brian Austen, James Nye, a Tunbridge Ware manufacturer who had been in business as early as 1757, had a son Edmund who, on his father's death in 1809, went into partnership with William Fenner, who was the man selected to make the Tunbridge Ware work- and writing-table for Princess Victoria in 1826 which has since been mislaid. There was a John Fenner who leased a shop on the Pantiles from 1782 to 1787, the year of his death, and traded as a turner and toyseller. The relationship between John Fenner and William Fenner is unknown, says Austen, but William's business opened very shortly after John's had closed. Could John be the blacksmith father of William Fenner? The date of his death is a problem. If he really died in 1787, he could not have executed the indenture dated 1 March 1790; on the other hand the document describes him as 'since deceased'. William Fenner subscribed five guineas in 1792 towards the re-paving of the Pantiles and a trade card has survived proclaiming the sale of print-decorated wares 'in the TURNER or CABINET line' at his Pantiles shop. This probably dates from 1796 and the next year Fenner was associated with James Nye's business. 'It is possible', comments Austen, 'that Nye was elderly and realised the advantages of taking the young and active Fenner as a partner'. He is surely right for James Nye died in 1809 and it seems that Edmund took his father's place in 'Fenner & Nye'. All this is thoroughly consistent with the theory that William Fenner of Tunbridge Ware fame was the great-grandson of Nicholas Wood and came into the *Blue Anchor* premises through family inheritance. What is puzzling is what came later. 'William Fenner appears to have retained a shop under his own name', says Austen (page 145), 'possibly the one shown on Barrow's map of 1808 near Mount Sion Grove and described as Fenner's Turnery.' The Fenner-Nye partnership was dissolved in 1817 and Austen then suggests that this occasioned the surrender by Fenner of his Mount Sion premises in favour of the 'Chalet' on Mount Ephraim which had been used by the partnership from 1808. There seems to be no direct evidence for the surrender of the Mount Sion premises in 1817, nor indeed that they had anything to do with William Fenner. Two things only are certain: James Nye was using a turner's shop in part of the old *Blue Anchor* buildings in 1790; and 'Fenner's Turnery' is shown on the Barrow map of 1808. On this foundation we can if we like erect a theory that Fenner and Nye moved from the *Blue Anchor* to Belgrove and thence to Mount Ephraim. We might also recall one item of newspaper testimony from the end of chapter 7: in the *Compasses* on Mount Sion in December 1787 there was a turner who had a fight with a carpenter and the turner's name was Fenner.

I have no information on the occupiers of the old *Blue Anchor* after Nathaniel Wilmshurst in 1797 until 1841 when the census shows Jane Akers and a second household living at Burlington House; but the second household was I think living in the *Blue Anchor*. It consisted of a 50-year-old widowed schoolmistress, Mary Battman, 11-year-old Eliza and her young sister Elizabeth and two older brothers John and Nathan. Nathan is 15 years old and a cabinetmaker! There will be more to say about the occupants and eventual fate of the *Blue Anchor* in a later chapter; but the Tithe map springs a surprise on the question of ownership. Burlington

House was owned as noted above by Ann Friend's daughter Mary Ann Hodgson, having been purchased by husband Isaac from Ann Friend in 1827; but the property includes the *Blue Anchor* building. Furthermore when the whole property came to be auctioned in 1873 on the death of Mary Ann, the *Blue Anchor* was part of the estate. In other words either I was mistaken in my interpretation of the Miles Garage deed of 1805 or Isaac Hodgson bought the *Blue Anchor* portion back from William Fenner perhaps with the main house in 1827. It is perfectly possible that the 1805 deed conveyed only a leasehold interest to William Fenner. I still do not think so; but the wording is so long-winded and repetitive that it is easy to lose the thread and misunderstand. If so, my apologies. On the other hand the repurchase theory is not impossible. Either way, however, it is certain that by 1841 and until 1873 the whole property, *Blue Anchor* included, belonged to the Wood descendant Mary Ann. The *Blue Anchor* building incidentally is described in the 1873 Sale Particulars as 'containing Five Bedrooms, Sitting-room, Kitchen, Pantry, Coal Cellar and WC, adjoining which are Stables for Four Horses, Coach-house with Lofts over and Stable Yard' – fairly cramped for a bustling hostelry.

What about the Miss C. Strange said by the *Courier* in 1933 to be the last occupant and from a family which had lived in the *Blue Anchor* building for 130 years? The *Directories* confirm that a Mrs Strange described as a dressmaker lived at 65 Mount Sion continuously from 1886 until 1931 and it is possible that the story could go back to 1800. The lady (or ladies of more than one generation) can be picked up in the census returns from 1881 back to 1851. In 1881 she is living at 65 Mount Sion and is named Eliza Strange, a widow of 50 and dressmaker, born in Tunbridge Wells. Living with her are her son Nicholas, an unmarried accountant of 22; two unmarried daughters, both described as dressmaker's assistants, Annie aged 18 and Clara aged 14; and a schoolgirl daughter of nine, Caroline. Ten years earlier this family was living in a house 'near the Grove' and enumerated immediately after Cumberland House. I have no doubt this was the *Blue Anchor* house. Eliza's husband Nicholas was living at this time and was described as a builder's clerk of 60, born in Tunbridge Wells. There were then two older sons living at home: Edwin S. a paperhanger and Henry S. a postmaster's assistant; and a daughter Eliza J., a schoolgirl of 14. In 1861 the family is living at 'Cumberland Cottage', again enumerated immediately after Cumberland House (hence its name at this time?) and again undoubtedly the same house in my estimation. Father was then described as an upholsterer and paperhanger and mother still as a dressmaker; and there were four children, from Edwin to toddler Nicholas. In 1851 comes the interesting census discovery. In a house on 'Mount Sion' enumerated immediately after Cumberland House lives a family headed by a 60-year-old widow and schoolmistress, Mary Battman, and living with her are her 22-year-old seamstress daughter Eliza and her son-in-law Nicholas Strange, aged 40 and described as a cabinetmaker. There were as yet no children of this marriage (Edwin the future paperhanger would be born the following year) but the schoolmistress had a son and daughter, a grandson and a four-year-old visitor living with her. The story can be taken back in time another ten years. In 1841 Nicholas Strange, cabinetmaker aged 30, is living at Fountain Cottage on Mount Sion (now Walmer Cottage – see chapter 17) with his 25-year-old wife Sophia and sons Thomas aged five and Sidney aged one-and-a-half. He has two lodgers staying with him, a widow and her daughter, and three female servants. Now this must surely be the same Nicholas Strange; but whatever happened to his wife and two sons? Were all three carried off by a tragic bout of disease or did he desert them for the charms of a 20-year-old seamstress? She, as 11-year-old Eliza Battman, is to be found living with her schoolmistress mother, young sister Elizabeth and older brothers John and Nathan. Nathan aged 15 is a cabinetmaker; could he perhaps have been working for or with Nicholas Strange?

The census enumerator entered the Battmans as a second household living at Burlington House with Jane Akers but my guess is that they were occupying the *Blue Anchor* house and that therefore the Strange connection with the *Blue Anchor* started when Nicholas moved in with his young bride around 1850. If this is so, then there is a gap between Wilmshurst and Mary Battman in the record of tenants of the *Blue Anchor*. For the story of Nicholas Strange and the inscription in Sion House see chapter 17. Mention of Nicholas can be found in the family history by C.H. Strange. 'Nicholas Strange, b. 1810, married a lady of the name of Bridger and lived in Tunbridge Wells. Their children were: Edwin Sidney, Harry, Jane, Nicholas, Annie, Clara and Carrie. There are two sons of Edwin Sidney now living in Tunbridge Wells – Sidney and Alfred. Also of Nicholas who married Edith Stringer there is a son, Fred. The married names of the daughters were: Jane Kenward, Annie Neale (deceased) and Clara Killick.' The book was written in 1920. If there are any members of this family who know more on this story I should be glad to hear. There is no doubt this is the right Nicholas. The 'lady of the name of Bridger' must be his first wife; but his date of birth matches and the children (of the second marriage) correspond exactly: Edwin S. is Edwin Sidney, Henry S. is Harry, Eliza J. is Jane and Caroline is shortened to Carrie. Eliza née Battman must be the Mrs N. Strange, dressmaker, who appears in the *Directories* from 1886 but by 1931 she would have been 102 years old and I think Johnson or the *Courier* would have mentioned a centenarian occupant of the double centenarian *Blue Anchor*. Did Nicholas junior marry a dressmaker – he was surrounded by them in his own family? Or have the *Directories* got it wrong and was it Miss Carrie who carried on her mother's trade at the old *Blue Anchor*? The *Courier* did say that Miss C. Strange was the last occupant. She would have been 60 in 1932.

There is no direct evidence who bought the *Blue Anchor* whether in 1873 or 1878; but David Johnson names Frank Hobbs as the owner in 1932 and Mr Miles has said that his father bought it from a Hobbs and there seems no reason to doubt them. William Hobbs & Son, builders, occupied Grove Lodge on the opposite side of Mount Sion in 1878 and William G. Hobbs was beginning his stint as landlord of the *Compasses* in 1878 – see page 75 for a photograph. To complete the picture, mention must be made of William Pearce who was sharing the *Blue*

Anchor building with Mrs Strange from before 1873. In fact the Sale Particulars of 1873 name him as the only tenant, paying £18 per annum on yearly terms; and it may be that Mrs Strange was his sub-tenant. At this time the house was numbered 33 Mount Sion (Mansfield House was 29 and Cumberland House No 31?) but after the development of the Bowling Green site it had two numbers, Mrs Strange being at 65 and William Pearce at 67 where he continued to be listed until 1899. In the 1870 *Kelly* he is shown as 'Pearce William, licensed to let horses, Mount Sion'; in 1871 he is enumerated after the Stranges and like them 'near Grove'; while in 1881 he is at number 67, living with his wife Abigail and his 22-year-old son William who is a fly-driver. All in all it seems certain that he was living in the *Blue Anchor* building from at least 1870. This being so, it might have been expected that he would have made use of the stables, coach house and yard at the back of the *Blue Anchor* but the Sale Particulars say that these (together with the empty corner plot on which Ansell was to build his factory) were occupied by a Mr Taylor (at eight guineas a week) who was, however, under notice to quit. Perhaps he did quit after 1873 and the Pearces could then have used the stables. A final point of interest from the Sale Particulars is that the purchase of Lot 2 (the *Blue Anchor*) was subject to a right of way from the garden of Burlington House into Mount Sion between the northern boundary of Cumberland House (now 63A Mount Sion) and the *Blue Anchor*. The Ordnance Survey map shows clearly how this used to be the back way into Burlington House. What happened to the Pearces after 1899 is uncertain but the *Advertiser* article suggests that Miss Strange was the sole occupant in 1931. How soon after demolition of the old building Miles built his workshop on the site I do not know but it lasted until 1994 when the present Mr Miles decided that a complete rebuild was necessary. Some of us were horrified to see a steel framework rise on the site but it was soon clad and the building which finally appeared was honoured with a Civic Society award.

Miles Garage workshops on the Blue Anchor site

Chapter 13

Philip Seale

The next three chapters deal with the strip of land adjacent to Martin's strip on the southern side of Little Mount Sion but which encroached on it at the top. This chapter is devoted to its early history and to Philip Seale and his two lodging houses which developed into the historic row in the photograph below. Chapter 14 looks at the story of the Presbyterian Chapel and one of its pastors, Thomas Bayes; and chapter 15 deals with the Seale inheritance and the later history of Sion Crescent also known as Queen Anne's Mansion.

Queen Anne's Mansion or Sion Crescent – Camburn postcard – about 1910

The story begins with the lease to Robert Brooke and Richard Constable of several pieces of Inhams Heath in 1684 for £7 per annum. As we saw on page 15, these two soon decided to partition and, in the process I suppose, or before it, they sub-let a strip of land to Thomas Moyce at £3 per annum. Anyhow, it is separately marked on the partition plan which was reproduced in chapter 2 and now shown here again in part on the next page. I do not have any information on Thomas Moyce unless he is the 'boy I keep' mentioned in Anne Ashdowne's will (see

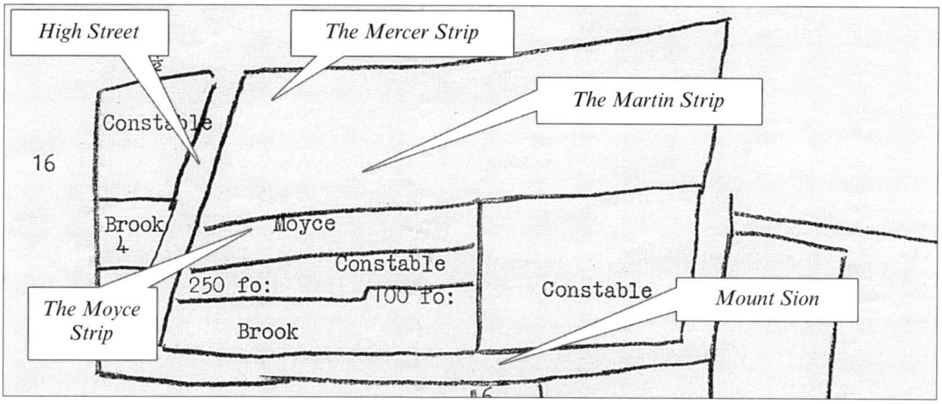

Part of 1686 Partition Plan

chapter 16) – not that this helps very much. Anyway, it cannot have been long before Philip Seale came on the scene. He took a lease which was to run, presumably to make its termination coincide with that of the main lease, for 47 years 11 months and 20 days from Michaelmas 1687. The rent was 20 shillings, indicating that perhaps about one third of the Moyce lease was involved and we can be sure where this third was, at the top of the strip, because the Bowra plan shows us where the house was located. Philip Seale started paying rates by May 1689; so we can surmise that the house was built mainly in 1688 and was ready for the 1689 season. It was evidently a success because Philip soon wanted to build another one next door. But there was a problem. Next door was not his land. So in 1692 he leased a bit of Martin's land. With the lease went 'the privilege of a way for Carts and Coaches leadeing from the house of the said Philip Seale up to the Common way beyond the Bowleing green and from thence a foote way leading up to the Grove for use of himselfe his servants and lodgers.' This seems to explain the shape of Little Mount Sion. The road could not continue straight uphill because there was a house in the way and Philip negotiated himself a right of way for his and his visitors' coaches to reach the Woodsgate Road (the original London Turnpike) without going down the hill and up round Mount Sion.

The Poor Rate record shows that Philip started paying rates on his second house in 1694. All this building and furnishing cost money and Philip had to borrow on mortgage. He is always described as a plumber and glazier and indeed the Chapel Vestry books show him doing odd glazing and painting jobs there from time to time; but whether he actually dirtied his own hands with paint and putty I rather wonder. In 1693 his wife died; but this may have been an equivocal tragedy because four years later he married again. I hesitate to say that he married the daughter of the Groombridge mercer for her money; but the fact is that she was able to help him. A Deed of Assignment dated 6 August 1700 shows that she sold two houses and a piece of land in Chiddingstone to pay off the encumbrances on her husband's property and to supply his 'other occasions' – in return for which the houses on Mount Sion were put in trust for the spouses and their children – and as a bonus for us the deed provides additional information.

By the end of 1700, therefore, Philip must have been feeling quite pleased with life. Here he was with a new wife and two new baby daughters his houses free from debt and money pouring in from the fashionable company. By the end of 1702 he must have been feeling even better: his wife had just presented him, at last, with a son, baby Thomas, christened on 10 November, and on the 28th he had signed the deed which gave him the freehold of his property. Word must have been going round the little community on the hill for some time that the lord of the manor, John so-called Earl of Buckingham, wanted ready cash and, if you were a chief lessee, there was a good chance of buying the fee simple and freehold. Philip was not the principal lessee of his lands but, by a lucky chance, his new father-in-law was the brother-in-law of Richard Constable who was – and on 28 November 1702 the deed was done. On the left you can see what he wrote on the outside of the parchment, his pride in his land-owning status shining through the dirt and dust of centuries: 'Philip Seale his Deed of Purchase of his houses and lands on Mount Sion'. You can see it at the Tonbridge Reference Library in the same bundle as the 1700 Deed of Assignment. Philip paid £150 to the Earl of Buckingham for five pieces of land, three of them coming from the land originally leased to Brooke and Constable and two from that leased to Edward Martin. It was standard practice for a field for grazing purposes to be given with a building plot in the town centre and two of Philip's five pieces were probably fields now occupied by houses in the Madeira Park area (the large rectangle marked 'Moyce' on the Partition Plan?) and the narrow strip connecting it to the top of Mount Sion. Of the remaining three the first was the main strip going up from the High Street. 'One piece or parcel of land being part of a certain ground called Inhams and bounding to a new way there leading from the Wells to South Borrough towards the north and containing in breadth against the said way three rods and ten foot and an half [= 20 yards or 18.29 metres] and bounding to other part of the said Inhams demised to Edward Martin towards the east and to a place where a dyke formerly was and a bank planted with birches towards the south and to lands demised to and in the occupation of Richard Constable towards the west on which said parcels there are several messuages tenements and other buildings now erected'. This is how the Deed of Purchase describes it; and if we look at the partition plan above and only assume that north is to the left the accuracy of the wording can be appreciated. To the

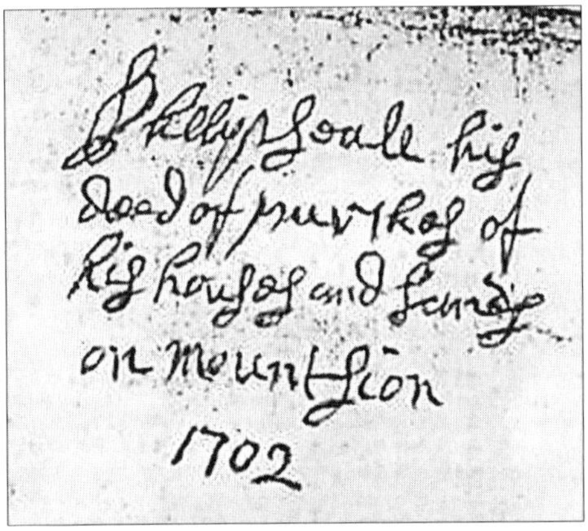

Inscription on Philip Seale's deed

north is the 'new way' i.e. the High Street; to the east is the Martin strip; to the west is Frog Lane land leased to Richard Constable; and to the south is 'a place where a dyke formerly was and a Bank planted with Birches'. I think the bank was the one which still exists behind the Toc H Hall – see the photograph below. The 1702 deed gives no measurement from north to south (for more on this point see page 160) but this strip, unlike the Mercer and Martin strips which went right up to the top of the hill, had to stop at Constable's square plot containing the Bowling Green; and, as a later chapter will show, Murray House was on Constable's plot and the present Spencer Mews replaced Murray House – see chapter 16. Spencer Mews can be seen at the top of the photograph and incidentally the bank was planted with lime trees until the developer of Spencer Mews cut them down.

Bank at back of Toc H Hall

If only the descriptions of Philip's final two acquisitions were as precise and clear as that of the main strip! These were pieces of land taken from the Martin strip and the first was described in the Deed of Assignment of 1700 as follows: 'whereas Martin and Gardner leased to Philip Seale on 28th March 1692 a certain small parcel of ground being part of lands called or known by the name of Inhams containing by estimation sixteen rods whether more or less as it was then and is now marked and bounded out and then in the tenure of the said Edward Martin but now in the tenure of the said Philip Seale or of his assigns and situate lying and being in Tonbridge aforesaid which said parcel of ground six rods and four feet part thereof lyeth to the north west bounding to the grounds of the said Edward Martin and six rods more thereof lyeth to the south east bounding to the grounds of Thomas Potten the said parcel of ground containing four rods in breadth against the head of the said Philip Seales house and at the end of the four rods in length from the house of the said Philip Seale to contain two rods and an half in breadth towards the grounds of the said Thomas Potten and at the end of the said six rods and four feet in length to contain fourteen feet in breadth towards the grounds John Mercer together with the privilege of a way for carts or coaches leading from the house of the said Philip Seale up to the common way beyond the Bowling Green and from thence a foot way leading up to the Grove for the use of himself his servants and lodgers.' The Deed of Purchase of 1702 repeats this description closely but the 'grounds of Thomas Potten' have become the 'land of Mr Amherst'; the intermediate measurement of 2½ rods has been excluded; and we are told the amount of rent payable – 25 shillings per annum – and that several buildings are erected and now in the possession of Philip Seale. What are we to make of this?

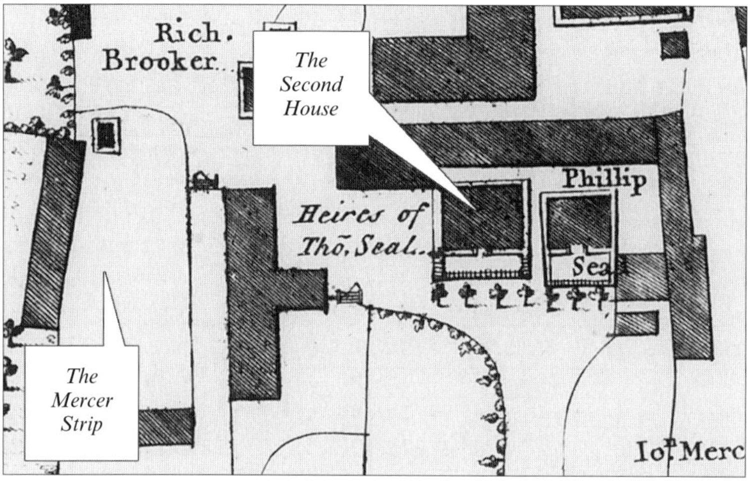

Detail from Bowra plan 1738

We know where we want to arrive! This has to be the bit of Martin's strip Philip needed to build his second house; but can this be reconciled with the words on the parchment? Firstly, I think there is a potential confusion between rods as units of area and of length – at least my *Pear's Encyclopaedia* says the same word can be used for both. 'Containing by estimation 16 rods' therefore must refer to area or square measure. A (square) rod measures 5½ by 5½ yards and contains 30¼ square yards. The plot on which Philip built his second house seems to have measured (using Bowra's scale) roughly six rods on each of two longer (horizontal) sides and four rods tapering to less than one on the other two (vertical) sides. If it measured the full four all the way the area would amount to 24 square rods. If the taper were regular from four to zero the area would be half this – 12 rods. Since the taper is somewhere in between, can we not conclude that 16 **square rods** is a fair estimate. How does this fit onto the map – or the ground? The distance from the right-hand side of the house to the 'o' of Tho Seal is by Bowra's scale more or less seven rods which is 38½ yards (check it for yourself!). On the Ordnance Survey 1/500 map roughly the same points are 28 yards apart. There seems, therefore, to be some discrepancy in the longer dimension. The shorter one is difficult because, although the back of the site is clear enough, the front of the garden on the Ordnance Survey map is not. The distance might vary from about 15 to 28 yards. On Bowra, the distance from the front of the garden (behind the trees) to the stables behind is approximately 3 rods or 16½ yards. If we measure from the front of the houses, the differences more or less disappear. Taking one thing with another, I think we can safely say that the description in Philip Seale's Deed of Purchase must refer to the site of his second house. The reason for the taper from 66 feet against his first house to 14 feet at the other end is of course apparent from the plan. It allows for a road through to what is now the top of Little Mount Sion and for access to the Grove. The reference to John Mercer is explained by what we saw in chapter 7 about the Mercer strip. The references to Potten and Amherst can I think be explained by assuming that Amherst is a mistake for Ashenhurst. The

1701 deed to which reference was made on page 86 tells us that Edward Martin sub-leased part of his land on 16 January 1687 to Thomas Potten of Speldhurst, innkeeper, and Susan his wife; and they mortgaged their holding on 16 July 1688 to widow Mary Allen of Marden for £100. Unfortunately, no clear description of the sub-division of Martin's land is given, reference being made to descriptions contained in recited documents. It seems clear, however, that, by way of several interconnected mortgages, Thomas Ashenhurst took over some or all of Thomas Potten's sub-leases. The fact that Potten's land in 1700 becomes 'Amherst' land in 1702 reinforces my theory. It is after all the same piece of ground which, from unrelated evidence, is known to have been in Ashenhurst's possession at a later date. The land to the south-east must surely be the ground *above* the two Seale houses shown on Bowra as a continuous range of stables. This range actually spans two strips, those of Martin and Moyce – or Martin and Seale, if you prefer. We must now turn to the second of the two parcels of land which Philip Seale bought in 1702 and which were part of the lands demised to Edward Martin from Michaelmas 1684 for 50 years at £5 per annum.

This was described as follows in the Deed of Purchase but was not mentioned in the Deed of Assignment: 'And also one small piece or parcel of land lying near thereunto the last mentioned piece and containing against the way there used towards the west three rods and against the south three rods and seven feet and against the land of the said Edward Martin towards the east four rods [and] fourteen feet and towards the north three rods and thirteen feet.' Notice that we are back to plain cardinal points – north, south, east, west – although the previous plot of land was described in the more accurate terms of north-west, south-east etc. Let us assume that north is the same as for the main strip i.e. straight down the hill – or, looking at the Bowra plan, east is to the left and west to the right. The plot is near the site of the houses; it bounds to Martin's land on the left and to 'the way there used' to the right. The only thing that fits the bill is the plot labelled 'Second Parcel' below. The 'way' is Little Mount Sion and to the left (east) is the back garden of Martins Upper House. Acording to the document, the longest dimension is the vertical one

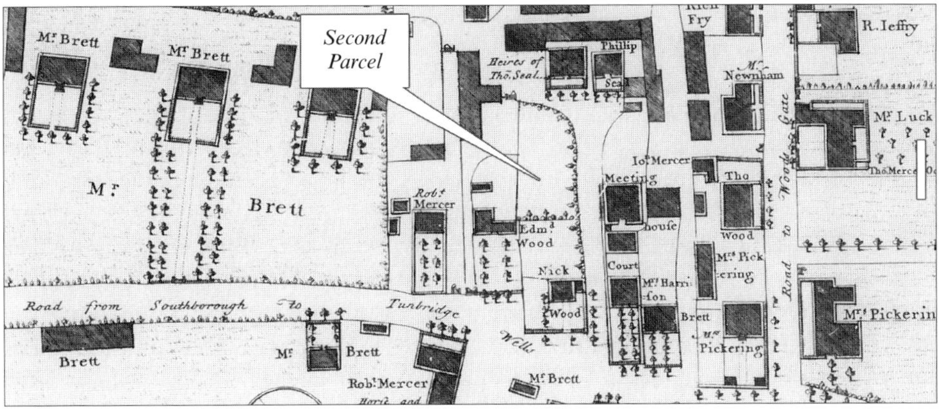

Bowra plan 1738

Little Mount Sion Car Park

on the left (against Martin's land) measuring 4 rods 14 feet or 80 feet. Top and bottom are roughly the same, about 60 feet; and the one on the right (against Little Mount Sion) is less than that on the left because the road curves. A check on the Ordnance Survey map (surveyed 1866) permits a similar conclusion – the site of Rosebury Place and its garden fits the old words well enough – and the place is now this: the Little Mount Sion Pay-and-Display car park – not a pretty sight now but Philip Seale used it for a front garden to his lodging houses.

There is one further tiresome question of measurement to be considered before we come to the two legends of Little Mount Sion. You remember that at the beginning of this chapter we surmised that Philip Seale took over the top third of Thomas Moyce's sub-lease and built his first house thereon. The two documents in the case, those of 1700 and 1702, describe the plot but in slightly different ways. The wording from the Deed of Purchase of 1702 was given at the bottom of page 156; the Deed of Assignment dated 6 August 1700 describes it in these words: 'One piece or parcel of heath ground part of certain lands called Inhams bounding to certain lands demised to the said Richard Constable towards the south and east and to a new way leading from Tunbridge Wells to Southburrow towards the west and to certain lands demised to Edward Martin towards the north and containing 4 rods and 2 feet in length and 3 rods 10½ feet in breadth …' The two descriptions agree precisely on the width of 60 feet and on compass points provided we make the familiar adjustment; but the 1700 deed gives a length measurement of 4 rods 2 feet (68 feet) whereas the 1702 deed simply says the plot bounds to the 'new way' (i.e. the High Street) suggesting the plot extended all the way down to the High Street. Must we assume that between 1700 and 1702 Philip took over the remainder of Moyce's land or perhaps that the remainder was included in the 1702 purchase? There are two pieces of evidence we might bring to bear on this problem: the Poor Rate record and, more speculatively, the legend of the Queen, the Quaker and the Actress.

The Poor Rate record for the house at the bottom of the strip (Mrs Harrison on Bowra) starts with Mr John Streeter in July 1685. I do not know who he was but presumably he had some arrangement with Constable and Brooke before their partition in 1686. Thomas Moyce then comes on the scene in 1687 and continues for ten years, to be replaced by his widow until 1700. After this the name Philip Seale appears. For the full sequence see Chapter 14 page 178. The conclusion is by no means clear-cut but the Poor Rate record does suggest that Thomas Moyce's widow might have made a change in about 1701. This would solve the problem of the 4 rod 2 feet dimension. The house at the bottom of the strip was perhaps lived in by the Moyce family at first. After Philip Seale, in 1704, the Harrisons take over – first Widow Harrison and then, after the gap, Mrs Mary Harrison who goes on until 1740 – and is marked as Mrs Harrison on the Bowra plan. The second point concerns the Meeting House.

The Presbyterian Chapel or Meeting House on Little Mount Sion was opened in 1720 and here to prove it is the cover page of the published version of the sermon preached on the occasion. The story was told by C.H. Strange in 1949. 'Early in the history of Tunbridge Wells we find a strong body of Presbyterians, but they had some difficulty in establishing themselves. So opposed were all parties to their principles that no person would sell them an inch of ground. Having no better accommodation, the ballroom of Mount Ephraim House was licensed for their use, and here they regularly assembled on the Lord's Day. A temporary pulpit was affixed to the wainscot by iron hooks, but this arrangement was soon found to be both inconvenient and objectionable. To their rescue came Mr Jordan, the manufacturer of Tunbridge Ware, of Jordan Lane (now Church Road). Mr Jordan belonged to the Baptist persuasion, and being on friendly terms with Mr Seal, the owner of property on Mount Sion, purchased of him the piece of ground on which they were able to erect a chapel. A map of 1739 shows a plot of ground on Mount Sion to be the property of 'heires of Tho Seal'. Mr Thomas Seal had retired from the hop-growing industry at Maidstone and was a Quaker in religious belief. He was ignorant of Mr Jordan's real intent in the purchase, doubtless supposing he wanted it for an extension of his business of Tunbridge Ware making. The conveyance was therefore made out in Mr Jordan's name, but shortly after transferred to Trustees for the use of the Presbyterian congregation.'

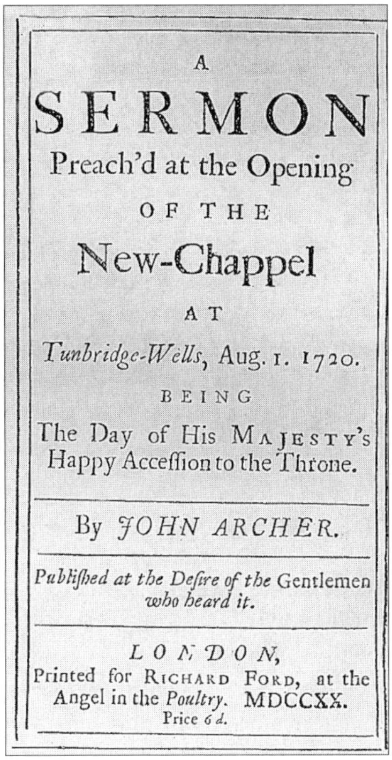
A

SERMON

Preach'd at the Opening

OF THE

New-Chappel

AT

Tunbridge-Wells, Aug. 1. 1720.

BEING

The Day of His MAJESTY'S Happy Acceffion to the Throne.

By *JOHN ARCHER*.

Publifhed at the Defire of the Gentlemen *who heard it.*

LONDON,
Printed for RICHARD FORD, at the Angel in the *Poultry*. MDCCXX.
Price 6 *d*.

Cover Page

What better illustration could be found of the proverb that a little learning is a dangerous thing? The map of 1739 is of course the Bowra plan of 1738 and the reason for 'Heires of Tho Seal' will be dealt with soon; but we already know a lot about the ownership of land on Little Mount Sion and it was Philip if anyone. As for Mr Jordan I have no idea why he comes into the picture. There certainly was a Thomas Jordan connected with the eponymous house at the corner of Church Road, later used by Burrows of Tunbridge Ware fame; but this may be Jordan's only conection with the industry and his religious beliefs and his role, if any, in the purchase of the chapel site are mysteries. The story, by the way, hardly reflects great credit on Jordan or the Presbyterians; nor does it fit the idea that Mr Seal was a Quaker, for as such he would surely have had no objection to selling his land to Nonconformists; indeed a chapel would have been preferable to the Tunbridge Ware workshops he was given the impression were to be built on his land. The source of the story about the hop-growing Seal of Maidstone on the other hand is known. It appeared locally in Colbran's 1840 *New Guide for Tunbridge Wells* but it originates in the autobiography of the 18th-century actress George Anne Bellamy. George Anne's stage career lasted from 1742 to 1770. She played in Dublin and at Covent Garden and was associated with Sheridan and Garrick. Her position was 'below the greatest actresses of her day' but she was petite, fair, blue-eyed and very beautiful. The story goes thus:

> Mount Sion was once the property of the mother of the celebrated actress George Anne Bellamy, who was the daughter of an eminent farmer and hop planter at Maidstone, named Seal. He was one of the people called quakers and grew so opulent as to be enabled to purchase an estate at Tunbridge Wells, called Mount Sion. Dying young and intestate, his whole fortune fell into the hands of his widow who married a second husband, named Busby, who was so involved in debt that his wife's fortune was not adequate to pay them, and herself and daughter were left destitute of support. Before this sad reverse of fortune, she had furnished her houses on Mount Sion and let them during the season to persons of the first distinction. One of those who occasionally occupied these houses was Mrs Godfrey, sister to the great Duke of Marlborough, who contracted such a friendship for Mrs Busby and her daughter that she offered to bring up the latter in every respect like her own. This offer, though declined at first in the prosperous circumstances of Mrs Busby, was now gratefully accepted.

The puzzle is where George Anne Bellamy, who certainly existed, got the story of Mr Seal the hop-planting Quaker for whose existence there is no evidence. There may well have been a rich hop farmer of Maidstone whose daughter dared to elope from her boarding school and his name may have been Seal but neither I nor the people at Maidstone have heard of him. A William Seale appears in the Rate Books of Maidstone in 1698 paying a bit above the average but there is no will at Maidstone or at the PRO. Martine Seale of Yalding left property to his brother William in a will dated 6 July 1699. Another line of enquiry which rapidly runs into the sand is the Quaker connection. It appears that all the early registers of births and deaths of the Society of Friends in Kent have been lost and this promising source of information is unavailable. The *Dictionary of National Biography* mentions an incident in George Anne's life when 'An abduction by Lord Byron led to a severe illness after which she took refuge with some Quaker relatives in Essex'. In the headquarters of the Society of Friends in London there is a letter which mentions a donation to George Anne by Dr Fothergill (who was a Quaker). In his youth he had known some of her relations on her mother's side and had received testimony of her character from her 'former lively intimate', Mary Wordley, a teacher and preacher among the Quakers. All this helps little in connecting the Quaker Seals with Mount Sion; but somehow or other George Anne made the connection.

The story goes on to recount how George Anne herself came into existence. Mrs Busby's daughter, Miss Seal, was placed in a boarding school in Queen's Square, London, presumably by Mrs Godfrey. Before marrying Colonel Godfrey, Arabella Chruchill had attracted the Duke of York, later James II, by a fall from a horse and fortuitous display of upper leg; and perhaps acting in character she does not seem to have been as careful in supervising her new ward as she might, for it was not long before the teen-age schoolgirl eloped with Lord Tyrawley. He set up his mistress in elegant apartments in Somerset House, where he was all attention. After a while, however, he had to visit his family home and was there persuaded to engage himself to some sort of dynastic marriage. He wrote to Miss Seal, explaining that he was forced to go though with the marriage for family reasons, but he loved only her and would find a way of returning. By some incredible mishap this letter was delivered into the hands of his intended wife, so that not only did the family marriage fall through but also his relationship with Miss Seal, who then married a ship's master, Captain Bellamy. Confronted, however, by the untimely arrival of a baby daughter to his new wife, the Captain cast off in a huff.

The birth took place, according to the actress, at Fingal, in Ireland, on St George's Day 1731 and she was christened George Anne in mistake for Georgiana. Lord Tyrawley acknowledged the paternity of the baby and placed her in a convent in Boulogne until the age of eleven when she returned to England and began to mix with her father's associates. How this led to her acting career can be read up by those interested; but we must face the prosaic facts of Little Mount Sion – and its second legend.

Philip Seale's two lodging houses became in time a continuous terrace which was known as Sion Crescent or Queen Anne's Mansion. I have not seen any use of the second name before the 20th century and cannot say when it was first used or why; but it certainly featured in Luke Pearce's *Historical Associations of Royal Tunbridge Wells from 1606 to 1909* where he says: 'The historic building at Mount Sion facing the High Street is known as QUEEN ANNE'S MANSION'. Camburn then referred to it, perhaps taking his cue from Luke Pearce or perhaps not, in the caption to the postcard photograph which heads this chapter and which illustrated an article in the *Kent & Sussex Courier* in 1913. 'Local tradition has it,' said the reporter, 'that in the house with the Georgian porch Queen Anne lodged when a visitor at Tunbridge Wells.' This would be very slender proof on its own but a little indirect backing is provided by the story of Miss Seal. The link with Queen Anne is through Sarah, Duchess of Marlborough, who was very close to the Queen. So, if the Duke's sister Arabella (Mrs Godfrey) stayed on Little Mount Sion, why not the Duchess? There are several stories about the Duchess and Beau Nash but they are much, much later; and there is the myth about the Duke of Marlborough having stayed in a house which did not then exist on the top of Mount Sion where Marlborough House was later built (see chapter 20). Two half-truths, however, do not have to add up to one whole and three dodgy stories do not necessarily reinforce one another. No harm in speculating, though; and if Sarah's sister-in-law stayed on Mount Sion, why not Sarah's friend Anne, although it has to be said that Arabella and Sarah did not get on well together, the Duchess referring scornfully to Arabella's 'Train of Bastards'. However, Anne certainly did visit Tunbridge Wells, not as Queen but as Princess: in 1670 at the age of five and 1674 aged nine; in 1684 the year after her marriage to George Prince of Denmark; in 1686, possibly 1687 and certainly 1688 the year of the 'warming pan' birth; in 1691, possibly 1696, and then in 1697 which is probably the year her son, the Duke of Gloucester, slipped on the muddy Walks; and possibly in 1698 to discover that the paving she had commissioned was not done; and never again. Whether Princess Anne ever stayed with Philip Seale, who knows? It is not impossible. In 1688 she might just have enjoyed the brand-new first house; in 1696-8 she could have stayed at either. The Camburn postcard says she stayed at the one with the big porch and that was the second house. From flights of speculation, it is time now to return to the dull and bourgeois world of map and document, not, however, before wishing that someone sometime will explain how George Anne Bellamy came to associate the name Seal with Mount Sion.

Philip Seale seems to have emerged into the local community, whether from Tonbridge, from one of the surrounding villages or from further afield, without revealing any traces of his background. There were other Seales around in the late 17th century. Children of one Richard Seale were christened at the Chapel of King Charles the Martyr in the 1690s; John Seale was paying rates in 1692 and in 1694 he was named in the register as reputed father of Jane Bartlemer's bastard son John; and William Seale of Maidstone and Martine Seale of Yalding with his brother William have already been mentioned. John Seale, a Tonbridge cordwainer, possibly the reputed father and ratepayer, leased from Sir Thomas Meeres in 1709 a small farm which bounded to the east on a highway called 'Leawe' (Lew?). This suggests a connection with the Southborough cordwainer, William Seale who, with his six children, was mentioned in 1763 in Mary Seale's will. No relationship was specified but I suppose a distant one existed. This hint excepted, I have found no evidence of relationships between any of these other Seales and Philip at the turn of the century. Philip must have been born around the 1660s and seems to have married twice. By his first wife, Elizabeth, he had a son William, whose baptism I have not found but who was a cordwainer in East Greenwich when Philip wrote his will in 1737. Perhaps this is where the family originated. By 1687 they were in Tunbridge Wells and two sons and a daughter were born in 1689, 1691 and 1693. Philip's second wife, as we have seen, was Mary Combridge from Groombridge; and since the next child was a girl called Mary, born in 1697, it can be assumed that she was the first child of the second marriage. Two more daughters followed and finally, to crown Philip's triumphal year, a son Thomas was born in 1702, the year when he became a landowner – see the family tree in chapter 15, page 185.

Separate records for Tunbridge Wells christenings start only in 1729 but the Tonbridge register names Mary as daughter of 'Phil Glazier of the Wells' and Thomas as son of 'Phil and Mary of the Wells'. Although cordwaining seems to have run in the family, Philip himself was a plumber and glazier by trade. He also did some painting. By 1709, from which year the Vestry Books of King Charles the Martyr survive, 'Mr Seale' is well established and payments of from shillings to pounds appear each year for glazing work (and in 1712 for glazing and painting) until 1730 when his son Thomas takes over. Philip was evidently a useful, responsible chap, for in 1714 he is repaid the five shillings he had paid to Henry Walker 'for Carrig for a pack of cloth'; and much earlier, in 1698, his name appears in the Tonbridge Parish Overseers' Accounts:

Paid to Philip Seale for Reliefe of a Travailer brought to bed at the Wells of two children	£00 15 07
More for her reliefe and for a coffin for those children	2s 6d

Remember also that in 1718 Philip signed the Probate Inventory of Thomas Mathews of the *Compasses* and probably wrote out the whole thing on his own whereas William Baines could only make his mark (see page 72).

Richard Constable was buried at Speldhurst on 27 October 1702 and it seems more than a coincidence that the sale of freeholds by the Earl of Buckingham to Philip Seale and to Winefrith Brooke took place less than a month later. The executor of Constable's will, made a few days before his death but not proved until 1 November the following year, was Francis Combridge, father-in-law, as we have seen, of Philip Seale and, according to the will, brother-in-law of Richard Constable himself. Richard had no surviving children and left all his freehold property to his brother John, who must have been around the same age. Be that as it may, the conjunction of events turned out favourably for Philip Seale who was able to lock away the precious piece of parchment, having first written his name on the outside as shown on page 156 above. Straggling and untidy as the handwriting is, I have no doubt, comparing it with Philip's signature on his will and with the 1718 Inventory, that it is his.

The 1700 Deed of Assignment says that the two houses are occupied by Philip Seale and William Fry and the Poor Rate record confirms that William Fry paid rates on the second house in 1704. William Fry was married to Philip's sister and it seems that these two took on the running of the second lodging house until they moved to their own Sion Lodge (see chapter 22). After them one Edward Waggon (or Waghorne) took over for a few years to be followed by Philip himself. These were prosperous years and young Thomas was growing up and following his father's trade. Then in 1721 he married Priscilla Wagon. She was the daughter of Samuel Wagon, a bricklayer of 'the Culverdens', and it may be coincidence that Edward Waghorne (the spelling seems to have been discretionary) had been living next door as Thomas grew up – but I suspect not. He was only 19 and I daresay his parents thought he was a bit young. We can imagine the arguments … but anyway it happened. On 17 November 1721 a marriage settlement was executed and on the 19th they were wed. Luckily for us the settlement provides a few interesting details. The second house was vested in Philip in trust for Thomas and Priscilla and any subsequent family. They were to have half the 'garden plot lying next over the way by the front of the said messuage' – the whole garden being divided in two equal parts at the joint charge of the owners. This refers of course to the present parking lot. The wording 'next over the way by the front' leaves no doubt, to my

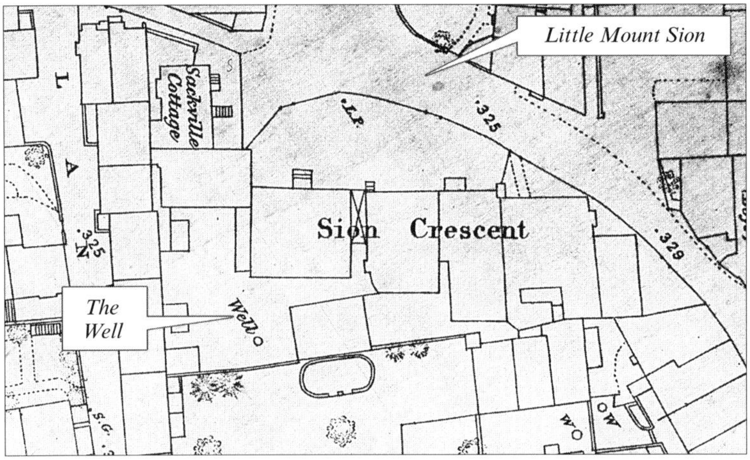

Ordnance Survey 1866

mind, that it was used as a garden. By this time it must have been well established. What did they plant? Flowers or vegetables or both? And how did they divide the planting after the Settlement? It would be nice to have a picture. True there was a road between house and garden but it was only an earth track and not much used I imagine. The newly-weds were also to have free use of the 'draw well' of Philip's house, keeping the bucket and kerb in proper repair. The Ordnance Survey map surveyed in 1866 shows where it was. Next came two stables, each fit for four horses, and a coach house and hayloft next to the north-east end of the house – that is, looking at Bowra, the left-hand side of the house. Finally, Thomas and Priscilla were to have the three-acre field abutting the lands of Thomas Goodall Esq. on the west and those of Nicholas Wood on the east (i. e. the field in the Madeira Park area marked 'Moyce' on the Partition Plan of 1686).

Whatever the parents' feelings may have been about their son's marriage, they were no doubt solaced by the prompt arrival on 4 September 1722 of a grandson, baby Thomas, guarantor of the continuation of the line. Two granddaughters followed – Mary in 1723, and another Priscilla in 1725. Business must have been flourishing. This was the period of Bell Causey, before the arrival of the great Beau Nash in 1735; but there were plenty of aristocratic hypochondriacs and pleasure seekers with money to burn. The Prince of Wales, for instance, came in 1724. Philip had a shop on the Walks as well as his lodging houses; and he continued to do odd glazing jobs for the Chapel of Charles the Martyr but, by 1730, he was perhaps feeling his age, as his son's name starts to appear in the Vestry accounts from that date. Then, in 1735, the very year of Beau Nash's arrival, tragedy struck.

In September Thomas junior died and a month later his father – their ages 13 and 33: both Thomases gone, the male line extinguished at a stroke. Philip sat down and wrote his will in 1737; in November 1739 his wife died and in April 1740 he joined her. All this explains, of course, why Bowra's map, made in 1738, shows Philip Seale in his own house but the second house attributed to the heirs of Thomas Seale; and the events behind the bare label, 'Heires of Tho Seal', must have been fresh in the mind of the mapmaker as he went about his business. Let us, however, in a new chapter turn from these scenes of sorrow back to the year 1731 and to the Presbyterian Chapel or 'Meeting House' just down the hill. This was the year when a new minister took up his post – Thomas Bayes, to my mind the greatest man to have lived in Tunbridge Wells.

Chapter 14

Thomas Bayes

The story of the founding of the Presbyterian Meeting House in Little Mount Sion was told in the previous chapter, page 161. The date of opening was 1 August 1720. This is certainly the date on the printed copy of the sermon preached by the Rev. John Archer on the occasion. Further circumstantial details are given in an article on 'Early Presbyterianism at Tunbridge Wells' in the *Journal of the Presbyterian Historical Society of England*. 'The day of the opening of the chapel happened to be the anniversary of the accession of George I and Mr Archer, in his sermon, took occasion to express the loyalty of the Dissenters to the throne'. Queen Anne did die on 1 August, on a Sunday morning in 1714, and so I suppose the Rev. Archer did his stuff on 1 August 1720. He relinquished the pastorate in 1731 and died two years later; and was replaced by the man I have called the greatest Tunbridge Wells resident.

The Presbyterian Chapel drawn by JJ Dodd about 1830

Thomas Bayes was born in 1702, the son of the Rev. Joshua Bayes, a Presbyterian pastor in London. There has been a great deal of interest in his life recently in mathematical circles; but the first in the field perhaps was J.D. Holland of Standard Telephones and Cables who gathered together as much as was then known in a scholarly article published in 1962 in the *Journal of the Royal Statistical Society* (the Tunbridge Wells Reference Library has a copy). Thomas Bayes was the eldest son of the Rev. Joshua Bayes, a Presbyterian pastor who finished his career at Leather Lane in Hatton Garden, London, where Thomas assisted his father before moving to Tunbridge Wells. Joshua Bayes was a man of some wealth and gave his son a 'liberal education for the ministry', probably at a dissenting academy called Coward's in Moorfields, London, followed by a time at Edinburgh University. His Tutor in London was John Eames, FRS, who was a friend of Isaac Newton and later, in 1742, was to be a sponsor for Thomas Bayes' election to the Royal Society. Interestingly, one of Bayes' few published works was, in 1736, a defence of the logical foundations of Newton's calculus against attack by Bishop Berkeley. It is not known why Bayes came to Tunbridge Wells; but it was a fashionable place at the time and also not too far from Thomas's home, London. He would have been able to converse with some of his intellectual equals when they visited the Wells. These included the mathematician Robert Smith, Master of Trinity College, Cambridge; the second Earl of Stanhope, one of Thomas's sponsors to the Royal Society, who, according to Mrs 'blue-stocking' Montague, was 'always making mathematical scratches in his pocket book'; and William Whiston who succeeded Newton as Professor of Mathematics at Cambridge.

Whiston met Thomas in 1746 as recorded in his memoirs: 'On August 24th this year 1746 … I breakfasted at Mr Bay's, a dissenting Minister at Tunbridge Wells … and a very good mathematician also'. It is a pity no one recorded where Thomas Bayes was living. Bayes was interested in electricity: in notebooks found after his death there are references to an 'electrifying machine' on which he seems to have written a report in Paris dated July 4th 1746. He was also a Greek scholar – 'the best …he had ever met' in the words of the Rev. Onely, rector of Speldhurst. Despite his abilities Thomas does not seem to have been a great success as a minister. A 19th-century church history calls him 'a gentleman of fortune but not a popular preacher'. In 1746 his father died and he inherited his father's library and £2,000 – about half a million, say, in today's money; but Thomas must have been of frugal habits. He never married and left most of his inheritance to be divided among family and friends. Among his bequests was one which throws an enigmatic light on his life in Tunbridge Wells. By his will, made in December 1760, he left '£500 and my watch made by Ellicot and all my linen and wearing apparel and household stuff to Sarah Jeffery daughter of John Jeffery (a holloware turner) living with her father at the corner of Jourdains Lane'. You can imagine that there has been much ribald speculation in academic circles about the reason why bachelor Thomas should have left a small fortune, not to mention his best watch and all his household stuff, to a local girl; but I have put forward a theory which is equally romantic in a different way – for in the course of other researches I had met this Sarah Jeffery. The striking thing about her is that she was evidently proud of her family name, because when she married she chose a wheelwright named Jeffery and when he died she married a tallowchandler named Jeffery – so that maiden, wife and wife again, she remained Sarah Jeffery from the cradle to the grave.

Now, Thomas Bayes' will indicates that Sarah was unmarried at the time it was made in 1760 and her father's will of 1769 says she is married to Robert the wheelwright. If we assume that she married half way between these two dates and was 20 years old, then it follows that she was sweet 16 when Thomas Bayes died. Thomas was, as we have seen, a bachelor and, rather than set up house on his own, probably lived in lodgings; and the Jeffery home on the corner of Jordans Lane was a lodging house. Jordans Lane is, of course, the old name for Church

Road and the house on the corner is the present no.69 London Road – see the photograph below.

No. 69 London Road

The Jeffery family were Nonconformists (see chapter 24 page 350) and the religious affiliation of the lodging house keeper might well have recommended this house to the newly arrived minister in 1731. If this speculation is correct, then the picture begins to take shape of the bachelor mathematician being a member of the household when Mrs Jeffery gave birth to a baby girl around 1740 and his then taking a fatherly interest in her through infancy and adolescence to the nubile stage at which he took his farewell with the gift of a small fortune. You may be interested to know that these speculations have received worldwide dissemination through correspondence with one statistician at the University of Natal and an article in the *IMS Bulletin* by another from the University of Western Ontario – such is the fame of our Little Mount Sion minister of long ago.

Be all that as it may, Thomas retired in 1752 but seems to have continued to live in Tunbridge Wells and perhaps it was during this period that he wrote the essay for which he is famous. He died in April 1761 aged 59, and is buried in the family vault at Bunhill Fields, in London. He left his papers and valuable library to his successor, William Johnston, and it seems to have been lucky that his essay was rescued for posterity. His friend Richard Price was going through his papers in 1763, found the essay and read it to the Royal Society. It is called 'An Essay Toward Solving a Problem in the Doctrine of Chances' and is the foundation of what is now known as Bayesian Statistics. For those interested, Bayes' theorem states 'Under the observation S the (conditional) probability of the hypothesis H is proportional to the product of the (a priori) probability of H and the probability of S, if H is true'. Which I think has something to do with working out the probability of something occurring again if it has happened before.

After Thomas Bayes the Presbyterian Chapel entered upon the most prosperous period of its history. The new minister, William Johnston, was a Scotsman, born probably in Dumfries in 1715 and ordained on 8 June 1737. He was then minister at Wisbech, Cambridgeshire, before coming to Little Mount Sion in 1752. I have always imagined that he brought a Scots accent with him. Colbran, 1840, says that he was a native of Scotland and praises his literary acquirements and gentlemanly deportment. In the understated terms of the *Presbyterian Historical Society Journal* his 'ministry was acceptable'. He lived, I am pretty sure, in Belgrove House (see pp.64-5); at least he paid the Poor Rate between 1765 and 1776 on a house in that location. It was, I suppose, conveniently close to his chapel and to those of his flock who lived on Mount Sion; it also had to be large enough for the six children who are buried with him at Speldhurst – for Johnston was no bachelor like his predecessor. Anyway he seems to have been a success. During his ministry the chapel was well attended and even patronised by some of the nobility, among whom was the Duke of Leeds, no doubt driven there in his famous coach and six. Johnston died on 2 March 1776, at Belgrove House apparently, and was buried at Speldhurst. A sample of Johnston's pulpit style has survived at Dr Williams's Library; and provides, as bonus, a sidelight on the story of Fairlawn House (see

Museum catalogue entry and photograph

chapter 24). The photograph on the previous page, of the tomb in Speldhurst churchyard, was brought into the Museum by the great-granddaughter of William Johnston in the 1930s – as shown by the label at the top of the photograph. If any reader, by the remotest chance, should know anything about this lady or her relatives, please come forward because the statisticians of the world are desperate to know what her ancestor did with the library left to him by the great Thomas Bayes. Johnston's death marked the beginning of a decline in the fortunes of the Meeting House, punctuated nevertheless by five occasions of celebrity when John Wesley preached there – although maybe there are not so many places where he did not preach! For example, his Journal for Monday, 6 December 1784 reads: 'I preached at Tunbridge Wells, but not without difficulty; part of the road being made scarcely passable through the abundance of rain. I preached in the large Presbyterian Meeting House, but the violent rain thinned the congregation'.

After Johnston the Chapel entered a period of decline. The Wesleyans used it in the early 19th century but, being denied its use after a while, built their own chapel in Vale Royal where a successor building still stands. In consequence the congregation fell off and 'the Chapel in Mount Sion, after being closed in 1814, appears to have year after year advanced in dilapidation'. Then on 9 March 1830 a new beginning was announced in the *Maidstone Journal*: 'It has long been a subject of regret to see the venerable edifice on Mount Sion, called the Presbyterian Meeting House, falling rapidly into decay, in consequence of the discontinuance of divine service there for several years past; but we are at length happy to find that it is soon likely to be rescued from the ravaging hand of time, by being put into thorough repair and converted into an Independent Chapel which (according to the plans and specifications) is to be completed in July next, under the superintendence of John Davies Esq., architect, Devonshire Square, London.' According to Colbran's 1840 *Guide*, it was Thomas Wilson Esq. of Highbury who was responsible for the idea. He was shown the Chapel while on a visit to the Wells and, having obtained the agreement of the surviving trustees for the use of the Chapel by the 'Congregational body – commonly called Independents – ', he organised the work and paid most of the bill which came to 'upwards of £700'. The Rev. Benjamin Slight, formerly of Highbury College, preached his first sermon in the Chapel on 8 August 1830 and the following year was confirmed as minister, which position he still held (living in Grove Hill Road) at the time Colbran's 1840 Guide was written and where he remained I assume until the Independents built 'the present beautiful structure on Mount Pleasant' (now Habitat). In 1854 the Primitive Methodists engaged the Chapel but only for three years until they had built their own chapel in the Camden Road. After 1857, therefore, the religious function of the building can be said to cease. Luke Pearce says somewhat elliptically that the 'Friends also appeared on the scene prior to 1887' but I think it was Mrs Murrell's Mission Hall at 63, Mount Sion, that was patronised by the Quakers – see chapter 19 page 279. The chapel building did, however, continue in use as a school for the nonconformist community. The renovation of the building in 1830 involved the placing of a gallery the whole length of the building in front (presumably the Little Mount Sion side), the removal of a vestry and the building of a schoolroom. Colbran, 1840, gives a good description but does not explain the gallery: 'The Chapel is a plain substantial building, nearly square – 40 feet by 34, it is distinguished by no architectural attractions; but its interior is comfortable and commodious. It is capable of seating 450 persons; allowing 400 for the Chapel itself, and 50 for the adjoining schoolroom, which is separated from the Chapel by sliding shutters ... During the week the schoolroom is used for a Female School, on the plan of the British and Foreign School Society; the average attendance at which is 60 girls'. National schools, like Murray House, were for Church of England children: British schools were for dissenters. The chapel is clearly marked 'British School (Infants)' on the 1/500 Ordnance Survey map. A report in the *Tunbridge Wells Gazette* of 6 July 1860 shows that the school was flourishing at that date and gives a picture of its activities.

> British School Examinations. The examination of the children taught in these schools took place last Friday evening, at the old chapel, Mount Sion. The chair was taken by Mr Finch and the examination of the scholars conducted by Rev G Jones, Rev WP Lyon and the teachers. The subjects upon which the children were questioned were as follows: The Oak – its properties and uses; rivers, their origin, characteristics and usefulness; scripture knowledge; mental arithmetic; grammar; general history; and domestic economy, including household management generally, and the work of domestic servants and housewives; upon which latter very useful and necessary branch of female education the girls showed a degree of proficiency which spoke well, not only for their capacity in receiving instruction but for their teachers' perseverance in imparting it. Several pieces of music, having reference to the subjects on which the pupils were examined, were sung; and an address was delivered by Rev George Jones to the parents upon their responsibilities in connection with the work of educating the children. At the end the National Anthem was sung and cheers were given for Mr Finch and the teachers.

The school continued probably until 1875. *Mathieson's Directory* in 1867 lists the 'British and Infants School' in Little Mount Sion and the 1871 census shows the 'District Schools' next to the *Jolly Sailor*. In 1873 however the Trustees decided to sell the whole property. An application dated 6 August 1873 was made to the Charity Commissioners explaining that a new chapel was to be built in Albion Road using the proceeds from the sale of the Little Mount Sion chapel. This was expected to raise £1,000 and the new chapel, the land being given free, would cost £2,000. The Commission asked for a copy of the original Trust Deed of 1758 but no trace could be found of it. A public meeting was advertised in the *Tunbridge Wells Gazette* of 18 December 1874 and was held at the Chapel on 26 December under the chairmanship of Mr John Remington Mills. The sale of the old chapel and application of the proceeds to the new building were approved. An order under the Charitable Trust Act, in respect of the 'Protestant Dissenting Chapel at Mount Sion', was issued on 5 February 1875 and a sale was held on 11 June the same year. The Sale Notice and Particulars are in the Reference Library and the

Sale Notice is reproduced below. The Conditions of Sale declare, surprisingly, that the vendors are to retain all the title deeds, although the purchaser may ask for attested copies at his own expense. Reference is made to indentures of 22 and 23 February 1758 but in such a way as to suggest that the documents themselves are lost. This would be the original Trust Deed which could not be found for the Commission; but why it was not dated earlier than 1758 is a puzzle. The two dates suggest a conveyance by Lease and Release. This was just into the beginning of William Johnston's pastorate and the congregation was flourishing. Perhaps it was nothing more than a change of trustees. I do not know the outcome of the sale. The 1881 census gives no indication what happened; indeed the building seems to have been empty. In the 1886 *Directory* however, next to the *Standard* (the *Jolly Sailor* under a new name) is to be found Timberlake's Tricycle Works. An advertisement in a guide book published without a date, but probably of about 1897 (*Tunbridge Wells of Today* by Martin and Row), gives some information on this attractively named enterprise:

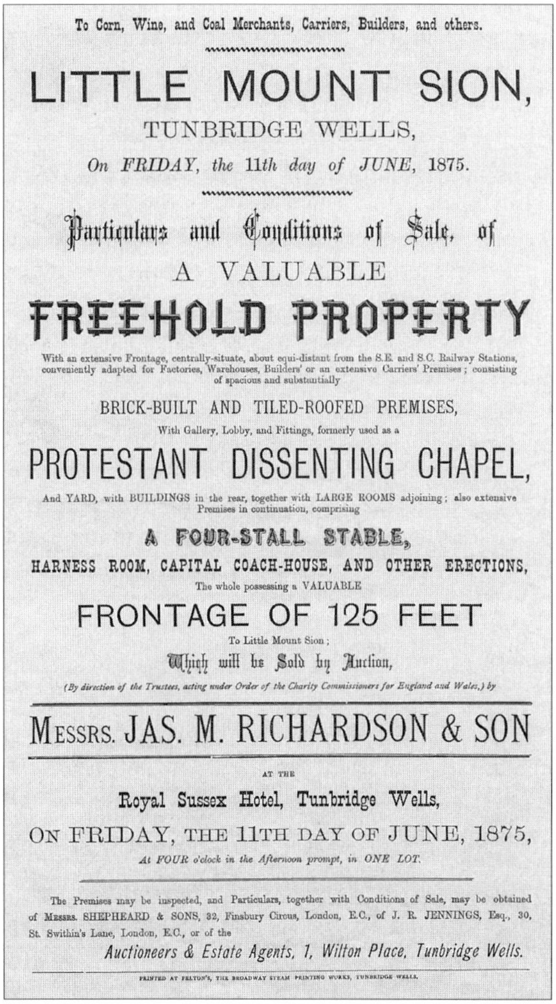
To Corn, Wine, and Coal Merchants, Carriers, Builders, and others.

LITTLE MOUNT SION,

TUNBRIDGE WELLS,

On *FRIDAY*, the 11*th day* of *JUNE*, 1875.

Particulars and Conditions of Sale, of

A VALUABLE

FREEHOLD PROPERTY

With an extensive Frontage, centrally-situate, about equi-distant from the S.E. and S.C. Railway Stations, conveniently adapted for Factories, Warehouses, Builders' or an extensive Carriers' Premises; consisting of spacious and substantially

BRICK-BUILT AND TILED-ROOFED PREMISES,

With Gallery, Lobby, and Fittings, formerly used as a

PROTESTANT DISSENTING CHAPEL,

And YARD, with BUILDINGS in the rear, together with LARGE ROOMS adjoining; also extensive Premises in continuation, comprising

A FOUR-STALL STABLE,

HARNESS ROOM, CAPITAL COACH-HOUSE, AND OTHER ERECTIONS,

The whole possessing a VALUABLE

FRONTAGE OF 125 FEET

To Little Mount Sion;

Which will be Sold by Auction,

(By direction of the Trustees, acting under Order of the Charity Commissioners for England and Wales,) by

MESSRS. JAS. M. RICHARDSON & SON

AT THE

Royal Sussex Hotel, Tunbridge Wells,

ON FRIDAY, THE 11TH DAY OF JUNE, 1875,

At FOUR o'clock in the Afternoon prompt, in ONE LOT.

The Premises may be inspected, and Particulars, together with Conditions of Sale, may be obtained of MESSRS. SHEPHEARD & SONS, 32, Finsbury Circus, London, E.C., of J. R. JENNINGS, Esq., 30, St. Swithin's Lane, London, E.C., or of the

Auctioneers & Estate Agents, 1, Wilton Place, Tunbridge Wells.

PRINTED AT FELTON'S, THE BROADWAY STEAM PRINTING WORKS, TUNBRIDGE WELLS.

Meeting House sale notice 1875

> C.Timberlake – Cycle Manufacturer – Wholesale Factor & Agent – Has a tremendous stock of every good make of Cycles, Sewing Machines, Perambulators. Mail carts, Invalid Chairs, Pianos, Organs etc A large number of second-hand Cycles from £1 upwards and in good condition – Cycling taught by efficient instructors – Large Riding School – Repairs by skilled workmen on the premises.

It seems that the firm was manufacturing bicycles and tricycles in the old chapel and using the large unobstructed floor space for a Cycling School! For whatever reason however Timberlake's Tricycles never became a household word. The 'bicycle factory' was still there in 1889 but by 1892 Benoy and Sons had taken over the Chapel building. In 1892 they were builders, in 1893 it was a paperhanger's stores and in 1895 it was the Benoy workshop. By 1898 things had changed again and the occupiers were Dunkley and Rogers, mineral water manufacturers, and so it went on. When Johnson took an interior photograph in 1934 it was the Tunbridge Wells Gas Company which was using the old chapel as a workshop and it continued in gas company ownership until quite recently. Splendidly refurbished in the 1980s by the Tunbridge Wells Typesetters, it is now in use by a firm of accountants. Let us hope it continues to find a useful function.

It can be seen from the Sale Notice reproduced above that the Chapel building itself was not all that was on offer in 1875. There were 'extensive Premises in continuation', consisting of stables and a coach house. These seem to have become an undistinguished building, called 'The Forge', which stood until recently on the site of the old cottage and garden shown on the Tithe map between the Chapel and the Twitten leading from Sion Crescent into Frog Lane. This was presumably the 'garden and cottage adjoining' which is mentioned in Colbran's account of the transaction between Jordan the Baptist and 'Mr Seal'. Curiously Bowra does not show the cottage on his map and Barrow shows only a narrow row of stables at the back of the site. The Tithe map shows the building also at the back of the site and the Award describes it as a cottage and garden, belonging to the Chapel Trustees and occupied by Mrs Brisenden. The 1841 census records Rebecca Brissenden, a 75-year-old widow living with Fanny Wells, aged 30, and her five-year-old daughter Fanny in Frog Lane. This refers I assume to the chapel cottage although it was not strictly in Frog Lane. In 1851 a house is enumerated in Frog Lane between Henry Peerless (York Villa – see chapter 16) and Jane Lipscomb (Frog Cottage); this house, occupied by one James Wraight, might perhaps be Rebecca Brissenden's old home but I cannot be sure. In 1861 the situation is no better. A cottage and a

Little Mount Sion by David Johnson 1934

shoemaker's shop are listed between Henry Peerless and Sackville Cottage: the cottage is occupied by a young journeyman butcher named Thomas Burr and might be the chapel cottage. By 1875, anyhow, the cottage and garden had disappeared and in their place was the 'Forge' building of recent memory, comprising the 'Four-stall stable, harness room, capital coach-house and other erections' proclaimed in the Sale Notice. There is a plan and elevation of this building in the Planning Records. The index shows '1870, Stephens, Stables ...'; but there is no attached application form and no other date and the marking of some, mainly internal, walls in red suggests that the application was for alterations rather than new building. The plan can be related to Johnson's photograph above. Where Johnson shows the little hooded car sticking its nose in there were four horse stalls with a harness room and corn bin at the back; where 'E. Powell' is written over the doorway was the coach-house. Alongside and behind the coach-house was a large 'warehouse for beer' and a dung-pit adjoined the public footpath or twitten. The name Stephens echoes the notes at the bottom of the Sale Particulars which say that the Chapel and Vestry Rooms are 'in hand' but that the remainder of the property is in the occupation of Mr Horatio Stephens who is under notice to quit at Midsummer next. The Sale Particulars, having described the Chapel and adjoining 'Vestry Room 27 ft by 22 ft, with a spacious Room in the rear 21 ft by 14 ft' go on to say: 'Contiguous are the Schools now fitted up as a Four-stall Stable' and so on. This is curious because, as we have seen above, Colbran, 1840, said that the schoolroom was connected to the Chapel by sliding shutters. It seems, therefore, that this schoolroom must have become, by 1875, the 'vestry room with spacious room in rear' of the Sale Particulars. The dimensions given, taken together, correspond reasonable well with those of the building shown on the Ordnance Survey map; and which can be seen in Johnson's photograph, next to the Chapel, with the little sporty car nosing into the large open door. This building was demolished in the recent renovation of the Chapel and has been replaced by an open garage with living accommodation over. If these suppositions are correct, then the 'forge' building next door was used as 'the Schools' before being 'fitted up as a Four-stall Stable'. The building could have replaced Mrs Brissenden's cottage between 1841 and the date of the Ordnance Survey map on which the present building is clearly shown. On the other hand, the 'Female British and Infants School, at Mount Sion Chapel' is listed among the charitable institutions in *Colbran's Guide* as early as 1840. An alternative theory is that the auctioneer simply got it wrong and the 'Forge' never was the 'Schools'. How did this building acquire the name 'Forge'? This question has arisen recently in connection with an application to demolish it. The answer, as far as I can see, is that in 1898 and 1900 (*Kelly's Directories*) it was in use by Richard Roberts FRCVS as a 'veterinary shoeing forge' – rather a far cry from the spreading chestnut image that the conservationists were hoping for. What happened to the building between 1875 and 1900 is difficult to tell from the evidence of the directories. Perhaps Horatio Stephens continued in occupation but his name does not appear at this location in any census or directory;

it does, however, appear in *Kelly's Directory* in 1874 and 1878 when he was living, in somewhat grander style than the 'Forge' connection suggested, in Grove Villa. One problem is that I am not sure whether the street number 16, Little Mount Sion, refers to the 'Forge' or to Sackville Cottage. In chapter 11 I assumed that No.18 was Sackville Cottage but it may well be the house with the tall chimney between Sackville and Sion Crescent. The chapel never had a number and no 14 was certainly the *Jolly Sailor* (*The Standard*).

Having finished the story of the Chapel we must now look at the lower part of Moyce's strip of land going up Little Mount Sion, between the Chapel and the High Street. This was touched on in the previous chapter. Bowra shows the position

Bowra plan 1738

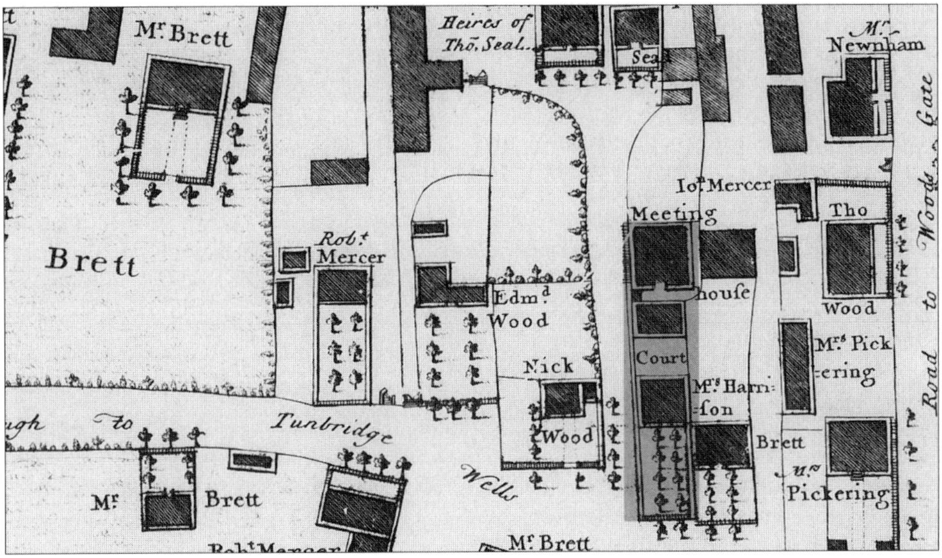

in 1738 see above, shaded grey. At the bottom is 'Harrisons' set back from the High Street with an avenue in front of the house. The labelling is not very happy but 'Mrs Harrison' refers to the house on its left – not the one below, to which the label 'Brett' belongs. The Poor Rate record for 'Harrisons' starts with Mr John Streeter in July 1685, as mentioned before. Thomas Moyce then comes on the scene in 1687 and continues for ten years, to be replaced by his widow until 1700. After this Philip Seale (or tenant for Widow Moyce) takes over. The possibility that the top piece only of the strip was sub-let by Thomas Moyce to begin with and then his widow about 1701 released the whole strip to Seale was advanced in the previous chapter (page 160) to solve the problem of the '4 rod 2 feet' dimension given in the 1700 deed. The house at the bottom of the strip was perhaps lived in by the Moyce family at first. After Philip Seale, in 1704, the Harrisons take over; first Widow Harrison and then, after the gap, Mrs Mary Harrison who goes on until 1740 – and she is obviously the 'Mrs Harrison' of the Bowra plan. Here is the Poor Rate sequence:

1685	Mr John Streeter
1686	Mr John Streeter or Thos Moyce
1687-1697	Thomas Moyce
1698-1700	Widow Moyse
1701-1703	Philip Seale or Tennant for Widd Moyses
1704	Mr Harrison wid for Philip Seale for late widow Moyce
1708-1714	Wid Harryson for Philip Seales
1728-1735	Mrs Mary Harrison for Mr Philip Seale
1736-1739	Mrs Mary Harrison
1740	Mrs Harrison or occ
1741-1742	Mrs Elliott for Mrs Harrisons
1743-1744	Mr Elliott for Mr Harrison
1745-1756	Mrs Knight for Mrs Harrisons
1757-1758	Mrs King for Harrisons
1759	Leonard Scotchburn for late Mrs Harrisons
1760-1797	Leo Scotchburn for late Harrisons

Widow Martha Harrison of Tonbridge made her will on 13 February 1713 giving her son Jonathan £20 and leaving the rest of her real and personal estate to her daughter Mary Harrison who proved her will on 7 May 1717. The witnesses, interestingly, were Philip Seale, Sarah Scoones and Elizabeth Constable. The *Sprange Guides* confirm and continue the Poor Rate sequence for this property and with the Barrow map provide additional confirmation of location. 'Leonard Scotchburn' is listed by Sprange as a lodging house in 1780 and 1786 but in 1797 and 1801 the entry has changed to 'Mrs George Fry, widow, late Scotchburn's'. The transfer is not surprising since Elizabeth Scotchburn married George Fry on 13 May 1770 and George Fry died in November 1791. In 1808 Sprange lists another member of the Fry family, John, in place of George's widow and Barrow's map locates Mr J. Fry at the bottom of Little Mount Sion on the southern side – where we had placed the property anyway on other evidence.

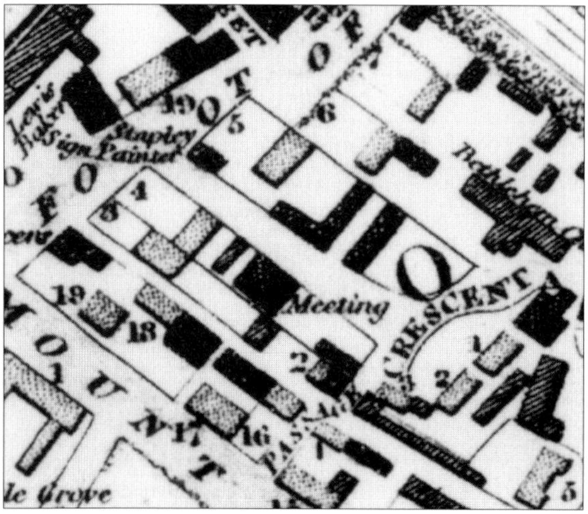

Barrow map 1808

In 1811 Sprange lists Mr Trice as the lodging house keeper for 'Harrisons' but it is in 1817 that the significant change occurs: between York House and Rosebury House Sprange shows 'Montgomery House, Mr Stapley' and 'Wilment Lodge', Ditto'. It seems quite clear that Michael Stapley took over 'Harrisons', renaming it Montgomery House and perhaps built a new house in the back garden. There is a bit of a problem here. On the Bowra map (page 177 above) a building is shown below the 'Meeting House' outlined with a double line. Bowra says in his 'References' that 'The Houses have Double Lines and the Stabling Single Lines round their Plans' and so the building between the Chapel and the court should be a house; but then the Chapel itself has a double line and it is not a house. It is certainly not stabling, however; so the place below might be an adjunct to the Chapel or a private house. Below this he marks a 'Court'. Why should Bowra so label this little area when all over his plan there are spaces which might surely be labelled 'court' with equal justification? If now we look at Barrow's map (previous page), number 4 indicates 'Harrisons' (Mr J. Fry) and between it and the 'Meeting' is a narrow building which looks rather like stabling. Barrow uses dotted shading to show Lodging Houses, black shading for 'Other Houses' and diagonal shading to indicate 'Coach houses, Stables etc'. The trouble is we cannot tell what the shading below the Meeting House is; it looks black, if anything. All in all, then, it seems that there was a building below the Chapel, not necessarily the same in 1808 as in 1738; and there certainly was one in 1817 when Michael Stapley gave it a name and we can follow its history – and perhaps he built it. I do not know where the name 'Montgomery' came from; probably picked from the air by the proud owner like so many other grand names. The name 'Wilment', however, is more interesting and informative, because the Goulden deeds reveal that one of Michael Stapley's sons, who was a half-brother only to the other children, was named William Wilment Stapley. I suggest, therefore, that 'Wilment Lodge' celebrates the maiden name of one of Michael Stapley's wives.

The main house seems to have been demolished between 1828 when it still appears on the map of the Calverley development of that date, and the time of the Tithe map which shows the new development – see right. This consisted of the shops on the High Street between York House and Little Mount Sion (nos 65-69 High Street) which still stand as the Coffee House and the *Dragon Inn* and a row of five cottages climbing the hill behind, which were demolished for car parking in recent years. The shops were known as Montgomery Place and the cottages as Montgomery Cottages.

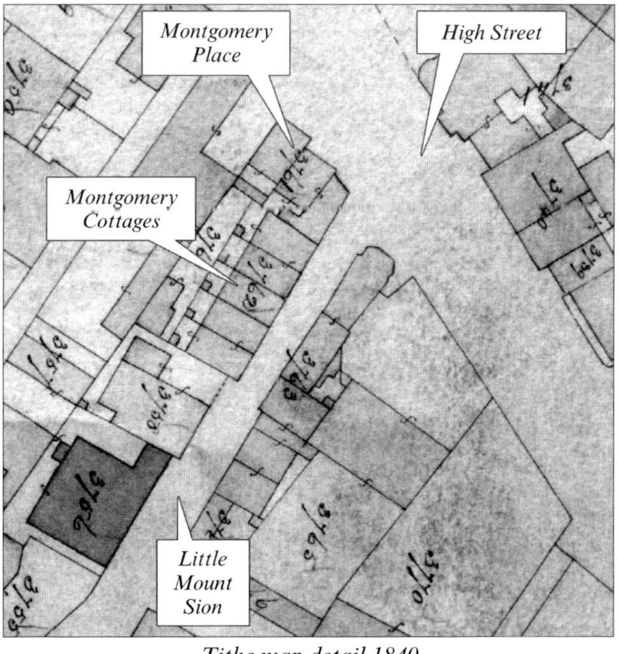

Tithe map detail 1840

Since Michael Stapley died between 1834 and 1837, it seems probable that he was responsible for this scheme and also that it was sold as a consequence of his death. The Tithe Award shows the property in the ownership of Thomas Hodges who was the younger brother of William Hodges the Younger of the *Compasses*. William's great-great-granddaughter, by the way, recently walked into the Reference Library on a visit from Suffolk in search of information about her family – for more on the Hodges connection see page 71. One result of this visit was a copy of the will of William Hodges the Younger. A codicil dated 2 December 1854 reveals that his brother Thomas had died since the making of his original will only a month before; and the Holy Trinity register records the burial of William on 10 January 1855. The brothers, therefore, died within two months of each other. The will shows that the 'several messuages or dwelling houses hereditaments and premises known as the Montgomery houses situate and being on Mount Sion' were owned by William, not Thomas. Either, therefore, the Tithe Award was wrong in attributing ownership to Thomas or Thomas sold to his brother between 1840 and 1854. The name 'Montgomery' is not used in the Tithe Award nor does the Ordnance Survey map show it; but it does appear in the censuses from 1841 onwards and there can be no doubt about its identification. William Hodges left his Montgomery houses in trust for his widow and then his daughter whose husband delighted in the name John Martyr Luck. After his daughter's death they were to pass to the Luck children as tenants in common. What actually happened to the houses subsequently I do not know. The shops were numbered 1, 2 and 3 Montgomery Place. In 1841 number 1 (now 69 High Street) was occupied by James Phippen, a bookseller, and his wife who was a 'Daily Governess'. The Reference Library has a copy of some private research carried out on this gentleman who was a writer and journalist. Born about 1795, Phippen was responsible for a poetic text, beginning with the word 'Infidel' and dated March 1831 which can be seen carved on the High Rocks. In 1835 he wrote an account of the planting of the Royal Victoria Grove on the Common and more particularly of the dinner which followed; this can be seen in the Reference Library. In 1836 he wrote *The Road Guide from London to Tunbridge Wells* and, of particular interest to local historians, he edited Colbran's 1840 *Guide* and I guess wrote most of the text himself. In this task he acknowledged special assistance from Mr Bembridge who was a partner in the Stone firm of solicitors. In later life he left Tunbridge Wells and was for some years Rochester correspondent of the *Maidstone Journal*, before he died in 1862. All three of the occupants of the Montgomery Place shops are of interest. At no 2 (now 67) was Charles Gardiner, the chemist, who later split Rosebury House with John Colbran and built the shop which became Dunkley and Rogers of recent memory. No 2 seems to have been in use as a butcher's shop from 1861 onwards, as it was until 1988. No 3 (65 High Street) was in the continuous occupation, from 1841 to 1881, of Thomas Cripps, described in 1841 as a florist and in 1861 as a nurseryman having 40 acres of land and employing 25 to 30 men. The deposited plan for the South Eastern Railway, 1844, shows that Thomas Cripps had a 'Planted Nursery' and two pieces of 'Wood, Nursery Ground and Stream' on land belonging to the Marquess Camden located roughly where Banner Farm Road now is. It is plainly marked 'Cripps Nursery' on the deposited plan and can be seen on a more accessible map, the one made by Stidolph showing the Tunbridge Wells Local Act District in 1838. The boundary of the nursery coincides in fact with that between South Frith Manor land and the land of the Marquess Camden, a line represented by the eastern extent of the Claremont School grounds and the bottoms of the gardens of the houses at the end of Claremont Gardens and also of Claremont Close. There is in the Frant Road Cemetery a handsome marble obelisk which commemorates 'Thomas Cripps, Founder of Tunbridge Wells Nurseries, who fell asleep on the 17th April 1888 in his 79th year' and two of his sons who died much younger. Colbran's 1850 *Guide* says that Thomas Cripps 'cultivated the rose to a high state of perfection' and I daresay some people would be content to have that as their only memorial.

The *Jolly Sailor* started as the house called Wilment Lodge which it was suggested above was probably built by Michael Stapley between 1811 and 1817. I cannot believe that it was either of the buildings shown by Bowra or Barrow for three reasons, not counting hunch. Firstly, the Barrow map shows a thinner building, possibly stables, in this position; secondly, what can be seen of the building on Johnson's and other similar images does not look like such an old building; and thirdly, because the name proclaims the Stapley family in a way which would hardly have been appropriate to the mere naming of an old building. Be that as it may, there can be no doubt of the connection between Wilment Lodge and the *Jolly Sailor*. The 1841 census shows 'Wellment Lodge' as a beer shop in the charge of Elizabeth Beadle; but in 1851 the enumerator wrote 'Wilment House' and then added underneath, in quotation marks, 'Jolly Sailor beer and lodging house'. The owner in 1841 according to the Tithe Award was Thomas Beeching and the house was empty. Since Beeching was a banker rather than a publican I suspect his interest in the house was connected with a mortgage and very likely with the Stapley family's disposal of its interest. The house obviously came under new management in 1841 and it may be that its history as a beer house, as well as a lodging house, dates from this year. In its time anyhow the *Jolly Sailor* was quite a place. It was much more than a pub; and, although the customers for beer and refreshing liquors may have left no mark on the sawdust of history, the censuses furnish five snapshots of the lodgers at ten-year intervals. It started fairly quietly. In 1841 Elizabeth Beadle was in charge with Mary Diplock, her 20-year-old servant, and there were ten lodgers, nine men and a boy of 12 – four hawkers, three tailors, two engravers and one labourer. In 1851 Richard Apps was the landlord and with him were his daughter, his son who was a coachman and his son's wife; and again there were ten lodgers, eight male and two female – three painters, three labourers, one flyman and three 'unknowns'. In 1861 William and Sarah Hickmott were in charge and had their teenage children, two sons and a daughter, living with them; but the number of lodgers had increased incredibly to forty. There were 19 men, 14 women and seven children making up six families, one with four children, one with three and one with one; and their occupations included hawker, travelling tinker, clerk, painter, servant, bricklayer, sawyer, coal miner and mason. It is difficult to imagine how they all fitted in. The *Sprange Guide* of 1817 gives Wilment Lodge three sitting rooms, three bedrooms and stabling for three horses. This would suggest that only a portion of the house was available for lodging visitors in 1817; or it might revive doubts whether the house of 1817 was not entirely rebuilt or considerably extended before 1861. About this period references to the *Jolly Sailor* appear in the local press. Without looking deliberately I have found two reports and there are probably others. In November 1860 the *Tunbridge Wells Gazette* (which was being produced as we saw on page 99 just on the other side of Little Mount Sion) reported the case of Jane Smith who was found by a policeman on a Monday morning, sitting asleep opposite the *Jolly Sailor*; and in August 1864 Alfred Caffyn, keeper of the *Jolly Sailor*, was prosecuted at the Petty Sessions for being open for the sale of beer during the hours of divine service on Sunday 31 July. Landlords of the *Jolly Sailor* do not seem to have lasted long until Thomas Neale took over. He is to be found in charge in 1871 and again in 1881. In 1871 the place is still swarming with lodgers. Thomas Neale was 30 and his wife was 25; he had a young visitor staying with him and a married couple as servants. The lodgers consisted of 20 men, six women and six children, making up seven families including one father with his six-year-old son. Their occupations included hawker, traveller, bricklayer, stableman, carpenter, labourer, pensioner and gardener. By 1881 the pressure had eased and the lodgers were mainly single men; there were 15 of these and one married couple and their occupations included labourer, carpenter, servant, painter, excavator, frame maker, tailor, paper maker, stableman, porter and seaman. Thomas Neale was still there with his wife, his mother and a widowed servant. The house was not given a name in the 1881 census but in the 1886 *Directory* it appears under a new name as *The Standard*. Perhaps the old sailor had acquired altogether too jolly a reputation. It must have been Thomas Neale who made the change. He appears in the directories until 1892 when Mrs Thomas Neale is listed. She was till there in 1899. According to Hetherington the trade in 1913 was two barrels a week, bringing in a profit of £1 6s. 0d.; and the licence was taken away in 1920. The brewers were Smith and Company of Lamberhurst and they received £1,237 as compensation. The house nevertheless continued as what seems pejoratively to be called a 'common lodging house' and its reputation can hardly have been enhanced by a report in the *Kent and Sussex Courier* of 20 January 1928; a divorce had been granted on the grounds of adultery with a woman at Little Mount Sion. Mr E.J. Fish of Little Mount Sion 'proved the charge of adultery'. Since the place was known in its latter days as Bish's Doss House I think the *Courier* made a mistake – the informant was Mr Bish. Anyway it was the erstwhile *Jolly Sailor* that was in use, it would seem, as a cheap substitute for a week-end in Brighton. The run-down building eventually succumbed to the imperative of the motor car in the 1960s and its empty site now provides lodgings for the cars of a building society. I did ask to see the old deeds but the Building Society could not find them.

Chapter 15

Queen Anne's Mansion

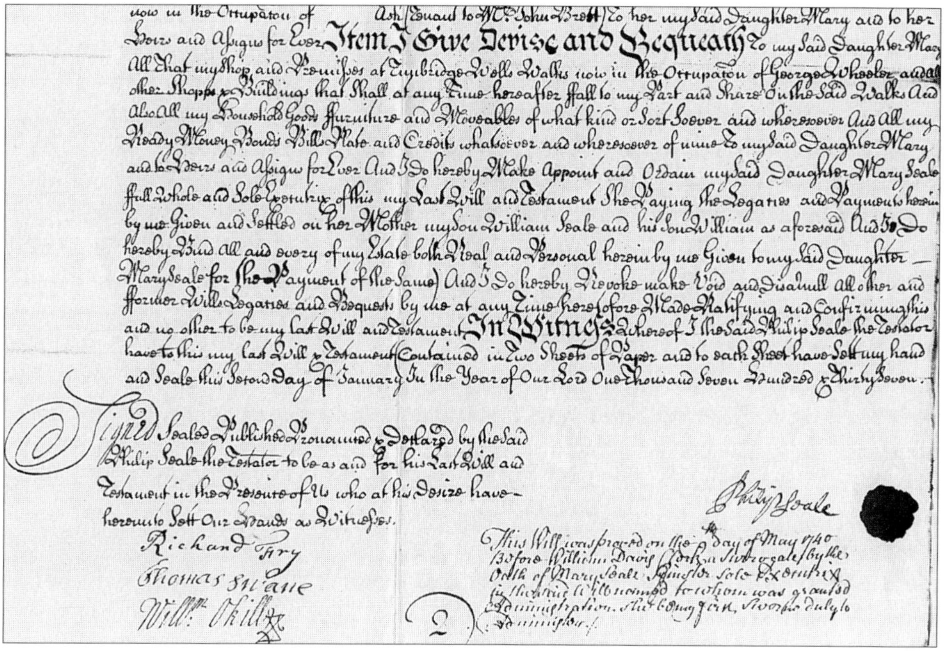
now in the Occupation of Ash Tenant to Mr John Brett To her my said Daughter Mary and to her Heirs and Assigns for Ever Item I Give Devise and Bequeath to my said Daughter Mary All that my Shop and Premises at Tunbridge Wells Walks now in the Occupation of George Wheeler and all other Shopps or Buildings that shall at any Time hereafter fall to my Part and Share On the Said Walks And Also All my Household Goods Furniture and Moveables of what kind or Sort Soever and wheresoever And All my Ready Money Bonds Bills Plate and Credits whatsoever and wheresoever of mine To my said Daughter Mary and her Heirs and Assigns for Ever And I do hereby Make Appoint and Ordain my said Daughter Mary Seale full Whole and Sole Executrix of this my Last Will and Testament She paying the Legacies and Payments herein by me Given and Settled on her Mother my Son William Seale and his Son William as aforesaid And I do hereby Bind All and every of my Estate both Real and Personal herein by me Given to my said Daughter Mary Seale for the Payment of the Same And I do hereby Revoke make Void and Disannull All other and former Wills Legacies and Bequests by me at any Time heretofore Made Ratifying and Confirming this and no other to be my last Will and Testament In Witness whereof I the said Philip Seale the Testator have to this my last Will & Testament Contained in Two Sheets of Paper and to each Sheet have Sett my hand and Seale this Second Day of January In the Year of Our Lord One thousand Seven Hundred & Thirty Seven.

Signed Sealed Published Pronounced & Declared by the said Philip Seale the Testator to be as and for his Last Will and Testament in the Presence of Us who at his Desire have hereunto Sett Our Hands as Witnesses.

Richard Fry

Thomas

Willm Okill

Philip Seale

This Will was proved on the 9 day of May 1740 before William Davis Clerk a Surrogate by the Oath of Mary Seale Spinster Sole Executrix

Part of the Will of Philip Seale proved 1740

Philip Seale's will is a rather beautiful document, the calligraphic handwork, I am sure, of William Okill who signed with a flourish as third witness. 'In the name of God Amen I Philip Seale of the Parish of Tonbridge in the County of Kent Glazier being in Good Health of Body and of a Sound Memory and Understanding Praise be given to Almighty God for the Same And calling unto Mind the Mortality of my Body and knowing it is Appointed for All Men once to dye but the time uncertain when …' he gave to his wife for life, and then to his daughter Mary, a Rent Charge of £4 per annum out of a farm and lands called Cold Harbour in Penshurst and to his wife only for life an annuity of £12. These provisions for his wife were, of course, nullified by her death before him. Then to his son William, the cordwainer of East Greenwich, he gave fourscore pounds and an unmarked silver tankard; and £20 to William's son William. To his daughter Mary (still living and still single) he bequeathed his 'lodging house and dwelling apartment' (rooms set apart in the lodging house for the owner and family?) and a two-acre field in the Calverley area (later to attract the attention of John Ward) which Philip had received from the Rev. John Elton in exchange for a three-acre field in Rusthall and which was occupied by Richard Fry the butcher. The house and field were to go if, as seemed likely, Mary had no children, to granddaughters Mary and Priscilla, the daughters of dead Thomas, as tenants in common. Philip's two stables (behind the lodging house I assume) and the 'mead' near Mount Sion (the three-acre field) were to go, after his wife's death, 'to the Use of the Settlement' on his son Thomas – which means, a reading of Thomas' will suggests, that they were then to go to granddaughters Mary and Priscilla when they reached the age of 18, in 1741 and 1743.

Daughter Mary was next to receive 'All that my Hayhouse Plat' and a small piece of ground adjoining it 'together with all the buildings thereon (now in the occupation of _______ Ash (Tenant to Mr John Brett)'. I cannot identify this 'Hayhouse Plat' but the name which can hardly have been used of more than one piece of land is to be found in the deeds of Marlborough House (now called Cecil Court, see chapter 20) and I think it must have been near Marlborough Villa; indeed the buildings referred to might be the origins of Marlborough Villa itself. Mr (Metcalf?) Ash was certainly in occupation of Forest Prospect (Ivy Chimneys) in 1737 (see chapter 20). The final item in Philip's will was his 'shop and premises at Tunbridge Wells Walks now in the Occupation of George Wheeler'. Who George Wheeler was and what he sold I do not know; but the shop and all Philip's furniture and personal effects were given to his daughter Mary who was appointed sole executrix. The witnesses were Philip's nephew, Richard Fry the butcher, Thomas Swane and, as mentioned already, William Okill, the schoolmaster at King Charles. The will of Thomas Seale, of course, came earlier than that of his father but it does little more than confirm the marriage settlement of 1721. What it does tell us is that Thomas must have known that his illness, whatever it was, might prove fatal. He signed the will on 18 October and on the 30th he was buried. He was only 33 years old.

As a result of these deaths the scene at the top of Little Mount Sion in 1740 had changed completely. Mary, Philip's 43-year-old spinster daughter, reigned in her father's original house and her brother's widow Priscilla, three years younger, was mistress of the other. At least the two women must have got on well enough together, since Mary, when she came to make her will, gave a bigger cash bequest to her 'sister' Priscilla than to anyone else, besides leaving all her property to Priscilla's daughter; and there is no reason to suppose that Mary and Priscilla did not make an efficient, even formidable, pair of lodging house landladies at the height of the Beau Nash period. In 1746 Priscilla's daughter Mary died at the age of 23 leaving young Priscilla the sole surviving heiress to Philip Seale's little empire; and she, in 1750, married Edward Mercer. This was a marriage of local dynasties, since the Mercer family, as we saw at the beginning of chapter 7, owned the *Compasses* and the strip of land down to the High Street and Edward was the son who was to be apprenticed to a trade by John Mercer's executors. He described himself as a glazier in the marriage settlement which was signed on 19 January

1750. The Trustee was Edward's brother Robert, owner of the *Compasses*, and the settlement covers the same ground as the 1721 settlement. It therefore includes the Mount Sion 'mead', the abuttals of which at this time were the lands of John Brett to the west and those of Thomas Wood to the east. Even more interestingly, a solicitor has at some unknown date written a note alongside the description of the field which says: 'now in lease to Mr Bingham' – additional confirmation that this is the Sion Lodge field (see chapter 22).

The marriage settlement unfortunately did not ensure that the marriage would bear fruit. Aunt Mary, when she came to make her will on the last day of 1763, may have had some lingering hope that her 38-year-old niece would produce an heir – but not much. Anyhow, she left her share of the Seale inheritance to her niece who then owned both houses. A settlement dated 8/9 February 1765 appointed Edward Mercer's brother-in-law, Edmund Baker, bookseller, of Speldhurst Parish, trustee for Mary Seale's bequest. The whole of the Seale inheritance and Edward's share of the Mercer one now rested with Edward and Priscilla; but there were no children. In 1773 the widow Priscilla died at the age of 73 and was followed only two years later by her 50-year-old daughter. The widower Edward Mercer lived until 1790 but, for lack of children of his own, had to leave all his land and houses to his sister Jane who had been married to the bookseller but was by now a widow with an only child, the maiden Jane. The only remembrance of the Seale family in Edward's will was a bequest of £5 to William Seal of Southam and £56 to his sister – whose name Edward could not even remember. In 1801 the widow Baker died and for the next 30 or so years Miss Baker was the queen-pin on Little Mount Sion. A family tree may help to clarify these events.

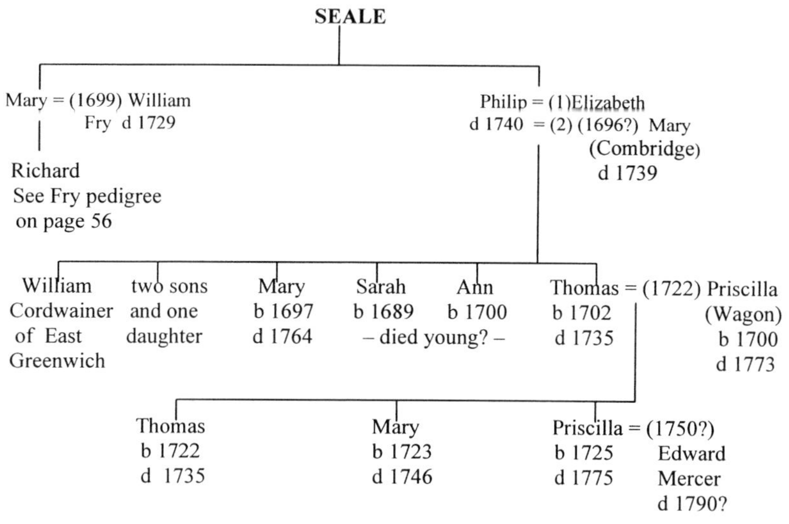

This whole family tale is more than confirmed by the Poor Rate record and later by Sprange's *Guides*. Here is the Poor Rate record for Philip Seale's two houses:

The First House

1689 (May)-1714	Phil Seale
1728-1729	Phil Seale
1730-1739	Mr Philip Seal
1740-1755	Wid Seal Senr
1756-1761	Mrs Seale Senr
1762-1766	Mrs Mary Seal
1767	Mrs Mary Seal now Edwd Mercer's
1768-1790	Edwd Mercer for late Mrs Seal's
1791-1793	Baker Wo (or Occ) for late Mercers before Seals
1794-1797	Baker Widw (or occupr) for late Mercers

The Second House

1694 (Apr)-1703	Philip Seale for Wid Rottenbridge
1704	William Fry for Widow Rottenbridges
1708	Edward Waggon for Mr Rottenbridges
1709-1710	Edw Waghorne for Rottenbridges
1711-1714	Mr Seal for Rottenbridges
1728-1738	Thos Seale
1739	Widow Seal
1740-1756	Wid Seal Junr
1757-1761	Mrs Seal Junr
1762-1767	Wid Seal
1768-1774	Widow Seale for her House & Lands
1775	Widow Seale or occ
1776	Widow SEALE
1777-1790	Mercer Edwd for late Widow Seal's House & Lands
1791-1793	Baker Wo (or Occ) for Wo Seals House & Lands late Mercers
1794-1797	(Combined with First House)

There is no reference elsewhere to the Widow Rottenbridge; perhaps she financed the building of the second house, despite an inauspicious name. There are some minor discrepancies in dates in these Poor Rate records but these are fairly common and can probably be explained by legal delays or lags in the recording of information by the Poor Rate collectors; but the nagging inconsistency concerns the Widow Seal Senior who is recorded as successor to Philip Seal at the First House in 1740. The junior widow should, of course, be the relict of untimely deceased Thomas and Philip's 'widow' should be the senior but she died before her husband. There is a bundle of deeds in Box 13 of the Ward Papers relating to the two-acre field which Philip Seale received in his exchange with the Rev. John Elton on 15 June 1720; and in the bundle is a 'Pedigree of Philip Seale' together with some related extracts from the Tonbridge Parish register. The pedigree shows the dates of burial of the other two Marys, daughter and granddaughter, in 1746 and 1764 and includes the burial of a Mary Seal on 22 November 1739. This must be

Philip's wife who died a year before him. How then is the ratepayer from 1740-1755, Widow Seal Senior, to be explained? The only guess I can offer is that the daughter was at first mistakenly thought to be a widow, perhaps because of her mature age or perhaps simply for honorific reasons – this is certainly the reason why she was later given the title Mrs Seale Senior and Mrs Mary Seal although she was unmarried.

The *Sprange Guides* list, in 1780 and 1786, (1) Mr E. Mercer, late Seal's; and (2) Mr E. Mercer's small house, late Seal's. By 1797, repeated in 1801, this has become (1) Mrs Baker, late E Mercer's Great House; (2) Mrs Baker, Middle ditto; and, interestingly, (3) Mrs Baker, Small new ditto. In 1811 Sprange shows: 'Mrs Gilbert'; 'Sion Crescent (Miss Baker)'; and 'Ditto (Large House)' – reversing the order. In 1817 the lodging house listing is reduced to: 'Sion Crescent No 1, Mrs Gilbert'; and 'Sion Crescent No 2, Miss Baker', the 'Large House' being omitted altogether. A different light on the scene is cast by Sprange's figures for the numbers of rooms in the houses. In 1797/1801 the Great House had three parlours, five chambers and six garrets; the Middle House two parlours, three chambers and four garrets; and the small new house two parlours, two chambers and three garrets. In addition there was accommodation for 3 coaches and 11 horses attached to the two original houses. In 1817 the total of 14 rooms in the 'Large House' is no longer advertised as available for letting to visitors. The obvious explanation for this is that the rooms were permanently taken by local residents. The fact is that, as the 18th century turned into the 19th, a social development was taking place which, I am sure, would have been a severe disappointment to Philip Seale.

When Philip built his houses the road system on Mount Sion Hill was embryonic; in fact, as we have seen, he was himself responsible for the present shape of Little Mount Sion. Visitors at a later date remarked on the haphazard way in which buildings were scattered amongst fields and orchards; and Philip had thrown down his houses in what seemed an ideal location, half-way up the hill with a view westward over the valley to the Common and sheltered to the rear and east by the hill. The houses up Mount Sion road by contrast tended to stare at each other across the street. Little Mount Sion, however, grew into the street where ordinary people lived and had their shops and beer houses while Mount Sion Road was lined exclusively with lodging houses for the fashionable visitors. Although (as will be remembered) Fanny Burney noticed the dirty little lanes where the shopkeepers lived as early as 1797, Barrow's map shows no greater development than one straight and one L-shaped row of cottages on the north side of Little Mount Sion in 1808. Perhaps Fanny Burney's shops were so ramshackle and temporary as not to merit mapping. At the same time a second development was taking place. Tunbridge Wells was losing its fashionable status to Brighton and the seaside generally and, by way of recompense, permanent residents such as Richard Cumberland and Lord North were settling in the town; but what retired gentleman or annuitant spinster would wish to make a home on Little Mount Sion? So began, I conjecture, the slow decline of Philip Seale's lodging houses and the piecemeal extensions which were to lead to the unbroken row of buildings which we see in Camburn's postcard.

The process can also be traced on maps. We have seen that as early as 1797 a new small house appears in the Sprange list. By 1808, the time of the Barrow map, see the detail below, there are two houses at the Frog Lane end of the crescent, one marked as a lodging house – numbered rather unclearly '3' – and the other as a private house – shaded black, between '3' and '2'. Barrow's key says:

Sion Crescent 1. Miss Baker – Great House 2. Do – Middle do 3. Mr Gilbert.

At the other end of the crescent the Barrow map shows another new building marked clearly with the letter 'A' which is identified by a key at the top of the map saying: **A** By Sion Crescent, Fry's Boarding School.

Barrow map 1808

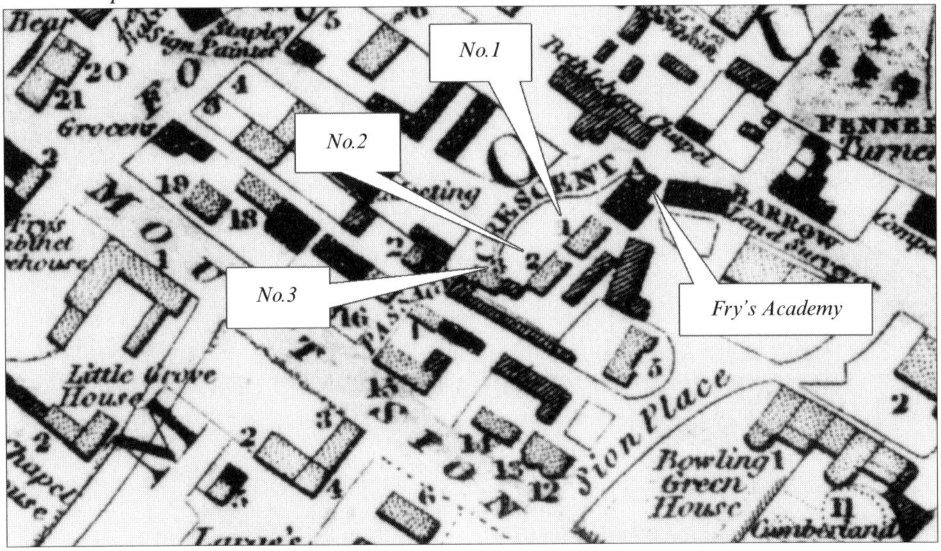

Exactly when Thomas Fry started his school I do not know but it may have been as early as 1804, for the *Tunbridge Wells Gazette* in 1860 printed an 'Address to the Volunteers' on the anticipated invasion of England by Napoleon, composed by Thomas Fry, formerly principal of Sion Crescent Academy, 1804.

Brave fellow soldiers, who undaunted stand
Prepared to vindicate your native land,
Permit a comrade simply to impart
The genuine feelings of a British heart …

We cannot follow him through all his 62 lines. He praises freedom, he lambasts the tyrant, he recalls ancient heroism and more recent success in Egypt (Trafalgar was yet to come) and, confident in victory, he dreams of its rewards.

If you, ye fair, from violence we save
Your rescued charms shall recompense the brave.

It fires his heart in freedom's cause to take an active part.

Our cause is just – away unmanly fears!
Unite like Britons! Fight like Volunteers!

They never did have to fight, although the danger was real enough; but I am sure they received their recompense from the fair ladies of Mount Sion all the same. Quite why the *Gazette* editor saw fit to print this piece 56 years after its composition he does not bother to tell us. Was Thomas Fry still alive? I doubt it. We next hear of him in 1806 when he inserted an advertisement in the *Maidstone Journal*:

> Mr Fry's School, No 29, Mount Sion, Tunbridge Wells, will open after the Christmas Vacation, on January 19th, where Young Gentlemen are taught the English Language Grammatically, Writing, Arithmetic, Merchants' Accompts, and Geography. Terms for Boarders – Eighteen Guineas per Annum, French – Ten and Sixpence per Quarter.

On 12 July 1808 he advertises again: 'Mr Fry returns thanks to his Friends for the liberal Patronage he has received, and begs leave to inform them and the Public, that having made very considerable Additions to his House, he is now enabled to accommodate a larger number of pupils…' I think this must refer to the building marked 'A' on the Barrow map (see above) which can be seen again, more clearly, on the Tithe map in 1840, marked '3779' – see page 190 below. Philip Seale's two lodging houses are next to it, numbered '3780', and it can be seen what a substantial 'extension' has been made – indeed a 'very considerable Addition'. Part of it can be seen on the left-hand side of Camburn's postcard at the head of chapter 13 and it can be seen clearly on the left of the house with the porch in Baker's painting on page 194.

For a long time I was puzzled about no 29 Mount Sion. You see, it had cropped up in an entirely different context – that of William Okill and his lodging house. This is a well known 'legend' of early Tunbridge Wells history – or so I thought. Here is how Bracket tells it on page 51 of his *The Spa Hotel and Tunbridge Wells through the Centuries*: 'In 1737 the Clerk at the chapel was one Okill. He kept a lodging house at No. 29 Mount Sion, and at times used the chapel for business purposes. Whenever he had rooms to let he gave out a hymn containing repetitions of the Psalmist's line 'Mount Sion is a pleasant place', adding 'especially No. 29'. Now we know that Mr Fry gave his school the number 29, Mount Sion' in his first advertisement in 1806. This seemed quite extraordinary. We know where it was because Barrow (who was living next door at the time!) has put it on his map; and anyway it was not called the Sion Crescent Academy for nothing – but how and why, for crying out aloud, could it be numbered 29 when not a single house anywhere in the locality is known to have been numbered until around 1870 at the earliest. It beat me; and what I thought must be more than coincidence was that this was the very same number which Mr Brackett pulled out of a hat as the number of OKill's lodging house of pleasant memory.

There is the hint of a relationship between the Seale, Fry and Okill families in the will of Edward Mercer, 1790. £5 was bequeathed to each of the children of Edward's uncle Robert Fry and one of these children seems to have been named Ann Okill by the time she received her five pounds. The fact that the Okills were schoolmasters as well as Chapel Clerks might be significant but, on the other hand, William Okill the younger was appointed master at the King Charles School – in succession to his father who moved to a newly built school at Crowborough as early in the century as 1744; the connection with Ann (Fry's) husband in 1790 could be rather tenuous therefore. Anyway the puzzle of no.29 was solved when I found in the Museum a list of lodging houses published by Mr Sprange in 1802 and nos 28 and 29 Mount Sion are marked Mr T. Fry. So at least that little problem is solved. Number 29 has nothing to do with the post office or mail delivery; it was part of Sprange's private system for identifying the lodging houses in the town. But we do know exactly where it was. And I think we can safely conclude that this is also where Mr Okill's pleasant lodging house was situated.

Thomas Fry's Academy continued at least until 1832 but the Tithe Award ten years later than this shows:

		Owner	**Occupier**
3779	House and Yard	Ann FRY	Charles PAINE
3780	2 Houses and yard	Edward MERCER	NOVIS and others

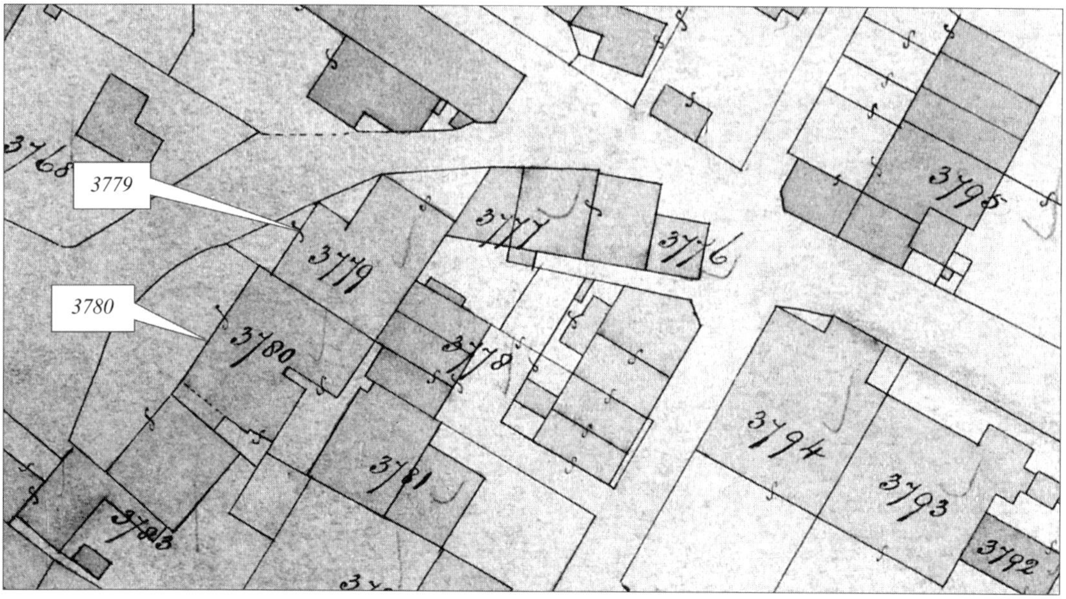

Tithe map 1840

'3780' covers Philip Seale's two houses; 3779 is the substantial addition referred to on the previous page. Ann Fry was, I assume, related to Thomas Fry the schoolmaster but I have no evidence on fact or degree. Edward Mercer is not, of course, to be confused with the one who died in 1790, Priscilla's husband. There must, I am sure, be a relationship but I do not know what. Priscilla's husband's sister, Mrs Jane Baker, as mentioned previously, had one child only, a daughter also Jane, to whom in her will, proved on 8 May 1800, she left everything. This was the Miss Baker whom we met in chapter 7, making suggestions to her solicitor concerning the house called Philpots at the bottom of Warwick Road. She never married but, as evidenced by the *Sprange Guides*, carried on the lodging house business as 'queen-pin' of Little Mount Sion. As such she got a rocket from the Court Leet of Southborough in November 1820. The ditch adjoining the garden belonging to Miss Baker was a nuisance: 'not being arched over, in all heavy rains [it] throws the water on the publick road adjoining and renders the same dangerous'. This may well have been the least of Miss Baker's maintenance worries! She carried on until about 1830 and, according to the Toc H deeds, was residing at Sion Crescent at the time of her death. 'All those two messuages or tenements being contiguous to each other situate at Mount Sion ... in one of which Jane Baker previously to and at the time of her decease resided...' I do not know exactly when she died but inside a copy of her mother's will, bundled with the Abstract of Title concerning the Great House or Goldstone's Field (see chapter 9 page 91), is an account of the estate of Miss Jane Baker, amounting in total to £650 out of which, as residuary legatees I assume, Edmund Mercer received £67 5s. 7½d. and John Baker £70 5s. 7½d. – not much to show in the end for the entire Mercer and Seale inheritances. The real estate would have gone, however, to the 'right heir' and this might well have been Edmund Mercer who may have been the one named in Edward Mercer's (1789) will as his nephew, the son of his brother Joseph; and 'Edmund Mercer (Sion Crescent)' appears in the Holy Trinity Burial Register (aged 82) on Christmas Day 1836. The Edward Mercer who owned the two old Philip Seale houses in about 1840 could therefore have been Edmund's son or even, considering his venerable age, his grandson.

I suggested above that it was between 1811 and 1817 that the old houses began to change from lodging houses for the wealthy visitors (shades of Princess Anne!) to year-round lodgings for the less well-to-do locals. What is certain is that the transformation was complete by the time of the first detailed census in 1841. In that year there were 13 households living in the various parts of Sion Crescent (excluding Sackville Cottage) comprising 36 adults and 12 children under fifteen. The table below gives the figures for the censuses 1841-1881

Sion Crescent (excluding Sackville Cottage)

Census Year	**1841**	**1851**	**1861**	**1871**	**1881**
Households	13	16	12	19	15
Adults	36	32	30	43	35
Children	12	10	11	31	15

The difficulty with the censuses is that there is no consistent identification of the different parts of the Crescent. The Ordnance Survey map gives a good plan view and the postcard pictures show pretty well what it looked like. The parameters are set by Sackville Cottage, which is named in all the censuses, to the south and

Bonham House, in one of its guises (see chapter 11), to the north. The most informative description is to be found in the 1861 census: Sackville Cottage; House-no-name; Sion Crescent Lodging House; Bakehouse – back of Crescent; Carpenter's shop and Lodging House; Sion Crescent; Crescent Cottage; and Laundry. It so happens that an equivalent number of parts (i.e. 8) can be distinguished on the Ordnance Survey map (see page 198 below). The bakehouse at the back of the Crescent is possibly the rectangle to the north of the well; but the map does not differentiate open spaces from buildings and on the Tithe map this space does not appear as a building at all. The remaining seven parts can be distributed in order starting with Sackville Cottage whose position is, thanks be, indisputable. The house without a name is then the tall-chimneyed building next door, formerly stables; Sion Crescent Lodging House is Philip Seale's first house in its entirety; the Carpenter's shop and lodging house is part of Philip Seale's second house and the other part, with the grand porch, is 'Sion Crescent'; Crescent Cottage is the academy building; and the laundry is the bit tagged on in the triangular plot at the end. In 1861 the 'laundry' was inhabited by Thomas Sears, a 69-year-old coachman and his 47-year-old wife Alice who was appropriately a laundress; and in 1871 'Crescent Cottage No 2' was the home of John Maynard and Harriett his wife, both aged 44. He was a labourer and she a laundress and they had one daughter and four sons aged from ten to one, not to mention two older men as lodgers. In 1881 Harriett was widowed and living at 32 Little Mount Sion with her three teenage sons but not William who should have been 11 – what had happened to him? She is still a laundress and indeed appears in the 1886 *Directory* as 'Maynard Mrs mangling' at 32 Little Mount Sion; and in 1890, as we shall see towards the end of the chapter, the 'laundry' was demolished. All this suggests that the 1861 descriptions do correspond in order with the buildings on the ground. Crescent Cottage was so named in 1851, 1861 and 1871, becoming no 30, Little Mount Sion in 1881; but in 1841, together with the future laundry, it was Sion Crescent No.4, the first head of household listed in the census being the 60-year-old Ann Fry. I assumed at first that she was the widow of Thomas Fry the schoolmaster; and the fact that the other members of her household were Susannah Rogers, a 30-year-old schoolmistress, and Emma Young, a young teacher of 15 years of age, would suggest a link with the pedagogic profession. However the Toc H Abstract throws some doubt on this. Its description of Crescent Cottage runs: 'All that messuage or tenement situate near to the premises first thereinbefore described and wherein Robt Fry formerly dwelt and his son afterwards dwelt called Crescent Cottage and the small yard ... used therewith ... formerly in the occupation of John Mackellow...' It is tempting to suppose that Thomas Fry, Robert's son, was the schoolmaster; but the premises described first in the Abstract were said to be occupied one by Jane Baker and another by 'Thomas Fry Schoolmaster' as if to distinguish him from others of the same name. Besides which he could not occupy two places at the same time – not that we can be sure that the times were not different. Anyhow, the name John Mackellow (coal dealer) appears at Crescent Cottage in the 1851 and

1861 censuses and, significantly, the 'cottage adjoining' Crescent Cottage in 1851 is occupied by Mary Chapman and her daughter Emma, both dressmakers, and the 1841 census shows Thomas Chapman (painter) and Mary his wife with their daughters Sarah and Emma living at No 4 Sion Crescent. What is more, Thomas and Mary appear in the Toc H Abstract which describes, thirdly, 'all those rooms or apartments and premises situate at Mount Sion ... formerly in the occupation of Ann Mercer and William Elliott and Susannah his Wife afterwards of Thomas Chapman Mary Chapman Mrs Ashby and the Widow Hunt ... and being contiguous to the premises thereinbefore described'. It is undoubtedly the future 'laundry' building which is being described in such a way as to suggest it formed an extension to the Crescent Cottage building. I find it difficult to understand, however, why no reference is made to the building's previous use as a school; for I cannot believe that Barrow was mistaken in his location of Fry's Academy. True the Toc H Abstract is reciting documents of about 1890 but the occupiers whose names it quotes are of a much earlier vintage. The other two households, it is interesting to note, which occupied No 4 Sion Crescent in 1841 consisted of John Chapman, schoolmaster, and his schoolmistress wife; and Elizabeth Clifford, schoolmistress, aged 45, living with Nathan Merry, aged 40, journeyman painter. Where I wonder were all these teachers teaching? And why this concentration of pedagogic power in one residence? As for the main part of the Crescent, the two original lodging houses later joined together, it is difficult to reconcile the different designations given in the five censuses from 1841 to 1881. The description in the Toc H Abstract, quoted in part twice already, runs in full as follows: 'All those two messuages or tenements being contiguous to each other situated at Mount Sion ... in one of which Jane Baker previously to and at the time of her decease resided and the other was then in the occupation of Thomas Fry Schoolmaster and which said messuages or tenements were afterwards respectively as to part thereof in the respective occupations of Sarah Mercer, Richard Novis and Sally his wife and since let in lodgings and as to other part thereof formerly used and let as lodgings and since in the occupation of Mrs ______Haywood and which said messuages were then in the occupation of ________ And of and in the front Court or Crescent outbuildings yards and appurtenances to said messuages or tenements belonging'. This description refers to a period when there were two, and only two, distinct parts; and divides this period into three stages, as shown below:

	Part A	**Part B**
Stage 1	Jane Baker	Thomas Fry Schoolmaster
Stage 2	Mercer & Novis	let as lodgings
Stage 3	let in lodgings	Mrs _______ Haywood

Unfortunately none of these names appear in the 1841 census but 'Novis and others' are shown as occupiers in the Tithe Award. The Award was passed by the Tithe Commissioners on 3 March 1841 and the census was taken on 6 June 1841. Maybe Sarah Mercer (listed by Pigot in 1832 as a straw hat maker) and the Novises did move out between these dates? The Tithe Award talks of two houses but, as we have seen, this seems to have become three parts by 1861 and indeed the censuses of both 1841 and 1851 refer to Sion Crescent Nos 1, 2 and 3; but unfortunately they seem to reverse the order. In 1871 on the other hand the whole of Sion Crescent is lumped into one! By 1881 house numbers have come in and Sion Crescent spans from 20 to 28 (even numbers and omitting 22 altogether!). If there were but one family, like the Dentons in chapter 11, which lived in the Crescent through the whole period, it might serve as an anchorage point. The Buckwell family almost serves the purpose; but they were in a house called Slow Cottage, at the bottom of the hill below the *Jolly Sailor*, in 1851 and who can say that they moved back to the same part of Sion Crescent afterwards? Anyway, in 1841 George Buckwell, a brushmaker aged 50, was living at No 1 Sion Crescent with his wife Phillis (30), children Rosina, Edmund and Ellen (12, five and two) and 80-year-old Charity Buckwell. In 1851 the whole family, less the old lady, is living at Slow Cottage. George is now a 'day labouring man'. Rosina is a dressmaker and Edmund an errand boy. In 1861 they are back in the Crescent at the 'Sion Crescent Lodging House'. George, at 75, is a brushmaker again, Rosa and Ellen are both dressmakers, Edmund has left home and the family is completed inexplicably by Annie Smith, a three-year-old granddaughter. By 1871 George has gone to a better home and the head of the household at 'Sion Crescent' is Rosa Buckwell, still a dressmaker, and with her are her mother, her brother Edmund, back again and now a brushmaker like his father before, a nephew called Clifford Buckwell and a boarder, the 35-year-old tailor James Atkins. In 1881 we catch a final glimpse of Rosa and her mother at 20 Little Mount Sion. Rosa is now Mrs Atkins and has suddenly lost six years to make her the same age as her tailor husband and former boarder James, while 'mother-in-law' Phillis is 80 years old. With them is Clifford F. Buckwell, now 18 and a compositor and printer – and no longer a nephew but the son of the family! If we assume that, when at Sion Crescent, the Buckwells always stayed in the same part, then that part was Philip Seale's first house, called No 1 Sion Crescent in 1841, Sion Crescent Lodging House in 1861 and 20 Little Mount Sion in 1881. However, we really wanted to know whether this part was called no.1 or 2 in 1851 and the Buckwells do not help. It would be interesting to know more about the bakehouse at the back and the carpenter's shop but the lack of bakers and carpenters to use them is their most striking characteristic. In 1861 the bakehouse was occupied by a labourer and a charwoman and the carpenter's shop by a charwoman and a

Sion Crescent upper part – prominent porch marks Philip Seale's second house

stableman. By the 1900s Mr Love, the builder, might have found a use for a carpenter's shop but as far as I can tell from Camburn's photograph (see chapter 13 page 154) his signboard is on the first Seale house whereas I thought the carpenter's shop formed part of the second.

Anyway, all this has given some flavour of life in Sion Crescent in the latter part of the 19th century: certainly a far cry from the upstairs and downstairs bourgeoiserie which had befallen the lodging houses built by Philip Seale's contemporaries on Mount Sion Road. As far as Sackville Cottage is concerned, it was the home of the Gilberts for most of the period, from 1841 to 1871. Until 1851 the occupiers were Sophia Gilbert and her younger sister Sarah; then Sarah and her brother Edward. Something more will be said about the Gilbert siblings in chapter 21. Sophia Gilbert was ten years older than her sister but was either sick or feeble-minded or both because a deed of 1852 had first been explained to her in the presence of Thomas Walker, solicitor. This deed conveyed Edward's third share in Brunswick House to his two sisters. Edward died about 1873 because that is the year when, on 28 October, his trustees offered Brunswick House for sale. Since Sarah was two years older than her brother I assume she died about the same time. At all events, in 1881, no 18 Little Mount Sion which I take to be Sackville Cottage was occupied by a young cabinet maker called Fred Kew and his wife and five small children.. Sackville Cottage and the adjoining building and yard behind were owned in 1841, according to the Tithe Award, by William Gilbert who also owned York House with its shop at the bottom of Frog Lane (see chapter 16). From this I conclude that William Gilbert of York House was somehow related to the Gilberts of Sackville Cottage. The sisters Gilbert described themselves as 'House Proprietors' or 'of Independent Means'; in other words they derived an income from Brunswick House (and perhaps other property) and lived rather more modestly in the cottage by the twitten. Edward described himself as a Land Surveyor and Accountant and seems to have been an active professional. In 1841 Sackville Cottage was occupied not only by the two sisters but also by the families of widow Mary Mercer, painter William Waghorne and farriers Richard Smith father and son, comprising in all 16 adults and six children! Perhaps the sisters were short of money at the beginning; but from 1851 to 1871 there were never more than three in the house.

At the time of the Tithe Award in 1841 there were, as we have seen, three owners of Sion Crescent and Sackville Cottage: William Gilbert, Edward Mercer and Ann Fry. Forty years later, in 1882, most of the property belonged to William Arnold of Bartley Mill, just off the Bayham Abbey road from Tunbridge Wells to Lamberhurst and some years ago brought back into use as a working water mill. How did this come about? The evidence I have is contained entirely in the Toc H Abstract of Title. The earlier stages in this transformation are therefore unclear. What is clear is that Ann Fry's property was divided into two parts, Crescent Cottage and the 'laundry' extension, and the resulting four parts (adding those of Gilbert and Mercer) were singly or in various combinations divided into five shares, either by will I presume or by sale. Then on 28 July 1856 a certain Charles George

Carpenter began a long process of re-uniting the parts and shares in his own hands. His first acquisition was a fifth share belonging to James Mercer in the hereditaments 'secondly and fourthly described'. This seems to refer to Crescent Cottage and Sackville Cottage, the 'firstly described' property being Edward Mercer's two houses and the 'thirdly described' being the 'laundry'. I am not entirely confident that this numbering transfers correctly from the original documents (presumably lost) to the Abstract. It certainly seems odd that James Mercer, whoever he was apart from being a Mercer, should have been selling a share not in Edward Mercer's property but in property in which Edward Mercer had no interest, at least in 1841. Be that as it may, Charles George Carpenter had to wait 16 years before making his next move, the purchase of one fifth of Part 4 from Edwin and Harriett Walsh and Caroline Standen. In the next two years he acquired more fifth shares from William Evans, from John Chapman and from Obediah Wickens. None of these names has on the face of it any connection with the 1841 owners. By sometime between 1874 and 1882 the position was that Carpenter had purchased a lot of shares, that he apparently owned in his own right one fifth of Part 4 (how I do not know but this may have been his original motivation), that his wife had inherited a fifth share in all four parts from her mother, Frances Collier; and that all these shares taken together amounted to the whole of Sackville Cottage and four-fifths of the remaining parts. Carpenter then contracted to sell his holding to William Arnold but died shortly afterwards and it was his widow, Mary Stronghill Carpenter of Wadhurst, who completed the transaction on 7 July 1882.

William Arnold described himself in his will as a miller and farmer of Bartley Mill, Frant, but he did not confine his activities to this place or trade. He founded a firm specialising in mechanical engineering amongst other things at Branbridges, near East Peckham; and not only does this firm still exist but also a granddaughter of William Arnold is living nearby. What William Arnold was doing buying up property on Little Mount Sion I cannot think. I was hoping that his granddaughter might know but neither her memories nor an initial survey of the company papers have revealed anything; and it is assumed that William and his sons were engaged in some private speculation having nothing to do with the firm. However I live in hope that a more thorough examination of the family papers may still come up with something. Whatever his grand plan (if such he had), William Arnold did a little rebuilding in 1889. The plan on the next page will help to explain.

There used to be an almost continuous line of buildings from the *Grove Tavern* down to the lower end of Sion Crescent but with a bit of a gap in the middle. The gap was partially closed by Sarah Bonham's construction of the present no 30 but there still remained a triangular space, so shaped because of the differing alignments of the Sion Crescent and Bonham House buildings. In this triangle was built at some time before 1840 a rectangular building joined to Sion Crescent but not fronting directly on the road. This was part of the Academy building discussed on page 189 above. In 1889 William Arnold decided to knock down this building, then numbered 32 Little Mount Sion and shown on his plan with that number and a note saying 'The Etched part shows the present building'. In its place he proposed to fill up the whole of the resulting triangular gap with a shop house. All this can be seen clearly on the plan. Although the shop and parlour on the original plan have been altered over the years to accommodate the present barber's shop and separate living accommodation and there are now two entrances, the plan of 1889 is substantially what is to be found today. There is a large cellar in the eastern corner and ground and first floors above with several rooms of triangular shape to fit the space available. Of special interest is the indentation on the plan where the new building adjoins the end of Sion Crescent; this looks like a chimney on the outside of Sion Crescent and it corresponds with the chimney shown on the Ordnance Survey map (see next page). There is indeed an unused chimney behind the wall of no.26 (present-day numbering) which comes out to a chimney on the roof some foot or so inside the external wall of the still existing building. The painting of Sion Crescent (see page 194 above) shows that this situation existed before Sion Crescent was demolished. The explanation seems to be that the new building was built into the old at this point. The other interesting feature of the building is the arched passageway leading from the road to the back yard. This

Block Plan June 1889

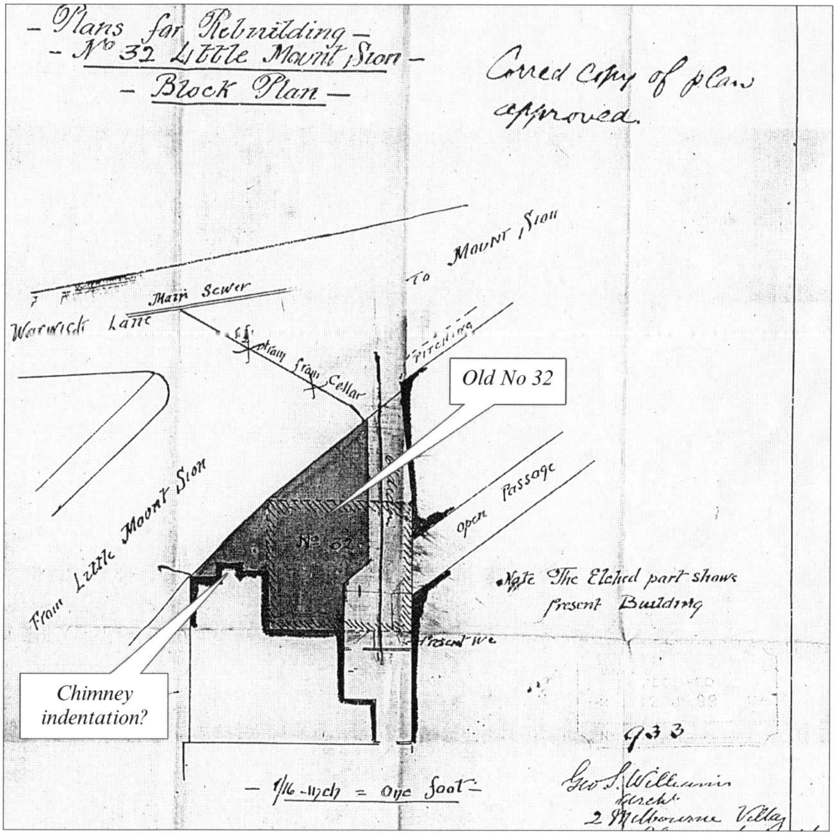

passage, wide and high enough to take a horse and cart, was obviously needed for access to the back of William Arnold's main property, Sion Crescent – for what precise purpose is not clear but some of the uses of these buildings were discussed on page 192 above. This passage has an archaic, coach and horses flavour about it which has led to mistaken notions about the antiquity of the building. The planning archives, however, leave no room for doubt; and in any case it is obvious (when you know the answer!) that nobody would have planned a building of this shape – the shape was dictated by the space left between the existing buildings.

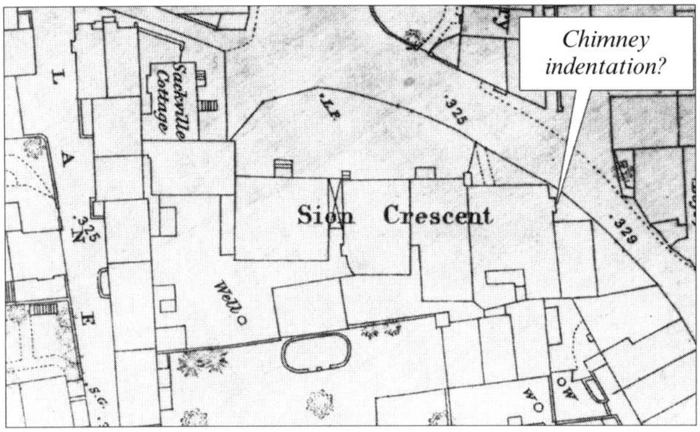

Ordnance Survey map 1866

William Arnold died at East Peckham on 18 October 1897 and left his property to his sons Walter and George as tenants in common. The next year on 3 February Walter and George (still described as millers of Bartley Mill) bought the remaining fifth share of Parts 1, 2 and 3, thus completing the assembly of the whole site. The vendor was Joshua Robert Gower, then described as a house agent of Tunbridge Wells and father I imagine of the more celebrated knight and mayor. He had acquired the share (perhaps by way of mortgage redemption?) from Elizabeth Standen deceased, a name which rings more of a bell in the Mount Sion context – see page 101 above. Some additional information dated 1897 is obtainable from the deeds of the present Nos 26/28 Little Mount Sion – John the barber's. Included is a 'certificate of Redemption of Land Tax' dated 1 June 1897. The owner, William Arnold, Bartley Mill, Frant, Gentleman, redeemed for £4 10s. 0d. the tax on 'All that piece of land with the several messuages, shops, outbuildings and appurtenances thereto belonging situate at Little Mount Sion, Tunbridge Wells, Borough of Southborough West … known as Sion Crescent'. The following details which must refer to an earlier date were given:

Name of Proprietor	**Occupier**	**Description**	**Rateable Value**
Mercer's Heirs	Various	Sion Crescent	£3 p.a.

The reference to 'Mercer's Heirs' is tantalising but suggests at least that some of those who sold to C.G. Carpenter obtained their shares by inheritance from Edward Mercer.

The triangular building which William Arnold and his architect G.S. Williams of Claremont Road created in 1889/90 and which involved the partial demolition of the 'laundry' was obviously built into or butted onto the 'laundry' remains and the side of Crescent Cottage; and it seems unlikely that they would have done this if they had in mind the demolition of the adjoining buildings. Remember, however, that this was Arnold senior; his sons at a later date had a different perspective no doubt. The 'horse and cart' passage at the rear of the new building remains a puzzle. The Tithe and Ordnance Survey maps seem to indicate that the passage would lead to a blank wall; yet we know that Sackville Cottage was in separate ownership and egress from that end of the Crescent would therefore be difficult; so that, if the Crescent inhabitants wanted access to the rear of the Crescent (and we know that there was in 1861 at least a bakehouse at the back), they would have to look to the northern end – and this might explain the incorporation of the 'horse and cart' passage in the new building. Perhaps there was already a passage under the old 'laundry' which had to be maintained. Earlier documents (see page 166) show that stables and coach houses for the original lodging houses were located on the north-eastern side. The 'Academy' building and the 'laundry' must therefore have replaced or perhaps in part incorporated the stables and some of this provision for equine transport may well have remained in place. It is an interesting commentary anyway on the history of Philip Seale's houses that stables and coach houses should have been abandoned. At least until the advent of the railway about the middle of the 19th century it was essential to provide for the horses and carriages of wealthy visitors; and the abandonment of such provision must suggest the abandonment of any pretension to cater for the fashionable visitors – a further indication of the change in the function of Sion Crescent in the first half of the 19th century. One effect of this change was evidently a decline in the standard of maintenance of the buildings (or a simple lack of any maintenance?). No doubt the division of ownership in the later part of the century did not help and the situation went from worse to worse until the lower parts only were inhabited and the upper parts were in what the printer of an article published in 1912 was pleased to call a very 'dilapitated' condition. This was Luke Pearce's *Historical Associations of Royal Tunbridge Wells from 1606 to 1909* to which I have already alluded on page 163. He has given the best, indeed the only, description that exists apart from pictorial testimony. He says. 'The historic building at Mount Sion facing the High Street is known as QUEEN ANNE'S MANSION'.

> The facia sign of Messrs Love and Son, builders, will identify it. We take it that at one time the whole of the buildings at the corner formed one mansion. Traces of doorways leading from one to the other are distinct evidences of this.
>
> It is said that when migration from Bishop's Down to Mount Sion took place these buildings were among those removed. Strange as it may appear, the medical profession decided that Mount Sion was the healthier of the two positions.
>
> On the left hand section may be seen the remains of an old porch over the main entrance, on which are traces of some beautifully carved work, and until recently bore the date of 1612 worked in with what appeared to be a representation of the Sun emitting rays of light.
>
> The grand old oak staircase, some six feet wide, comes in for general admiration. The lower part of the house is inhabited by several tenants who encourage visitors to view. The upper part is in a very dilapitated [*sic*] condition.

The windows, especially those of the right-hand section, afford fine views of Mount Ephraim, Rusthall Church, and further on to Crowborough.

An eye-witness account of the state of nos 30 and 32 Little Mount Sion, just before their renovation a few years ago, paints a similar picture. Ceilings had collapsed, 50-year-old newspapers lay on the floors which were rotten or honeycombed with rat holes covered in layers of lino, skirting boards were gnawed, nothing seemed to have been lived in within living memory. Some inkling of what was to come seems to have surfaced in the local press at the beginning of 1913. On 21 February came the report of a meeting of the St John's Church of England Missionary Society at which Mr F.J. Brampton read a paper on the town's history and stated (without committing himself!): 'It is said that the oldest house in the town is now occupied by Mr Love, in Little Mount Sion'. On 14 March the *Courier* noticed Luke Pearce's book on the *Historical Associations* from which the quotation above comes; and finally on 21 March 1913 came the report of impending demolition. It was headlined 'Vanishing part of Old Tunbridge Wells' and was illustrated by the Camburn photograph reproduced at the beginning of chapter 13. 'These picturesque old tiled houses on Little Mount Sion, which are reputed to be the oldest in the town, except some portions of the Pantiles, are to be demolished, and the tenants have this week received notice to quit. Local tradition has it that in the house with the Georgian porch Queen Anne lodged when a visitor at Tunbridge Wells. The disappearance of these quaint old houses will be a matter for sentimental regret, as they represent one of the few remaining portions of old Tunbridge Wells.' It would surely be a matter for a little more than sentimental regret today; and who could have imagined that the site would remain more or less derelict to this day – however worthy the work of the Toc H and delicious the cakes offered weekly by the Women's Institute? Johnson copied the Camburn photograph with his own camera but surprisingly left no comment.

When the deed was actually done, I do not know – not long after I presume, but have found no report. I was once told (and I wish I could remember by whom) that an American millionaire had bought the remains and shipped them to the States for re-erection; but I daresay this would have merited a newspaper report. If anyone knows differently please let us know! The gaping hole in Little Mount Sion is anyway mirrored by a hole *in Kelly's Directories*. Love and Son, builders, at no 20 and the other inhabitants of nos 22 to 26 appear in 1913 but not in 1914. What were Walter and George Arnold thinking of when they gave the order for demolition? I suppose they had some scheme of redevelopment in mind but perhaps the outbreak of war in 1914 put a stop to their plans – or maybe it was Walter's death in 1916. William Arnold had paid Charles Carpenter £1,400 in 1882 and the sons had put in another £210 in 1898 plus whatever the demolition cost. For this the surviving brother George got back £850 when he sold the empty site in December 1921. The purchasers of an absolute freehold (with a few safeguards for the neighbouring nos 26-28 Little Mount Sion) were trustees of the First Church of Christ Scientist – Marian Bartrum, a spinster from Calverley Park;

Arthur Higgs, a farmer from Edenbridge; and Brigadier William Hodgson Suart of Rusthall Cottage, heir to the Manor of Rusthall who however died before the life tenant, Frank Osborne Baird. Whether George Arnold was a Christian Scientist or whatever other reasons may have underlain this transaction I can only speculate. The deeds of 26/28 Little Mount Sion reveal that George Arnold died in April 1925 and in October his widow, Agnes, of Hale Place, East Peckham, and her trustees sold the triangular building which William had erected in 1889/90 to the man in occupation, Frederick Rickwood, newsagent and tobacconist.

A temporary hall for the use of the Christian Scientists appears to have been constructed soon after the acquisition of the site in 1921. In 1923 the Tunbridge Wells branch of Toc H was formed at a meeting held in the old Cadena Café; but the Christian Scientists were still in possession in 1931 – the Abstract of Title records the replacement of trustees on 24 October (Brigadier Suart had died in 1923 and there were other changes) – and Toc H do not seem to have taken over on Little Mount Sion until 1933 when they are listed there by Kelly. Quite what use the Christian Scientists had made or intended to make of their new property I do not know; but for whatever reason they came to a surprising agreement with the Toc H organisation. The property was transferred to Toc H by Deed of Gift with a covenant that, should it ever be sold, the proceeds would return to the Christian Scientists at Tunbridge Wells. This explains why the site has remained undeveloped to this day. Toc H derives a small income from hire of the hall and parking spaces and has no incentive to sell. I think it must have inherited the temporary structure and this is probably what Richard Cobb describes as 'a little corrugated-iron shed painted cream, with a roof painted red, and that belonged to Toc H, with a flame coming out of a saucer painted on its front ... it always seemed to be shut.' In 1938 an application was made to convert the temporary building into a permanent structure. This application was made in the name of Miss Ada Carr as owner. Quite how she came into the picture I do not know but she was a local benefactress, having money derived I think from the manufacture of biscuits; and at all events a plaque is still to be found inside the existing building which says: 'This building was the generous gift of Miss Ada Carr of 8, Broadwater Down in memory of her brother Ellis Carr'. One of Miss Carr's many bequests when she died in 1943 at the age of 89 was £100 to the Tunbridge Wells Branch of Toc H. In 1947 Kent County Council came on the scene with an application to make minor alterations to the hall so that it could be used as 'dining and kitchen accommodation' for the Murray House School. This use no doubt died with Murray House and the Toc H Hall seems set fair to continue its present tranquil existence for the foreseeable future, untroubled even by the ghosts of teeming Sion Crescent or apocryphal Anne or the founding phantom of Philip Seale himself, clutching the shadow of his Deed of Purchase of his Houses and Lands on Mount Sion, dated 1702.

Chapter 17

Frog Lane and Murray House

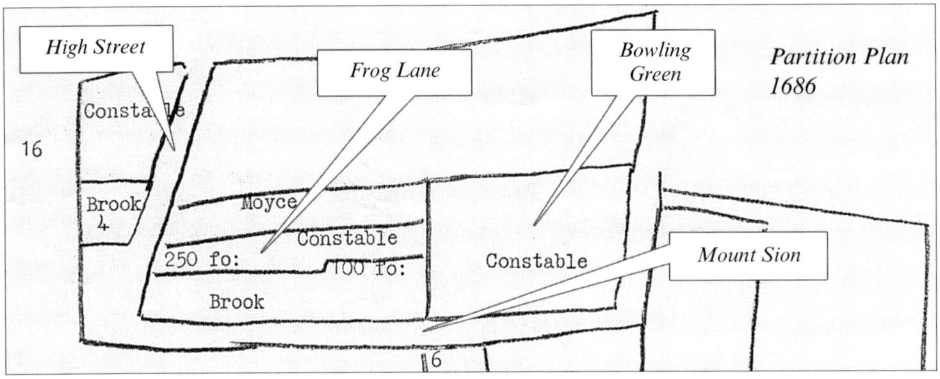

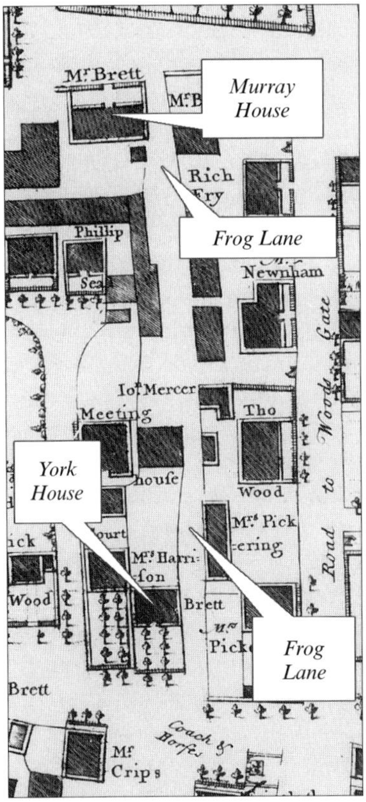

Bowra plan 1738

In her diary for October 1779, Fanny Burney, having commented on the 'strange, wild manner' in which Tunbridge Wells houses were scattered about, as if dropped where they stood by accident, mentions three dirty little lanes where the shopkeepers live, 'much like dirty little lanes in other places'. One of these lanes was surely Frog Lane and is the subject of this chapter. Essentially it is the narrow strip of land (not the rectangular plot) marked 'Constable' on the Partition Plan which you should recognise from chapter 2. The strip measures 350 feet from one end to the other, as marked on the plan itself; but what is not stated is the description of the adjoining strip of land sold to Winefrith Brooke. This is to 'contain in length from north to south 350 feet or thereabouts and in breadth at the north 80 feet and continuing of the same breadth in length 250 feet and at the south end containing in breadth 92 feet and so continueth of the same breadth in length 100 feet to the upper end thereof'. In other words we have here the width on the other side of the fence, as it were. Winefrith's Mount Sion strip is wider along its top 100 feet and therefore Constable's Frog Lane strip is correspondingly narrower. The difference is 12 feet. See the Bowra plan on the previous page. The narrowing at the top shows more or less clearly here and in the maps of succeeding periods which flank this chapter.

Let us begin by recalling that two portions of the land leased to Richard Constable were sold by the Earl of Buckingham in 1702 but anything else fell into the lap of John Brett in 1715. The Frog Lane strip we are here concerned with therefore belonged to John Brett from 1715 which explains why his name is to be found alongside the big house at the bottom of the lane on the Bowra plan of Mount Sion. This is, in fact, York House which still stands there today. Mirabile dictu! We have seen in the previous chapter that we must avoid confusion with Mrs Harrison – she belongs to the house on the left which is no longer there but whose ancient position can be judged in relation to the back of York House as it exists today. The right-hand (or south-west) boundary of the Frog Lane strip is the right-hand edge of the lane itself: all the buildings between it and Mount Sion Road were Winefrith Brooke's domain – see next chapter. It can be seen, then, that there was not much to Frog Lane in 1738 except York House, a square building adjoining the Meeting House or Chapel and a few stables next to Philip Seale's first house. The 350-foot length of the strip finishes short of the top of the lane. This can be measured approximately on the maps according to their accuracy; but it must follow anyway from the ownership of properties. The two houses marked 'Brett' on both sides at the top are so marked because they belong to the square 'Bowling Green' plot. 'Rich Fry' on the other hand is the topmost house in the Winefrith Brooke strip up Mount Sion Road. The house at the top on the left, however, although not properly belonging, will be considered in this chapter as part of the Frog Lane strip because the lane was for long called Murray Lane after the house which became Murray House School.

Two general questions which spring to mind at the mention of Frog Lane are unfortunately difficult to answer in a satisfactory manner. The first is the name 'Frog'. At least there is one piece of evidence here. The 1866 Ordnance |Survey map labels the lane 'Frog Lane'. Otherwise no names are ever given. There is a document dated about 1813 which seems to refer to it as the way leading to the Bowling Green and this may well have been the common nomenclature for the 18th century. The story has been well propagated which claims that 'frog' is an old name for a brake used on a carriage wheel to stop it slipping on a steep hill; and I suppose Frog Lane is steep enough to support the story but I have found no lexicographical authority for the usage. Anyway, it is I think unarguable that this lane was the back service road for the big lodging houses on Mount Sion and was lined with stables and coach houses with hay lofts and rooms for stable folk above – although as we noted just now not much appears on the Bowra plan by way of such buildings. Of course, some are on the Winefrith Brooke side of the boundary. The other question is the road surface. Frog Lane is famous for its spalls but when were they first laid? There are maybe a few photographs of them but only in the late 19th or 20th centuries and I cannot recall any documentary references ever. The photograph below clearly shows the spalls as they were about 1920 perhaps, as well as illustrating Frog Lane from its intersection with the Twitten upwards, with Caxton Cottage on the right and on the left Frog Cottage, a row of stable buildings and Murray House at the top. The identity of the two ladies is unknown.

Frog Lane about 1920

It has been commonly believed that these spalls were unique to Tunbridge Wells in that they were limestone pieces split horizontally and laid with the flat side upwards, as distinct from the cobbles of Mermaid Street at Rye, for example, which present an uncomfortably bumpy surface. This is still very much the case but insistence on calling the material limestone seems to be unnecessary since Kentish Rag falls within the classification limestone. Frog Lane was completely relaid within the last ten years and much of the new material was Kentish Rag. Some of us felt that this was a historical mistake but John Fuller, who is a geologist as well as historian of the Church of King Charles the Martyr, states that a sample of the old Frog Lane spalls in his possession is identical with ragstone specimens from a quarry in the Upper Loose valley. It seems reasonable to assume that a commonly available local material would have been used by those who first laid the spalls in Frog Lane – and in other places. Little Mount Sion was certainly spalled within living memory and other roads now asphalted – Mount Sion even – may have been so surfaced, although traces at the side of Mount Sion Road may represent no more than drainage channels. The whole subject of road surfaces is curiously lacking in historical evidence or comment. The one comment that is heard is a complaint about the dust. Rain was welcomed to lay the dust and when rain did not come water carts were used for the comfort of the company. This suggests, of course, that a dirt surface was common rather than stone spalls.

Let's begin at the bottom of Frog Lane with the large lodging house which became known later as York House. As explained already, this came into John Brett's possession by his foreclosure on the Earl of Buckingham in 1715 and is simply marked 'Brett' on Bowra, telling us nothing of the individuals who lived there and ran the business. For this reason I have been unable to identify a Poor Rate for the house but what is certain is that a large house was there in 1738 and here is what it looks like today, viewed from Little Mount Sion which gives the best impression of its size. Note the large tile-hung side wall.

York House from Little Mount Sion

We have a good description of what it was like in 1831 when it was advertised for auction in the *Maidstone Journal*. In the basement were a good kitchen, housekeeper's room, butler's pantry, scullery and domestic offices; on the first floor a large entrance hall and staircase, a dining room 20 feet by 12 feet and breakfast parlours; on the second floor a drawing room also 20 feet by 12 feet, with glass folding windows opening on a verandah in front of the house, three principal airy bedrooms, dressing room and water closet; and on the upper floor five servants' bedrooms. There was an extensive back lawn and another lawn in front of the house which commanded a fine view over the much admired Common called Tunbridge Wells Common and also Mount Ephraim. The premises were well calculated for the accommodation of a genteel family or at a trifling expense might be converted into a genteel and comfortable residence. There must, of course, have been some changes since the house was built 150 years earlier (the water closet perhaps?) but essentially I think the auction particulars give a good picture of York House in its initial lodging house phase. I have no information on how it left the Brett ownership; it may have been unchanged in 1764 when John Brett the Elder and John Brett the Younger mortgaged among much else a messuage situate on the 'east side of the road leading from the Wells to Mount Sion and now in the occupation of John Lewis' – but the description is so vague it is hardly possible to be sure that York House is intended. From 1780 to 1817 evidence from the *Sprange Guides* becomes available as follows:

1780/1786	Dunage	3 parlours, 5 chambers, stables for 8
1797/1801	Mr Jones	3 parlours, 4 chambers, 6 garrets, 2 coach houses, stables for 8
1808	Mr Peerless	3 parlours, 4 chambers, 6 garrets, 2 coach houses, stables for 6
1811	Mr Peerless	- as above -
1817	Mr R Delves	3 sitting rooms, 4 York House bedrooms, stables for 6

Mr Peerless is confirmed on the Barrow map of 1808 which also shows the location as that of York House, a name first used in 1817 whether thanks to Richard Delves or not is uncertain. Auction particulars point to 27 February 1822 as the date when it was acquired by Richard Delves. His career will be dealt with in chapter 20 but he was certainly in a bullish mood at this time, expanding his list of lodging houses. In fact, he overreached himself and was bankrupted in 1830 which is why the sale of York House took place in 1832 ('by order of the Commissioners named in a Commission of Bankruptcy lately awarded against Mr Richard Delves'). The outcome of the auction is not known but the house was probably bought by the Gilbert family who appear as owners on the Tithe map and Award in 1840 – no 3759 Dwelling House, York House and Shop – Owner and Occupier William

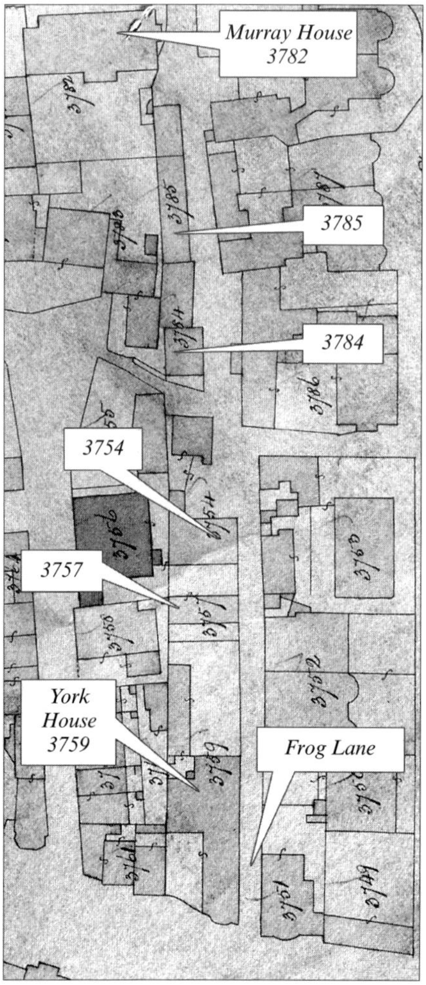

Tithe map 1840

Gilbert. William Gilbert was recorded by the 1841 census enumerator as an Ironmonger aged 55 and living with him were his wife Sarah, 50, son John, 30, daughter Elizabeth, 25, twins George and Emma, 15 and 12-year-old Mary and two servants. The Tithe map also shows dramatically the extension which must have been made to the façade of the old house between 1832 and 1840 – and which is a feature of the building today. No doubt this changed the building from lodging house to Ironmonger's shop; a change consistent with the demolition of 'Harrisons' ' and the Montgomery development next door at about the same time (see page 179 above). Ten years later William Gilbert has died, the widow Sarah is still there and in charge are master ironmongers, employing eight men, John, aged 44 (a son by a previous marriage apparently), and George aged 27. The two girls, Emma and Mary, are there both unmarried (like their brothers) but there is also an unrelated assistant and apprentice and an errand boy and a house servant. George seems to have been the heir and he willed one third of the property to his mother and two-thirds to his sisters. Sarah died in 1866 and George in 1867 and Mary had in the meantime married John Mason, another ironmonger. The two sisters then owned the entire property between them but in 1869 Emma sold her share for £1,250 to her sister's husband so that he became effectively the sole owner. John Mason died in 1888 and his son, named Gilbert after his mother's family, inherited his father's half share in the property (paying however £1,500 for the ironmongery business of Gilbert & Co) and the other half came to him on his mother's death in 1894. It is, I am sure, no coincidence that the name Mason crops up later in connection with the sale of York Villa – see page 209 below.

The two lawns, front and back, which were put forward as recommendations in the 1831 Sale Particulars were no doubt lost in the change of use. The front lawn was half or more taken over by the new extension and the extensive back lawn would surely have been taken over for the storage needs of the business. Certainly no vestige of the lawns remains today. Just above the York House property the Tithe map shows (3757) stables owned and occupied by William Gilbert and one of the earliest applications for planning approval in the town relates to this property. On 29 November 1865 W.L. Wright, Town Surveyor, approved the Plan and Elevation of a Cart Shed and Loft for Mr Gilbert in Frog Lane, subject to proper drainage from the dung pit. A drawing shows a brick building with a slate roof and two doors, one double and one single. Above this is a

Front of York House showing on right the 19th-century extension bisecting the façade

property (3754 on the Tithe map) described as 'Stabling, Cottage and Yard' owned and occupied by Henry Peerless. This shows clearly on the map as two distinct buildings of which one is undoubtedly the present picturesque cottage numbered 4, Frog Lane and the other is located on a level with the Presbyterian Meeting House in Little Mount Sion. Looking back at the Bowra plan there is a square building in just this position but no sign of the cottage in 1738. In 1808, however, the Barrow map shows the cottage and the building near the Meeting House albeit looking a bit smaller. The key to Barrow's map under the heading 'Crescent Passage Mount Sion ' lists 'Mr Peerless Glover etc' and 'Parman's Cottage'; but seems to have got the figures 1 and 2 the wrong way round. Caxton House in Mount Sion was at the time called Parman's Lower House (see chapter 18) and it seems evident that 'Parman's Cottage' must be the present Caxton Cottage and Peerless must be at the 'Cottage' (no 4 Frog Lane) which is where the Tithe map and other evidence place him.

The Twitten

Peerless is also mentioned in annotations by David Johnson to a well-known photograph of the 'twitten' leading from Mount Sion to Frog Lane showing the 'Cottage' which was his home as a boy from 1867 to 1874. He says that the cottage was previously owned and occupied by Mr Peerless a 'dealer in sheepskins' and that the weatherboard building below was used for storage. All this evidence establishes the presence in this location of the Peerless fellmongering family. John Peerless appears as ratepayer for the Fellmonger's Yard (see page 143) in 1784 as does William Peerless in the 1790s; and the Tithe map shows Henry Peerless in partial occupation of the yard in 1840. Henry Peerless is shown in Frog Lane also in 1840 and the census of 1851 provides a little more detail. He is then 48 years old, unmarried and living with his sister Mary. He would therefore have been five in 1808 so that the glover of that year was probably his father. The 'Cottage' was called 'York Villa' in the 1871 census which might be connected with the fact that Mr Peerless had a shop in York House in 1808 and may indeed have owned York House. Still more speculative is the possibility that the cottage might have been built for the Peerless family. We know it was built between the dates of the Bowra and Barrow maps, that John Peerless was working as a fellmonger in 1784, that Mr Peerless, glover, was in occupation in 1808 and even more definitely that Henry was owner and occupier in 1840 and that his property extended down the lane.

The house seems to have been built as two cottages shown clearly on the 1866 Ordnance Survey Map (see next page) but not so clearly and orientated at right angles on the Barrow map – and not shown at all on the Tithe map. In 1861 I have no record of the occupants of York Villa but Henry Peerless is to be found in Little Mount Sion next to the *Jolly Sailor* in what is called appropriately enough the 'Leatherseller's Shop' without his sister but with a hotel porter and his wife and two infants. The 1871 census lists the Johnson family at York Villa: father James Johnson, aged 48, born in Ticehurst, occupation 'Greengrocer shop'; mother Lucy, aged 38 born in Frant; and the future photographer David aged nine. With them are a lodger, 19-year-old unmarried needlewoman Jane and her five-year-old brother Albert. When the Johnson family moved out I do not know but Pelton's and then *Kelly's Directories* show no.4 Murray Road occupied by Moses Milner, a groom, and W. Powell and described as a shoeing forge and coachworks – perhaps they lived in the cottage and worked at the forge in Little Mount Sion – and in 1892 as a lodging house run by Moses Milner. In 1908 Mrs Chandler takes over, followed by George Fermer in 1915, Frederick William Quinnell in 1919 and Alfred followed by Mrs Hicks from 1922 until 1936. During this last stage the first conveyance recorded in the existing collection of deeds took place. On 31 May 1929 John Weyman Mason conveyed to the Tunbridge Wells Gas Company 'all those messuages or dwelling houses known as nos 3 and 4 Murray Road together with the plots of land forming the respective sites thereof'. No description of John Mason, the vendor, is provided but I refuse to believe that he had no connection with the ironmongery business in York House. Notice that no 3 went with no 4. No 3, now called 'Toad Hall', is below the tall building on the right in the photograph above This is the one, taken by David Johnson on 19 September 1934, showing the buildings below York Villa, to one of which Johnson referred as 'the weatherboard building below'. He says: 'The building on the right and the one below it stand on the site of an old Forge and yard where tyres were put on Coach wheels. The higher building was erected about 1873'. This note does not seem altogether consistent with Johnson's statement about the weather boarded building below York Villa used for storage but is worth quoting all the same. This photograph will be used again in chapter 17 to illustrate building on the opposite side of the lane. The 'lantern' on

Lower Frog Lane by D.J. Johnson. Front right is the building which may have been used for storage.

top of the nearer building on the right has come in for much comment. My theory, based in part on Johnson's comment, is that it served to ventilate a space used for storing sheepskins. It is now an office. Nos 3 and 4 continued in the same ownership until Mrs Brain, who bought them from SEGAS, died in 1972. For a long time, in a reversion to the 18th-century method of naming houses, York Villa was known as Mrs Brain's Cottage. She filled it with cats and bric-a-brac until she had to use her no.3 for sleeping accommodation.

At this point on the lane, as has been illustrated in two images above (*Frog Lane about 1920* and the *Twitten)*, a footpath crosses Frog Lane leading from Mount Sion to Little Mount Sion. This along with other local footpaths is known as a twitten. Prominent in the first of these two pictures is tile-hung Frog Cottage, no 5 Frog Lane. The cross-roads formed by the Twitten and Frog Lane and the four buildings at the corners form one of the most picturesque, 'touristique' spots in the town – aided by the spalled and brick surfaces. The two buildings on the southern side belong properly to the Mount Sion strip and the next chapter. They are Crescent Lodge on the lower side of the Twitten and Caxton Cottage above. York Villa, no 4 Frog Lane has just been discussed. Let us now look at the northern side of Frog Lane, above the Twitten. Bowra (see page 202 above) shows only a short row of stables joining at right angles those behind Philip Seale's houses. The ownership must, however, be different unless Philip bought or leased from John Brett at an early stage – for which there is no evidence. Further up at the top of Frog Lane is Murray House which belongs to the Bowling Green plot – see the 1686 plan at the start of this chapter. The exact boundary line is probably that shown on the Ordnance Survey map of 1866 on the left, just above the well at the back of Sion Crescent. Today this line marks the bank at the back of the Toc H Hall.

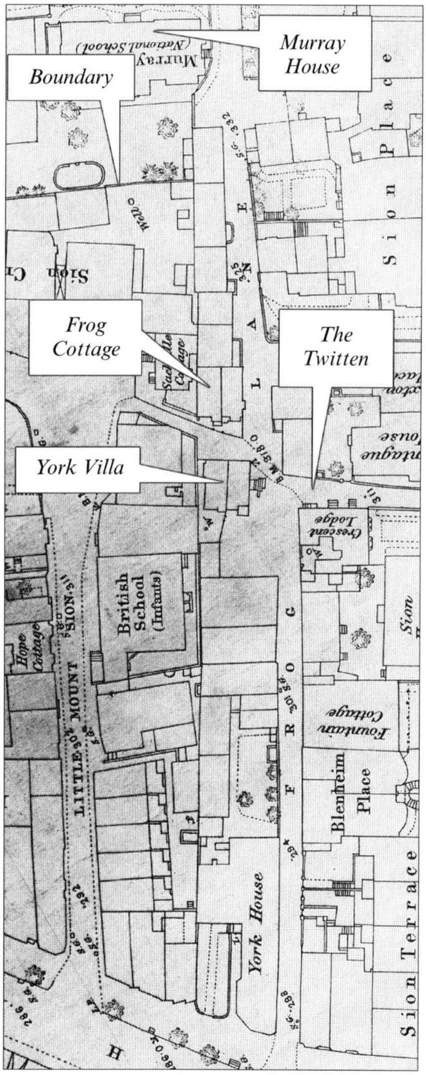

Ordnance Survey 1866

The Ordnance Survey map shows Frog Cottage just above the Twitten divided into two parts parallel with the lane and above it a row of stables. The topmost stable belonged to Murray House and is not shown on Bowra, doubtfully on Barrow but clearly on the Tithe map. From the evidence of the maps, therefore, we can surmise that the northern side of Frog Lane from the Twitten upwards was originally a row of stables to which one was added at the top in mid-19th century and one at the bottom converted to a cottage perhaps about the same time. One of these stables survived in what would seem to have been its original form until about 1970 when it was replaced by a small house numbered 6 Frog Lane. Before this it was used as a garage but consisted of an open space at ground level with a hayloft above to reach which a ladder was needed. Below this are two garages and an extension to Frog Cottage all of which used to be stables. The story of the topmost stable will be detailed shortly. On the other side of the lane also it may be noted there were stables in the 18th century one of which, at the back of no 23 Mount Sion, survived as a garage until the 1960s with a projecting brick high up one wall on which presumably the groom placed his candle at night. The stables above the Twitten on the south side of the lane, however, became Caxton Cottage.

Frog Cottage was owned at the time of the Tithe map by Edward Groombridge and occupied by Edward Lipscombe. Lipscombe appears in the 1841 census as a coachman aged 50 living with his wife Jane of the same age and two children. By 1851 Edward has gone but Jane Lipscombe is still there with her son George aged 23 described as a grocer and tea-dealer. The name 'Groombridge' stuck with the cottage until 1903 when the house deeds describe it as 'All that piece of land with the messuage or dwelling house and buildings erected thereon situate in Murray Road ... and now or lately called 'Groombridge House' and known as Number 5 Murray Road'. Unfortunately this is the earliest deed in the collection and nothing is to be found about the earlier history of the place. Perhaps it was Edward Groombridge who built it – certainly a well-known local name but unidentifiable in particular. When the house name changed to Frog Cottage I have no definite information.

The Tithe map (see page 206 above) shows that a block of stables just above Frog Cottage went with the cottage (3784) but the next block (3785) was owned by Mary Chatterton and occupied by James Hollamby. Mary Chatterton was owner of Mansfield House, no 29 Mount Sion, which will form a topic in the next chapter. The final stable in the row climbing Frog Lane is the one which was built later and belonged to Murray House, the house at the top of Frog Lane to which we will now turn our attention. It took its name from General Murray but he acquired it only some hundred years after its construction. It was built, I am sure, soon after the lease in November 1684 of the Bowling Green plot to Brooke and Constable which Constable took over after the partition of 1686 and there is a Poor Rate sequence which almost certainly applies.

Murray House Poor Rate:

1689-1692:	Mr Horsey or Rich Ashdowne
1693-1713:	Rich Ashdowne
1714:	Rich Ashdowne or Occ
1728-1754:	Alexander Ashdown
1755-1757:	Alex Ashdown or Occ

1758:	Jno Fry for Alex Ashdowne
1759-1784:	Jno Fry for late Alex Ashdowne
1785-1793:	Fry Mrs Mantua Maker for late Ashdowns
1794-1795:	Fry Mrs for late Ashdowns
1796-1797:	Fry Mrs Mantua Maker for late Ashdowns.

Richard Ashdowne's widow Anne left a will dated 30 November 1713 and proved on 13 December the following year:

> I Anne Ashdowne wife of Richard Ashdown of Chitting Stone in the County of Kent I the said Anne Ashdowne Living on Mount Sion in Tunbridge in the said County being very sick and weak in Body … give and bequeath unto my son Alexander The end of my House towards Mount Sion Grove containing Three rooms with two beds The one a feather bed and the other a Flock bed with all belonging thereto and Three Chairs and a Table to each Room and likewise the little brewhouse at the backside of the House and the little Shop in the Yard and the lower Stable and likewise the Heath field on Calverley plaine and to have the use of part of the Yard and likewise my will is that if my said son Alexander dye that then his son Alexander now living do have and enjoy the same Item I give and bequeath unto my daughter Sarah and her heirs and assignes for ever all the other part of my House with all my Linnen and Peuter together with all the goods and Furniture therein with the other Stable and Coach House my will is that my said daughter Sarah may have the use of the Brewhouse Item my will is likewise that my son Alexander and my said daughter do equally between them pay the ground rent Item my will is that my said daughter Sarah do take care and put out Thomas Moyse to a Trade a Boy which I now keep … I desire my Cousen Seal to be Overseer of this my will desireing him to Assist my Executrix in the management and execution of this my last Will.

One of the witnesses was Thomas Mathews, the landlord of the *Compasses*. Notice these points also. Firstly, the reference to the end of the house 'towards Mount Sion Grove' suggests that this is Murray House, the orientation of the house and its proximity to the Grove supporting this supposition, and the division into eastern and western parts corresponding with later usage. Secondly, the relationship between Richard and Alexander Ashdowne is a reasonably convincing demonstration that this will and the Poor Rate sequence are linked. Thirdly, there were two Alexanders, father and son. Fourthly, the reference to ground rent confirms that the freehold of the land lay elsewhere, although it is a pity that Anne does not give the landowner's name. In 1713 it would, I think, be Thomas Constable. In addition to the will there is a Probate Inventory – a fairly rare find.

ANNE ASHDOWNE late of Mount Sion widow deceased taken 16 November 1714

1	Wearing apparel and money		£2-0-0
2	*Kitchen*	16 pewter dishes, 42 plates, 1 fork, 1 pair Andirons, fire shovel and Tongs	£3-5-0
3	*Brewhouse*	One fornace, 2 tubs, 2 kettles, 1 pot	£1-5-0
4	*In 3 Chambers and 2 Garretts*	5 feather bed bolsters and pillows blanket quilts and Curteyn beddstedds and all thereunto belonging	£15-0-0

5	4 sutes of hangings	£2-0-0
6	12 cane chairs 3 Turkeywork chairs 2 arm chairs 6 rushbottom chairs	£2-0-0
7	7 tables 2 pairs Andirons	£1-0-0
8	10 pair Sheets 4 pair pillows 24 napkins 6 towells	£3-5-0
9	1 Case of Drawers and 2 chests	£0-15-0
10	Things out of sight forgotten and unseen	£0-10-0
	TOTAL	£31-0-0

Appraised by Tho Mathews
Thomas Combridge

Notice that the *Compasses* landlord appears again, this time as appraiser, along with a name that should ring a bell. Philip Seale's second wife was born Combridge – see page 164. If Anne Ashdowne was related to the Combridge family the reference to 'Cousin Seal' in her will might be explained.

It is perhaps difficult to reconcile the inventory with the will but there can be no doubt that they belong together. Does the inventory tell us anything about the lodging house business in the early 18th century? For that is the business the Ashdownes were in I am sure. It was evidently on a very modest scale. The total value might come to £3,000 in today's terms but the equipment was sparse – mainly beds, chairs and tables with linen to suit. The beds and their furnishings form by far the most expensive item. There are 'hangings' – for walls I presume – but no mention of floor covering. The inventory mentions three chambers and two garrets, while the will bequeaths three rooms with two beds in just one end of the house. Then there do seem to be some omissions. What about lighting? Surely there must have been a few candlesticks? And the little shop mentioned in the will, why is the stock not mentioned in the inventory? And the stables and coach house, did they not boast any equipment worthy of a place on the inventory? Provision for one's guests' horses was after all even more important than car parking today. It is interesting that Anne Ashdowne was 'living on Mount Sion' when she wrote her will in November 1713. This suggests (remember that the landlord of the *Compasses* had to come and witness) that there was, by this time, a small community living on the hill throughout the year.

The Poor Rate record quoted above shows that occupancy of the house changed from Ashdowne to Fry in or about 1758; but documents among the Ward papers show that the house belonged to John Brett the Younger at least until 1777 when property conveyed to Trustees as part of his marriage settlement included 'those two messuages on the west side of the Bowling Green fronting east on the said Bowling Green, the one formerly occupied by Richard Fry butcher, afterwards his widow, and now or late Joseph Delves, the other now or late occupied by John Fry blacksmith'. The house occupied by Richard Fry was Mansfield House, no 29 Mount Sion (see chapter 19); the other one was Murray House. We have seen in chapter 6 that John Brett senior died in 1784 and his son sold the Grove Houses in 1786 and it seems very likely that Murray House would have been sold about the same time and no doubt to John Fry the blacksmith. All available records show a Fry in occupation: Sprange lists John Fry in 1780 and 1786 and Mrs Jane

Fry in 1797 and 1801; and Barrow's map of 1808 shows 'Mr John Fry – Union Hall'. This name was undoubtedly given to the house for a time and I suppose it was in commemoration of the 1801 union with Ireland. It was used by Barrow in a design for gift wrapping paper from which the detail on the left is taken. The appearance of the house is unmistakeable as can be seen by comparison with the photograph at the bottom of the next page or at the end of the chapter.

Murray House about 1808

I do not know whether the blacksmith John Fry was one of Richard's family (see pedigree in chapter 6). Anyway it seems likely that he acquired the freehold of the house and proceeded to lease it to Thomas Murray at the beginning of the 19th century. Tunbridge Wells historians have been remarkably reticent or curiously uncurious about General Murray. Not even his Christian name is mentioned which is awkward because the Army List for 1808 contains three generals of this name – two Johns and one Thomas. Colonel and Mrs Murray are to be found amongst the 'Company at Tunbridge Wells' in 1797 on a poster in the Sprange collection but again there is no Christian name. However a perusal of the Minutes of the King Charles Vestry revealed the presence at meetings in 1797, 1803-5, 1808-9 and 1811 of one 'Thomas Murray'; and a visit to the PRO at Kew uncovered some notes on the career of General Thomas Murray, Colonel of the late Royal Veteran battalion. He was an infantry officer, first commissioned as an ensign into the 45th Foot on 2 October 1765 and promoted to Lieutenant on 22 September 1769. As a captain he was commanding a company of the 16th in 1780 and on 17 February 1781 he was promoted major in the 84th Foot. There is at Kew a Muster Roll of 'His Majesties 2d Battn 84th Regt whereof Lieut Colonel John Small is Commandant' in which the entry 'Thos Murray Major' is to be found. There are some references to individuals 'on command in Newfoundland' and 'on duty in New York', while one private is a 'prisoner with the Rebels & not yet joined'; but the muster, for the period 25 December 1782 to 10 October 1783, was taken at Windsor on the latter date and the career notes say that the 84th was disbanded in 1783. Thomas Murray was then on half pay for the next twenty years. This would account for his joining the fashionable company at Tunbridge Wells in the 1790s but it does not seem to have prevented his promotion to colonel on 21 August 1795 and major-general on 18 June 1798. On Christmas Day 1802 he was appointed Colonel of the 7th Veteran Battalion and three years later received the rank of lieutenant-general. Finally on 4 January 1814 when he must have been at least 65 years of age he became a full general – a sort of retiring handshake perhaps? Or was he on active service when he died, two years later, 'in foreign parts'? For that is what is recorded against his name in the PRO wills index.

Anyhow his will gives an immediate clue to his family history by naming as legatees his brothers Sir Robert and Sir David and his nephew Sir John Murray

Bart. *Burke's Peerage* 1842 lists a number of noble Murrays but in only one family were there three brothers, David, Robert and Lt Gen Thomas, whose nephew John was the present baronet. These were the Murrays of Stanhope in the County of Peebles (Peebleshire is located between the Scottish border and the Firth of Forth). The family traced its descent from a Scottish chieftain known as 'The Outlaw Murray' who was around in the late 16th century and features in a Scottish ballad. From him descended David Murray who was knighted by Charles I and acquired the Stanhope lands in Peebleshire. His eldest son William supported the King in the Civil War and was rewarded by Charles II with a Baronetcy of Nova Scotia. Continuing the Cavalier tradition a later Sir David fought for Bonny Prince Charlie at Culloden, was captured, condemned and exiled, his lands and title forfeit. The title was however assumed once more, following the 'Act of Revisal', by John Murray who died in 1777 and was General Murray's father. Doubts as to the legitimacy of this assumption did not deter the general's two elder brothers and his nephews from enjoying the title. Sir David, of the Royal Navy, died in 1791, without an heir, and was succeeded by Sir Robert who died before Thomas made his will in 1811 but had two sons who succeeded in turn, the younger one, John, being the baronet at the time of General Murray's death. This explains the situation when the will was written. Loyalty to the family is the characteristic which emerges from the will. High hopes were evidently centred on the present baronet's seven-year-old son and heir, Master John. Thomas gave annuities to him and his father and further annuities went to the widow of the general's brother Robert and to the 'reputed' (i.e. illegitimate) daughters of his father and of his brother David. Thomas and his wife Mary appear to have had no children and the residue of the estate (the annuities would have required a capital fund of some £10,000) was left to trustees for the benefit of his wife during her life and then to young Master John – or his sisters if he should die. The residue included 'the house and premises I now occupy together with the leases thereof with all my furniture plate linen china carriages and horses'. In other words, as evidence elsewhere confirms, he did not own the freehold of Murray House but must I guess have had a longish lease to justify the extensive alterations of which Amsinck speaks. Paul Amsinck took over as Master of Ceremonies on the Pantiles in 1805 and in 1810 wrote and illustrated a very informative book *Tunbridge Wells and Neighbourhood* in which he has this to say about Murray House: 'In the vicinity

Murray House (near left) in September 1934. Berkeley Place is the ivy-clad house on the right.

of the Grove House but higher on Mount Sion, Lieutenant-General Murray has for many successive years (except when diverted elsewhere in the service of his country) taken up his abode. Having long experienced the advantages of the situation, he has recently so improved it as to have actually renovated his dwelling; and at the same time, from the taste displayed in the execution, made it a principal ornament to this part of the place.' On the previous page is a photograph of the house taken by David Johnson in September 1934.

I think General Murray was responsible for the 'twin towers' which can be seen here and in the previous little image. At any rate we have Amsinck's word that some considerable remodelling went on and in this of course General Murray would have been following a general movement towards the refronting of houses which can be seen elsewhere but Amsinck's is the only specific reference to be found in any contemporary local historian. One thing is certain. Such an impression must have been created that the name 'Murray House' stuck to the building for the next hundred years and more.

Thomas appointed two trustees to his will: one was a personal friend, John Peter Addenbrooke, of Stratfield Saye in Hampshire (where a grateful nation was soon to purchase a property for the hero of Waterloo); the other was a local man, Thomas Pinckard Bingham, who lived at Sion Lodge (see chapter 22) and was a JP and whom we met on page 94 as a trustee of the Girls' National School. The will was written in Tunbridge Wells in August 1811 and witnessed by John Bullin, surgeon, and John Nash, stationer, both of Tunbridge Wells, and by Thomas Sizer, servant to General Murray. This is all fairly straightforward but in December 1815 comes the 'Mystery of Warren's Hotel'. On 30 December the general was in London, staying at *Warren's Hotel*, Charles Street, St James's Square, when he decided to add a codicil to his will: £500 to his beloved wife Mary Murray 'to be by her received immediately after my decease out of the monies in the house or to be made up … out of the balance in my banker's hands'; another £60 per annum to Master John Murray, now eleven years old, an attractive age; and £500 to his most worthy friend John Peter Addenbrooke as a testimony of confidence esteem and regard. He called in the owner of the hotel, William Warren, to witness the codicil together with his servant Sizer – not Thomas this time but William Paul – a son perhaps? The next day, or New Year's Day or whenever, he departed for … Did he have a premonition? Was he on a dangerous mission? This seems unlikely. For one thing he was touching seventy; for another, the war was over, Europe was at peace and Wellington was being lionised in Paris. Admittedly everyone was making a rush to visit France once more – perhaps he was just one of those. Or a trip to the field of Waterloo? Why leave Mary at home then? Be that all as it may, one thing is certain: within a few months he was dead … and 'in foreign parts'.

On 19 July 1816 his will was proved at London by his widow and his worthy friend. She continued live in Tunbridge Wells. In 1819 and 1820 she is paying the Poor Rate – but only £10 where the General had paid £30. Was this because of changed circumstances or a change of residence? Then in 1827 *Pigot's Directory* shows 'Murray Mrs General' living on Mount Sion, so perhaps she lived on in Murray House. As for the Murrays of Stanhope, things did not go according to plan. 'Master' John married in 1824, at the age of twenty, a girl called Elizabeth Fletcher but two years later he was dead – who knows how? – without producing any baby heir or even daughter. Old Sir John, on the evidence of *Burke's Peerage*, lived on until 1850 at least; but when he was eventually laid to rest the baronetcy went with him. Two daughters married, Emily a Howell and Frances a Gyll, and had children but that is another story; I should be interested to hear if anyone out there knows it.

In 1840 the Tithe Commissioners made a rare mistake and wrote the name of the house as 'Merry House' – or was this a local joke? At least we have definite confirmation that the freehold belonged to the Fry family. The owners and occupiers are recorded as Thomas Jenks and George White who also owned Bedford House (not Place) and Sion Cottage in Chapel Place. Now the hatches, matches and despatches column of the *Maidstone Journal* of 12 January 1830 announced the death on 5 January, at Sion Cottage, Tunbridge Wells, of Mr John Fry, many years upholsterer of that place. A few years later (strange to relate!) his two daughters were married – Charlotte Susanna to Thomas Jenks, looking glass maunfacturer of Fleet Street London, and Eliza to George White, upholsterer of Canterbury. It is fairly clear, therefore, that John Fry the cabinetmaker (on Barrow's map he is in Chapel Place as 'Manufacturer etc') was the owner of Murray House also – probably by virtue of being the son of John Fry the blacksmith – and his property passed to his daughters and their husbands. At all events Murray House was let at the time of the 1851 census to William Beane, a 50-year-old coal merchant hailing from Cumberland. With him were his wife Mary from Banbury and eight little Beanes ranging from 21-year-old Kate Beane Beane to five-year-old Isabella, all born in London and most in Peckham. Eventually however, in 1858, Jenks and White decided (or were persuaded) to sell – by which time, according to the deeds, the house had been 'for some time past untenanted'.

The purchaser was that popular Poo Bah and public-spirited Panjandrum of Mount Sion, the Reverend William Law Pope who had been installed as incumbent of the Chapel of King Charles the Martyr in 1829 and in 1848 had built himself a sparkling new villa which can still be seen, thankfully, closing the vista of Eden Road; although the view on either side has changed somewhat, and not for the better, with the disappearance of the old Brunswick House on the left (see chapter 21) and the more recent demolition of Eden House and Cottage on the right (see chapter 20). Anyway the Reverend Pope had but a short walk to Murray House to visit the Girls' School for which he had purchased the house. A Charity School for Boys and Girls had existed as long as the Chapel itself, using part of the Chapel as a schoolroom. A good account of the school is given in 'The Story of the Church of King Charles the Martyr' by Col Waring. He says that the Girls' School separated from the Boys' only when Murray House was purchased but this is incorrect. We have already seen (on page 94) that the girls moved in 1813 to new premises in Little Mount Sion. Two Girls' School Committee Books have survived. The first says that the school was established in 1813 and transferred to Murray House in 1858 and contains an extract from the 'Trust Deed belonging to the Female National School on Mount Sion' dated 1813 which witnesses agreement between John Lloyd and Thomas Pinckard Bingham (General Murray's trustee also) to permit the 'Chapel Ground tenement and hereditament' to be used as a Charity School – and the Chapel Ground is the so-called Bethlehem Chapel at the top of Warwick Road. The Committee minutes go on to record that out of the purchase price of £850 for Murray House £418 2s. 6d. was raised by subscription and £330 was obtained by sale of the old school the new occupiers of which were the boys of Christ Church, as clearly shown on the Ordnance Survey 1/500 map surveyed in 1866.

The second Committee Book contains copies of deeds written in a very fair italic hand. The first deed, dated 20 December 1858, is the conveyance to the Rev. William Law Pope by James White and others but notes that this was for the purpose of convenience only and the premises were really purchased by the Trustees of the Girls' National School who were Thomas Mayo of 56 Wimpole Street, doctor of medicine; David Jean Robertson of Tunbridge Wells, Esquire; and Walter Sprott. Thomas Mayo is the doctor who built Grecian Villa and moved to London when he sold it in 1834; so that it is worth noting that he is continuing to take an interest in Tunbridge Wells affairs twenty years later. By the second deed, dated 25 June 1859, the Rev. Pope conveyed the east end of the house (nearer the Grove) to Dr Mayo and Walter Sprott as trustees (David Robertson having died in 1859). On one page of this copy has been drawn a plan showing the site coloured blue and the house uncoloured. There is no writing on the plan but part of the blue area is a rectangle which must represent the stable on Frog Lane. The third deed is dated 27 March 1874 and is the conveyance of the west end by Pope to the Trustees. Why the gap of 15 years is not stated but it was probably to do with the fact that the west end had in fact been occupied by Alfred Diggens, the Master of the Boys' School, until he moved to Cumberland Villa in Cumberland Walk in July 1880. He was in occupation at the time of the 1861 census, along with the schoolmistresses and the soup kitchen. Diggens came from Hambledon in Hampshire and was 37 years old. His wife Mary was seven years his senior and originated from Norfolk. Their children had all been born in Presbury, Cheshire. Fourteen-year-old Emily was already a pupil-teacher and William, Georgina and little Alfred were aged 11, nine and seven. Their 29-year-old servant, Eliza Worth, seems to have followed the family from Cheshire for that is where she was born. The schoolmistresses were Miss Sarah Barnes and her 17-year-old sister Mahala who was a pupil-teacher; and Caroline Winder, another 17-year-old who, as we learn from the Committee Minutes, came from Dublin and established the Infant School in 1860.

The Minutes recount that the school opened on 24 December 1858 with a dinner prepared in the kitchen which was intended for the instruction of the girls in cooking and 'which is now used for a Soup and Dinner Kitchen for the poor'. Mary Leigh was the cook according to the census; she was a widow and must have been glad of a job and a home for herself and 7-year-old Walter and baby Louisa. The headmistress was Miss Harriett Parrott 'from the Home and Colonial School in London' who was appointed in 1863 and remained until 1895 at least. She was followed until the First World War by the Misses Allsop, Wiltshire, Kempthorne and Hazelwood. Between the wars the school appears in *Kelly's Directory* as King Charles School (senior girls) and after the Butler Act of 1944 as King Charles C. of E. Modern Girls' School; King Charles C. of E. Secondary Girls' School and Bennett Memorial C. of E. Secondary Girls' School (Murray House). The Murray House Soup Kitchen is recorded in 1895 and again in 1899 when Mrs Leigh, for all her 75 years, was still in charge. The new classrooms at the east end of the house which can be seen in Johnson's photograph were added, according to Col Waring, in 1908 and must have necessitated some purchase of adjoining property.

A glimpse of life at the school is afforded by a letter written to the editor of the *Tunbridge Wells Gazette* by an anonymous lady in February 1860 when Mary Leigh (surely it was she) prepared the annual dinner for the girls.

> I read with pleasure your account of the boys' annual dinner at the Chapel School, and I looked in this week's Gazette for some account of the girls' dinner, which took place last Thursday, at the national school, Murray House, but your reporter was not I suppose present.
>
> I was much pleased to see the children, upwards of 90, assembled. Looking so clean and orderly, and so happy. They did ample justice to the well-cooked meat, and excellent plum puddings, placed before them. After grace was sung, the prizes from the Duchess of Kent were given, as in the boys' school; but something more was in store for us. A treat was provided in the room above, which I confess I enjoyed as much as the little ones. The Christmas tree was got up in good old German style, beautifully lit up (daylight being quite excluded), and decorated with fruit and all kinds of suitable presents for the children – and more happy faces I never saw than in the double circle round the tree.
>
> We had some pretty songs before the presents were given and the tree stripped, and then plenty of hearty cheering, and ended, as all loyal subjects should, with 'God Save the Queen' which, by the way, the children sang particularly well, they concluded with the last verse of our Evening hymn.

Site of Murray House in use as car park

Things continued in this more or less happy vein until the Second World War when the Butler Education Act of 1944 introduced big changes in the whole local education scene. Murray House School eventually became part of the Church of England Bennett Memorial School for Girls taking children of secondary ages, the new Primary Schools hiving off the younger children who had previously been part of the Murray House scene. This was obviously an inconvenient arrangement since the distance from the main school was considerable, although former pupils of the Murray House section retain happy memories of the place and have kept up an Old Girls' Association. By the 1950s, however, the writing was on the wall and on 12 July 1961 Murray House, along with the boys' school buildings in Chapel Place and the Victoria School off the Camden Road, was sold by auction, Murray House fetching £3,000. The Charity Commissioners hold a report from the surveyors Bernard Thorpe of Oxted which describes Murray House as being in a very dilapidated condition. Demolition followed probably in 1967 and there was then a period when the site remained vacant and was used as a car park – see the photograph on the previous page which gives some idea of how the Common appears from the top of Mount Sion hill without intervening buildings. A row of town houses was then built which unfortunately did not commemorate the old name but was called Spencer Mews after the architect; the Murray House Old Girls have, however, fixed a plaque to the wall at the Grove end of the building in memory of their old school.

As we saw earlier, Murray House had a stable or coach house of its own at the top of the row, built sometime after Bowra and before the Tithe map. On the left is a photograph annotated by David Johnson as follows: 'Photograph taken by Mr Spencer. Probable date 1900-1905. Foreground building was used as a Coach Builder's workshop 1869 onward by Harriman, employed by Wm Powell, Fly Proprietor; afterwards by Wm Crossland and then became stores of the Tunbridge Wells Gas Company.' Behind this picture lies a curious tale of squatters' rights and proprietorial insouciance. The stable was demolished, by mistake, at the same

The top of Frog Lane about 1900; the sign above the doors reads 'W. Crossland Fly Proprietor'.

time as Murray House itself. I was there but I cannot remember the details too well. The demolition men were using a winch and cable and somehow the cable snagged the roof of the stable and brought it down together with the roof of the adjoining building, the dormer window of which can be seen to the right of the lady walker. Quite how this combination of events could have come about, whether the cable was attached to a bulldozer or not, where the bulldozer or whatever was placed, what the cable was supposed to be pulling, all this is quite obscure in my memory; but I am quite clear that this is what happened. Whichever way it was, Patrick Harbour who had the possessory title to the building was left with a ruin, from which (razed to ground level at the beginning of his operations), almost single-handed, and largely re-using the original materials, he created a small dwelling with a living room on the upper level lit by three dormer windows and a kitchen and garage on the ground level – the whole conserving the character of the old building. But how did Patrick Harbour come to hold a possessory title?

It started in 1954. Kenneth Child, a sculptor and, inter alia, restorer of Chichester Cross and of gargoyles on Chichester Cathedral, tells the story in the 1968 affidavit by which he claimed the property. He first took possession in January 1954 and paid rent of 2s. 6d. a week to the Estate Agents Parris and Quirk. The rent went to the Church Commissioners who, as he understood, owned the property together with adjoining Murray House School. On 1 January 1955 collection of rent was undertaken by the Commissioners and was to be delegated to the 'Vicar'. In the middle of 1956 Kenneth Child went to the vicar and offered him £2; but the vicar knew nothing of the matter. The affidavit does not say which vicar he saw: King Charles the Martyr or Christ Church? Murray House had very close ties with King Charles the Martyr, as we have seen, but is actually in the parish of Christ Church. Anyhow Kenneth Child, in his words, 'realised that this land did not belong to the Church' and he had been paying rent unnecessarily. If you have occupied land unchallenged for a dozen years you can register a provisional title and after a further 15 years the Registrar can make the title absolute. So in 1968 Kenneth Child

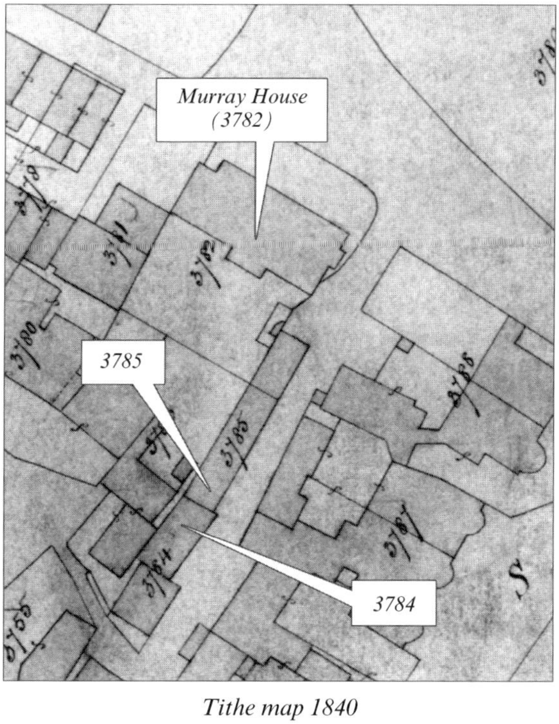

Tithe map 1840

registered a provisional title. In 1970 Patrick Harbour bought the property, taking the risk that it might be claimed before the title became absolute. In 1975 his application for planning approval for a conversion was approved. In 1983 the title was made absolute. The registrar may – but is not bound to – issue notices and make enquiries before granting the title. Whether in this case he served notices on owners of adjoining properties, advertised in the *Gazette* and locally or made his own enquiries I do not know.

If the Registrar had made enquiries he might have started with the Tithe map of 1840 – see the previous page. This shows Murray House (described as 'Merry' House, Garden and Stabling) with the stable (or Crossland coachworks in Spencer's photograph) in the corner of the site and two blocks of property below. The lower block (no 3784) includes the present Frog Cottage and adjoining stables, all owned by Edward Groombridge and occupied by Edward Lipscomb. The middle block (no 3785) covers the present no 6 Frog Lane and the squatter property and was owned by Mary Chatterton and occupied by James Hollamby. Mary was the daughter of Joseph Delves and owner at this time of Mansfield House – see chapter 19. Then in 1858 Murray House was bought by the Rev. Pope for the Girls' School. A plan in the School Committee Book, already mentioned on page 218 above, on a scale roughly double that of the Ordnance Survey (i.e. about 1/250), seems to show that not only the Murray House Stable but also the squatter property (approximately half Mary Chatterton's stable block) was conveyed to the Church. This would, of course, explain the collection of rent on behalf of the Church Commissioners. The description in the deed seems to fit: 'the Stable and Coachhouse yard and premises in the rear of and adjoining the said … dwelling house then or late in the occupation of ______ Powell or his undertenants'. William Powell featured in David Johnson's note on the Spencer photograph. One problem is that there is no evidence that Mary Chatterton or her successors did or did not sell half the stable block to the Church. We do know, however, that part at least of the block continued to go with Mansfield House because on 29 December 1883 Henry Goodrham conveyed to John William Rush 'All that Coachhouse and stabling situate

North-east side of Frog Lane – drawn by Gill Twells about 1970

on the north-east side of Murray Road Tunbridge Wells'. This reference is to be found in the Abstract of Title of Mrs E.A. Pickering which forms part of the Frog Cottage deeds. The north-east side of the lane is quite certainly the one on the right-hand side of Spencer's photograph and the sketch on p.222.

From this point alternative hypotheses have to be followed. (1) The squatter property was in fact sold to the Church. In this case the mystery is easily solved. Lack of communication between the Church Commissioners and 'the Vicar' and lack of follow-up by the Commissioners meant that the property was first lost sight of and then ... lost. It is not as if, after all, Murray House by this time was any concern of the local church: it had long been absorbed into the State secondary education system. (2) The second theory has to assume first of all that the plan in the School Committee Book is erroneous or conceivably that the squatter property appears on the plan because the Church was using it but was not the formal owner. Some support for this theory may be found in a letter held by the Charity Commissioners dated 18 June 1973 about title to the Coach House and Stables which states a problem in that these were not included in the deed of 1859. Either way Mrs Pickering's Abstract tells us that J.W. Rush died in 1920 and left his property amongst his sons. Frank Owen Rush, a Crowborough builder, received the coach house on the north-east side of Frog Lane as part of his share; and in 1944 he sold it to Forwells Limited for £250. What sort of company Forwells was is obscure but its registered office at 25, High Street, Tunbridge Wells, was the office of a firm of accountants, Clarke Pickering & Co, who had a London address at 23 Bedford Row and one of whose partners was Ronald R. Pickering FCA. We also know from her Abstract of Title that Mrs Eva Adams Pickering was a director of Forwells.

Murray House about 1970

At this point the story becomes so confusing, involving the deeds and garages of Crescent Lodge as well as those of Frog Cottage and Durnford House, that any certainty disappears. More progress might be made if the original documents came to light because the conveyance of 1883 contained a plan of the coach house on the north-east side. What emerges from the clouds of confusion is that in 1961 Kenneth Child, as we know, was squatting in the upper part of Mary Chatterton's erstwhile stable block while the lower part was in regular use as a garage by the owners of Crescent Lodge who had bought it with the house and knew nothing further. It has since been demolished and replaced by no.6 Frog Lane. Here is a photograph of Murray House shortly before it was demolished, taken by one of the 'old girls' of the old school.

CHAPTER 17

Winefrith's Strip

We move, in this chapter, from Frog Lane to the adjoining strip of land shown on the Brooke/Constable partition plan of 1686. This strip today forms the north-eastern side of Mount Sion Road from no 1 at the bottom to no.25 at the top and was sold to Robert Brooke's widow, Winefrith, in 1702. The description given in the Chancery case of 1708 runs as follows: 'one piece or parcel of ground whereon divers messuages houses stables and other buildings are erected and was heretofore a parcel of certain heath ground called Inhams in Tonbridge aforesaid near Tunbridge Wells and bounding towards the north to a new way there laid out and leading from the Wells to Southburrough and to a new way leading to the Bowling Green towards the west to other lands intended to have been sold to the said Richard Constable towards the east and south and doth contain in length from north to south 350 feet or thereabouts and in breadth at the north 80 feet and continuing of the same breadth in length 250 feet and at the south end containing in breadth 92 feet and so continueth of the same breadth in length 100 feet to the upper end thereof'. An echo of this wording is to be found in the 'Deed Poll' of Winefrith Brooke. The original of this document was dated 30 March 1710 and a copy made in January 1718 (29 January 1717 Old Style) was included in the

Brooke/Constable Partition plan 1686

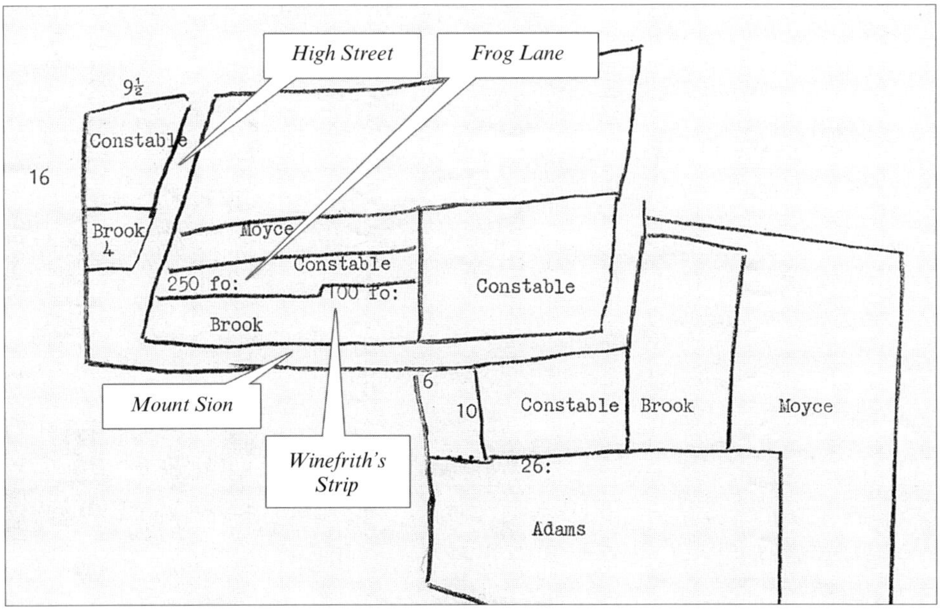

deeds of Sion House, no.15 Mount Sion. This valuable 18th-century collection has most unfortunately been lost between one owner of the house and the next. The outgoing owner left it in the house for the incoming owner who denies having found it. Fortunately I was able to examine the deeds before they were lost and to make transcriptions, notes and a few photocopies, so the content has in the main been preserved. Here is the opening of the Deed Poll.

> To all Christian people to whom these presents shall come I Winefrith Cullen wife of Thomas Cullen of Tonbridge in the County of Kent yeoman Greeting Whereas I the said Winefrith by the name of Winefrith Brooke of Tonbridge … widow by indentures of lease and release bearing date the 27th and 28th days of November in the first year of the reign of our Sovereign Lady Queen Anne or by some other good conveyances in the law for and in consideration of a certain sum of money in the same indentures mentioned did purchase to me and my heirs of the Right Honourable John Earl of Buckingham Thomas Lake Thomas Weller and George Weller or some or one of them One piece or parcel of land whereon divers messuages and other buildings were erected late parcel of certain lands called the Inhams and divers other parcels of land lying near Tunbridge Wells in Tonbridge aforesaid and bounding as by the same indentures is set forth …

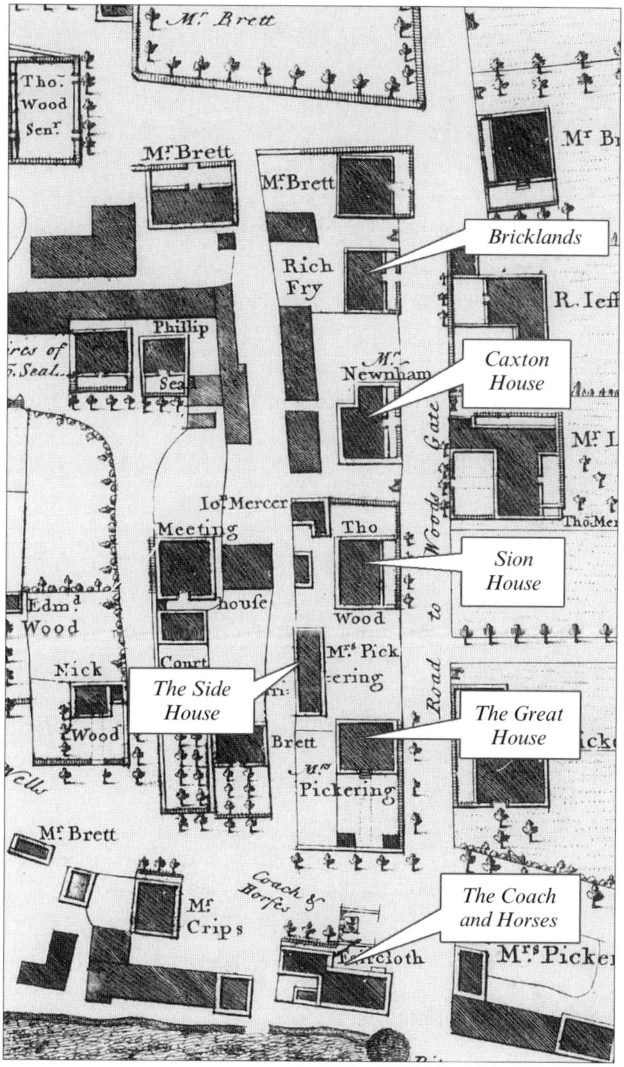

Detail from Bowra plan 1738 illustrating Winefrith's Strip.

Having laid claim to the property 'in fee simple' Winefrith proceeds to determine how it should be distributed following her remarriage and then her death. By a conveyance dated 6 and 7 August 1703 (when she married yeoman Thomas Cullen of Aylesford, Kent) she leaves everything to two trustees, yeoman Christopher Dobson of Bidborough and periwig maker Sherrard Dixon of London, using the 'Deed Poll' as a kind of combined Marriage Settlement and living will. Firstly she reserves for herself 'without the power and control of my husband' the house at the lower end of the street called the 'Coach and Horses' occupied by John Tomsett and 'by him used as a Victualling House with the stables outhouses and other appurtenances thereunto belonging'. The 'Coach and Horses' can be seen clearly on the Bowra plan (see previous page); it must have occupied the island site used until recently by the Midland Bank (now a restaurant) and its neighbours. The rest of her property is to be for the use of her husband during his life (no doubt she hoped he would look after her!) and then her own use. These are normal marriage settlement terms, the only difference being that no mention is made of children; evidently the begetting of babies on the wife's body (the usual elegant legal language) was not the anticipated outcome of this marriage. The final disposal of the property was at her nomination in writing. This occupies the bulk of the document; and provides us with information on the property. 'Now know ye,' she says, 'that in pursuance of the same indenture of bargain and sale and the power thereby to me assured and reserved and for the better settling the premises therein mentioned to come after my decease I the said Winefrith Cullen do by these presents direct limit and appoint …'

Starting at the bottom of the hill then, the alert reader will have noticed a problem: the *Coach and Horses* is not part of the strip shown on the 1686 partition. A small square of land, measuring four rods in one direction or another and marked 'Brook', is shown on the plan on the other side of the High Street and this may be the solution, although the position does not correspond. Nevertheless, the Deed Poll speaks specifically of the *Coach and Horses* and I cannot believe it is not the place shown on Bowra. The victualling house with its yard and garden is left to Edward Dixon, son of Sherrard Dixon, one of the trustees. Next comes the Smith's Forge in the occupation of Edward Hilder 'and the room over it' which is left to Susan wife of (first name blank) Harman, of Speldhurst, tailor. I assume this must be one of the outbuildings adjoining the *Coach and Horses*. There is a forge (Bodles) shown on Bowra but this is located on the Common, in the Parish of Speldhurst and the Manor of Rusthall. Smith's Forge must be a different one. Then there are the 'stables adjoining to the little new stables built by John Tomsett and by me formerly settled'. These seem to bound to 'a certain watercourse towards the north and to Richard Constable's land towards the east'. There are words missing here either in my transcription or in the original but the description would make sense if north were interpreted as downhill towards the Common. The watercourse would then be the Vale Stream and Constable's land would be that shown on the Partition Plan measuring 16 and 9½ rods. Anyway the stables are bequeathed to Martha Kitchingham daughter of William Kitchingham whom we shall meet a little while later. After the stables come 'the two shops in the lower yard adjoining to the way one in the occupation of William Bewley the other in the occupation of Edward Whiteing with the appurtenances'. Looking at the Bowra plan above, these shops appear to be the two small squares looking like overgrown gateposts at the bottom of the Great House garden behind the row of trees … unless you have a better idea? Here is a detail from Kip's engraving of 1719 showing them with pyramidal roofs and positioned as on Bowra's plan.

Detail from Kip's engraving 1719

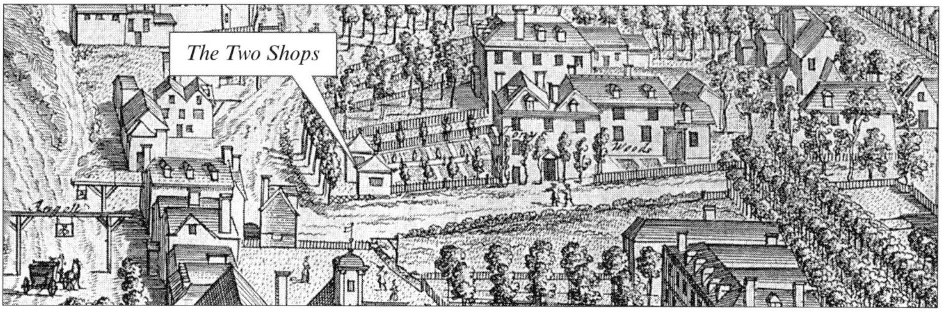

They certainly 'adjoin the way' or road or street and could be called in the 'Lower Yard'. The two of them are bequeathed to Christopher Mountain, son of John Mountain late Minister of Brenchley. After the two shops come two pieces of land which are difficult to locate. One contains four acres and adjoins certain new ways towards the east and north and lands of Edward Allen towards the west now occupied by Edward Allen. We shall meet Edward Allen in a later chapter in connection with Jerningham House. This land is left to Philip, Elizabeth, Christopher and Alexander Mountain, sons and daughters of the late Minister of Brenchley. The next piece of land is also occupied by Edward Allen and bounds Waterdown Forest to the west and other lands of Edward Allen and lands occupied by Thomas Cullen to the east and north. This land is left to Robert Brooke, son of gentleman Francis Brooke of Rochester, who I guess was a brother of Winefrith's late husband. There is a rectangular piece of land marked 'Brook' on the Partition Plan, but it cannot bound Waterdown Forest nor can it be as large as four acres. The location of these two pieces of land is therefore uncertain.

Now we begin to climb Mount Sion proper. The two shops at the bottom have already been noticed set in the Lower Yard of the 'Great House'. This was one of the row of large lodging houses which looked over the High Street (the new way from the Wells to Southborough) to the Common (Bishops Down). Next were York House, then 'Harrisons' and Rosebury (Martins Lower) House flanking Little Mount Sion, then Warwick (Martins Upper) House and finally Camden House. All these have been noted in previous chapters. The 'Great House' was variously known as the Mansion House, White's, Bolton's and Stone Court before it was demolished in the mid-19th century. The Deed Poll of 1710 refers to it in these words: '… the Great House and the Side House now in the occupation of the said Thomas Cullen and the Yard adjoining to the same and the backyard and the walk towards Waterdown Forest between Mr Bretts land and lands in Edward Allen's occupation and the Coach House and stables in the Upper Yard with the appurtenances' and bequeaths all this to the London tailor John Kitchingham together with a gift of £100 on condition that he 'shall pay with it all such money as I have mortgaged or engaged the same to pay' and also makes certain small payments including £5 to the poor of Tonbridge Parish. The 'Side House' I take to be the building backing onto Frog Lane between the Great House and Sion House which is now the back part of Nos 9, 11 and 13 Mount Sion. This is marked 'Mrs Pickering' on Bowra (see above). The stables and coach house can be assumed to fill some empty spaces but the 'walk towards Waterdown Forest' is a puzzle. The Forest is up the hill and beyond and Brett's land might refer to Frog Lane but Edward Allen's land was on the other side of Mount Sion Road – named by Bowra the 'road to Woodsgate' (Pembury).

Bowra also shows the Great House and the Side House in the ownership of John Brett's widow, Mrs Pickering. which means that John Kitchingham must have sold soon after inheriting the place from Winefrith. I do not have a precise date for Winefrith's death but it must have occurred between 1710 and January 1718 when Sarah Jeffery (née How) had a copy of the Deed Poll made. There is a Poor Rate sequence which seems to fit the 'Great House' but this transaction would have taken place during the 1714-28 gap or in 1713-4 when no occupier's name is given. Here is the sequence:

Great House Poor Rate Payers

1686-1695	Robert Brooke
1696-1698	Mr William Brooke
1699-1704	Mrs Brooke
1708-1712	Mr Culling
1713-1714	The Occr of the house late Mr Caltons
1728-1729	Mr John White
1730-1736	Mr John White or Occ
1737-1757	Wid White or Occ
1758-1764	Wid White or Occ Mr Geo Lewis
1765-1767	John Knight for Widow Whites
1768-1775	Widow Lewis for Whites
1776-1782	Gratton Wm for Whites
1783	Gratton Widow
1784	Mitchell for Whites late Grattons
1785-1792	Mitchell Henry
1793-1797	Mitchell Henry for Whites

Quite why John Brett's widow should have wanted to extend her property from the Chapel Place block across the road I have no explanation but there is no doubting the evidence of Bowra and a linkage with the George Lewis in the Poor Rate sequence can be established. The suggested Poor Rate record therefore makes sense on certain assumptions. It begins in the year of the Brooke/Constable partition with Robert Brooke and continues with William Brooke – a relative no doubt – followed by Mrs Brooke perhaps showing that Robert had died in 1699. We know that Winefrith married Thomas Cullen in 1703 and then in 1713 it seems that perhaps both husband and wife had died leaving an unnamed occupant of the house. Some time during the gap years Mr White became the tenant. We know he was not the owner because the Chancery Court case records (see chapter 5) show that from 1719 to 1742 rent for 'Mr White's House at Tunbridge Wells' was received by Margaret Pickering. The connection with George Lewis then is that when Margaret eventually died in 1743 she still had no children of her own and left all her property to trustees for the benefit of a niece, Hester, who at the time of her aunt's will was married to a certain Josiah Newton but was later to marry a George Lewis. White and Lewis were succeeded by their widows until 1776 when William Gratton (whom we know as landlord of the *Gloucester Inn* on the Pantiles among other things) presumably bought the house. Another widow then followed and another purchaser, Henry Mitchell, who completes the series. George Lewis and Henry Mitchell feature in the deeds of Walmer Cottage which we shall come to in a short while.

The 'Great House' or 'Whites' was used in the 18th century I am sure as a lodging house for the summer visitors; but as the new century drew on I think it became more and more a boarding house for local people. The evidence for this is the census of 1841 which shows it occupied by a draper, his family, apprentices and servants and an independent family, amounting to no fewer than twenty persons in all. The draper was named Henry Corke and the place was known as Stone Court after William Stone (another player in the Walmer Cottage deeds) who seems to have owned the house for a time from perhaps 1797. He had some relationship with the Stones of Mayfield one or more of whom later became partners in the solicitors Buss Stone now Buss Murton. *Sprange's Guides* list Stone's 'largest' and 'smaller' house in 1797 and 1801, Stone's 'large' and 'small' houses in 1808 (although Barrow's map shows Mitchell in that year), Mr Stone and Bolton House in 1811 and Fountain Place and Bolton House in 1817. The name 'Bolton' seems to supersede 'Whites' at this time but is replaced by 'Stone Court' later. The whole picture is confused because construction of Walmer Cottage and Blenheim Place was taking place about this time and both Stone and Mitchell were involved in related conveyances and mortgages. Be that as it may, the owner in 1840 was Richard Corke who may or may not have been the same as the Henry Corke of the 1841 census. Here is the Tithe map. No 3750 is

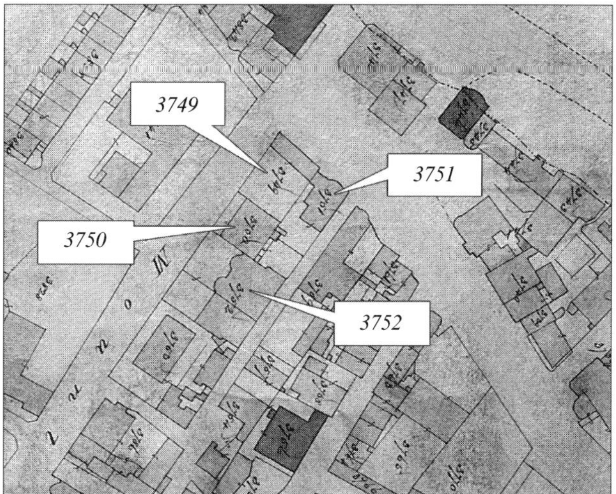

Detail from Tithe map 1840 showing Stone Court

'Stone Court house and Yard' (the old house itself); no 3749 is called 'House Shop and yard' and is the garden or yard in front of the house and one or both of the little shops merged into one building; and no 3751 is a new building on the Frog Lane corner. All are owned by Richard Corke and all also occupied by him except 3751 whose occupier is one James Dampier, a hairdresser, who with his wife and child had a narrow escape in the fire of 1857 about which more in a minute. No 3752 is listed as Blenheim Place 2 houses and Fountain Cottage owned and occupied by Thomas and Frederick Taylor. Perhaps it was this new construction abutting the old house which sealed its fate. At any rate a note appeared in the *Sussex Agricultural Express* of 22 September 1849 reporting that Mr J. Dadson had given a dinner to the builders employed on erecting three large houses on the Stone Court property which he had just purchased. The 'Great House' had been pulled down and Sion Terrace, Nos 3, 5 and 7 Mount Sion as we know them now, was in course of erection. The new building did not, however, extend right down to the corner. Maybe Corke the draper wanted to keep his shop on the High Street? If so he had his wish for eight years but then fate took a hand. About two o'clock in the morning of Wednesday 18 March 1857 PC James Judges was on duty in the High Street when he observed smoke coming from Mr Corke's shop. He soon saw that the place was on fire and, in the words of the *Gazette*'s report, 'gave an alarm'. How, we are not told. Did he run to the fire station? Did he blow a whistle? Did he send a small boy who happened to be walking down the High Street at two in the morning? All we can say with certainty is that he did not use his police radio. The building was of largely wooden construction, like many on Mount Sion at the time, of course, and the fire soon took a hold. A number of townspeople had heard the alarm and were giving what assistance they could. About £10 worth of drapery goods were rescued from the flames, albeit damaged. On the Pantiles newly married Mary Agnes Strange was woken by her six-weeks-old baby and saw the red glare and her husband, Edward Hilder, got up and woke his father E.J. Strange who was later spotted by the *Gazette* reporter among those at the scene; but no one else on the Parade heard anything of it.

The fire engine arrived and was soon in full play, using water from a pump at the Kentish Hotel yard, from the *White Bear Inn* and other places; but the exertions of the fire brigade were almost futile, the timber building being well alight when they arrived. Fortunately no one was sleeping on Corke's premises; but this was not the case in the adjoining building occupied by J. Dampier, hairdresser, his wife and child. They were startled from sleep by the cries of alarm but found their normal exit blocked by flames and smoke. No time was to be lost but the only means of escape was by the window of the bedroom which was at the rear and some fifteen feet from the ground. The child was dropped from the height and was dexterously caught by Mrs Standen from Fountain Cottage. Mrs Dampier then jumped from the window and was taken to the *White Bear*. Finally Mr Dampier jumped and all three miraculously escaped serious injury. In the meantime Mr Crundwell, watch and clock maker, and his family of ten who lived next door to the Dampiers had succeeded in clearing their house of furniture, tools and stock-in-trade which was taken over to the *White Bear Inn* and otherwise strewn about in the vicinity of Mr Dadsford's photographic carriage. Watches were taken for safety to Fountain Cottage whose Mrs Standen was a tower of strength. This house was then left to share the fate of Corke's and Dampier's. Just across the bottom of Frog Lane York House, the premises of George Gilbert, furnishing ironmonger, were in danger but survived unlike the furnished lodging house called Sion Cottage behind Corke's which was soon a burning mass, throwing out intense heat. The house was occupied by Mr Joy, boot maker of Chapel Place, a relative of Mr Heather, the owner, and his wife and child. They were awakened by the suffocating smoke and barely escaped with their lives. The building was completely gutted – those pieces of furniture that could be extricated being removed through the windows and placed on the lawn in front of Dr Trustram's residence. He was instrumental in stopping the spread of the fire into Sion Terrace. Its progress was being checked by the wall of the recently erected brick building; but No 3 Sion Terrace was also in the occupation of Mr Heather and, presumably because he owned Sion Cottage also, there was a communicating door. The wall became so intensely hot that it was feared the wainscoting on the other side and a sash window nearby would ignite and the whole of Sion Terrace would be at risk. Fortunately the brick wall checked the fire and, on Dr Trustram's instructions, the connecting door and its wooden frame were ripped away with an axe and the aperture stopped with a palliasse copiously saturated with water poured out at intervals and at considerable personal risk to those involved. By this means the extension of the fire up Mount Sion was prevented.

The local people had rallied round to do what they could, working indefatigably at the fire engine and carrying buckets of water from the Kentish Tap pumps. They were assisted and encouraged by police-sergeant Swift and by constable Judges who had been the first on the scene. Foremost in endeavouring to check the progress of the devouring element were Mr Gilbert, ironmonger of York House, and his staff. In the words of the *Gazette* report, Mr Gilbert stimulated 'to active exertion all those who required stimulating on the distressing occasion by throwing open his beer-cellar, which, we have since been informed, was emptied of its contents'. Among those spotted by the *Gazette* reporter were Joseph Delves from Blenheim Place, E.J. Strange from the Pantiles, Mr Forman the solicitor and Mr Broadwood the MP from Jerningham House, Messrs Haines father and son from the *Kentish Hotel*, Mr Stidolph from Cumberland Walk and many others. At the suggestion of E.J. Strange apparently a main from the waterworks was opened and a copious supply of water was obtained with little or no labour. It was not until five o'clock in the morning, however, that the fire could be considered under control and the adjoining properties out of danger. The whole of Mr Corke's premises were razed to the ground; nearly the whole of Mr Dampier's and Mr Crundwell's were lost; Sion Cottage was completely gutted, nothing but the bare walls being left, and the adjoining property was damaged by the intense heat. Mr Field, watch maker, found it necessary to keep the shutters of his front shop, which were thirty or forty yards from the blazing mass, well applied with water and the shutters of Mr H. Edwards, butcher, on the opposite side of the street, were also damaged. Fortunately there was little wind. Total damage was estimated at £4,000 but most of the property, stock-in-trade etc was insured. The cause of the fire was not known.

Corner of High Street and Mount Sion about 1910

All this evidently left a large hole at the bottom of Mount Sion and Frog Lane. So what filled the hole? Well the photograph above, although taken some fifty years later, supplies the answer on the Mount Sion side. It was taken about 1910 by 'Wheeler and Fisk Moore' but copied by David Johnson with the commentary: 'At top of centre house with steps up, The First Studio in Tunbridge Wells occupied by Lawrence 1860'. I think he is pointing to the weather-boarded sort of attic up high which makes sense because the early photographers needed good daylight, so the top of the house was a good place. There is a marvellous book, by the way, to be made out of the photographers of Tunbridge Wells. The date 1860, three years after the fire, is perhaps significant. The two-storey bit fronting the High Street with the decorative gable was the Studio Tea Rooms in 1910, as can be seen. It seems that the first floor became a more conventional photographic studio operating under various practitioners until well into the 1900s and gave its name to the tea rooms below. All this is confirmed by the large-scale Ordnance Survey map which shows in 1866 on the Frog Lane side of the devastated area two narrow properties parallel with the lane and presumably having shop fronts onto the High Street. These later became the pub named *Eclipse*, after a famous stallion I believe, which survived until the last twenty or thirty years to be replaced by the present modern shop with offices above. The buildings shown in the photograph did not last so long being replaced in 1927 by the National Provincial Bank which became the Natwest and is now the Pizza Express.

There are two points to notice about Sion Terrace. Firstly, it used to have a magnificent balcony and canopy running along the whole front. This can be seen in the background of the photograph below which shows the girls of the Girls Public Day School Trust in the garden of Jerningham House in about 1894 – see

Girls and staff of Girls' Public Day School Trust in garden of Jerningham House about 1894. Sion Terrace with balcony and canopy can be seen on the right.

chapter 25. Secondly no 7 Sion Terrace was the residence of Dr William Webber in 1864 when the 'Webber Riots' took place outside. For more on this story see chapter 27.

Let us now proceed one step up the hill and confront contradictory evidence from Kip and Bowra. The detail from Kip is repeated on the next page. For Bowra see page 225 above. The building abutting and to the rear of the Great House, on the right, seems to correspond with the slim building marked Mrs Pickering and level with Frog Lane on Bowra; but Kip marks it 'Woods' which should indicate the building above marked Tho Wood on Bowra which is in fact Sion House. My explanation, unsatisfactory though it may be, is that Kip has misplaced the label 'Woods' which should apply to the house further up the hill as indicated below. The gap below this house seems too great certainly but against this the position of the Side House tight up to and behind the Great House supports my theory. The name Kip gives to the Great House is 'Tovy' and John Tovey is in fact named in one of the Sion House deeds dated 18 May 1719 as occupier of the neighbouring house. What Kip should have put on the Side House as a label is anyone's guess. Be this all as it may, I have more faith in Bowra's accuracy than Kip's bird's-eye view. Anyway, the deeds of Walmer (formerly Fountain) Cottage confirm Mrs Pickering's position; and if you look at the Tithe map above you will see that the Cottage as well as Blenheim Place are forward extensions of the 'Side House'. The

Kip's engraving 1719 - detail

main document in the Walmer Cottage deeds is dated 1813 but appended is a Schedule of Deeds the first of which dated 29/30 January 1753 records the purchase of the property by Hester Lewis, wife of George Lewis, from William Ashdowne, son of the survivor of two trustees and executors of Margaret Pickering. Hester, it may be recalled (see page 229 above), was Margaret's niece and her son, John Newton, was a party to the deed. Thus far the Poor Rate record is confirmed but the next event, the purchase by William Gratton, is not documented. However a conveyance from Eleanor Reed to William Stone on 16/17 July 1801 is in the Schedule and Eleanor Reed was the remote heiress (first cousin to Mrs Gratton) who inherited Great Mount Pleasant House (the *Calverley Hotel*) *inter alia* when Mrs Gratton died in 1790. This confirms that William Gratton must have bought the property (consisting presumably of the Great House and the Side House) and that it was sold to William Stone in 1801; and that Sprange's listings (page 229 above) are largely correct.

I have a full transcript of the main document in the Walmer Cottage deeds. The original was in the hands of Mrs Riches now deceased and may or may not be in those of the new owner. The document, long and involved, recounts how William Stone, described as a draper, grocer and confectioner, acquired the property from Eleanor Reed in 1801, immediately mortgaged it, was unable to keep up payments, became insolvent, was rescued by a composition agreement with Henry Mitchell who in turn was unable to meet his obligations, turned to his relatives including the Mayfield surgeon Nicholas Stone for help and eventually sold out to Thomas Taylor. The Tithe map (see above) tells us that in 1840 Thomas and Frederick Taylor owned Fountain (Walmer) Cottage and Blenheim Place while the Great House was owned by Richard Corke. I have no direct evidence on the sale of the Great House but it seems reasonable to suppose it was sold to Corke at about this time. The puzzle is whether Blenheim Place was part of the sale of 1813. The description in the 1813 document is as follows:

> All that new erected Messuage or Tenement and shop adjoining to the Court Yard or Garden at the side of a Certain House called Bolton House and formerly called Whites House with the yard garden and Backside thereto belonging and Used therewith and the Ground in front thereof fully to the Highway leading from Mount Sion to the Wells and abutting to a Lane leading to the Bowling Green House on Mount Sion between the said new Erected Messuage and the Messuage or Tenement Yard and Garden of Henry Peerless and formerly of the Reverend Mr Brett on the east or north east to a Messuage or Tenement called the little Lodging House and the Court Yard before the same on the north (the Boundary Line towards the said Courtyard being in a straight line from the north west Corner of the said new Erected Messuage hereby Granted and Released to the said Highway) to a Tenement and premises late of Thomas Wood deceased on the south or south east and to the said highway leading from Mount Sion to the Wells on the west or south west which said messuage and premises are situate lying and being at Mount Sion Tunbridge Wells aforesaid in the parish of Tonbridge in the said County of Kent late in the Tenure or Occupation of the said William Stone since of Thomas Wightwick and now of George Trice his undertenants or assigns …

A pencil note in the margin of the original, alongside this description, reads: 'this is explained to be Walmer Cottage in later deeds PH' – but was it Walmer Cottage alone or was 'PH' only interested in the cottage? Again the problem of compass points crops up. The lane leading to the Bowling Green House must be Frog Lane with Henry Peerless's property on the other side and it is 'on the east or north east'. North-east would be accurate, as would also south-east for Thomas Wood's premises (Sion House) and south-west for the highway from Mount Sion to the Wells (Mount Sion Road). The 'little Lodging House' which is the problematic part of this description would then be at forty-five degrees as it were down the hill and the boundary line mentioned would be from the downhill corner of the new building nearest Mount Sion Road. My interpretation of all this is that the 'little Lodging House' is the Side House or what remains of it and therefore Blenheim Place was built later – and the document refers to Walmer (Fountain) Cottage alone. A glance at the Barrow map (see page 178) shows that some forward extension of the Side House had taken place by 1808 – no.18 is listed as 'Mr Mitchel – small House'. The incontrovertible fact remains anyway that by 1840 Blenheim Place had been constructed alongside and belonged to Thomas Taylor – and Frederick, perhaps his brother or son?

Thomas Taylor was a plumber and I am sure must be the man who first supplied piped water to the Pantiles and Mount Sion areas from the Tangier Spring. On the next page is a view of what Blenheim Place (and Fountain Cottage) looked like when new. Shame that the splendid balconies and canopies have disappeared. At least the bow fronts still adorn the Mount Sion street scene even if less prettily than might be. I have no evidence on the building of Blenheim Place but it must have taken place about 1820. Who was responsible for the design is equally unknown but some credit must be due to the two Taylors who were the owners in 1840. The use to which these new buildings were put seems to have been the usual one –

lodgings mainly for visitors but sometimes for more permanent accommodation. For instance the 1861 census found No.1 Blenheim Place occupied by James Sayers, a butler, and his wife Caroline, a lodging house keeper, while No.2 was occupied by Joseph Delves and his family. Joseph was one of the old unelected Town Commissioners and at their last meeting in August 1860 he commented on the state of the road. 'He was sorry to say that he had never seen the roads in such a filthy, dirty state as they had been within the last 12 months ... There was the back of the Parade, why it was hardly fit to go along, and there was Mount Sion, you were hardly able to go up Mount Sion it was in such a state. He never saw Mount Sion in such a disgraceful state at any time, that he would say without fear of contradiction.' Mr Gates: 'You live there, Mr Delves.' Mr Joseph Delves: 'Yes I do live there, Mr Gates, I do live there.' By 1871 Joseph Delves had gone, however, and Mrs Jordan, a lodging house keeper was in occupation at No.2.

Blenheim Place and Fountain Cottage in about 1830

Time to move up the hill again, to Sion House, no.15, which Winefrith's Deed Poll disposed of in these words: 'One Messuage Called the Upper House alias Mrs Powells House with the Brewhouse Yard and Stable thereunto belonging ... To the use and behoof of Sarah How Spinster now liveing with me and her heires and assignes for ever'. It may be recalled that in chapter 8 I quoted the example of the Poor Rate for Sion House and bragged that all my Poor Rate sequences tended to be confirmed by the subsequent discovery of Sarah How in the house deeds. Well, here is that sequence again.

1686-1692	Mr Powell
1693-1695	Mr Robert Brooke for Mr Powells
1696-1698	Mr William Brooke for Mr Powells
1699-1704	Mrs Brooke for Mr Powells
1708-1713	Mr Culling for Powells
1714+	Thomas Wood for Mr Powells
1728-1758	Thomas Wood for Sarah Hows
1759-1761	Widow of Tho Wood for Sarah Hows
1762-1771	Widow Wood for Sar Hows
1772-1778	Wood John for the Green Pales
1779-1797	Strange Edward for the Green Pales

Compare the first entries for 'The Great House' (page 228 above): 1686-1695: Robert Brooke – 1696-1698: Mr William Brooke – 1699-1704: Mrs Brooke – 1708-1712: Mr Culling. They are the same except for the period 1686-92. I do not know who Mr Powell was. Maybe he built the house; maybe he financed its building. Anyway, he soon disappears, leaving, however, his name behind. As can be seen, the house was called after him for many years. Then it was called 'Sarah Hows' for an equally long period before becoming the 'Green Pales'. The whole story of the house is here. It was built by Mr Powell in 1686, just two years after the first leases of 1684. Then the Brookes come on the scene but the house is still called Powells. Then Winefrith marries Thomas Culling. Then Thomas Wood appears as tenant at first and the house name changes to Sarah Hows. I was mystified by Sarah Hows when I first saw the Poor Rate – but of course it all became clear when I saw the Deed Poll. She must surely have been a companion to Winefrith Brooke and the house her reward for faithful service. Anyway, it will come as no surprise to find that she did not remain a spinster for long after inheriting the house! The copy of the Deed Poll was made in 1717 for 'ye benefit of Sarah How spinster – now ye wife of Jon Jeffery'. It is possible that this was the John Jeffery who owned 69, London Road – but there were always so many Jefferies around that it is difficult to be sure. If so, it would explain why the newly-wed couple did not want to live in Sion House and proceeded to sell it in 1719 to William Banes the brewer who first owned the 'Central Station' brewery. The story of Sion House is continued in a series of title deeds the originals of which are now lost – although I have not altogether lost hope that they may come to light somehow. John and Sarah Jeffery did not, however, sell the whole site to Banes. They kept the bakehouse for themselves. This may have been because John was a baker. It may also explain why they almost immediately mortgaged the bakehouse for £30 to another baker by the name of John Riplingham. The mortgage deed describes the bakehouse. 'All that Bakehouse formerly a Stable with the Oven thereto belonging And also part of the yard thereto adjoining Conteyning Thirty Foot one way and Five and Twenty Foot another way …' This arrangement itself did not last long. In February 1721 the bakehouse was sold for £43. The purchaser was William Mercer, described as a tailor of Speldhurst parish.

Now the interesting thing about this is a comment made on a conveyance document some forty years later. 'The said William Mercer,' it reads, 'after making the aforesaid purchase erected and built upon the said purchased premises or some part thereof a Messuage Tenement or Lodging House ... ' I don't think there can be any doubt that the photograph below shows the messuage referred to — Crescent Lodge.

Crescent Lodge, 17 Mount Sion

It is not often that we can date a building with such precision. If confirmation were needed, look at Bowra (page 225 above). Sion House is flagged and just above it, to the left, is Crescent Lodge – and the owner is 'Ion Mercer'. Why not William Mercer? Well, the Sion House deeds told the story. William Mercer died in 1735 or 1736. He had three sons, William, the eldest, Edward and John and one daughter, Mary. William was to have the family home and Edward its coach-house and stables and Mary was to have the lodging house on Mount Sion provided she did not marry without her father's consent ... but that, of course, is just what she did. She married a London innkeeper called Richard Smith; and so John was given Crescent Lodge on condition that he paid his sister and his brother Edward £50 each and allowed his mother to live in the lodging house. This, then, is how the name John Mercer appears on the Bowra plan of 1738.

The next year, 1739, John and his wife, Ann, proceeded to borrow £80 from a certain Samuel August – who described himself as a citizen and weaver of London but whose first name suggests to me where his main interests lay. He seems, however, to have been a decent sort of a Jew because he could have caused trouble a few years later but didn't. What happened was that John Mercer died in June 1744 before redeeming the mortgage – which meant that Samuel became the legal owner of Crescent Lodge and could have turfed the widow out. Instead he agreed to accept late payment and she borrowed the £80 from Robert Mercer, a relative I presume. So here's widow Ann on Mount Sion with an urgent payment to be made in London. What to do? A cheque? Electronic transfer? Helicopter? Well, not exactly – she sent William Okill to London with the money – and good old Samuel put his stamp on it all with a splendid Deed Poll of which we do have a photocopy, if no longer the original.

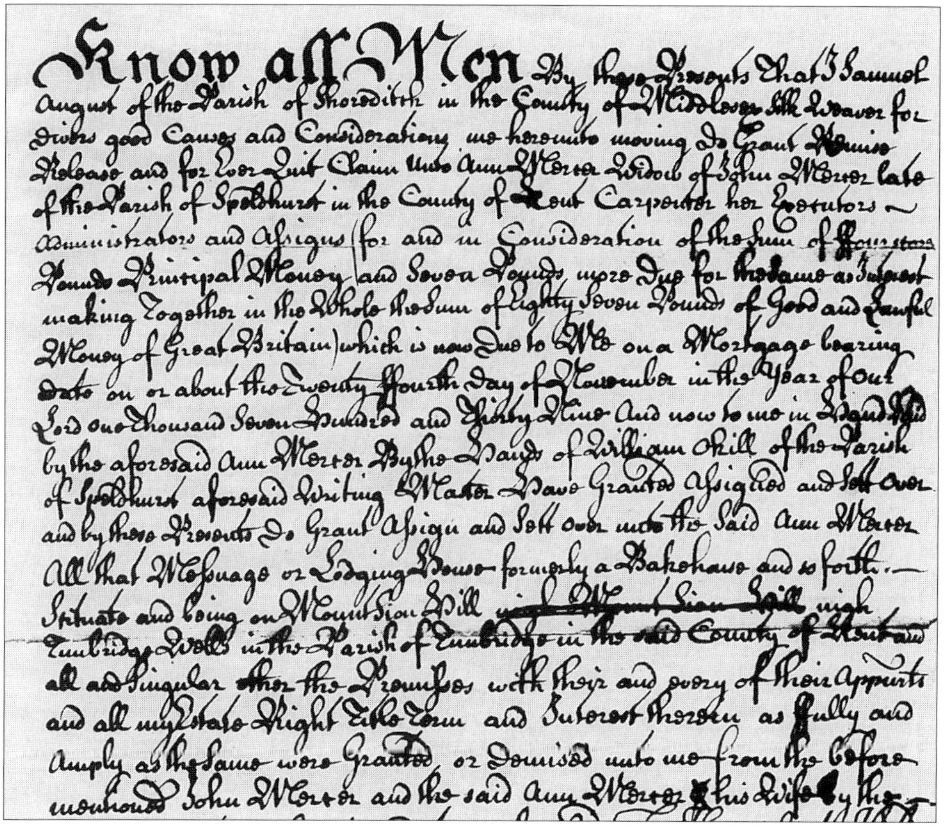

Deed dated 20 December 1754

Know all men by these presents that I Samuel August of the parish of Shoreditch in the county of Middlesex silk weaver for divers good causes and considerations me hereunto moving do grant remise release and for ever quit claim unto Ann Mercer widow of John Mercer late of the parish of Speldhurst in the county of Kent carpenter her executors administrators and assigns (for and in consideration of the sum of four score pounds principal money and seven pounds more due for the same as interest making together in the whole the sum of eighty seven pounds of good and lawful money of Great Britain) which is due to me on a mortgage bearing date on or about the twenty fourth day of November in the year of our Lord one thousand seven hundred and thirty nine and now to me in hand paid by the aforesaid Ann Mercer by the hands of William Okill of the parish of Speldhurst aforesaid writing master

> have granted assigned and sett over and by these presents do grant assign and sett over unto the said Ann Mercer All that messuage or lodging house formerly a bakehouse and so forth situate and being on Mount Sion Hill nigh Tonbridge Wells in the parish of Tonbridge in the said county of Kent and all and singular other the premises with their and every of their appurtenances and all my estate right title term and interest therein as fully and amply as the same were granted or demised unto me from the before mentioned John Mercer and the said Ann Mercer his wife by the deed of mortgage bearing date as aforesaid To have and to hold the same unto the said Ann Mercer her heirs and assigns to do therewith at her and their free wills and pleasures ... in witness whereof the said Samuel August hath sett his hand and seal this twentieth day of December in the eighteenth year of the reign of our sovereign lord George the Second by the grace of God of Great Britain France and Ireland King defender of the faith and so forth and in the year of our Lord one thousand seven hundred and forty four.

That's what I call LANGUAGE! I wonder whether you noticed in the middle of all that the phrase 'by the hands of William Okill of Speldhurst writing master'? So there can be no doubt that our William Okill took to London cash amounting to almost the full value of the house – it was sold fourteen years later for £110. So that would be about £200,000 today? How did he travel? By coach – crammed inside hoping no one would pick his pocket – or on top hoping he wouldn't fall off? I don't think so. I think he took a horse and I think he had a companion. The deed is witnessed by two men – William August, presumably Samuel's brother or other relative – and John Pack. Now Pack is a local name and I am sure he was the travelling companion. They took with them in addition to the money the original mortgage deed which was endorsed on the same day, 20 December. And what else do you suppose they took with them – apart from a clean pocket handkerchief and a toothbrush? How about a brace of pistols?

On top of everything else I think our William sat down and wrote out the splendid Deed Poll we see here. This is a shot in the dark; but I think I recognise his hand. I have seen it on wills to which he was a witness – and we shall see what I think is another example in a minute. To continue the story – in 1750 the friendly relative, Robert Mercer, died and his son and heir, John, wanted the money his father had lent. Ann and her son Thomas had to scout around for another lender and found one in the owner of the house next door – Thomas Wood – whose motives I guess were not entirely disinterested, as we shall see! Seven years later Thomas Mercer conveyed the house to his mother 'in consideration of his natural love and affection' and for her 'better maintenance livelihood and preferment' in the words of the document on the next page (detail only) which is the one I said just now I think is in the hand of William Okill. Is it the same hand? I think it is, but anyway the real story behind it is to be seen on the fifth line where Thomas describes himself as a yeoman '*but now a soldyer*'. He was off to the wars and not sure that he would come back. The wars in question would seem to be the Seven Years War which started in 1756. I wonder what happened to our hero. Did he see action on the continent or overseas – was he perhaps with Wolfe at Quebec? We do not know his fate – but what his mother did on the other hand we do know – she sold the house in 1758. And I think it could be guessed to whom – to Thomas Wood next door, who I am sure had had his eyes on it all along. He was now able to reunite the two parts of what had been a single property and this is how it remained until 1921.

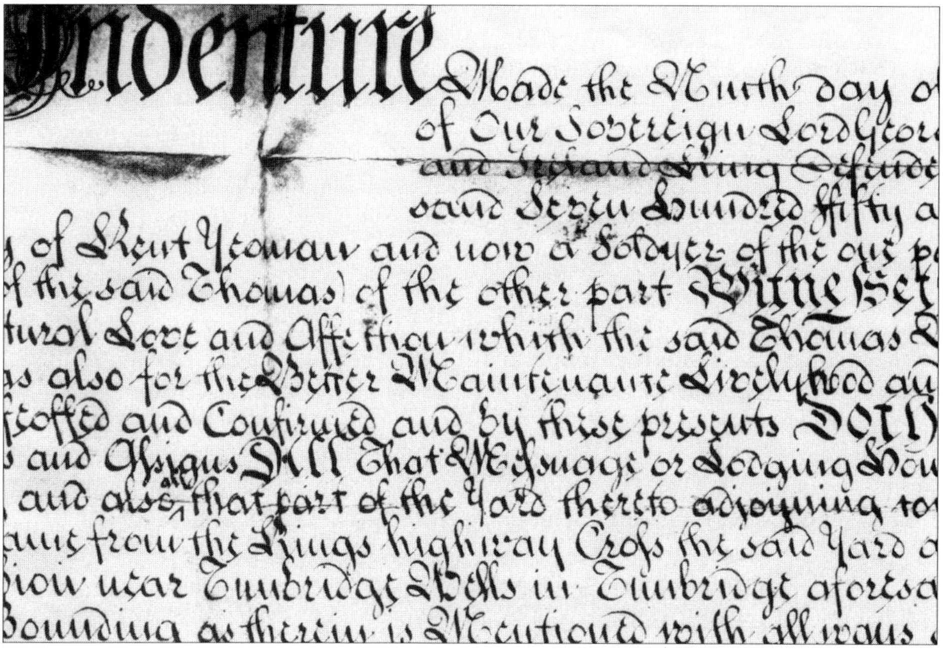
Indenture Made the Ninth day of
of Our Sovereign Lord George
and Ireland King Defender
and Seven hundred fifty a
of Kent Yeoman and now a Soldier of the one p
f the said Thomas of the other part Witnesset
tural Love and Affection which the said Thomas
s also for the Better Maintenance Livelyhood an
feoffed and Confirmed and by these presents Doth
and Assigns All That Messuage or Lodging Hou
and also that part of the Yard thereto adjoining to
ance from the Kings highway Cross the said Yard
Sion near Tunbridge Wells in Tunbridge aforesa
bounding as therein is Mentioned with all ways

Conveyance dated 9 May 1757

In about 1790 Edward Strange seems to have taken over the tenancy of Crescent Lodge in addition to that of the main house. I shall have more to say about Mr Strange a little later but his connection with Crescent Lodge is confirmed on Barrow's map of 1808 under the label 'Strange, Bow Window' … and by the records of the Court Leet of Southborough Manor which, on 4 November 1796, complained that 'Edward Strange permits or suffers the Soil of his Necessary-house belonging to his Lodging-house called the Bow Window-house on Mount Sion hill Tunbridge Wells near the King's Highway within the jurisdiction of this Court Leet to run down the same to the great Annoyance of the King's Subjects – he is therefore commanded to remove or stop up the same within Six Weeks from this Day or that he be amerced 13s 4d.' Does this mean that there was an overflowing toilet at the end of the garden on the Mount Sion side or does the King's Highway refer to Frog Lane?

Edward Strange died in 1807 and his place was taken by John Stapley who first appears in Sprange in 1811 and then in 1817 with the name Crescent Lodge attached. The Stapley family remained at Crescent Lodge for the rest of the century. Ann Friend's will of 1831 names John Stapley as her tenant and he or his family are to be found in the censuses from 1841 to 1881. In 1851 he described himself as a

Tunbridge Ware maker, aged 67 and born in Tunbridge Wells; with him were his wife, Fanny, aged 68, and his daughter, Rose, aged 28. Rose was a 'visiting governess' and in particular a teacher of the guitar. She seems to have died in 1902, when she must have been 79, and the photographer David Johnson, commenting on the Twitten photograph reproduced in chapter 16 (page 208) said: 'On left, part of Crescent Lodge occupied from 1869 until her decease by Miss Rose Stapley, teacher of the mandoline and guitar'. On 22 June 1923 Crescent Lodge was sold, separately from Sion House, to an Army captain and since then it has been used as a private residence.

We can now turn our attention to the main house once more which we left in 1719 when it was sold to the brewer William Banes (see page 237 above). Both he and his wife, however, died within two years of the purchase and the house descended to their daughter who was married to a barber and wigmaker of Chatham called Thomas Duplex. He mortgaged the house for £100 but failed to pay the interest and eventually, in 1729, called it a day and sold out to the sitting tenant for £260. The sitting tenant had been since 1714, as the Poor Rate shows, Thomas Wood – and thus 'Sion House' came into the ownership of the Wood family with whom it

Sion House, 15 Mount Sion in 1934

remained for the next two centuries and this is probably why the house had such an unusually good set of title deeds – at least until we in our day succeeded in throwing them away.

Thomas Wood was by trade a 'hollow ware turner' but I doubt whether he spent his time turning out wooden bowls. His will, made in 1755, speaks of his lodging house 'wherein I now dwell' and I see no reason to suppose that it was not his home throughout the period of his ownership which happened to coincide to within a few years with Beau Nash's reign as Master of Ceremonies from 1735 to 1761. A house so important and conveniently located as Sion House can scarcely have been wanting clientele during the season. Many prominent personalities must have stayed

Sion House in 1998

there but it is frustratingly impossible to discover who or when or whether.

The one thing of note that Thomas Wood did was to build in the tiny space between the back of Sion House and Frog Lane. He refers in his will to 'my new built Messuage or Tenement standing behind my … Lodging House called Green Pales with the usual and accustomed Ways and Passages to and from the same now in the occupation of the Reverend Mr Johnson …' If you doubt that it was possible to squeeze a building in such a place, there is evidence both photographic and cartographic. On the previous page is a photograph of Sion House taken by David Johnson in 1934. To the extreme left of the picture a glimpse can be caught of a weatherboarded first floor and a window. It cannot be seen today. What you can see now is the building on the other side of Frog Lane – see the photograph taken in 1998. If this is not enough, have a look at these two photographs. The one on the left was taken by David Johnson in 1934, from the

Frog Lane by Johnson in 1934 (below) and in 1998 (right)

Twitten, half way up Frog Lane. The black wall on the left is the back of Crescent Lodge and immediately below it is Thomas Wood's building. The photograph on the right was taken in 1998. It shows clearly that the back cottage has been demolished since Johnson's photograph – leaving only the sloping wall as a memento of the lean-to roof below the first floor window. More evidence is to be had from maps – take a look at the Tithe map on page 229 or at this detail from the Ordnance Survey map, showing the back cottage and just room in the courtyard in between for two trees!

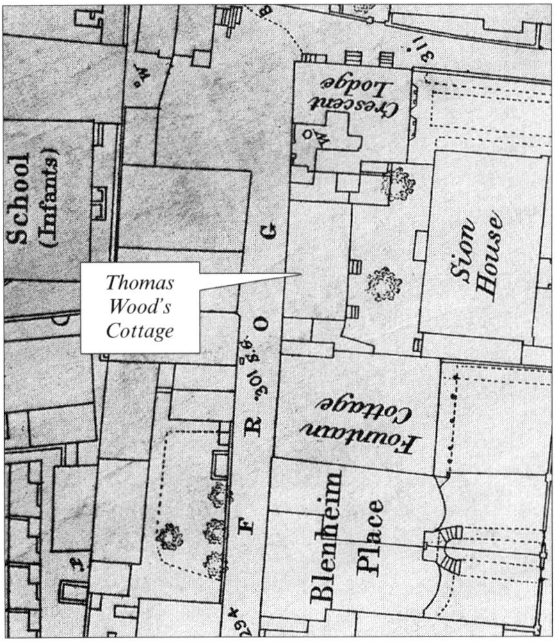

Ordnance Survey 1866

Thomas Wood died in 1758, survived by two sons, Thomas junior and John who was under age. Thomas junior was already living at Burlington House and was given Ashenhurst's Great House and some land. Sion House, together with the back cottage and Crescent Lodge, went to the widow Elizabeth for her life and then to the other son John. Evidently Elizabeth Wood, helped I am sure by young John, ran the lodging house for the next 13 years since the Poor Rate record shows the Widow Wood as ratepayer from 1759 to 1771. Curiously, the rate collector (harking back as far as 1718 or earlier) called the house 'Sarah Hows' but Thomas Wood in his will in 1755 was already calling it 'Green Pales', a name first used by the Poor Rate collector in 1772 when John Wood took over as ratepayer until 1778. I have not found John's will but the Poor Rate record shows that Edward Strange took over the Green Pales in 1779.

Edward Strange's reign at the Green Pales deserves special recognition, if only because his descendants have played a notable part in the history of Tunbridge Wells; and one of them, the chronicler of the hardships of chimney sweeps' apprentices, was living in the town till her death. There was evidently some connection by marriage between the Stranges and the family of John Hilder, the tenant of Crescent Lodge (see above), since one of Edward's sons was named Edward Hilder. On the facing page is a family tree which may help explain this story. One of Edward Strange's sons was named Edward Hilder Strange and became proprietor of the *Angel Inn*. He married a Jane Jeffery, who carried on the hotel business with great success after his death, and they had a son called in commemoration Edward Jeffery Strange who founded the building business from which the name is best known; he married his cousin, Mary Strange Mathew, and is the ancestor of our Kathleen. He also had a daughter Jane who married Joseph Delves of Chapel Place – and a son Nicholas about whom a story in a minute.

THE FAMILY OF STRANGE

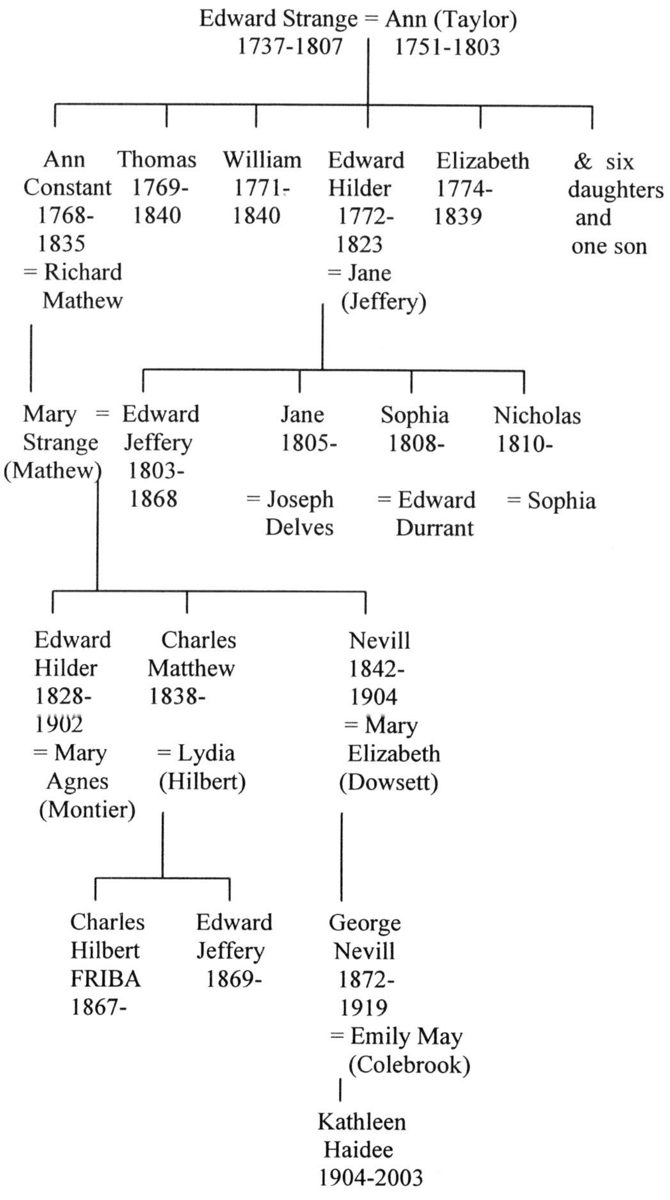

Then there was a second Edward Jeffery, born in Cumberland Gardens in 1869, managing director of Strange & Sons Ltd and mayor of the town in 1936; and his elder brother Charles Hilbert, architect of the Homeopathic Hospital and other buildings and author of a family history. Both were great-great-grandsons of Edward of the Green Pales. The family history says that Edward married in 1767, at the age of 30, a remarkably pretty girl of 16 named Ann and they lived at the Green Pales on Mount Sion.

The 1841 census shows Fountain Cottage occupied by Nicholas Strange, cabinetmaker, aged 30, his wife Sophia aged 25 and his sons of five and one plus two lodgers. This Nicholas Strange must almost certainly be the man who left his mark in the house next door. When the last owners but one of Sion House were having interior decoration done they discovered an inscription on the wall of a first-floor bedroom. This is what it said: 'N Strange hung this room St Swithins Day 1845'. (He didn't say whether it was raining or not!) Well, as you can imagine, the owners were quite excited about this; and left strict instructions to cover the inscription with a glass panel so that it should remain visible for ever. When they returned in the evening it was the story of Queen Anne and the pantiles all over again; their instructions had been ignored! Well, there's only one N. Strange who fits the bill – and he's Nicholas the cabinet maker of Fountain Cottage in 1841 – I suppose there's no reason why a cabinet maker shouldn't help out his next door neighbour with a bit of papering, is there? Particularly when his grandfather used to be 'Edward Strange of the Green Pales'! It may be remembered that the life story of Nicholas Strange featured in chapter 12 pages 151-2.

Information from the *Sprange Guides* becomes available from 1780 and sure enough in that year Edward Strange is shown at the Green Pales and in succeeding editions of the *Guide* until 1808. According to C.H. Strange, Ann died in 1803 and Edward in 1807. They had 12 children (born during a 24-year period from 1768 to 1792) and their great-great-grandson wonders where they were all stowed! The answer must be, I think, that in common with all the lodging house families on the hill they had to pack like sardines (or move elsewhere) during the season; but it was only for four months or so and during the rest of the year they could expand. Sprange shows that in 1780 there were in the Green Pales five parlours, nine chambers and no stabling; and subsequent editions show in a little more detail five parlours, seven chambers, seven garrets, no stables and no coach houses. The Green Pales must have suffered some disadvantage from having no in-house provision for horses and coaches; but John Jeffery with his bakehouse and its sale away from the main house and Thomas Wood with his back cottage had removed any scope for stables and coachhouses.

The name Green Pales continued in use until some time between 1811 and 1817. It was surely Thomas Wood senior who gave the name to his lodging house in the 1750s or earlier, even though the rate collectors were reluctant to use it at first; but why Thomas chose it is a matter for speculation. Perhaps it had a wooden fence or palings painted green; in which case it is interesting to speculate on the origins of the present iron railings. In 1811 a Mrs Cave is listed by Sprange; and the Green Pales is shown split into two 'apartments'. In 1817, however, the name has changed to Sion House. During the next century or so Sion House saw a variety of tenancies and occupiers, for the Wood family ceased to take a direct interest in 1807 when Thomas III died unmarried and his sisters Sarah and Mary followed in 1811 and 1818 – leaving only Ann married to the brewer Robert Friend. Another glance at the family tree from page 142 may help:

THE WOOD FAMILY OF MOUNT SION

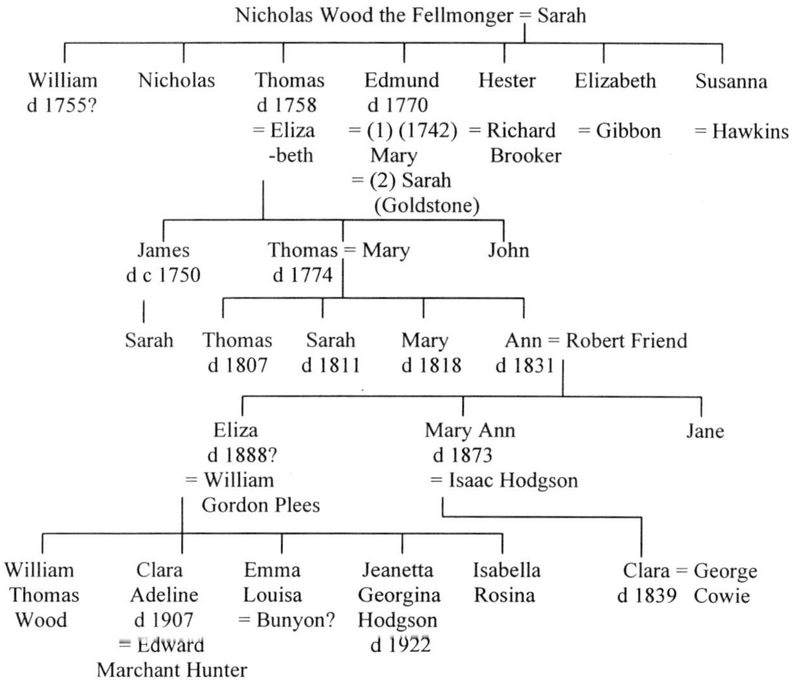

As indicated above, the Green Pales became Sion House sometime between 1811 and 1817 and in 1817 Mr Roots is listed by Sprange as the lodging house keeper, so that perhaps it was he who changed the name. John Roots is named in Ann Friend's will as tenant of Sion House and he appears in the 1841 census but not in *Bagshaw's Directory* of 1847. This is not surprising because in 1841 his age was given as 75. His occupation was that of farmer and he had living with him two daughters, aged 25 and 30, one female lodger of fifty years and independent means and two female servants, one of whom Fanny Buss did not know her age! Sprange in 1817 shows Sion House 'in Apartments' and this might mean that, like Mrs Cave in 1811 (see above), John Roots let a sizeable part of the house, comprising two reception rooms and three best and three servants' bedrooms, as the sort of permanent residence, unconnected with the fashionable season and probably unfurnished, which was at this period coming into demand. If so, this would explain an otherwise puzzling notice of sale which appeared in the *Maidstone Journal* of 10 September 1833.

Headed 'Sion House, Mount Sion', it announces the auction on the premises of 'Elegant and Costly Furniture' by order of the proprietor 'who is leaving for the Continent'. There was a 'double-seated Pony Phaeton, recently new, (builder, Wright, Westminster Bridge)', and 'a complete Pony, 7 years old, quiet in harness, and has been driven by a lady'; there were an elegant drawing room suite and a cabinet piano-forte (by Broadwood); there were a superior chimney glass in a gilt frame 51 by 46 ins, a set of 12 rosewood chairs and two couches with matching drab moreen curtains and ornamental velvet cornice, a pair of wainscot oak book cases, fitted up in a superior style, 8ft high by 5ft , a carved mahogany four-post bedstead with chintz furniture lined, more beds, tables, carpets, chests of drawers, a Brussels stair carpet with brass wires, a hanging hall lamp, a guitar and case, a handsome set of sideboard ornaments in alabaster, six Don Quixote prints and 'the usual domestic and culinary requisites suitable for a gentleman's establishment'. But whoever was the gentleman leaving the country and his elegant furnishings behind? It can hardly have been 67-year-old farmer Roots. It is possible to envisage the furniture fitting into an apartment of two reception rooms and three best bedrooms but the identity of the fastidious gentleman must, I am afraid, remain a mystery.

Bagshaw's Directory of 1847 lists 'Forbes Mrs Mary, Sion House' and 'Heather Mrs, Sion House (lodging house)'. Furthermore the 1851 census shows William Heather and his family living in one part of Sion House and Elizabeth Forbes with a visiting friend and servant living in another. William Thomas Heather was listed separately as a cabinetmaker on Mount Sion. This evidence reinforces the theory that the house was divided between a lodging house and a (probably unfurnished) apartment. Mrs Forbes was described as a 'fundholder' or lady of independent income. William Heather was described as a carpenter and a farmer of 33 acres employing two men; with him were his wife, and two Harrietts, one a cook and the other a housemaid.

In 1861 the same general situation applies. William T. Heather, aged 55 now, has married Harriett the housemaid and they have a son of five and a daughter of three; what happened to Mary his former wife is a mystery. His new wife's widowed sister, Emily Joy, is employed as housekeeper and has her five-year-old son with her. In the apartment are living Hester Beauchamp, the 55-year-old wife of an officer of the Indian Civil Service, herself born in India, three daughters of whom Mary, aged 22, was born in Marylebone and the two younger both in India, a twelve-year-old son also born in India and a parlour maid from Reading. William Heather continued at Sion House until sometime between 1886 and 1889 when the directories show a change to Thomas Woodward. In 1874 the place was described as a lodging house but by 1882 it had become 'first class furnished apartments'. Whether or not this implies some internal rearrangement or refurbishment I cannot tell.

It was some time in the early 1870s that William Heather struck a deal with John Brown which eventually led to the creation of the John Brown Dairies (see chapter 10). Johnson comments on his photographs of Sion House and Lower Frog Lane (see pages 242 and 243) respectively as follows: (I) 'Occupied at one time by Mr Heather who carried on a small dairy business from the cottage showing at the back, on left-hand side. John Brown joined him in a partnership as Heather & Brown and from this small beginning originated John Brown's Dairy Co Ltd.' (II) 'The building below with white window frame stands at the back of Sion House, Mount Sion. John Brown joined Heather of Sion House who had a small milk walk and from this connection started the John Brown Dairies Company. The Heather & Brown partnership was formed about 1870-1-2.' John Brown's granddaughter has some evidence that the Browns' eldest child, Alice (see chapter 10), was born at Sion House. This is contradicted by the census record but it does suggest that the Browns may have lived in the back cottage of Sion House in the early 1870s before moving to Wood's Cottage. At the same time as providing accommodation the Sion House cottage was used as the base for the 'milk walk' operations. Perhaps William Heather's 33 acres, wherever they were, provided the milk which was transferred from churns to pails in Frog Lane.

From 1889 for the next twenty years or more Sion House was let out in apartments by Thomas Woodward and then, in 1912, by his widow Mary Ann; and it continued in this use under a number of occupiers until the early 1970s when it became a private residence with antique business connections and then, refurbished and resplendent, a private residence pure and simple, in which state may it long continue! On St Valentine's Day 1923 meanwhile a significant event in the history of the house had occurred: the house was sold to the sitting tenant, Mrs Alice Young, for £1,250. The price included Crescent Lodge and the back cottage. The description runs: ' ... the two messuages or dwelling houses ... known as Sion House with the cottage and stabling in rear thereof and Crescent Lodge as the same were then respectively in the occupation of the Purchaser and of Mrs Anna Maria Reader and their sub-tenants.'

As explained above, the Sion House property had by 1830 come into the hands of Ann Friend. Thomas Wood I had given it in his will to his widow for her life, then to his son John, then in default of issue to his son Thomas II and finally to Thomas III, his grandson. John had evidently died without issue. Thomas II did not mention Sion House in his will, presumably relying on the provision in his father's will, and Thomas III had no children and left everything to be shared between his three sisters. He died in 1804 and was followed in 1811 by his sister Sarah and in 1818 by the second sister Mary, both sisters dying intestate and unmarried. Everything, therefore, came to the third sister Ann, who was married to Robert Friend the brewer. She had three daughters, Eliza, Mary Ann and Jane.

Mary Ann was married to Isaac Hodgson and her story was related in chapters 10 and 12. For Jane and the *Compasses* see chapter 7. Eliza was married to William Gordon Plees who was described in Mary Ann Hodgson's 1843 will as a schoolmaster of Bristol; and it was Eliza to whom her mother bequeathed Sion House and Crescent Lodge. Presumably she went to live in Bristol and it is for this reason, therefore, that the Mount Sion properties were left in the hands of tenants. The bequest to Eliza was a life interest only, however, the reversion going to all her children equally as tenants in common. This entailed the formation of a trust. The first trustees were the executors of Ann Friend, already mentioned: Thomas Fry, the Sion Crescent schoolmaster, and William Jewhurst. A succession of trustees took their places over the years: Mary Jewhurst; William and George Hinds; William Gordon Plees, Eliza's husband; Edward Marchant Hunter, a local banker who seems to have married one of the Plees girls; John Read of Jerningham House, accountant; and William Henry Delves of neighbouring 23 Mount Sion (see chapter 21).

Eliza Plees seems to have lived until 1888 (unless there was an intervening generation about which I have no information) and at the time had five children: William Thomas Wood Plees (commemorating the old family name); Clara Adeline Hunter, married, I assume, to the banker; Emma Louisa Bunyon; and two spinsters, Jeanetta Georgina Hodgson Plees (another family name!) and Isabella Rosina. Clara Adeline was living at 'Beechville' Tunbridge Wells when she died in 1907 and Jeanetta Georgina Hodgson, living at 1, Lyndhurst Gardens, survived until 25 September 1922. This was evidently the trigger for winding up the trust and selling the property; and completes the story of Sion House and the first part of that of Winefrith's Strip, from nos 1 to 17 Mount Sion, which will be continued in the next chapter with Caxton House and Bricklands, nos 19 to 25.

A recent discovery is worth a final mention. In the basement of Sion House its latest owner has unearthed a well. The 1866 Ordnance Survey shows wells in the grounds of other houses on Mount Sion but this one is not shown (see page 244 above), presumably because it was within the house. The well has been cleaned up and clear fresh water is available at a depth of six feet. It may be remembered (see page 93) that one of the advertised attractions of the old chapel building on Little Mount Sion in 1812 was that excellent water could be had at a depth of 39 feet. I wonder whether this could be the same level as six feet at Sion House. In any case an additional interesting light is thrown on the daily living of the inhabitants of 18th-century Mount Sion.

Chapter 18

Caxton and Bricklands

In the previous chapter we learned about the strip of land which Winefrith Brooke bought from the Earl of Buckingham in 1702 (see page 224) and we studied the buildings on it as far up the hill as Crescent Lodge, no 17, Mount Sion. This chapter continues up the hill as far as no 25. Now the remarkable thing about the description of the strip contained in Winefrith's Deed poll is that there is no mention of the house labelled Mr Newnham on the Bowra plan (see page 225) which we now call Caxton House and is numbered 19 and 21 Mount Sion. The reason must be that in 1710 this house did not exist – but in 1738 it did. In the Deed Poll the site is referred to as the 'Upper Yard' and the deed skips straight from Mrs Powell's House (Sion House) to a messuage in the occupation of Mr Brickland abutting the Upper Yard and Stables towards the north – which is the house marked Rich Fry on Bowra. Fortunately the Poor Rate record amply confirms this supposition.

Caxton House Poor Rate

1738-1744	Mr Rich Newnham for a New House
1745-1773	Mr Richard Newnham or Occupier
1774-1776	Newnham Robt
1777-1778	Fry George for Newmans House
1779-1791	Parman Saml for Newmans
1792-1797	Parman Widow

A collection of deeds belonging to Caxton House recently deposited with the Tunbridge Wells museum expands the story. In 1778 Mary Fry married Samuel Parman and a Marriage Settlement dated 16/17 June conveys to George Fry of Tonbridge, butcher and William Foley of Speldhurst, hollowware turner, as trustees, hereditaments of which Mary the bride was 'seized'. They are described thus: 'All that Brick messuage or tenement theretofore built by Richard Newnham deceased on a certain piece of ground purchased of Margaret Pickering adjoining Mount Sion together with coach house stables and buildings; the ground adjoins at one end several messuages late occupied by Elizabeth Wood and at the other end a messuage occupied by Sarah Fry widow; and abuts backwards on the road leading to stables belonging to Mr Brett then Sarah Fry (110 feet long by 78 feet broad) then or late occupied by Mary Fry'. The houses occupied by Elizabeth Wood are Sion House and Crescent Lodge, that by Sarah Fry is Bricklands and the back road is Frog Lane. My guess is that George Fry bought the house for Mary about 1777 when it came on the market following the death of Richard Newnham. The Newnhams were brewers. Bowra's general map shows Newnhams Brewhouse along the Eridge Road opposite the Brighton Lake. It was later called the Victoria Brewery. Richard Newnham, the Elder of Speldhurst, salesman, died in 1748 and bequeathed to his sons Richard and Robert his 'large messuage or lodging house situate on Mount Sion Hill with all and every the Stables and Outbuildings ... furniture goods and moveables'. Robert did not live long to enjoy his share for in April 1748 the will was proved by Richard Newnham 'son and surviving executor'. Presumably the Richard who paid the Poor Rate was the surviving son and he died about 1773 and the Robert who followed was of a later generation. There is at the Centre for Kentish Studies, Maidstone, an indenture, otherwise irrelevant, which contains a description of 'that one large brick messuage ... or lodging house ... on Mount Sion Hill ... heretofore in the occupation of Richard Newnham deceased and now of Richard Newnham'. Notice the stress placed on 'brick' in this and in the Marriage Settlement description. The earliest lodging houses built in the 1680s and 1690s were timber-framed and the fact that Caxton House was brick-built reinforces the idea that its construction came later – and certainly it has retained its brick-built appearance to the present day – more or less unaltered, I believe. It is a puzzle that Margaret Pickering owned the site purchased by Newnham. I can only assume that she bought it from Sarah How or one of the later owners of Sion House in the same way as she had acquired the Great House and the Side House.

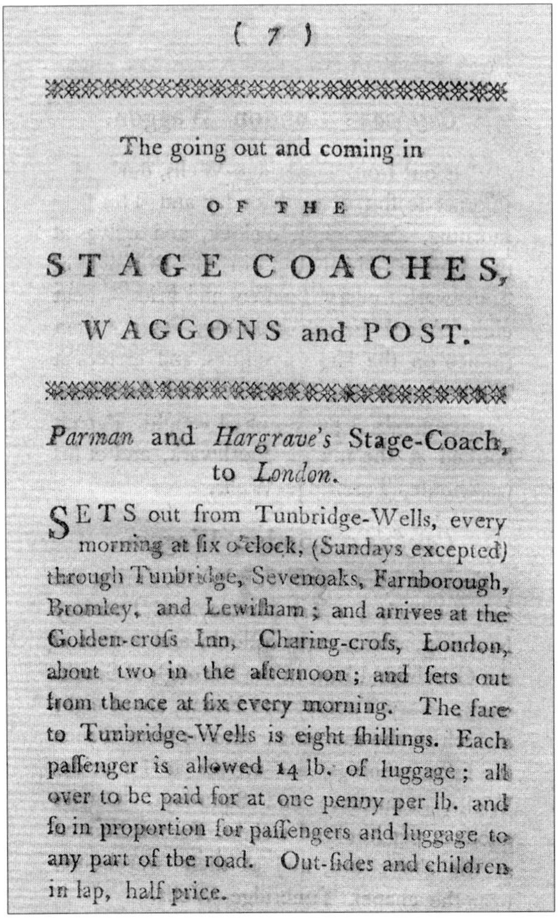
(7)

The going out and coming in

OF THE

STAGE COACHES,

WAGGONS and POST.

Parman and *Hargrave's* Stage-Coach, to *London*.

SETS out from Tunbridge-Wells, every morning at fix o'clock, (Sundays excepted) through Tunbridge, Sevenoaks, Farnborough, Bromley, and Lewifham; and arrives at the Golden-crofs Inn, Charing-crofs, London, about two in the afternoon; and fets out from thence at fix every morning. The fare to Tunbridge-Wells is eight fhillings. Each paffenger is allowed 14 lb. of luggage; all over to be paid for at one penny per lb. and fo in proportion for paffengers and luggage to any part of the road. Out-fides and children in lap, half price.

Page from Sprange Guide *1780*

In 1780 Sam Parman acquired (in what precise way I have no information) the next house up the hill, Bricklands, which had probably been his wife's childhood home and all seemed to be going well; but something was wrong with Mary. In August 1780 she made a will and added a codicil in February 1781. By 1784 she was 'deceased without issue'. Was it illness or childbirth? Her will leaves an annuity of £20 to her 'sister' Susannah Delves which means that she was a daughter of Richard Fry of 'Bricklands' because we know that Susannah Fry, another daughter, married Joseph Delves. In that case who was the George Fry who we thought bought the house for Mary and became a trustee of her marriage settlement – her eldest brother perhaps? The will also mentions brothers Edward, George, James and John and a married sister Elizabeth – all this (except the married sister) is consistent with the family tree on page 56. Where the bridegroom Samuel Parman lived before marriage I do not know. The Parmans ran coaches – see the illustration from Sprange's 1780 *Guide* on the previous page.

In 1783 Samuel married again – another Mount Sion girl, this time Elizabeth, the 18-year- old daughter of Richard Delves of Home House, later Eden House. Then in 1784, for £400, he bought Caxton House from his late wife's brother, innkeeper John Fry. The two adjoining houses became known as Parman's Upper and Lower Houses. The second marriage produced three sons and two daughters but after eight years it was over. March 1791 found Samuel closeted with his father-in-law, his brother-in-law Joseph Delves and Joseph's wife, Susannah, sister to Sam's first wife. These three were witnesses to Sam's hurried and incoherent will. 'I give to my wife Elizabeth all my freehold and copyhold estates together with all my Household Goods, Debts and moveable effects by her firstly to be possessed and enjoyed her life at her Death an equal Division to be made among such of my children as shall then be alive.' In August 1792, no executor having been named in the will, administration was granted to Elizabeth. By 1798, however, when Richard Delves came to make his will, his daughter was dead (she could not have been more than 33) and he was showing a grandpaternal concern over difficulties he feared might arise among the children 'as to the construction and fulfilling of the will of their late father'. His solution was to leave £1,600 to his executors to be shared out on condition that the sons, when of age, should join in 'the necessary conveyances for Equalising the distribution of the Real Estate'; but if they refused then the whole sum was to be divided among the daughters only. By March 1799, as is shown by an agreement with the Land Tax Commissioners, Joseph and Thomas Delves (sons of grandfather Richard) were guardians of the infant children of the late Samuel Parman. In 1808 relations between the two families were strengthened when Henry Delves married the eldest Parman girl Ann and then in 1809 a younger Richard (both he and Henry were sons of Joseph and Susannah, the sister of Sam Parman's first wife Mary) agreed to buy all Sam Parman's estates for £2,000. This agreement was put into effect by a conveyance by Lease and Release dated 16/17 September 1811 to which all concerned were parties, including the infant heir to the Marriage Settlement Trustee William Foley, to whose participation the Master of the Rolls had to give approval. Richard Delves paid out £2,000 in various portions for the 'messuage formerly called Parmans Lower House but then Montague House'. However, I think the deal must have included the Upper House as well, for while the Barrow map and Sprange show Parmans Upper House in 1808, in 1811 this has changed to Sion Place Nos 3 and 4 (Mr R. Delves). In the same year the Lower House entry has changed to 'Montague House (Mr R. Delves)' and at the same time a sub-division seems to have taken place for also listed is 'Montague House (2nd Apartment)'. Each part had two parlours, three chambers, three garrets and no coach house or stable, indicating presumably that the cottage and equine facilities at the back (now Caxton Cottage) were no longer available for visitors' use. In 1817 (Sprange again) the name has changed to Montague Place Nos 1 and 2. A description contained in the deeds held by the owner some ten years ago confirms the division: 'All that messuage or tenement then and for several years past converted into and used as two dwellings respectively numbered 1 and 2 and called or known by the name of Montague Place.' Anyway, it seems likely that Richard Delves was responsible for the conversion. The double doors which still remain under the porch testify to the division although internal arrangements have changed again with later conversions.

Richard Delves, no doubt, did not wish to continue the Parman name and to use his own name for all his properties would have been confusing to his contemporaries let alone future historians. In any case it was becoming fashionable to choose a grandiloquent name for one's house. The obvious local association with the name Montague is the notorious blue-stocking about whom we may read at length in Barton and Melville. Now Elizabeth Montagu is known to have stayed on Mount Ephraim, at the Stone House, and herein lies perhaps a clue, for Richard Delves owned a fifth share in the Stone House Estate. Is this why the name 'Montague' was chosen? We only know about this piece of Delves property because of a notice in the short-lived *Tunbridge Wells Visitor* announcing its sale by auction on 11 October 1833 for reasons which we have already met in connection with York House – see chapter 16. Whatever the origins of the name, Richard Delves proceeded in 1812 to mortgage the house (or houses?) to Richard Jones Esquire of Frant for £3,000 and again for £800 to Walter Sprott the solicitor. On the last day of 1817 he was in trouble for he could not pay off the £3,000, only £1,000, and was rescued by five friends. Finally in 1830, as we know, the blow fell. He 'became indebted to William Gilbert of Tunbridge Wells ironmonger in the sum of £100 and was declared bankrupt'. For more on the 'Delves Dynasty' in general see chapters 20 and 21. Caxton House among other lots was auctioned at Garraway's Coffee House, Cornhill, on 15 April 1831 and the successful bidder was Stephen Farley. The description of the property, in addition to mentioning the 'messuage for several years past in two dwellings, Nos 1 and 2 Montague Place' included: 'And also all that piece or parcel of ground situate next a lane or Byeway called Frog Lane with the buildings thereon then consisting of 2 stables with lofts respectively over the same and a double Coach House … behind the Messuage …'

By an unusual stroke of luck the deeds include the plan used at the auction – see the next page. It provides a splendid insight into the layout in 1831 of Caxton House and the present nos 23/25 Mount Sion, which was then called Sion Place No.3 (no.25) and Sion Place No.4 (no.23) and was included in the sale as Lot 3 (the main house) and Lot 6 (stables and cottages at rear?). Caxton House was, of course, Nos 1 and 2 Montague Place (No.1 on the downhill side) and was

Lot 4 (the main house) and Lot 5 (stables and coach house at the rear). Notice how in a short space of Frog Lane frontage there are four sets of stables (for 15 horses), one coach house and two cottages. Montague Place also has two more coach houses one of which has since disappeared and the other appears now to be incorporated in the main house. Notice also the two pumps in the Montague Place garden or yard indicating an underground water supply – apparently lacking in the house next door!

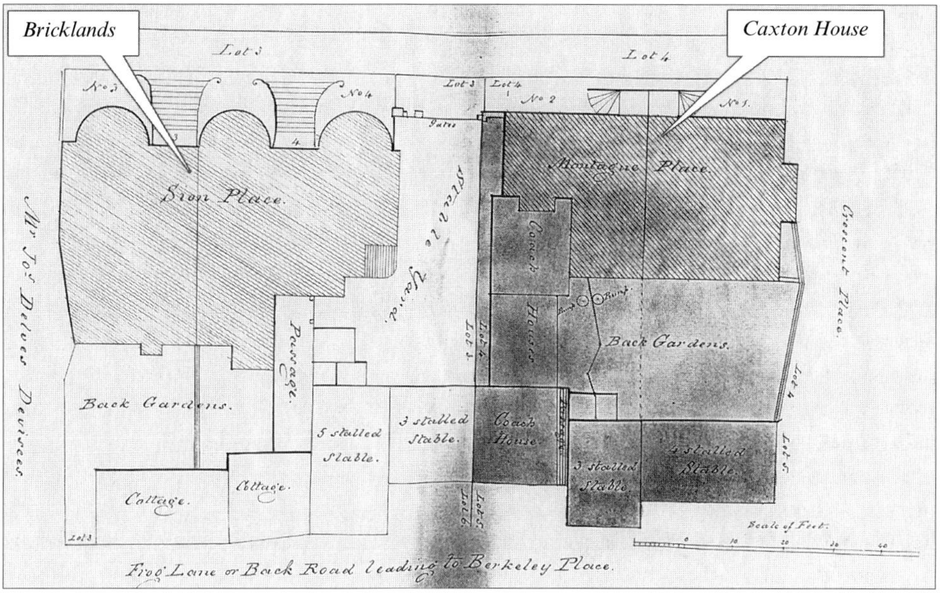

Auction plan 15 April 1831

The 1841 census, for reasons unexplained, does not show Montague Place but it is in the Tithe Award as 'Montague House and Yard, House Yard and Stabling', owned and occupied by Stephen Farley. Contradictorily the house deeds state that Stephen Farley died in 1833 predeceased by his wife and leaving three children, John, plumber and glazier of Tunbridge Wells; William, 'bachelor' of Tunbridge Wells; and Jane, wife of Edward Piper, plumber and glazier of Mayfield. A second daughter, Mary, died in 1843 married to Thomas Bonham, engineer of Oxford Street, London. I am afraid I cannot disentangle what went on amongst this lot in the next ten or more years but pedigrees were invoked, wills were made and deaths took place, a Statutory Declaration by widow Sarah Bonham (any connection, I wonder, with Little Mount Sion – see chapter 11?) mentioned events of 1775 and 1802 and finally the Court of Chancery was involved in 1857 and ordered Montague Place to be sold, which it was on 22 May 1860 to Henry Edwards for £1,100. The 1851 census shows the two halves of the house named Caxton House and Montague Place, Caxton being the upper part (No.2) and unoccupied in 1851. These two names continued in use until 1903 when the 'Montague' dropped out. Montague Place in 1851 was occupied by Richard Turner, surgeon to the Tunbridge Wells

Dispensary, who later moved to Howard Lodge and whose death was lamented in the local press in October 1860. In 1851 he was a widower of only 34, living with his sister, five small children, his dispensing assistant, a lady visitor and her maid and his own four servants, a household of 14 in all. The visitor was a Miss Tibbs who must surely be the same lady whose maid stole from her mistress £25 in notes and allowed the suspicion to fall on poor Liz Waters from Hastings; but this took place in Jerningham House and the story belongs to chapter 25.

The new purchaser, Henry Edwards, was the butcher whose excavation of the cellar outside his shop at Russell Place on the London Road had revealed the drain which occasioned the Webber Riots of 1864 – see chapter 27. The purchase was probably an investment since he did not live in the house himself. He took out in April 1861 a mortgage of £800 (followed by a further charge of £600 in 1867) from the 'Tunbridge Wells Tonbridge and Weald of Kent and Sussex Permanent Mutual Benefit Building Society' whose resounding title was supported by a worthy band of trustees including Charles Trustram, the doctor who lived at Bedford Place just down the road; Thomas Robert Allfree of the Romanoff House Academy; William Willicombe the builder; and William Charles Cripps the lawyer. In 1861 Montague Place was occupied by Miss Augusta Tunne, a gentlewoman of 55, and her Scottish lady's maid, Janet Polson; and Caxton House by William Brackett, his wife and two-year-old son, Arthur W., two apprentices, one shop assistant and two servants. William Brackett, born in Suffolk, gave his occupation as printer and stationer, employing five men, four apprentices and five errand boys. When Arthur William Brackett, full of years and prestige, came to write the centenary history of the family estate agency business in 1928 he did not allude to his father's previous activities, only to his purchase of Mr Henry Sawyer's business in 1866.

In 1873 Henry Edwards died leaving Caxton House and Montague Place in trust for his wife Jane and his three married daughters, Jane Harris, Elizabeth Bates and Sarah Pochin. The trustees were Jane Harris's husband James and John Colbran, the latter being replaced in 1883 by William Brackett. I wonder whether William Brackett had in fact worked for John Colbran 20 years before. The 'Montague' half of the house was occupied successively after 1874 by Mrs Simmonds, the clothier whose shop at that time occupied the Hall's Bookshop premises in Chapel Place; Robert Barton, a veterinary surgeon; Mrs Edwards, presumably the widow of Henry; and Thomas, followed by Mrs, Maynard who ran a lodging house until 1903. The other half, 'Caxton', was occupied from 1874 until 1894 by the butcher's son-in-law, John Frederick Bates, who seems to have found a home conveniently near his work as secretary to the Tunbridge Wells Corn Exchange Co. Ltd of Cumberland Yard, dealers in corn and coal. 'Caxton' was rented later by the curiously named Fairchild Huxtables who took over the whole house in 1903 and ran it as what they called their Christian Boarding Establishment – see the postcard copied on the next page.

In 1913 the trustees on behalf of the surviving daughters, Elizabeth and Sarah, decided to sell to the sitting tenants at a price of £1,600. The conveyance describes

Henry Fairchild Huxtable as a Free Church Minister and *Kelly's Directory* for 1916 has him living at no.19 while 19 and 21 form the Caxton Boarding Establishment (Mrs Fairchild Huxtable, proprietress). The 'Church News' column in the *Courier* for 27 January 1928 mentions the Rev. H. Fairchild Huxtable, minister of St John's Free Church, and Mrs H. Fairchild Huxtable, President of the Ladies' Social Committee. By this time the lady seems to have laid down the labours of landlady and for the next forty years or so Caxton House provided private (furnished) suites under various proprietors. Until change of ownership in 1964 it is worth noting that Caxton Cottage was under the same ownership as the main house, although it had clearly outlived its coach-and-horses connections long before. Caxton House is now, although very different from the 18th-century lodging house it was under the Newnhams and Parmans, still the one house on Mount Sion Hill that approximates most closely to its original use; and perhaps, despite the loss of its chimneys, the one which has most nearly retained its original appearance.

Caxton House about 1920

We now turn to the next house up the hill – Bricklands or Parmans Upper House or Sion Place Nos 3 and 4 – or 23 and 25 Mount Sion as it is today. Winefrith's Deed Poll described it as 'One other Messuage or Tenement now in the Occupation of Mr Brickland a Cook bounding to the way to the Bowling Green towards the west to the said Upper Yard and Stables towards the north'. If we take 'north' to mean the straight down the hill direction then the Upper Yard is the site of Caxton House and the way to the Bowling Green must be Mount Sion Road itself. This makes sense but does not tell us much about the house itself. The Poor Rate record confirms the presence of Mr Brickland the cook and shows how his name clung to the house for half a century or so – and corrects any initial impression that the name may derive from the material of its construction (the original house was certainly timber-framed). However, the first entry dated 1694 shows the house named after 'John Seale' and occupied by the Widow Frye. This is a puzzle. 1694 was of course in the period when the land had been partitioned and Robert Brooke was the sole owner, but this hardly helps. John Seale may have been related to Philip Seale of Little Mount Sion but I have no information about him; and the Widow Frye may have been related to Richard Fry who appears as rate payer much later and is confirmed by Bowra – but again I have no evidence on the widow. Here anyway is the full Poor Rate record alongside a detail from Bowra.

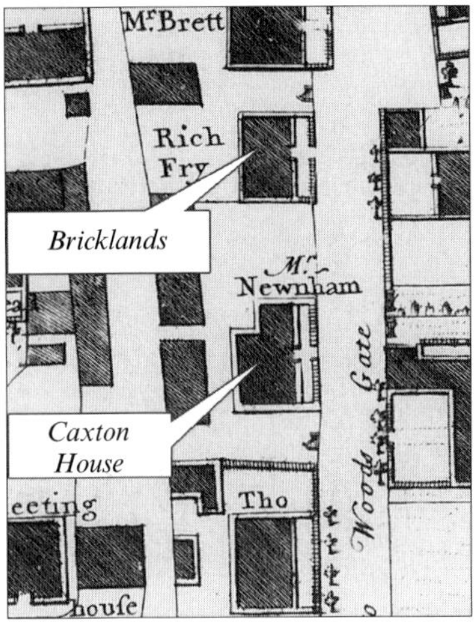

Bowra plan 1738

1694-1697	Wid Frye for John Seales
1698-1704	Mr Brickland for John Seales
1708-1710	Mr Brickland
1711-1712	Mr Brickland or ye occupier
1713-1714	Richard Taylor for Mr Bricklands or occupier
1728-1736	Sarah Randal for Bricklands
1737-1742	Rich Fry for Bricklands
1743-1751	Mr Frye
1752	Richd Frye for Brickland
1753-1761	Mr Fry for Bricklands
1762-1771	Mr Rich Fry for his own House
1772-1779	Fry Widow for her own House
1780-1791	Parman Saml for late Mrs Frys
1792-1797	Parman Wd for late Frys

Richard Taylor was a lawyer, I think, but Sarah Randall, I have a suspicion, may have married Richard Fry – anyway Richard's wife was a Sarah! Bowra, of course, ties in well with the Poor Rate record in 1738. Richard Fry the butcher continued at Bricklands until he died in 1768, leaving ' all that my … Lodging House … situate on Mount Sion' to his widow for her life and then to be divided among the children. Since these numbered nine, the outcome was inevitably the sale of the house and we know that Sam Parman took it over in 1780 and called it Parman's Upper House.

Looking at Bowra, it is noticeable that the house in 1738 was little more than half its present size. This can be demonstrated by scaling up the Bowra image about three times and comparing the result with the Ordnance Survey 1/500 map. This assumes, of course, that Bowra is accurate but he does appear to be. The scaled-up plans of most houses fit reasonably well and in particular that for the well-defined L-shape of Jerningham House. Bowra does not, on the other hand, seem to be so accurate for the distances and bearings between the houses. Another fact is that the bottom third or more of the present house is brick-built whereas the remainder, at the rear, is of timber-framed construction with either tile-hanging or weather-boarding. Furthermore, the whole front of the building has been remodelled at some time giving it the three prominent bow fronts it features today. My guess is that the extension and the new façade were all part of the same scheme and probably date from between 1811 when Richard Delves took over Parmans Upper House and 1817. There is a significant development in nomenclature in *Sprange's Guides* for this period.

From the *Sprange Guides*

1808	Delves Bow Window 1	Delves Bow Window 2	Parmans Upper House	
1811	Bow Window No 1	Bow Window No 2	Sion Place No 3	Sion Place No 4
1817	Sion Place No 1	Sion Place No 2	Sion Place No 3	Sion Place No 4

Nos 23 & 25 Mount Sion

Bow Windows 1 and 2 refer to Mansfield House which will be a topic in the next chapter. The point to note is that it always had a bow window and was known thereby; and it belonged to Richard's father, Joseph Delves. This I think was the inspiration to repeat the bow-window theme down the hill when Richard got his hands on Parmans Upper House. Here are the three bow fronts on nos 23 and 25 Mount Sion. The white building on the right is no 27, a later in-fill between 25 and 29. Evidently the Delves' tried to impose some unity on their property, giving it a single name with four sub-divisions in addition to architectural harmony.

The next event in the story is the bankruptcy auction of 15 April 1831 at which, as we have seen, Caxton House was sold to Stephen Farley and Sion Place Nos 3 and 4 (Lots 3 and 6) went under the hammer to Edward Colsill Edlin, turner and joiner of New Bond Street. This was a new name in Tunbridge Wells history but perhaps a Sussex link can be found in Henry Edlin who proudly proclaimed his proprietorship of the *St Leonard's Hotel* in the *Tunbridge Wells Visitor* of 1834. The Tithe Award shows E.C. Edlin as owner and occupier of 'Sion Place and Yard, Cottages and Stables'. 'Sion Place 3 and 4' is the designation in the censuses of 1841, '51 and '61. In 1841 No 4 was occupied by James Moneypenny 'Clerk', his wife and six children, a governess and four female and one male servants. In 1851 the occupiers were a Cambridge MA landed proprietor and fundholder, his wife and five children, governess, nurse and four servants while No.3 housed a lady fundholder and two sisters, a niece and five servants including an 84-year-old housekeeper. In 1861 No.4 was empty except for a sawyer from Frant and his wife who was in charge of the house and No.3 was occupied by 26-year-old Miss Amelia Haly, a proprietor of houses from Hartfield, a cook and a housemaid. The house name changed to a simple '3 and 4 Mount Sion' in the census of 1871; and also in a Sale Notice of 1859 announcing the forthcoming auction of 'a valuable freehold estate, known to the fashionable visitors of Tunbridge Wells as Nos 3 and 4 Mount Sion'. It appears from the particulars of this and a subsequent sale in 1874 that E.C. Edlin died in 1844 and left his property in trust until his youngest child reached 21, which happened in 1859. The successful bidder in 1859, whose identity I do not know, does not seem to have occupied any part of the building. No.3 (the present 25) was at the time of the sale let by the year to 'a highly respectable and responsible tenant at the very low rent of £60 per annum'; this was almost certainly the Miss Amelia Haly, mentioned just now, who continued to live there until around 1890. No.4 (the present 23) was sold furnished and in January 1864 it was occupied, according to the visitors' list in the *Tunbridge Wells Gazette*, by Lady Repton and family while the 1871 census lists Henry Yetman, lodging house proprietor; in other words the visitors, fashionable or perhaps not always so, were still being accommodated in this part of the house. All this changed in 1874 when the 'Two Commodious Freehold Residences (Land-Tax redeemed) known as Nos 21 & 23 Mount Sion (now 23 and 25) were offered for sale, No.21 being let on a lease which expired on Lady-day next and No 23 let to a 'highly respectable yearly tenant of many years standing'.

It so happened that about this time William Henry Delves, the grandson of Richard the Spirited, was living at the top of the hill in Forest Prospect (the present Ivy Chimneys) but was going to be obliged to move because the Court of Chancery had ordered the winding-up of the family trust of Joseph Delves – see chapter 21. I cannot be sure that William Henry bought 23 Mount Sion at the 1874 auction; but the fact is that he lived there from about this time until his death in 1922 when, as the overcoat-scorning, tricycle-riding, nonagenarian chairman of the Town Council's Finance Committee and grand old man of Mount Sion, he was certainly the owner of the house. A point of interest in both these Sale Notices is that the root of title quoted is a mortgage by Richard Delves in 1812. Around 1890 Miss Haly presumably died and the vacant No.25 appears in *Kelly's* and *Pelton's Directories* until 1915 under the name 'Royton House' in the occupation of Mrs R.W. Weekes. Messrs Weekes (of the department store now Hoopers) have in fact confirmed that R.W. Weekes owned Royton House and that it was the 'family home'. After a short spell as the 'Royton Nursing Home' (I have heard at second hand of ladies who remember 'lying-in' there – and tales of its use as overspill

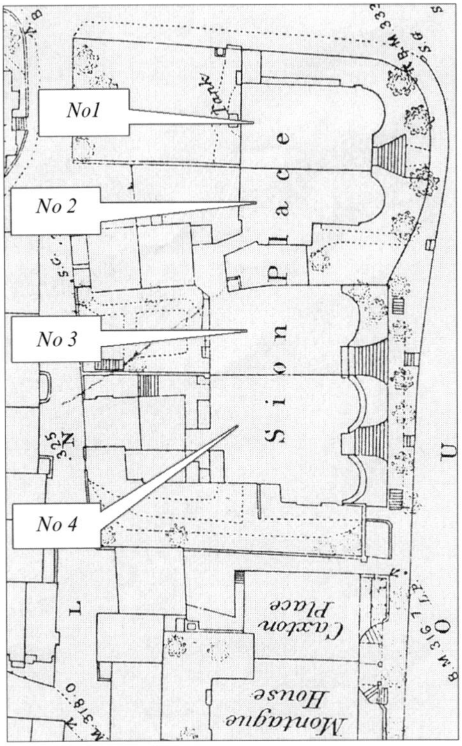

Ordnance Survey 1866 showing 'Sion Place'

to the Eye and Ear Hospital across the road), the house was within the last half century christened 'Nash House' and claimed as Nash's 'Gaming Establishment'. The evidence for this theory is two-fold: firstly, there is a sort of niche in the wall of the entrance hall where, it is said, a footman or doorkeeper stood; and secondly, the two main rooms on the first floor open one into the other in a way which would be suitable for gaming. Judge for yourselves. When I came to Mount Sion in 1960 someone told me (I wish I could remember who) that 23 was Beau Nash's house and part of my motivation has been to confirm this story. Of course there is no point in differentiating between 23 and 25 since they were one and the same house in Beau Nash's time; but it is equally pointless to look for a house belonging to Nash. The Master of Ceremonies made only a fleeting visit each year and, although he must have laid his head and wig somewhere at night, there is little reason to suppose that he had any regular lodgings. Maybe the Pantiles … but who knows? A little more substantial is the story I was told at the same time that Edgar Wallace lived at 23 – but it wasn't him, it was his deserted ex-wife. Mrs I.M. Wallace is recorded at 25 Mount Sion in *Kelly's Directory* of 1926.

Finally a brief comment on front steps. In Bowra's time (see above) and for the 18th century generally there was a flat façade to Bricklands and the entrance seems to be in the middle, although at what level it is impossible to be sure. When the three bows were built an arrangement was made which is well illustrated in the 1831 Auction Plan (page 255). Steps led up to the first floor (the 'piano nobile') between the bows providing two main entrances to Nos 3 and 4 Sion Place. The steps to No.3 (now no.25) are still there and can be seen in the photograph above; but owing to the slope of Mount Sion hill the steps to No.4 (now no.23) had to be much higher and were abandoned some time ago in favour of a side entrance. At one time, in about 1870, an elevated walkway connected the sets of steps and further steps led from the walkway to street level. This arrangement can be seen in the Ordnance Survey map on the previous page while the situation in 1808 can be seen on the Barrow map on the right which shows that the 'bow-window' development at Bricklands had not then taken place. Barrow gives Bricklands the number 14 which can be made out indistinctly and calls it 'Parman's Upper House'. The story of Bricklands or Parmans Upper House or Sion Place Nos 3 and 4 or nos 23 and 25 Mount Sion is partly connected with that of the house next up the hill, Mansfield House, which is itself linked with that of the Bowling Green plot to which we now turn.

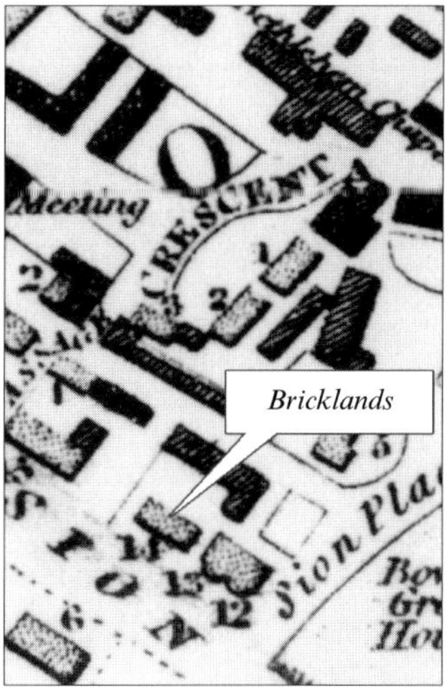

Barrow map 1808 (enlarged)

CHAPTER 19

The Bowling Green

This chapter is concerned with the rectangular 'Bowling Green' plot which was part of Richard Constable's share in the 1686 partition with Robert Brooke. This plot took in the Bowling Green itself, the 'Ballroom' or Bowling Green House and two houses on the other side of Berkeley Road as can be seen on the detail from Bowra's plan on the next page. One of these was Murray House at the top of Frog

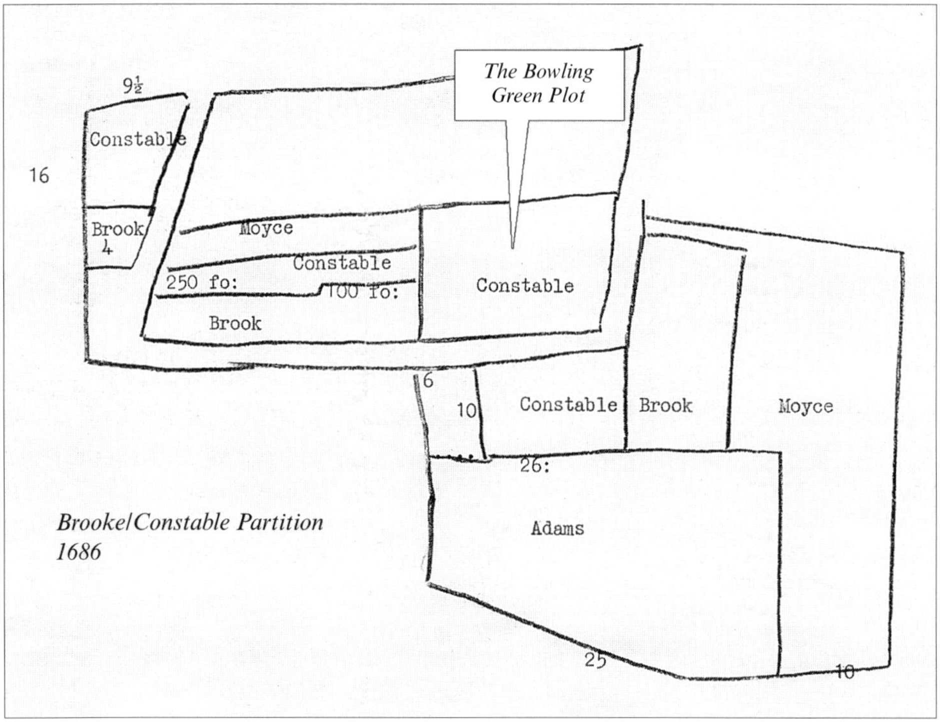

Brooke/Constable Partition 1686

Lane which was dealt with in chapter 16; the other was Mansfield House, no.29 Mount Sion, known as the 'Bow Window House' inspiring I guess the bow windows of Sion Place, as discussed in the previous chapter. I shall, therefore, follow on with Mansfield House and then deal with the Bowling Green.

The reason why Mansfield House (and Murray House equally) are marked Mr Brett on the Bowra plan is hardly worth repeating. As part of the land leased to Richard Constable but unsold in 1715 they fell into the hands of John Brett. The three houses marked Mr Brett to the south of the Bowling Green are, of course, a similar case; but they formed part of a separate plot leased to Constable as can be seen on the Partition plan above and will form the subject of the next two chapters. Identification of occupiers is more difficult in these cases but nevertheless a Poor Rate sequence is discernible for the 'Bow Window House' as follows:

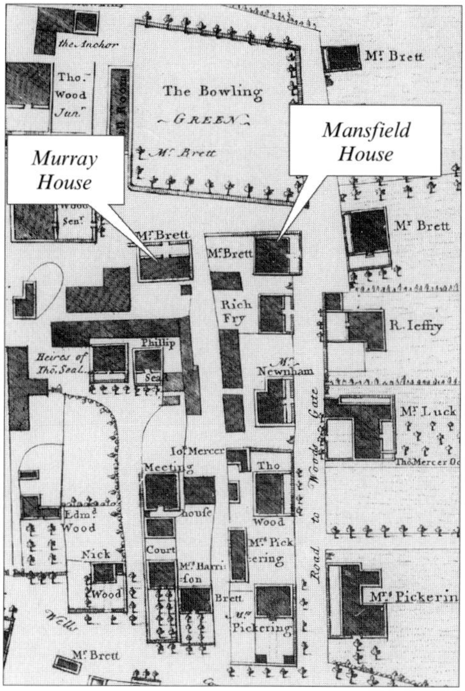

Bowra plan of Mount Sion Hill 1738

Poor Rate for Mansfield House

1689-1690	John Waghorne
1691-1692	Mr Cooper for John Waghornes
1693	Mrs Cooper
1694-1703	Mr Jas Callant for Mrs Coopers
1704-1708	James Callant for Mr Hoopers
1709-1714	Madam Chatharine Ashenhurst for Mr Hoopers
1728-1737	Mrs Walton for Mr Hoopers
1738-1752	Mrs Carter for Mrs Waltons
1753	Mr Fry for Mrs Waltons
1754	Mrs Fry for Mrs Waltons
1755-1761	Mr Fry for Mrs Waltons
1762-1771	Mr Rich Fry for Waltons
1772-1779	Fry Widow for Waltons
1780-1797	Delves Joseph for Mrs Frys late Waltons

Most of the names mean nothing to me until we come to Mr Fry. A John Waghorne was one of the bricklayers and masons who worked on building the Chapel of King Charles the Martyr. Indeed, he obtained an extra payment 'in consideration of overwork and the hardship he lay under by his contract'. Richard Constable bequeathed £100 to Mary Waghorne, the daughter of John Waghorne of Groombridge, carpenter. There may be some links here but it is all speculative. Madam Chatharine (*sic*) Ashenhurst must be the sister of Thomas Ashenhurst but what she was doing at the Bow Window House, who knows? Maybe she lived there after leaving her brother's Great House – the dates would fit – and maybe also, as I suggested in chapter 10, she married Mr Walton between 1714 and 1728 – but, if so, what became of him? Anyway, a Mr Fry took over in 1753 followed by Mrs Fry the next year. This may be merely a misreading of the Poor Rate volume – it is sometimes difficult to distinguish Mrs from Mr; or perhaps Mrs is Mr's widow succeeded swiftly by a younger Mr Fry who may or may not be the Mr Richard who comes next. With Richard we know where we are. He was the butcher who had been living and raising his large family (see family tree in chapter 6, page 56) in Bricklands since 1737. His daughter Mary had married Samuel Parman and died young and his daughter Susannah had in 1775 married Joseph Delves whose sister Elizabeth had become Samuel's second wife. Richard died in

1768 but the Poor Rate collector seems to have been a bit tardy in registering the fact. It might be thought that the year 1753 when 'Mr Fry' took over is significant because of the disposal of Brett property in 1752 by Chancery Court decree; but, as we shall see in the next chapter, the 'two messuages on the west side of the Bowling Green' were not included in that sale and in 1777 they were still Brett property because they were conveyed to trustees as part of the marriage settlement of that year and Mansfield House was described as 'now or late in the possession of Joseph Delves'. We have seen moreover in chapter 6 that the Rev. John Brett, after the death of his father in 1784, sold the Grove Houses and land to George Fry and it seems plausible that he might have sold the two houses on the west side of the Bowling Green at about the same time, although I have no direct evidence. Anyway, it seems that it must have been Joseph Delves who bought the freehold of Mansfield House, not any of the Fry family, and it may be that Joseph was responsible for giving it the name 'Bow Window House'.

Bow fronts on the north-eastern side of Mount Sion – photograph by D.J. Johnson about 1930

The first recorded use of the name 'Bow Window House' seems to be in *Sprange's Guide* for 1797. Bowra shows a flat front. Does this mean that Joseph Delves created the bows? Not impossible. In that case all the bows are down to the Delves family. Here is a photograph taken by David Johnson in about 1930 which illustrates the magnificent march of bows down the hill. What idiot put that ridiculous cap on the second bow and when I do not know but I wish he hadn't. Another innovation by Joseph Delves was to split the house into two. He died in 1827 and bequeathed his two 'lodging houses Nos 1 and 2 situate on Mount Sion aforesaid called the Bow Window Houses' together with all the contents to trustees who were to pay the profit arising therefrom (after deducting an annuity of £50 for his widow Susannah) to his daughter Mary, the wife of Edward Chatterton, and eventually to convey the property to any children of the marriage absolutely. The will says that one of the houses was let as a lodging house and the other was in the occupation of Dr Mayo, presumably the same Dr Mayo who built Grecian Villa in 1824 and whom we met as a trustee of the Murray House Girls' School in 1858 – see chapter 16. The Tithe Award shows Mary Chatterton as owner and occupier of '2 houses, yard and cottage at back'. The name Chatterton appears again in the house deeds which fortunately exist, at least from 1866, in the hands of the owners. They tell us that 'two messuages or tenements Numbers 1 and 2 at Mount Sion … called the Bow Window House' were conveyed in 1866 to Robert Wilsher Weekes, draper, by Harriette Chatterton of the Mile End Road, London. Harriette was the widow of Joseph Delves Chatterton (note the name!), son of Mary Chatterton. Let us notice here that Mary who married Edward Chatterton of Rye in 1801 had seven children of whom one, Henry Delves Chatterton, emigrated to the USA with his family of eight in 1852 and founded a New World branch of the family. Henry, born in 1812, was a man of parts, having been a midshipman, clerk of customs, schoolmaster, trained as a chemist and studied to become a missionary. He held a religious position at Lewes Prison and occasionally preached at Ringmer Church. In 1833 he married Mary Ann Gasson, a musician who was offered a job as music teacher at a religious academy in Twinsburg, Ohio, and Henry decided to go to America as ill-health prevented his becoming a missionary. Together with their eight children and Mary Ann's brother Thomas Gasson they sailed in the *Northumberland* and arrived at New York in April 1852. They settled in Cleveland, Ohio, and their last child, Charles William, was born in 1853. The next year Mary Ann died in an epidemic of typhoid and Henry died the same month, November 1854. Nevertheless, a total of 840 descendants spread across the United States has been recorded by a grandson of Charles William, Arthur Chatterton of Indiana, who took a close interest in the family history, visited the UK for that purpose in 1999 and was able to see the family home on Mount Sion; but he has since, sadly, died.

The name 'Mansfield' has been applied to the house since 1860 or earlier and is supposed to celebrate the residence of the 18th-century Lord Chief Justice of that name. The first mention I have found of the name 'Mansfield House' is in an advertisement in the *Tunbridge Wells Gazette* for 27 July 1860. R.W. Rogers Long BA announced the opening of his Tunbridge Wells Classical and Mathematical School at Mansfield House Mount Sion. However the enterprise seems to have been short-lived for the 1861 census makes no mention of Mr Long at '1 Sion Place' and in 1862 there are references in the *Gazette* to visitors staying at 'Mansfield House'. In the 1866 conveyance there was no mention of Mansfield but in the 1871 census R.W. Weekes is living at 'Mansfield House' while '2, Mount Sion' is unoccupied. A mortgage deed of 1872 still talks of Nos 1 & 2, Bow Window Houses but in 1874 Kelly gives 'Weeks Rob' at 27 and a 'Harding, Mrs' at 29, Mount Sion. In 1876 R.W. Weekes sold both houses to the brothers Goodrham, upholsterers, formerly of Bedford Terrace, and this time the names 'Mansfield House' and 'Durnford House' are in the conveyance.

In 1896 the Goodrham family sold the houses separately, Durnford going at auction to J.W. Rush, a butcher, for £1,200 and Mansfield for £1,410 to R. Missing, a fishmonger. From 1914 to 1923 the Weekes family was back again at Mansfield

House, this time in the persons of S.S. Weekes (the local tennis star) and his family. All this summarises the development of the name 'Mansfield House' – but what evidence is there for the presence of the Lord Chief Justice? Hardly enough, I am afraid, to ravel a single curl in his Lordship's wig. Barton says that he was a frequent visitor to the Wells, stayed on Mount Sion but spent much of his time on Mount Ephraim with his 'old flame', Mrs Johnson. John Evans writing in 1823 says that 'Earl Mansfield, that luminary of the law' once resided in one of the mansions on Mount Sion. Savidge says that he came to Mount Sion and later to stay with Mrs Johnson with whom he had once been in love; he lived till 1793 and was often to be seen on the Walks. This is undoubtedly true. There are newspaper references. The *Maidstone Journal* reported in September 1786: 'Lord Mansfield is daily upon the walks, by seven o'clock in the morning, to take the waters from which his Lordship has experienced so much benefit, that he appears perfectly recovered from his late indisposition …' And in 1788 the same journal reported that Lord Mansfield again goes for a few weeks to Tonbridge. *Colbran's Guide* 1884 says that Mansfield stayed for the season of 1784 only, a statement belied by the newspaper accounts. Whatever the truth about his visits, they do not prove that he stayed in a particular house on Mount Sion, even if that house has borne his name for a hundred years and more. There is another possibility. The Church of St Mark in Broadwater Down was built by Mansfield the builder in about 1864. Could this perhaps explain the assumption of the name by no 29 Mount Sion at about the same time?

There is a tale attached to the name 'Durnford House' also. This name was first used apparently in the conveyance of September 1876. It applies to no.27 Mount Sion, which was part of an infill of the space between nos 25 and 29 which had been partially closed by the time of the Ordnance Survey map surveyed in 1866 – see page 260. 'Durnford' is not one of those grand names like Berkeley or Burlington which are promiscuously bestowed all over the country nor does it refer to any character of local anecdotage, so where did it come from? There was a General Durnford of the Royal Engineers who was buried at Holy Trinity in Tunbridge Wells in 1850 and a related Col A.W. Durnford (one of the family at least served continuously in the Sappers from 1755 to 1926) who died a heroic death in an engagement with a Zulu army at Isandhlwana in January 1879 and is buried at Pietermaritzburg. He is said to have been loved by the Basutos whose chief Hlubi sent a letter of condolence to the Colonel's parents, saying: 'I grieve deeply for the loss of the 'Inkos' and things will be very different now for me and my people. While HE lived we were happy and protected … The Colonel always treated me as kindly and well as though I had been a white man, and where shall we find another 'Inkos' who will do that?' The trouble with all this is that it took place three years after the naming of Durnford House. Enquiry had to be made elsewhere.

Colbran's Guide for 1884 says that: 'Dr Durnford the late Lord Bishop of Chichester aptly called Tunbridge Wells the Fashionable Metropolis of Kent'. As Richard Durnford was bishop of Chichester from 1870 to 1895 perhaps this was the vital clue; but the present bishop's librarian was unable to trace any connection between Bishop Durnford and Tunbridge Wells. A descendant of the bishop, however, put me onto the Eton connection. The bishop had married a daughter of the celebrated Dr Keats of Eton and his younger brother, the Rev. F.E. Durnford, was a master whose Punch-like proboscis is still commemorated in 'Judy's Passage' and who was the first housemaster of Durnford House until 1864; to be succeeded from 1876 to 1879 by the bishop's younger son, Walter, who eventually became Provost of King's College, Cambridge. Unfortunately for my theory the only residents of 27 Mount Sion at the relevant time who might have wanted to commemorate happy days at Eton seemed to be the surgeon Robert Gream (1841-1862) and R.W. Weekes (1866-1876) and neither name occurs in the Eton registers. However, while searching microfilm copies of the *Tunbridge Wells Gazette* for some reference to Col Durnford and the Zulu war (without success) I came upon the name 'Durnford House' in a list of residents for the year 1876. It appears for the first time on 3 March and continues until 4 August when it drops out for no apparent reason. The residents during this period were 'Mrs H Verschoyle, Mr F and Miss Verschoyle'; and lo and behold! on revisiting the Eton registers I found that Arthur Verschoyle was in the Fourth Form in 1874. Mystery solved? Surely the name is so out of the way that there can be no doubt.

Before leaving Mansfield House let us look at a revealing piece of evidence which came to light not long ago. Among the relics left behind by David Johnson, the photographer, were a few glass negatives (many more have, I am afraid, been lost) and I had prints made. Among them was this photograph which must I guess

Mansfield House – print from glass negative about 1900. Murray House is on the far right.

have been taken about 1900 and shows Mansfield House with a flight of steps leading up to what is now the first floor, demonstrating the position of the 'piano nobile' in this and, by extension, in many other houses in the 19th century. The evidence of maps and plans has already been seen in the case of Bricklands, nos 23/25 Mount Sion (see chapter 18).

Let is now turn to the Bowling Green. It seems clear that the idea for a Bowling Green on flat ground at the top of Mount Sion must from the beginning have been in the mind of Thomas Weller or whoever planned the lease plots of 1684. The square plot dictated the shape of the building plots and the roads all around. Just glance at the Partition plan of 1686 and at Bowra. I wonder what the area was like originally and what efforts were needed to level it and lay turves or sow seed. Macaulay's history described it as 'elastic' although, as we shall see in a minute, some commentators have painted lyrical pictures of the ladies and gentlemen dancing in the evening sun on grass as smooth as any in the world. 'Elastic' suggests springy rather than smooth – good for dancing perhaps but not so perfect for bowls. We shall never know. What we do know is that the Bowling Green or 'Alley' first appears in 1690 in the Poor Rate record which runs as follows until the usual gap in 1714:

1690-1694	Mr Ashenhurst or Mr Reynolds for a new house and Bowling Alley
1695-1697	– do – for a new house and Bowling Greene
1698-1710	Mr Thomas Ashenhurst for – do –
1711	Mr Blamire for – do –
1712-1713	Mrs Thompson for – do –
1714	Mr Blamire or occ of the new house and Bowling Green

I do not know anything about Mr Reynolds or his association with Thomas Ashenhurst but I think it is fair to assume that Ashenhurst was the leading light. Chapter 10 (pages 106 et seq) dealt at some length with what I know about him and with his houses and his quarrel with his sister; and with the problem of the 'two great houses'. I concluded that the second great house must be the one marked 'Ballroom' on the Bowra plan (see the beginning of this chapter) and the 'new house' of the Poor Rate sequence above. I argued that there was a separate sequence for 'Berkeley Place' and that Katharine Ashenhurst recorded in her accounts a payment of ground rent to Mr Constable which makes sense because the 'Ballroom' was on Constable's Bowling Green plot. The counter argument was that Bowra shows a ballroom not a lodging house on his plan – but on the other hand I showed a detail from Bowra's general map where the building looked more like a normal house. Some additional evidence is provided by the Sun Insurance register kept at the Guildhall Library. Fire insurance is recorded in about 1727 for a 'House on Sion hill near Tunbridge Wells Walks occ. Mrs Thompson; adjoining part of Mrs Thompson's house occ. Mrs Ashenhurst; house called the Bowling Green house on Sion hill near Tunbridge Wells Walks occ. ______'. Mrs Thompson was of course the widow lady to whom Thomas Ashenhurst willed his – probably depleted – real estate in 1713 and it is interesting to see Katharine Ashenhurst occupying the adjoining part of Mrs Thompson's house – presumably 'Berkeley Place', so they must I suppose have been on speaking terms. Thomas Ashenhurst incidentally subscribed five guineas between 1688 and 1696 to the Chapel building fund as can be confirmed by anyone with good eyesight who cares to climb the gallery stairs in the Church of King Charles the Martyr.

There are contemporary references. Celia Fiennes (1697) says:

> There are several bowling-greens about the Wells one just at it on Mt Sion, and another up the hill called Mt Ephraim … ; they have all houses to the greens so the Gentlemen bowle the Ladies dance or walke on the green in the afternoons, and if wet dance in the houses there being Musick maintained by the Company to play in the morning so long while they drink the waters, and in the afternoon for dancing …

Another, more imaginative, picture is painted in the *Memoirs of Count Grammont* (published 1713 but of uncertain temporal reference): 'As soon as the evening comes, everyone quits his little palace to assemble on the bowling-green, where, in the open air, those who choose dance upon a turf more soft and smooth than the finest carpet in the world'. Lord Macaulay says that 'on fine evenings the fiddlers were in attendance, and there were morris dances on the elastic turf of the bowling green'.

Would Celia Fiennes have said that the Bowling Greens had 'all houses to the greens' if these appendages had been ballrooms and nothing more? Taking all the evidence into account, I have no doubt that there was a lodging house overlooking the bowling green on Mount Sion and that the house continued in that use even after the dancers had deserted the ballroom on the hill for a more sophisticated assembly room; which happened about 1739 when the public room on the Upper Walk of the Pantiles was enlarged just after Beau Nash had taken over as Master of Ceremonies. The Bowling Green House is described in a deed of 1752, for whatever the standard legal terminology is worth, as a 'messuage or tenement commonly known by the name of the Bowling Green House together with a Bowling Green thereunto belonging containing by estimation ¾ of an acre'. This 1752 deed (see chapter 20) was the one by which some of the property disposed of to satisfy the demands of John Brett's will was, at one remove or two, sold to William Camfield. The deed says that the house was in the possession of Metcalfe Ashe (occupier of Forest Prospect) 'by virtue of an Indenture of Lease at the yearly rent of Twenty Six Pounds and wherein there is yet to come little more than two years'. The Ashe tenancy, alongside other as yet unexplained occupancies, is reflected in the Poor Rate record which, after the 1714-1728 gap and with some simplification for the sake of brevity, runs as follows:

1728-1736	Mr Betts or occ for a new house & Bowling Green
1737-1749	Mr Ash for – do –
1750-1753	Wm Fry for ye Bowling Green House
1754-1757	Occr of ye Bowling Green House
1758	Capt Ash for the Bowling Green House
1759-1760	Mr Lincoln for – do –
1761-1778	Mr/Widow Gosling (or occ) for – do –
1779-1780	Goodwin widow (or occ) for – do –
1781-1782	Richardson ________ for the Bowling Green late Goodwins
1783	Fry John for the Bowling Green late Richardsons
1784	Fry John for 2 New Houses late the Bowling Green

The Poor Rate record really comes up trumps here, furnishing a quite precise date for the transformation of the Bowling Green House. A few comments should be made, however, on the earlier entries. The name 'Betts' in the first entry suggests a possible mistake for 'Brett'. There can be no doubt that 'Betts' is a correct transcription since it occurs not once but each year for eight years; but the overseer himself might have got the owner's name wrong – not altogether unlikely in the state of Brett affairs at the time; but on the other hand I doubt if any member of the Brett family would have been taking a personal interest in running the Bowling Green House at this time. In 1750 the description 'house & Bowling Green' changed to 'Bowling Green House', suggesting that the bowling green might have ceased to be used as such. Thirty years later the description changed again to 'for the Bowling Green' – which could be taken to mean that the house had become more a plot of land than anything else. Barton, in fact, painting a picture of Tunbridge Wells in 1779 says as much: 'The Bowling Green, from ceaseless cutting and rolling since the days of Lord Rochester, had changed only for the better. It was enclosed on three sides by symmetrically planted rows of fine tall trees, and on the fourth by the Assembly Room of pre-Nash days, now in 1779 standing empty and neglected'. She does not, of course, cite any evidence; perhaps she was letting her imagination embroider Bowra's plan. All this is very speculative; but what followed is one of the best authenticated facts in Tunbridge Wells history (few and far between in the 18th century!) concerning particular houses and their occupants. Two houses were contrived on the Bowling Green site and before very long Richard Cumberland and his friend Sir James Bland Burgess had settled in as pioneering permanent residents. There is plenty of primary evidence in the case of Cumberland but for Bland Burgess the sources are secondary and disagree not only on the number of 'S's in his name but also on whether he occupied Burlington or Bowling Green House. The Poor Rate record bifurcates after 1784 as follows:

(1)	1785-1797	Fry John for a new house lett to Mr Cumberland
(2)	1786-1787	Wogan Mrs Eliz for a New House
	1788-1790	Wogan Mrs Eliz or occ for a New House
	1791-1797	Fry John for late Elizabeth Wogans

Sprange is silent for the years 1780 and 1786 and in 1797 and 1801 shows the Bowling Green House (three parlours, five chambers, seven garrets, one coach house and four stables) and Cumberland House (two parlours, five chambers, five garrets, no coach house and no stables – does this mean that Cumberland was letting rooms to visitors?); while the Barrow map shows the two houses by name not occupier. There can be no doubt then of the names and positions of the two houses – see the detail from the Tithe map on the next page. 3789 is the Bowling Green House and Pleasure Ground and 3790 is Cumberland House, Pleasure Ground, Stable, Coachhouse and Yard.

This is what Cumberland had to say in his memoirs about the house 'which I rented of Mr Jn Fry, at that time master of the Sussex tavern, partly new and partly attached to old foundations'. He says that it was sufficient for his family and

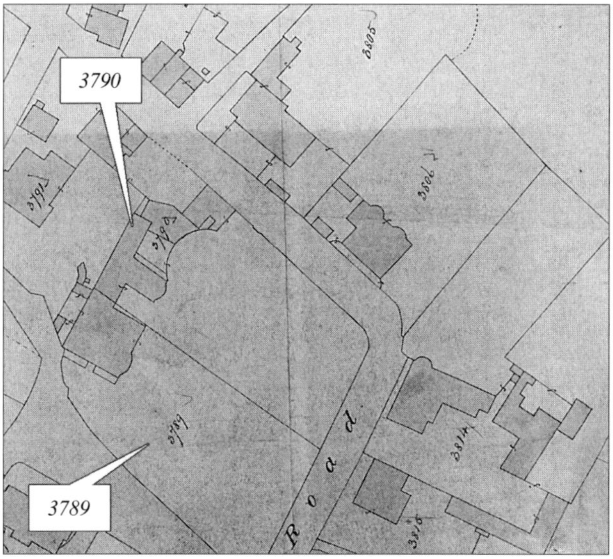

Tithe map 1840

that he fitted it up with part of his furniture and pictures; and, as to the garden, there was a square patch of ground in front of about ½ acre, fenced, and planted round with trees and this he converted into a flower garden encircled with a sand walk. Elsewhere he says: 'For more than twenty years I lived at Tunbridge Wells inhabiting the same house, and cultivating a plot of garden ground, embowered with trees, and amply sufficient for a profusion of flowers ...' A further description is quoted by Melville from Mrs Pitt Byrne: '... a quaint old tenement, rather imposing from its dimensions and the site it occupied on the brow of the hill, standing back among the chestnut trees which overshadowed it and railed off from the London turnpike road on the north side, opposite Culverdens'. Mrs Byrne's *Gossip of the Century* was published between 1892 and 1898 and her description must refer to a period later than Cumberland's occupancy. The reference to Culverdens is puzzling: the only thing truly to the north (or better north-east) of Cumberland House was Burlington House; and the turnpike road ('the highway leading to Woodsgate' – see Chapter 20 about the Cecil Court site) followed if anything the line of present-day Mount Sion. However, a wider reading of Mrs Byrne's chapter on Tunbridge Wells reveals that her father (Hans Busk) had a house called Culverdens and when she says 'opposite Culverdens' she must be looking, as it were, across the town towards the Mount Ephraim ridge. A final description of the bowling green houses (from his own recollections presumably) is to be found in Brackett's *Tunbridge Wells Through the Centuries*: 'Some will remember a pair of large old-red-brick houses with gardens that stood at the top of Mount Sion which were known as Cumberland House and Bowling Green House'. From all these descriptions a picture begins to emerge of what the place was like; and which may be further complemented from maps. Bowra shows a fence and a row of trees on three sides while the Ordnance Survey (see next page) shows the outer ring of trees still standing and inside this the arrangement of shrubs, flower beds and paths which dated perhaps from the horticultural designs of Richard Cumberland. An interesting detail is the flight of steps, ten perhaps in number, which led from Mount Sion onto the end of the Bowling Green garden, showing that the old bowling green probably stood above the level of the road at this point.

From studying the positions of Bowling Green and Cumberland Houses on the Ordnance Survey map and comparing them with the position of the ballroom on Bowra and from Cumberland's statement that his house was 'partly new and partly attached to old foundations', I conclude that John Fry in 1783/4 used part of the old building to form the rear of his new house and built as far again in front to complete the renovation. The proportions of old and new are very speculative but it is fairly certain that at least the rear wall was not demolished. The reason for this certainty is two-fold. Firstly, Nicholas Wood in his will of 1724 (see chapter 10) mentions the encroachment made upon his land for which the landlord of the Bowling Green House had to pay him 10s. a year; and secondly the Sale Particulars of Burlington House (in 1873) stated that 'on the south side of this lot are two buttresses supporting the north wall of Cumberland House and

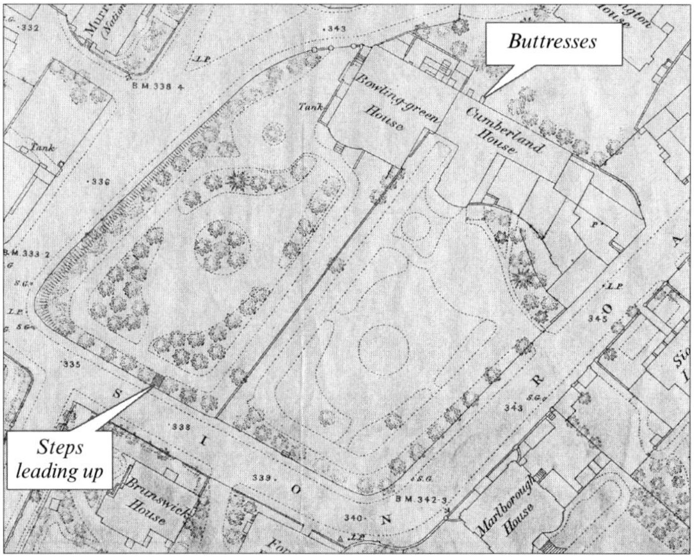

Ordnance Survey 1866

for which the owner of Cumberland House pays a rent of 10s per annum'. Note that the rent had not changed in 150 years! This, by the way, is surely further proof that the 'Ballroom' was more than a single storey high. The position of the buttresses can be seen clearly on the Ordnance Survey map. Perhaps this tells us something also about the standard of construction of the original house.

Richard Cumberland can therefore be put firmly in his place and time; but Sir James Bland Burgess is somewhat elusive. Melville says that he 'lived in one of the houses on the site of the bowling-green on Mount Sion, called Bowling-Green House, and about 1786 no less a person than Richard Cumberland settled down next to him'. Barton, on the other hand, says: 'Immediately opposite to Cumberland in Burlington House was Sir James Bland Burges, a man after his own heart, pompous, studious and vain'. Savidge seems to follow Barton but I am sure Melville is right. I know that Thomas Wood (see chapter 12) was living in Burlington

House and I cannot see him sharing his home with the likes of Sir James – or vice versa. Compared with Cumberland his neighbour Sir James cuts a nugatory figure. How long he stayed at Bowling Green House is not clear nor whether he was more than a summer visitor. He seems to have collaborated with Cumberland for several years on an epic poem called the 'Exodiad' which was published in 1806 to total lack of acclaim.

The usual stories about Cumberland may be culled from Melville and Barton; but a few deserve to be dusted out. He had, in his own words, a 'most excellent wife' whom, it is recorded, he used to call 'mamma' and four sons and three daughters. His eldest daughter was married to 'one of the best and most amiable of men', Lord Edward Bentinck, who shared an ardent enthusiasm for cricket with his brother-in-law, Richard's son Captain Charles Cumberland, a renowned fast bowler and member of the Kent and All-England elevens of his day. This fascinating sidelight on the family life of the apparently staid and solemn figure of the dramatist and model for Sheridan's 'Sir Fretful Plagiary' is to be found in the excellent history of the Tunbridge Wells Cricket Club compiled by Carl Openshaw for the club's bicentenary in 1982. He quotes the *Sussex Weekly Advertiser* of June 1786 as follows: 'A match of cricket was played on Monday, June 12th on Tunbridge Wells Common, eleven on a side, and the successful men had each a hat given by Lord Edward Bentinck and Mr Cumberland; a supper was likewise provided for all the players'. Hat-tricks all round! Cumberland and Bentinck were active in organising local cricket and in a match between Tunbridge Wells and Brighton in 1790 the Tunbridge Wells team reads like a roll-call of local history – Chapman, Strange, Nye, Cripps, Newnham, Mercer ... Cumberland took six wickets, all apparently clean bowled, and made 17 runs, the second highest score in a losing innings of 74.

Richard Cumberland's daughter, Sophia, was married to one William Badcock who died in 1802 leaving five children 'awarded to my care by Chancery and looking to me for their education' in the words of Cumberland's *Memoirs*. If these children resided at Cumberland House and the cricketers were around too (Charles did in fact live for a time in Sion Lodge opposite) then the house can hardly have been the grim place suggested by local mythology – and no mention has yet been made of the dramatic dimension. Richard Cumberland's claim to fame (and he was buried in Westminster Abbey!) is as a dramatist, and although his plays today are condemned unread as unreadable, 'The Jew' is not half bad and helped the reputation not only of Mrs Baker's company but also of her principal actor and son-in-law, William Dowton, when he took the title role at Drury Lane in 1794; and his plays were regularly performed in Tunbridge Wells. Research by Norma Hodgson has pointed out some inaccuracies in the accounts of Melville and Barton on this topic; but at the same time has shown a remarkable coincidence in the date of arrival of Cumberland on Mount Sion (1785) and the building of Sarah Baker's first theatre in Tunbridge Wells in 1786. This was humorously known as 'The Temple of the Muses' and was situated on Mount Sion and apparently not yards away from Cumberland House – but where, oh where, was it? Mrs Baker is known to have toured the Wells for years before 1786 and Cumberland had written plays (e.g. 'The West Indian' and 'The Brothers') many years before 1786 which, however, were regularly in the repertoire when the company had its own theatre at Tunbridge Wells. It is therefore reasonable to suppose that Cumberland was acquainted with Mrs Baker before he and she settled on Mount Sion; and surely not unreasonable to suppose that it was more than coincidence that they became neighbours. A second coincidence is revealed in a quotation from 'The Diary or Woodfall's Register' taken from the same article. 'Mrs Baker's little playhouse on Mount Sion is pulled down and another is to be erected for her on the site of Fry's tavern at the Sussex, and to have communication with some of these rooms …' John Fry was of course Richard Cumberland's own landlord and I like to think that John Fry offered Sarah the site for an enlarged theatre as they and Richard Cumberland were strolling beneath the chestnut trees of the old bowling green, to the sound of bat and ball as Captain Charles and Edward Bentinck and assorted grandchildren disported themselves on the remains of Grammont's finest carpet of turf. Obviously Cumberland found it convenient for his play-writing to have actors and a theatre on the spot but there was an additional advantage in the arrangement. Sophia's prolific husband William Badcock 'used to tread the boards' according to Savidge or was, according to Barton, a 'good-for-nothing son-in-law' who 'could amuse himself harmlessly by strutting the boards as Hamlet or Richard'. So I should like to complete my picture of the Cumberland House garden with a figure histrionically rehearsing in the shrubbery beside the bow-window.

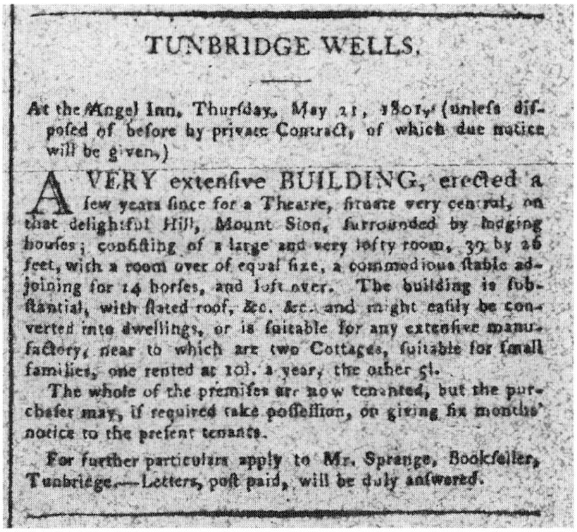

TUNBRIDGE WELLS.

At the Angel Inn, Thurſday, May 21, 1801, (unleſs diſpoſed of before by private Contract, of which due notice will be given,)

A VERY extenſive BUILDING, erected a few years ſince for a Theatre, ſituate very central, on that delightful Hill, Mount Sion, ſurrounded by lodging houſes; conſiſting of a large and very lofty room, 39 by 26 feet, with a room over of equal ſize, a commodious ſtable adjoining for 14 horſes, and loft over. The building is ſubſtantial, with ſlated roof, &c. &c. and might eaſily be converted into dwellings, or is ſuitable for any extenſive manufactory, near to which are two Cottages, ſuitable for ſmall families, one rented at 10l. a year, the other 5l.

The whole of the premiſes are now tenanted, but the purchaſer may, if required take poſſeſſion, on giving ſix months' notice to the preſent tenants.

For further particulars apply to Mr. Sprange, Bookſeller, Tunbridge.—Letters, poſt paid, will be duly anſwered.

Maidstone Journal

The mystery of the location of the 'Temple of the Muses' was deepened if anything by my discovery of an advertisement for its sale in the *Maidstone Journal*, as follows:

Tunbridge Wells

At the Angel Inn, Thursday, May 21, 1801 (unless disposed of before by private Contract, of which due notice will be given,)

A VERY extensive BUILDING, erected a few years since for a Theatre, situate very central, on that delightful Hill, Mount Sion, surrounded by lodging houses; consisting of a large and very lofty room, 39 by 26 feet, with a room over of equal size, a commodious stable adjoining for 14 horses, and loft over.

> The building is substantial, with slated roof etc etc and might easily be converted into dwellings, or is suitable for any extensive manufactory, near to which are two Cottages, suitable for small families, one rented at 10l. a year, the other 5l.
>
> The whole of the premises are now tenanted, but the purchaser may, if required take possession, on giving six months' notice to the present tenants. For further particulars apply to Mr. Sprange, Bookseller, Tunbridge. – Letters, post paid, will be duly answered.

It is very difficult to see where a building of this size, plus a 14-horse stable and two cottages could be fitted in near Cumberland House, unless they were all on the other side of the road where Marlborough House would be later built. Possibly, just possibly, the large room might be part of the Cumberland House complex itself as shown on the Ordnance Survey map. There is a rectangular building adjoining the road which has the right proportions but is a bit too small for 39 by 26 feet. What then about the stable and above all the two cottages? Of course 'Woodfall's Register' said that the playhouse was pulled down in which case it would hardly feature on a map of 1870; but why was it offered for sale? Again it would scarcely be for sale if it was virtually part of Cumberland House; but then it was built about the time when John Fry was carrying out substantial alterations to the Bowling Green House – and John Fry did help Mrs Baker with the site for the replacement on the Pantiles. The 'Temple of the Muses' will, I fear, remain a mystery.

On 7 May 1811 Richard Cumberland died in Tunbridge Wells and was buried in Poets' Corner in the Abbey; and in the same year Sprange shows both houses, Cumberland and Bowling Green, in the occupation of Richard Delves. This was the period when Joseph's eldest son was extending his lodging house empire to what seems in the event to have been unwise limits and I suppose he was glad to snap up these Mount Sion tenancies when they fell vacant. The old Bowling Green House or Ballroom was purchased in 1752 by William Camfield and in 1801 John Fry willed a freehold messuage occupied by Mr Cumberland to his wife for life and then to his sons John and Henry as tenants in common. Since he started paying the Poor Rate in 1783 it is a fair guess that he owned the house then but how and when it changed hands from Camfield to Fry I have no evidence. A further mystery is the ownership of (the new) Bowling Green House at the time of John Fry's will. Fry mentions also his two messuages on Mount Sion ('late the Widow Fry's') – as will be discussed in connection with Sion Lodge in chapter 21 – but I do not think the description fits the Bowling Green House. The purchaser was probably the Mrs Elizabeth Wogan who started paying the rates in 1786 and whose name appears in the Vestry Minutes of King Charles the Martyr as the donor of £200 by her will dated 23 June 1786. Confirmation comes in *Sprange's Guides* which in 1796 describe two 'elegant new brick houses' on the top of Mount Sion Hill, one the property of Mrs Wogan and the other, adjoining, the residence of Richard Cumberland, both 'situate on the Bowling Green where formerly the Assembly-room stood'; and in 1797 change the description to 'late the property of Mrs Wogan'. On the other hand John Fry re-appears in the Poor Rate record 'for late Elizabeth Wogans' from 1791 to 1797. In 1817 Richard Delves is still shown in Sprange as occupier of both houses. In 1827 *Pigot's Directory* lists Daniel Webb Esq at Bowling Green House but makes no mention of Cumberland while in 1832 the situation is reversed and James Deane Esq is shown at Cumberland House. The Tithe map (see page 271 above) confirms James Deane as owner and occupier of Cumberland House and gives James Hoppe as owner and occupier of the 'Bowling Green House and Pleasure Ground'. In 1850 *Colbran's Guide* lists Mrs Kemp at the Bowling Green House and the 1851 census gives more details. Augusta Kemp was a 49-year-old widow from London living with her daughter of 23 and staff of butler, ladies' maid, housemaid and cook. By 6 January 1860 Mr and Mrs Broadwood had moved in and they were to be the last occupants of the Bowling Green House as Mr and Mrs Deane were to be of Cumberland House.

Henry Broadwood described himself to the enumerator in 1851 as a Member of Parliament with income from the Funds and House Property. He was born in Hanover Square and his wife, Frances, who at 32 was 26 years her husband's junior, was born at St James'. In 1851 they were living at Jerningham House with Alfred aged two and three local female servants and a manservant born in Antwerp; but in 1861, at Bowling Green House, Henry was away from home and Mary aged eight and Alfred aged four made up the family. Alfred must have been the second child of that name. In 1871 the house was unoccupied at the census, although Henry Broadwood is listed in *Kelly's Directory* for that year. Cumberland House was the home of James Deane for over thirty years, from at least 1832 until, in March 1865, his funeral at Eridge was reported in the *Tunbridge Wells Gazette*. As early as 1833 his name is to be found amongst the notables serving on the Local Act Committee and in 1834 it appears in the *Tunbridge Wells Visitor* among those present at the laying of the foundation stone of the Victoria National School and dining with the Duchess in the company of Decimus Burton and others. In August 1834 the deputation to present a loyal address to Princess Victoria and her mother included, from Mount Sion, Aretas Akers, the Rev. W.L. Pope, Robert Foreman (of Jerningham House), Joseph Delves and James Deane. In 1851 he and his wife Harriet, both aged 62, were living with their 25-year-old daughter Harriet and son William of 23. James was born in Marlow, Buckinghamshire, his wife in London and the children both in Buckinghamshire. He described himself then as a fund-holder but ten years later as a magistrate; and in the *Tunbridge Wells Gazette* in November 1860, an example already mentioned in chapter 14 (page 182), is to be found a report of the Petty Sessions when, before Messrs Elers, Deane and Musgrove, Jane Smith was charged with being drunk and pleaded guilty. She had been found by the policeman on Monday morning, on Mount Sion, sitting asleep opposite the *Jolly Sailor*. The *Jolly Sailor*, as we saw in chapter 14, was actually in Little Mount Sion, just below the Presbyterian Chapel. Jane was ordered to pay 5s. or in default go to prison for seven days. In 1861 the Deanes were looking after four grandchildren, Mary, Alexander, Emilie and Alfred de Bylandt, aged from one to seven, and their Belgian governess. In his will James Deane left all his real and personal estate to his wife for life and then to be equally divided between his son William Henry and his daughter Harriet, wife of Alexander de Bylandt. A witness to the will was one Charles Prince 'lodging house keeper, Tunbridge Wells' who had been the family butler in 1861 – a married man of 57 born in Canterbury. Brother and sister or maybe brother and Belgian brother-in-law seem to have fallen out over the estate for amongst the Brackett sale catalogues is a notice of the auction in 1894 of no.61 Mount Sion and the adjoining Mission Hall when would-be purchasers were informed that the title was to commence with a conveyance dated 20 February 1877 made under a Chancery Court order following a suit for the administration of the estate of James Deane deceased. Harriet Deane, the widow, aged 81, was still living in Cumberland House in 1871 but on 1 September 1876 the following notice appeared in the *Tunbridge Wells Gazette*:

> VALUABLE BUILDING SITES – MOUNT SION
>
> The ground at present occupied by Bowling Green and Cumberland Houses To be let in Plots on Lease for 99 years. Plans may be seen and further particulars obtained at Messrs Weeks and Hughes, Architects, Grove Hill Rd or of Messrs Jull & Co, Auctioneers, Parade, Tunbridge Wells.

Quite when the old houses were demolished is unclear but new building cannot have been long delayed. Another Sale Notice in the Reference Library (1897) refers to a semi-detached pair numbered 39 and 41 Mount Sion, the title for which was said to commence with a conveyance dated 20 February 1877 – the same as that for no.61 quoted above. It is evident, therefore, that the whole Cumberland House site was sold on this date – to whom I do not know but a planning application dated 17 August 1877 names Francis Peek Esq of 4 Fenchurch Street, London, as owner of the Bowling Green Estate and, since he is known to have worked with the architects Weeks and Hughes on a number of Tunbridge Wells developments, it is likely that he bought the Cumberland House estate also. Hughes is William Barnsley Hughes, the most notable of Tunbridge Wells architects, and his partner was James Weeks – not I think connected with the department store Weekes family. The odd thing is that the two parts of the development are so different. If the same firm of architects were used a similarity of architectural style might be expected but no! the two could hardly be more different. Facing Berkeley Road, on the Bowling Green site, is a terrace of dark-red brick houses with fanciful gables and finials while facing Mount Sion are plain stuccoed villas, two pairs and a terrace of 11, with a large brick building on the corner of Berkeley Road and Mount Sion. Yet one of the stucco pairs is on the Bowling Green site and the other on that of Cumberland House. The latter was referred to above as nos 39 and 41 Mount Sion while the Bowling Green pair is stated in the conditions of sale by auction on 17 June 1887 to be part of an estate called Bowling Green House whose title was to start with a conveyance dated 12/13 January 1824 – an interesting piece of information but tantalising because I have no clue to the identity of vendor or purchaser – too late for Mrs Wogan and 18 years before Hoppe is known to have been the owner. Yet the pair 35/37 is in outward appearance (have a look yourself) and in internal description (drawing room, dining room, five bedrooms, kitchen, pantry, coal cellar and three WCs) exactly the same. In other words the style was apparently dictated by the position of the houses not the site. This suggests that one mind was behind the whole two-site development and perhaps the red brick of Berkeley Road was chosen to blend with the architecture

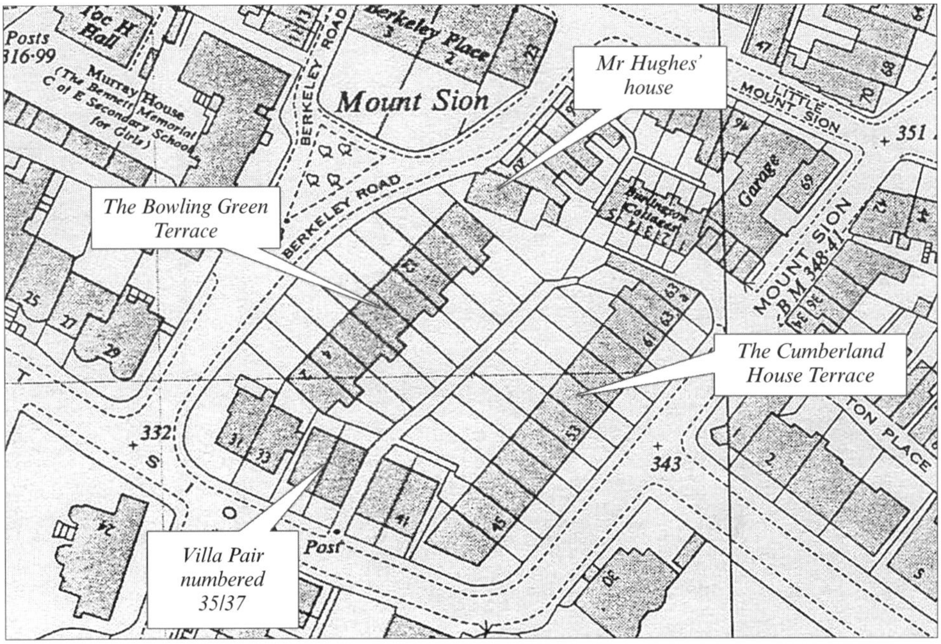

Ordnance Survey about 1950

of surrounding buildings such as Berkeley Place, while the stucco blended with the classical façade of Marlborough House. What do you think? Reference to the detail from an Ordnance Survey map (see above) of a somewhat later date (about 1950) and comparison with the older map on page 272 above may help. The back path serving the two terraces provides another indication of a unified plan. I used to think that it marked the boundary between the Bowling Green and Cumberland House sites but a glance at the two maps shows clearly that it does not – the old boundary shows that the Bowling Green House site narrows towards the north and the Cumberland House one widens; but the present back path is equidistant from the back of each terrace or even tends the other way. Another boundary was that between the old Bowling Green plot and Nicholas Wood's Burlington House grounds; and this boundary can be seen to be very much preserved today at its eastern end between the Miles Garage car park and no.63a Mount Sion – of which more in a moment. Reference to the 1866 map on page 272 will show, however, that at the other end the straight line of this boundary is interrupted by a jumble of buildings at the rear of Bowling Green House which evidently came within the grounds of that house. In this position was built a house, now numbered 18 Berkeley Road, which in another document showing the Burlington House development was labelled 'Mr Hughes' House' and I have marked accordingly. The photograph below shows it as it is today with no.16 of the red-brick terrace beside it. Evidently William Barnsley Hughes lived in this house or even built it for himself while supervising the rest of the development.

Berkeley Road: No.18 on the left, No.16 on the right.

Finally, before leaving the transformation of two large old houses formed from the Bowling Green Ballroom or lodging house into more modest dwellings for 25 or more families, a small development at the far end of the Cumberland House terrace is worth consideration. In 1884 a Mrs Murrell owned nos 61 and 63, the two end houses of the new terrace, and, for reasons best known to herself, wanted to make no 63 with an extension into a Meeting Room or Mission Hall. She therefore submitted an application to the Town Council of which a partial copy is reproduced on the next page.

The plan involved extending no.63 right up to the boundary wall with the Burlington House site and amalgamating the two parts by taking down the original outside wall of 63. This plan was evidently carried out and the hall was hired out at £1 per month from 7 February 1886 to the recently formed Quaker Meeting for worship every Sunday morning and evening until autumn 1887, when Mrs Murrell, who was not herself a Quaker, indicated that the room was required for other purposes. The Friends moved to the Mechanics Institute in Dudley Road in October 1887 and remained there until they built themselves a grander Meeting Hall in Grosvenor Park which opened in September 1894.

What Mrs Murrell's other purposes were I do not know but the enterprise did not last long. The Mission Hall was offered for sale a few years later. The sale was to take place on 16 February 1894 and the Sale Notice describes the hall as a Freehold Chapel, known as 'The Mount Sion Mission Hall, Tunbridge Wells',

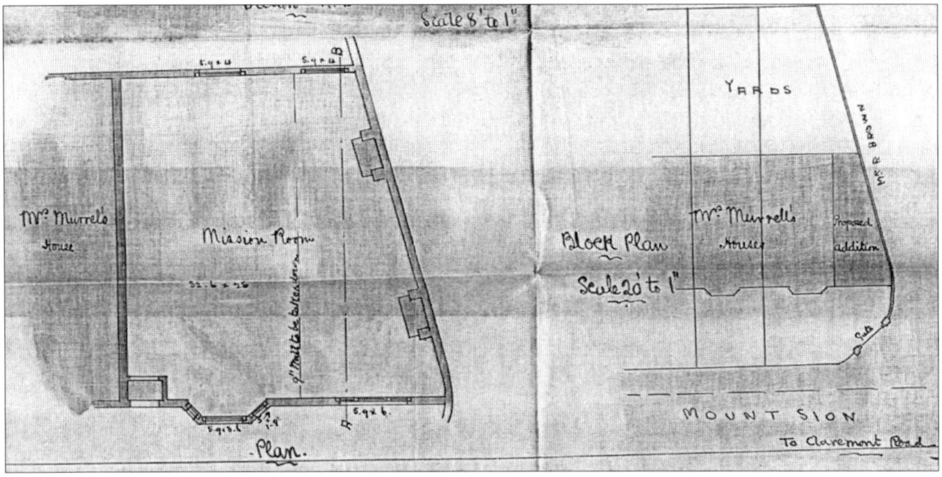

Mount Sion Mission Hall plan 1884

substantially built of brick with slated roofs. 'The Chapel, which has a separate Entrance Lobby, Forecourt, WC etc is a bright and cheerful Building of good pitch available for SEATING 250 persons (More or Less), it measures 31′ 6½ in length (exclusive of bay) by a mean width of about 28′ 6½ and is nearly 20′ in Pitch. Adjoining is a FREEHOLD RESIDENCE known as 61, Mount Sion'. The Property offered an unusual opportunity to persons interested in Religious, Philanthropic or Educational Work, who might require Premises of this description in so remarkably central a position where it is extremely difficult now to obtain the requisite space for their construction and the purchaser was to have the option of buying the chairs, harmonium and furniture at a valuation – but even this was not enough to tempt the auctioneer's audience, and a second auction was held on 31 October 1895 when the attractions were extended to possible uses as Chapel,

Cumberland Terrace with no. 63a on the right

Mission Room or School, or for conversion into a Factory, Warehouse or Business Premises. Even this was insufficient to attract a buyer of the hall as such and the solution that can be seen on the ground today was reconversion into dwelling accommodation. The extension of no 63 was numbered 63a because 65 (the *Blue Anchor*) already existed next door. The photograph above not only gives a general impression of the 'Cumberland House Terrace' but shows no 63a at the right-hand end. The casual passer-by sees no distinction but a closer look reveals two differences: the bay does not extend to the first floor; and there is that dormer window in the roof. A style of building similar to that of the terrace was used for the two semi-detached pairs round the corner and, as a matter of incidental interest, nos 39 and 41, the auction of which was mentioned on page 277 above, failed to find a bidder and the auctioneer pencilled in the prices, £620 and £630, at which he withdrew the two lots in 1897. They were described as pleasantly situated (with a southern aspect), brick and slated, semi-detached, bay-fronted, Villa residences; and no 41 was let at £42 per annum to the Misses Fooke, who could be turned out, however, at three months' notice after March 1898.

A later resident worthy of notice lived at no.59 Mount Sion, one of the villas of the Cumberland Terrace. He was David Johnson, the photographer, who left a photographic record of Mount Sion which is now in the Museum. The house forms the subject of one of his photographs (see on the right) dated 1 August 1938, which has been annotated by another hand: 'Mr David James Johnson resided here until his death June 16th 1945.' Johnson left long historical notes on the backs of some of his photographs but on this one there is none. This is strange because, of all places on Mount Sion Hill, it is the back gardens of this terrace which fancy may justifiably people with ghosts of the past: Richard Cumberland tending the flowers in his garden or, a century earlier, the ladies and gentlemen dancing by twilight on the elastic turf of the Bowling Green.

No 59 Mount Sion

CHAPTER 20

The Delves Dynasty

The theme of this chapter should rightly be the three houses to the south of the Bowling Green marked Mr Brett on the Bowra plan and later named Forest Prospect, Brunswick House and Eden House – see below. However, Forest Prospect (the present Ivy Chimneys) and Eden House together with the later Marlborough House are so linked with the Delves family, of which we have heard already, that I am taking the opportunity of dealing with the 'Delves Dynasty' in tandem. As with Murray and Mansfield Houses before, 'Mr Brett' appears on Bowra against these three houses because they were on land leased to Richard Constable (see the 1686 Partition plan at the head of chapters 16 and 17) and unsold at the time of the 1715 foreclosure. This does not mean that 'Mr Brett' had much to do with their stories; the name simply stands in the way. Let us start with Forest Prospect which was so called because it stood at the top of the hill with views towards Waterdown Forest to the south and east. It was a well-chosen name and should never have been changed! It has been singled out as one of the oldest Mount Sion houses but the Poor Rate seems to show, as expected, that it is similar in date to all the other original lodging houses. Terence Davis calls it 'an early 18th-century tile-hung timber-framed house'. The sequence runs as follows:

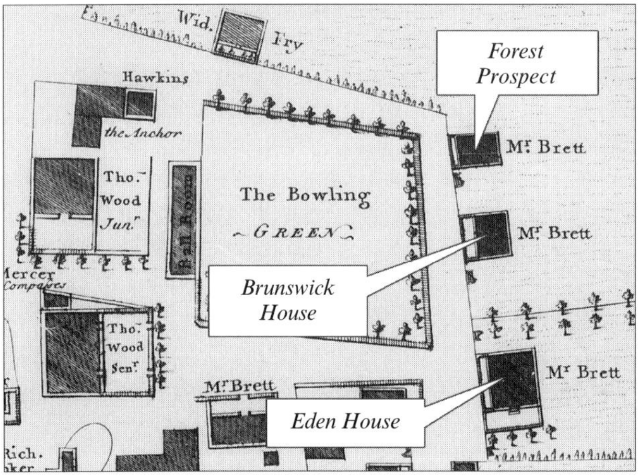

Bowra plan 1738

1689-1690	Hills
1691-1714	Thomas Hills
1728-1736	Mrs Chapman for Hillses
1737-1748	Mr Ash for hillses
1749-1758	Mrs Ash for Hills's
1759-1769	Ash for Hills
1770-1775	Ash Mr his Heirs for Hills's
1776	Delves Ric for Hills
1777-1797	Delves Ric for late Ash's

The house was called Hillses for about a hundred years, so who was Thomas Hills? He left a will but it does not leave us very much the wiser. It was made on 21 May 1717 and proved by his daughter and executrix Anna Hills on 22 June the same year. He called himself a husbandman of Tonbridge – meaning the parish of Tonbridge, of course – and he 'would disspous of that Little goods I enjoy in This world so as no disspuites May Arise Amonngh my children after my deseas'. He enjoins his daughter to take care of his beloved wife Elizabeth and 'to provide all things necessary for her the terme of her Life' after which he leaves to his daughter 'all and Every of my goods and chattels as well houseall goods as other' after paying funeral expenses and legacies. Of houses and land, however, there is no mention. The legacies indicate that he had two sons, both dead, four daughters all married except Anna and at least two granddaughters. Witnesses to the will interestingly were Nicholas and Sarah Wood (from Burlington House) and William Ashdowne (Murray House). I do not understand why his will made no mention of his house. The freeholder at the time of construction was the Manor of South Frith and the leaseholder was Richard Constable; but the first occupier was Thomas Hills who may well have arranged and financed the construction in the first place. Certainly the continuance of the name Hillses for such a long period points to something of the sort. Why then does the house not feature in the will? Not far away we have seen (page 212) that Anne Ashdowne felt free to bequeath the two parts of Murray House, subject only to the payment of ground rent. Old title deeds might help but those for Forest Prospect, like so many others, have totally disappeared. It seems very improbable that Richard Constable built houses himself on the land he leased in 1685 but he could not have given building leases for a longer term than the 50 years he himself had been granted; so that the various sub-tenants would have been obliged either to renegotiate their leases around 1735 or surrender the house to the John Brett of the day.

The name which follows Thomas Hills in the Poor Rate record (after the 1714-1728 gap) is a Mrs Chapman who might just possibly be Anna Hills under a married name. She had been made executrix and legatee of all her father's goods with instructions to take care of her mother and pay some small bequests to children and grandchildren. Thomas had a married daughter, Elizabeth Morley (perhaps connected with Morleys Coffee House on the Walks?) who is mentioned in an earlier will which throws an interesting light on Thomas, his wife and his dwelling house. Thomas Tilden was a Tonbridge mercer who was surely related somehow to the City of London merchant, Daniel Tilden, who figures in the Earl of Buckingham proceedings. In his will, dated June 1704 and proved a month later, Thomas Tilden left £5 to his sister Elizabeth, now wife of Thomas Morley, and to his son John a feather-bed and bolster, two feather pillows, two pairs of fine sheets and a pair of blankets 'now abiding and being in the house of Thomas Hills my Father in Law situate on Mount Sion Hill in Tonbridge in Kent'. He asks his mother 'now wife of Thomas Hills' to look after his son John and allots income from lands in Westwell and Charing in Kent for the purpose; so that it is clear that Thomas Hills was the testator's step-father, not father-in-law, and that he and his widow wife brought up her grandson John Tilden in the house on Mount Sion. This will was witnessed by Thomas Scoones of Fairlawn House and a John Moorhouse who could from his name be the husband of one of Thomas Hills' daughters.

After Mrs Chapman in the Poor Rate record for Forest Prospect comes the name Ash about which I have no information except to note that, as we saw in the previous chapter, Mr Ash from 1737 to 1749 and 'Capt Ash' in the one year 1758 paid rates for the Bowling Green House. Mr Ash's occupancy in fact coincides to within a year with his time at Forest Prospect. It is difficult to avoid speculation that the location of the house right next to the Bowling Green had something to do with the matter. Mrs Ash, presumably the widow, took over the house until 1758 which is the one year when Capt Ash appears on the Bowling Green list. Perhaps he was a son and gave up the Bowling Green but retained the house (Ash for Hills) from 1759 to 1769 when his heirs took over for five years. The Poor Rate record suggests that Mr Ash bought the house in 1737 but we know from the Brett story that all the Brett lands and houses remained untouched until part was sold on Chancery orders in 1752 – see next paragraph. The unfortunately imprecise descriptions in these documents suggest that the three southern houses formed part of this transaction, Eden and Brunswick Houses being sold to gentleman William Camfield of Speldhurst, and Forest Prospect possibly to the occupier Metcalf Ash. I think that Metcalf was Ash Junior and his name appears as purchaser although his mother was paying the rates at this time.

The Chancery documents form two conveyances. The first is dated 5 August 1752 and recites the whole story of how the bequests in John Brett's 1719 will were insufficiently covered by cash in hand; how part of the real estate was ordered to be sold, to the value of £1,670, and completes the sale taking account of interest and legal costs and with the agreement of all parties. The purchaser was named as William Davids, gentleman of Holborn, but he was acting in trust for James Davenant Esquire of St Luke's parish Middlesex. Neither of these men seems to have any local connections; they were intermediaries or property developers or the like, I suppose. Finally the various properties sold are listed and described with their abutments – but there is, of course, no plan to help us today! Eight items, comprising houses and fields in varying combinations, are listed. The next conveyance is by Lease and Release and is made up of the two related documents dated 10 and 11 August 1752 and effects the sale for the sum of £1,405 by James Davenant to William Camfield, gentleman of Speldhurst, of six of the eight items he had bought a few days before. The six items are described in exactly the same words as in the conveyance of 5 August. They include one item of two houses and two fields on Mount Sion Hill and another item is the Bowling Green House; the others are elsewhere in the town. The two items not included in the sale to William Camfield are both on Mount Sion; one is at the foot of Mount Sion near the Chapel; the other I take to be Forest Prospect.

This house is described as 'a messuage situate on Mount Sion Hill with the garden and orchard and with a slip of land thereunto adjoining and belonging together with the outhouses Coachhouses and stables thereunto belonging abutting north east on Woodsgate Road together with a field of three acres and abutting south on land of Lord Abergavenny west and north on lands now or late in the possession of Widow Mercer and east to Wybournes Wood. It is now in the possession of Metcalf Ash at the yearly rent of £23.' If you look at the Bowra plan you will see that Mount Sion Road is called the 'Road to Woodsgate'. This is because this route was commonly used by coaches travelling from or to the 'Wells' to or from Pembury linking with the Turnpike Road to London. There can therefore be no doubt on the meaning of this part of the description. 'Abutting this road to the north east' is an accurate description of the location of Forest Prospect. The other abutments are less certain. Abergavenny land is certainly on the other side down the hill towards the Grom valley. Wybournes Wood I cannot pinpoint; but if we assume that the Widow Mercer had Brunswick and Eden Houses, then the abutment west and north makes sense. The first item in the sale to William Camfield is described as two messuages on Mount Sion Hill and two fields. The houses and one field abut north on the Woodsgate Road which makes sense if we are talking of Brunswick and Eden Houses; they abut west on lands in the possession of Richard Jefferys – immediately below Eden House on the Bowra plan, also making good sense; they abut south on Abergavenny land, similar to the Forest Prospect case; and east on lands in the possession of Mary Seale – this might make sense when we come to consider Marlborough House. In summary then I am happy to assume that the two houses sold to Camfield are Brunswick and Eden houses and that Forest Prospect was not sold to Camfield – in which case is it not reasonable to suppose it was sold by James Davenant to Metcalf Ash, the sitting tenant? The Bowling Green House was another item in the sale to Camfield which means that the only houses not considered as possibilities might have been Murray and Mansfield houses; but we have seen in chapters 16 and 19 that these two houses 'on the west side of the Bowling Green' were still in Brett hands as late as 1777 and perhaps a bit later still. The Chancery decree documents refer not only to the 'messuage on Mount Sion Hill' which we take to be Forest Prospect with its slip of land and a three-acre field occupied by Metcalf Ash at the yearly rent of £23; but also, it is worth noting, to the reservation to Metcalf and Elizabeth Ash (and to the heirs of Elizabeth Ash) of a right of way to their field; and again to a lease of the Bowling Green House to Metcalf Ash at £26 p.a. with two years left to run.

The Ward Papers provide no direct evidence on the sale of Forest Prospect although it seems probable that it was sold to Metcalf Ash some time after 1752. Anyway, whatever the uncertainty about this sale, there can be no doubt that the house ended up in Delves' ownership and the Poor Rate record puts the date at 1776; and Richard Delves must have been the purchaser. He was the founder of the Delves dynasty in Tunbridge Wells and was the son of Thomas Delves of Ringmer in Sussex and Elizabeth from Waldron in the same county. Most of their children were born in Waldron, including Richard who was born in 1727 and evidently came to Tunbridge Wells in his early 20s, marrying Dorothea Mercer at Pembury in 1752. The first documentary evidence for the family is the entry in the Charles the Martyr baptismal register on 10 November 1753 – 'Joseph, son of Richard and Dory'. Dick and Dory had ten, but in total some 70 baby Delveses were to be trundled into the Chapel for their christenings between 1753 and 1872. The family lived, as far as I can tell, in mother-in-law's house which was Eden House. The Poor Rate sequence which I connect with Eden House runs as follows:

1734-1742	Jos Pulling for Mr Bretts
1743-1746	Joseph Pulling or Occ for Mr Bretts
1747	Jos Pullen or Occ for Mr Bretts Mrs Mercer ('Mrs Mercer' added later?)
1748	Wid Mercer
1749-1757	Wid Mercer for Bretts
1758	Rd Delves for Bretts
1759	Delves for Wid Mercers
1760	Richd Delves for late Widow Mercers
1761-1797	Richd Delves for a house and Lands

The immediately striking thing about this sequence is that it begins some 50 years after the first houses were built – a bit later and it would not have appeared on the Bowra plan. What the explanation may be I cannot say. It was called 'Mr Bretts' from the beginning which might mean that Dr John Brett had it constructed; but there is no evidence that he ever did anything of the sort. Here is a photograph taken shortly before demolition in 1969. I hazard the opinion that the style of

Eden House in 1969. The bay of Mansfield House can just be seen on the far left.

construction is more consistent with 1730 than 1690. Another feature which distinguishes it from the original houses is that it faces west, down the hill, not across the road. Joseph Pulling or Pullen is unknown to me. I assume that Mrs Mercer and the widow Mercer are one and the same; and I make a bolder assumption that she was the mother of Dorothea whom Richard Delves married at old Pembury Church in 1752. The Delves family papers seem to make much of this marriage and it may be that it contributed largely to the foundation of the Delves fortune. It is, however, difficult to pin down the Mercers, it being a common name, and not all Mercers, I am sure, being related. Dory's father was Thomas Mercer and a 'Thomas Mercer' can be found on Bowra maps in two places – as occupier of Jerningham House and also of Lord Percival's house, later the *Calverley Hotel* now the *Hotel du Vin*. Certainly if the widow Mercer was leaseholder of both Eden and Brunswick Houses in the mid-18th century, as the Chancery documents suggest, she must have been a member of a substantial family. However, the Poor Rate record for Brunswick House does nothing to confirm that Mrs Mercer had any interest in the house:

Poor Rate Sequence for Brunswick House

1689-1691	Of her (Mrs Mitchell?) or Mr Young for an other house
1692-1700	Mr Mitchell or Wm Young Esq for another new house
1701-1714	Mr Mitchell or Wm Young Esq for a new house
1728-1731	Mr Goodall for a new house
1732	Mrs Goodall for a new house
1733-1734	Mrs Goodall or Mr Elliott for a new house
1735-1741	Mr August
1742-1746	Mr August or Occ
1747	Mr August or Occ Peat Latter
1748-1757	Peat Latter
1758-1782	Docr Willett for Peat Latters
1783-1789	Mrs Willett
1790-1797	Rev Joseph Langley

I am not entirely confident of the beginnings of this sequence, particularly before the gap; but I am quite sure that the end, from the Rev. Langley working backwards to Mr August in 1735, applies to Brunswick House. It is very likely that the Delveses, sitting on either side of Brunswick House, would dearly have liked to take it over; but they never did and I propose to treat this house as a separate item at the end of this chapter and concentrate now on the Delves family and its property.

We left Richard Delves, newly arrived in Tunbridge Wells, and newly married, living with his bride's mother in Eden House and filling the house with a regular input of babies. He was a butcher by trade and almost certainly had a shop on the Pantiles, although I am not sure where it was. As such he prospered and I think he used the fields behind Eden House for grazing animals before slaughter. Meat surely played a much larger part in diet then than it does now – at least among those who could afford it, which the summer visitors certainly could; and the butcher's trade must have been profitable. There is some confirmation in a curious passage in Benge Burr's history of Tunbridge Wells, advocating standardisation of prices amongst tradesmen. 'One set of men', he says referring to butchers, have 'by this conduct raised themselves, without incurring the reproach of extortion, to a very considerable degree of eminence in this place' – and I am sure Richard Delves was one of those he had in mind.

The other business, of course, to profit from the summer visitors was that of the lodging house and I am sure Richard threw himself into assisting what I assume was his mother-in-law's business, so that when time overtook her, about 1758 judging from the Poor Rate record, it was natural for Richard and Dory to assume the reins. At some stage Richard built a smaller house for himself and his family alongside (to the south of) Eden House and called it his 'Home Cottage' or later Eden Cottage. This enabled him to let out the whole lodging house and yet be on hand to sort out his tenants' everyday problems. In his will in 1798, he refers to 'my present dwelling house in the yard belonging to the … Great House' and he gives to his wife 'the Bed and Bedstead … which stands in the New Room just built and wherein we now sleep'. When in 1776, as we assume from the Poor Rate record, he bought Forest Prospect he adopted the same policy and built behind the house a substantial home house which still exists and was called Marlborough Villa – see the aerial photograph below which was taken in 1959 when Eden House and Cottage were still standing. Note that the Brunswick House of this photograph is not the one that was there in the 18th century and the terrace below is equally new. The building of Marlborough Villa may have happened

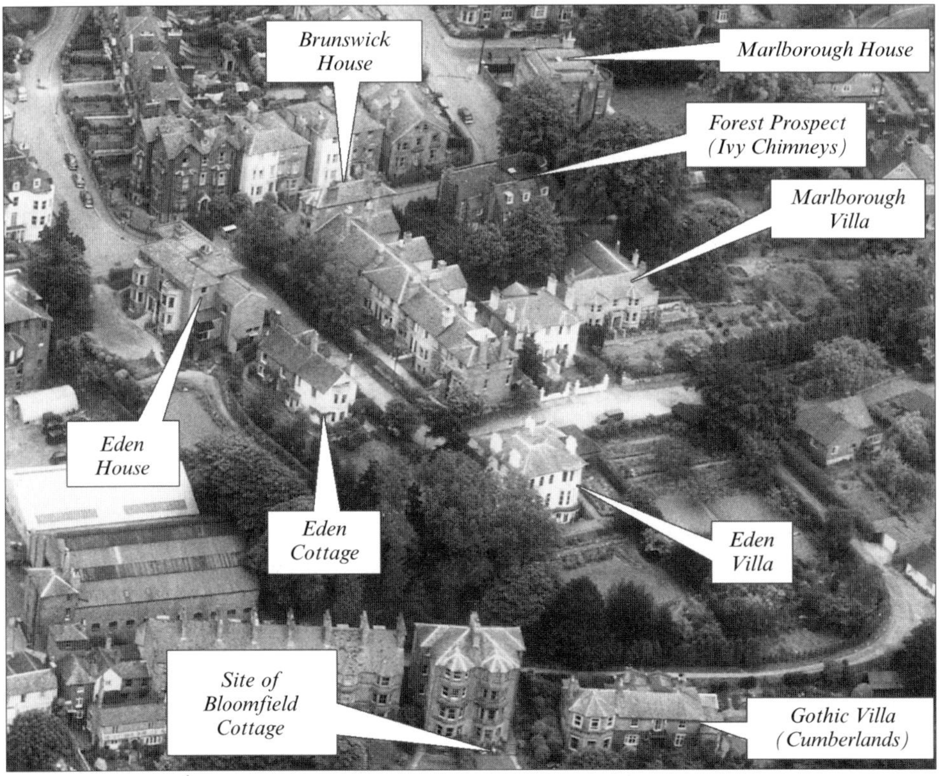

Mount Sion from the air 1959

between 1783 and 1784 when the rate payment for Forest Prospect increased from £10 to £12 10s. 0d. The rates for Marlborough Villa as for Eden Cottage were, I assume, included with those for the main houses – anyway, I have never found separate sequences. Marlborough Villa was built alongside the coach houses and stables of Forest Prospect as was shown clearly when the two houses were sold separately a hundred years later (see the next chapter) and the villa had three coach houses and stabling for six horses while the main house had none and the purchaser of the Villa was required to build a seven- foot brick wall across what had been the common drive to the coach house and stables. The two 'Home Houses' can be dated within wide parameters by their not showing on the Bowra plan or map but appearing on the Barrow map of 1808, clearly labelled Mr Joseph Delves and Mr T. Delves and shaded to indicate that they were not lodging houses. It may be remembered that in the Chancery document Forest Prospect was bundled with a slip of land and a three-acre field and I think this may account for the fact that the Delveses later owned land running down from their two houses towards Cumberland Walk and Abergavenny land. Elizabeth Mercer also had a lease on two fields totalling seven acres which went with Eden and Brunswick Houses.

Meanwhile Richard's children were growing up. In 1775, as we have seen, his eldest son Joseph married Richard Fry's youngest daughter Susannah; his daughter Elizabeth, as we have seen also, married Samuel Parman as his second wife; and his daughter Dorothea tragically married Alex Goate one day in 1788 and was widowed within the week. 'A most melancholy circumstance occurred the beginning of last week. Mr Goate whose marriage to Miss Delves of Tunbridge was mentioned in our last paper,' reported the *Maidstone Journal*, 'was taken suddenly ill a few hours after his marriage – the next day he was so bad that his friends were obliged to call in the Faculty and on Tuesday last he died at his lodgings in Gloucester-street, Queen Square. He has left a very genteel fortune to the lady to whom he was married.' Thomas, the youngest son, whom I imagine as a page boy of six at his eldest brother's wedding, married in 1799 but seems to have anticipated his wedding by a few years. He went to live in Shoreditch with a girl called Mary Ann Mills. They had a daughter Sarah baptised at Shoreditch in 1796. Three years later they married in Shoreditch Church; but the next child was christened in Tunbridge Wells, at the Countess of Huntingdon's Chapel in February 1800. By this time Richard was 73 and, although still going strong buying farms and adding codicils to his will, he died in 1804.

One glimpse into Richard's private and social life is provided by his will. He gave a gold ring each to the brothers William and Stephen Woodgate of Summerhill 'as a small token of my great regard and respect for those gentlemen'. The Woodgates were lords of the Summerhill mansion and estate from 1712 until the early 19th century; and one of the family has written a history of *The Woodgates of Summerhill* which gives us further glimpses of Richard's hobnobbing with the local squirearchy. In 1769 he leased a farm in Chiddingstone from one of the Woodgate family, the Reverend Francis of Mountfield. In 1773 the reverend gentleman's son wrote to him and I quote from the letter: 'I mistake Mr Thompson was at Ton[bridge] on Monday at our Turnpike Meeting, who said he was pure well. I desir'd Mr Delves to acquaint you of it on his journey to Battle. I shall be up with him again to-morrow afternoon.' What Richard was going to Battle for I have no idea; but on his way he could certainly have called on the vicarage at Mountfield to deliver the message that Mr Thompson was 'pure well'. Three years later another of the Reverend's sons, Henry, was writing to him: 'My Bror says Delves thanked him kindly for recommending such a customer ... Delves told my Bror that he discounted a Draft of Lord Ash[burnha]ms for £200.' Richard was actually related, distantly by marriage, to the Woodgates. His nephew William, son of Richard's elder brother who was Vicar of Frant (and Waldron also), was Vicar of Ashburnham near Battle, but he was unlucky with his wives. The first died in 1791 and in 1795 he married Mary, the elder daughter of Thomas Swayne, a Tonbridge lawyer, whose father, George, married Rose Woodgate as his second wife. There are two references to Mrs Mary Delves. An undated letter from Maria Woodgate to Stephen Woodgate (page 352) says: 'Mrs Delves has been given over for the last fortnight and I am afraid before this the scene is closed.' Another letter (page 172) dated 8 July 1800 says: 'Poor Mrs Delves I understand was buried at Ashburnham.' The reverend gentleman consoled himself by marrying Maria Eyles the following year. Another aspect of Richard Delves' life is revealed by the Court Book of Southborough Manor. It might have been expected that Tunbridge Wells would come under the Manor of South Frith, for as we have seen that is where much of the land – and certainly all that on Mount Sion – came from; but by the second half of the 18th century, if not earlier, Southborough seems to have assumed the manorial functions of public supervision in the Southborough east and west divisions of Tonbridge Parish which between them covered Tunbridge Wells (the Poor Law nevertheless being administered by the Parish). Regular appointments were made to the posts of Constable, Borsholder for east and west Southborough, Ale Conner and Street Driver. Richard Fry was Borsholder for the west division in 1754 and in 1760 Richard Delves appears as a member of the Jury of which he was Foreman in 1774, '76, '77 and again in 1780. He was a Borsholder (west) in 1777; and his name last appears, as a Jury member (along with Samuel Parman), in 1786. Joseph Delves was on the Jury five times from 1781 to 1793 and he was Borsholder (west) in 1795. In the 19th century, as we shall see, other Delveses were to play a part in local government.

When he died Richard had well and truly founded the fortune of the family. Exactly where the money came from it is difficult to judge but it must have been a combination of Delves money, Mercer money and the fruits of business. Its extent can be seen from what he left to his heirs. When he died he had two surviving sons: Joseph, his first-born; and Thomas who made an honest woman of Mary Ann in 1799. The brothers were left the bulk of the land and property jointly. Not long afterwards, however, they entered into a Deed of Partition which gives us a good idea of the extent of Richard's possessions. There were eleven farms, all purchased by Richard, with a total acreage of about 600. Two of them were purchased in 1802 and 1803, necessitating codicils to the will; and in 1803 he also bought the *Boar's Head* on the road to Crowborough. Most of the farms were in the Rotherfield area, a few in Withyham. One of them, purchased in 1797, was the 60-acre Huggatts Farm which became Tuttys Village and the nucleus of present-day Hawkenbury. Another purchase was Jack Woods Spring and Quarry which had once belonged to our old friend John Brett and was later sold to John Ward to provide stone and water for the Calverley estate. Another purchase of which Richard was sufficiently proud to single it out in his will was 'the estate of George Weller gentleman which I purchased by public auction'. George Weller died in 1785 and the estate later came to be known as the Grosvenor Estate – at the top of the town.

Most of the property was allotted to one or other brother but the Grosvenor Estate they decided to keep in their joint names. The main effect of Richard's will was that Joseph and his descendants had Forest Prospect and the villa behind; and Thomas and his family had Eden House and Cottage. Not that they lived alone – oh no! The butcher's youngest, prettiest daughter produced regularly, from the year after her marriage to Joseph, almost every year for the next 14 – 12 babies in 14 years actually; and Thomas was not to be outdone, though he needed two wives – his total was 19 over 27 years. In those days women had no time for feminism. Nowadays, they can please their husbands (and themselves, I hope) and

THE DELVES FAMILY OF MOUNT SION – AN ABBREVIATED FAMILY TREE

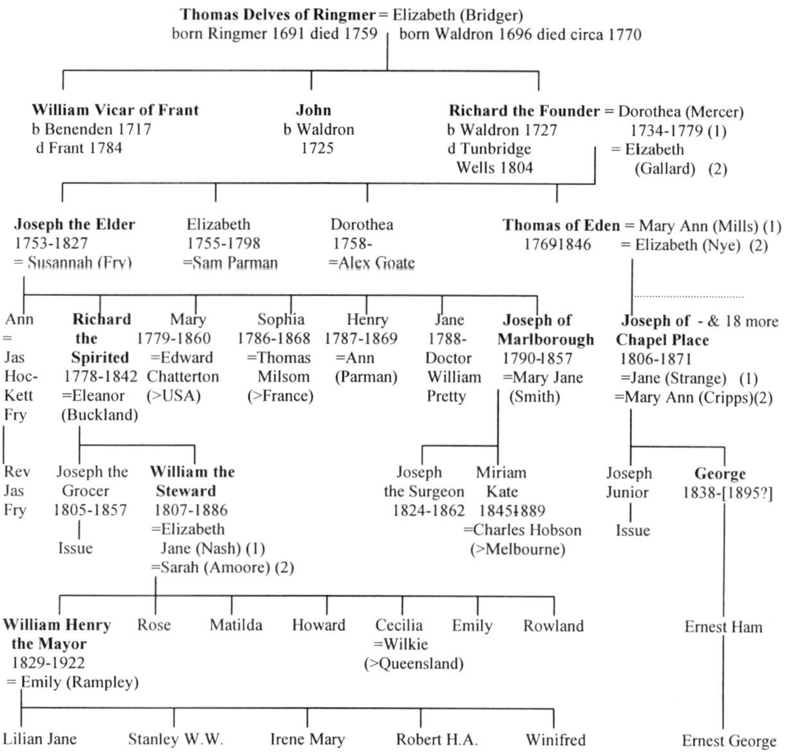

still have time to spare; but then it was a baby a year and at the end of all that they were shattered and could not care less about women's liberation.

When Joseph married Susannah in 1775 I think they lived in the Bow Window House but I assume that at some stage, possibly after Richard's death in 1804, the family moved into Marlborough Villa and Forest Prospect. A look at the shortened family tree on the previous page may help to clarify the situation. The eldest offspring was Ann who married a cousin, James Hockett Fry, and had a son who became the Rev. James Fry and inherited the Grosvenor Estate. Next came Richard junior whom we have met already in connection with York House and Bricklands and about whom there will be more to say in a minute. Then there was Mary who inherited the Bow Window (Mansfield) House, as we saw in the previous chapter, and whose son founded the American Chattertons. Sophia, born in 1786, started another foreign connection. She married a Thomas Milsom at Speldhurst Church in 1810 and had a son Edward and a daughter Emma. The son emigrated to France where he entered the silk business in Lyons, married Mlle Louise Poinset and, with 11 children, founded the French branch of the family. The Delves Family Papers contain a letter written in 1953 to Uncle Stanley (Stanley W.W. at the bottom of the chart) from a Major Milsom DSO of Devon saying that he had met, the previous month, in Switzerland, a Monsieur George Milsom, Chevalier de la Légion d'Honneur, a senior official of the Red Cross in Geneva, and been royally entertained by him as an English link with the French Milsom family. I have written several times to the Red Cross in Geneva but have been unable to trace a French Milsom. The major said there was a Milsom vault at Mont Parnasse but I am afraid I have not tried to find it. I did try to find a Milsom relative in Devon but without success. I have a suspicion that the gallant major got his dinner under false pretences. Back to the family tree! Henry, born the year after Sophia, married his cousin Ann Parman but lived to 82 without having any children. Jane,

Marlborough House in 1915

the next year, married a doctor, Pretty by name and perhaps by nature; and finally in 1790 came another Joseph – at one time I reckon there were five Joseph Delveses wandering around Tunbridge Wells! This particular Joseph Delves took over Marlborough Villa when his father died in 1827 and turned out to be another prolific parent, to the number of 11, from the day he married Mary Jane Smith at Speldhurst Church, needing a special licence since she was under age – not to mention pregnant – the christening of yet another Joseph taking place five months after the wedding ceremony! Meanwhile, Thomas had been living in Eden Cottage since 1804 and populating it with his numerous progeny; but continuation of the story of that branch of the family will have to be postponed to a later page.

One major event during this period was the building of Marlborough House now known as Cecil Court. David Johnson photographed it in 1915 (see the previous page) and commented as follows: 'I knew this house in boyhood as Marlborough House. A private residence, later it became Cork's School. At the early part of "The Great War" report stated that it had been presented to the Government who had it converted into flats for the widows of officers killed in the war. I received instructions to photograph the front from the foreman of the London firm who were carrying out the alterations.' Richard Cobb in his autobiography called it 'The Widows' Flats'. It was owned by the Housing Association for Officers' Families which amalgamated in recent years with Haig Homes. It still looks much the same today as it did in 1915 – rather severe and forbidding from the Mount Sion side but on the other are two bows and a delightful canopied balcony the restoration of which won a Civic Society award in 2000. Here is a print which must date from about 1880 when it was a school. Forest Prospect and the corner house of Cumberland Terrace can just be glimpsed at the right-hand edge but what is striking is the open expanse below the house which explains why Forest Prospect was given its name and why both houses face in that direction.

Marlborough House in about 1880.

Marlborough House is the only house on Mount Sion for which a set of deeds from its building to the present-day exists. I only wish the message they contain were clearer. The first document is a conveyance by Lease and Release dated 19/20 May 1801 from Jane Baker to Charles Stevens and Richard Hunter, both 'turners' of Tunbridge Wells, of 'the Garden Ground or orchard … on Mount Sion Hill … adjoining to the highway leading to Woodsgate and opposite to the garden in the occupation of Richard Cumberland Esq containing in length towards the said highway on the north 110 feet … and in depth from the same said highway along the fence of Mr John Fry towards the east 160 feet …'. So far so good. This describes the site of the house perfectly well. We know the Woodsgate Road and we know Cumberland's garden. The frontage is 110 feet and the land on the east (or better north-east) is John Fry's and is marked off by a fence of 160 feet. We are told in the Lease that Jane Baker is the spinster daughter of Edward Mercer's sister and we know her. She was the 'queen-pin' of Little Mount Sion whom we met in chapter 15 and who, from lack of fecundity, inherited Philip Seale's little empire. We know also that Philip Seale bought a field in this area in 1702. So Jane was selling off a bit of her inheritance. She got £100 for it.

The difficulty comes with the next deed which is dated 20 January 1802. Richard Hunter had given his share by Deed Poll to Charles Stevens who sold to William Knight for £550 the field described above and also

> all that the aforesaid new erected Messuage or Tenement Workshops and other buildings lately erected and built thereon or on some part thereof which said piece … of land was lately in the occupation of John Turner as Tenant thereof but is now together with the said buildings in the tenure … of the said Charles Stevens Together with a Free Way or Passage to and from the said piece … of land on the west containing in length 156 feet … along the road leading to the field occupied by the said John Turner … William Knight keeping the said road open and in good repair …

The 156-foot 'Free Way' will come up for consideration in a minute; but an immediate question is whether the new messuage was Marlborough House. For one thing eight months is remarkably quick for such a building; for another I am convinced that the creator of Marlborough House was Joseph Delves who comes on the scene later. If I am right, then the new buildings of 1801-2 must have been more or less temporary or located away from the main site. In the conveyance of 20 January 1802 James Fry the Elder, butcher of Tunbridge Wells, is named as a trustee for William Knight and he (or rather his two sons since he had died in the meantime) are vendors along with William Knight to Duncan John Cameron of Brownings Farm, Rotherfield in the next conveyance dated 30 November/1 December 1803, which was witnessed incidentally by Richard Delves Junior. One of the Fry brothers is James Hockett Fry whom we saw just now as the husband of Joseph Delves' eldest daughter Ann. The price was £210 and exactly the same amount was paid three years later when Cameron sold to Jospeh Delves Esq on 7/8 March 1806 – note how Joseph had adopted the title Esquire after the death of his father in 1804. The next document in the series comes somewhat later, on 4 April 1822, when Joseph Delves bought a 'slip of land adjoining late Camerons' from Thomas Pinckard Bingham for £30 –

> all that slip ... of land being the south-western end or part of a certain field heretofore called the Hay House Platt ... extending in length from Mount Sion Road to a certain piece ... of Meadow land called Mercer Field or The Meadow and used as a Roadway to and from the said Mercer Field or The Meadow and containing ... in length 156 feet in breadth at the upper end next ... Mount Sion Road 17 feet and at the lower end next the said Mercer Field or The Meadow 15 feet ...

Bingham was at the time tenant of the house next door (away from Forest Prospect) – No 10 on the Barrow map below and marked 'Wid Fry' on Bowra.

The field name 'Hayhouse Platt' occurs in Philip Seale's will of 1840. He bequeaths to his daughter Mary his mead near Mount Sion (I guess this is the garden or orchard that Jane Baker sold in 1801) and 'All that my Hayhouse Platt And also a Small Piece of Ground Adjoining the Same with All and every of the Appurtenances thereunto belonging with All Buildings on the Same now in the occupation of __ Ash (Tenant to Mr John Brett)'. The next document in the sequence of Cecil Court deeds is dated 4 May 1826 and entitled a 'Deed of Gift Joseph the Elder to Joseph the Younger'. Joseph Esquire gives to Joseph Gentleman, out of his 'natural love and affection and for his promotion and advancement in the world',

> All that piece or parcel of land being part of a certain field heretofore called The Hay House Platt situate ... on Mount Sion Hill ... adjoining on the north or north-west to the Highway leading to Woodsgate and opposite to the garden late in the occupation of Richard Cumberland Esq and now of Richard Delves his Undertenants or Assigns and which said piece ... of land is the same piece ... of land (with the exception of a small portion thereof lately sold and conveyed by the said Joseph Delves the Elder to Thomas Pinckard Bingham Esq) which was purchased by ... Joseph Delves the Elder of and from Duncan John Cameron Esq And also all that slip ... of land being the south-western end ... of the said field called the Hay House Platt and formerly used as a roadway but now thrown into and forming a part of the said heretofore first mentioned piece ... of land and was lately purchased by the said Joseph Delves the Elder of and from the said Thomas Pinckard Bingham Esq and which said pieces ... of land are now in the occupation of the said Joseph Delves the Younger And all Houses Outhouses New Erections and Buildings ...

A year after this gift of land to his son Joseph, in May 1827, added a second codicil to his will revoking a bequest of £300 because he had 'on occasion of my said son building a new house given him the sum of three hundred pounds considering it most for his interest so to do at the present time'.

All the evidence I have is now before us and to my mind there can be no doubt about the broad picture. Joseph Delves the father bought the piece of land next to his house, Forest Prospect, and gave it to his son in 1826 together with £300 in cash in 1827 and the new house was built in those years. The maps on the next page confirm the hypothesis. The map on the left is the Barrow map of 1808 and

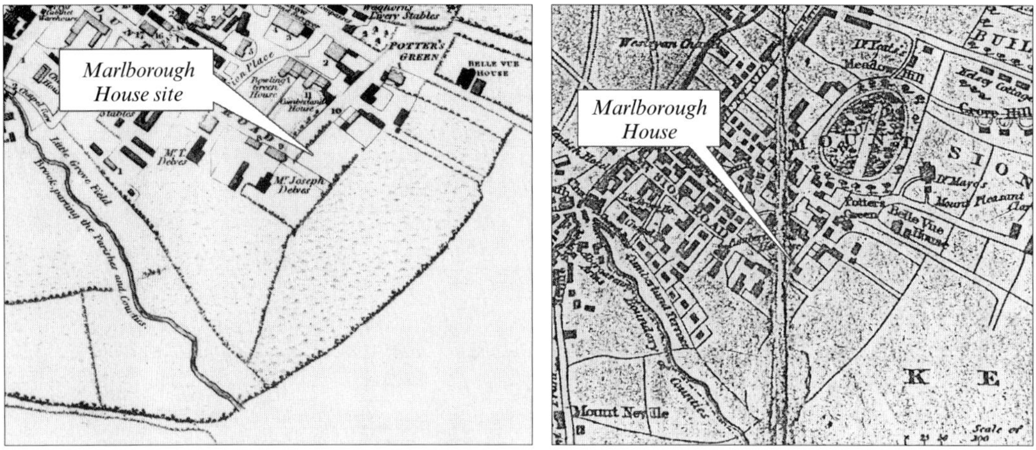

Barrow map 1808 (left); map dated 1828 (right)

there is plainly no sign of any building on the site or indeed in the fields around it. The house on the right is Sion Lodge about which there will be more to say in chapter 22. The map on the right is one which appeared in Britton's *Descriptive Sketches* in 1832 but the Reference Library has a fair framed copy dated 1828. A house is clearly to be seen in the Marlborough House position. The trouble with the broad picture is that it is not entirely consistent with the documents of 1801 and 1802 and some of the later field descriptions are problematic. First of all, there is a direct conflict if the 'new erected messuage etc' of 1802 was on the site of Marlborough House. The only way out then would be to suppose that the new erections were demolished. However, I suspect that they were built on another adjoining field or on part of the 110 by 160 foot 'garden' ('built thereon or on some part thereof') because a 156 foot long 'free way or passage' is required to access the field; and this same 156 feet is specified in the conveyance of April 1822 of the south-western part of the Hay House Platt where the slip of land leads from Mount Sion Road at a width of 17 feet down to the Mercer Field or The Meadow at a width of 15 feet. The Garden which was sold in 1801 was 'part of' the Hay House Platt and the slip of land 156 feet long was on the side nearest Forest Prospect, Mount Sion Road being on the north-west. The 156 feet long slip was bought by Joseph Delves Senior in 1822 and by 1826 had been 'thrown into' the 'Garden' and was part of the gift to Joseph Junior. Down the hill was the field called Mercer or The Meadow which was not part of these transactions; but which seems to be the field occupied by John Turner – except that it is now 'with the said buildings' in the tenure of Charles Stevens – see the exact wording on page 294 above. These considerations reinforce my view that the 'new erected messuage' and other buildings of 1802 were not built on the site of Marlborough House. Have a look at the Barrow map detail above and see what you think.

Finally there is the curious case of 'Marlborough', the name. There is a tradition or myth that the house was built on the site of one occupied a century earlier by the great John Churchill, Duke of Marlborough. This story was, I think, first printed by W.R. Knipe in his *Tunbridge Wells and Neighbourhood*, 1916. He says that the Duke came to the Wells in 1717 and 'it is supposed' that the house named after him on the top of Mount Sion marks the site of his residence. He does not name a source and a supposition hardly needs a source; but he does acknowledge more generally the provision of much valuable information by Mr W.H. Delves 'who has lived in Tunbridge Wells since his birth [1829]'. Did William Henry, through the family, know something about Marlborough which we shall never know? Of course the bestowal of a grand name on a house needs no linkage at all and in the absence of further information we must guess that one of the Joseph Delveses, father or son or both together, liked the sound of the name for their new house and bestowed it at the same time on the family home, Marlborough Villa. Father Joseph died in 1827, the year of his gift of £300 to his son.

The Delveses began to spread themselves about the beginning of the 19th century. In 1805 Joseph the Elder had bought Fairlawn House just down the hill which will be the topic of chapter 22. Then about 1810 young Richard (aged 32) really got the bit between his teeth. The *Sprange Guides* reveal an astonishing development. In 1808 there are only half a dozen Delves' properties on Mount Sion plus the Grosvenor one at the top of the town. In 1811 there are 23; and in 1817 there are 25. In 1811 Mr R. Delves appears all of a sudden, not only at Sion Place and Caxton House, but also at Burlington, Bowling Green and Cumberland Houses around the old Bowling Green at the top of Mount Sion – and in other parts of the town: Warwick House and Great and Little Merryvale in the High Street; Heath Cottage and Rock House on the London Road; Great and Little Mount Pleasant (the *Calverley Hotel* building and the house that used to stand where the cinema recently was); and Wellington Place on Mount Ephraim. In addition we have Joseph Delves at Grosvenor House and his son-in-law in the Lodge and Cottage. In 1817 there were 25 family properties and out of these 19 appear against the name of Richard rather than other members of the Delves family. You might wonder whether Richard was not merely acting as agent or just renting; but subsequent events show that he owned the freehold. So, where had he found the money? Or had he borrowed – as the eldest son of aging Joseph, Richard's expectations and credit must have been good?

He was evidently riding high at this time. Three extracts from the local press give a hint of his standing in the town. We all know, of course, about the state of the royal marriage in 1820 – the King was trying to get Parliament to convict the Queen of adultery. Eventually he failed; and the *Maidstone Journal* reported in November:

> Tunbridge Wells was illuminated last evening in honor of the Queen; and we understand that in the course of the week, Mr R.Delves, an eminent house-agent at that place, intends giving a bullock, which is to be roasted on the common, and at the same time to distribute six butts of good old stingo, to drink her Majesty's health.

Then in 1826 the Duchess of Kent came with her seven-year-old daughter Victoria to stay in Calverley House also known as Great Mount Pleasant. The town decided to give the little princess a leaving present of Tunbridge Ware and guess who was one of the organising committee of three? Mr Richard Delves, of course. Finally, consider this extract from October 1827: 'Amongst the numerous improvements made here by our spirited fellow-townsman, Mr.R.Delves, may be classed the extensive building now erected in the market place, which will shortly be occupied by his son, as successor to Messrs. Fry and Delves, butchers, who are about to retire from business. We are also glad to find Mr.R.D. has taken Great Mount Pleasant for a term of years the arrangement of which maybe productive of considerable advantage to the place.' It would be of interest to know which building it was that Mr R.D. erected in the market place – by which I assume is meant not the Fishmarket but Bath Square. My guess is no.9.

The precise story of Richard's interest in Great Mount Pleasant House has yet to be unravelled. Eleanor Reed gave a 21-year lease in 1792 to Richard's uncle, John Fry; and when he died in 1803 Richard was assigned the residue of the lease and then in 1812 reached an agreement with the trustees of Eleanor Reed's will to purchase the house for £4,500. However, he had to borrow £3,700 on mortgage from the trustees and it rather looks as if he could not keep up the payments. Anyway, in 1819 William Lushington took over the mortgage and bought the place himself; but he died in 1825 and his daughter Charlotte immediately sold out to John Ward – who therefore was the owner of the house in 1826 when the Duchess of Kent and Princess Victoria made their first visit; but he, in December 1827, as the *Maidstone Journal* had forecast, gave a 14-year lease to Richard Delves; so that when the royals came again in 1828 there is no doubt that Richard was their landlord. This seems to provide the best explanation of the seven-shilling print. One of the Delves family heirlooms used to be a print of the Duchess of Kent and Princess Victoria which had been given to a member of the family in gratitude, according to family legend, for the loan of a piano for the Princess's use. Unfortunately Uncle Stanley included this precious heirloom among his furniture and effects when he auctioned them in 1955. All that remains is a Brackett's catalogue showing that the print was sold for seven shillings.

Be that as it may, we are now in what I call the golden age of Delvian history.

> *La famille Delves devait avoir une grande fortune. Elle habitait une propriété donnant sur le parc de Kensington, dont le jardin était limitrophe de la propriété de la Duchesse de Kent, mère de la Princesse (depuis reine) Victoria. C'est le fait de ce voisinage des deux jardins que ma mère jouait et se disputait avec la future reine Victoria. Par testament le grand-père Delves laissa toute sa fortune à son fils cadet. De là une scissione complète dans la famille. Le docteur Delves et nos grands-parents restèrent dans une position très modeste.*

> The Delves family must have had a large fortune. The family house overlooked Kensington Park and its garden ran alongside the property of the Duchess of Kent, mother of Princess (later Queen) Victoria. It is because the two gardens adjoined one another that my mother used to play and quarrel with the future

Queen Victoria. By his will grand-father Delves left all his fortune to his youngest son. Hence a complete rupture in the family. Doctor Delves and our grand-parents remained in very modest circumstances.

This letter which is undated is to be found among the Delves Family Papers and gives a contemporary, but maybe distorted, glimpse of the golden age. The writer was one Edward Gruner whose mother, Emma, was a daughter of the marriage of Joseph the Elder's daughter Sophia with Thomas Milsom in 1810 as recounted on page 292 above. Emma's brother Edward had emigrated to France where he entered the silk business in Lyons, married Mlle Louise Poinset and, with 11 children, founded the French branch of the Milsom family. Emma joined her brother in France and married a Frenchman Louis Gruner, their son Edward being the author of the letter.

It is clear that the Grand-father Delves of the story is Joseph the Elder who stood, therefore, in the grand-paternal relationship to the first generation of the French Milsoms – Edward and his wife Louise and his sister Emma; and Doctor Delves must be the Doctor William Pretty who married Jane Delves. Some fanciful stories evidently enlivened the French kitchens; but there is enough truth to give an insight into the feelings of the time. 'The Delves family must have had a large fortune' ... well, there is some truth in that – but how large is large? Now we come to the really fanciful bit ... 'They lived in a house looking over Kensington Park and their garden adjoined that of the Duchess of Kent ... that's how my mother used to play and quarrel with the future Queen Victoria.' Well, Emma must have been born about the same year as Victoria (1819), so the timing is consistent – but what about the place? So far as I know there never was a Delves residence in London – and certainly not next to Kensington Palace. I can only speculate that what we have here is a third-hand memory of games played in the grounds of Great Mount Pleasant House – which might to Richard's little niece have seemed those of a palace ... well, can you think of a better interpretation?

However, what about the size of the fortune and its distribution? A rough comparison of Joseph's estate with that of his father shows that Richard left eight items of real estate, about £2,000 in money and £100 per annum in annuities; while Joseph left 29 items of real estate, about £10,000 in money and £800 per annum in annuities. Some allowance must be made for inflation and the fact that some of Joseph's real estate items are simply sub-divisions of Richard's bequests. On the other hand something like half Richard's estate went to Thomas of Eden. All in all, there seems no doubt that Joseph made good use of his inheritance; but the resulting fortune was hardly commensurate with properties in Tunbridge Wells and Kensington Park and familiarity with duchesses and princesses. Nor is it fair to accuse Joseph of leaving everything to his youngest son to the neglect of the rest of the family. Each member of the family got about £2,000 (worth perhaps a quarter of a million in today's money) or the equivalent in property, out of an estate valued according to Inland Revenue records at £18,000 – a couple of million today? It is true that Joseph the Younger was to have Forest Prospect and

Marlborough Villa provided he made a home for his mother; and he gained an influential role as executor with his uncle Thomas and his brother-in-law James Hockett Fry, the grandson of Richard Fry. The eldest son Richard might well have felt aggrieved; he got just the standard £2,000 with additional provision for his children – but he had property a-plenty anyway. None of the remaining members of the family was neglected. The first-born, Ann, married to James Hockett Fry (who must have been on good terms with his father-in-law), received the most valuable bequest – the Grosvenor estate which Richard had bought at public auction in 1785 – see above. Mary received the Bow-Window House; Sarah Gorringe £100 for each child plus assistance with education and apprenticeship fees and an annuity for herself so long as she lived separate from her husband; Sophia received the income from £1,300 plus the cancellation of her husband's, Thomas Milsom's, debt of £700; and Jane, married to Dr Pretty, the income from £1,500. It can be seen from these details (an inevitably imprecise abbreviation of the excessively long, complex and repetitive will which John Stone produced for his client) that the story of favouritism is partially justified but to say that everything was left to the youngest son is untrue; it could equally be maintained that the eldest daughter Ann and her husband were unduly favoured. Nevertheless, the very existence of the story bears witness to an ancient family quarrel – and the fact, as we shall see in the next chapter where the Delves story continues, that this will was one document which turned up in Australia shows how important it was considered.

Chapter 21

Alderman Delves

If Richard the Younger, 'eminent house agent and spirited townsman', had been banking on his father's will to rescue him from trouble, he must have been disappointed. It is evident that his father did not trust him an inch. He got the standard £2,000 but it was to be dished out in dollops of £500 a year over four years – and a codicil dated 1826 reveals that Richard had just borrowed £250 which was to be deducted from the first £500. Perhaps it was the fact that his younger brother, as one of the trustees, was going to dish out his allowance that stuck in his gullet. Not that there is any evidence that Richard complained. It was the minor members of the family who seem to have been upset – the Milsoms and the Prettys. Richard, fresh from playing landlord to the royals, found further cause for rejoicing in 1828. On 11 November his son William married Elizabeth Jane, the eldest daughter of John Nash, the Pantiles bookseller and postmaster; and a year and a week later a son was born who was to become Mayor of Tunbridge Wells in 1900. Another year and a week after the birth, however, disaster struck. A meeting was announced to take place at eight o'clock in the evening of 26 November 1830 at *The Duke of York* on the Pantiles. The creditors of Richard Delves were asked to attend 'for the purpose of investigating and ascertaining the amount of the debts owing by him and the assets and effects to meet payment of the same; and generally to consult upon the best method to be adopted for arranging and adjusting his concerns'.

What followed revealed the extent of Richard's assets. By the end of 1831 a series of auction sales 'by order of the Commissioners in Bankruptcy' had disposed of most of the houses I mentioned just now; and the lease on Calverley House, as this building was by then known, was taken over by the assignees. All this must have been a terrible blow to Richard's pride; but he seems to have retained something of his former pugnacity, popping up once or twice more in the newspaper to object strongly, for instance, to the rate set by the new commissioners in 1835. In 1841, a year before his death, he was living with Grace, apparently a new wife, at Pelham House.

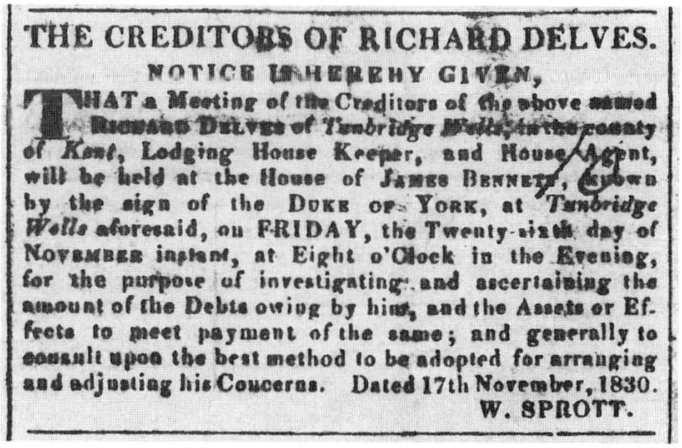
THE CREDITORS OF RICHARD DELVES.

NOTICE IS HEREBY GIVEN,

THAT a Meeting of the Creditors of the above named RICHARD DELVES of *Tunbridge Wells*, in the county of *Kent*, Lodging House Keeper, and House Agent, will be held at the House of JAMES BENNETT, known by the sign of the DUKE OF YORK, at *Tunbridge Wells* aforesaid, on FRIDAY, the Twenty-sixth day of NOVEMBER instant, at Eight o'Clock in the Evening, for the purpose of investigating and ascertaining the amount of the Debts owing by him, and the Assets or Effects to meet payment of the same; and generally to consult upon the best method to be adopted for arranging and adjusting his Concerns. Dated 17th November, 1830.

W. SPROTT.

Maidstone Journal

The Nevill Street/London Road junction in 1830. Pelham House is the building on the corner where the sign Delves House Agent may be read.

Here is Pelham House in 1830, on the right, where Barclays Bank now is. With a little imagination you can see the sign 'Delves House Agent' above the shop. Richard had two sons who survived, Joseph and William. Joseph was known as 'Joseph the Grocer' to distinguish him from other Josephs and I think he ran the Delves' shop on the Pantiles, until recently 'Todds Vintry'. William, possibly prevented from following in his father's footsteps because of the bankruptcy, became steward to Lord Abergavenny in which role he distinguished himself. In 1833 these two obtained a lease of Bedford Place and the old Little Grove House at the bottom of Mount Sion from their uncle Henry Delves who had married Ann Parman but had no children. Bedford Place was listed in *Sprange's Guide* 1817 under the name Richard Delves but how it came into Henry's hands I do not know – maybe he bought it at a bankruptcy auction; but the evidence of ownership and leasing is unmistakable in the will of Henry who died in 1869. The result of this transaction was the construction of Bedford Terrace, one of the architectural ornaments of Tunbridge Wells, for which the family can claim some credit. The *Tunbridge Wells Visitor* reported in June 1834 that '... a few old houses have been taken down and a row of houses built called Bedford Terrace'. On the next page is a recent photograph.

During all this time Joseph the Elder's younger brother, Thomas, had been enjoying the life of an urban country gentleman on his 'Eden' estate. He did purchase Grove Lodge (see chapter 23) in 1806 but otherwise made no additions

Bedford Terrace in 1993

to his inherited property except to permit the building of Bloomfield Cottage (since demolished) and Gothic Villa (the present 'Cumberlands') at the bottom of his meadow. Both these houses had been built by 1840 – see the Tithe map on the next page. Gothic Villa still stands but not Bloomfield Cottage. Gothic Villa and the replacement for Bloomfield Cottage can be seen on the aerial photograph in the previous chapter. By 1840 Gothic Villa and the plot of land alongside had been sold to a Mary Ann Malcomb but the house was occupied by a Mrs Smart and the plot by William Pankhurst. Bloomfield Cottage remained in the ownership of Thomas Delves and was occupied by George Bennett who also owned and occupied a cottage and garden next to it on the Fairlawn House side. Thomas Delves owned and occupied the Home Meadow whose extent can be seen on the Tithe map. Bloomfield Cottage is still there on the Ordnance Survey map surveyed in 1866 and is listed by Mathieson (1867/8) as the home of Lady Maria Meade about whom I know nothing except that she was a co-exhibitor with her neighbour Joseph Delves of hot-house plants at the Horticultural Society shows – see page 306 below. Bloomfield Cottage figures in the 1871 census and the 1874 Electoral Roll but the roll for 1877 shows 'late Meade's Trustees, Cumberland Walk' and by 1886 the houses now numbered 11 to 19 are listed with their various new residents. I do not know the details of this redevelopment but the physical presence can be perceived on the ground or in the aerial photograph.

To judge from the evidence of his will alone Thomas valued books, particularly those of a religious tendency. He left to Sarah 'my works of Josephus and a piece

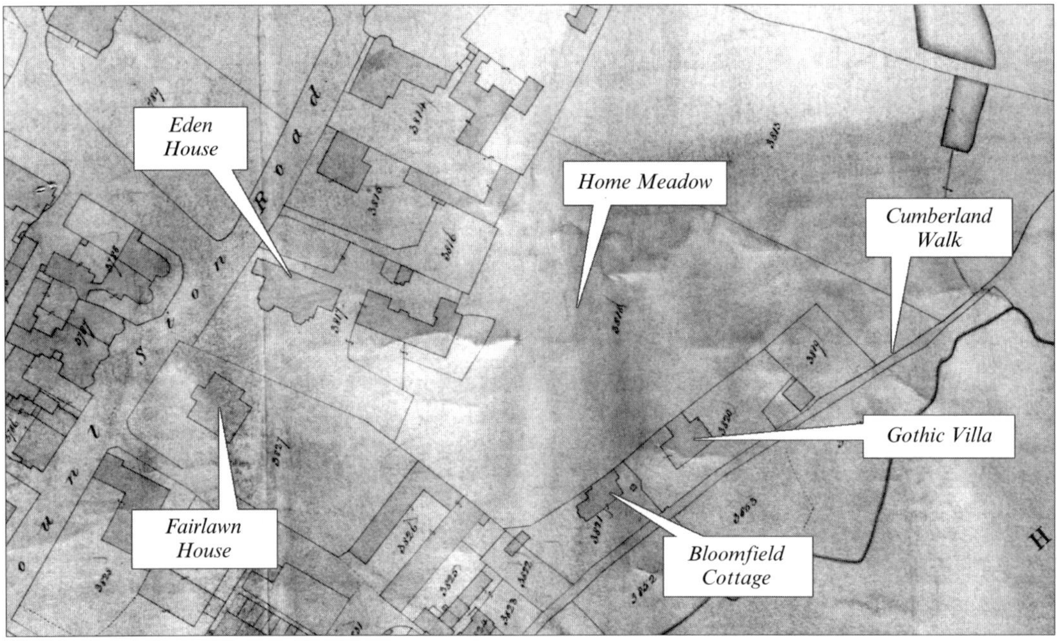

Tithe map 1840

of her own needlework the subject being the flight into Egypt'; to Henry Fenner all the works of the Reverend William Huntingdon in his possession; to James one volume of the works of Mrs Baring (to be kept by his mother until he came of age); to Elizabeth 'Spencer's folio History of England'; and to Emma Peacock Bunyan's *Pilgrim's Progress*. His first five children were baptised at the Chapel of the Countess of Huntingdon's Connexion but after 1806 he patronised the King Charles Chapel.

His first wife, Mary Ann, whom he had married, according to the Delves family papers, at Shoreditch Church died in 1815, having borne him 11 children; and he married in 1817 Elizabeth, daughter of James Nye of Mount Ephraim, Tunbridge Ware manufacturer. This seems to have led to some stepmother trouble, for Thomas begins his will by directing that his son Joseph 'shall not interfere or have any power in respect of any provision herein made in favour of my wife and my children by her'. The animosity, if such it was, might possibly be not unconnected with the circumstances of the remarriage, for it is a curious thing but this respectable, religiously-minded gentleman of 48 years seems – if we are to trust the registers – to have married a woman who was five months pregnant. The wedding took place at Speldhurst Church on 10 September 1817 and was witnessed by William Fenner. On 4 December 'Henry Fenner Delves son of Thomas and Elizabeth' was christened at the Tunbridge Wells Chapel but on 2 May 1818 Henry Fenner Delves was buried at Frant aged four months. On 7 March 1819 twin sons of Thomas and Elizabeth were baptised in Tunbridge Wells and named Henry Fenner and Benjamin. Did Thomas marry to legitimise another's child? Fenner and Nye were partners in the Tunbridge ware business at about this time: could this be significant?

Be that as it may, Thomas and Elizabeth had another seven children together and during most of his 77 years Thomas seems to have lived comfortably in his Home Cottage near the lodging house which used to be called the Home House but had, at the time of his will, 'for some years past' been called Eden House. In addition to the usual stables, coachhouses, granaries and outbuildings there was a brick-walled garden and shrubbery, woodhouse, well and pump; and three and a half acres of meadowland, called the Home Meadow which, with its old stable, his son Joseph was to be permitted to use for pasturing horses and sheep 'subject to a right for the occupiers of Home Cottage and Eden House to walk therein at reasonable times as they have been used to do'. Sloping southwards, it must indeed have been a pleasant spot for a saunter; although it used to be called, says the will, the Slaughterhouse Field which is a source of confusion with Slaughterhouse Fields in other parts of the town but may be significant in relation to the Delves' trade. I do not know whether Thomas ever practised the trade himself but his father Richard who occupied the house and cottage before him certainly did; and Thomas' eldest son, Joseph, followed in turn by his two sons, ran the Delves' butcher's shop in Chapel Place until it was sold to J.W. Rush later in the century. Amongst other bequests to his trustees Thomas left 'the muniments of title and other papers and writings' relating to what he called his 'Home Estate'. I wish I knew what had happened to them since! I wish also I could trace some of the heirlooms which were named in the will of Thomas' son Joseph: his father's portrait; the portraits of Joseph and his first wife; Joseph's 'Yeomanry' picture and his old family Bible and iron chest to keep writings in; grandmother Strange's likeness; the four pencil drawings made by Jane (born 1840) and 'her father's and mother's small likenesses in cases; and the likeness of Arthur's uncle William (I can find no such uncle on the Delves side unless the reference is to cousin William, the Abergavenny steward who was 16 years older than Arthur). If there are any Delves descendants out there who recognise any of these descriptions I should like to hear. Another thing Thomas might have told us is why he changed the house name to 'Eden'. Maybe he thought it was a paradise, as well he might; otherwise the only theory is that it commemorates the Eden family. A Mrs Eden conversed with Lady Jerningham on the Pantiles in 1806 (see page 376) and one other family member at least is known to have been staying somewhere in Tunbridge Wells in 1817 and 1826.

Thomas died in 1846 at the age of 77, directing his trustees (his son Joseph, Edward Kine of Frant and Charles Trustram, the surgeon who lived at Bedford Place) to sell all his land and houses for the benefit of his family. There is some incomplete documentation in private hands which suggests that preparations were made for a grand sale but whether it ever took place I do not know. Seven lots were planned. Lot 1 was Eden House and the Home Cottage and also Bloomfield Cottage at the bottom of the site – which was later demolished. This lot was sold 'in or about the year 1848' to a Steven Jones but then some time later bought back from him by Joseph Delves, son of Thomas. I imagine there were rules against a trustee selling to himself. By this time the number of trustees had been reduced to Joseph Delves and Trustram the surgeon, Edward Kine dropping out. Then on 6 May 1848 Lot 2 was bought by the Rev. Pope. This is deduced from the Sale Particulars of 1879 which say that the title to Eden Villa should commence on that date. Lot 3 was a field adjoining the Eden Villa site and bounded by Eden Road. Lots 4 to 6 were fields on the other side of Eden Road (part of the 'Home Meadow') and Lot 7 was Gothic Villa (the present 'Cumberlands'). All these lots were purchased from Charles Trustram and Joseph Delves on 26 May 1851. I have a copy of an extract from a conveyance of that date which shows that a Joseph Delves entered into covenants with Charles Trustram and Joseph Delves and their heirs as Trustees (and with the same Joseph Delves as owner of Lot 1) not to erect any house on Lots 3, 4, 5 and 6 costing less than £800 or £500 in the grounds of Gothic Villa and to share in the use and maintenance of the private road and the barrel sewer and such like. The purchaser was undoubtedly cousin Joseph of Marlborough who built no houses but created a miniature park with a small lake at the bottom to enhance the view from his residence, as can be seen in the detail below from the plan which accompanied the Sale Particulars of 1874 – see page 316 below.

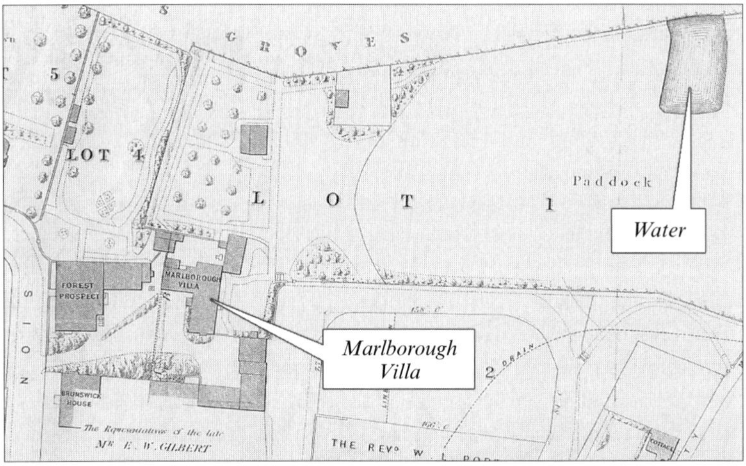

Sale Particulars 1874

Several greenhouses can be seen on this plan and demonstrate the importance to Joseph Delves of the frequent flower shows held by the Tunbridge Wells Horticultural Society from 1833 onwards. These took place in Mr Nash's Assembly Rooms on the Pantiles and in May at the first show of the 1834 season, for instance, the reporter noticed 'a very chaste collection of turban rananculus, azalia Indica, erica mirabilis etc from J.Delves Esq, Mount Sion'. By the next year Joseph had invested in a greenhouse and was exhibiting grapes; and in June 1836 the 'hot-house plants of Lady Meade and Mr J.Delves excited universal admiration'.

On his Lot 2 the Rev. Pope built a sparkling villa, seen on the next page from the back garden. It can presumably be dated to 1848/49 and its name will be considered in a minute. Thomas mentions Grove Lodge in his will but only to offer the contents to his daughter Sarah and her husband Edward Butler for £150. The house must have been sold but this story belongs to a later chapter. Finally the Tuttys Estate (Hawkenbury, that is) which Thomas had inherited from his father was sold to Lord Camden for £2,500 in 1847. I suppose the proceeds of all these disposals were distributed among Thomas's numerous progeny but I have no evidence of this. At all events the upshot was that Joseph of Marlborough had acquired most of the Home Meadow to add to his back garden and Eden House and Cottage remained in Delves' hands and continued to be rented out; which is why Eden House was able to enjoy its moment of greatest glory in 1849 when the Queen's mother came to stay for three months from August to October.

Eden Villa

On 21 July that year the *Sussex Agricultural Express* announced the Duchess's impending visit and said that Grecian Villa was to be taken for two months and was undergoing repairs for the purpose; while Eden House had been reserved for part of Her Royal Highness's suite. By 4 August, however, Sir George Couper, comptroller of the household, had fixed on Eden House for the Duchess's residence. Had he, I cannot help wondering, discovered a skeleton in one of the Grecian Villa cupboards? Anyway, where was the Duchess's suite to go now? The obvious answer was Fairlawn House next door – and there is some evidence that it was actually used. The granddaughter of Robert Russell, the Tunbridge Ware manufacturer, related how her grandfather (and I quote) 'served the Duchess of Kent with many things when she stayed at Eden House on Mount Sion. My mother has often told me how her mother and father would have to go to 'Fairlawn' ... members of the Duchess's household lived there and my grandparents would set out the Tunbridge Ware in a large room there and leave it. Then the Duchess would walk through and select what she wanted and all the business would be done by her Equerry'.

Another piece of evidence comes from the obituary of one of the Delves family, William Henry, who was born in 1829: 'He well remembered Queen Victoria visiting Tunbridge Wells. She used to stay with her mother at Eden House, Mount Sion, and her suite lived at Fairlawn House close by.' I am afraid that William Henry was talking to a journalist at the end of a very long life and he cannot be right about the Queen. She and Prince Albert came on a day trip in June 1849 but the Duchess of Kent did not arrive at Eden House until August. So can we believe what he said about Fairlawn House? What cannot be doubted is that the Duchess of Kent did stay for three months at Eden House from August to October 1849 because it is fully reported in the press and very pleased the inhabitants of the town were about it. When the Duchess departed by train in mid-October she told anxious enquirers that she would come again 'if spared'.

Among the deputation which presented a welcoming address to Her Royal Highness at Eden House on 11 August were the Rev. Pope, Joseph Delves and Joseph Delves of Chapel Place. The Duchess's birthday was 17 August and there is a contemporary account of what happened on that day. It is in an old exercise-book containing the 'Remembrances' of a member of the Strange family which the late family member, Kathleen Strange, kindly lent me. To quote: 'A procession of all the schoolchildren and Sunday schoolchildren, to the number of two thousand, passed the house, headed by the Magistrates, Clergy, Ministers and many others. A grand dinner was given to the children on the Common. In the evening there were fireworks, which owing to the rain coming on were a failure, but the day was altogether a successful and delightful one'.

Born in 1806, Joseph Delves, son of Thomas, ran the butcher's business in Chapel Place, married Jane Strange (of the local family) and then Mary Ann Cripps (of the legal family) and had a family of nine by his first wife. In 1851 he was living with his family in Chapel Place over the butcher's shop which was until recently the florists; but by 1861, having set up his sons Thomas Hilder and Joseph in a partnership to run the shop, he had moved to No 2 Blenheim Place (see chapter 17 page 236) and pursued a more gentlemanly career as house agent and Town Commissioner. He had been elected one of the 24 town commissioners under the new dispensation of 1860 and he appears from time to time in the newspaper reports one of which was quoted in chapter 17 – he had never seen Mount Sion 'in such a disgraceful state ...' Perhaps this is why he moved to Heath Villa, next to the old Vale Road Post Office, where he died in February 1871. Eden House and Cottage, after an unsuccessful attempt in 1878, were eventually sold in 1881 for £2,995. The proceeds from the sale of Joseph's estate had to be split seven ways. When the butcher's shop was sold, Thomas Hilder ran a wine and spirit shop in the High Street (where the *Eclipse* pub later was, I think, on the opposite corner of Frog Lane from York House) and never married. Joseph married and had a family; and another son, George, moved to Exeter and opened a chemist's business and it is one of his descendants, a Delves living in Suffolk, who has provided the testamentary information.

There is some confusion over the name 'Eden Villa'. Both Eden Cottage and the Rev. Pope's new villa seem to have used the same name. By coincidence the Rev. Pope died in 1879, just a year after Eden House and Cottage were put up for sale for the first time and consequently there are two sets of Sale Notices. The first is for the sale of Eden House and Eden Villa on 25 October 1878 at the *Royal Sussex Hotel* by J.M. Richardson and Sons 'who have been favoured with Instructions from the Trustees of the Will of the late MR JOSEPH DELVES' and the second is for the Freehold Residence known as 'Eden Villa' on 11 July 1879 at the same hotel by the same auctioneers 'By Direction of the Trustees of the Will of the Late Rev William Law POPE'. Obviously, we are talking about two different houses. In the testamentary accounts we find that Joseph owned three houses and they are named as Eden House, Eden Villa and Heath Villa and payments are made for rates and insurance and for repairs and gardening and so on, as would be expected, and payments of rent for Eden House and Villa are regularly recorded; and eventually the three are sold, Heath Villa in 1873 and the other two, as I said just now, in 1881. Why is Eden (or Home) Cottage not named? The answer is obviously that it has taken on the name 'Eden Villa'. The Sale Notice of 1878 for Eden House and Eden Villa says that the villa (Lot 2) adjoins the house (lot 1) and the description tallies better with that of the Cottage than the Rev. Pope's house – both can be seen in the aerial photograph on page 288 of the previous chapter. The tenant of the house called Eden Villa in the accounts was a Miss Jacques and there are references to her at Eden Villa and the Rev. Pope at No 2, Eden Villa – for instance in the *Tunbridge Wells Gazette* of 6 January 1860 and the 1861 census. In the 1851 census there are two houses named Eden Villa side by side: one occupied by Jane Jacques and the other by William L. Pope. In Colbran's 1850 *Guide*, however, the list of Resident Gentry shows Miss Jaques at Eden Cottage and the Rev. Pope at Eden Villa. I conclude from all this that the house owned by Joseph Delves and sold in 1881 after his death was Eden Cottage and the Rev. Pope owned the house built on Lot 2 until his death in 1879 when it was put up for auction. Who bought it, I do not know. On its subsequent history I have no information until 1897 when it was sold by Augusta Puckle to Henry Wild who sold it in 1917 to Mrs Nicolaidi who called it 'Acropolis' – at all events it had nothing to do with the Delves family. Thankfully the present owners have reverted to the proper name Eden Villa, numbered 4 Eden Road.

Demolition of Eden House 1969

Eden House and Cottage were sold to Henry Denton Montague Williams, a coal and corn merchant, but their subsequent story is undistinguished. Let it be noted that in 1858 the Shakespearian actor Sir Frank Benson was born in Eden House and in 1862 the Earl and Countess of Mount Edgecombe stayed briefly. In 1922 the house was used as a hostel by the Tunbridge Wells High School which had occupied Fairlawn House until 1900. Eventually the area of land accompanying the house and cottage attracted the attention of developers. The owners of Eden Cottage were made an offer they could not refuse, despite promises to neighbours that they would not sell, and the Council did not consider that the visit of the Queen's mother in 1849 was good enough reason to refuse planning approval. Demolition followed in September 1969 and two terraces of town houses now grace the grounds.

So much for the Thomas of Eden side of the Delves family. How about starting on the other side with Joseph of Marlborough (see the Family Tree on page 291 above)? As mentioned already, he had married, at the age of 34, in 1824, Mary Jane Smith of Speldhurst and during the next 20 years of what was to all appearance a happy and successful marriage eight daughters and three sons were born. When the census enumerator called on Marlborough Villa in June 1841 the household consisted of Joseph aged 45, Mary Jane, ten years younger, and seven children ranging from 14-year-old Susanna to one-year-old Catherine who was not to survive the year; but the eldest son, Joseph, was not there. Ten years later father Joseph is there aged 57 with Susannah, Clara, Isabella, William Percy and five-year-old Miriam Kate; but mother Mary Jane is away and son Joseph turns up as house surgeon at the Tunbridge Wells Infirmary. He died a bachelor aged 38 in 1862 and of the other boys, Charles died at 13 and William Percy at the age of 21, mysteriously in Australia on the very day he made his will leaving an annuity of £250 to one Eliza Brown Smith; and two of the girls, Marian and Catharine, share with their father a shady tomb in the Trinity Arts grounds which commemorates also Isabella who died a spinster in 1900.

The youngest girl Miriam Kate is the most interesting. In 1865 she married an Australian, Charles Perry Hobson, and a letter which I found among the Delves family papers began to reveal the story of the Australian connection. Miriam's family included a daughter who married a Major General Johnston and one of their sons wrote a letter in 1939 to Stanley W.W. Delves (Uncle Stanley – see Family Tree). He wrote from the family home, 'Yerangle', in Melbourne, asking for information about his grandmother's family and saying that he and some cousins were planning to write a history of the Hobson family and publish many old letters which they had. Thinking that the old letters might contain valuable Mount Sion information, I followed up this lead but for ten years failed to find any trace of the old letters or any descendants of the letter-writer or any family history beyond what the letter-writer of 1939 vouchsafed. He was Roy Luttrell Johnston, son of Major General Johnston, who had married a daughter of Miriam Kate; and he included in his letter the family tree reproduced on the next page: I contacted the Genealogical Society of Victoria and they put an advertisement in the Melbourne newspaper *The Age* for me, asking descendants to come forward. No response. I found out that Charles Perry's father was well-known as a pioneering biologist and founder of Melbourne Hospital; and Hobsons Bay on which Melbourne stands was named after his uncle, Capt William Hobson, who made

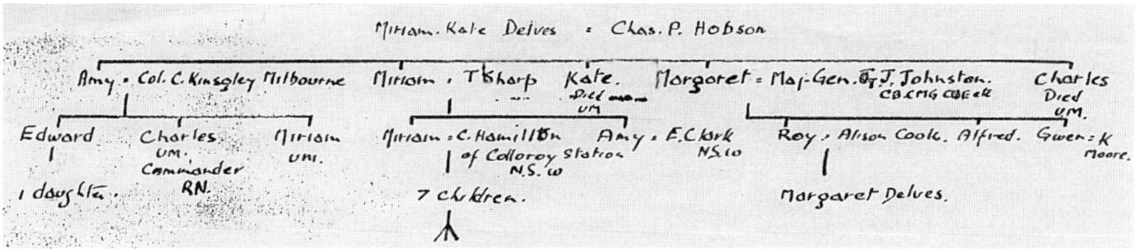

Roy Johnston's family tree

the first official charting of Port Philip in HMS *Rattlesnake*. The La Trobe State Library, the Caulfield and the Kilmore Historical Societies and others were most helpful and I found out quite a bit about the Hobsons and their houses but no hint of the descendants of Roy Johnston. Then one day in 1993 a lively Australian lady came to Tunbridge Wells seeking information about a 'Delves' in her own family tree and the Reference Library directed her to me. There seemed to be no link between her family and the Tunbridge Wells Delves but I gave her some details about my Australian problems. She and her husband were off on a year's sabbatical to study bats in Malawi but she said she would bear me in mind on their return to Canberra. On a visit a year later to her parents' home in north-east New South Wales she and her husband stopped for the night at a half-way village and she thought to check whether they were anywhere near the Colloroy Sheep Station which features in the little family tree above. To her surprise it was on the road map and they were quite close. Neither the police nor the post office nor the camping ground manager knew of Johnstons or Hamiltons and unfortunately they had to move on; but knowing where the Colloroy Station was she was able on her return to Canberra to find the telephone number and contact a helpful bookkeeper who said that she often had correspondence with people enquiring about ancestors or family who had worked at Colloroy and one of these, she thought, was a Hamilton connection who now lived in Canberra. She tracked down the name and address and telephone number of this person, a Mrs Lyn Bowman. A telephone call soon revealed that this was one of the descendants of Miriam Kate but not of Roy Johnston – see the family tree on the next page.

So far so good; but there was a difficulty. Lyn's mother, Mrs Crocker, knew about the Johnstons – in fact she used to correspond with Roy but after his death (she could not remember the date) she had lost touch with the daughters. She could not remember their names but thought they lived in the Melbourne area. How were Lyn and my helper going to trace two women whose married names they did not know out of the population of Melbourne? Here I was able to come to the rescue. I had been working through the Victoria Genealogical Society since 1992 and eventually they found out for me when Roy Johnston had died and the La Trobe State Library produced copies of newspaper funeral notices – including the married names of the two daughters: Mrs Gordon McCreadie (Del) and Mrs Craig Macauley (Robin). I immediately passed on this information and Lyn and my helper set to work, she on the telephone directory looking for McCreadie and

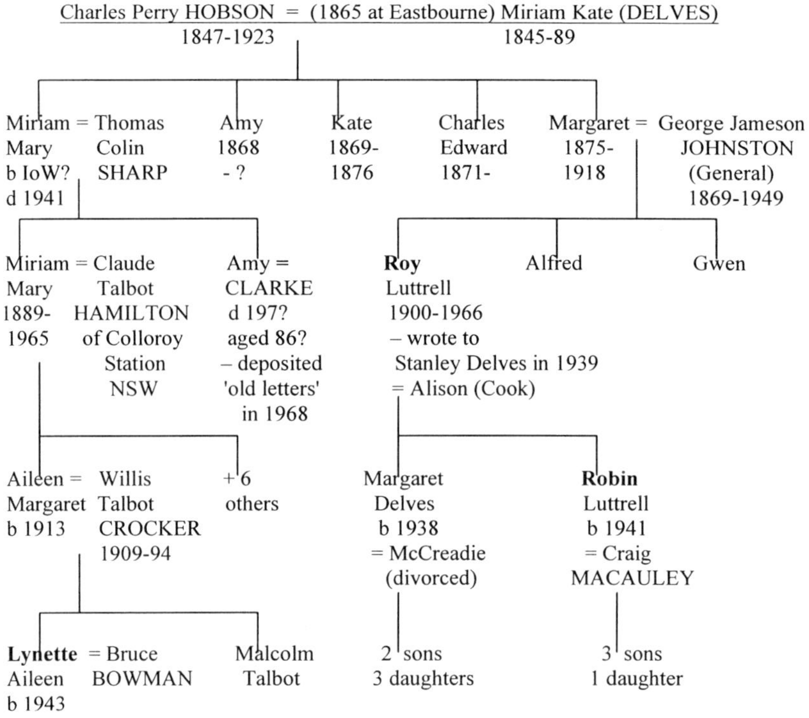

Lyn on the electoral roll for the whole state of Victoria looking for Macauley. It turned out that the search for McCreadie was hopeless since Del had divorced and no longer used the name; but Lyn on the other hand, undeterred by the number of Macauleys on the roll and variations in their spellings, at last found a name which rang a very loud bell: Mrs Robin Luttrell Macauley – Luttrell being the family name which Roy Johnston also used, derived from the maiden name of Miriam Kate's grandmother by marriage, Malvina Luttrell.

So she wrote and Robin replied enthusiastically – yes, she was Roy Johnston's daughter and, no, she had not seen the notice in *The Age* (although she did look sometimes!) and, well, what a pity, they had been in England last year and had planned to be near Tunbridge Wells but had changed plans and gone hunting Macauleys in the Outer Hebrides instead! And there is a Johnston family history written not by Roy Johnston but another family member and published in 1980. So, the unknown members of the family had been traced and brought together (Lyn met Robin in Melbourne in May 1995) and the family tree thoroughly clarified and general rejoicing prevailed; but what had been achieved for the history of Mount Sion? The published family history deals strictly with the Johnston family starting in Aughakilmore, County Leitrim, in 1750 and is the work of a cousin of Roy Johnston – the daughter of his father's sister – Phyllis Ashworth who has died subsequently in her 90s. The book is of general interest but sheds no light on Miriam Kate. There are good photographs of Roy, the general and Yerangle, the family home from where Roy wrote in 1939 but which is now a bowling green, Lyn says! The book is not, however, the one projected by Roy in 1939. On the other hand the 'old letters' have been found. Lyn's great aunt, Amy Clarke (see the family tree above), gave 'a suitcase full of papers' to the Victoria State Library, Melbourne, in 1968. It seems likely that the publication project was aborted by the war; and all thought of using the old letters was abandoned after Miriam Mary Hamilton died in 1965 and Roy in 1966. I do not understand why the Library failed to tell me about these papers when I enquired in 1992; however, Lyn had a look when she visited Melbourne in May and reported: 'The old letters are fascinating to look at but unbelievably difficult to read. Most of the handwriting is a terrible scrawl and some of the ink has faded a little. There were personal letters, business letters, accounts and newspaper cuttings. The majority of the material relates to Dr E.C. Hobson. Also in the box is the Last Will and Testament of Joseph Delves of Tunbridge Wells, dated 6 April 1825'. This is, of course, the will in all its repetitive length which seems to have caused a family row and it is highly suggestive that it has found its way to Australia and been preserved.

Much has come to light, from Australia, not least the photograph below which tends to confirm what Lyn's mother said (see next page) that the baby was born on the Isle of Wight where the photograph was taken. Secondly, the marriage of Charles Perry Hobson and Miriam Kate took place, not from the bride's home on Mount Sion, as I always imagined, but in Eastbourne; and I have (via Australia) a copy of the certificate to prove it. The date was 30 January 1865 – and she was 19 but he was only 17. The address given for both partners is 'Eastbourne' but banns had been called. The two witnesses are not from the family, as far as I know. Miriam's father had died eight years before, in 1857, but her mother was only about 60 – did she know what was going on? The other surprising information to emerge from Australia was that Charles Perry came to England 'for his education' in 1854 and did not return to Australia until 1874. This means

Charles Perry Hobson, Miriam Kate and baby Miriam Mary born 1866, photographed in Ryde, Isle of Wight.

that he had been in England for ten years when he married and must then have seemed more English than Australian. Who was looking after him? Where did he get his education? One possibility that sprang to mind was Christ's Hospital at Horsham where two Delves cousins went; but enquiry showed that this was not the case. The other curious fact is that three of Miriam Kate's children must have been born in England – or at least not in Australia. Lyn's mother says that Miriam Mary was born on the Isle of Wight and the family lived in France for a while and she went to a boarding school in Germany! There is a lot we do not know. Charles does not seem to have been an altogether admirable character and Miriam Kate, according to Roy Johnston in his original letter, had 'rather a sad life'. Her husband received a lot of money from his mother and inherited a farm and large house from his father but he ran though most of his resources, and his wife's, and in the end she left him to live with his mother who gave her money to compensate for what her husband had squandered; and she died at the youngish age of 44. He remarried and lived on to be 76.

Delves family photographs from Australia

One other interesting thing to come out of Australia is a set of four old photographs of which I reproduce two above. Unfortunately none of the subjects is identified but the one of the couple on the right bears the photographer's name – Edward Sims of Tunbridge Wells. Could this be Miriam Kate's parents? The trouble is that Sims is first recorded as a photographer in the *Court Guide* of

1865/6 – and father Joseph died in 1857. Perhaps a historian of photography in Tunbridge Wells (a book that needs to be written) might solve this one. The lady on the left looks remarkably like others in Aunt Lily's album (see below) but they are of a generation younger than Miriam Kate – could this be her all the same? It is time, anyway, to leave Australia and return to Tunbridge Wells in about 1830.

In 1829, you will recall, a grandson was born to Richard Delves at the height of his lodging house career which was promptly wrecked by bankruptcy the following year. The father William had married into the Nash family but, after giving birth to William Henry and two daughters, Elizabeth Jane died in 1835 aged 26 and in 1836 William married again and in 1844 started a new career which was to last for forty years. He became steward to Lord Abergavenny and moved to a house built in 1846 on Broadwater Down called Hargate Lodge. In 1851 he was enumerated at Hargate Lodge, Frant Forest and described as a farmer of 130 acres employing 11, with a household of nine: his second wife, Sarah, his widowed sister Ellen Turner, daughters Rose (18), Matilda (17), Cecilia (five), Emily (three) and three-month-old son Rowland and two servants. Missing were 12-year-old Howard who was presumably away at Christ's Hospital and William Henry who was a 21-year-old banker's clerk living at Gordon Villa with his uncle Robert Nash the postmaster. The 130-acre farm was the one marked on maps as Delves Farm located roughly where the Nevill Cricket Ground now is; but William seems to have left the day-today running of the farm to a manager or tenant. Howard was admitted to Christ's Hospital in 1848 and died in 1853 at the age of 14. The school records tell the story. '1853 July 5th. Howard Delves having had leave to visit his parents at Frant nr Tunbridge Wells on the 20th ulto after Scarletina, died there on the 3rd inst of 'cerebral congestion and convulsions' as appears from a letter from his medical attendant dated Tunbridge Wells July 4th 1853.' His younger brother Rowland born in 1850 was admitted in 1860 and left in 1865 – the year of Miriam Kate's marriage in Eastbourne. Rowland helped his father with the management of the Eridge Estate but he died unmarried at the age of thirty. Here is a photograph of William 'the Steward' in later life. Is there a resemblance with the man in the Edward Sims photograph above? When he died in 1886 the newspaper obituary stated that two important pieces of development in the town, Hungershall Park and Broadwater Down, both on Abergavenny land, were 'of his creating'.

William Delves 1807-1886

William Henry, the first-born, rose from bank clerk to be manager of the Lewes Old Bank on the Pantiles (otherwise Whitfield, Molineux and

Company) and, I think, he was living at Forest Prospect in 1872 when Mary Jane, widow of Joseph of Marlborough, died. This seems to have triggered a demand from the family for the winding-up of the trust which Joseph had set up by his will in 1857. I speculate that this might account for the fact that Miriam Kate and her family did not leave for Australia until 1874. The Trustees were William and his son William Henry and the Rev. James Fry, son of James Hockett Fry, and William's aunt Ann (see Family Tree). Perhaps the Trustees merely wanted to protect their backs or perhaps William Henry did not want to move from Forest Prospect. Anyway, the case went to the Court of Chancery which decreed that the estate should be sold. The auction took place under the gavel of James Mannington Richardson at the *Sussex Hotel* on 16 April 1874. Marlborough Villa, a plot of building land adjoining, Gothic Villa, Forest Prospect, Marlborough House and the White House Farm, Rotherfield, were on offer, as well as 32 shares in the Tunbridge Wells Gas Company. The results of the sale have not survived but Marlborough Villa went to Thomas Guilford (remember his Little Mount Sion exploits from pages 95-96?) and Forest Prospect to Alfred Tulk MRCS (and in 1895 to the Rev. Walter Octavius Peile MA who had the arrogance to change the old name to Ivy Chimneys). Marlborough House did not fetch the reserve price at auction and was later sold by private treaty to the schoolmaster William Henry Corke who used it for his 'Classical and Commercial School' from 1877 to 1888. On 19 June 1874 a second auction was held on the Forest Prospect premises to sell the whole of the 'Excellent Household Furniture and Effects' ... and that was virtually the end of old Richard's and Joseph's empire, started some 120 years before. There was still Fairlawn House which will be considered in chapter 24. The Bedford Place properties were sold, after the death of Joseph the Grocer in 1857, to William Stone and John William Roper – see chapter 26.

Lilian Jane Delves

William Henry, as we have seen in chapter 18 page 260, moved into 23 Mount Sion which had belonged to his grandfather, whether through sentimental attachment or the opportunity of the moment is unclear, and stayed there until he died in 1922 aged 93. He had married about 1865, somewhat late in life, a widowed lady, Emily, and they had five children together. The first was a girl called Lilian who later compiled a family photograph album. Here she is when very young.

William Henry was for many years a mainstay of the Literary Society and Reading Rooms on the Pantiles. He was Secretary to the Walks Estate. He was Secretary of the Freehold Tenants of the Manor of Rusthall. He was Chairman of a Building Society and manager of a Penny Bank. He became a Town Commissioner in 1882, an alderman in 1892, a JP in 1899, mayor in 1900 and a Freeman in 1910. His particular interest on the Town Council was finance. He was called 'The Statistical D'. The *Courier* likened him to the 'skid' of the municipal coach – meaning that he was always putting the brakes on! He was Chairman of the Finance Committee for many years and indeed was preparing to move the General District and Borough Rate when death overtook him at the age of 93 the day before the Town Council Meeting. He still rode a tricycle round the town in his 80s and considered it effeminate to wear an overcoat.

The Gas Company had been founded by Joseph of Marlborough Villa and two years after his death in 1857 William Henry became a director and was then Chairman from 1887 to 1920, never mssing a single meeting for 21 years. It was his great aim to bring gas within the reach of every household. A penny off the price of gas was as important as a penny off the rates, he said. He was Chairman of several more local companies, including the Pump Room Company and S.E.Haward Limited. His hobby was target shooting and here he is, in the photograph on the right, 'at the butts' – somewhere on Broadwater Forest, I should guess. The photograph, as you can see, is dated 1873 and comes from the studio of Henry Peach Robinson, our most famous local photographer. William Henry joined the Tunbridge Wells Rifle Volunteers in 1859 and rose to the rank of colour sergeant, winning trophies for shooting on the way. As Mayor of Tunbridge Wells in 1900/01 he laid the foundation stone for the Opera House (together with Sir H. Beerbohm Tree) on 10 October 1901; and proclaimed the accession of Edward VII (see next page photograph).

William Henry Delves

It is time now to leave the houses associated with the Delves family and indeed the family too and turn our attention to the Brunswick property which intervened between Forest Prospect and Marlborough Villa and Eden House and which the Delveses were never able to acquire – although I have no evidence that they ever made the attempt. There was a 'hate wall' built along the boundary but I think this was erected to hide the new terrace from the enraged residents of Eden Cottage or Eden House – and this would have had nothing to do with the Delveses since the terrace dated from 1875 or later. I have already commented on these matters on page 287 in the previous chapter and set out there the Poor Rate sequence which I take to apply to the house, with the proviso that I am not too confident

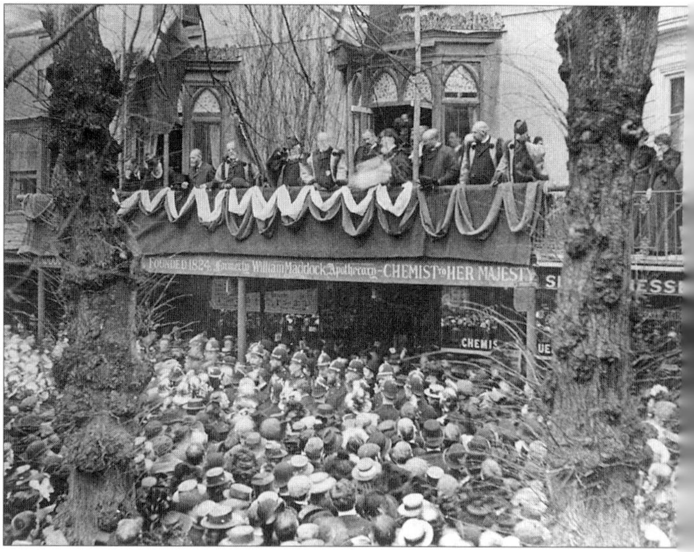

Proclamation of Edward VII on the Pantiles 23 January 1901

of the earlier stage, before the gap especially. The names Young and Goodall occur also in the Poor Rate record for the Grove Houses – see pages 52-54 for more detail. In fact 'Mr Young for a field' is the first entry in December 1687 followed by 'Mr Young for a field & 3 new houses' from 1689 to 1698; and then in 1728, after the gap, comes 'Mr Goodall 'for a field and 3 houses' until 1732 and then from 1733 to 1734 'Mrs Goodall or Mr Elliott' followed by Mr Elliott on his own. The detail from Kip's engraving of 1719 on page 53, chapter 6, shows the Grove Houses labelled Mr Goodals. Of course Brunswick House is 'out of shot' for Kip; but all this does show some tie-up between the two properties, although its explanation is quite unclear. Beyond this I know nothing of Goodall or Young – or for that matter of Mr August unless he is the Spitalfields financier who helped out Ann Mercer with Crescent Lodge (see chapter 17 page 238). With Peat Latter we are on firmer ground because of links forward to facts that can be confirmed. Peat Latter appears as the son of widow Mary Latter of Mount Sion whose will was made and proved in 1716. After bequests to other sons and grandchildren she says: 'And considering my daughter Mary Latter and Peat Latter my son are unprovided for and have been much at home and very helpful to me in my Business, I give and bequeath to them … all the rest of my goods …'. We know from this that the widow was 'of Mount Sion' and had a business and we know that Peat Latter, probably her son, was paying rates on Brunswick House some thirty years after Mary Latter's death. Was she perhaps managing the lodging house for Mr Goodall and did her son continue to do so until he was in a position to pay the rates himself? Speculation, speculation! Anyway he was sufficiently associated with the house for it to be called 'Peat Latters' in 1768 when Doctor Willett took over.

I have a few scattered facts about the ownership of the house from this point onwards but it is difficult to make a coherent story from them. Edward Willett, named as a trustee in the will of Thomas Wood, junior, made in 1762, was described as a surgeon of Withyham and the testator's brother-in-law. Thomas was married to a Mary who we can assume, therefore, was the doctor's sister. The Poor Rate record suggests that Dr Willett died in 1782 and his widow, named as Mary in the conveyance of 1852, took over the house until 1789 although in fact she died in

1786. Then, surprisingly, Sarah Langley left the house in her will dated 19 June 1790 to her husband the Rev. Joseph Langley for life and then to be sold to provide income for her sister Mary Gilbert and her children after her. The children were named Edward Willett Gilbert, Sophia Gilbert and Sarah Ann Gilbert and in 1831 Ann Friend (daughter of Thomas Wood junior) left a legacy of 19 guineas to each of them in her will (naming Edward schoolmaster of Frant). In 1852 Edward Willett conveyed to his two sisters for £284 his third share in 'All that messuage tenement or lodging house with the coach house outhouses stables yard gardens backsides lands ... and appurtenances situate on Mount Sion Hill ... opposite ... the piece ... of land formerly used as a bowling green ... in ... occupation formerly of Edward Willett ... since of Mary Willett ... afterwards of James [should be 'Joseph'?] Langley...' Sophia 'made her mark' with the endorsement 'Signed sealed and delivered by the within named Sophia Gilbert the contents and the object of the deed having first been explained to her in the presence of Thomas F. Walker, solicitor, Tonbridge' – see the earlier reference on page 195. The sisters then mortgaged the property which was described as 'commonly called Brunswick House'. In 1869 Edward Willett Gilbert, now a 'Land Surveyor', swore a Statutory Declaration concerning the ownership of Richmond and Cumberland Villas in Cumberland Walk in which he said that he was then 72 years of age, had lived in or near Tunbridge Wells all his life and 'for the last 40 years and upwards' he had known all the different properties on Mount Sion. In 1871 (census) he was living at Sackville Cottage (next to Frog Cottage) with his aged and still unmarried sister Sarah Ann and a 15-year-old servant girl. He died in 1873 and I assume his sister was already dead. In any case Brunswick House was put up for auction on 28 October 1873. The Conditions of Sale refer to the 1790 will of Sarah Langley but state that no sale was made in pursuance of the trust and the property became vested as real estate in the children of Mary Gilbert.

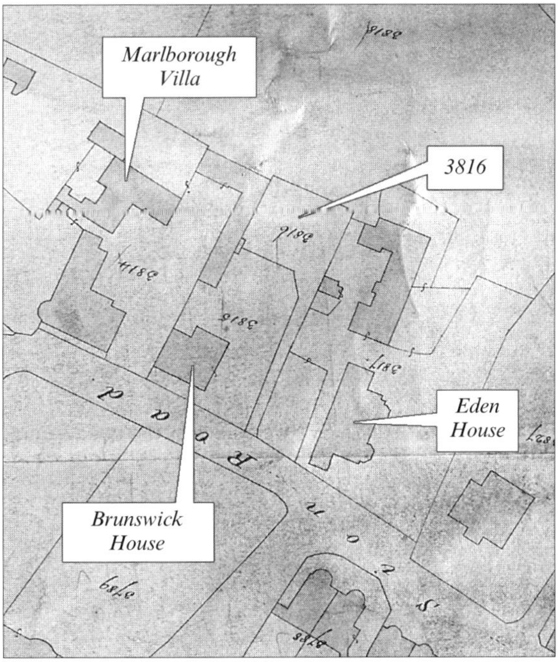

Tithe map 1840

The snag in these scattered facts is the relationship between Dr Willett and the children of Mary Gilbert, one of whom took the name 'Willett' as a forename. The obvious explanation would be that this was his mother's maiden name. If so,

Mary Gilbert and her sister Sarah Langley were the daughters of Dr Willett. The house must then have been willed to daughter Sarah – perhaps Mary already had a suitable house and Sarah and her reverend husband were living at Brunswick House and had nowhere else to go? Anyway, Sarah certainly had it in her gift but did not live long to enjoy it, dying four years after her mother. It would then make sense for her to pass it on, since she had no children of her own, to her sister and her sister's children after her husband's death. There is evidence for this scenario in the record of a mortgage dated 13 July 1787 between John Gilbert, shopkeeper of Groombridge, and his wife Mary (late Mary Willett spinster) and Sarah Willett spinster, Mary and Sarah being administrators of Mary Willett widow deceased who was the sole executrix and residuary legatee of Edward Willett. Spinster Sarah must then have married the Rev. Langley shortly after this date.

Anyway the *Sprange Guides* show that the Rev. Langley continued in occupation until 1811 at least but for unknown reasons gave the house the name Norwich House which appears on the Barrow map of 1808. Then in 1817 it is Mrs Gilbert; from 1827 to 1832 it is Mrs Harriett Cipriani; in 1840 Edward Willett Gilbert is owner and occupier of Brunswick House and Garden and Road; and in 1847 Miss Gilbert is at Brunswick *Lawn.* The outcome of the 1873 auction has not survived but less than two years later an application was before William Brentnall, the Town Surveyor, for construction of a terrace of nine houses and one large one. Weeks and Hughes of Tunbridge Wells claimed to be the owner and architect but I suspect that Francis Peek was behind them, as we saw in chapter 19, page 277. Anyway, the result was a new Brunswick House and adjoining terrace of nine houses which can be seen today – or on the aerial photograph on page 288 of the previous chapter. The first occupants of the terrace houses were recorded in *Kelly's Directory* of 1878.

A peculiarity of the arrangement which persists today is the fact that there is a dead-end road in front of Brunswick Terrace and alongside it at a lower level, separated by a brick wall, is Eden Road. The Tithe Award lists two separate plots both owned and occupied by Edward Willett Gilbert and described as (3815) 'Brunswick House and Garden' and (3816) 'Garden and Road' and these can be seen in the detail on the previous page – and in particular the road leading to the plot at the back of the house. There does not seem to have been a road in 1840 where Eden Road now is; but when the Rev. Pope built Eden Villa he must have been given a way in and in 1852 when the land was laid out in plots for disposal the 'carriage road' was drawn in just as it is today. Exactly when and in what circumstances the so-called 'hate wall' was erected I have no information. An unknown contributor to a discussion of such walls wrote to a newspaper, in the early 20th century I think, and I have the cutting but there are no dates or names. The remains are still to be seen today but a number of feet must have been cut off the top since it was built. On this somewhat unsavoury note it is time to leave the three Brett properties on the south-western side of the Bowling Green and consider the house on the south-east marked 'Wid Fry' on the Bowra plan.

CHAPTER 22

Sion Lodge and Madeira Park

The house marked 'Wid Fry' at the top of the Bowra plan of Mount Sion Hill (see page 5) was later known as Sion Lodge and, demolished, made way for Madeira Park. That is what this chapter is about. The Barrow map of 1808 shows it as a lodging house occupied by Mrs Canning and Sprange lists Mrs Canning in the same year, with three parlours, six chambers, five garrets, two coach houses and stabling for six horses. The Sprange listings for the earlier years are: 1780 – Mr Richard Fry – 4 parlours, 5 chambers and stabling for 7 horses; 1797 – Mrs Gilbert – 4 parlours, 5 chambers, 4 garrets, 2 coach houses and stabling for 9. In 1811 and 1817 I can find no corresponding house in Sprange. The Poor Rate sequence which links least inadequately with this limited evidence runs as follows:

1709-1710	William Fry
1711-1714	William Fry for a new house
1728-1736	William Fry for a new house
1737-1756	Wid Fry for a New house
1757	Wid Frye for a house
1758-1794	Wm Fry for a House
1795	Fry Wm or occ for a house
1796-1797	Gilbert John for late Willm Frys

The problem is to tie this sequence with certainty to the proposed location. The Widow Fry in 1738 certainly ties in with the house above the Bowling Green on Bowra's plan; and the Barrow map's 'Mrs Canning' can with some confidence (taking the number of rooms among other things into consideration) be linked with a Sprange sequence leading back to the names Gilbert and Fry. True, Richard Fry should be William, and John Gilbert is not the same as Mrs Gilbert; but the male being given precedence over the female is not unheard of, even today, and we do know that Richard and William Fry were brothers. This information comes from the will of William Fry, dated 1728 and proved the following year. Unfortunately, he did not specify the house and land which he left to his wife for her life, with instructions to look after their two younger sons, Nicholas and John. There were two elder sons, William and Richard, and all four were to share the property eventually. Now Richard was almost certainly the butcher who lived at Bricklands (see chapter 18) and whose daughter married Joseph Delves. The evidence is indirect but the argument is persuasive. On 28 November 1699 William 'Frey' married Mary Seale at Tonbridge. Philip Seale, the glazier of Little Mount Sion, had a daughter Mary who died a spinster in 1763 and left small legacies to her 'cousin Richard Fry of Tonbridge butcher', to his daughter Mary who was her god-daughter and to William Fry, son of her 'cousin William Fry of Tonbridge bricklayer'. 'Tonbridge', of course, refers to the parish and includes Tunbridge Wells. Richard Fry of Bricklands did have a daughter Mary and William the son was named as a bricklayer in the mortgage deed which will be considered in a minute. All the relationships mentioned in this will can be explained on the assumption that the bridegroom of 1699 was William Fry of Sion Lodge and his bride was Philip Seale's sister. As further corroboration Philip Seale and his wife witnessed the will of 1728. The date of William Fry's death does not correspond as neatly as might be hoped with the change to 'Widow Fry' in the Poor Rate sequence (1737) but it does tie in with Bowra (1738) and, moreover, the fact that the two elder sons were William and Richard might explain why the Poor Rate record gives one name and Sprange the other.

The Widow Fry, with or without the help of her bricklaying eldest son, seems, on the evidence of the Poor Rate, to have run the lodging house until 1757 when her son took over. He died some time before 1782 and his widow, another Mary, carried on the business with the help of their son, another William. All this appears from a mortgage deed of 1782, whereby 'Mary Fry of Tonbridge widow and relict of William Fry of Tonbridge Bricklayer deceased' and 'William Fry of Speldhurst Taylor and Salesman only son and heir of the said William Fry' borrowed £200 from John Start of Tonbridge victualler. The loan was secured on 'All that messuage or tenement or lodging house with the coach houses stables buildings Yards Backsides Gardens and Orchards … on Mount Sion late in the tenure and occupation of the said William Fry deceased and now of the said Mary Fry and William Fry'. The money was repaid by 1786 but nine years later the house was up for auction. A rare insight into contemporary proceedings is afforded by the three sale posters which form part of the Tunbridge Wells Museum's collection of Sprange's printing work. In charge of all three sales was 'E. Strange' who was probably Edward Strange of the Green Pales doing a little

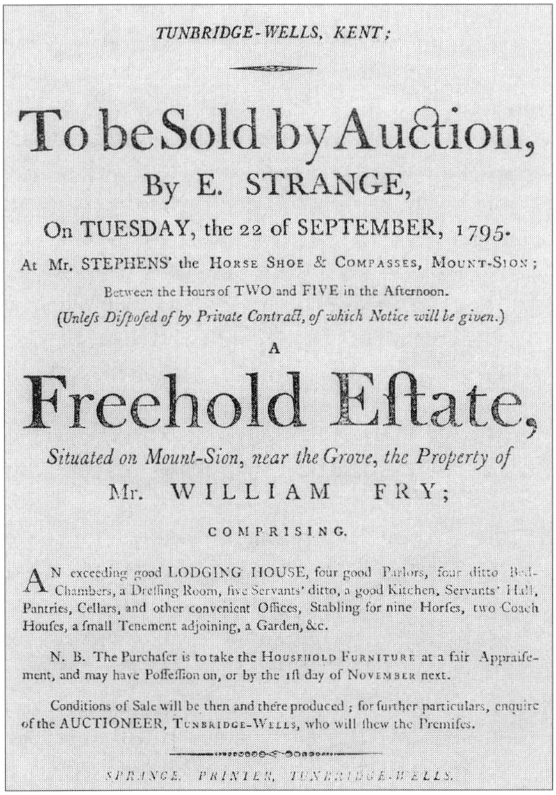

TUNBRIDGE-WELLS, KENT;

To be Sold by Auction,

By E. STRANGE,

On TUESDAY, the 22 of SEPTEMBER, 1795.

At Mr. STEPHENS' the HORSE SHOE & COMPASSES, MOUNT-SION;

Between the Hours of TWO and FIVE in the Afternoon.

(Unleſs Diſpoſed of by Private Contract, of which Notice will be given.)

A

Freehold Eſtate,

Situated on Mount-Sion, near the Grove, the Property of

Mr. WILLIAM FRY;

COMPRISING.

AN exceeding good LODGING HOUSE, four good Parlors, four ditto Bed-Chambers, a Dreſſing Room, five Servants' ditto, a good Kitchen, Servants' Hall, Pantries, Cellars, and other convenient Offices, Stabling for nine Horſes, two Coach Houſes, a ſmall Tenement adjoining, a Garden, &c.

N. B. The Purchaſer is to take the HOUSEHOLD FURNITURE at a fair Appraiſement, and may have Poſſeſſion on, or by the 1ſt day of NOVEMBER next.

Conditions of Sale will be then and there produced; for further particulars, enquire of the AUCTIONEER, TUNBRIDGE-WELLS, who will ſhew the Premiſes.

SPRANGE, PRINTER, TUNBRIDGE-WELLS.

auctioneering on the side – no other member of the Strange family seems to fit the bill. The first two sales were held at the *Compasses* (landlord Mr Stephens). On Wednesday 11 March it was the lease which was on offer 'eight years unexpired Lady-day next' and the house was described as situated on Mount Sion Hill and in the occupation of Mrs Powell and J. Reynolds who were presumably sub-tenants to an unnamed lessee. William Fry was certainly the owner since a second poster (reproduced above) announces the sale on 22 September of 'A Freehold Estate, situated on Mount Sion, near the Grove, the Property of Mr William Fry'. How the Fry family obtained the freehold I do not know: their name does not appear in the list of original leases of Lady Purbeck and if the house had been one of those acquired by John Brett Bowra would have marked it so and it would have been mentioned in one of the Ward Papers – as was the case with the houses round the Bowling Green considered in recent chapters. The description of the estate on the poster corresponds convincingly with that given in the *Sprange Guide*, the only discrepancy being that the *Guide* lists five chambers and four garrets as against four good bedchambers and five servants' chambers in the sale description. It is surprising, however, that no mention is made of the field below the house (unless 'a garden etc' embraces the field) since the field was quite large, about three acres, and it shows clearly on the Barrow map of 1808 as if belonging to the house, which in any case it did by the time of the Tithe map in 1840. At all events the field is important to this story because, a hundred years after the auction of 1795, it was to provide the major part of the land for the Madeira Park development. What happened at the two auctions is a matter for speculation; but the successful bidder in September evidently rejected the Household Furniture, even at 'a fair appraisement', and a third sale was held, this time on the premises, on Guy Fawkes Day 1795 and the following day, beginning at Eleven o'clock. The household goods and other effects consisted of: 'Nine Goose and other Feather beds, Four-post and other Bedsteads and Furniture, Mahogany Chairs, Tables, Chest of Drawers, Pier and Swing Glasses, Carpets, Bath and Pantheon Stoves, Festoon and other Window Curtains, an exceeding good Eight-day Clock, Linen, Pewter, Kitchen Range, Smoke-jack, Copper Boilers, Stew and Saucepans, Brewing Copper etc with every kind of useful Kitchen Furniture'. The whole was to be sold 'without reserve, as the estate being sold, the premises must be immediately cleared'. This list can with interest be compared with Anne Ashdowne's inventory at the very beginning of the 18th century – see chapter 16 page 212.

Mrs Gilbert can perhaps be assumed to be John Gilbert's widow and more speculatively still she may have been the Mary Gilbert whose sister Sarah married the Rev. Joseph Langley and who seems to have inherited Brunswick House, as we saw in the previous chapter. The Poor Rate record suggests that it was John Gilbert who purchased the house but it is not impossible that he and Mrs Gilbert and then Mrs Canning were tenants to some other purchaser; and there is some evidence that the house remained in the Fry family. In the first place a sharp-witted reader may have remembered that the site of Marlborough House (see chapter 20 page

294) was described in the conveyance of 1801 as bounded on the east by the 160-foot fence of Mr John Fry. This almost certainly refers to the boundary with Sion Lodge, although of course the direction is more north-east than north; but Cumberland House is said to be to the north and it follows that Sion Lodge must be to the east. Another piece of evidence is to be found in a mortgage deed of 1822 amongst the Ward Papers. John Fry of Tunbridge Wells in the parish of Speldhurst, gentleman, has borrowed £500 on the security of 'All that messuage tenement or lodging house with the Coach Houses Stables Buildings Yards Backsides Garden and Orchard ... on Mount Sion Hill ... formerly in the ... occupation ... of William Fry since of John Gilbert but then and for some time past unoccupied'. A comparison of this description with that in the mortgage deed of 1782 already mentioned (see page 322 above) shows how the phraseology persists unchanged. In the 1822 deed the three-acre field is included. It is difficult to disentangle one Fry from another but I think the John Fry of 1822 must be the one who had become the Rev. John Fry when he took belated administration of his father's will in February 1823. His father was the John Fry, landlord to Richard Cumberland and some time master of the *Sussex Tavern*. The 1822 deed contains a reference to a conveyance of 1799 or 1800 by which William Fry sold his house to his cousin John but to which the widow and daughter of John's eldest brother George were also parties. In his will of 1801 John the father left his 'two messuages on Mount Sion (late the Widow Fry's)' to his sons John and Henry on trust to apply the income for the benefit of his wife, his son George and his seven daughters. One of these houses is surely Sion Lodge but the second one is a puzzle. John Fry left in all four freehold houses – the house occupied by Richard Cumberland, 'Lord North's House' and the two which were late the Widow Fry's – and a half share in the Great Grove House. The only possibility for the puzzling second messuage seems to be Bowling Green House. In chapter 19 (page 275) I speculated that Mrs Wogan had bought the house but noted the conflicting evidence of the Poor Rate record in which John Fry re-appears 'for late Elizabeth Wogans' from 1791 to 1797. At any rate, as far as Sion Lodge is concerned, the *Maidstone Journal* provides incontrovertible evidence of the situation in 1805. Until then it had been the residence of Captain Charles Cumberland, Richard's cricketing son, but I cannot be sure how long he had lived there. He is listed as a visitor to the Wells as early as 1786 when his father took Cumberland House and in August 1787 the newspaper reported his victory in the Horse Races on the Common. 'Lord Sackville's chestnut mare, rode by Capt Cumberland, beat Capt Cookson's chestnut horse, rode by Lord Sackville, one mile, for 25 guineas'. He married in 1799 and perhaps it was then that he started his own establishment. In March 1805 however the auction of all the elegant furniture at the house of Charles Cumberland Esq. 'removing to town' was advertised; and in July the auction of the house itself was announced, by order of the trustees under the will of the late John Fry deceased. 'The above house was lately the residence of Charles Cumberland Esq. and now of Mrs Stratford Canning, and subject to a lease of

which four years will be unexpired on 1st November next' – remember that Mrs Canning was firmly located at Sion Lodge on the Barrow map. It seems that Mrs Canning stayed until the end of the lease but the mortgage deed of 1822 suggests that once again the auction was unsuccessful and John junior and Henry Fry were formally the owners at least until 1822. Sprange's silence in 1811 and 1817 and the reference to lack of occupants in the 1822 deed all suggest that the house stood unoccupied for twenty years. About 1830 the house seems to have come into the ownership of Thomas Pinckard Bingham, whom we met in chapter 16 (page 216) as a trustee to General Murray's will. Indeed since the will was dated 1811 I wonder whether Bingham may not have been living in the house from that date until he died, which was evidently about 1830, because the Poor Rate record shows Aretas Akers whom we shall meet in the next chapter as ratepayer for 'house late Bingham's' in 1831 and in 1834, to the tune of £57, for 'Sion Lodge, House, Buildings, Garden & Land'. The letter books of Akers (to be considered in the next chapter) confirm that he bought the house from the executors of Thomas P. Bingham. Then the Tithe Award shows that in 1840 it was the home of Captain Green, about whom I have no information, but was owned by the equally unknown Miss Catharine Groves. The 1841 census does not show the house or its inhabitants in any recognisable form although one uninhabited house near Marlborugh Villa is shown which may or may not be Sion Lodge. Similarly in 1851 there is no sign of Captain Green or Miss Groves but one uninhabited house is recorded between Marlborough House and Knocklofty Cottage which is where Sion Lodge would have been on the route which the enumerator seemed to be taking up the right-hand side of Mount Sion and on to Claremont Road.

On the north-west side of Sion Lodge was the lane which is now a cul-de-sac called Clifton Place – see detail from the Tithe map on the next page. It used to lead about a quarter of a mile downhill to premises known as Knocklofty – once called 'Not Lofty' by the enumerator! The name seems to be of Irish origin but otherwise is a mystery. It survives as the name of a house near the tennis club in Upper Cumberland Walk which is no accident. In 1873 the lane was described in the Sale Particulars for Burlington House and the Fellmonger Estate as 'the road leading to Knocklofty farm' but in the 1851 census Knocklofty Cottage was the only mention of the name and in 1841 'Knocklofty' appears on its own. The Tithe Award refers to 'Knocklofty House and Yard' owned by Mary Ann Hodgson and occupied by Peter Hutchingson. Now in the 1841 census Peter Hutchinson is shown, living at 'Knocklofty' and described as a 55-year-old sweep. Living with him were Ann Bishop, a woman of the same age as him and three boys, John Nash, aged 14, and the brothers Ephraim and William Taylor, aged eight and nine, all three described as Sweep Apprentices. The boys' ages and a reading of Kathleen Strange's *The Climbing Boys* leave little room for doubt that this is what they were. Let us hope that Peter was one of the better masters. Ten years later he was still a chimney sweep but seemed to be living on his own in 'Sweep's Lane' (Clifton Place?) along with two other householders, one a farrier and the other a journeyman upholsterer;

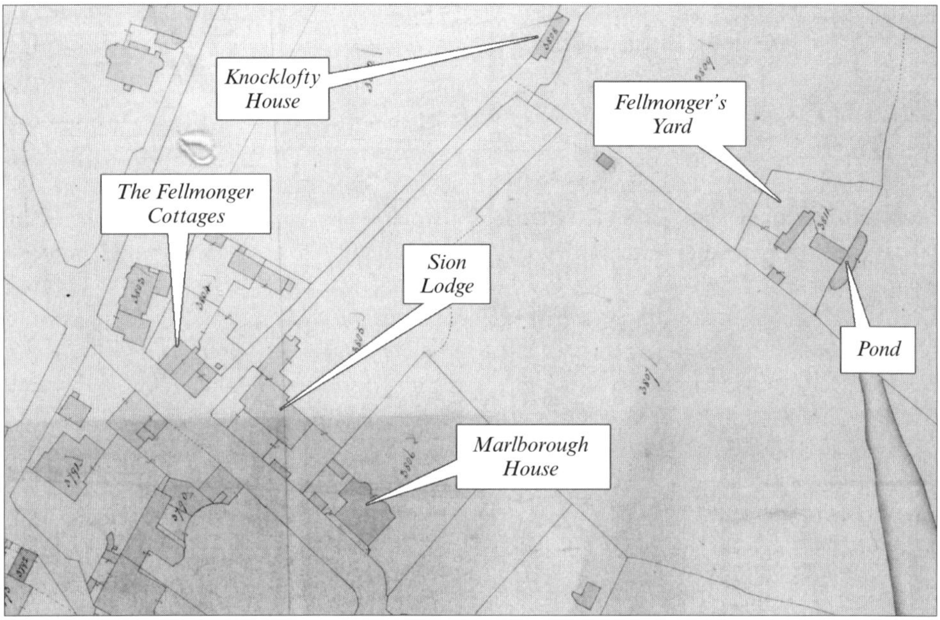

Tithe map 1840

while 'Knocklofty Cottage' was occupied by Mary Tracy, a railway watchman's wife of Irish birth.

If in 1840 you walked down the lane to Knocklofty House and then turned right, a further quarter of a mile or so would bring you to a group of buildings used by Henry Peerless. He was a fellmonger and these were no doubt the premises originally created by Nicholas Wood for his trade (see page 141) and which, together with the fields on either side, were still in the family ownership, by this time in the person of Mary Ann Hodgson by virtue of the will of Ann Friend in 1831, bequeathing 'all that fellmongers yard and the several pieces or parcels of land thereunto adjoining and belonging situate near Mount Sion as the same are now in the occupation of Henry Peerless ...' Immediately below the southernmost building was a large pond, one of a number of stretches of water which seem, on the evidence of the Tithe map, to have formed a marshy tributary to the stream which ran down to the Pantiles and which 'divided the counties of Kent and Sussex'. One of them formed the 'ornamental water' which embellished the bottom of Joseph Delves' paddock – see chapter 21 page 306. Now, according to an 18th-century definition 'fellmongers are those who buy skins of all sorts, with the wool on, from the country people, which they take off, and sell the skins dressed to the glovers etc and the wool to the woolstaplers'. The first process in removing the wool was to soak the skins in a solution of water and lime and this is where the Knocklofty pond came in. Another reason why the site was chosen was perhaps the smell. The lime water was used for months without renewal and smelled foul, so the further away from houses the better. After a while the bacteria in the solution begin to eat the roots of the wool which becomes easy to remove – a process carried out on a special curved bench with an 'unhairing knife'. Then, of course, the depilated skins and the wool had to be dried; and I have speculated rather wildly that a tiny tall building in Clifton Place, sometimes called the smallest house in the town, was a drying shed – as also was the weatherboard building with a lantern roof in Frog Lane to which reference was made in chapter 16 page 208. As already noted on page 141, fellmongers still operate and under the same name. There is a Company of Fellmongers in Richmond, Yorkshire, and a United Kingdom Fellmongers Association in Bradford and there are a dozen or so companies working in the UK. They take the skins, particularly those of sheep and lambs, remove the wool and sell the wool to wool-processors and the skins to tanners.

The fellmongering premises must have stood within the circle of present-day Madeira Park and Knocklofty House perhaps in the back garden of no 10. In 1851 the 'Fellmonger's Yard' was occupied by James Hook, a 40-year-old Fellmonger's Journeyman; but by this time the business must have been in decline. Dramatic changes had already occurred to the landscape and more was to come: the railway had arrived. There were two phases. Around 1845 the skimped tunnel was driven under the Grove and by 1852 the line had been pushed through to Hastings; but it was the later link, in the 1860s, between the rival stations of the South Eastern Railway and the London, Brighton and South Coast Railway that definitely disturbed the bucolic backwaters of nether Mount Sion. Connecting with the Hastings line near Knocklofty House (already a railway watchman's abode in 1851), the line curved below the Fellmonger's Yard (for which the South East Railway was paying rates in 1852) and disappeared into another tunnel under the Frant Road. The cacophony and confusion of construction scarcely bear contemplation. Perhaps it was all too much for Captain Green, sitting up in Sion Lodge surveying the mayhem at the foot of his meadow, and by 1851 he had gone. By 1860, however, the Misses Dawkins had moved in, as tenants of Miss Groves whose name appears, as owner of the adjoining field, on the plan annexed to the Delves auction notice of 1874. Perhaps the advent of the Dawkins can be dated a little earlier since the minutes of the Murray House Girls' School Committee record that one of these spinster sisters 'had been added to the Committee in 1856'; and in January 1873 the school had sustained a great loss in her death. She had 'laboured heartily' for 17 years and she 'gave the clock in the school'. The other Miss Dawkins then lived for a while in Sion Lodge with her former neighbour, the widow of James Deane JP who had occupied Cumberland House (see chapter 19 page 276). The name 'Sion Lodge' seems to date from the Dawkins period, appearing first in the 1860 Residents' List and then in the 1861 census which provides some information on the sisters. Juliana H. Dawkins was then 68 and Augusta A. was three years younger. The elder had been born in Wiltshire and the younger in Oxfordshire. Both were described as 'Fundholders'. Living with them in 1861 were Mary, a 17-year-old niece born in Corfu, and four servants. *Kelly's Directory* for 1878 does not show Sion Lodge but in 1882 the occupier is given as

Robert William Weekes. The founder of the department store, Robert Wilsher Weekes, had five sons of whom Robert William was the second and had confusingly the same initials as his father. The evidence from directories, Kelly and Pelton, becomes difficult to interpret at this point because of rapid changes in the numbering of houses. In 1886 Robert William was at Sion Lodge, no 18 Mount Sion; in 1892 he was at no.20; from 1893 to 1900 Thomas Weekes was at no.22 and in 1901 he was at no.34. 34 is the present-day number of the first of the three 'fellmonger' cottages beyond Clifton Place which however was numbered 26 in 1873; and who Thomas Weekes was I do not know. However some reliable evidence comes to the rescue here in the form of plans and drawings of the builder Louis Beale, deposited with the Centre for Kentish Studies.

Louis Beale was the builder who was responsible for most of the earlier houses in Madeira Park and whose sturdy workmanship has been admired ever since. The Archives collection, rescued not long ago from Beale's office by Mr Julian Fall, late of Goulden and Curry, contains some very handsome drawings of Madeira Park houses; but what is of interest in the present connection is a drawing of a new porch which Beale prepared for Ernest B. Weekes as owner of Sion Lodge in February 1893. 'EB' Weekes was the eldest of the five sons but why Kelly should list Robert William at Sion Lodge while 'EB' was planning a new porch is difficult to explain unless the younger brother was tenant to the older. Perhaps – speculation again – it was over a discussion of the alterations to Sion Lodge in 1893 that builder and owner hit upon the idea of developing the hinterland. In the bundle of drawings for the new porch is a rough plan of the Sion Lodge land with a precise note of its area: 6 acres, 3 roods and 36 perches. Such an area implies that the field long attached to Sion Lodge had been extended, and perhaps with deliberate intent, to include the Fellmonger's Yard and its adjoining fields all of which had belonged to Mary Ann Hodgson. Her will directed all her real estate should be sold but the 1873 Sale Particulars do not mention the fields which may therefore have been sold earlier. Be that as it may, all the land required for the development seems to have come into one ownership by 1893; and amongst the Beale papers is a 'Plan of Sion Lodge Estate' which shows the house and land behind with a road lay-out pencilled over it. Attached to this plan with a paper clip is a typed note which suggests that the plan had at some time formed part of an exhibition – perhaps in the late 1940s. There were originally three plans, numbered 1382 A, B and C; but only A has survived. The subsequent story can be told in the words of the typed note:

> MADEIRA PARK. This group shows some of the pre-history of this compact development. 1382A which must date from soon after 1890 shows the area as the garden, kitchen garden and fields attached to SION LODGE, on Mount Sion. A preliminary road lay-out is sketched over it. 1382B shows another road lay-out and plots fairly carefully planned, with a drainage lay-out. At this time it appears that Sion Lodge was going to be kept, with only part of the ground beside the house used to provide access. 1382C shows a further revision, nearer to the road as it exists today, and this plan was approved by Tunbridge

> Wells Works Committee in September 1897 … Although building began before 1900, it continued over the next 40 years, always of very well-built houses, in the style of the day … The high quality of these houses, and of those further out built by the same firm, helped to make the south-western quadrant of the town a particularly pleasant place to live, as it continues to be. The major snag of the older part of the road is the lack of car-parking space at each house.

In connection with the last sentence – which can bear repetition! – I cannot resist giving a pat on the back to the owners of no.41 who have managed to build a garage under their front garden and surround it with original stone work in a style of which Louis Beale himself might have been proud.

The quotation above suggests that building started after 1897 but *Kelly's Directory* of 1895-6 lists one house in Madeira Park. In 1896-7 there were four and by '98-9 thirteen including Louis Beale himself and his estate office at no.6 and Richard Pelton JP at no.5. The original plan for Madeira Park envisaged a circular road with entry and exit only from Mount Sion. The reason was that it was bounded on the north and west by existing houses, on the east by the railway line and to the south by the lands of Lord Abergavenny who had his own ideas for the development of his Warwick Park estate. At what stage the Marquess's Rodmell Road condescended to link with Madeira Park I do not know; but if you have ever wondered why Madeira Park suddenly becomes Rodmell Road before the junction with Warwick Park Road this is the reason. To cross the divide is to pass from the ancient estates of the Abergavennies into the Forest of South Frith, erstwhile domain of the lords of Summerhill. The Marquess, by the way, named his roads – Rodmell, Blatchington, Roedean – after parts of his Sussex estates; what Madeira Park was named after is a mystery. 'EB' Weekes was reputed to be a fan of ocean cruising and possibly, just possibly, it was a cruise to Madeira that inspired the choice of name.

Early view of Madeira Park printed from a David Johnson glass negative. Note the 'Madeira Park' signboard.

It is a pity that David Johnson did not take a photograph of Sion Lodge before it was demolished since he was around Mount Sion at the time; but on the previous page is one of the block with the corner tower and spire which took its place. Printed from a glass negative, it must date from early in the century. Just beyond the block is Clifton Place and in front is the road through the site of Sion Lodge which gives access to Madeira Park. So far as I know there is no surviving image of Sion Lodge, if there ever was one. Pity! But before moving on to Grove Lodge this is a convenient point to consider the 'Fellmonger Cottages' – and appropriate in view of the discussion on fellmongering above. Here they are,

The Fellmonger Cottages

numbered 34 to 38 Mount Sion, with recent unsightly scaffolding over Grove Lodge next door. There is no evidence of a precise date for their construction but, since they are not on the Bowra plan or map and they are on Barrow, a guess at mid-18th century seems reasonable. In view of their ownership by the Wood family and their location near the Fellmonger's Yard I have no doubt they were erected for workers at the yard – but I could be wrong. Just out of shot on the right but with its roof showing is the 'smallest house'.

The only documentary evidence concerning these cottages comes in the will of Ann Friend of 1831 and the Sale Particulars of 1873 when all the old Wood family properties were sold on the death of Ann Friend's daughter Mary Ann Hodgson. Ann Friend left to her daughter 'all that fellmongers yard and … several pieces … of land thereunto adjoining … situate near Mount Sion as the same are now in the occupation of [Henry] Peerless and all those my cottages and barns …

near the fellmongers yard'. The cottages were Lot 4 in the 1873 sale and were described as '3 Capital Brick, Timber and Tiled Cottages known as Nos 26, 28 and 30 Mount Sion Road with large productive gardens and a well of capital spring water. Nos 26 and 28 each contain Two Bedrooms, Sitting Room, Pantry, Wash-house and Coal Cellar with WC adjoining, and are in the occupation of Mr J Keansley and Mrs Johnson at rentals of 4s 6d per week each. No 30 contains Two Bedrooms, Sitting Room, Mangling Room, Wash-house, Pantry, Coal Cellar and WC and is let to Mrs Simmons at 5s per week. [This lot has a frontage to Mount Sion Road of 62 ft and a frontage to the road leading to Knocklofty Farm of 67 ft 9 in].' There were at the time two more cottages to the rear which can be seen on the Tithe map above but have since disappeared. Notice incidentally that there is no mention of anything fitting the description of the 'Little House'. The house or houses adjoining the end of the Fellmonger Cottage terrace, as noted above in connection with the scaffolding in the photograph, was Grove Lodge which together with Belle Vue House will be the subject of the next chapter.

Chapter 23

Potter's Ghost

Barrow map 1808

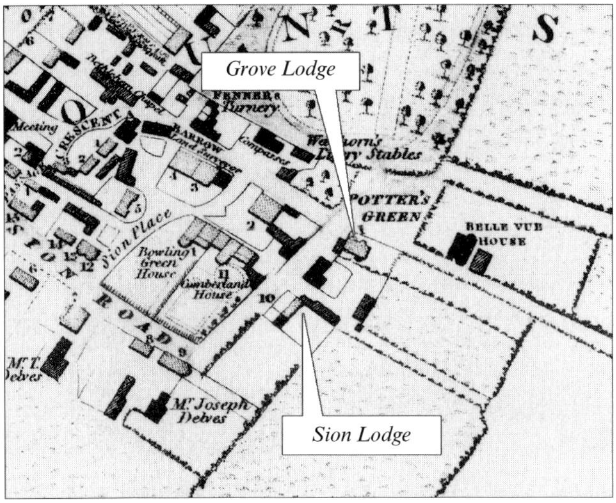

The detail below, from Barrow's map of 1808, shows the area of interest in this chapter. Grove Lodge, Belle Vue House and Potter's Green. This is as far as my definition of Mount Sion will permit in this direction and indeed is pushing fuzziness a bit far. The house labelled '1' on the map is Grove Lodge, since called Percy House, and marked by Barrow 'Potter's Green Mount Sion – Mr T Delves'. Belle Vue House is shaded to show that it is not a lodging house and no owner is therefore given. No.10 is marked 'Mrs Canning' and is, of course, Sion Lodge, the subject of the previous chapter, and the Fellmonger Cottages are shown between it and Grove Lodge. The area is beyond the boundary of Bowra's plan of Mount Sion Hill but his general map shows the owner of Grove Lodge as Edm Wood and of Belle Vue House as Mr Brett. The Partition plan of 1686 falls short of this area and the vague verbal descriptions of bounds and borders contained in the Chancery papers have not helped me to discover the original lessees of the land. It might be supposed that Martin's strip continued across the road since the Wood family seems to have ended up with property there; but I do not think so. For one thing the dimensions of Martin's strip are known and its 40 rods takes it as far as but not beyond the road. For another, I am sure the plots were planned with the roads in mind and would not therefore have ploughed across a projected road. The fact that Bowra labels the house 'Edmund Wood' means that it is difficult to disentangle from other Wood properties in the Poor Rate record. However there is evidence concerning the 18th-century history of Grove Lodge which was set out in some detail on pages 90-2 of chapter 9 in connection with Martin's Upper House and Edmund Wood. I suggested that Grove Lodge was built by Edmund Wood after the death of his father but (obviously because it is on the Bowra plan) before 1738. It is referred to in a deed of 1742 as 'newly erected'; but of course this could point back quite a few years. Grove Lodge is called in the deed 'The Little Grove House', otherwise Doyle's Upper House, otherwise Goldstone's Bow Window House and is said to have been occupied by Edmund Wood, then Richard Waghorne, then Sarah Fenner and 'now' Andrew Fenner. Sarah Fenner was the granddaughter of Nicholas Wood and Andrew was her son. The Fenner connection with Tonbridge Ware and the *Blue Anchor* building across the road from Grove Lodge was noted in chapter 12 and there is more on the house in chapter 9; but the main point is that in 1806 it was bought by Thomas Delves and remained his until he died in 1846.

The later history of Grove Lodge is somewhat simpler than the earlier. Why Thomas Delves bought the house in the first place is unclear; but it happened two years after his father's death and he may have had money to invest. He continued to live at Eden Cottage and no doubt let out Grove Lodge either to families or to a tenant to run as a lodging house. The Tithe Award shows 'Grove Lodge, 2 Houses and Yard' owned and occupied by Thomas Delves and in the 1841 census it is occupied by one of the *Belle Vue Magazine*'s 'contiguous' families whom we shall meet in a moment. John Daniel described himself as 60 years old and a man of independent means; and the family consisted of his wife Mary, aged 50, and four children with ages ranging from 20 to 30. The 1844 railway reference book (see later) lists the house as unoccupied. In 1846 Thomas Delves died. His will does not refer to Grove Lodge as a specific item of real estate but it does provide, as mentioned in chapter 21 pp.306-7, for the sale of all his 'household goods fixtures furniture and other effects which shall be in or about the lodging house situate in Tunbridge Wells aforesaid called Grove Lodge' to his son-in-law Edward Butler and daughter Sarah, within one month, at £150, if they so wished. Whether they took up this, presumably favourable, offer and when the house was sold I have no evidence; but *Bagshaw's Directory* of 1847 lists Mrs Beale at Grove Lodge lodging house and the 1851 census gives more detail. The head of the household was Joseph, aged 50, a master carpenter employing ten men and born in Frant. His wife Mary, aged 41 and from Norfolk, was evidently running the lodging house and had at the time of the census one guest, Harriet Bedford, a 70-year-old house-owning spinster who did not know or would not say where she was born. Joseph and Mary had a son aged three, Henry, born in Tunbridge Wells when his mother was 38. Ten years later Joseph the carpenter was dead but his widow was still

Grove Lodge seen from the Grove across Potters Green

employing three carpenters and looking after three lodgers and her only child. By 1871 Henry had flown the nest but his mother was soldiering on, with the help of an 18-year-old servant girl, looking after four boarders. In 1877 another family of carpenters was in occupation, William Hobbs and Son. On 25 August that year William Hobbs, as owner of Grove Lodge, applied for permission to erect a lean-to shed to shelter timber in his yard – about where the office building is now between Nos 44 and 46. The accompanying plan shows what is now No.44 (Percy House) as 'Grove Lodge' and the extension which is now Grove Lodge seen from the Grove across 'Potter's Green' No.42 is labelled 'Old Shop'. To the rear is shown the cottage which still exists, with the crooked chimney, and behind that another shop. Who ran the shops and what they sold is a mystery; but it is clear that the western extension of Grove Lodge pre-dates 1877, although the present bay windows are not shown on the plan. The land to the east is labelled 'Mr Bright' who is listed in the 1882 and 1886 directories at Jerningham Villa (Mr Tracy's house) followed by 'Miss Bright' in 1889; and to the south are 'Mr Clifford's Wall' and the property of Mr Clifford. The transitions in house numbers and names can be clearly seen in the directories. The present 42 and 44 used to be 30 and 32 from 1886 to 1900. In 1898 Hobbs Builders were at no.30 and at no.32 were W.R. Hobbs (Grove Lodge) and Miss Gunnell (Percy House). In 1901 Hobbs Builders were at no 42 (Grove Lodge) and Miss Gunnell was at no.44 (Percy House). In 1902 'W. Hobbs' (Clifton House)' came on the scene, filling in the gap alongside the Fellmonger Cottages; and there were no more changes until 1932.

Belle Vue House, which used to stand away to the left, out of shot, in the above photograph is another of those houses to which it is difficult to assign a Poor Rate sequence. *Pigot's Directory* for 1827 lists John Lloyd Esq of Belle Vue among the Nobility, Gentry and Clergy of the town (we have met him in chapter 16 as co-trustee with Thomas Pinckard Bingham of the Murray House Girls' School) but his death on 13 August 1826 was reported in the press and an auction of the contents was to be held on the premises on 14 March 1827 and the following days. In 1827 Pigot shows Mrs Akers at Burlington House and it was perhaps the propinquity of the house which decided her son to take advantage of the vacancy at Belle Vue House. Pigot places him there in 1832 but he must already have been living elsewhere in the town since his daughter (see below) was baptised at King Charles in 1822. The name Aretas Akers obviously goes with a certain staccato swing and was enjoyed by the first-born son through at least five generations. The surname is not uncommon but 'Aretas' does not even find a place in Chambers' list of common first names. The *Oxford Dictionary of English Christian Names* does have it but the entry reads like a history of the Akers family as if no one else ever used the name. It originates as the name of a series of kings of the Nabataeans, one of whom is mentioned in the Bible. 'The daughter of Aretas Seton, Governor of the Leeward islands, married at the beginning of the 18th century Edmund Akers, ancestor of the present Lord Chilston, and from that time the name has been in regular use in the Akers (now Akers-Douglas) family.' To the general historian Aretas Akers of Mount Sion is of interest for his maternal grandfather, the Rev. James Ramsey, who was a pioneer in the anti-slavery movement; and for his grandson, another Aretas, who served in Balfour's cabinet as Home Secretary from 1902 to 1905 and in 1911 became the first Lord Chilston. Chilston Park, near Maidstone, was the seat of his wife's family of Douglas. To the local historian, however, the Mount Sion Aretas is of outstanding interest not so much for what he did but for the fact that his letter book and family magazine have survived and provide a rare insight into the daily life of the period. A letter book was the forerunner of yesterday's file of carbon copies. Having written a letter, the author (or clerk in a business) would make a copy in the letter book whose pages could be numbered and an alphabetical index made for easy reference. Aretas Akers did not go as far as this. Important letters he copied carefully and comprehensively but routine or trivial ones he summarised in a sometimes hurried hand. Letter books must have been widely used but a family magazine was a far less common phenomenon. This one had an obvious function in the education of the young Akers family and no doubt it pandered to some literary pretensions on its editor's part; but it flourished also because its circle of contributors and readers included three neighbouring families. As the editor said in the final number (the magazine lasted from 1840 to 1843), 'We knew and well appreciated the rare advantage we possessed at our outset in the close neighbourhood and intimate union of four families under almost contiguous roofs'. The other families were the Daniels, literally neighbours at Grove Lodge; the Offleys at Forest Prospect; and the Blencowes across the Grove at Middle Grove House. It is noticeable that, although the Offleys and Daniels rented their houses from Joseph and Thomas Delves respectively, there is no hint of any social intercourse with the Delves' family. The few letters and references are restricted to business matters.

Aretas Akers

Aretas married in 1821 and his first child, Isabella Dorothea, was baptised at King Charles the Martyr on 25 February 1822. The minister who performed the christening was a relative on the mother's side, the Rev. Lambert Larking, vicar of Ryarsh and founder secretary of the Kent Archaeological Society, who also wrote several articles for the *Belle Vue Magazine*. Aretas must have been living somewhere in the town in 1822 but I have no evidence where. During the next twenty years and more he raised a family and occupied himself with local affairs, with the duties of a magistrate and with administering his own financial and family affairs. In 1833 he moved an amendment at a public meeting held in the *Sussex* hotel to discuss the lighting of Tunbridge Wells by gas. In 1834 he was a member of a deputation presenting a loyal address to the Duchess of Kent and Princess Victoria. In a letter dated 26 November 1844 he asked to be relieved from the job of superintending the Grove which he had done on behalf of the Trustees 'for a few years past'. Other jobs were: trustee of the Victoria School; Guardian of the Tonbridge Poor Law Union; member of the board of the Medway Company; and Chairman, Treasurer and Collector for the Tunbridge Wells Conservative Registration Committee. He was educated at Christ Church, Oxford, took a commission in the 18th Hussars, served in the Army of Occupation in France and retired to practise at the Bar 'but an attack of brain fever compelled him to retire to the country. So he came to Tunbridge Wells where his widowed mother lived.' Despite a seemingly agreeable life-style in near-idyllic surroundings, however, the letter book is full of the search for a new home, anywhere in the region it seems, rather than Tunbridge Wells. Perhaps the reason lay in his mother's death, at Burlington House, in 1842. No doubt the house was cramped with so large a family and the condition of the building clearly left something to be desired. Towards the end, despairing of finding a suitable alternative, he engaged Decimus Burton to prepare a scheme of extensions and renovations for Belle Vue and a letter written to the architect on 20 March 1844 goes some way to explain his dislike of the house. 'Besides the additional best bedrooms proposed to be added I shd require 2 more servants' rooms. The present pantry is v damp & requires a fire even in Summer to keep things from rust and mildew, the walls quite running down w moisture. It is likewise not at all conveniently fitted up, requiring water to be laid on & a sink besides conveniences for keeping glass etc etc. The larder too is so damp that nothing can be kept there without contracting mould in a day or two. It shd also be separate from the dairy & the scullery apart from both & nearer the kitchen, much inconvenience arising from the steam reek & bad smell from the latter.'

No inkling is to be found in the letter book of what the family thought about moving house. Aretas does not refer once in the letter book to his wife. In the *Belle Vue Magazine*, however, there is a story whose opening paragraphs reveal that one at least of the children had quite other emotions. Contributors to the magazine protected their anonymity by initials, the secret of which was revealed in the last number of the magazine. Two stories, Patty Moon and Potter's Ghost, were the work of 'MAB' who turned out to be 'Miss Akers' – the eldest daughter whose christening in 1822 has already been mentioned, making her 18 years old when she wrote 'Potter's Ghost'. She starts by inviting her gentle reader to think of a favourite spot on the globe. She has such a spot in mind. 'In my heart of hearts, among the richest treasures of my memory do I look for it. It is the fairest, pleasantest, healthiest and dearest, that the two counties of Kent and Sussex can boast of, and they contend for it accordingly.' The description which follows may seem a little fulsome but is in fact well identifiable and quite accurate. 'Near the summit of a gentle slope (the top of Mount Sion) sheltered on the north-west by a magnificent grove of oaks and beech, that have outlived six or seven of the frail generations of men (the Grove) is a house (Belle Vue) of very moderate size and pretensions surrounded, with its lawns and flower beds, by a shrubbery where the nightingale loved to pour forth its song, and the thrush and blackbird delighted to haunt. To the south that mixed kind of wild and domestic scenery (the paternal pastures now buried beneath the houses of Banner Farm and Madeira Park and sliced by the railway) which forms the beauty of the Weald of Sussex, spread out in wide and distant perspective (the stream dividing Kent from Sussex and the forest beyond). To the west lay an open and breezy common, covered in the proper season with the golden and fragrant blossom of the furze (the Common which used to be almost bare of trees); while the bright meadows, clustering hops and extensive plantations cheered the eye with an assurance of plenty and peace (perhaps these were beyond the Common to the south-west?). The description focuses next on the Belle Vue garden 'bounded in front by a paling overshadowed with acacias, whose snowy pendant blossoms I can now see drooping over it and rocking in the breeze; and beyond the paling a small delta shaped open space of turf separating it in that direction from the road'. Did the 'editor', reading these lines, have any qualms, I wonder, about uprooting his children from the place of their birth and childhood?

The 'delta shaped' space to which the first-born of those children refers is to be seen on the 1/500 Ordnance Survey map as part of the Belle Vue garden with a triangular path defining its shape; and on the Tithe map it is shown to be owned by Aretas Akers, suggesting that the legal battle hinted at in the next part of Isabella's story had already been resolved. On Bowra's and Barrow's maps by contrast the Belle Vue garden clearly does not include the space which Barrow labels 'Potter's Green' – see the map at the start of this chapter. The origin of this name is indeed the sparking point for Isabella's story which is therefore a mixture of fact and fiction in unknown proportions. The opening paragraphs, as we have seen, are flowery but factual: what may the proportions be in the following paragraph?

> One blustering equinoctial day … my governor took me by the hand, while he went round his narrow domain. We had just arrived at the spot in question, which he stood measuring with his eye, when we were unexpectedly joined by old Digges who owned a bit of land separated from this only by a carriage road. Digges was a morose rough mannered sturdy yeoman, full of the contradictions which belonged to that fast failing class. Loyal to the constitution but a sour critic of men in power, attached to his church but perpetually complaining of the indolence or rapacity of the clergy, a friend to order and the gradation of ranks, but a stern resister of the smallest encroachment, or what he deemed so, of his rights. 'And so sir, you mean to enclose this piece of land'. 'Yes', said my governor, 'unless you can show me what right you have to prevent me'. 'Why it will ruin my property, and I can't have my view blocked up by your shrubs'. 'I have no such wish or design', replied my father, 'but I cannot relinquish my claim, for no better reason than this'. 'Well, you will do

as you please', said Digges. 'All I know is, it has never been enclosed in my memory, or that of my forefathers, and it shan't now, while I have a sixpence to try the right with'.

Now, it is certainly true, on the evidence of Bowra and Barrow, that the 'green' had never been enclosed. It is also true, as a glance at the map will show, that there was a house overlooking the 'green', whose view would have been spoiled by any planting or building on the open space of turf. What is really intriguing, however, is the identity of the house owner. The house was Grove Lodge and the owner was Thomas Delves. This is historical fact but what relation does it bear to 'old Digges'? Why did Isabella, faced with an unlimited choice of pseudonyms, choose one that began with a 'D', ended with 'es' and had the same number of letters as 'Delves'? Perhaps the name alone, not the character, was suggested by 'Delves'. On the other hand, Thomas Delves would have been 71, he was religiously minded and had changed his church, and if we think of the 'Delves' as sons of the Sussex Weald (and Thomas was only one generation away) rather than the professional gentlemen they later became, the idea is not so fantastic. The story continues with

Belle Vue House from the north – painted in about 1840 by one of the Akers children

sidelights on the Akers family routine and allusions to the head of the household's legal training: 'He presently left us and we soon after returned home and dined; after which the youngsters were admitted, and the conversation turned upon what I had witnessed in the morning. My father explained to my good mother the mysteries of the law upon the case, talked of Steel versus Prickett – opinions of the recorder of London and various other matters as unintelligible to me as then would have been a chorus of Sophocles. When a pause at length ensued, I ventured to ask why the land in question was called, as I heard it was, 'Potter's Green'.' The 'Governor's' answer in short was that a man named Potter used to live in Belle Vue House when it was 'little better than a poor cottage'. I have no evidence that any Potter (or potter for that matter) lived at Belle Vue. The name does occur twice in the Poor Rate records. Stephen Potter was paying rates from as early as 1670 until 1708 when Mr Hill took over 'Potter's Farm' and was succeeded in 1711 by John Beeching; but the trail goes cold in 1714 and I do not know where Potter's Farm was. The name William Potter occurs much later, from 1756 to 1765, in connection with a property known as 'Druetts' which Nicholas Wood (junior) occupied (or paid rates for) from 1728 to 1734; but I have been unable to locate the property. The trouble about Belle Vue is that it was not used as a lodging house and therefore is not listed by Sprange; and Bowra, the other source capable of linking ratepayers with particular houses, shows only the ubiquitous Mr Brett. Barrow, equally unhelpful, shows 'Belle Vue House' as the map detail above shows.

The story of Potter's ghost, sparked off by questions on the origin of the name 'Potter's Green', continues in the *Belle Vue Magazine* in ever more fictional vein. Potter was a farmer who had lived in the cottage a hundred years before and by dint of hard work and frugal and parsimonious habits began to amass money. He became a hop planter and found an opportunity to purchase at a moderate price the land which had brought him 'such a harvest of gold'. He distrusted any form of investment apart from land. The South Sea speculation was fresh in men's minds and he refused to invest in the funds or embark on trade or lend on mortgage. He was exceedingly reserved about his money and regarded all who broached the subject as actuated by sinister design. 'If I ever save a little at the year's end I shall bid for neighbour Jones's shaw that joins my hop ground; but none of your bubbles or bonds for me', he said. In this way his acres grew but so secretly did his guineas. The whole world might see the farmer at work himself or urging on the labourers he employed; but no one saw, though many suspected, his secret visits to a corner of his roof where he concealed his hoarded gold. He slept in an attic where he had constructed behind the bed a moveable panel which he could push aside and find in the thatch the tin box where he put his gold. He was not married. How could such a man indulge in the expensive luxury of a wife or trust the secret of his soul to a woman's keeping? Instead he relied on an old woman to act as cook, housekeeper, steward and nurse – for he grew infirm with years but worked outdoors in all weathers. One day he was laid up with rheumatism and could not move hand or foot. Saturday night came and four men and a boy were to be paid. His bag contained a little silver but it was not enough. 'Had Old Molly a guinea about her?' No indeed, she should be glad to know where she should get so much. She was sure it would not have been in Master Potter's service where she had toiled for 16 years. The men had to be paid and the farm could not do without them. He was finally driven to call on Old Molly to get out the box which he assured her contained but eleven guineas; but she noticed its weight and knew that all these pains were not taken for silver and base metal. Old Potter recovered sufficiently to go about his farm the following week but when on Wednesday he proceeded as usual to make an addition to his hoard his dismay was unspeakable when he found that the contents of the box had been replaced with heaps of copper coin. Molly was nowhere to be found and when the constable was charged to apprehend her he learned that an old woman answering her description had mounted the London wagon with a bundle under her arm. She was traced to Monmouth Street where she had purchased various articles of dress of both genders, as it was thought for disguise; but she was heard of no more by Potter. The old miser was distracted. His farm was neglected, he no longer attended market, he was no longer to be seen at earliest dawn following his own plough or trenching his garden. He passed his days and a great part of his nights in wandering up and down his house, a pale emaciated shadow. His only care seemed to be to restore his loss by saving. He let his farm. In food, in clothing he restricted himself to the coarsest and scantiest allowance. He never again trusted another in his house. He concealed his savings elsewhere but the habit never left him of visiting the corner of the attic which had served as his treasury. Here his neighbours used nightly to observe the dim reflection of the farthing rushlight which lit his search for his lost guineas; and when after a few months of a miserable existence he was missed in his usual places of resort and sought for at his cottage his attenuated corpse was found stretched along the floor of that room grasping a tin box full of the copper coins. There are those who say that for years after the long thin figure of the old man might be seen traversing the room, that his tread might be heard as he advanced to the panel and the rattle of the metal as he took the box and glanced despairingly beneath the lid … the young author rounds off her story by telling how her sleep was disturbed that night, how a storm blew up, how she heard ghostly footsteps and rattling sounds, only to realise that it was the butler who had come to gather up her clothes to brush and clean them.

The story of Potter's Ghost may not add much to our knowledge of the early history of Belle Vue House but, by contrast with the paucity of early material, a lot of detail is available about transactions in the years 1843-45. When he begins his letter book Aretas Akers is showing an interest in the purchase of 'Mitchell's estate near this place' (the present Holmewood House School) but there were legal snags. Then in 1843 Mrs Mary Ann Hodgson evidently let it be known that she would consider selling some of the land at the back of Mount Sion which had come down to her from old Nicholas Wood. Her land bordered some of the Akers acres and Aretas had ideas for improving the approach to his house. Besides there was a distinct potential for building development in the combined acreage and a good price should be obtainable if he later sold. In September he offered Mrs Hodgson £1,200. He used incidentally the Tithe Award numbers (3800, 3802 etc) to identify the land in question. On 28 December 1843 a letter to Scoones & Alleyne announces that Mrs Hodgson has agreed to sell 'at v high terms' and that a memorandum of agreement had been signed on the spot. 'It is fee simple property and has been she tells me in her family for more than a century'. Two days later Aretas tells his solicitors that Mrs Hodgson has assured him that the property has been in her family 'as she thought not much less than 200 years'. 150 years would have been a more accurate figure but Mrs Hodgson, though that much closer to the events than we are today, was evidently quite vague about the story of her great-grandfather. What price Aretas eventually paid is not revealed but several nuggets of information can be mined from the correspondence which ensued before completion of the purchase in June 1844. Firstly, as was noted in chapter 22 (page 325), Sion Lodge used to belong to'Bingham' who must surely be Thomas Pinckard

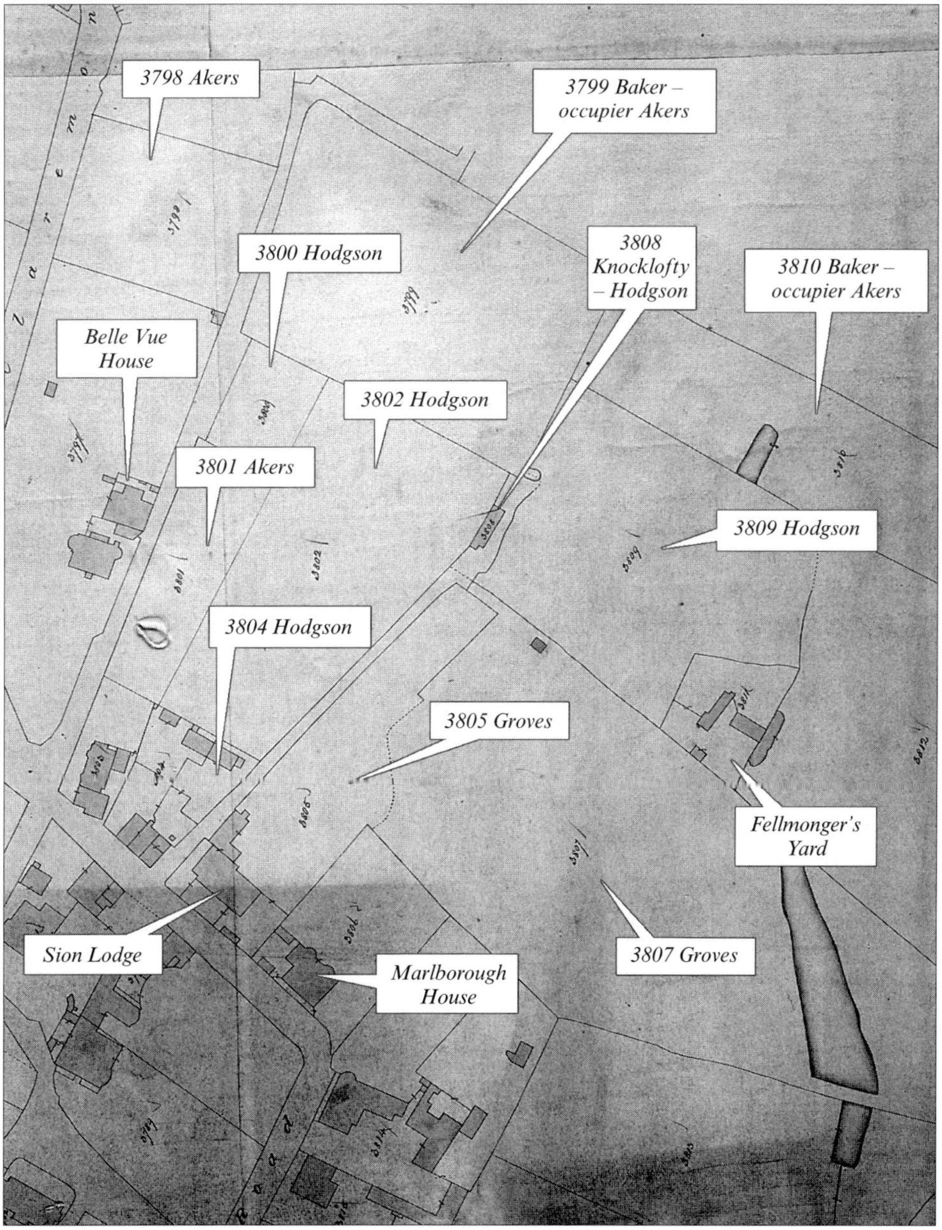

Tithe map 1840 showing owners

Bingham; and Aretas Akers bought it from Bingham's executors. Miss Groves must have bought it subsequently. Secondly, T.P. Bingham made an encroachment on Mrs Hodgson's lane (leading to Knocklofty – now Clifton Place) near its outlet into Mount Sion, in order to enlarge his stable yard. He also used her lane and a gate opening into it near Knocklofty House (described in the correspondence as 'Hutchinson's Cottage') as a way into his field without going through the garden of Sion Lodge. Hutchinson was the chimney sweep mentioned in the previous chapter, page 325. This can all be seen clearly on the Tithe map on the previous page. For these two concessions Bingham was paying Mrs Hodgson 10s. per annum and the arrangement was continued with Aretas Akers and then with Miss Groves, although Mrs Hodgson had wanted to withdraw both concessions. Thirdly, the field to the north-east of Knocklofty House (3799) and the adjoining one to its south, shown in the Tithe Award as the property of Edmund Baker, but occupied by Akers, had, by January 1844, been acquired by the occupier. Fourthly, Aretas was planning to use the Knocklofty lane as part of a new approach to Belle Vue House. He might want to improve and widen the lane and wanted no restriction on his freedom of action. In the end a compromise was reached. Aretas would have a right of carriage way over the part adjoining Sion Lodge and would take the 'soil and freehold' of the remainder down to the Fellmonger's Yard. Such is my interpretation, in the absence of the plan to which reference is made in the letter book. In general, the vendor's solicitors, Messrs Stone and Wall, adopted a rather scornful attitude to the agreement which Aretas and Mrs Hodgson had signed at the outset of the negotiations but Aretas shows himself anxious to complete the purchase despite legalistic objections. A further point of argument, the outcome of which is not revealed in the letter book, was custody of the deeds, depending on whether he or Mrs Hodgson retained the major part of the property covered by the deeds. I wish I knew what became of them, whoever was the eventual custodian.

As the deal moved towards completion, Aretas Akers wrote to several prospective purchasers of Belle Vue: Miss Groves herself was interested in the land but Aretas said that it was the sale of the house he desired and was indifferent to that of the land; there was a George Lynch Esq and a Mr Pullen whose offer to lease Belle Vue House for use as a school Aretas rejected, offering instead to sell with half the price left on mortgage at 4 per cent. The asking price was variously stated as £7,500 or 7,000 guineas; or, for the house alone with 1¼ acres, £2,500. The house could be let on a seven-, 14- or 21-year repairing lease for £125 p.a. The whole property was described as consisting of the house and adjoining cottage with coach house and stable, another small cottage which could be used for a gardener or bailiff, the garden and meadow and pasture land amounting to about 23 acres. The small cottage and 13 acres was at the time let at £100 p.a., and the rest of the land (worth about £50 p.a.) was in the owner's occupation. From the Tithe map and the Railway Deposited Plans it is possible to see the extent of Akers' acres. The boundary between Tithe maps for the southern part of Tonbridge parish and for Tunbridge Wells at a much larger scale runs along the eastern edge of upper Claremont Road and south from there to the (old) county boundary. The land to the east of this line from (and including) Claremont Lodge, as far as Poona Road and to a depth indicated by the present grounds of Claremont School, up to the boundary with Camden Park, was owned in 1842 by Mrs Hodgson but was not included in the sale to Aretas Akers. The land, to an equal depth, to the south of Mrs Hodgson's, as far as the stream dividing the counties, was owned by Aretas Akers. Between these two holdings was one field (at a guess, the present south side of Claremont Gardens) which belonged to William Hodges, with whom Aretas had some correspondence regarding a right of way into his field. The fields between this Akers holding and the rear grounds of Mount Sion (Thomas Delves' meadow, the gardens of Forest Prospect and Marlborough House, the Sion Lodge garden and meadow and Grove Lodge garden) had three owners in 1842; but, by 1844, Aretas had acquired Edmund Baker's fields and by the purchase from Mrs Hodgson, which included Knocklofty House and the Fellmonger's Yard, he had consolidated in his ownership the whole area now covered by the south-western half of the Banner Farm estate and by the eastern side of Madeira Park. Aretas never omitted to tell prospective purchasers that his land was very eligible for building and would advance in value if Tunbridge Wells increased 'as is expected'. He would hardly have predicted the present pullulation of premises on his pastureland.

Running down from the edge of the Belle Vue garden to the Knocklofty lane was a row of allotment gardens. These are not shown on the Tithe map but can be made out on the 1844 Deposited Plan, although unnumbered, if you know where to look. There were seven of them, rented by John Barnard, Peter Monrow, James Standing and the Hutchinsons senior and junior, not forgetting James Denton and the Widow Mary Mercer who both had pig sties as well. They were all on Mrs Hodgson's land and Aretas was insistent that she should give notice to all her tenants before completion; although 'not decided on taking the land into his own occupation he yet wishes to have it in his power'. Rent was due from these tenants (Peter Hutchinson had to pay for Knocklofty House too) and from a few others including Henry Peerless who was paying 22 guineas a year for the Fellmonger's Yard and two fields; and the proceeds had to be split between purchaser and vendor as from 4 June, besides which some of the tenants, Hutchinson in particular, were reluctant payers and had to be threatened. It seems unlikely that Aretas wanted the view from his house to be dominated by allotments and pig sties because, while still dallying with prospective purchasers, he was meanwhile pressing ahead with marking out his new drive and discussing his house improvements with Decimus Burton. It seems that he was planning to build a new coach house and stables near his boundary with Grove Lodge and to run his new entrance drive via Knocklofty Lane to the front of the new coach house. On 14 July he writes to Burton saying that he likes the proposed coach house and stables but suggests '3 feet more to the E on acct of Delves's fence' and two days later he says that 'Delves sets his boundary at 3ft on my side of his fence'. The reference can only be to Thomas Delves and Grove Lodge. The next stage in the plan would have been, it is possible to guess, the closure of the present Farmcombe Lane. The Tithe map, of course, does not attribute ownership of roads to anyone; but the Railway Plan and Reference Book show the lane in front of Belle Vue as an 'Occupation road from Mount Sion to Lands' and in the ownership of Aretas Akers. There is no doubt that Aretas would have been quite prepared to close the road for his own purposes. He had after all shown no compunction over 'Potter's Green'. His letter of 29 September says that his acreage 'includes the slip of green enclosed in front of original purchase which I think can hardly exceed 25 to 30 perches'. So much for old Digges! By closing the lane and eliminating the allotment gardens he could have contrived a lovely landscape sloping southwards through fields to the tree-lined stream, with upland vistas of primordial forest beyond. The envisaged improvements to house and grounds might in time have reconciled even Aretas to life on Mount Sion; I am sure his children would have been delighted.

These dreams were, however, to be swiftly shattered. On 29 September 1844 he is writing to Alleyne 'giving one or two heads of information to assist in framing the Draft Agreement with the Railway Comy'. The letter book does not reveal exactly what happened but I suppose the railway surveyors appeared on the horizon one fine autumn morning. They can hardly have hoped to map out the tunnel which was to skirt the foundations of Belle Vue and the track cleaving the fields without giving the landowner some inkling of what they were up to. So on 30 November 1844 'at 15 minutes before ten o'clock' Mr Apsley Ranger, the Company Surveyor, deposited the plan with the Clerk of the Peace. From this point the sale to the Railway Company went ahead without serious problems. On 24 May 1845 Aretas writes that the company has put off the final settlement for a few days longer but, although the letter book ends on 30 May without indicating that the sale has been completed, it must have been very soon. There were difficulties and delays. Aretas becomes extremely irritated by the slowness of the company's responses. He calls attention to the 'suspension of my building & repairs which would have been covered in & secure from the weather' and complains at the delay in hearing anything from the SE Company. There are problems with Mr Barrett the builder. Shall he be paid off by Aretas or shall the Railway Company take over the liability and, if it wishes, the building operations? Decimus Burton must certify for the work done to date. Shall he sell his furniture and the cattle on his land? Mr Brandram wants to buy some land. The family appears to be living temporarily at Murray House but in December Aretas plans to move to his house in Dover. George Down, the gardener who acts as agent for Aretas in his absence, is recommended to the Company 'in the strongest terms as a person every way competent to look after the land ... should they require such a person'. In the meantime shall he continue to occupy the cottage on the property, which he now lives in free of rent, making 'what he can of the garden in return for looking after the house, garden and land'? And will the Company pay his wages at 18s. a week? All these questions await a final decision from the South Eastern Railway. A preliminary agreement is reached whereby the Company takes over the profits and liabilities of the estate from 1 December, pending completion. The sale is to include all the land as well as the house but – an interesting detail – is to exclude Rectorial Tithes because Aretas wishes to retain them as a qualification to vote for this division of the county. As noted above, the family seem to have lived at Murray House for a period. The evidence for this is, firstly, a letter dated from Murray House on 4 October 1844; and, secondly, a note dated 22 December to Mr Nash (the postmaster who acted as local banker) to pay Joseph Delves for Delves & Jull (the agents) £46 1s. 0d. for the rent of Murray House. The first letter is of additional interest for its reference to drains. Addressed to Mr Apps, one of the Surveyors of Highways for the parish of Tonbridge, it gives notice to 'take measures to remove a certain nuisance which has recently been brought on my land by means of an underground drain which conveys night soil, refuse and various offensive matters into a pond of mine used for watering cattle'. In December the family removed to the house in Dover and were still there on 30 May 1845 when the letter book ends. The sale is still not completed, the Railway Company having 'put off their final settt w me for a few days longer'. A penultimate letter tells J. Burke Esq that Aretas cannot subscribe for his paper 'The Patrician' as he is going abroad. When the family returned their new home was to be the somewhat grander Malling Abbey. In 1854 Aretas took his daughters on a grand tour of France, Switzerland and Italy; but in April the following year, on the way home, he died in Paris at the age of 56. There is a pencil sketch of him (see page 335 above) in the *Belle Vue Magazine* bearing the epitaph: 'We shall not look upon his like again'.

It was fortunate in the event (although Aretas could not have foreseen it) that he did not complete his improvements only to have a railway driven through the middle of his beautiful view. The exact timing of tunnel and track construction and house demolition I do not know but 'Belle Vue' is to be found in the 1851 census, occupied by the fittingly named civil engineer, Henry Buttress, and his wife, five children and sister-in-law. I guess he was working on the railway. Although it might have been expected that the Railway would sell land surplus to its requirements as quickly as possible, the loop line plans which were deposited by the Lewes Uckfield & Tunbridge Wells Railway in November 1852 show that the South Eastern Railway had retained all the land to the west of the Hastings line which it had bought from Aretas. Miss Groves owned the Sion Lodge garden and meadow as before; Henry Peerless continued to rent, but from the Railway now, the Fellmonger's Yard and buildings together with some pasture land; while Knocklofty House (occupied in 1844 by Aretas' gardener and factotum, George Down) and much of the remaining land on this side of the railway was rented from the Company by Andrew Tracy. He appears in *Mathieson's Directory* of 1867 as a 'Cowkeeper & Dairyman'; and a planning application of 1877 shows 'Mr Tracy's New House' in the position occupied by the present Jerningham Villa. The application is for Mr R.W. Weekes, owner of Sion Lodge, to build a 'vinery' in his kitchen garden, on the other side of the lane from his house, behind today's 'Little House' and the Fellmonger Cottages. By this date, therefore, R.W. Weekes must have acquired at least part of the land purchased by the South Eastern Railway from Aretas Akers; and it seems very likely that he had bought all the land the Railway did not want to the west of the new loop line. The 1866 Ordnance Survey map shows the site of Belle Vue House occupied only by five trees and a well, with a raised (or sunken?) area between it and Claremont Road, probably the lawn which forms the foreground of the *Belle Vue Magazine* painting. This site was not built on until 1927, when 'Thomas Isard (The Bungalow)' – later numbered 71, Claremont Road – appears in *Kelly's Directory*; followed in the next few years by nos 73 and 85. On the other side of the old Belle Vue site, however, two grand new houses had risen by the 1860s. These are the houses which still stand and are now numbered 67 and 69, Claremont Road. No.69, nearest the old house, was called Belle Vue and no.67, named Claremont House, became the Christ Church Vicarage and remained so until the 1930s. Confusingly, no.69 is now called Claremont House and no.67 has no name. There are some auction Sale Particulars for Belle Vue (the new one) in the Reference Library. The Conditions of Sale are unfortunately missing – they usually contain some clues to earlier title – but the remaining papers give some information. Ten properties, the estate of Charles Cripps, were for sale by order of the Master of the Rolls in the Chancery Division, in a testamentary dispute involving Hannah, the widow, and William Charles (the son, I assume) as defendants and her daughter Mary Ann as plaintiff. This was the Mary Ann Cripps who became the second wife of Joseph Delves of Chapel Place. Charles Cripps was, I think, a builder and developer who started out as a bricklayer and fathered the better-known W.C. Cripps. At any rate, by the time of the Tithe map he owned land and houses to the east of Poona Road and he also owned Mount Calverley Lodge, which was not far away in Prospect Road, roughly between present-day Park Street and North Street; and in 1843 he increased his holding in the area by buying from Charlotte Lushington the field on which Oakfield Court was built – see chapter 9, pages 90 and 92.

The case of Delves *v* Cripps commenced in 1871 but the sale was scheduled for 13 July 1877: included were Cambridge House, Cambridge Lodge, Clifton Villa, Claremont House and Belle Vue, Mount Calverley Lodge, the *Royal Oak* public house and six cottages in the Windmill Fields. Evidently Charles Cripps was the owner of Claremont House and Belle Vue when he died. In the deeds of no.65 Claremont Road reference is made to covenants concluded by the South Eastern Railway, Mary Ann Caballero, Charles Cripps and others on 3 September 1858; and the Sale Particulars of 1877 refer to indentures dated 19 October 1859 and to a 21-year lease running from 29 September 1863. From this evidence I assume that the two houses were built around 1860 and maybe Charles Cripps was the builder. The Sale Particulars allude also to a dispute with Madame Caballero over ownership of part of the garden; and to a quaint arrangement whereby the South Eastern Railway added to the gardens of Claremont House and Belle Vue the strip of land occupied by the hedge bounding the railway on condition that the hedge was kept 'free from weeds and clipped'. The new Belle Vue was occupied first by a Colonel Stewart; then and until 1908 by Rear Admiral F.S. Tremlett and his widow after him; and by Baron Dulwigk until 1914. Claremont House ceased to be the Christ Church Vicarage only in 1937 when it was divided into three flats. The vicar moved into no.22 Claremont Gardens and then into the present vicarage, no.63, which with its pair no.65 was built in 1929/30 on land purchased from the estate of John Leshley, heir to Madame Caballero.

Chapter 24

Fairlawn House

In the last few chapters we have travelled via the old Bowling Green and the houses on it or surrounding it to the top of Mount Sion hill and to the borders of Mount Sion as I have defined it and beyond. It is time to begin the last stage in our tour and descend the hill as far as the house just below Eden House. Here it is photographed by David Johnson in 1934. The original lessee from Viscountess Purbeck was one Henry Adams. He leased three pieces of land for 50 years at £1.10 per annum on 10 December 1689; but curiously the Brookes and Constable Partition Plan which we have seen before (see page 224) shows the site in the name of Adams as early as 1686. The Poor Rate record begins, however, with 'Mr Scoones' who was probably the original developer of the building.

Fairlawn House Poor Rate

1690-1704	Mr Scoones
1708=1714	Widdow Scoones
1728-1730	Widdow Scoones
1731	Wid Scoones or occupier
1732-1791	Rich Jeffery
1792-1793	Stevens the Revd Mr for late Rd Jefferys
1794-1797	Stephens the Rev Thos

I have no information why Henry Adams disappeared from the scene; it happened in other cases that the original lessee was not the purchaser of the freehold

Fairlawn House in 1934

in 1702. Henry Adams, yeoman, of Speldhurst, made a will in 1714 but its contents do not help. Thomas Scoones was another 'yeoman', this time of Tonbridge parish, and he evidently found the lodging house business sufficiently attractive to warrant the purchase of the freehold when it was offered in 1702. A copy of the conveyance by Lease and Release dated 27/28 Nov. 1702 is in the Ward Papers. John Ward's interest was not in the lodging house on Mount Sion but in the four-acre field which was part of the same transaction. This field and adjoining land belonging originally to the Mercer family was situated towards the bottom of Camden Road and was required for the supply of stone and water to the Calverley development. The description of the Mount Sion property and its abuttals is of some interest:

> One piece or parcel of land heretofore part of certaine land called Inhams on which a Messuage Tenement and other buildings are now erected lying on Mount Sion hill bounding to a new way there leading from the Chapell to the Bowling Green towards the north-east to a parcel of the same Inhams in the occupation of William Younge Esquire heretofore demised to Richard Constable and Robert Brooke and now parted by a pale towards the south And to other part of the same Inhams demised to Edward Allen toward the west and north which said piece contains by estimation half an acre and lyeth in breadth against the said new way 5 rods and 10 feet and is in length from the said way to the land of Edward Allen 15 rods ... All which premises are ... now in the occupation of Thomas Scoones by virtue of a lease made by Lady Purbeck and Sir Thomas Meeres to Henry Adams from Michaelmas 1689 for fifty years at thirty shillings per annum.

The 'new way' is clearly Mount Sion road to the north-east; the parcel occupied by William Young to the south is, I guess, future Eden House land but not yet built on; and Edward Allen's land to the north-west is Jerningham House property. The dimensions given correspond well with the frontage of Fairlawn and the depth back to Cumberland Walk; and a plot of these dimensions would contain a little more than half an acre – if *Pear's Encyclopaedia* and my arithmetic are correct.

Attached to the bottom of the parchment document bearing witness to the sale were the signatures and seals of the Earl of Buckingham, his trustees Thomas Lake and the two Wellers, Thomas Scoones himself and, acting as his trustee, Nicholas Wood the fellmonger who lived just by the top entrance to the Grove; for the Grove was already valued and used by Mount Sion residents, although the formal Trust Deed was not to be enacted until the following year. Indeed, the conveyance which Thomas had just signed, even though his lodging house was a quarter of a mile from the Grove, contained a covenant binding all the signatories: 'That the Grove standing and being near unto the above bargained premises formerly called Inhams Bush and now called the Grove alias Mount Sion Grove adjoining to the land of Mr Younge shall be preserved for a Grove for the use of the Inhabitants and lodgers of the premises above bargained with others to walk and the trees there growing preserved for shade and not any of them to be cutt downe nor any buildings to be there erected'. The date of the Grove Trust Deed is 20 April 1703.

Thomas Scoones died some three years after this transaction. He made his will on 8 August 1705 and probate was granted to his widow on 27 November the same year. He left the house with its furniture, brewhouse, stables, coach houses, garden and lands to his wife Sarah for her life; after her decease it was to go half to his eldest son John and half to his daughter Sarah, on condition that they paid £100 to each of their younger brothers, Thomas and Henry. Their mother was to maintain and educate the youngest son, Henry, and 'till Thomas and Henry or either of them shall soo dispose of themselves either by marriage or sett up in a way and bussiness to live when they are out of imployment I would not have them destitute of a home but my mind and will is that they have a being in this my dwelling house till they got into imployment not paying anything for their houseroome'.

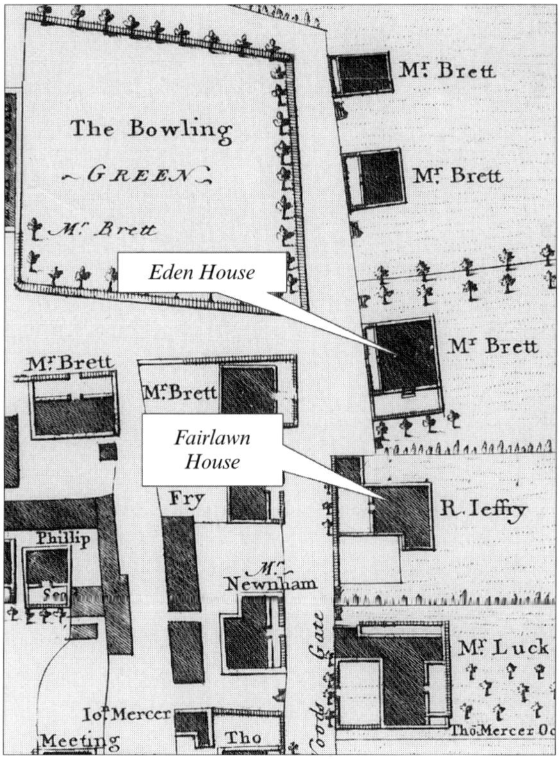

Bowra plan 1738

Old Thomas evidently expected his wife to carry on the lodging house business because the will continues: 'If it please God to prosper Sarah my said wife in her present bussiness so that she make an addition to her present estate I leave it wholly to her to augment my children's portions as she finds them most deserving.' He need not have worried. John became a fell-monger and glover, Thomas a 'salesman', Henry a tallow chandler and they all married girls called Mary. Henry had no children, John two daughters and Thomas three daughters and a son (named Thomas, of course!) who was the first of the lawyer Scoones whose successor firm flourishes today as Thomson, Snell and Passmore. The widow Scoones carried on the business with evident success until it was taken over by her daughter and son-in-law Richard Jeffery; and it is 'R Jeffry' who appears on the Bowra map in 1738 as the owner of the house on Mount Sion – see above.

Two years before this, in July 1736, Thomas Wilson DD, son of the Bishop of Sodor and Man, visited Tunbridge Wells and his diary contains a rare reference to lodgings. The road from Sevenoaks was indifferent and 'plagued with touters' but, arriving at the Wells 'at about 7' a clock' on Wednesday 14th, he agreed for lodging at £1 5s. 0d. per week 'at one Knights at the front of Mount Sion'. This house was perhaps situated in the High Street (Foot of Mount Sion), roughly where the Bedding Centre now is, and is possibly the building marked 'Blans' on Kip's engraving of 1719. On 3 August the Rev. Wilson made a diary entry of more immediate interest. 'Jeffery's very good lodgings and so are Woods and Brothers upon the top of Mount Sion near the Bowling Green. A very handsome house.' The handsome house must be either Burlington House or, more probably, Berkeley Place. 'Jeffrey's' could refer to the lodging house on Mount Sion or to that of John Jeffery, now 69, London Road, on the corner of Church Road. The context perhaps favours Mount Sion.

In 1726 Sarah Scoones and her four children and their spouses came to a family arrangement. This involved a number of houses and some land in Tonbridge; but, as far as the Mount Sion lodging house was concerned, the eldest son John gave up his half share in favour of his sister and brother-in-law and their children. When the widow Scoones died in 1730 (apart from bequeathing pieces of gold to two sons and 'my Wedding Gold ring' to Henry the youngest) she left her half share of the lodging house in trust for Richard and Sarah Jeffery and their children. As a result the whole place came effectively under the one ownership and the Jefferies ran the business throughout the Beau Nash period and the prosperous latter years of the 18th century. The house must have seen many interesting personalities and incidents but (unless anyone knows differently?) no record has survived. In 1770, however, misfortunes began to arrive in more than single spies. Richard, the paterfamilias, was buried on 10 November and Sarah, his widow, followed within weeks. She died on 15 December and on the 23rd a sermon was preached in her memory at the Presbyterian Meeting house in Little Mount Sion by the pastor, the Rev. William Johnston (see left and chapter 14 page 171).

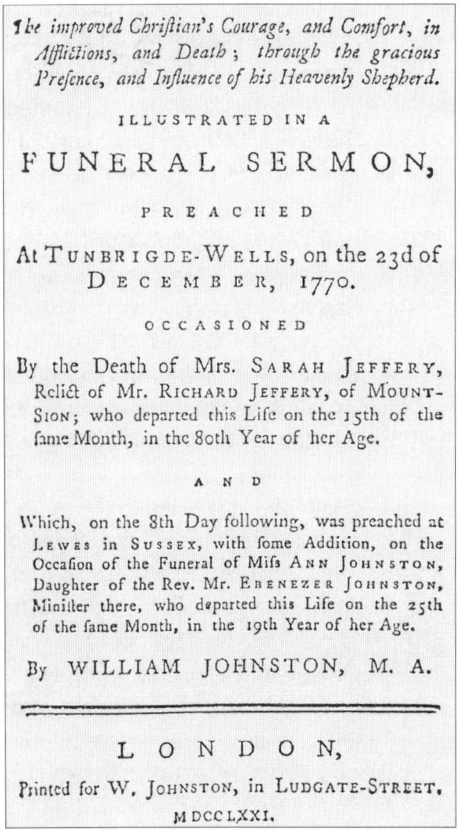
The improved Christian's Courage, and Comfort, in Afflictions, and Death; through the gracious Presence, and Influence of his Heavenly Shepherd.

ILLUSTRATED IN A

FUNERAL SERMON,

PREACHED

At TUNBRIGDE-WELLS, on the 23d of DECEMBER, 1770.

OCCASIONED

By the Death of Mrs. SARAH JEFFERY, Relict of Mr. RICHARD JEFFERY, of MOUNT-SION; who departed this Life on the 15th of the same Month, in the 80th Year of her Age.

AND

Which, on the 8th Day following, was preached at LEWES in SUSSEX, with some Addition, on the Occasion of the Funeral of Miss ANN JOHNSTON, Daughter of the Rev. Mr. EBENEZER JOHNSTON, Minister there, who departed this Life on the 25th of the same Month, in the 19th Year of her Age.

By WILLIAM JOHNSTON, M. A.

LONDON,

Printed for W. JOHNSTON, in LUDGATE-STREET, MDCCLXXI.

Sermon for Mrs Jeffery

As to the character of our greatly esteemed and departed sister, Mrs Jeffery, there is great reason to think she was a truly worthy and excellent person, that she was sincerely pious towards God, having constantly attended the public

> ordinances of his house, while her bodily health and strength enabled her, and since they were impaired by a stroke of the palsy, disabling her from attending them, spending generally several hours daily in reading and conversing with the Holy Scriptures, and in other acts of devotion. She fulfilled the relative duties of life, as a wife, a mother, a mistress and a neighbour, with unblemished reputation and honour. She was of a remarkably meek, peaceable and healing temper; and as might be expected in a person of this character, she was generally cheerful, composed and easy. As these characters are the ornaments and glories of her sex so they are highly worthy of her sex's imitation … Especially doth it become children to imitate the virtues of their parents; and I am persuaded this intimation will have weight with the children of the deceased …

Sarah Jeffery's will, unaltered since it was made some thirty years before, left her half share of the house to her two daughters and their heirs; but this was to be a pious hope. Elizabeth died two months after her mother and Sarah in March 1777, both unmarried and intestate. This meant that the brothers, Richard and Thomas, as co-heirs in gavelkind firstly to their parents and secondly to their sisters, became joint owners of the whole property. The brothers both married girls called Sarah (like their mother and grandmother!) but these did not emulate their namesakes in fecundity. Thomas and his Sarah managed to produce one daughter, Ann; but Richard was still trying when he made his will in 1788: 'I give and devise my part of a Messuage … in the Parish of Penshurst unto my Brother Thos Jeffery except I shall leave Issue of my own body then to my own Child I give …'. His half part of the Mount Sion lodging house and the land that went with it he left to his wife for her life but forgot to provide for the subsequent inevitability, so that his brother became heir in gavelkind. Richard died in December 1788 and his brother's death nine months later left 16-year-old Ann as sole heiress and led to perhaps the most dramatic incident recorded in the entire history of Mount Sion. Her mother had been one of three sisters, granddaughters of William Wilkin, 'citizen of London' as he liked to call himself and a feltmaker by trade, who owned the *King's Arms and Hands* in Bermondsey and the *Three Pigeons* near Whitechapel church as well as the Great Lodge estate near Pembury which he had acquired during the Earl of Buckingham's great South Frith sell-off in 1702. Sister Hannah had married a learned clergyman, the Rev. Samuel Morton Savage DD, but they had no children; while the other sister Ann had remained a spinster and, probably from that fact, had been left the bulk of the family fortune. Ann Jeffery had been christened after the spinster and now found herself the expectant heiress, on the death of her mother, of the Wilkin fortune, as well as enjoying an immediate income from some £10,000 in the funds. On top of this she would inherit all her father's and uncle's property – all in all a fortune of £50,000 – which means millions today – but perhaps she was not thinking of this as she lay in bed that morning. There was that clever clergyman she had met. He was quite a bit older than her but … he had been very attentive.

Tunbridge Wells Sept 7', ran the story in the *Maidstone Journal* of 15 September 1789,

A most daring violation of the law was attempted here today which threw the inhabitants and company at this charming place into the utmost confusion. About half after eight in the morning a post-chaise, with two men in it (for of course they cannot be called gentlemen, although they were well-dressed) drawn by six horses, followed by a shabby looking servant, out of livery, with a cockade in his hat, stopped on Mount Sion, a little above the house of the late Mr. Jeffery, who died last week, and was buried on Thursday; the whole party entered the house, at the back door, and demanded of the housekeeper where Miss J___y was, who informed them that she was not up; they insisted upon her being immediately called, as she must go with them; this the housekeeper refused, adding that Miss J___y was ill, and should not be disturbed; at the same time she called in some of her neighbours, who, sending for a constable, the Gentlemen and their Valet were conducted to the Sussex Tavern, and from thence to Tunbridge to a Magistrate, to be charged with the assault, escorted by a number of horsemen, (a Rescue being apprehended) and by several post-chaises, carrying the insulted parties and their friends. Mr J___y dying worth Fifty Thousand Pounds, which will come to Miss J___y at the death of her mother, stimulated those adventurers to this audacious attempt. Miss J___y is only sixteen years of age.

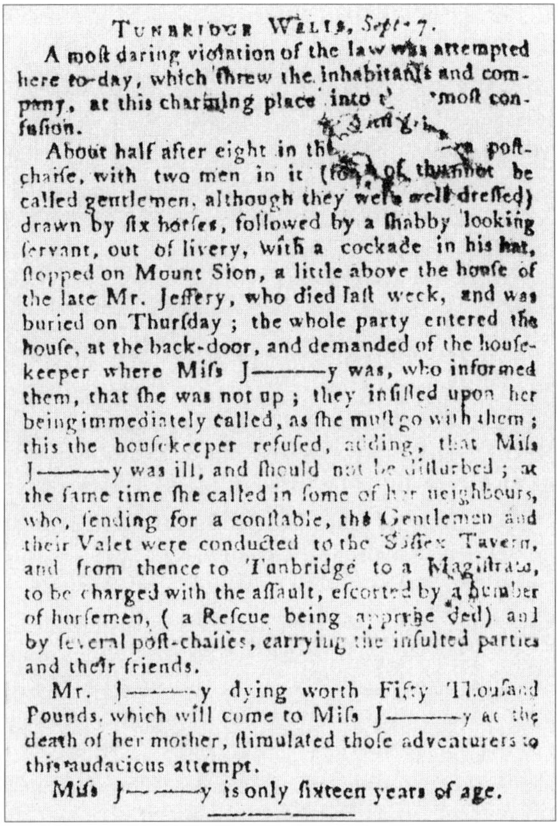

TUNBRIDGE WELLS, *Sept.* 7.

A most daring violation of the law was attempted here to-day, which threw the inhabitants and company, at this charming place into t[he] most confusion.

About half after eight in the [morning a] post-chaise, with two men in it (for of course they cannot be called gentlemen, although they were well dressed) drawn by six horses, followed by a shabby looking servant, out of livery, with a cockade in his hat, stopped on Mount Sion, a little above the house of the late Mr. Jeffery, who died last week, and was buried on Thursday; the whole party entered the house, at the back-door, and demanded of the housekeeper where Miss J——y was, who informed them, that she was not up; they insisted upon her being immediately called, as she must go with them; this the housekeeper refused, adding, that Miss J——y was ill, and should not be disturbed; at the same time she called in some of her neighbours, who, sending for a constable, the Gentlemen and their Valet were conducted to the Sussex Tavern, and from thence to Tunbridge to a Magistrate, to be charged with the assault, escorted by a number of horsemen, (a Rescue being apprehended) and by several post-chaises, carrying the insulted parties and their friends.

Mr. J——y dying worth Fifty Thousand Pounds, which will come to Miss J——y at the death of her mother, stimulated those adventurers to this audacious attempt.

Miss J——y is only sixteen years of age.

Maidstone Journal

There is no doubt that heiresses of this and earlier periods were in some danger of abduction because, once a marriage was official, the husband had absolute control of any part of his wife's wealth that was not protected by having been, for instance, vested in trustees. The law recognised the crime, particularly where the motive was 'for lucre thereof'. In 1702 an improvident Danish timber-dealer called Haagen Swendsen was hanged, much to his surprise, for abducting Miss Pleasant Rawlins and making her believe that she had no choice between marrying him and being thrown into a debtors' prison. After 1753 banns or a licence were necessary for English marriages but the problem could be overcome, and was, by going to Gretna Green. Thus in 1791 (some 18 months after the Mount Sion attempt) Richard Vining Perry drove Miss Clementina Clarke, 15 years old and heiress to her uncle's Jamaica fortune, from Bristol to Gretna Green and was tried in 1794 for 'Forcible Abduction or stealing an Heiress From the Boarding-School of Miss Mills'. Fortunately his pregnant wife was allowed (after opposition from prosecuting counsel!) to depose that she had been making eyes at him from the school crocodile and the elopement had been arranged with the help of Eliza Baker of the school's domestic staff. The book of the Perry trial mentions also the case of Lucy Ramsay who was forced from her coach in Hyde Park, carried to lodgings in the Strand and married to her abductor under threat of being carried out of the country if she would not comply. It seems, therefore, that there were ways and means of overcoming the abductor's problem of persuading a reluctant girl to go though a marriage ceremony. What the three Mount Sion miscreants had in mind I cannot think; nor do I know what their fate was, although I have tried to find out.

Escape to Gretna Green – after Rowlandson

One other thought may have been occupying Ann's mind as she lay in bed that autumn morning. Had her father made a will? Her aunt Hannah and Uncle Savage, the Doctor of so-called 'Divinity', had produced a will – not a scrappy death-bed thing, but a proper document all legal phrases and everything; and it was dated the day before poor Papa went to heaven ... but it had not been signed. They said it would be approved and already they were behaving as if everything belonged to them, even though the will apparently said no such thing, and they had taken possession of all the writings concerning the family property; and Aunt Sarah seemed to be in with them too. Ann had not been told anything really, but what she had picked up from overheard conversation was worrying. Her thoughts went back to the Rev. Stephens from Frant who had been briefly incumbent at the Chapel of King Charles the Martyr until the Rev. Martin Benson took over in 1786. He seemed to know about legal things. He talked like a Welshman and like a Welshman he talked! She liked that. Perhaps he could help. My guess is that he did help. At all events, a complaint was entered into the Court of Chancery on 23 September for Ann Jeffery by her 'next friend' (she being a minor) John Jeffery, tallow chandler of Tonbridge. John Jeffery was family, a status to which Thomas Stephens could not yet aspire; but I am sure Thomas was somewhere in the picture. No doubt he would have been surprised, and everyone else, if he had known that a quarter of a century later he would be coming to John Jeffery's rescue with a mortgage loan of £500, only to find himself within the year acting as his assignee in bankruptcy – but that is another story. The question of Thomas Jeffery's will was soon decided in favour of Ann but before the Court had finished with this matter it was ordering, on 5 December the same year, that Thomas Stephens be at liberty to propose terms for a settlement on the marriage then intended between Thomas and Ann.

The young heiress and her clever clergyman were in too much of a hurry, however. Before any further Court proceedings could take place, the wedding had been solemnised. The Reverend Thomas Stephens was about thirty-two years old at this time. He was the son of William Stephens, gentleman, of County Pembroke. Perhaps it was his maturity that appealed to Ann and maybe also to her mother who was no doubt missing the masculine support to which she had been accustomed. Moreover, he did know a bit about the law: some years later he was to receive the degree of Doctor of Law and, not long after the wedding, he revived the case, speaking now as 'next friend' for his own wife. On 11 June a Master in Chancery filed a statement of the facts. Briefly, Ann was entitled to certain farms and lands in Kent and Sussex of an annual value of about £80 as heiress to her father; and under the will of her aunt, Ann Wilkin, after the death of her mother, to other property in Kent, Sussex, Surrey and Middlesex of an annual value of £125, together with some £24,000 in Bank and South Sea Stock and New and Old South Sea Annuities; and an immediate income for her own use from £9,500 Bank Annuities 4 per cent under her aunt's will.

Articles for a marriage settlement were agreed on 18 June 1790 and embodied the usual provisions for handing the estates to trustees. The one unusual point was that the arrangement had to wait until the bride reached the age of twenty-one; in fact it was not completed until 1799. Meanwhile the honeymoon continued. Mother-in-law was ensconced at Great Lodge and the happy pair divided their time between this, their country seat, and Devonshire Place, in the Marylebone district near the future Regent's Park. Great Lodge was a 'Mansion House' with 130 acres of grounds which included the Robingate Wood on the other side of the A21 from Pembury Hospital. Thomas Stephens seems to have taken to his role as country gentleman like a duck to water. In 1792, for instance, he was one of those in the locality who took out a Game Certificate entitling him to shoot over his property; and in 1828 William Clapson, who had been bailiff on the Reverend Doctor's farm for many years, was sentenced to be transported for seven years for selling lambs to Joseph Delves and others without handing the money to his master.

A strangely similar but conflicting incident of abduction is reported by two early Tonbridge historians, John King in his *Chronology of Events* and Arthur Neve. According to these sources, there was a court case in 1789 concerning a teen-age girl, Elizabeth Jefferys, who eloped from her home in Tonbridge with one George Ashworth. They were, however, intercepted and the girl later married the Rev. Dr Stevens. I cannot believe that there were two Rev. Dr Stevenses. On the other hand the story, based on the court case at which William Scoones was clerk, is so circumstantial as not to be doubted. The only way out of this dilemma seems to be to suppose that the elopement with Ashworth is true but the later marriage of Elizabeth was substituted by mistake with that of Ann Jeffery and Thomas Stephens. In any case there is so much reliable documentary evidence to substantiate the Ann Jeffery version of the story that there can be no doubt of its veracity.

After Ann's marriage the lodging house on Mount Sion was no longer required by the family and an era in its history was at an end after almost exactly one hundred years. On Tuesday 18 January 1791 and the two following days Messrs Cheesman and Skinner auctioned on the premises the 'entire HOUSEHOLD FURNITURE of the LODGING HOUSE, late belonging to RICHARD and THOMAS JEFFERY, both deceased, situate on MOUNT SION HILL', consisting of 'Twenty-one Feather Beds, four-post and other Bedsteads; Furniture, Counterpanes, Quilts and Blankets; Chests of Drawers, Tables, Chairs, Pier and other Glasses; Carpets; an eight-day Clock and a large assortment of Kitchen Furniture together with a great quantity of Linen.' Despite the sale of its contents the house was advertised in *Sprange's Guides* for 1797 and 1801 as a lodging house offering four parlours, five chambers, five garrets, two coach houses and stabling for 12 horses. It was certainly better placed than Sion House to accommodate horses and coaches. Perhaps Henry Fry was the tenant who took on the lodging house business during this period; at any rate in March 1805 the Trustees of the Marriage Settlement (with the approval of Mr and Mrs Stephens) contracted to sell the house to Henry Fry. For whatever reason, Henry Fry did not wish to, or could not, proceed with the purchase (he became bankrupt in 1811) and agreed to sell to Joseph Delves for £1,900, of which £1,192 went to the Trustees and the balance to Henry Fry. Before changing his mind, however, Henry Fry had concluded a 21-year lease of the house (at £120 per annum) with William Large who was a Tunbridge Wells stable keeper; and this lease had to be honoured. I guess William Large was particularly interested in the stables and coach houses at the back. Horse hire was at any rate part of his business because in 1802 one of his customers rode away with a horse and he had to advertise in the *Maidstone Journal*:

> Tunbridge Wells, May 12. FIVE GUINEAS REWARD. Rode away with on Sunday last, by a person answering the following description; – Dark complexion – dark hair, powdered – about 5 feet 6 or 7 inches high –had on a dark coat, plain buttons – striped waistcoat – yellow leather breeches – new boots, with turned down tops, a pair of military steel spurs – and a new hat, the MARE he hired of Mr LARGE, to go to Brenchley, and to return in the evening, is a stout, boney, light chestnut MARE, with a large blaze down her face; her hind legs white; and a singular mark on the near haunch near her tail, occasioned by a wound from a bullock's horn; another mark by a bullock on her wind pipe. The person that is suspected, but a few days ago sold a horse on the Hastings road. Whoever will give information, so that the above-mentioned MARE shall be recovered, will be paid the above Reward, and a further Reward of FIVE GUINEAS, on conviction of the above-mentioned person, by W.LARGE.

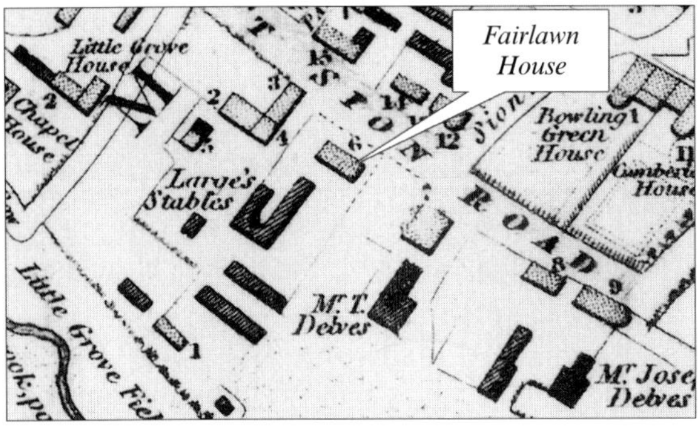

Barrow map 1808

Perhaps William Large was already at this time, as a tenant, using the stables of the Mount Sion lodging house; his advertisement unfortunately gives no address. In any case he took on the house and stables in 1805 and in 1808 the Barrow map shows 'Large's Stables' as a large three-sided block to the rear of the house, suggesting that a business separate from that of the lodging house had been established. This later became 'Hodges Yard' and clearly represents the beginning of the process which has led through many variations of non-residential use of Cumberland Yard to the latest residential development. Also shown on the Barrow map for the first time (and in *Sprange's Guide*) is the name 'Fairlawn House'. The naming of houses was certainly becoming fashionable about this time but it was surely the new owner of 1805 or the new tenant who chose the name: my guess is that it was Joseph Delves.

The name 'Fairlawn' might have been adopted in imitation of any number of Fairlawn Houses in the country (there was a 'Fairlawn' in Sandrock Road in 1908); but it would be nice to think that there was indeed a fair lawn behind the house. The Ordnance Survey map shows a long flight of steps, leading down to a tree-lined path encircling what was surely a sunny sward where persons of quality used to perambulate and until recently Peugeots and Porsches stood on black asphalt to await new exhaust pipes. The asphalt seems destined to remain but happily the garage complex behind has been replaced by a block of 'mews' houses. The change of name might have been symbolic of a face-lift for the old house. At about this time it must have been given the rather severe classical façade which remains today in spite of enlargements and which is to be seen in Johnson's photograph. Alternatively the old house could have been knocked down and rebuilt; but this I do not

Fairlawn House – a mid-19th-century reconstruction by Gill Twells

believe. Inspection of the exposed interior during the most recent refurbishment suggested that the original building was still there. To my mind there is a remarkable similarity between the centre section of the building, as shown on the photograph, and the house shown on page 292 of chapter 20. We there concluded that Marlborough House was built about 1820 by Joseph Delves junior and it is not therefore unreasonable to attribute the façade of Fairlawn House to the same inspiration, whether that came from the owner, architect or builder. This development may well, however, have awaited the end of William Large's 21-year lease.

Thomas Stephens and young Ann in the meantime were enjoying her inheritance. They produced a pigeon pair: William Wilkin, born about 1792 and christened in grateful commemoration, and Georgina Isabella. This took up some of their time I suppose, but not overmuch in view of the domestic assistance available; and the demands of the London season and the country estate no doubt took up some more. Thomas must, however, it would seem, have been devoting some of his leisure to study; because in December 1807 the following announcement appeared in the *Maidstone Journal*: 'The Rev Thomas Stephens, of Magdalen College Oxford and of Great Lodge, in Kent, has been admitted by that University, to the accumulated degrees of bachelor and doctor of civil law; upon which occasion his numerous friends were entertained with his accustomed hospitality and kindness.' Unfortunately the newspaper got the college wrong: it was Magdalen Hall, later merged with Hertford College, and records earlier than 1849 are missing.

On 31 January 1815 Mrs Jeffery, 'last surviving sister of the Wilkins, formerly of Great Lodge near Tonbridge', died at the Devonshire Place house in her 85th year, thus permitting Ann and her husband at length to enter into full enjoyment of the inheritance. In 1822 Thomas undertook what seems to have been a rare exercise of his clerical functions and performed the marriage ceremony, at Speldhurst Church, of the son of Lieutenant-General Smith RA to the eldest daughter of the late Robert Woodman Esquire of Montague Square; having apparently accumulated another degree since 1807, that of Doctor of Divinity. In October 1826 he hit the headlines again in less happy circumstances:

> On Monday evening an accident of an alarming nature occurred at Pembury, but though considerable injury was incurred, we are happy to state that no lives were lost. About half past ten a post-chaise containing three gentlemen, who were returning from Robertsbridge fair, came in contact with the gig of Thomas Stevens esquire containing that gentleman and his lady. The post-chaise was overturned by the violence of the concussion and Mr Stevens was thrown out of his gig and considerably bruised, as also the post-boy, but they are both now in a fair way of recovery. Providentially Mrs Stevens and the gentlemen in the post-chaise sustained no injury beyond the fright consequent on so alarming an occurrence.

Perhaps this incident, and advancing age, persuaded Thomas to move house. About 1828 the Great Lodge estate was bought by Sir Edward Colebrook Bart. and became known as Colebrook Park after improvements had been made for the new owner. A list of pictures at the Royal Academy Exhibition appeared in the

Maidstone Journal in 1829 and included one of 'Alterations and additions to an old house (formerly called Great Lodge) at Colebrook Park near Tunbridge Wells, the seat of Sir Edward Colebrook Bart by CR Ayres'. By 1840 Thomas Smith was the owner and the enlarged house is shown on the Tithe map as three sides of a square open to the south-west and looking onto a large sheet of ornamental water: today this is the North Farm Sewage Works and the whole area is bisected by Longfield Road and covered by the ever-expanding Industrial Estate. In 1869 W.A. Smith had sold part of his land to the Town Commissioners for the sewage farm and moved his own residence to a new house, called 'Colebrooke', much nearer the main road – and further from the sewage! The 'Home Farm' to the south and its 26 acres 'formerly occupied by Edward Mercer then Thomas Chambers' at an annual rental of £8 5s. 0d. are commemorated in the name of the housing estate adjoining the Industrial Estate. The new country residence for the Stephens family was Southfield Park which also has found a new use: today it is the playing fields of Skinners School between the lane which used to run down to the Powder Mills and the Yew Tree Farm, where the Southborough Fire Station and Library now are. In 1838 when it had become 'the seat of the Rev William Wilkin Stephens, MA', Southfield Park was described as 'an ancient house, sheltered on the west by thriving plantations, and surrounded by extensive and fertile grounds'; and somc indication of the standard of living of the family is given by the fact that the interior was 'ornamented with a small collection of paintings by Sir Joshua Reynolds, Sir Peter Lely, Spagnoletto, Romney, Hogarth, Francesca, Mola and others'.

In 1823 The Rev. Dr, Mrs and Miss Stephens had been spotted by the local reporter at Nash's Race Ball at the Assembly Rooms on the Pantiles but the fond parents' efforts to bring out their daughter do not seem to have borne fruit until 1831 when, on 5 January at St Marylebone Church, their son performed the marriage ceremony for his sister; and on 24 September the lady of William Samuel Jones of Brunswick Square presented Thomas and Ann with a grandson. Less than a year later, however, the proud grandfather died at his London home in his 79th year. In his will he left the income from £3,000 each to provide for his dear wife Ann and his daughter (unmarried at the time of making the will), the money to be raised by sale or mortgage of property. His 'Capital Messuage or Dwelling House with its coach house and stable situate in Devonshire Place, Marylebone, with its contents' went to his widow; and 'all my Library of Books' to his son together with the residue of the freehold property. The executors were his friend William Allfree Esquire of Herstmonceux in Sussex and his widow and daughter; and probate was duly granted to the three of them on 4 July 1832. What became thereafter of Ann, the Mount Sion heiress, still no more than 59 years old when she became a widow, I do not know – any more than I can be certain that her ever-after had really been as happy as, from what we know of her life, it deserved to be. The subsequent career of her son, however, forms a curious sequel to this story.

William Wilkin Stephens never married, it seems. He was perhaps more active as a clergyman than his father; at least he ws reported in August 1833 as the preacher of a sermon at Tonbridge. Southfield Park was an old house of some importance with no passages but rooms leading one from the other; and there he lived in lonely splendour with his servants and his pictures and the one lodge keeper at the end of the long drive which curved past the house and then back to the main road. He had one great friend, however. This was a London lawyer who rejoiced in the name John Stephen Spindler Hopwood and practised with his son under the name Hopwood and Son; becoming an Under Sheriff of London and Grand Deacon in the Grand Lodge of Masons. In 1846 William Wilkin found himself failing in health and went to live with his lawyer friend at 10, Montague Place, behind the British Museum in London; taking with him some furniture, plate, books and pictures and letting out Southfield Park to a succession of clergymen. In 1860 a son was born to one of the sons of J.S.S. Hopwood and William Wilkin stood Godfather to his friend's grandson who took the forenames Francis John Stephens. Eight years later William Stephens died and for the third time the Wilkin fortune became the object of envy and controversy.

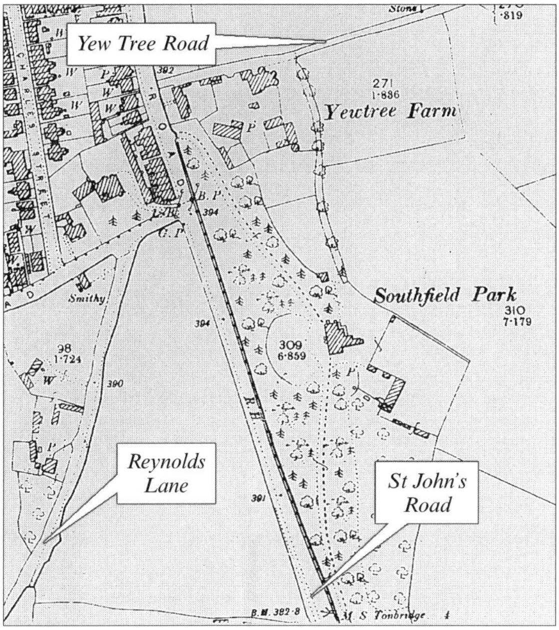

Ordnance Survey c.*1870 showing Southfield Park*

John Stephen Spindler Hopwood had five sons and one daughter and I suppose it was natural that during the twenty or more years that William Stephens spent at the Montague Place house they should have become a sort of surrogate family for the bachelor clergyman. At all events they benefited under his will. Four sons received £1,500 each and one £2,000 while Hannah, the daughter, was given a handsome £5,000. 'My young friend Walter William Hopwood of Pembroke College Oxford M.A.' received £300, in addition to his £1,500, to enable him to purchase a 'library of standard works'; and Charles Henry, one of the executors, in addition to his £2,000, was rewarded not only with the collection of books at 10, Montague Place (Thomas Stephens' library, I suppose) and the largest silver salver but also with the farm, pub and tenements at Bell's Yew Green which had been Jeffery property. The gardener and lodge keeper at Southfield Park and the daughter of William's former housekeeper were remembered with legacies of £500 and £300 and his friend and medical adviser, John Rowland Gibson, had another £300. After all this the residue of the personal and real estate (and there was no suggestion that it had to be mortgaged or sold to pay the legacies amounting to some £15,000) was left to his friend J.S.S. Hopwood and his heirs. The Jones family of Brunswick Square evidently felt left out in the cold and thought they should have had some share in the Jeffery and Wilkin inheritance. Whether sister Georgina was still alive in 1869 I do not know but the case of 'Hopwood and Others against Jones and Others' came to be heard in the Court of Probate early in the year. Well, there may have been some doubt about the morality of the will but of its legal validity there could be none; and the judge so decreed and in course of time William Stephens' godson prospered and was elevated to the peerage and took the title Lord Southborough. The late second holder of the title recollected that his father and uncle and their cousins all had a say in the disposal of the land, practically all of which was sold by the time his father was made a peer; but a plot or two remained which he was forced to sell to the Council after his father's death. He remembered also that, when they used to visit Southborough together, his father mentioned that the house at Southfield Park had been let as a school. What Lord Southborough did not know, however, was the story of his benefactor's father and his whirlwind wedding to the young heiress of Mount Sion back in 1790. What he did say was that William Wilkin Stephens was apparently a man of affluence and the belongings which had been left to his great-grandfather were of very good quality. He possessed two handsome gold seals with Stephens' coat of arms engraved on them, the crest being a stag's head. A memorial to this story survives in the naming of two roads in the town: Stephens Road and Hopwood Gardens. There used also to be a Wilkin Road but it disappeared some years ago.

Nancy Storace

William Large, in the meanwhile, carried on at Fairlawn House until 1830, four years beyond the term of his lease. In August 1827 and again in July 1829 Sir William Pringle stayed there and in July 1828 it was occupied by Mr Braham, 'the celebrated vocalist'. John Braham, although aged 54, was then at the height of his powers as a tenor. Two years before he had sung in the first performance of Weber's 'Oberon'; but his career had been helped in its early stages by another English singer, Nancy Storace, who had been the first Susanna in the 'Marriage of Figaro' in Vienna in 1786. There are those who say that Susanna's last act aria in the garden was a love song from Mozart to Nancy. Be that as it may, another sort of love developed between Nancy and the young tenor, John Braham, in 1797 (although she was nine years his senior) and they went off on a joint five-year concert tour of Europe at the end of which Nancy bore the tenor a son. The story ended unhappily for Nancy because he would not marry her and she died in 1817; but we at least can bathe in a small amount of glory reflected from the fact that the father of the son of the first Susanna actually stayed in Fairlawn House. But any bit of reflected glory from Susanna is enough for me. On the previous page is a picture of Nancy with a hat. It is not a good picture but I think I can understand why Mozart and indeed half Vienna, including the Emperor, were said to be in love with her. John Braham had appeared in 1806, as Sesto in 'La Clemenza di Tito', in the first performance of a Mozart opera in England and was the original Max in Weber's 'Der Freischütz' at the Lyceum in 1824. He had already accumulated a large fortune during a career of forty years; but a few years after his visit to Tunbridge Wells he was to lose most of it in speculations involving the Colosseum in Regent's Park and the building of the St James's Theatre at a cost of £30,000; forcing him back to the stage where in 1839 he sang Don Giovanni, his tenor having suffered somewhat from the ravages of time.

Whether these visitors used the whole house and how long they stayed it is impossible to be sure. Other activities continued also at the back of the premises: in September 1828 the newspaper announced that the 'first pocket of new hops sent to London this year, was received on Friday last, by Messrs Nokes, Rose and Nokes, factors, Borough, from Mr Large, of Tunbridge Wells', although on Saturday after a bidding of £4 10s. 0d. it remained unsold. No doubt Mr Large was busy also hiring out horses and supplying hay and corn. In November 1830, however, an auction sale, on the premises, Fairlawn House, Mount Sion, was announced for Guy Fawkes Day and the following day. Genteel Household Furniture, Chimney and Pier Glasses, etc. etc., were to be sold 'by direction of the Proprietor, Mr Wm. Large, who is removing': bedsteads; 12 'excellent seasoned feather beds'; dimity and moreen curtains; mahogany tray-top night commodes; wash hand stands, basins and ewers; dining tables with oval ends; Scotch and Kidderminster carpets; register, pantheon, elliptic and other stoves; kitchen range with smoke jack; and so on. Joseph Delves died in 1827 and left Fairlawn House to his son Joseph and his son-in-law James Hockett Fry in trust for Henry, his son, and Henry's wife Ann, who was a daughter of Samuel and Elizabeth Parman. If Henry and Ann had no children – which proved to be the case – then the property was to go to his grandsons, Joseph and William, sons of his son Richard. Since this Joseph Delves (there were three of them even after the death of Joseph senior!) died in 1857 and Henry and his wife were dead by 1869, the effect of this testamentary provision may well have been to pass ownership to William Delves alone: but this is to anticipate. I assume that Henry or some division of Delveses undertook the re-furnishing of the house or even, as suggested above (page 357), the renovation and re-fronting of the building if this had not been done at the earlier date. The idea could have been to upgrade the house for use not as a lodging house but as a furnished house for letting undivided. Anyhow, this seems to have been the trend of the times.

On 27 July 1833 Octavia Harvey Boys died 'of a rapid consumption' at her mother's residence, Fairlawn House, at Tunbridge Wells, 'deservedly beloved and regretted by her family and friends'. She was in her 21st year and was the youngest daughter of the late William Boys Esquire, Colonel of Marines; the granddaughter of the late Admiral Sir H. Harvey and niece to Rear-Admiral Sir Thomas Harvey KCB. In 1836 the house was the scene of a happier event. The arrival of the Rev. William D. Johnstone and his wife at Fairlawn House was announced in the local press on 3 May and on 13 September a son was born to the lady. In 1841 the house was occupied by Bartholemew Jeffery (no connection as far as I know with the 18th-century owners), a gentleman of independent means, his wife, three children in their thirties and three servants. In 1847 the occupier was a gentleman named Theophilus F. Johnson; and in 1849 came a brief moment of muted glory. On 30 June that year the Queen and Prince Albert had come on a hurried and, it would appear, unpremeditated visit to the Queen Dowager who was staying at the *Calverley Hotel*, scene of the Queen's earlier and (by the good citizens of the Wells) nostalgically remembered sojourns. The poor stationmaster at the *Bricklayer's Arms* had been given but a few hours notice to prepare a suitable reception before the special train consisting of the Royal Saloon, two first-class carriages and a break van had set off at half past two, arriving at Tonbridge in less than an hour where the engine had to be changed and a dish of grapes was hastily rustled up. On arrival at the Jack Woods terminus, a quick visit to the hotel was followed by a circular drive to the High Rocks and back by the Eridge Road, a short inspection and purchase of Tunbridge Ware for the children at Nye's Repository, and a 'déjeune' at the hotel before departing at six o'clock. Maybe it was a gossip with mother about this trip which prompted the Duchess to renew her acquaintance with Tunbridge Wells. What certainly did not happen was any meeting between mother and daughter at Eden House or anywhere else in the town. The subsequent visit of the Duchess of Kent and her suite's use of Fairlawn have been noted already in chapter 21 (page 307) – after which Fairlawn settled back into its habitual ways for another decade or two.

In 1851 Selina Still, an unmarried fundholder of 52 years from St George's Parish, Middlesex, was in occupation with her young niece and nephew (an ensign in the 65th Regiment), a governess, lady's maid, butler, nursery maid, cook, page boy of 14 and female servant; and in January 1860 Mr and Mrs Fletcher were occupants of the whole house. However, in July 1860 there was another furniture auction, this time 'in consequence of the house being let on lease, unfurnished', and by the end of August the Misses Mary and Harriet Seeley had arrived to set up their ladies' school. In 1861 their ages were 32 and 24; and, as well as a cook and two housemaids, they had a young French teacher from Switzerland and just five scholars, two of whom, sisters of 18 and 16, were named Seeley! This enterprise did not last very long for by 1871 the house was in domestic use again. David Johnson wrote the following comment on his photograph: 'Used as a private residence by Mr Gibbons and daughter 1873-4 onwards. Afterwards as the High School for Girls. Then as the Eye and Ear Hospital.' Johnson is not quite accurate for Kelly gives Robert Kenrick Gibbons as early as 1871 and in January 1882 the *Tunbridge Wells Gazette* listed the Misses Gibbons. The stables and buildings at the rear of Fairlawn House, presumably with the good will of the business, had been sold just before William Large left the house in 1830 and the purchaser was William Hodges junior, of the *Compasses*. This was the start of an association which lasted for fifty years and which gave the name 'Hodges Yard' to the premises; although the name 'Cumberland Yard' was in use in 1835 as is shown by an advertisement which appeared in the *Maidstone Journal* in April 1835:

PARTICULARS
OF VALUABLE
FREEHOLD BUSINESS PREMISES,
So exceptionally situated on The Mount Sion, Tunbridge Wells, and so widely known as
CUMBERLAND, OR HODGES' YARD,
Comprising Substantially-constructed
EXTENSIVE RANGE OF
Coach-Houses with Stabling,
OVER WHICH ARE
Spacious Lofts and Fodder Rooms,
HAVING AN AREA OF ABOUT 3450 SQUARE FEET.
These ample and exceedingly well arranged Premises are the most extensive of the kind in the Town, and have for upwards of 60 years past met all the requirements of Messrs. HODGES & Co. and their predecessors, who have carried on very Extensive and Lucrative Businesses as
Coal, Corn, and Forage Merchants, and Livery Stable Keepers.
THE ACCOMMODATION IS AS FOLLOWS:—
7 LOCK-UP COACH HOUSES
A DOUBLE DITTO,
A Four-Stall Stable
Two Three-Stall ditto
Four Two-Stall ditto
Most of these Stalls are convertible into Loose Boxes.
Large Forage Warehouse 93ft. by 18ft. 9in. fitted with Corn Bins.
Hay and Straw Loft 91ft. by 18ft. 9in.
Attached to these Buildings is a Coachman's Living Room, Bedroom, and Harness Room; also a W.C. and Manure Pit,
THERE IS
A LARGE AND WELL PITCHED STABLE YARD,
With Well of Soft Water and Pump, and also the Right of Way over the broad road leading from Mount Sion to these Premises, subject to a stipulation to contribute towards the repair of the same. Attached is
A CONVENIENTLY ARRANGED OFFICE,
AND ADJOINING IS
A SUBSTANTIALLY CONSTRUCTED RESIDENCE,
Containing 4 Bedrooms, 2 Sitting Rooms, Kitchen, and Domestic Offices.
GAS & WATER ARE LAID ON.
All Trade and other Fittings and Fixtures, the Property of the Vendors, are included in the Sale.
This Property is situated in the Centre of TUNBRIDGE WELLS, and offers exceptional advantages to those requiring Spacious and Commodious Premises for the carrying on successfully of a large Business of a similar character to that which, under the name of HODGES & Co., has become so well known in the Counties of Kent and Sussex. The whole is now let under a Lease to Mr. H. D. WILLIAMS, expiring on the 24th June now next, at the low
Annual Rental of £145 0s. 0d.
The Lessee covenanting to leave the Premises in good and tenantable Repair and Condition.
Possession will be given on Completion of the Purchase.
The Plan accompanying these Conditions is believed to be substantially correct, but is furnished more for the purpose of shewing the position and site of the premises than for its accuracy in detail.

1894 Sale

> To be sold by auction. A PAIR of handsome BAY PONIES, rising 5 and 6 years old, 13 hands high, (the property of a gentleman having no further use for them), have been driven regularly together, in Harness, for these last two years past, and are also quiet, and acknowledged to be in single Harness without a compeer. They may be viewed … at Mr WILLIAM HODGES'S, Cumberland Yard …

William Hodges seems to have lived in a house which he built at the end of the southern row of stables and which still exists as 'Woburn House' (somewhat altered after the latest development) and was until recently used as offices and a spare parts store by Stephenson's Motors. In his will he refers to his 'freehold messuage and dwelling house wherein I now reside and the Coach houses Stables Buildings … and premises thereto belonging situate … at or near Mount Sion'.

The business evidently flourished, as witness the auctioneers in 1884: 'These ample ... premises ... have for upwards of 60 years past met all the requirements of Messrs Hodges & Co and their predecessors who have owned a very extensive & lucrative business as Coal Corn & Forage Merchants & Livery Stable Keepers ...'. The extent of the premises is surprising, as shown by the 1884 sale notice above. William Hodges lived there until he died in 1855 and his son took over until his premature death from pneumonia in 1870, after which the trade was carried on firstly as John Hodges & Co and then as the Tunbridge Wells Corn Exchange Co Ltd, whose secretary was J.F. Bates of Caxton House. The old stables and premises were replaced about 1920 by a large covered workshop which was recently demolished to make way for the present housing development. See the Tithe map plan of Hodge's Yard below.

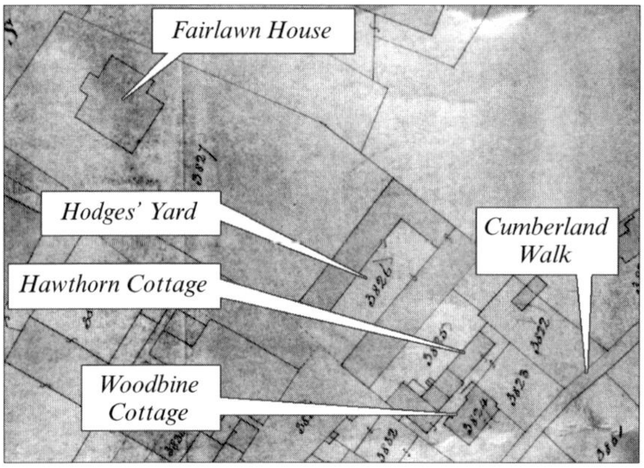

Tithe map 1840

Also shown on the Tithe map are two cottages facing Cumberland Walk – or Patty Moon's Walk to give it its older name. One of these cottages dates from before 1808 when it appears on the Barrow map as Mr Stidolph's Cottage in the 'Little Grove Field', numbered '1' – see detail on page 356 above. This must have been sited on part of the plot of land leased to Henry Adams in 1689; but I have no information on when Stidolph or whoever came before him acquired the land. By 1840 (see Tithe map detail above) there were two cottages, facing Cumberland Walk, on the 'Adams plot' and both were owned by Stidolphs: Woodbine Cottage, the original cottage from 1808, was owned and occupied by Thomas; and Hawthorn Cottage by William Stidolph. Now 'T', presumably Thomas, Stidolph was a Land Surveyor who announced in the *Tunbridge Wells Visitor* in 1834 that he was to publish a map of Speldhurst, made a map of the 'Local Act District' in 1838 and called himself 'Surveyor to the Commissioners'; and made a map of waterworks for Lord Abergavenny in 1838, calling himself 'Surveyor etc' of Cumberland Terrace – a former name for Cumberland Walk. Then in 1850 a map of the Manor of Rusthall was published by 'Stidolph & Sons'. In the census of 1841 the occupier of Woodbine Cottage was entered as Thomas Stidolph, a schoolmaster aged 50. Hawthorn Cottage, however, had changed its name to 'Cumberland Cottage' (which it still bears) and the occupier was John Jenner, a shoemaker. In 1861 the 'Superintendent Registrar' for the census was 'E Stidolph'. From these scattered facts it is impossible to do more than guess that there was a senior 'Stidolph' who owned the cottage in 1808 and had a son Thomas born about 1790 and perhaps another son, William, who was living next to his brother in 1840 but by 1841 had moved on – or he may have been a son of Thomas who, with another son, was helping his father to make maps by 1850. Where 'E' Stidolph, the Registrar, fits in is difficult to say. Anyhow, Thomas had left Woodbine Cottage by 1861 to be replaced by Thomas Stapley, an 82-year-old retired butcher and his three daughters; and a 'Miss Stapley' continues to be listed in directories until at least 1900.

Fairlawn House meanwhile, in 1883, entered upon a new era, as a school; but this time it was no fly-by-night spinsters' pastime. The Women's Educational Union, an early augury of the feminist movement, was constituted in 1871 and formed the Girls' Public Day School Company which opened its first school at South Kensington in January 1873. In 1906 the Company was converted into a Trust which today controls schools over the country from its headquarters in London, although its Tunbridge Wells off-shoot closed in 1940 from lack of numbers, having moved from Mount Sion to Camden Park. There are still alumnae of the Girls' High School living in the town. I have not been able to discover for certain whether the school bought or leased Fairlawn House nor from whom. As already suggested, the owner was probably William Delves who lived at Hargate Lodge in Broadwater Down (see chapter 21). He died in 1886 but his will does not specify his property, leaving a residue in trust for his unmarried daughters Rose and Matilda. However, it is certain that the girls' elder brother, William Henry, the future mayor of Tunbridge Wells, who had already been living for ten years at no 23, Mount Sion, just opposite Fairlawn House, would have had a weighty voice in family matters; and there is in fact a family story saying that he was somehow influential in the foundation of the school and that one of his motives was to find a school for his daughter. In any case he certainly acquired some shares in the company which his grandson sold recently.

Whatever the truth of the Delves' family story, it is a fact that William Henry's eldest daughter, Lilian Jane (see photograph in chapter 21), along with Lucy Colbran and others, was one of the big girls of Form IV when the school opened its doors on 18 January 1883. She must actually have been 17 years old and cannot have stayed long. In later life she became an archery champion, introduced 'Papillon' dogs into the UK and married Howard, son of the founder of the YMCA, Sir George Williams. When the school celebrated its half-centenary a number of old girls and mistresses recorded their memories and impressions. The building was simply a large old private house, rather gloomy and shabby, with a plastered classical front and four storeys; and without the additions to right and to left of the central section which have since appeared. Behind was the garden, originally a grassy square surrounded by flowerbeds and 'delectable shrubberies for playing 'Prisoners' and other romantic games' – but no one remembered the stables at the back.

On that first day there were a mere 20 girls but numbers rapidly increased and after ten years there were one hundred and sixty-four. In 1894 the old house was bursting and Jerningham House next door was taken over, becoming the senior school. Previously the sixth form girls had been housed in attics on the top floor along with the staff room; and the other floors were used in a descending order of seniority. The Assembly Room was originally on the first floor at the head of a flight of shallow stairs ('irresistible for rushing up two at a time'). Later it was to become the Women's Ward of the hospital. At the bottom of the stairs was Miss Moberley's room (known as 'The Den') with a window overlooking the garden, which the headmistress would on occasions throw up to say: 'Girls, you may shout, but not SCREAM!' Miss Moberley's dreaded punishment for smaller misdemeanours was to stand girls under the hall clock in full view of passers by.

In 1887 a new Assembly Room was added, on the right of the building, where the Outpatients' Entrance can be seen on Johnson's photograph. This was described as an 'Iron Room' and remarkably was dismantled and re-erected in Cambridge Gardens when the school moved there: a pioneering pre-fab in fact. The external wall materials were brick, wood and iron and the builders were E.J. Strange and Sons, descendants of the 'Green Pales' lodging house keeper. There was a pitched roof running from front to back and at the far end a space was partitioned off for a laboratory with a sink and a 'stench closet'. Part rested on a new scullery and furnace at basement level and the outer part on stilts. Steps led down internally from the main building and more steps gave egress to the garden where a holly tree stood under a window. The 'fair lawn' at the back soon succumbed to the tip-and-run and hockey of the girls, despite their tight-buttoned bodices, high collars and flowing skirts, and was asphalted over. For years it seems to have served for hockey and rounders in winter and cricket and a little tennis in summer; but in 1892 use was obtained of one of the Claremont Road Tennis Courts and in 1895 a field for hockey was hired where Blatchington Road now is; and proved a great success even though it was under threat of being built on at any moment and there was a large oak tree in the striking circle. In 1898 the Claremont Road courts (where were they?) were used for a 'Strawberry Fête' in aid of the school's Children's Country Holiday Fund (held the following year in the Calverley Grounds with a military band in attendance); but by 1900 the courts had ceased to exist. The two hockey teams, the Scarlet Runners and the Blue Beans, performed successfully against other schools as far apart as Croydon, Sutton and the future Roedean at Brighton.

Scholastically the school also did well. There was a certain prejudice that girls should be learning to be housewives not blue-stockings and to counter this the girls threw themselves into cookery classes on a Saturday morning; but one year the three girls in the Upper Sixth Form managed to collect five University Scholarships between them and the school had a holiday. There was a compulsory entrance exam but the school eschewed prizes ('Honour before Honours' was a class motto) although at a later stage public examinations had to be accepted – and even a portly School Inspector, whose twirl in illustration of a planetary orbit remained in many a girlish memory. A few more scattered memories will perhaps complete the impression. Fraeulein was quickly dissuaded from making the girls learn pages of the Wellington College French Grammar by heart, rules and examples; it was not done in England, they maintained. The First Formers lined up every morning with sponges which were dipped in a bucket of water and had to last for their slates for the day; and some of them contrived to make appalling squeaks with their slate pencils. A Scripture lesson for two fourth forms was held in separate rooms at Jerningham House and the teacher stood in the doorway in between. Best of all perhaps was Zuleika, the cat, who regularly attended classes on one lap or another: 'Oh, yes, miss,' the girls would tell the new teacher, 'she much enjoys maths but will not listen to Greek lessons.'

This idyll – if such it really was – disappeared with the old century; or departed from Mount Sion at any rate. I do not know why the move was made: I guess a chance had arisen to house the school more conveniently under one roof. Anyway, a long line of girls wound its way one cold January day in 1900 up the hill towards Grove Hill Road carrying scientific equipment in waste paper baskets and everything except the laboratory sink and the stench in the closet. Even the 'Iron Room' was transferred to the new site in Cambridge Gardens. It could not be taken down until the beginning of the Christmas holidays and its reconstruction on the new site was a work of time. Progress was not helped by the terribly bad weather which greeted the new century and term did not eventually begin until 29 January. Even then the coal had not arrived and it was a bitter cold day and, after a brief 'Lord, behold us with Thy blessing' in the old Assembly Room on the new site, everyone trailed home again. The next day, however, the term got under way to the accompaniment of strange bangings in the newly-installed central heating pipes and occasional incursions of plumber or carpenter into the classroom. Back on Mount Sion, meanwhile, Fairlawn and Jerningham stood waiting in the desolate winter for new occupants.

Fairlawn House with proposed New Wing – Courier *1900*

The Eye and Ear Hospital had started life in 1878 in Vale Road and moved to Sheffield House on the Pantiles in 1888. Accommodation was cramped, however, and the departure of the Girls' School from Fairlawn House did not pass unnoticed. In April 1900 (see above) a sketch of the house with a new wing added on the site of the dismantled Assembly Room was to be seen in the *Courier* and under it was an appeal for money.

> The above sketch illustrates the proposal of the Committee of the Eye and Ear Hospital which for years has done good work on the Pantiles to obtain

> more commodious premises on Mount Sion. The building will be recognised as that recently vacated by the Girls' High School with a new wing added to it designed by Mr C.H. Strange. The rooms are spacious and are considered easily adaptable for their new purpose, while the extensive grounds for the patients' use will be an improvement on the present site. Another advantage is that the property will be freehold instead of leasehold. The cost is about £3000 and another £1000 will be required for alterations, furnishing and contingencies.

Whether the vendor was the Delves family or the Girls' School was not stated – I guess it was the Delves. Deeds there must have been until the 1950s or '60s or conveyances could not have been made; but enquiry shows that somewhere between Stephenson's Motors, Robert Stace, Seeboard and their respective solicitors the deeds have been mislaid or destroyed: but this is to anticipate.

The appeal continued:

> The statistics of the number of patients treated show that a larger number of beds is absolutely required, and the excellent work which this hospital in the special diseases it treats is doing in the neighbourhood will ensure sympathetic consideration for the present appeal. For the present week we notice there are 9 in-patients and 149 out-patients, and the last annual report records a large increase of work in every department.

The money was duly forthcoming, the list being headed by £500 from the Archbishop of Canterbury 'under the Marriott bequest' and £100 each from Lord Abergavenny and others. The Strange wing, in a classical style to match the Delves façade of Fairlawn House, became the Outpatients' Department, as can be seen on David Johnson's photograph. The 'Eye and Ear' deserves a chapter in the history of health provision in Tunbridge Wells. It is still vivid in the memory of many older citizens. 'I had my tonsils taken out there,' I was told only the other day. Dr Abbott, a well-known ophthalmic surgeon, was in charge on the Pantiles and moved with the hospital to Mount Sion. He was succeeded in the early 1900s by Dr David Davies who was primarily an eye specialist but also did ear, nose and throat work until after the 1914-18 war when Dr Walker Wood joined to do ENT surgery. In 1917 the hospital was open at 1.30 p.m. on Mondays, Wednesdays and Fridays and in 1921 it treated 303 in-patients and 2,339 out-patients. The staff in 1917 included David Davies (surgeon), Edwin Starling (anaesthetician), Edward Adeney JP (physician), William Trollope (surgeon-dentist) and Miss Emily Swindale (matron).

The matron was the aunt of Richard Cobb who sketches her with characteristically studied sarcasm in his memoirs. She never moved far from the hospital where she lived unless given a lift. Her extreme limit on foot was the Cobb house in Claremont Road which she visited several times a week, staying to watch and embarrass but never partake of her sister's lunch. Favours she received with 'an almost regal hauteur, as if they had been her due'. Her nurses were always giving her presents – 'little things to put on the mantelpiece of her sitting room; and they frequently put in extra hours of duty – all of which she accepted with rather an absent-minded grace'. When she retired she moved to a flat in the

Kentish Mansions (where the old *Angel* and *Royal Kentish Hotels* had been); and she died in the Kentish Nursing Home at Jerningham House, in the big room with its own balcony overlooking the garden. Perhaps this was the same 'light room looking across the garden down the hill' which had been the Lower Fourth classroom in the time of Miss Julian, the headmistress who succeeded Miss Moberley in 1892.

The Eye and Ear Hospital must at the beginning of the 20th century have seemed an enduring institution on the Mount Sion scene. It did last over thirty years but by the mid-1920s moves were afoot to expand the General Hospital, then in Grosvenor Road. In 1926 the Great Culverden site came on the market, on 19 July 1932 the then Duchess of York (our late Queen Mother) laid the foundation stone, on 11 August 1934 the first patients were admitted to the new Kent and Sussex Hospital and three weeks later patients from the Eye and Ear Hospital were transferred. Johnson's photograph, therefore, shows an empty building waiting to embark on a new and somewhat sadder career as an office block.

At first the building continued to belong to the hospital and was let out to the Ordnance Survey from 1937 to 1940. At the end of 1945, when the war was over, it was offered for sale and realised £5,115. At least this was a boost to the hospital's finances during a difficult period before the NHS took over in 1948. I do not know who the purchaser was but the directories show that the occupiers were the Ministry of Works (1948-50), Robert Stace the printers (1957-61) and Seeboard (1963-74). Subsequently, with the addition of a third storey above the old Out-patients' Wing (which spoils the view of the Jerningham House roof from down the hill), it was let out as offices by a Life Assurance Company which saw fit to dignify it with the 'name' TWENTY-TWO! It was then occupied by a firm of financial consultants who agreed to give it back its old name. Now after conversion and refurbishment on a substantial scale it is still called Fairlawn House, giving it a link with its varied, nay romantic past; but its use has reverted to the residential – a number of 'luxury' apartments.

Fairlawn House in luxury apartments – from the Sales Brochure 2001

Chapter 25

Jerningham House

This chapter takes us one step down the hill from Fairlawn House but still on the southern side of the road. Here is a postcard which proclaimed Jerningham House's use in about 1920 as a nursing home. The 17th-century lease plots on this side of Mount Sion ran at right angles to the road and as far as the boundary of South Frith land with that of Lord Abergavenny. It might be thought that this would also be the county boundary between Kent and Sussex but in fact Lord Abergavenny owned a strip of land on the Kent side of the stream marking the county boundary.

Jerningham House c.*1920*

I do not know the reason for this arrangement or how far back it went in time – certainly as far as the 17th century because it enabled him to participate in the development of the Pantiles on the Lower Walk side. Maybe he wanted to be able to fish from both sides of the stream but I do not think he would have had much luck in the little Grom brook. On Mount Sion the boundary between the two ownerships became in time a footpath which in the 19th century was called Cumberland Terrace, then Patty Moon's Walk and finally Cumberland Walk as it is now.

The record begins on 10 December 1689 when the Countess Purbeck leased several pieces of land to Edward Allen for 50 years – the same date as the leases to Henry Adams dealt with in the previous chapter. Allen started paying the Poor Rate on his Mount Sion property the very next year. His daughter Ann inherited from her father in 1720 and in 1729 married a widower named John Wells Luck. This explains 'Mr Luck' on the Bowra plan – see the next page. She was in her late 30s and he was six years older.

The Poor Rate record for Jerningham House runs as follows:

1690-1714	Mr Edward Allen	
1728	Mr Edward Allen	
1729	Mrs Anne Allen	
1730-1737	Mr Luck	
1738-1742	Tho Mercer for Lucks house	}
1743	Thos Mercer for Mr Lucks new house	} Mr Luck for a new house
1744	Thos Mercer for Mr Lucks house	}
1745-1759	Tho Mercer for Lucks 2 houses	
1760-1774	Wid Mercer for Lucks 2 houses & field	
1775	Wid Mercer or occ for – do –	
1776-1784	Delves Richd for Lucks 2 houses & field	
1785?	Latter Darius for two houses and land and Mercers field?	
1786-1792	Quinnell George for late Richd Delves's for Lucks two houses and Land	
1793-1797	Quinnell George for late Richd Delves	

The bifurcation in the record occurs because in 1738 Mr Luck built a new house. From 1730 to 1737 he paid the rates on the original house and then Thomas Mercer took over which is why we find 'Tho Mercer Occ[upier]' on Bowra in 1738. So from 1738 to 1744 there are two houses and two ratepayers (I think we can disregard the 'new' in the 1743 entry for Mercer). Then in 1745 Mercer took over the new house and paid rates for both until 1759. He was followed by the Widow Mercer until 1775 and by Richard Delves until 1785. Then a man called George Quinnell took over to the end of the century. Evidently the house was being used as a lodging house during all this period. *Sprange's Guide* for 1780 lists 'Delves, late Widow Mercer's' as a lodging house and in 1797, with Mr Quinnell in charge, the house has been divided into three. It is tempting to assume that Thomas Mercer was the father of Dorothea who married Richard Delves in 1752, as this would explain the succession Thomas Mercer/Widow Mercer/Richard Delves; but this assumption was discussed in chapter 20 (page 287); and the issue is by no means clear-cut. The Poor Rate record for Eden House suggests that the widow died in 1759 or '60 whereas that for Jerningham House has her paying rates until about 1774. Problem unresolved. Notice the shape of the house. It is basically L-shaped. Owners of the house keep telling me that it was

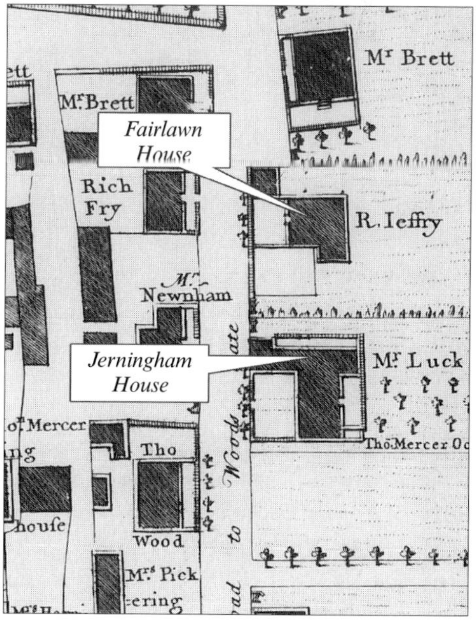

Bowra plan 1738

built in two stages but, as far as I am concerned, it was built as one L-shape and that's how it has always been. Some confusion is created by the fact that it has at various times and in various ways been sub-divided – as, of course, it is now into four. So we find references to Jerningham House and Jerningham Place and more than one house; but the solution to this lies elsewhere.

It seems that Ann and John Luck did not live in Jerningham House or even in Tunbridge Wells but in Wadhurst and when she died in 1768 and he three years later they were buried in Wadhurst Church – under a massive iron slab in the porch, so that anyone going into the church has to step on their bodies. Besides that there is a memorial on the porch wall. Ann had no children herself but her husband had a son and a daughter by his previous marriage and the children benefited under their step-grandmother's will. This provided for the transfer to her husband of a small lodging house on her estate in Tunbridge Wells which he had built 'at his own proper charge' (this must be the 'new house' of 1738) and the disposal of the remainder on her husband's death.

Memorial to Ann and John Luck in porch of Wadhurst Church

The sale of Jerningham House, however, did not take place until 1804 on account, it appears, of family and legal complications, and the purchaser was William Beale, described as a coach-master or coach proprietor. I wish I knew more about this character – did he crack the whip literally, I wonder. Anyway he died in 1808 and his four children inherited: two sons, William and John, and two daughters, Harriet and Emily.

The situation in 1808 is recorded by Barrow on his map. The legend tells us that the main house was divided into Mr Beale Nos 2, 3 and 4 while No 5 was

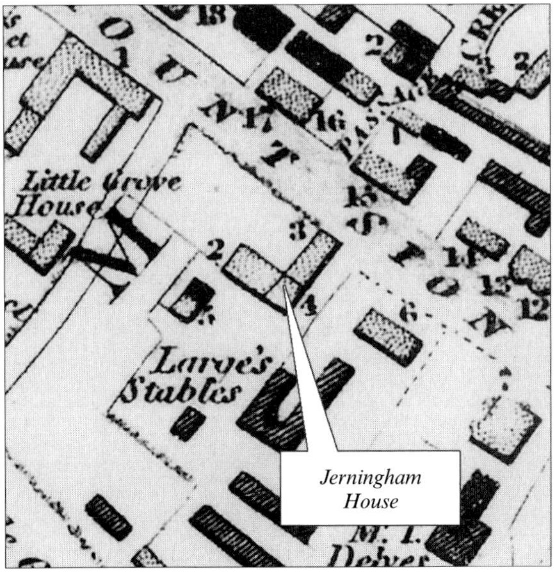

Barrow map 1808

called Mr Beale's Cottage. The deeds of Howard Lodge (kindly made available by one of the present owners), while dating some twenty years, later explain the various parts: Jerningham Place or the Great Lodging House, the Wing End and the Green Apartments forming the main house while the separate building, No.5 on the map (presumably Mr Luck's 'new house'), was split into two, one half of which, as indicated by the black shading, was the private residence of the widow Mary Beale and her daughters, Harriett and Emily, and was called Mrs Wilmot's Cottage in the deeds and the other half was let out and called the Small Lodging House. Quite which parts of the house were the Wing End and the Green Apartments is difficult to be sure. The Wing End could be the end of either arm of the L and (judging from the number 4 on the Barrow map) the Green Apartments might well be the corner which is now in fact numbered 4. Here it is.

Jerningham House – Cumberland Yard side. No.4 is on the far left.

The coachmaster William had died in 1808, intestate, and his widow was evidently soldiering on. The two sons, William and John, inherited as co-heirs in gavelkind but they had to manage a £1,000 mortgage provided in 1804 by one Henry Playsted of Wadhurst who was the husband of Philadelphia, Ann Luck's granddaughter. Things began to move in 1818 when Henry died and the mortgage was redeemed. Just before this, however, came the first appearance on the scene of Robert Foreman – described in the documents as a gentleman of Frant but in fact a solicitor.

Even earlier, however, in the first years of the 19th century, occurred the events which stamped their imprint on the house for ever after – the visits of Lady Jerningham and her husband. The Jerninghams were Roman Catholics who for reasons of past history were still somewhat discriminated against and unhappy about it. They were related to the Howards of Arundel (could that possibly have anything to do with the naming of Howard Lodge?) and the Honourable Frances who married Sir William was a Dillon and they had Irish connections – Catholics, of course, and famous for the 'Dillon Regiment' which fought for France. Lady Jerningham was especially proud of her elder brother Arthur, sixth and last Colonel of the regiment, who was guillotined in 1794 as an aristocrat. Sir William himself had served in the Household Cavalry of Louis XV before his marriage. They had many continental connections – particularly French – and the daughter Charlotte was sent at the age of 13 to a Convent School in Paris – hence much correspondence

Mrs Jerningham by Hoppner

between mother and daughter. Charlotte married a Roman Catholic baronet, Sir Richard Bedingfeld, whose castle was at Oxborough in Norfolk; and had a family of eight and continuing correspondence with her mother after her marriage. A selection of these letters was published in two volumes in 1869 but all the originals have survived and are held by Birmingham University who have sent me photocopies of all those written from Tunbridge Wells. Not much notice of these letters was taken by early Tunbridge Wells historians but a few extracts were published in Lewis Melville's *Society at Tunbridge Wells in the Eighteenth Ceentury – and After*, one of the standards of Tunbridge Wells history. If you haven't come across it, I recommend a read – or at least a browse. It's very good for background atmosphere. The picture above on the left is inserted among extracts from the letters and is labelled simply 'Lady Jerningham (from a painting by Hoppner)'. Hoppner portrays the lady as Hebe, cupbearer to eagle Jupiter; but unfortunately Melville has got it wrong. The book of correspondence published in 1869 shows that she is really the wife of our Lady Jerningham's eldest son, George William, and the correct caption is Mrs Jerningham.

On the right is the best we can find for the real Lady Jerningham – taken from the volumes of correspondence. Anyway, the fact is that in the early 1800s she did write some letters from Tunbridge Wells to her daughter, Lady Bedingfeld; and the vital question is whether they prove that she ever stayed at Jerningham House. The wretched woman, however, never had the decency to think of the historians of centuries to come by heading her letters with the address from which she was writing – or even to provide a hint like the name of her landlord. On 18 June 1802 she says that the season began the day before and that there is music three times a day on the Pantiles, 9-10, 1-2 and 7-8 – played by a harp and several wind instruments. It is what she has to say in 1803, however, that is not only interesting but ***new*** and this is what she says:

Lady Jerningham

Mount Sion, Tunbridge Wells – June 16 1803

MY DEAREST CHARLOTTE,

Here I am again on this pleasant Mount, in a very tolerable House, tho' not quite so pretty as that of Last year, nor so high up the Hill. I got here on Monday evening, and found your Father well and at the Sussex Hotel (tho' in possession of a House), for which they made Him pay accordingly. But He had forgot all Hotel keepers are audacious thieves. I brought Little Prissy with me for change of air, as she really looked ill in London, and was so. At the same time it is a Little Companion, whom I Can dispose of in any Closet when I want her Room. We have on the first floor four good Bedchambers, and two Closets with Beds in them, two Bedchambers below Stairs, and two Parlours, besides a Housekeeper's Room, Garrets, and offices Sufficient. The Price 7 guineas a week; I think this very reasonable. Lord and Lady Dynevor, and Children are in the House we had Last year.

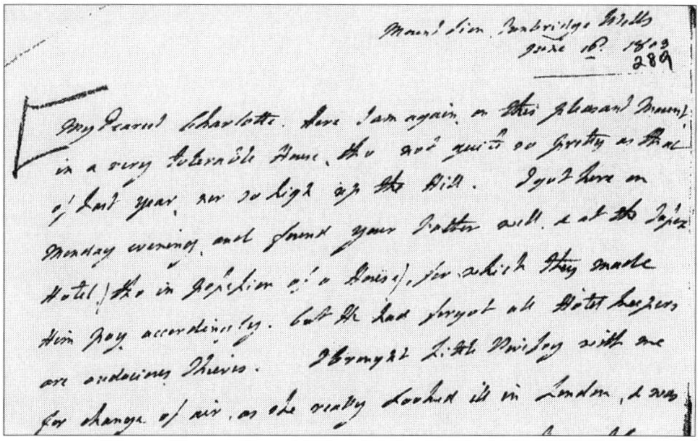
Mount Sion, Tunbridge Wells
June 16 1803
289

My Dearest Charlotte. Here I am again on this pleasant Mount
in a very tolerable House, tho' not quite so pretty as that
of Last year, nor so high up the Hill. I got here on
Monday evening, and found your Father well, & at the Sussex
Hotel (tho' in possession of a House), for which they made
Him pay accordingly. But He had forgot all Hotel keepers
are audacious thieves. I brought Little Prissy with me
for change of air, as she really looked ill in London, & was

Letter dated 16 June 1803

Does this previously unknown information help to pin-point Lady Jerningham's abode? Well, it certainly does not rule out Jerningham House; but it does not go as far as to rule it in either. Not 'so high up the hill' is certainly suggestive; and *Sprange's Guide* for 1797 shows that the main part of the house had three parlours, five chambers and eight garrets – whereas the lady's letter says two parlours, four good bedchambers and an unspecified number of garrets; but in addition two chambers below stairs and a housekeeper's room. What should we think? Making allowance for a degree of inaccuracy on either side it could well be a match, couldn't it? What else can we deduce? First of all, if she was at Jerningham House in 1803, she was not in 1802; or *mutatis mutandis*, supposing we could establish that the Dynevors were at Jerningham in 1803, then the Jerninghams were at Jerningham in 1802! The next visit was in 1804 and letters are headed Mount Pleasant. In 1806 her address was 'Tunbridge Wells'; in 1807 she was on Mount Sion but in a different house (different from when? the previous year or 1803?); and in 1808 the address was 'Tunbridge Wells' again. That was the last year because Sir William died in 1809 and it was for his sake mainly that they came to take the waters. What can we make of it all? Well, I think it very likely that they did stay at Jerningham House in 1803 – possible that they did a second year – and faintly possible a third … possibly also not at all; but if she never did, the question has to be answered – why the name? To the best of my knowledge it was first applied to the house in *Sprange's Guide* of 1817 – which certainly supports the idea that the house was named after Lady Jerningham and Sir William.

Daughter Charlotte was quite an artist and here is a drawing which she made of herself in Brussels in 1792. Back home at Costessy in Norfolk in 1803, Lady Jerningham recommends her daughter to read a novel by Mr Cumberland with whom she became particularly acquainted during her visits of that year and the year before. And in 1806 she mentions Mrs Eden whose husband was Lord Auckland's brother who converses with her in the Library while their respective daughters walk on the Pantiles. She then goes into a few society details:

Charlotte Jerningham later Lady Bedingfeld

> Every evening there are meetings at the Rooms or in private Houses. And the Hours are delightful: Dinner at four, meeting a Little after seven, and parting before eleven, so that Tunbridge is Like a Large Convent (not the usual story I must say!), every one asleep in their beds before twelve … To-night is the first regular Ball. On Thursday there was a hop at the Rooms, begun by your father and Lady Boyne. He is quite well and in great spirits; this place and the Company of this year particularly suits him.

This is the last we hear of Sir William Jerningham – in great spirits at a hop! From the Wells the lady went to Brighton (address given – 5, Pavilion Parade) but is writing to her daughter in Tunbridge Wells, 'that Elisium of quiet, pleasant, Sociable Intercourse' in contrast to 'great Staring, Bustling, Unsocial' Brighton where she goes to the Races and hobnobs with the Prince and Mrs Fitzherbert. Maybe it was all too much for Sir William.

After this Jerningham diversion we return to the story of the house which we left in 1818 with the death of the mortgagee Henry Playsted and the advent of Robert Foreman. John and William, the two sons of the coachmaster, were the legal owners of the property under their father's intestacy but William had his own trade of cabinetmaker and was willing to give up his interest, leaving the others to pay off the mortgage. However, they wanted to be legal owners first.

This is where Robert Foreman came in. A family arrangement concluded shortly before the repayment of the mortgage conveyed the property from the sons to Robert Foreman in trust for the widow during her life and then for John, Emily and Harriett. During this period our gentleman-solicitor was not letting the grass grow under his feet. The *Maidstone Journal* of 19 July 1825 was informed that Mr Robert Foreman 'who was admitted in last Hilary Term an Attorney of His Majesty's Courts of Law at Westminster and also a Master Extraordinary in the High Court of Chancery has commenced as a Practioner at the Wells'. He had also been busying himself in other directions – less than two weeks later he married Emily Beale. I wonder why he did not choose Harriett? Ah well, they could not both have him, I suppose! Harriett had the consolation of looking after her mother who died in 1829. Before this, however, the Beales' new business manager (sorry, Emily's new husband) made a start on maximising their assets. In February 1826 they sold part of a 'certain plot of land then known by the name of Mrs Beale's Plat' – see above my version of a sketch in the margin of an Abstract of Title.

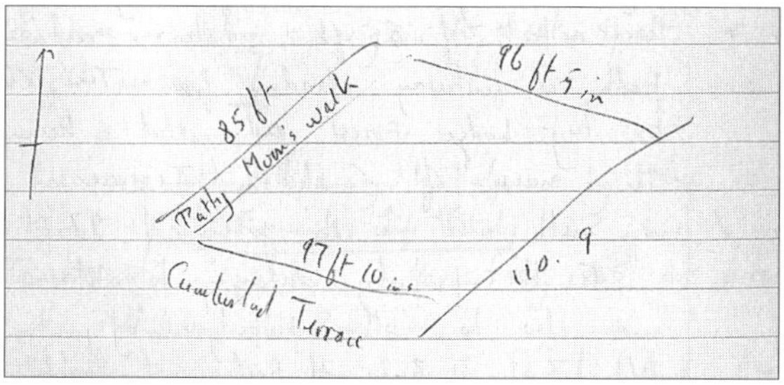

Mrs Beale's Plat

Remember that Edward Allen's lease plot of 1689 extended from Mount Sion Road back to Cumberland Walk; but note the change in nomenclature. The boundaries were: Patty Moon's Walk (which is now Cumberland Gardens) on the north-west (85 feet); a 'footway leading from Tunbridge Wells Chapel to Ivy Lodge Forest ... known by the name of Cumberland Terrace (the present Cumberland Walk as noted already) on the south-west (97 feet); property belonging to Mrs Jane Cripps and to the Beale family on the south-east (110 feet); and to the other part of Mrs Beale's Plat on the north-east (96 feet). The plot of land so described, Mrs Beale's Plat, is in fact the site of two of the architectural showpieces of the town – Richmond and Cumberland Villas. They are said, by the architectural cognoscenti, to have been designed by Amos Wilds (of Brighton fame) on account of the ammonite capital (his motif) on Richmond Villa – see right. Unfortunately, the dull old legal papers never reveal interesting details like this. The purchaser

Richmond Villa – ammonite motif

of the land was one Stephen Sawyer who had a nephew Henry who may well have been the man from whom Arthur Brackett purchased his estate agency in 1866. It was surely a building speculation, although Stephen and his wife Mary seem to have been living in one of the pair in about 1840.

Howard Lodge

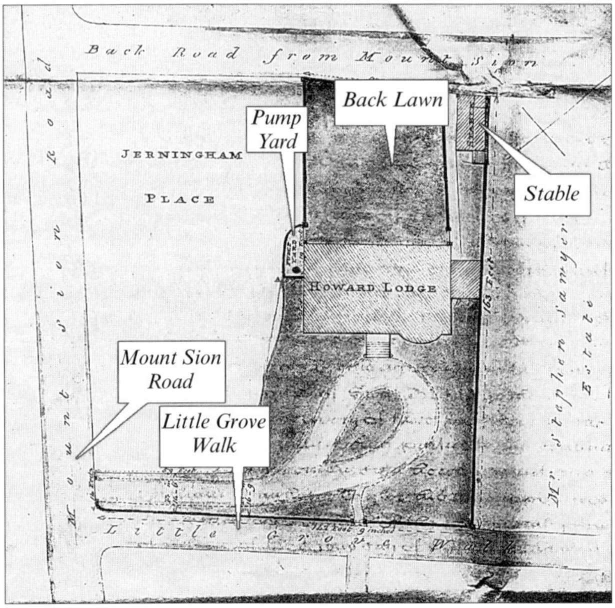

Plan from Howard Lodge deeds 1836

The two ammonite villas were not the only building work going on at this time. In the words of the Howard Lodge deeds, 'sometime in or about the year 1826 the two messuages occupied by Mary Beale Harriett Beale and Emily Beale and called Mrs Wilmot's Cottage and the other used as a lodging house were pulled down and upon the site thereof a messuage or Dwelling house and offices thereto were erected and built called Howard Lodge.' On the left above is Howard Lodge today and below is a plan which appears on the deeds showing a few points of interest. The date is 1836. The Howard Lodge building as you can see has not changed in its basic shape but new building has taken place since, fronting onto Cumberland Yard, on what the deed refers to as the 'Back Lawn'. A small stable is shown but the original stables for Jerningham House must have been much more extensive and located probably in the area which is marked Stephen Sawyer's Estate. Notice the Pump Yard which contained the well providing water also for Jerningham House although it belonged to Howard Lodge.

Mount Sion seems to have been a scene of frantic activity about this time – with our Robert in the thick of it. There are two parts of the original 1689 Jerningham plot not yet accounted for: a large area between Howard Lodge and the ammonite villas; and the space to the east of Richmond Villa up to the boundary with Woodbine and Hawthorn Cottages mentioned in the previous chapter. The first of these areas was soon developed by Stephen Sawyer who built a terrace of four houses now numbered Nos 1-4 Cumberland Gardens. I have no direct evidence when these houses were built (two owners have kindly searched their deeds without finding anything relevant) but the Tithe map establishes that they were there in 1840 owned by Stephen Sawyer. They are rather shy houses hiding behind long shady gardens. The two houses fronting Cumberland Walk next to Richmond Villa are among the curiosities of Tunbridge Wells architecture. The Tithe map gives these houses (now nos 8 and 9, Cumberland Walk) the enigmatic names 'Marine House' and 'Marine Cottage' owned and occupied by

Marine House (left) and Marine Cottage (right)

Jane Cripps. Here they are today. Why 'Marine'? Is it to do with the beach-like pebbles? Or with the architect Amos Wild who came from Brighton on the sea? I wish someone would come up with a convincing theory. Marine House by the way, no 8 Cumberland Walk, was from 1891 to 1904 the vicarage for the Church of King Charles the Martyr – and the cottage was bought by the church at the same time apparently. The conveyance of Mrs Beale's Plat in 1826 mentioned that it abutted on the land of Mrs Jane Cripps. This suggests that the two marine houses had already been built, probably about 1820. We are now in fact almost at today's position. The only additions since have been some cottages (built on the Back Lawn mentioned just now) and a very recent row of garages.

To return then to the past … in June 1830, after their mother's death, Harriett and Emily bought out brother John for £495 and divided the property between themselves. Then in September 1830 the mortgage was redeemed and in January 1831 Harriett sold her share to Robert Foreman for £1,980 and we never hear of her again. Robert, however, was at long last undisputed master of all. So what did he do? He tried to sell the old house for development, that's what – as if he had not done enough already! The year was 1833, one of the few years when the local newspaper known as the *Tunbridge Wells Visitor* was in circulation; and on the left is the beginning of the advertisement which appeared in the issue of 7 December.

> To persons inclined to speculate in building at this singularly favoured Watering-Place, this Freehold Estate offers peculiar advantages: it abuts at the upper end on a private road leading into Mount Sion Road, over which the purchaser will have a right; and consequently there is a second frontage of about 75 feet, admirably adapted for the erection of 5 or 6 small houses, which would produce a rental of at least £100 per annum. This consideration would probably induce the purchaser to pull down the present buildings, the materials of which would be found more than sufficient for erecting such houses. This being done, the purchaser would still have for appropriation the main frontage and beauty of his ground to an extent of 124 feet … The advertiser will not venture a single suggestion as to what might be here done; a survey of the spot and its localities will be a fair guide to better judges, particularly as the purchaser will not be fettered with any restrictive Conditions.

TUNBRIDGE WELLS.

To Builders and others.

To be Sold by Private Contract,

All those Three several FREEHOLD

Messuages or Dwelling-Houses,

Known by the Name of

Jerningham Place,

Nos. 1, 2, & 3,

Together with the Piece of Ground thereto attached and belonging, well situated on, and forming the most commanding part of

MOUNT SION.

The ground has a frontage towards Mount Sion Road of 150 feet, extending in depth from the said road at the upper part 75 feet; and at the lower part 65 feet; a straight line between the two points to form the south-west boundary mark.

Tunbridge Wells Visitor

Finally, it is mentioned that No.1 is let furnished for £150 per annum; No.2 is occupied by the Proprietor but could be let unfurnished at £40; No.3 is let at £16; and the furniture in No.1 might be taken at a valuation. Further particulars obtainable from the Proprietor, Mr Foreman, solicitor, Tunbridge Wells. No mention of Emily! What it was that saved Jerningham House from demolition I suppose we shall never know. Perhaps the developers of Tunbridge Wells had exhausted their resources by this time and were pausing for breath.

The next thing to happen was the sale of Howard Lodge, which took place in 1836. The purchaser was William Stanhope Taylor Esquire. And thereby hangs a tale … and a cartoon! The mother of Howard Lodge's first owner had in fact been Lady Lucy Rachael Stanhope, daughter of the 3rd Earl Stanhope, who rather spoiled her copybook by eloping at the age of 16 with the family apothecary and marrying him in 1796. He was Dr Thomas Taylor of Sevenoaks who is shown in a cartoon by James Gillray with some unmentionable medical thing hanging behind called a 'Clyster Pipe'. The good news was that his bride had an influential uncle who must have had a soft spot for his niece – none other than the Prime Minister, William Pitt, whose sister was married to the Earl. The aberrant apothecary became Controller General in the Customs Office and they had three sons and four daughters and Lucy died in 1814. William Stanhope Taylor was the eldest son and lived the life of a man of means. He was 'Major Stanhope Taylor', Chairman of the Town Commissioners when the railway came to Tunbridge Wells in 1845 and 'Treasurer of the Coal Fund' – whatever that was! His house was described as a 'residence of distinction'. As a matter of incidental interest, have you heard of the eccentric aristocratic lady who in the 19th century went to live in the Middle East and was fond of a hookah with the Tuaregs – or something of the sort!? She was the Howard Lodge owner's aunt – Lucy's big sister.

'Democratic Levelling—Alliance à la Françoise or The Union of the Coronet & Clyster Pipe' by James Gillray. A representation of Charles, 3rd Earl Stanhope, his daughter Lucy, Thomas Taylor of Sevenoaks, Charles James Fox, and Richard Sheridan.

Gillray cartoon

The Stanhope Taylors continued to live in Howard Lodge in some style for the next twenty years or so. In 1841 they had five children, from 10-year-old Elizabeth to four-year-old Stanhope (destined to be killed by Indian mutineers in 1857), and five servants; and in 1851 Lady Taylor was not at home but Elizabeth was, with a sister of 18 and two younger children of nine and seven – and the servants: Lady's Maid, House Maid, Nursery Maid, Cook and Footman. Ten years later the Taylors had gone (he died in 1858 and she a year later and they are buried in Rusthall Churchyard) and been replaced by Richard Turner (see also pages 255 and 406), the first of a number of doctors at Howard Lodge. By 1861 it was Dr Blackall Marsack who survived until about 1890 after which Drs Anderson, Adeney, Riley and Chisholm followed until 1965 when the building was sub-divided as it is now.

As for Jerningham House, its subsequent history seems a bit of an anti-climax after all that had happened before. The Foremans occupied the part of the building known as Jerningham Place for the next twenty years or so while the other part called Jerningham House was let. In 1851 it was the residence of an MP, Henry Broadwood, aged 58, his wife Frances aged 32 and little Arthur, born in Tunbridge Wells two years before; they were later to move to the Bowling Green House – see page 276. What happened to Robert Foreman and Emily is a bit unclear. In 1841 they were at Jerningham Place with their eight-year-old daughter Emily; but in 1856 Foreman sold the house to house agents who in turn sold to Thomas Read the next year. Thomas Read was a 60-year-old clergyman who made full use of his purchase by installing his accountant son, John, and family in Jerningham Place while his 62-year-old wife used Jerningham House as a school assisted by her unmarried daughter of 32 and three female teachers of whom one was Sarah Hutchinson – more of her in a minute. There were 12 scholars one of whose mother was living in the house and one aged 18 hailed from Australia. John Read was 30 and his family consisted of his wife of the same age, their one-year-old daughter, a monthly nurse and two servants of whom one was Jane or June Waters about whom a story appeared in the local press in 1864 under the headline 'A Suspicion Cleared Up'.

> An unusual domestic episode has lately come to light, by which a native of Hastings has been entirely exonerated from a suspicion attaching to her for some time. Elizabeth Waters, a domestic servant and a member of a family well-known in the old town, was apprehended at Tunbridge Wells early in November 1861 charged with stealing £25 in bank notes, the property of her mistress Miss Tibbs, a lady then residing at Mrs Read's Jerningham Place Mount Sion. She was brought before the magistrate and remanded on bail. At the fourth examination she was discharged for want of sufficient evidence to bring the charge home to her. The imputation thus cast upon the girl's character has remained until within the last month, when Supt. Glenister received a note from Mr J. Bartlett of Fleetwood, Lancashire, stating that a female who was Miss Tibbs' lady's maid at the time of the robbery had confessed to have been the thief and had also admitted having taken another £5 note belonging to Mrs Read. The object of the communication was to obtain the address of Waters in order that her late fellow servant might be acquainted with her tardy repentance. Supt. Glenister at once took the matter up and having ascertained the facts of the story found it to be correct. The result is that the guilty person has written the following letter to Waters. 'May 25 1864 – Madam, On the eve of leaving England for ever I feel that I cannot do so in justice to you without acknowledging my guilt with respect to the money lost while you were with Miss Tibbs. It was I who took it. How deeply and grievously you were wronged: can you ever forgive me? I have written to Miss Tibbs stating your innocence. Yours S. Hutchinson.

Now there are of course two discrepancies between the census record and the article; but does this cast doubt on the story? Firstly, the wronged girl is Jane or June in the census, Elizabeth in the article; secondly, the guilty party was a teacher

THIS PICTURE of Miss Read's school at Jerningham House, Mount Sion, Tunbridge Wells, which was taken in 1866, was given to the Courier by Mr. Alan Payne-Jenkins, who closed his photographic business in Grosvenor Road, Tunbridge Wells, last autumn. Mr. Payne-Jenkins has since moved to the West Country

Mrs Read's School

in the Jerningham House school, not a lady's maid in Jerningham Place. I find the gist of the story totally convincing – and as for the details I prefer to believe the census rather than the journalist. Here above is a photograph of Mrs Read's School.

The photograph was taken in 1866, as the caption says, and was given to the *Courier* by Alan Payne-Jenkins when he closed his shop in Grosvenor Road. Excuse the quality. The reproduction is taken from a photocopy of the *Courier*. Thomas Read died in 1873 and Mrs Read's school was succeeded until 1888 by the Ladies' Schools of the Misses Edwards and then for a few years of Mrs Robertson. In 1894 came an episode which we dealt with in the previous chapter – the Girls' High School from Fairlawn House next door overflowed into Jerningham House and stayed until 1900. For a few years thereafter the building became the office of the Surveyor to the Post Office and then, in 1905, the Kent Nursing Institution took over and stayed until 1939, the Matron, Miss Mottram, purchasing the freehold from the Trustees of Thomas Read's will for £2,200 in 1934. The picture at the head of this chapter is from a postcard of that period. The rest is recent history. In 1940 it became a Guest House and then in 1957 a Boarding House. There were fears of demolition but in 1973 it emerged as today's four splendid residential units. It has lasted three hundred years so far, survived a mortal peril in 1833 and long may it survive those to come! If proof of antiquity were needed, early 18th-century glass fragments were discovered in a rubbish pit uncovered during construction of a drive in June 1972.

CHAPTER 26

Chapel Place

In Chapter 2 we addressed the question where Mount Sion begins and ends and I suggested that the London Road was 'out' except for the *Angel Inn* (*Kentish Royal Hotel*) which with Chapel Place was largely relevant to the Mount Sion story. In practice this means that, following my usual procedure of dealing in turn with the plots leased out by Viscountess Purbeck, I should now turn my attention to the whole 'Chapel Place block' which runs from Cumberland Gardens to the London Road and from Mount Sion Road to Cumberland Walk. As far as I can tell this block was rented from South Frith Manor by John Wybourne by 1670 or earlier and then transferred to John Brett when (I assume) Wybourne died in about 1690. The Chapel was built in one corner starting in 1676 and around 1690 John Brett began amid controversy the construction of the *Angel Inn*. At some stage a large boarding house was built behind the Chapel and called 'Chapel House'. All this is well illustrated 'from the air' by Jan Kip in 1719. One of the

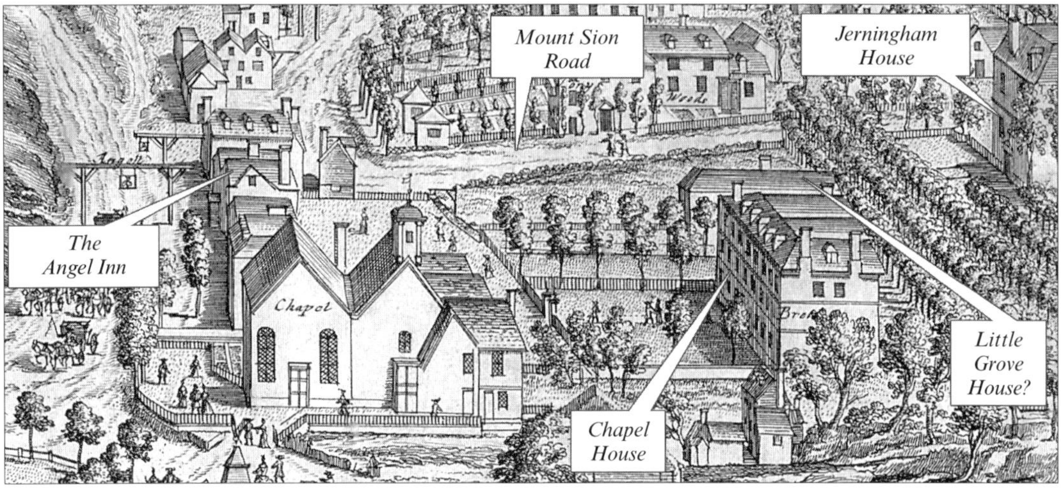

Kip's engraving 1719

three lines of trees on the right marks the line of Cumberland Gardens. The whole block is to be seen and there are just these three buildings: the Chapel, Chapel House (labelled 'Brett') and the *Angel*. Perhaps there may be something on either side of the *Angel* and possibly a building beyond and separate from Chapel House, maybe an original Little Grove House? What is not shown on Kip's engraving is the large open-square-shaped building marked 'Mrs Pickering' on the Bowra plan on the next page. It obviously follows that this building dates from between 1719

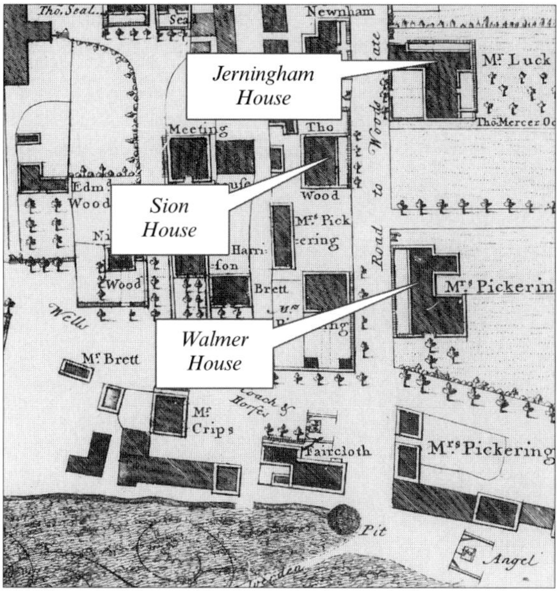

Bowra plan 1738

and 1738. The problem is what to call it. In the 19th century it used to be in two parts called Walmer House and Bedford Place; before that it was confusingly called Sion House and in 1780 it was nicknamed Bedlam and even called as much in *Sprange's Guide*. For simplicity's sake and because we still have a Walmer Cottage on the other side of the road I shall call it Walmer House. It is to this building that I propose to devote most of this chapter.

In the Poor Rate record it begins with the name 'Ye Great House' and the ratepayer is Mr Pickering who, I am sure will be recalled, was the second husband of John Brett's widow, Margaret.

Walmer House Poor Rate

1735-1742	Mr Pickering for ye Great House
1743-1757	Mrs Pickering for ye Great House
1758-1764	Mr Geo Lewis for the Great House
1765-1775	Widow Lewis for the Great House and field
1776-1780	Gratton Wm for the Great House
1781-1782	Gratton Wm for the Green House
1783-1790	Gratton Widow for the Great House
1791	Turner John for the Great House
1792- ?	Record merges with Grove House and one other and is lost

The start date is within our parameters if a little on the late side. The Pickering connection, of course, is plain to see on the Bowra plan; but the dates do not coincide too well with what we know from the Chancery records which show that Mr Pickering died in 1729 and Margaret Pickering in 1743 – at least the order of going is right. We have met George Lewis before (see chapter 17 page 229) in connection with the other 'Great House' (Boltons or Whites) and Walmer Cottage on the other side of the road. He was a second or third husband of Margaret Pickering's niece Hester for whose benefit Margaret left all her property in trust. The succession from Widow Lewis to William Gratton in 1775 also occurs in the Poor Rate sequence of Boltons (or Whites) on the other side of the road; I assume it was simple sale and purchase but there may have been more to it. William Gratton, it may be remembered, was landlord of the *Gloster Tavern* on the Pantiles and married the widow of the owner of Calverley House – or the *Hotel du Vin* if you prefer. In the case of Boltons we know that it was Gratton's heiress, Eleanor Reed, who sold the place in 1801; but in the case of Walmer House no such information has come to light. All we know is that John Turner started paying the Poor Rate in 1791. Now John Turner appears in Sprange's *Lodging House List* in 1797 as landlord of 'Sion House' and the Little Grove House – which may go some way to explain the last entry in the Poor Rate sequence above. A Turner also had a shop in the Chapel Place block; and I wonder whether by chance John might be the brother of Thomas Turner, the diarist of East Hoathly. This brother, John, was the eldest of the family, was born in 1717 and in 1777 was 'now in business for himself at Tunbridge Wells'.

Chapel Place about 1820

The table of lodging houses at the back of *Sprange's Guide* for 1780 shows 'Gratton's Bedlam-house' 10 parlours, 10 chambers and stables for 11 horses but an asterisk indicates that those thus marked 'are frequently divided into small apartments'! I think we can take it that this was the lower end of the lodging house market! By the next edition of Sprange in 1786 'Bedlam' had disappeared from the description of the house which had become: 'Gratton, Great House' but the room and stable details are unchanged. I am therefore quite certain that this is the house referred to in a *Maidstone Journal* report on the progress of the 'season' in 1787: 'On the Hills dwell the Great and the Fashionable – the Single men and the Smarts – The lodgings are nearly filled. There are great many people in Bedlam – a large boarding-house so called.' Above is a print (the original is quite tiny) which gives a good idea of what the place might have looked like at the time. The fact that it is captioned 'Bedford Place' must mean that it post-dates

1808 when both Barrow and Sprange use the name 'Sion House'. On the left is the Bedlam-house *aka* Sion House *aka* Bedford Place *aka* Walmer House. Behind it in the distance is the Chapel House boarding house (roughly where the old schoolroom was and the present Chinese Restaurant is) and on its right, of course, is the Chapel. In the right foreground is probably Mr John Fry's cabinetmaker's warehouse.

Sprange's Guide for 1811 omits the house – perhaps it was between owners; but by 1817 both name and owner have changed again. The *Guide* shows Bedford Place No.1, Mr R. Delves with three sitting rooms, six bedrooms and stables for seven; and Bedford Place No.2, ditto, with three, six and six. This was the time when Richard Delves was expanding his lodging house empire as recounted in chapter 20 page 297 and the story of Bedford Place and Bedford Terrace was continued in chapter 21 page 302. We have seen above that Bedford Place and Little Grove House seem to have gone together and perhaps Richard Delves bought the property from John Turner and then in 1830 it fell into the bankruptcy. The next we know is that on 29 April 1833 Richard's younger brother Henry grants a lease on this property to Richard's sons William and Joseph. How it came into Henry's hands I do not know – perhaps he bought it at a bankruptcy auction; but the evidence, as noted on page 302, is unmistakable in the will of Henry who died in 1869. The result of this transaction was the construction of Bedford Terrace, one of the architectural ornaments of Tunbridge Wells as already mentioned (see photograph on page 303). The *Tunbridge Wells Visitor* report of 28 June 1834 that a 'few old houses have been taken down and a row of houses built called Bedford Terrace' has already been quoted on page 302. It suggests to me that the old Little Grove House was demolished and the present Little Grove House was built as part of the whole development. Anyway, it looks to me like part of the whole, although some owners may disagree.

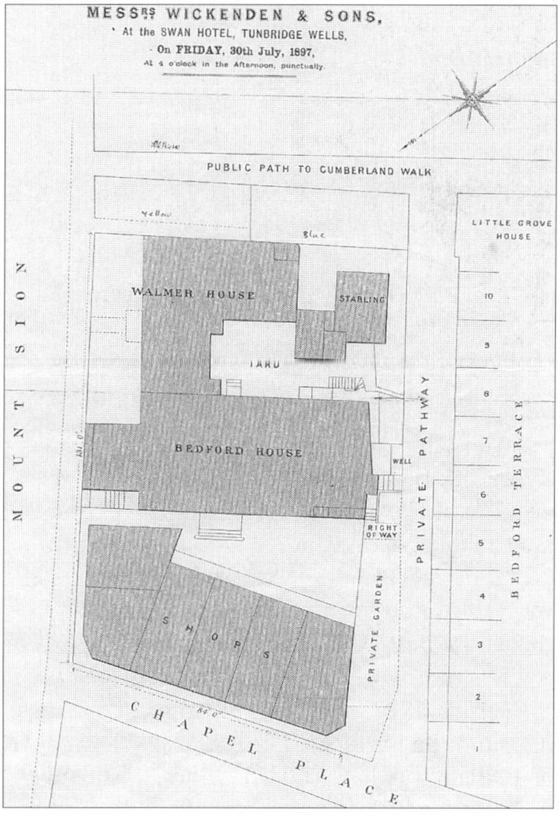

Sale Plan 1897

One thing is clear. The name for the new terrace comes from the name Bedford Place which was already in use, as we have seen, in 1817. About this time someone – and in view of their building activities in Bedford Terrace it seems reasonable to suppose it was the Delves brothers – made fairly large-scale alterations to the 'Great House'. This was discovered in the course of later investigations which I shall deal with in a minute. The lease to the brothers was for 99 years and contained an option to purchase which, however, was not taken up. Instead the Delves family in 1869 agreed a sale to William Stone and John William Roper (a couple of local solicitors). There followed a morass of mortgages, wills, trusts and family arrangements and eventually, for whatever reason, an auction sale was scheduled for Friday, 30 July 1897 at the *Swan Hotel* on the Pantiles and the plan of the property (see previous page) is of some interest. It can be seen that the shops on the Chapel Place side of the building and on the Mount Sion corner were already in place in 1897, from the old Mears Fishmongers (now the Italian Arte Bianca or White Arts) to the antiques shop on the Bedford Terrace corner, but the main frontage to Mount Sion was still clear. These shops occupied as it were the front garden of Bedford Place, the main steps of which can be seen on the plan – see the straggly trees in the photograph below.

Entrance to Chapel Place about 1880

One of the more interesting and longer-resident occupants of Bedford Place (note that the Auction Plan is wrong to call it Bedford House – that was a building on the other side of Chapel Place) was Dr Trustram. Charles Trustram was born in 1809 in Bedfordshire. After apprenticeship to a local surgeon, he studied at St Thomas's and Guy's and commenced practice at Tunbridge Wells in 1832. Perhaps it was the reminder of the county of his birth that attracted him to Bedford Place; anyway, he was there in 1841 with his wife and four small children and there he stayed until the evening of 24 June 1872 when, having visited a patient near the Parade, he returned home at 10 o'clock, went to bed as usual and died of angina pectoris early the next morning despite the presence of two colleaugues including Dr Fred Manser, who in 1874 was living in William Webber's old place in Sion Terrace just across the road. In 1833, shortly after his arrival in the town, he married one of the two only daughters of John Prince Esquire, formerly of Emmanuel College, Cambridge, and (in the words of the obituary) 'the leading surgeon among the fashionable society which resorted to Tunbridge Wells in the days of Beau Nash' His career was further enhanced by his success in restoring the use of her arm to a young lady from one of the county families of Cornwall whose father handed him a cheque for 100 guineas 'with which to buy a watch'. During his forty years on Mount Sion it was difficult to escape him, whether in the course of his professional work as GP and Honorary Surgeon to the Infirmary and Dispensary or as Town Commissioner, Chairman of the Tunbridge Wells, Tunbridge and Weald of Kent and Sussex Permanent Benefit Building Society or Trustee of the will of Thomas Delves or President of the South-eastern branch of the BMA, to name but some of his activities. I have indeed seen him named as the inspiration behind the digging of the Brighton Lake, a work of charity usually attributed to the Rev. Pope under the name 'Pope's Puddle', and his obituary emphasises his services 'largely and gratuitously bestowed on the poor'. He was one of those behind the foundation of the Building Society and having presided at its first annual meeting in 1851 was chairman until 1872 – in which role it is worth noting that he was followed by such local notables as John Colbran, William Henry Delves and two members of the Strange family, Charles M. and then his son Edward Jeffery, bringing us up to 1941. The first offices of the Society were at No 2, Bedford Place – although they moved about the town subsequently. Living where he did Dr Trustram was, of course, in the thick of the events of November 1864 when the Tunbridge Wells mob assembled in their thousands on the road between Bedford Place and Sion Terrace and disturbed the peace of Dr William Webber and his family. Quite what role the good doctor played is questionable. Perhaps (see the next chapter) he was not whole-heartedly on the side of his professional colleague.

Walmer House about 1900

The photograph on the previous page captioned 'Entrance to Chapel Place' demonstrates that the shops must have been built in the twenty years before 1897, since in the background of the original photograph which now hangs in Hall's Bookshop in Chapel Place can be seen the shadowy outline of the new *Royal Kentish Hotel* (present Kentish Mansions) built in 1878. During this period, in about 1889, Walmer House became the Technical Institute as seen about 1900 in the photograph by David Johnson above. The Technical Institute was one of the brainchildren of Dr George Abbott, the eye surgeon and amateur geologist. It

Walmer House in about 1970

moved in 1902 to the new building in the Monson Road and the move perhaps occasioned the construction of an untidy excrescence of shops on the Mount Sion frontage, as seen in the 1970s photograph above. The two-storeyed flight of fancy with the prominent gable was, of course, part of the earlier development but the shops with a sort of conservatory on top must have come after the Technical Institute moved. If you ignore the excrescence you can clearly make out the basic shape of the building – very square from this angle but actually, of course, an open square at the back.

Dr Trustram apart, much gossip mght be possible about the various occupants of the building and its surrounding shops – the baths underneath, the alleged suicide, the photographer Death, Don Roberts the hairdresser and his jazz band, the Christian Science Reading Room and the Toc H, The Servants' Registry, Oliver and Rush's Bedford Garage, Miss Avery's Four Ways Café and much more ... Bedlam it was and Bedlam, you may say, it remained to the last. I will however allow myself one bit of gossip. Behind those conservatory windows lived, in the late 1940s, the 'Mount Sion School of Dancing' – Principal Dorothy Conibear; and there I took my first lessons in ballroom dancing. Had I but known, I might have had a better look round the building! But imagine, if you can, neat little Miss Conibear and me up there doing the foxtrot.

Who the ultimate owner was who decided that a modern block of offices and shops would be preferable I do not know; but the situation has been so well summarised in a Civic Society report that I can do no better than quote:

> By far the worst case of the failure of those in authority to afford statutory protection to an important building ... has been that of Bedford House and Walmer House in Mount Sion. We devoted a very great deal of time and energy to that case; alas, to absolutely no avail ... The building was capable of restoration, be it for residential use like Jerningham House adjoining, or for commercial use, and the stuccoed treatment to the lowest storey of the Mount Sion frontage could have been reinstated after the removal of the shop fronts.

This would have been preservation and enhancement of the Conservation Area in a real sense ... Although the Department of the Environment indicated that they probably would have included the building in the statutory list had the shop fronts been removed, they thought that the building with its shop fronts was more suitable for the local list. Even so, this offered a prima facie case for confirmation of a Section 8 Direction which would have enabled the practicability of retaining this irreplaceable piece of old Tunbridge Wells to be investigated more thoroughly. However, officers of neither the County Council nor the Borough Council seemed to have much enthusiasm for the building, although I gather that the making of a Section 8 Direction could have been a possibility if the Borough Council had accepted responsibility for any financial liability arising from it. We could not ourselves see that the making of a Section 8 Direction would, of itself, have given rise to such liability but the very mention of those words seems enough to act as an effective deterrent to such action. In the event, therefore, the Borough Council although at first placing an embargo on office redevelopment on this site, eventually did approve a scheme for shops, offices and a basement car park for 33 cars, holding in the process a debate in secret session of full council during the period when representations had been invited by an official Public Notice. It is hard to believe that in these days when so many prominent people pay lip service to Conservation and to Public Participation in Planning that such a sorry saga can develop around a building of about 1730 situated in the most important sequence of Georgian buildings in one of the major historic towns in the Country. The case does show how far we are from being able to assume that the battle for the conservation of Tunbridge Wells is all but won ... I hope that it may serve to sharpen our resolve rather than drive us to despair.

Some compensation for the demolition of Walmer House was an archaeological investigation carried out during the process by none other than Dr Anthony Streeten, a young student at the time, and son of one time mayor Mrs Myrtle Streeten. He had two main findings: firstly, that the existing building could be

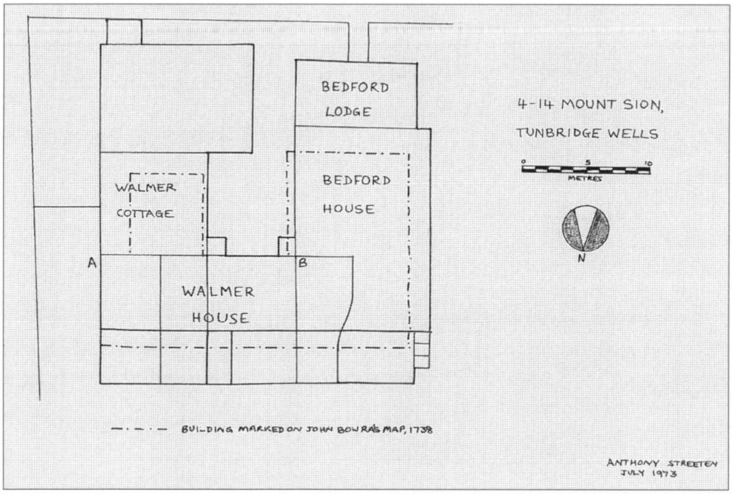

Walmer House – Dr Streeten's comparison with Bowra

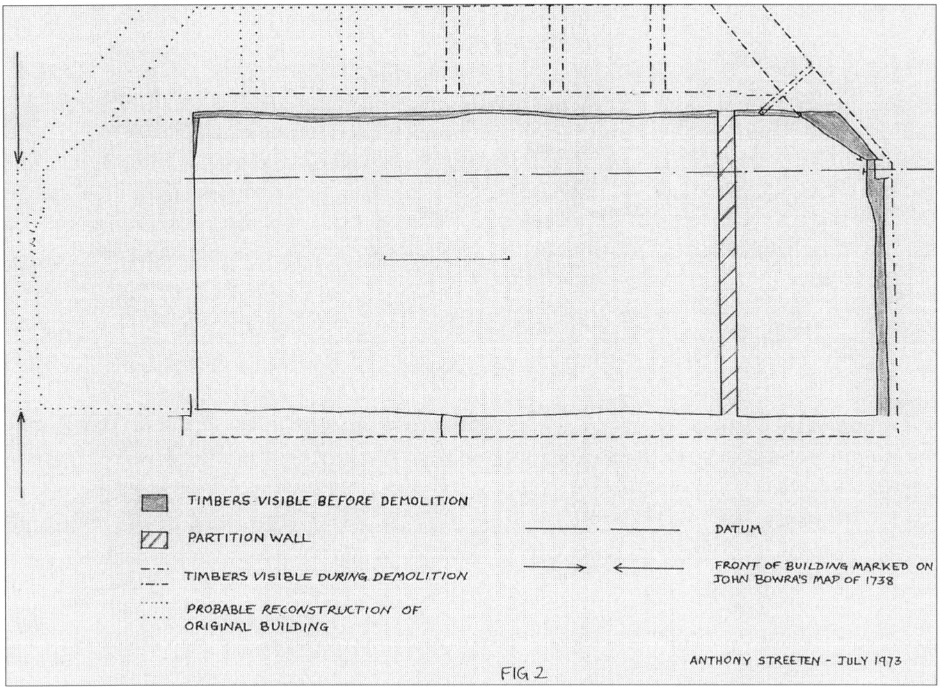

Walmer House – Dr Streeten's reconstruction

identified roughly with the one shown on the Bowra plan, as shown in the drawing on p.391. The dotted line is the Bowra plan superimposed on a modern plan. From this you can see the rough correspondence if we ignore Bedford Lodge – a later addition – and the unlabelled area behind Walmer Cottage which was originally stables. The front wall is immediately below the word 'house' of 'Walmer House' and all the subdivisions below this are the 20th-century shopfronts. The dotted line is then clearly in front of the front wall as it was and this points to Dr Streeten's second finding and his most interesting discovery, illustrated in the second drawing (above) which is a side view. To quote: 'John Bowra's map indicates that in 1738 the building had a width of approximately 7.16 metres; the width at present being only slightly more than 5.5 metres; but scale drawing shows that if a main post is reconstructed at 7.16 metres not only does the

Walmer House in about 1970

gable assume the correct pitch but also the roof construction becomes symmetrical and the floor girder lies at the centre of the building.' The arrows on the left of the drawing mark where the front of the building used to be. The dotted line shows a probable reconstruction of the original building. A photograph, taken from up the hill shows all this quite clearly. You can see how the slope of the roof at the front is shorter than that at the back; so all the façade was new work. Probably at about this time the rear of the building had been hung with mathematical tiles but in its original form I imagine that the old front wall was tile hung. Dr Streeten suggests also that the west end was classicised at the same time so that it looked like the print on page 386 with no sign of a gable. This must mean that the reconstruction was completed before the date of the print i.e. between 1808 when the place was called Sion House and 1817 when it became Richard Delves' Bedford Place. There was a *Sprange Guide* in 1811 but, as already mentioned and without explanation, the list of lodging houses omits the house concerned. Anyway, the refronting obviously took place earlier than Dr Streeten thought – he said 'probably *c.*1830'. It also means that the man responsible was our old acquaintance, Richard 'the Spirited' Delves. So a new Mansard-roofed block arose to replace Margaret Pickering's 'Great House'. There is perhaps one very small silver lining to this cloud. Without the demolition we should probably not have had the evidence about the refronting. If you really want to know the history of your house, start pulling it apart! But the final irony is that the new building has already outlived its use as an office block and has been converted back to its original residential use.

Let us now take a quick, incomplete look at the rest of the Chapel Place block. An enlarged detail from Barrow's map will help – see right. The map can usefully be visualised by reference to the print of Bedford Place on page 386 above. The dates diverge by a few years only. Dividing the Chapel Place block from Jerningham House land was the path we now call Cumberland Gardens but, in 1836 and no doubt earlier, was called 'Little Grove Walk' as can be seen on the plan on page 378 of chapter 25. This is because it led to the Little Grove or Little Grove Field as marked on the Barrow

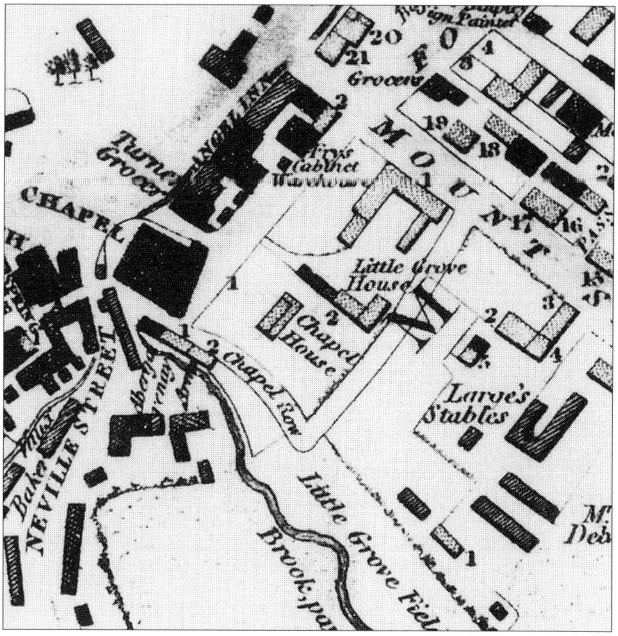

Barrow map 1808

map. The Grove proper was sometimes called the 'Great Grove' just to distinguish it from the little one. I suppose it had trees to make it a 'grove' and, with the stream alongside, it must have been a pleasant spot. The land actually belonged to Lord Abergavenny and later he let it out in parcels as gardens for the owners of the houses which sprang up on the other side of the, as yet non-existent, Cumberland Walk. The first of these houses, marked '1' on the map, was Stidolph's Cottage which has already been mentioned on page 364 of chapter 24. All this helps to explain why the house behind Walmer House and half way along Cumberland Gardens (or 'Little Grove Walk') was – and still is – called Little Grove House. Whether the house clearly marked on the 1808 map is the same building as the present Little Grove House is another matter. I have already opined that the present one was part of the Bedford Terrace development and so the old one was pulled down. According to Barrow's key or 'Reference to the Lodging Houses' (1808) the Little Grove House was in two parts as follows:

Little Grove Mt Sion. 1 Little Grove House
2 Do

(Mr Stidolph's Cottage came under a different heading – Little Grove Field). The '1' for Little Grove House seems to have got lost, however, although the '2' is plain to see. The '1' over to the left refers to Chapel House under the heading Foot of Mount Sion and No 2 under the same heading is 'Mr J Fry – Manufacturer etc' which obviously goes with 'Frys Cabinet Warehouse' just below on the map. The Foot of Mount Sion numbers then continue up the High Street. The '1' under the 'O' of MOUNT S(ION) refers of course to Walmer House called, as stated already, 'Sion House' in 1808. The '1' and '2' below the Chapel come under the heading 'Chapel Row' (now part of Cumberland Walk) and are assigned to Mr Hoskins (1) and Mr Strange late Newtons (2).

It may be that the old Little Grove House predated Walmer House. We have already seen, looking at Kip's engraving at the beginning of this chapter, that there appears to be a building hiding behind Chapel House. Be that as it may, I can find no Poor Rate sequence to assign to Little Grove House, very likely because it merged with that for Walmer House as we saw in the last entry for that house on page 385 above. The next record is in *Sprange's Guide* 1780 when we find Mr Gratton with three properties – his 'Bedlam House', the Little Grove House and its Second Apartment, confirming that these properties had the same owner. Gratton changes to Turner in 1797 and in 1817 to Richard Delves. Then bankruptcy in 1830 forces Richard to sell but somehow the property ends up in his younger brother's hands who then leases it to Richard's sons. They knock the old house down and build Bedford Terrace in 1834. The Tithe Award shows Joseph Delves 'grocer' as owner of Bedford Row, House and Yard, Little Grove House and Bedford Place – why William Delves was not included I do not know. The occupiers were Goodrham and others as tenants of the terrace houses, Joseph himself for Little Grove House, probably letting it as a lodging house, and Charles Trustram for Bedford Place. In 1860 Little Grove House was home to a short-lived venture called the Industrial Girls' School and in the 1880s and '90s it housed a veterinary practice under veterinary surgeons Barton, Hollinham and Roberts.

Turning now to Chapel House, there is a Poor Rate sequence which may fit but it begins with Mr John Wyborne in 1670 and changes to Mr Brett for John Wiborne's in 1690. There is a gap between 1670 and 1676 and another from then until 1683 but after that it is continuous until 1689. Since I certainly do not think that John Wyborne built the house in 1670, the question is when was it built and by whom. In chapter 3, page 23, I suggested that it was built by John Wybourne some time after the construction of the Chapel. Certainly it was prominently there for all to see in 1719 – witness Kip's engraving at the beginning of this chapter. The sequence continues with Brett or a Mr Witherden who may well have been his tenant until 1714 and then, after the usual gap, during which John Brett died, of course, we find the familiar sequence of Pickering, Mr and Mrs, and George Lewis. We know that the house belonged to the Brett family because there are two documents, cited previously, a mortgage of 1764 and the marriage settlement of 1777 which record the fact – in 1764 in these or similar words 'All that Messuage or Tenement in Tunbridge Wells called the Chapel House occupied by Hodges with outhouses buildings yards and appurtenances fronting west road leading to Mount Sion and east back path leading to Mount Sion north Messuage or building belonging to Mrs Lewis south lands belonging to Lord Abergavenny'. When and to whom a sale was eventually made I do not know; but Mrs Hodges continued as ratepayer 'for the Chapel House' through to 1797. This name is confirmed by Sprange who shows in 1780 and 1786 'Mrs Hodges, a boarding-house called Chapel-house' with seven chambers, eight parlours and no stabling; and in 1797 and 1801 'Mrs Hodge, a Boarding house' with four sitting rooms, 10 chambers, eight garrets and no coach houses or stabling. In 1808 and 1811 Sprange simply lists 'Chapel Boarding House (in apartments)' which may mean that after twenty years and more Mrs Hodges had given up. Anyway, in 1817 a Mrs Barron has taken over and evidently continues until 1832 when *Pigot's Directory* lists 'Barram Mrs Mary Chapel House' under

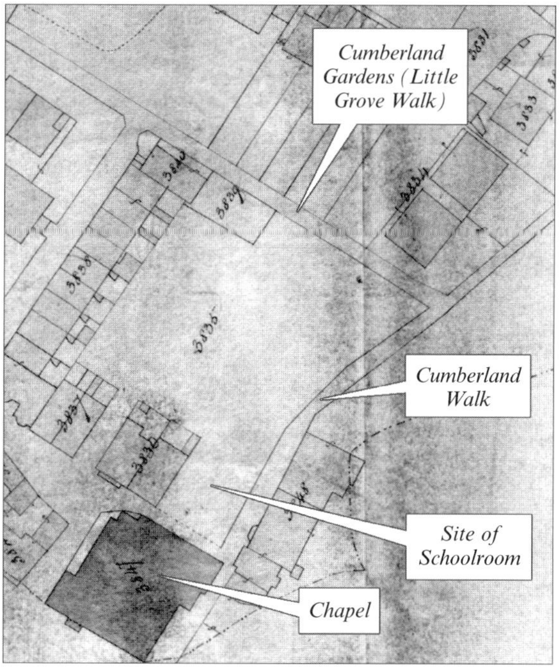

Tithe map 1840

Boarding Houses. This however was nearly the end of the line for the old Chapel House. In November 1833 a notice appeared in the *Tunbridge Wells Visitor* as follows: 'To be sold by tender. The materials of all that messuage or tenement known by the name of Chapel House near the Chapel Tunbridge Wells tenders to Mr Sprott solicitor'. Quite what Walter Sprott, the solicitor, had in mind is guesswork. He was acting on his own behalf since the Tithe map a few years later shows him as owner of the large square site where the Chapel House had been. All that had happened was the leasing to Joseph Delves of a piece of ground to act as a garden for his Little Grove House (it still does) and the erection of two pairs of shops, which still exist, facing Chapel Place with a passage between them. The one nearer the Chapel (until recently the florist's) was the Delves butcher's shop occupied by Joseph junior. The Tithe map (see previous page) shows the position. The large vacant 'Piece of Ground' numbered 3835 was owned and occupied by Walter Sprott. What was he to do with it? If he had a hefty profit in mind he was soon to find otherwise. It is a well rehearsed story. The Chapel School, by this time taking boys only since the girls had moved to Little Mount Sion, was confined to makeshift accommodation within the Chapel and wanted to expand. Mr Sprott was therefore approached in 1844 to sell a piece of his land for the purpose. He was offered £250 and he refused; but he had not reckoned with the Rev. Pope's persuasive tongue. Not only was Sprott persuaded to sell but also to donate half the £250 towards the school. The result was one large room and a classroom to which a further room was added in 1858. All this served the Chapel's educational needs for many years but post-war reforms took local boys elsewhere and the building now houses the 'Gracelands' Chinese restaurant whose patrons are sometimes entertained by impressions of Elvis Presley. An underground passage was built between the Chapel and the schoolrooms which was recently unearthed during repairs to the steps outside.

Two more buildings were to make use of the Chapel House site. Firstly, in 1851 a Baptist chapel named Rehoboth Chapel was erected using the passage between the two pairs of shops for access. It was – and still is – a substantial building in a classical style; but it has recently been abandoned by the Baptists and is now an antiques centre. Secondly, a very large pair of semi-detached brick houses was built in the southern corner of the site, called Sussex Villas 1 and 2. This happened sometime before 1886 when Frank Simmonds was listed in *Stevens' Directory* at No.2 – close at hand for the clothes shop which used to be where Hall's Bookshop now is. They are now called Sussex View – appropriate enough since they stand high and used to look directly over the stream dividing Kent from Sussex. One of them was Richard Cobb's home when he was five or six and he devotes a page or two of *Still Life* to rather confused memories of it and the boys of 'King Charles Choir School'.

The western or, better, north-western side of the Chapel Place block was dominated by the Chapel itself, of course, but even more by the *Angel Inn* and its associated buildings. The Tithe map (see next page) and Award show that out of five properties in this block three were owned by Thomas French, comprising the *Kentish Hotel*, tap, stabling and yard and three more houses and a yard. At the High Street end was John Fry's Cabinet Warehouse and at the other end near the Chapel was a shop labelled 'Turner Grocer' on the Barrow map. Let's start with the Cabinetmaker, continue with the *Angel* and finish with the shop and the Chapel. We are lucky to have a glimpse of the Warehouse on the right of the print of Bedford Place on page 386 above. Kip shows an empty yard but Bowra's plan shows a small building on the very corner. By the time of the Tithe map this has expanded and is described as 'Bedford House, Sion Cottage and Yard'. The map shows three parts to this complex extending almost as far as the Bedford Terrace path on the other side, all numbered 3842. Here we see a different orientation of the Tithe map with the London Road and the Common at the top. The little building attached on the left and numbered 3844 is described as a house owned by Thomas French and occupied by John Holyer. The Tithe Award names Thomas Jenks and George White as owners of the Fry complex which is not surprising as we have met them before as the husbands of John Fry's daughters – see chapter 16 page 217, where we learned that the newspaper announcement of John Fry's death at Sion Cottage in 1830 described him as 'many years upholsterer at that place'. What happened to the business and building subsequently I have no information except to note that the photograph of the entrance to Chapel Place reproduced above on page 388 shows what may well be Sion Cottage with the addition in the triangular space seen vacant on the Tithe map of a ground-level shop displaying the goods of 'E.F. Loof Gunsmith' – all now replaced by a solid building occupying the whole corner site down to the London Road. Bedford House (note 'House' not 'Place') was in the 1860s the Tunbridge Wells surgery of the dentist Quintin Hair who used to visit once or twice a week and who regularly advertised his expertise in artificial teeth – see page 407.

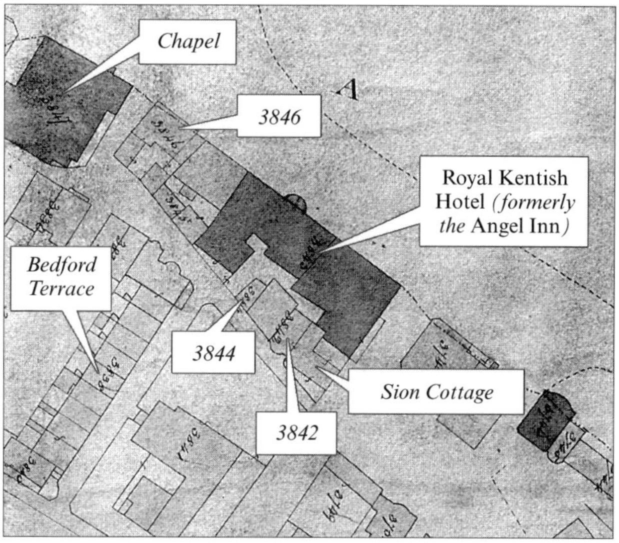

Tithe map 1840

The *Royal Kentish Hotel* started life in about 1690 as the *Angel Inn* and John Brett was much involved in its construction. The somewhat confusing evidence has already been set out in Chapter 3 and there is no need to go into it all again. Reference is made there to the Poor Rate sequence but since it was not given in full a complete version is provided on the next page. There can be no doubt that the inn had a busy history spanning the 18th century, nor that John Brett was its founder and that his widow took over after his death; but the other names on the list of ratepayers ring no bells except perhaps that of Riplingham who as John Riplingham is recognisable as a scrivener and probably part-time lawyer.

Poor Rate for the Angel Inn

1691	Mr Pottinger for Mr Bretts new house
1692-1694	Mr Brett for the Angell
1695-1696	Mr Brett or Frampton for the Angell
1697-1698	Mr Frampton for the Angell
1699-1704	Mr Frampton
1704	Mr Brett or the occ of Framptons
1708-1714	Mr Riplingham for the Angell
1728-1736	Mrs Pickering or occ for ye Angel
1737-1745	Jn Hazelden for the Angel
1746-1747	Jn Hazelden for the Angel or occ
1748-1754	Mr John Marlow for ye Angel
1755	Geo Hone for ye Angel
1756	Geo Hone or occ for ye Angel
1757-1764	Mr Marlow for the Angell
1765-1797	John Knight for the Angel

Print dated 1 May 1804 showing the Angel Inn

John Marlow seems to have had a substantial interest and John Knight reigned for over thirty years but these are no more than names. Ownership, however, remained with the descendants of John Brett at least until 1777 when (as happened with Chapel House also – see above page 395) the property was involved in the mortgage of 1764 and the 1777 Marriage Settlement of John Brett the Younger and was described as follows: 'All those three Messuages or Tenements 2 whereof adjoin each other called Angel Inn and Crown Ale House'(1764) and 'the messuage or tenement called the Angel Inn and Little Angel ... and also all those 4 coachhouses erected in the place whereon formerly stood a messuage called the Crown Alehouse which said last mentioned messuages are now or lately were in the occupation of John Knight' (1777). Again, as with Chapel House, I do not know when or to whom a sale was eventually made but it may well have been behind the make-over which the building undoubtedly suffered early in the new century. It is known that Edward Hilder Strange, son of Edward Strange of the Green Pales (see chapter 17 page 244), was landlord, probably proprietor, of the hotel in the early 19th century and it may well be that he was responsible for the refurbishment. His son, Edward Jeffery Strange, born in 1803, later founded the Strange building enterprise and may have had a hand in his father's building work. *Clifford's Guide*, 1823, says that the hotel 'has lately undergone great improvements, which have amply repaid the proprietor for his exertions'. In fact he died that very year and his wife, Jane, took over; so that the evidence suggests the work was completed before then. The *Maidstone Journal* reported the death: 'On the 12th instant [June 1823] in the 51st year of his age Mr Edward Hilder Strange of the Royal Kentish Hotel Tunbridge Wells leaving a widow and 7 children to lament their loss. Mr Strange's character for probity and goodness of heart was surpassed by few; and as an affectionate husband, a kind father and a valuable friend he will be long lamented'. It appears then that the original building shared in the refronting fashion of the beginning of the 19th century. As Savidge says '... the Angel became the Kentish Royal Hotel with a three-storey Regency front and a four-column porch'. The regency front included a typical bow whereas the original was surely flat-fronted. There is a small print dated 1 May 1804 which appears to show the original building with the Chapel to the right – see previous page. A later print, dated 1826 (see next page), used as an endpaper for Savidge's history shows the new frontage together with a clear view of Chapel House before its demolition about 1834. Note that the Barrow map still uses the name 'Angel Inn' and shows no sign of a bow front (see page 393 above). Later landlords, after Mrs Strange, were Edward Churchill 1832-1852; William Haines 1855-1867; J. Stuckey 1868-1870; and J. Braby 1872-1874. This information can be useful for dating photographs since the landlords were wont to display their names above the porch.

The Tithe Award records that the premises consisted of the hotel, the tap, stabling and a yard. The hotel itself was obviously behind and beside the bowfront and porch and Hetherington has a story of a coach running out of control down the High Street and hitting the window of the tap, breaking glass. The tap must therefore have been on the Mount Sion side of the premises, part of the ramshackle building visible on the right-hand side of the photograph on page 388 above. The stabling must also have been on this corner since access through Chapel Place was clearly not possible. A later photograph, however (about 1874 – see page 30), shows a two-storey building in this position marked 'Hot and Cold Baths'.

The Royal Kentish Hotel *and Chapel House from the Common in 1826*

The landlord at the time of the Tithe map, but not the owner, was Edward Churchill who also ran the *Calverley Hotel* which he had taken over in 1839 after its extension by Decimus Burton. The *Kentish Hotel* was involved in the goings-on of Dr Webber in 1864 which will be recounted at length in the next chapter. Webber's ambition to rebuild the hotel came to naught but in 1878 the joint efforts of Francis Peek as financier (see chapter 19 page 277) and Weeks and Hughes as architects accomplished what Webber had failed to do. The old building was completely demolished and replaced by the grand building we have today; but its days as a hotel were numbered. It started as the *Kentish Hotel*, became the *Grand Hotel* briefly in 1905 and then was converted into the Kentish Mansion flats which we now have.

Looking back to the Barrow map detail on page 393 above, the label 'Turner Grocer' can be seen against a building between the *Angel Inn* and the Chapel. I guess – but it is no more than a guess – that Turner the grocer of Chapel Place was the same John Turner whom we met on page 386 above as ratepayer for Walmer House and the Little Grove House. The only other deduction we can make is that there was then a shop on this corner, as no doubt there had been for many years and was to be until 1900 when Lloyds Bank came along, as witness the photograph on the next page which shows a typical old-style building with a

The Chapel and No 1 London Road before 1900

shop on the ground level which was in fact a greengrocer's at the time. There is still a very similar building on the northern corner of Mount Sion and the London Road. The identity of the mounted band and the occasion of its parade in front of the Chapel are unknown.

To the right of the corner shop, with the blind, is Simmonds clothiers at 22 Chapel Place; and Frank Simmonds, as we have seen, lived for a time at one of the Sussex View houses and Mrs Simmonds, in the 1870s (see chapter 18 page 256) lived at Caxton House. Hall's Bookshop opened in 1898 at 18 Chapel Place but moved to its present premises at 20 and 22 in 1938 when Simmonds moved uptown. The Tithe map (page 397 above) shows the whole corner site, numbered 3846, as 'House, Shop and Yard' owned by Hester Wighton and occupied by Thomas Mathews. The larger portion was on the London Road front and the smaller, with a yard alongside, on the Chapel Place side; which was the shop and which the house? Barrow's map does not help and Bowra's Mount Sion plan does not extend this far but his general map at small scale shows two buildings on the corner. Going still further back in time there is some evidence that John Wybourne had a shop here. This brings us to the whole saga of the tenements beneath the ante-gallery.

Much of this story was rehearsed in chapter 3 page 22. The business of the tenements came to a head in 1809 (see Waring's history) when general repairs to the Chapel were contemplated but it was concluded that repair of the ante-gallery was pointless until the tenements below were made safe; and the best thing would be to buy them. In the words of Col Waring 'they occupied the ground floor where the chancel and vestry now are, and also covered part of what is now the public pavement leading to Cumberland Walk and part of the present passage between the Church and the School'. Why part of the Chapel should ever have been built over John Wybourne's property is a mystery. I have ventured to suggest that it was simply because Wybourne refused to budge and the space was needed for the Chapel. The bulk of the tenements belonged to the Rev. John Brett of Norfolk and he agreed to sell. There is in fact an addition to the Marriage Settlement document of 1777 which says: 'MEMO 31 Dec 1810 within named John Brett sold 'All those vaults within mentioned near the Chapel at Tunbridge Wells formerly occupied by Ann Cripps now ______ Golding' to the Earl of Abergavenny and others on trusts therein mentioned.' As a matter of interest, part of the tenements was the shop, or dwelling, of a Mr Wighton. I should dearly like to know the connection, which I am sure must exist, between this man and Hester Wighton, owner of the corner property at the time of the Tithe map. I should also like to know whether I am right in supposing that 'the shed or building there late built by John Wybourne now standing and used for a shop towards the west ...' was in fact the forerunner of the corner property shown in the photograph above, now No.1 London Road together with Nos 18-22 Chapel Place.

So we have come full circle, from the earliest temporal extremity of our Mount Sion story when we dealt with John Wybourne and John Brett in our early chapters to its geographical extremity at the point where John Wybourne's problematic buildings had a chapel planted amongst them and where a century and a half later the Rev. John Brett came to the Chapel's rescue with the sale of John Wybourne's dilapidated tenements. In conclusion, come with me on a little temporal and geographical excursion – to the year 1810 and to Norfolk. The Vestry Minutes record that, after the dust had settled on the purchase of the tenements under the ante-gallery, it was resolved at a Vestry meeting on 23 July 1812 that certain deeds should be entrusted to the safe-keeping of Messrs Scoones. These deeds must certainly have included documents dealing with the purchase of the Brett property in 1810. The legal firm of Scoones has now become the somewhat larger firm of Thomson, Snell and Passmore; and so I wrote to them, as far back as 1987 in the first place, asking if they could trace these documents which had been committed to the safe-keeping of their predecessors in 1812. Some years later, after a polite reminder, I got a response. Mr Bertram wrote from the Tonbridge office (from where William Scoones used to operate) to say he could find nothing; and the Tunbridge Wells office suggested I get in touch with Mr Duncan Rawson-Mackenzie who was, he said, Secretary to the Parish Council. So I did and I discovered that he had two large tin trunks in the vaults of Cripps Harries Hall full of records of the Trustees of the Chapel and amongst them the documents I had been seeking for so long!

I had been hoping for two things from the 1812 documents; more information about John Brett and his property; and a more detailed description of the 'tenements under the ante-gallery'. I am afraid I was unlucky on both counts. The description in the conveyance of the Rev. Brett's property goes: 'All those Rooms and Vaults near the said chapel being partly underneath the Vestry Room or House and the Gallery belonging to the said chapel … formerly in the occupation of Ann Cripps, sometime of John Wyborn, since of John Brett, now or late of Alexander Wilmshurst Cordwainer.' Not very informative – and of course nothing in the way of a plan.

On the other hand, it is something to have handled the actual piece of paper on which John Brett's great-great-nephew wrote to William Scoones on 31 August 1809 and folded carefully and sealed and which then travelled by coach, I suppose, from Norfolk to the Wells. Let me quote a bit for you, because it gives a flavour of the man – and the times:

> I am obliged by the friendly wish at the conclusion of your letter in regard to my health of which I thank God I have no reason to complain. I hope you enjoy yours and long may. I will thank you to say the same from me to your neighbour, my old friend Mr Children, whom you mentioned as one of the Trustees of the Chapel and to give my compliments to him which with the same to yourself concludes me … Dear Sir … Your faithful and obedient humble servant … J Brett.

A year and more later, the Rev. Brett's solicitor, Mr Goodwin of King's Lynn, wrote to Scoones with somewhat less reassuring news about his client's health. He says he has explained the Draft Bargain and Sale to Mr Brett 'who resides seven miles from Lynn and who is now so infirm as not to be able to travel from home – the sooner the engrossment is sent me the better. I will then ride over to Grimston and get it executed. I will probably be in town in the course of a fortnight.'

So the story of Chapel Place comes to an end with a final look at the descendants of the John Brett who had so much to do with its beginnings; but Chapel Place itself and some of its traders and the *Kentish Hotel* were to play a part in the astonishing events of November 1864 with which, in a final flourish to our story of Mount Sion, we conclude in a chapter devoted to the 'Webber Riots'.

Chapter 27

The Webber Riots

Anyone looking for a model for Mr Grouser of Toytown or Mr Disgusted of Tunbridge Wells need look no further than a certain doctor who arrived in the Wells without a stir in June 1860 and departed in a huff and hurry and flurry of controversy four years later. Had he imagined that, on the hot Saturday evening of 2 July four years after his hopeful arrival, the post-prandial calm of his family and their living-in patient would be interrupted by the stuffed effigy of a pig burning upon his railings, volleys of stones breaking his windows and a crowd of a thousand or more milling around the bottom of Mount Sion, Dr William Webber, consulting surgeon, might have chosen some other town in which to recover from illness and the strain of practising in London for thirty years.

Yet Tunbridge Wells had the reputation of a quiet and pleasant inland resort and basked still in the reflected glory of those days not thirty years before when the dear Queen as a girl had sat in her peaked bonnet in the gallery of King Charles Chapel listening to the Rev. Pope or dreaming of donkey rides or dreading the return to Kensington in October. Mount Sion was in a way an epitome of the place. It encompassed lodging houses, gentry, doctors and schools. The houses had started their lives in the late 17th century to lodge the fashionable takers of

Princess Victoria in the Chapel 1834

the summer waters and had variously been renovated, rebuilt or replaced over the next century and a half. Those at the bottom of the hill were let out in rooms and apartments while those at the top enjoyed a superior social as well as geographical position. Either they had become private residences or they were let as whole houses for the season or longer. Thus, occupying the site of the old bowling green where the gentle company had bowled by day and danced by night, Bowling Green House was occupied by Mr Broadwood MP and his wife and Cumberland House by James Deane Esquire JP who on 14 October not long after Dr Webber's arrival, as we saw on page 276, sentenced Jane Smith for being drunk on Mount Sion. Both houses and their large, chestnut-shaded gardens were destined to disappear within two decades under the red brick or white stucco terraces of Berkeley Road and upper Mount Sion. On the other side of the road Marlborough House was let that season to the Hon. J.H. and Lady M. Knox while in 1861 and 1862 it was the family of the Rt. Hon. Sir Charles Edward Grey that was to enjoy its southerly aspect over the as yet virgin site of inconceivable Edwardian mansions in Madeira Park. It was Eden House, however, that retained from its association with the Duchess of Kent the real cachet of aristocracy. In 1860 it was the home of the Benson family whose claim to fame lay in the future of two-year-old Frank who was to become an actor and a knight; but 1862 saw the visits of the Marchioness of Abercorn and the Earl and Countess of Mount Edgcombe. Perhaps the present-day occupants of the town houses known as Sion Walk can still glory in some faint aura from the visit of the Queen's mother in 1849. If only the fabric of the old house could have been preserved. What else was incinerated in the demolition men's holocaust of 1969? Even the azalea pinched from the front garden lasted only a summer.

Did Her Royal Highness know that not a hundred yards down the little side road was Eden Villa, residence of the self-same Rev. William Law Pope, MA and former scholar of Worcester College, Oxford, to whose sermons her daughter had listened with less than rapt attention? Then he had been minister for a few years only; in 1860 he was still there and was to be until 1877, the Grand Panjandrum of education and Poo Bah of social welfare for the tiny parish which was to obtain formal recognition only after his death. It is hard to believe that he had not been there, on that great occasion in 1849, somewhere in the wings, taking a proprietary interest in the proceedings. Two years before Dr Webber's arrival a job creation scheme organised by the Rev. Pope resulted in the digging of Brighton Lake, nicknamed 'Pope's Puddle', and in the same year he raised £850 to buy Murray House at the top of Frog Lane which was to be used as a school for Girls and Infants, presided over by Miss Parrott, and as a residence for Mr Diggens who taught the Charles the Martyr boys. Well-cooked meat and excellent plum puddings were also to be had at Murray House, as we have seen in the account of the girls' dinner in 1860 in chapter 16. In addition to the Church schools there was no dearth of private schools on Mount Sion. On 27 July 1860 (the same day incidentally as was announced the arrival at Rock Villa of a certain Mr Thackeray W.M.) Mr James M. Richardson had the pleasure to announce to the Gentry, to

Families Furnishing, to Brokers and to the Public in General that he had been favoured with instructions to sell by auction on the premises of Fairlawn House, Mount Sion (in consequence of the house having been let on lease unfurnished), a quantity of very excellent and genuine household furniture, china, glass, earthenware and numerous other effects; and before the author of *Vanity Fair* left Rock Villa at the end of his short holiday the Misses Seeley had opened their Ladies' Seminary at Fairlawn House, thereby increasing to four the number of schools for ladies on Mount Sion; the others being carefully supervised by Mrs Allen at Burlington House, by Miss Billing at Brunswick House and by Mrs Read at Jerningham House. For pupils of unspecified, but probably male, sex Mr R.W. Rogers Long BA at the Tunbridge Wells Classical and Mathematical School, Mansfield House, Mount Sion, offered a thoughtful and careful education – either elementary or advanced – and received a few boarders. Finally the Tunbridge Wells Girls' Industrial School at Little Grove House in Cumberland Gardens trained girls of a different class for domestic service and included on its committee of management the wife of Richard Turner who lived at Howard Lodge on the other side of the walk and was a surgeon at the Dispensary in Grosvenor Road, forerunner of the present hospital. Mr Turner died in October and an auction sale was held to dispose of 26 nearly new iron bedsteads and many other items appropriate to the training of girls in domestic service. Mrs Turner and family left Howard Lodge and were succeeded, keeping up the medical tradition in house and hill, by Dr Blackall Marsack who stayed for thirty years. Indeed medical men inhabited Howard Lodge in unbroken succession until it was sub-divided in the 1960s. In the early 1900s there was to be a hospital on Mount Sion but in 1860 there were just three doctors, or four if we include Dr Webber. Dr Robert Righton Gream was living with his wife and family at 2, Sion Place, now Durnford House, and at Bedford Place (see chapter 26) was to be found, if not engaged on the affairs of the Town Commissioners, Dr Charles Trustram.

On the other side of the road was a recently erected pair of tall bow fronted villas with ornate ironwork balconies and canopies, now unfortunately missing – see the illustration in chapter 17 page 236. Number 1 Blenheim Place was a boarding house whose attractions Mrs George Gilbert had advertised at the beginning of the year as 'Situation healthy, sheltered and near the Common, the Parade and the Railway Station; terms moderate'. Number 2 was the family residence of Joseph Delves senior, house agent numbering his late father's Eden House among the properties on his list and father himself of Joseph junior who kept the butcher's shop in Chapel Place. In September 1860 the Town Commissioners were elected for the first time, not appointed, albeit on a limited plural franchise weighted in favour of the bigger property owners; and among the chosen 24, besides such names as Willicombe, Edwards, Colbran, Molyneux and Maingay, were Charles Trustram and Joseph Delves. On one thing at least these two could agree: that was the state of the roads. As we have seen on page 236, Mr Joseph Delves told the last meeting of the old Commission in August that he was sorry to say that he had never seen the roads in such a filthy, dirty state as they had been within the last 12 months. At the first meeting of the new Commission, in October, the following altercation was reported:

> Mr Jos Delves: (Blenheim Place, Mount Sion, speaking to Mr Trustram) You say Mr Delves. Please to say whether you mean Mr William Delves or Mr Joseph Delves. As we are beginning today, I should like it to be understood that it ought to be properly expressed whether it's Mr Joseph Delves or Mr William Delves (laughter).
>
> Mr W. Delves: I should particularly wish that also. (much laughter)

William Delves of Hargate Lodge was Steward to the Earl of Abergavenny and passed on his enthusiasm for local affairs to his son, young Mr William Henry, who was celebrating his 31st birthday in 1860 and whose career was dealt with in chapter 21.

In March 1860 Mr Haines, proprietor of the *Royal Kentish Hotel*, announced the installation at a large expense, in premises adjoining his hotel, of baths replete with every comfort and convenience – see the photograph on page 30. Hot and cold water was laid on in unlimited supply allowing bathing in water of any degree of temperature and hot, cold, warm and tepid shower baths and vapour baths were available in a variety of transmutations thanks to the complete and comfortable fittings provided by Mr Soper. The *Royal Kentish* was still at this time the pleasant three-storey Regency building with a single bow front which can be seen in old prints. In 1878 it was replaced by a new hotel, now the Kentish Mansions whose grandiose entrance flanked by the sale of packaged chicken bits on the one side and the hire of videos on the other serves a useful function as a bus shelter. Behind the *Royal Kentish*, then as now, was Chapel Place where the Delves brothers, Thomas Henry and Joseph junior, kept their butcher's shop where the florist recently was, Mrs Simmonds ran her clothier's business where Hall's bookshop now is, William Fox, chemist, supplied the needs of the local doctors' clientele not to mention his Celebrated Cough Jujubes, Digestive Ginger Candy and Magic Tincture, and Thomas Kinlan, watchmaker and jeweller, had recently suffered a robbery of £300-worth of stock from which disaster he had recovered only thanks to a whip-round amongst his fellow tradesmen. Here also, every Tuesday, Friday and Saturday in Bedford House, consultations could be arranged with Mr Quintin B. Hair, the 'Established Dentist at Tunbridge Wells During the Last 24 Years, Patronised by H.R.H. The Duchess of Kent, the Nobility, Clergy and Gentry of the Wells and Neighbourhood ... Perfection in Artificial Teeth ... All Charges Strictly Moderate'. In spite of Thomas Kinlan's misfortune or the occasional case of drunkenness the local newspaper was able in October to congratulate the district on its crime statistics – 'a fact which speaks well for the officers and men of the local police force'. Of 32 larcenies reported during the last 12 months no fewer than 26 criminals were detected – a decrease of 11 larcenies and an increase of 11 detections compared with the previous year, thus showing the remarkable immunity of Tunbridge Wells from danger.

Unto this mount of comparative tranquillity came then, between 1 and 8 June 1860, the Webber family: himself a man of 60 but showing no decline in physical or mental capacity, his wife and three daughters. Mount Sion was a suitable choice of locality for a medical man but No.1 Sion Terrace – which still exits as no.7, Mount Sion – was a modest residence compared with those enjoyed by Messrs Gream, Turner and Trustram; but William Webber's financial circumstances were modest also, as will be seen later. All the same a neighbouring house, No.3, must have had the same accommodation and this was offered for letting, unfurnished, on 27 July of that year and contained dining and drawing rooms, five bedrooms, two dressing rooms, two water closets and the usual domestic offices. Next door, up the hill, were the two bow fronts of Blenheim Place and down the hill, but replaced in 1929 by the National Provincial Bank, was a so-called 'cottage' attached to No 3, Sion Terrace and then the corner shop occupied by Mr G.H. Lawrence and his School of Photography. How the doctor got on with his new neighbours is a matter for speculation since for a while he managed to keep out of the news; but this was not to last.

In May the following year Dr Webber travelled to Buxton in Derbyshire to attend a medical conference. At the *George Hotel* he met a well-known surgeon, Thomas Spencer Wells, to whom, however, he was not altogether well disposed since he suspected Wells of being one of those who had blackballed him when he was up for election to the Royal College of Surgeons. Wells, on the other hand, was inclined to be friendly. He was feeling pleased with himself no doubt because he had given a lecture to the conference on the subject of 'Vesico-vaginal and recto-vaginal Fistula' and had printed copies of his lecture for private circulation adorned with necessarily explicit gynaecological engravings. Thomas Wells in his mood of conciliation or vanity gave a copy of his lecture to the 'Boots' of the hotel and asked him to deliver it to Dr Webber. The 'Boots', lazy or unaware of the nature of the bombshell he was carrying, left it on view in one of the public rooms addressed to Dr Webber. Perhaps it would be unfair to suggest that William Webber seized an opportunity to get his own back on his blackballing colleague. No doubt he was acting on the highest principles and in the interests of public decorum. Doubtless he was sincerely outraged. Thomas Spencer Wells ought to be ashamed of himself; it was disgrrr … aceful! It all went into a letter to the Editor of the *Medical Circular* accusing Wells of unprofessional conduct and a host of other crimes against society. The writ for libel was not long delayed and a report of the hearing appeared in the *Tunbridge Wells Gazette* on St Valentine's Day 1862. The local doctor had not appeared to give evidence in his own defence – this was to become an unfortunate habit – and the court awarded £300 damages to the plaintiff, an imposition which proved too much for the Webber finances. In July a dividend meeting of the London Court of Bankruptcy was held before Mr Registrar Hazlitt in re Mr Webber, surgeon and apothecary, and as a consequence of adverse legal proceedings in the suit with Mr Wells, surgeon. Debts amounted to £1,701 9s. 10d. The official assignee held a balance of £152 6s. 6d. which the creditors resolved should be divided among them. Quite how the doctor managed to weather this storm is unclear. He had applied for a re-trial but was apparently unsuccessful. He provided himself, however, with an excuse to write the first of numerous letters to the Editor of the *Gazette*, complaining on this occasion of various inaccuracies in the newspaper's report of his application. The paper suggested that he had retired: that was incorrect. He was ill after living in London but was now 'desirous of engaging in the more active support of my profession as a consulting practitioner and operative surgeon as has been my wont during the last two-thirds of the 45 years I have been a member' of the medical profession. At all events he continued to reside undisturbed at 1, Sion Terrace and the only presage of storms on the tranquil sea of relations between town and doctor occurred in connection with plans for the Royal Marriage Celebrations when Webber was the only opposing voice simply because, in the words of a later *Gazette* editorial, the Committee's measures 'would not dovetail in with his own ideas'.

At the beginning of 1864 events gathered pace. At this time two schemes were afoot for the rebuilding of hotels by the promotion of private companies which sought to attract finance from local shareholders. One company was interested in Mr Haines' hotel and called itself the Kentish Royal Hotel Company. The other, called the Tunbridge Wells Hotel Company, was planning to replace the *Sussex Hotel* on the 'Parade' with a building standing a little further back which would occupy an 'elevated site, conveniently placed between the two roads, and surrounded by about eleven acres of ornamental grounds and gardens tastefully laid out'. In January 1864 'Mr Webber' made a long speech at an early public meeting of the Kentish Royal Company. He claimed that it was he who had originated the 'idea of Hotel Companies' in Tunbridge Wells but he defended himself against certain charges that had been made. One of these was that he had introduced measures 'tending to injure lodging-house keepers'. It is unfounded speculation, of course, to suppose that lodging-house keepers at the bottom of Mount Sion or Joseph Delves the house agent were leading complainants or that there was any personal animosity involved; but it is certain that his early brush with the lodging-house lobby can have been no assistance to the doctor in the events of the summer. He had no desire, he said in closing his speech, on this occasion to injure anyone and indeed he had been unsparing in his efforts which were actuated – as usual – only by the highest motives and with the object of benefiting the town. Whether the local people were convinced is uncertain but the City men behind the embryo company seem to have been impressed for in early February a further meeting of the Kentish Royal Hotel Company was chaired by Mr Webber in his new capacity of 'local director'. It was perhaps in this capacity that he took an interest in the affairs of the rival Tunbridge Wells Hotel Company and attended their meeting in March. After the usual expositions, explanations, questions and answers had been exhausted and potential shareholders had been urged to put their hands in their pockets it was left to the Rev. W.L. Pope among other municipal big-wigs present to propose a vote of thanks to the chair. The vote was seconded by Mr Webber who took the opportunity to make some observations in the course of which he alluded to the increased use that might be made of the chalybeate waters of the

Wells – and to the share he had taken in drawing attention to their merits. He also said that in going to many watering places, Brighton, Hastings, Bognor and others, people who went for a dip in the sea found themselves immersed in the sewage of the town, whereas the salt could be brought from the sea to Tunbridge Wells and a genuine salt-water bath enjoyed without the drawback he had named … At this point there was an interruption. Mr Webb rose to his feet. 'I cannot allow the libel Mr Webber has endeavoured to put upon Brighton and Hastings to go forth in print without contradiction. I deny most emphatically that anybody ever bathes in sewage when they go down to Brighton (hear, hear!) and it ought not to be asserted by a gentleman professing to stand so high in the medical profession … ' William Webber must have wondered what had hit him. Here he was giving a boost to the town, not to mention a plug for the baths newly installed by his neighbour Mr Haines and what thanks did he get? Perhaps a suspicion of paranoia in the doctor's mind may be traced back to this moment. That he was disenchanted with the town was shown in the course of a public meeting also held in March. This was a public enquiry connected with the Local Government Act, 1858. Liberal ratepayers headed by the baronet rector of Frant and brother-in-law of Lord Abergavenny had been successful in achieving the 1860 election of Town Commissioners but they were now pressing for equal voting by ballot and incorporation as a borough. Dr Webber in his customary public-spirited way had gone along to the enquiry and had found that he was one of only three simple ratepayers present, the remainder being Commissioners. Not unreasonably he suggested that not enough publicity had been given to the enquiry; but the Inspector said that notice had been given in the prescribed form and Mr Trustram said that he had lived in Tunbridge Wells a long time and knew the ratepayers' opinions as well or better than Mr Webber who, seeing that he was out-gunned, decided to be conciliatory and said that he would not press his objection as he saw that there was a tendency to receive it in the quarrelsome spirit that always characterised meetings 'in that place'. Mr Wigg immediately jumped down the doctor's throat. Mr Wigg was later to double-barrel himself and as Stone-Wigg become a very big wig and chairman of the Board.

Mr Wigg: I call upon you, sir, to withdraw that expression.
Mr Webber: I am quite ready to leave the room and your society too.
Mr Pearless: Sit down, Mr Webber, that's the best thing you can do.
Mr Webber: What did you say, sir?

At the end of March or possibly on the first of April Joseph Delves senior moved house from Blenheim Place, next door to Dr Webber at 1 Sion Terrace, to Heath Villa on the London Road. No suggestion of cause and effect can be made. During April there appears to have been growing dissatisfaction with progress on the *Kentish Hotel* rebuilding project. On 29 April a letter from Webber appeared in the *Gazette*.

Sir, My attention has been called to two letters which appeared in your paper last week purporting to be written by two dissatisfied shareholders but in so covert a way as to bring to mind the old song of 'Two faces under one hood'.

Neither author has had the courage to append his name of which they may be justly ashamed. Both nevertheless make statements as frivolous as they are false and as senseless as they are sinister in their object. 'The Directorate' has ever been open and honest in ITS doings and when the party or parties who are so ready to attack it shall dare to be equally candid and straightforward, it will be prepared to answer frankly and truly any fair and business-like questions which any of the bona-fide shareholders may be desirous of asking; but the directorate will not condescend to reply to anonymous missiles, set forth by the pen of falsehood and dipped in the ink of malevolence. It has been more than once publicly stated by those whose word is their bond and who will not be driven to spend the shareholders' money hastily and lavishly that '*the hotel will be built*'. What right then has any importunately-disposed or loquacious shareholder or busybody to doubt their word or to ask them to 'commence building' operations? As local director (not offering myself but proposed and unanimously elected by the shareholders to an office I had not the desire to take) I have it would seem incurred the ill-nature of those opposed to the Kentish Company and the ill-will of the tradespeople and others whose interests I have sedulously endeavoured, regardless of any personal considerations, sacrifices or fatigue, to uphold and advance – no uncommon occurrence where a fearless independence and unselfishness are exercised.

Dr Webber in a donkey cart

Lengthy quotation from this letter may perhaps be forgiven for the flavour it gives of the Webberian style in indignation and self-righteousness. Its effectiveness on this occasion, however, was somewhat diminished by its author asking the editor to withdraw it and publish a different letter. The editor refused and for good measure printed an attack on Webber by one signing himself (or herself?) 'Marjorie'. None of this seems to have resulted in any speeding up of building operations as is shown by the following letter which appeared two months later, on 17 June, under the title

'The Hotel that 'Web' Built', and whose ironic eloquence maybe justifies the pseudonymous Celtic signature:

> Sir, I was confidentially informed this morning that our local director had really commenced proceedings and had workmen employed in the destruction of the old hotel, in anticipation of a large arrival of bricks alluded to so eloquently at the late dinner, and cleverly negotiated by this excellent business man. I need scarcely say I hastened down to Chapel Place with great impetuosity but found alas! The only proceedings an act of spoliation, for one of the imposing boards that now embellish the hotel that 'Web' built (?) instead of, I presume, the long-deferred and mythical arcade that our local director promised us – one of these boards, illustrated with letter-press, had been violently torn down and (cruel mockery and insult!) had been reared in front of Mr Webber's residence. This act of vandalism deserves the severest reprehension. I am glad to say, from sympathising enquiries, that the local director is as well as can be expected and that he will still carry on his acts of philanthropy which in this town at least are as distinguished as his urbanity, unselfishness and deference to public opinion. The police are unable to discover the perpetrators but it is suspected a group of infuriated shareholders fancy they have a right to some portion of the property and are willing even yet to divide it with the local director of the gasping and I fear dying Kentish Hotel Company. I am, Sir, Yours faithfully, Erin-go-bragh.

Now anyone signing himself 'Up with Ireland' cannot be surprised if his Irish provenance lays him open to suspicion and although, of course, there may have been many Irishmen in Tunbridge Wells at the time it is nonetheless a fact that Thomas Maxwell Kinlan, the jeweller of Chapel Place, and his young wife Mary (if not their five-year-old daughter Marion) were born in Ireland. If, however, it be thought that Erin-go-Bragh's epistle was beyond the powers of a simple tradesman the finger of suspicion might point a tiny bit further up the hill to the residence of Charles Trustram at No 1 Bedford Place. Here lived and worked as assistant to the doctor another native of Ireland, the 38-year-old bachelor and member of the Apothecaries' Hall, Robert Branigan ... or could it possibly be that the respectable general practitioner and respected Town Commissioner himself had a finger in the pie?

Be that as it may, these go-braghian goings-on were soon to be overshadowed by more noisome events. It might have been thought that William Webber had created for himself a delicate, not to say explosive, situation in which his best course was to lie low and attempt by a quiet efficiency in deeds rather than words to live down the unpopularity which he had, inadvertently or not, acquired. Was it, therefore, a cruel coincidence or deliberate trick of playful Nemesis that led the doctor across the London Road one fine morning towards the end of June? But then, as Thomas Kinlan was to say on a later occasion, Mr Webber was a man 'very much about'. He was bound to pass that way sooner or later and spot the excavated cellar. After all, it was only just at the bottom of Mount Sion on the London Road. Henry Edwards, the butcher, had applied to the Paving and Drainage Committee for permission to excavate the cellar and the workmen employed by Messrs Willicombe Son and Oakley had come upon an unused drain, formerly the town drain. Quite rightly they informed Mr Wright, the Town Surveyor, who found it sealed up with brickwork on either side of the excavation made for the cellar. On taking up a portion of the arch a deposit of 'drift' was discovered which had no doubt been there many years and was comparatively inoffensive. The main drain, therefore, being dry as a matter of course was perfectly innocuous. 'Drift' is presumably an euphemism for a nasty water-borne deposit although no such sanitary usage is indicated in the dictionary. Anyway, Webber passed by during the excavation and in his high-minded and high-handed way concluded that it was disgraceful and someone ought to be ashamed. He complained to the Town Surveyor and to the police. He may well have told Mr Wright that he should be ashamed of himself but he was not satisfied with the response and so he wrote a letter to Sir George Grey at the Home Office. He mentioned the lack of necessary precautions and spoke of the want of attention displayed by the Commissioners to their duties as the Sanitary Board of the town. He went so far as to state that he himself and some patients of his had been made ill from the effects of this very drain. It was perhaps a pity that he should have made this particular accusation if he could not substantiate it and this he never did although he left the town still promising to explain hereafter 'when the thirst for unjust vengeance has passed away' that he was not the first to publish the existence of the fever. Perhaps he was simply impulsive: he saw something wrong and he said so on the spot – besides, it was difficult to resist the temptation to write a letter. On the other hand, suspicion of the purity of the doctor's motives had arisen already over the gynaecological engravings. Maybe his public-spirited indignation concealed an urge to get his own back – and to hell with the consequences!

The Home Office was not slow to act. In these modern times, after a century and more of progress, a delay of weeks or months might seem reasonably expeditious but in 1864 an inspector, Dr Hunter, was knocking on the Town Hall door within a matter of days and before the Commissioners had even been consulted. The inspector's hunt for evidence and the report of his 'scientific enquiry' were equally swift and efficient. He visited Dr Webber and his patients; he inspected records of general sanitary conditions; and he attended a committee meeting at which Dr Webber was invited to appear but failed to do so. In his report Dr Hunter said that neither his examination of the drain nor his interviews with patients had produced evidence to bear out the allegations. Death statistics generally were satisfactory; there had been recently only two deaths from scarlatina and one from scarlet fever. A meeting of the town's medical gentlemen took place at which Dr Webber was condemned: he had made ungrounded allegations; he had done damage to traders and lodging house keepers; it was hoped that there would be no repetition of 'that officiousness and want of consideration which has characterised Mr Webber's proceedings in the present instance'. William Webber stood thoroughly condemned both by the authorities and by his professional colleagues but perhaps the matter was not so absolutely clear-cut as was publicly proclaimed. At a later Town Commission meeting the chairman, the Hon. F.G. Molyneux, said that Dr Hunter had given 'many small hints which would be useful'; but a good report was very satisfactory. The inspector would report to the Medical Board of the Privy Council. Tunbridge Wells might not receive a copy of the report although one had been requested. Charles Trustram thought that Tunbridge Wells should ask for the report; speaking from his own medical practice of many years he knew there was nothing to conceal. He then went on to comment on the state of the offending drain in words he may possibly have regretted on reflection. It was true, he said, that there was a sort of channel in that drain. There, probably, some monarch of the rats was used to hold his levée and his midnight revels; there perhaps the spoils from unprotected larders were brought; but anything else beyond that there had not been for the last 15 years. Mr Wigg wanted to know why the central government had acted without consulting local government first. Joseph Delves asked whether they could not see the letter from Webber … 'a person who had come very lately into the town'. The chairman observed that there had been extraordinarily few cases of scarlatina or typhus in the last 12 months. It should be remembered that water, sewage and public health were very live issues of the day especially in London. Nevertheless Trustram's talk of royal rodent revels passed unnoticed; not an editorial eyebrow was elevated; no commissioner commented; no colleague complained.

Meanwhile whisperings of another sort pervaded the town. It was later said that rumours had been flying for days and the police should have known. In due course the whisperings turned to action and the whisperers made their way in twos and threes or larger bands to the Common. Many of them were 'mere boys', as defending counsel was to plead later, but there was a stiffening of over twenties. One of them had made a kind of pig out of sacking and was a centre of subdued hilarity. It was a muggy sort of midsummer evening, the rain threatening but never coming – a Saturday, anyway, and time to celebrate the end of a six-day week. The twos and threes had swollen to hundreds and as twilight approached they made their way from the direction of the Wellington Rocks down the slope of the Common and across the London Road, skirting the hole in the ground that had started the trouble. Soon they were blocking the road between Sion Terrace on the north and Bedford Place and Walmer House on the south and were spilling up and down the hill, so great were their numbers – 500 at least at the beginning increasing to 2,000 according to some estimates by half past nine. Many of the latecomers were no doubt passive spectators like some of the Town Commissioners who were spotted by PC Fenner on the southern side of the road. Charles Trustram living in Bedford Place was certainly one of them and it may be guessed that Joseph Delves was there with his butcher sons. It must be presumed that these worthy citizens came upon the scene only later to see what the disturbance was.

Inside the Webber residence all was quiet. The family was in the parlour on the first floor: the doctor, his wife Eliza and two daughters. At the time three daughters, all unmarried, and a son, ages from 28 to 14, formed the family but this evening Henry, the youngest, and one of the daughters, Eliza, Emily or Ellen, were away from home. Their numbers were, however, made up by a living-in patient, Captain John Blake and his wife and sister. The 72-year-old housekeeper, Elizabeth Newson, and Mary Blyth, the cook who was 34, were about their normal concerns. There was also a housemaid, Natalia Etherton, but she was a local girl and probably had the evening off. The other two servants had come with the family from East Anglia. At ten to nine the first stone hit the front door. One of the servants went to see who was knocking. When she opened the door a potato flew past her. She called her master. Followed by the gallant captain, the doctor hastened downstairs and walked out onto the front steps. The pig effigy was attached to the railings. A policeman was there and a lot of boys and they were looking at the pig and talking about it. Webber told the policeman to take it away and the boys jeered. 'Why don't you take it away?' Webber asked the policeman and 'What is your name?' 'He hasn't got any!' a boy said and they all laughed. The crowd was shouting and yelling 'Webber' and hooting. Then the stones started flying. The doctor retreated indoors. Thomas Cole was standing on the opposite side of the road. He had a large stone in his hand and he threw it directly through a window in Webber's house. He turned to PC Forward, who was standing nearby in plain clothes being off-duty, looked up into his face and said, 'That's a good un'. 'It is, Tom,' said the constable. Alfred Taylor and Henry Butcher, a labourer, were there too. They all came from Tunbridge Wells. Taylor was dressed in a blue smock. Edward Beeney threw two stones. The first stone he threw the constable said, 'You know that is doing wrong, Ted,' but Ted said nothing and immediately threw another. He was a billiard marker. There were only three or four policemen there and there was not much they could do. Superintendent Emburey, in charge of the Tunbridge Wells police force, came on the scene. He saw Beeney with a large can. It was nearly full of beer. He kept pouring the beer into a small can and giving it to the people there. The superintendent remonstrated. 'Do you know you are doing wrong?' The only answer he got was a cheeky 'I suppose I can give away beer, if I like'. Soon there were no more windows to break and the pig was burned out. A second effigy appeared out of the crowd, was fixed to the railings and lit. A mat was set on fire and when it was well alight one of the crowd, with a violent effort and the encouragement of the by-standers, flung it onto the first-floor balcony which caught fire. Anyone looking at no 7 Mount Sion today will see that the original balcony is missing; for what reason is speculation. At half past ten the threatened rain at last came down and the

Sion Terrace 1997 – Dr Webber's residence in 1864 is that on the far right.

mob dispersed, leaving William Webber to dowse the flames, keep the rain out of his broken windows and sleep on his frustration and indignation. The Tunbridge Wells mob observed the Sabbath; at least they did not re-appear in Mount Sion until the Monday evening. This time, however, the authorities were ready for them. The Chairman of the Commissioners had been informed, so he said, only late on Sunday of the events of the previous day and had immediately summoned the Police Committee for 10 o'clock the next morning. Necessary steps had been taken, warrants had been issued against identified miscreants and a large force of County Constabulary had been drafted in under Supt Dance with the result that, although a good many assembled on Monday evening, there was no rioting. The necessity to call on the County Police, however, as was pointed out at a capacity meeting of the Commissioners in the Town Hall the following Wednesday, was a reflection on the ability of the town to manage its own affairs. Mr William Delves was critical of the police. Why had they not acted to forestall events of which they must have had warning? It was a matter of pride for Tunbridge Wells not to call in the County Police. There was the danger of amalgamation. The Chairman, the Hon. F.G. Molyneux, opening the proceedings, chose his words with dignified care. Scenes such as those of Saturday were a reproach and a disgrace and were even more injurious to the reputation of the town than reports of fever. He wished in particular to refute accusations that some Commissioners had stood idly by. Mr Maingay pointed out that the crowd had been plied with liquor at the expense of others. The obvious implication that someone of means had been behind the riot was curiously not taken up by succeeding participants in the debate. On the evening of the Commissioners' meeting an explosion was heard in Tunbridge Wells but it had nothing to do with Webber and caused little comment – two men had been killed at the powder mills in Tonbridge.

Tom Cole, Ted Beeney, Alfred Taylor and Henry Butcher were committed to the next Kent Assizes despite a valiant speech for the defence during which great excitement prevailed but was checked by the Chairman of the Bench, the Hon. F.G. Molyneux. The prisoners were accused that on 2 July together with divers other evil-disposed persons to the number of 500 and more they had riotously assembled to disturb the public peace and make a great noise, riot and disturbance, to the terror of Her Majesty's subjects. Mr Cripps for the defence said that he would not like to travel into matters causing the riot, it would not influence their Worships in the least, but when they saw a statement made which tended to deprive many persons almost of their daily bread (loud applause … threats to clear the court) he argued that they could hardly fairly commit persons holding high and good positions in the town simply because they were present at the riot. The Bench, however, was adamant. It was equally decisive but in a different sense at the next Petty Sessions which were concerned with private prosecutions brought by William Webber. The completely full court contained some of the most influential and respectable men of the town. The first prosecution alleged that Frederick Robert Ward, landlord of the *Camden Hotel*, had on 25 June in Chapel

Place and High Street used threatening and insulting words and behaviour towards Mr William Webber. When the complainant was called there was a general buzz and burst of laughter quickly suppressed. Mr Sperling, the Chairman on this occasion, said that the bench had received a communication from Mr Webber saying that he feared violence and asking for an adjournment. The case was therefore dismissed; the Bench would not agree to adjourn. Mr Browell, the third magistrate along with the Hon. F.G. Molyneux, said that they had tried to communicate with Mr Webber but 'business required him from home'. Mr Ward: 'He has bolted, sir!' (A noise) 'Order, gentlemen, order!' Upon the appearance of the defendants in the next case a general and very ill-suppressed laugh ensued. They were Thomas Henry Delves and his brother Joseph, butchers; Thomas Kinlan, watchmaker; William Fox, chemist, all of Chapel Place; and Edward Durrant, grocer, of the Parade. They were charged with taking part in the unlawful assembly and riot on 2 July. The Chairman said that as Mr Webber did not appear the case was dismissed and this decision was hailed inside with thunders of applause which were taken up by the hundreds of persons assembled outside and unable to gain admittance. The defendants, elated with their success, repaired to the near-by *Camden Hotel* of which one of their number, Frederick Ward, was landlord and

The Camden Hotel *and old Town Hall before demolition 1959*

enjoyed what was later described as a 'capital dinner' followed by some excellent after-dinner speeches. In exuberant, not to say merry, mood the influential innocents climbed into their carriages and followed the Town Band in a triumphal procession; and as they made their way towards the bottom of the town they flourished in a kind of regal acknowledgement what from a distance might have been taken for flags but on closer inspection turned out to be legal documents, the summonses served on them at the behest of their enemy. When they reached Mount Sion they were careful not to be too provocative but somehow the band was observed standing outside Number One playing what the watchmaker of Chapel Place later identified as 'The Rogue's March'.

These events were reported in the *Gazette* of 15 July. In the same issue appeared one notice and two letters which throw some additional light on the story. The notice said: Wells v Webber will shortly be published. A full report of the above trial. It will be distributed gratuitously. That the public may have an opportunity of studying character. The first letter was from William Webber to Joseph Delves junior and was printed at the writer's request for public information. 'Within the last 24 hours some circumstances have come to my knowledge which lead me to believe that you have not been actuated by any ill feeling towards me; that you did not participate in the atrocious attack made upon me and my unoffending family on the painful – and I fear tragical – night of the 2nd inst when through the malicious and wicked inclinations of evil-disposed persons whom I have never injured who can show no just ground of complaint against me my house and the lives of seven females – ladies and servants – and an invalid gentleman and myself narrowly escaped being destroyed.' Here we see perhaps the better side of the doctor endeavouring to be fair to one whom he believes he may have wrongly maligned. The second letter is signed 'Rowbentur'. Perhaps some expert deciperer of anagrams may be able to penetrate the anonymity. The absence of pseudonyms from our present-day correspondence columns may be commendable but it certainly detracts from their liveliness. 'Sir, If I were to ask what had best be done with a notorious, self-infatuated, bigoted, bellicose agitator ... summary ejectment suggests itself ... Having striven with no success for celebrity and failed at even gaining popularity, WW is determined to attain notoriety.'

A further occasion for celebration occurred during the following week when, by kind courtesy of the Hon. F.G. Molyneux, a marquee was erected in the grounds of Buckingham Place on Mount Ephraim and the annual dinner of the Amalgamated Friendly Societies was held with catering provided by Mr Ward of the *Camden Hotel*. During a speech of thanks Mr James Richardson, the auctioneer, said he believed Providence had especially favoured Tunbridge Wells 'although a black sheep may occasionally come amongst us'. (Mr Delves: Where's Webber?) 'Be quiet!' It may well be asked what Webber was doing during this period. He must surely have been agonising over his position in the town. His letter appeared in the *Gazette* on Friday, 22 July; but it seems that in those days of primitive technology printing deadlines were more flexible than they are today. He might, therefore, have popped his epistle into the *Gazette* office some time on Thursday. Anyhow, it is known where he was on Wednesday evening and what he was doing. He was in the porch of the *Kentish Hotel* with a seven-barrelled revolver in his hand and he was threatening to put its contents through Thomas Kinlan's heart.

During subsequent hearing of the cross-summonses taken out on Thursday by Kinlan against Webber and on Friday by Webber against Kinlan, the doctor was asked why he carried a pistol. 'It is because I have been warned,' he replied, 'not to go about without one as they intended me some harm. On a lamp-post I saw a picture – underneath it was 'Webber's End'.' During cross-examination Mr Langham, for Webber, held up a caricature 'representing about 10 individuals, an organ, policeman's staff, moustache etc' (Did the moustache perhaps symbolise Webber?)

> Langham: Did you sell any of these?
> Kinlan: Yes, sir. I will sell you one if you like ... There is a flattering likeness of the Doctor there. (A laugh)
> Langham: Did you also sell these prints? (holding up a song)
> Kinlan: No, they were hawked about the street.

The events of Wednesday evening became clear during the court hearing. Fox and Webber had passed each other outside the hotel but, after continuing a short distance, Fox turned back and accosted the doctor. Then Kinlan came on the

Royal Kentish Hotel *about 1880*

scene. Standing on the steps of the hotel porch and looking down on Webber, he wanted to know why the doctor had summoned him. 'Don't speak to me, sir,' said Webber, becoming excited. 'I have no answer to make.' 'You have taken away my character,' said Kinlan. 'It has yet to be shown what character is; you have no right to speak to me,' was the doctor's reply. 'Do you refuse to give me an apology?' 'I do.' 'Then,' continued Kinlan calmly and civilly, 'you are a coward.' Webber showed signs of great agitation. 'I am only reiterating what Mr Cripps said before the Bench,' Kinlan persisted. 'You are a coward because you have made a charge you can't substantiate and you refuse to give an apology.' Webber now became more excited than ever and went under the porch, climbing the step, with his fists clenched. 'I have got you now,' he said, 'I will have you up; you called me a coward.' He moved towards the door of the hotel and Kinlan followed. 'I am determined to have it out,' said Kinlan, clenching his fists in turn and moving a step nearer the doctor. 'Don't come near me, sir!' 'I am not going to touch you, Mr Webber,' said Kinlan calmly. 'Stand back, sir!' The doctor held up his hands in high excitement. 'Stand back or it will be the worse for you!' 'I shall have you yet,' said Kinlan, putting up his fists within striking distance of the doctor. Then Webber put his hand into his coat pocket and drew out a revolver. 'If you don't keep away from me, sir,' he shouted, pointing the weapon at Kinlan, 'I shall put the contents of this through your heart!' William Fox stood in horrified indecision. Alfred Weller, assistant at Mrs Simmonds, clothier in Chapel Place, saw the pistol in the doctor's hand but did not notice if it was cocked. Charles Bale, waiter at the *Kentish Hotel*, was standing in the foyer and heard Kinlan say, 'I shall have you yet' – or so he said. Counsel suggested that a promise of a job in the 'new hotel' had prejudiced his evidence. William Haines, the landlord, stood and stared. For a moment the frame was frozen. Then tragedy gave way to bathos. 'You call yourself an Englishman,' said the Irishman, 'to walk about with such weapons in your possession!' Webber replied that he was obliged to … for his protection. The landlord sent for a policeman. Kinlan walked away.

In the Magistrate's Court the bench decided to bind over both parties in their own recognisance of £10 and expressed the hope that this would put an end to all ill-feeling. This did not prevent someone signing himself 'Q' from protesting in a letter to the *Gazette*, arguing that all the wrong was on Webber's side and Kinlan should not have been bound over. At the Kent Summer Assizes His Honour was inclined to be understanding in the case of the rioters. The Tunbridge Wells Four were ordered to pay £5 each for the broken windows although Webber estimated the cost at £45. This is to anticipate, however. On 22 July the doctor's farewell letter appeared in the *Gazette*: 'As it seems to be the pleasure of the mob-dictators of Tunbridge Wells that I should keep more honourable and creditable society, I beg to express my ready acquiescence in their views, not that I recognise their right to dictate. I am actuated by a higher motive – a regard for the peace of the town. I can have no desire to prolong my stay. I certainly was astonished to see among the ruffianly assailants those whom I had aided in their hour of sickness and those whose covert proceedings incited to this outrage. All this too in the absence of any sound or qualified charge – for I was *not* the first to publish the existence of the fever, as I shall hereafter explain when the thirst for unjust vengeance has passed away. My parting words to the town – which I shall leave with one regret, namely that I ever entered it – will be Peace to it and may it cease to look for a crop of prosperity from seeds sown in the hot-bed of injustice, tyranny and wrong.' The editor in the same issue welcomed the intelligence conveyed in Mr Webber's 'parting words' and endorsed on behalf of everyone his regret of ever having entered the town. The last dying speech of a criminal would create more sympathy than the parting words of this 'pseudo-benevolent director' who made his exit after performing a variety of madcap freaks. He had been tried at the bar of public opinion; the punishment was greater than he could bear and he beat an ignominious retreat. Ever since he entered he had sown the seeds of discord. His connection with the *Kentish Hotel* had not been a success as the proprietary had discovered. His last effort dated back but two months. By a most unlucky accident he happened to be passing an innocuous drain. Now, Mr Webber had thought, for sweet revenge on the town that would not have him to reign over them. Incited by feelings of the deepest abhorrence of the author of the great calumny some of the aggrieved and injured industrial classes had burnt Mr Webber's effigy.

It might be thought that the doctor's farewell letter was the end of the matter as far as Tunbridge Wells was concerned; and indeed from the date of the letter the name of Webber no longer appears against No.1 Sion Terrace in the *Gazette*'s weekly list of residents and visitors. On the other hand, however, he was at the *Kentish Hotel* at four o'clock on Tuesday 2 August for the purpose of rendering an account of his stewardship, having announced to the Board his retirement from the directorship of the company. The following week's *Gazette* takes the opportunity for another sarcastic swipe at 'Mr Webber Again in a Novel Position'. The paper had intercepted a 'Round-Robin to Shareholders' sent to a few subservient shareholders only. Seven or eight out of a possible 50 or so shareholders attended. Webber said the press must leave and rejected all protests. He then made a speech lasting about one hour in which he said that the hotel would be built but on a limited scale. The capital would be nearer £13,000 than £50,000 as before. The rump voted unanimously in favour. The *Gazette* commented in the words of the song: 'I care for nobody, no, not I, and nobody cares for me'.

The affair reached the national newspapers. On 12 August the local paper reprinted an article under the headline 'The Morning Herald's Dose for the Meddlesome Doctor'. 'The sensations of a respectable gentleman who, at a time of profound peace, looks out of his parlour window on a hot summer afternoon and perceives attached to his railings the ignited effigy of a pig furiously blazing, while in the background is an indignant mob, some 2000 strong, must certainly be curious.' A Liberal newspaper had written an article representing Webber as a martyr to truth; but the *Morning Herald* took the opposite view. A final echo of all this was heard in the *Gazette*'s review of the previous year which appeared on 6 January 1865. Allusion was made to the collapse of two schemes and the demise of the Royal Sussex and Kentish Hotel Companies, 'the one fading noiselessly and honourably into oblivion; the other leaving behind it footprints of a less honourable and satisfactory character'.

In the meantime the doctor had not departed so soon as expected. There was the Great High Street Fire on 26 August 1864 and its aftermath when Dr Webber made an unexpected reappearance. At about five o'clock on the day in question, which was a Monday, Llewellyn Diplock was heating glue in Mr Strange's carpenter's shop near the *White Bear* (now Barzia) between the bottom of the High Street and the London Road. A moment's carelessness and some wood shavings near the fire were alight. Soon the fire had spread to Waghorn's stables three yards away, recently tarred and full of hay and straw. PC Forward happened to be near the spot and he called for the Tunbridge Wells engine and a telegraph was sent to Tonbridge for theirs and a messenger on horseback for the Withyham engine. The town brigade arrived within half an hour and, obtaining a good supply of water from a pipe opposite to Mr Gilbert's, the ironmonger's shop (York House), was able to reach the seat of the fire. Unfortunately the buildings were of wooden construction and it was thought, with a brisk wind fanning the flames, that the entire block would succumb. On the London Road side a string of 50 or 60 men were passing buckets from hand to hand to be carried up a ladder to the top of the three-storeyed houses. The local people and shopkeepers began to carry their belongings and their stock out of the threatened houses and barricades were set up to enclose a stretch of the High Street from Castle Street to the *White Bear* in which were bundled higgledy-piggledy piles of cheese, coffee, tea, soap, baking powder, matches, British wine, loaf sugar, ginger nuts and loaves of bread not to mention furniture and household stuff. At twenty-five past six the Tonbridge engine arrived to cheers and took up position on the London Road to be supplied with water from a pipe opposite No.3 Vale Place. The fire was eventually brought under control by eight o'clock but not before considerable damage and personal loss had been inflicted; and it was with the charitable purpose of mitigating the suffering that a public meeting at the Town Hall was held on the Friday afternoon. The Hon F.G. Molyneux, chairman of the Town Commissioners, instanced cases of hardship: Mr Baker, the fly-driver had lost everything he possessed; Miss Gladwin, one of three ladies living in Vale Terrace, had recently lost her father, Sergeant Gladwin, and had applied the money he left her to equip the house for lodgings. All had gone and with it her means of subsistence. Her case was a particularly hard one. Mrs Long had lost a soda-water machine worth £100. And so on. The Chairman moved that it was desirable to alleviate distress caused by the fire and the Rev. Pope seconded. Further motions followed, to open a subscription and to appoint a committee. At this juncture Dr Webber rose and attempted to address the chairman. 'I think some special provision should be made for those who distinguished themselves at the fire', he said but was interrupted by Town Commissioner Edwards, the butcher whose drain had been the original occasion of the riot of 2 July. 'Get out. Go down stairs – that's the proper place for you', he said amid hammering of sticks on the floor. The chairman tried to restore order but Edwards left his seat and walked over towards Webber, speaking to those around. 'I am now told something about having forged a will', said Webber, evidently much annoyed. 'I won't allow these things to go on. I shall summons you for saying that I forged a will.' 'Yes', countered Edwards, 'but you won't appear' (loud laughter). Webber then left the room, deliberatedly, and the meeting concluded with the signing of a subscription list headed by £40 from the residents of Chancellor House, the ex-Queen of the French, Marie Amélie, and her family.

Perhaps Dr Webber was the victim of bad behaviour from Henry Edwards on this occasion but the doctor's activity reported in the following week's *Gazette* was of a more reprehensible character. He was behind an attempt to raise money for a Riot Prosecution Fund the object of which was to bring to justice 'the *deliberate* Plotters and Ringleaders of the late Riot'. Two apparently respectable gentlemen were recruited as figureheads, a Mr Ranger of the Manor House, Ashurst, and Richard Wetherall Esq. JP, of Grove Hill Road; but the man behind it was William Webber evidently hankering after revenge. This is made plain by a lengthy correspondence which filled most of one page of the *Gazette* on 30 September and which was submitted to the paper by an aggrieved gentleman from London, Mr Mansfield, who had been employed by Webber to canvas subscriptions from traders on the Parade. He had come down from London by train, booked a room nearby for a week and been sent off by Webber to raise money for the Fund. One day's work was enough to convince him that the project was hopeless. The people on the Parade left him in no doubt of that and so he told the doctor that evening in the coffee room of the 'Kentish'. How Mansfield and Webber subsequently quarrelled can be read at great length in the *Gazette*. They were a match for each other in their long-winded and high-flown self-righteousness. The matter was discussed by the Tradesmen's Association and by the Town Commission and some remarks by Dr Charles Trustram may be of incidental interest. 'I have a garden', he said, 'on both sides of my house and I found that it gave me as much as – nay, more than – I could do, to keep the people constituting that mob from treading down and spoiling my plants and flowers, and breaking my fences.' A commissioner caused some merriment by suggesting that a claim should be made on the Riot Prosecution Fund but the Chairman considered the matter of the fund beneath his notice or that of the Commissioners.

A summary of Dr Hunter's report was read to the Commissioners on 5 October and it was considered a very satisfactory vindication of the town in matters of public health. It throws a light of incidental interest on the history of the town's drains. Long ago, it said, an old water-course which divides two parishes was the original drain for the use of the small population but it was 'by piecemeal covered up and even built over by the various adjoining owners'. This must, in my opinion, have been the stream which used to run from the Calverley grounds area down Vale Road to join the Grom Brook near the Chapel. This stream may certainly be said to have divided the parishes of Speldhurst and Tonbridge. Then, in the words of Dr Hunter, 'an excellent new drain was made under a high road, and the old one, neglected and dried up, is now almost forgotten. In many parts it is filled up, in others it forms part of cellars'. The new drain was built, I think, in 1838; but a remnant of the old one surely lies at the bottom of the events of 1864. Dr Hunter allowed himself some mild criticism of the town for not having sufficient information on the line taken by the old drain. On Friday 14 October a public 'indignation' meeting was held at the Town Hall to consider Dr Hunter's report, to discuss the welfare of the town in general and condemn the Riot Prosecution proposal and to hear a personal explanation from Mr Mansfield of London. The hall was crowded to excess and, at the request of a large number of gentlemen, C. Trustram Esq consented to preside. He revealed that the youth said by Dr Webber to have died from 'miasma' had in fact died from cricket. The young fellow 'from his own inadvertence and indiscrimination of an attack of scarlatina, that was upon him, and having promised to stand umpire at a game of cricket, had remained in the wet all day, came home, and died at night from congestion of the lungs and heart, and had no more poison in his system ... from any drain than the man in the moon' (hear, hear and laughter). After more, much more from himself and others and motions moved, seconded and carried, Dr Trustram announced that a letter from Dr Webber had been placed in his hand and 'carrying out that justice and fairness which they all loved, he would at once read it to the meeting'. The letter called Dr Hunter's report an inauthentic, erroneously-drawn, cooked account, claimed that he was prepared to show that his allegations had been amply proved and complained about Mr Mansfield and the 'Crusade' in the *Gazette*. None of this cut much ice and the meeting concluded with a long, inconsequential statement by Mr Mansfield which the meeting declared 'vindicated his character for uprightness and probity'. Dr Webber had, according to one of the speakers, left the town for a while after the riot but had returned, although in fear of further trouble on Guy Fawke's Day, as he told the magistrates on 24 October, a scene which the *Gazette* reported in humorous vein as a Farce in Seven Acts. The two magistrates said they knew nothing of threatened disturbances on 5 November but the police would take whatever action was necessary; and in fact special constables were sworn and took care to patrol the bottom of Mount Sion – but of course nothing occurred. Two weeks later Webber was in court again, this time contesting the expenses of £2 8s. 7d. which Mansfield claimed – and was granted with costs.

Despite the failure of the Riot Prosecution Fund, there was a civil prosecution. The trial took place before the Nisi Prius Court in Maidstone on Wednesday 14 March 1866 when eight Tunbridge Wells worthies pleaded Not Guilty to charges of trespass, damage, showing an effigy with gallows etc. They were William Willicombe, builder, Levi Catt, ironmonger, George Elliott, publican, ____ Isard, chandler, Robert Jull, house agent, Frederick Ward, publican, William Henry Wright, town surveyor and Joseph Delves, butcher. The outcome was that damages of £25 each were awarded against Catt and Elliott with costs while the other defendants were simply required to pay their own costs. The costs to be paid by Catt and Elliott were computed at about £300 – the plaintiff (unnamed but presumably Dr Webber) having subpoenaed more than 50 witnesses. Webber's muted £50 triumph did not last long. In the first place Catt and Elliott declared themselves bankrupt after the trial and therefore could pay neither Webber's damages nor costs; while in the second place an arbitration award had been made against Webber following cross-summonses for libel made by him and Charles Trustram and Webber found himself unable to pay the damages and costs and was arrested on 21 June 1866 and imprisoned. At a hearing of the Court of Bankruptcy on 11 October it was revealed that his debts amounted to £422 and his principal creditor was Dr Trustram; but he had failed to prepare accounts. His house was expensively furnished but as a result of his previous bankruptcy in 1863 the furniture belonged to his daughter or her trustees and the household bills were being paid by his wife who enjoyed a settlement bringing in £450 per annum. Webber complained that he had no access to advice, that he was suffering from heart disease, could not lie down in bed and his life was being shortened; and he left the court saying he had suffered quite enough. Mr Commissioner Goulburn at the next court hearing on 7 November said that Webber had been sufficiently punished and signed an order for his release which, however, would not come into effect for 31 days.

Where the good doctor went on his release the local newspapers do not vouchsafe. His name certainly does not appear on the list of Mount Sion residents in 1867 or 1868. He makes, however, one final appearance in *the Tunbridge Wells Gazette*. On 27 May 1867 a case was heard at the Court of Common Pleas, Westminster, when Mr Chambers QC for Dr Webber argued that all the defendants in the Maidstone trial had conspired to agree to the verdicts in the knowledge that Catt and Elliott fully intended to go bankrupt, thereby defrauding Dr Webber of his damages and costs, and that the case should be retried. Plausible as this scenario may appear, Lord Chief Justice Bovill and three judges were not impressed. Webber had produced no evidence of fraud and anyway he was out of time. The application should have been made within the first four days of the ensuing term, not more than a year after the trial. No account was taken of Webber's own bankruptcy and imprisonment.

I used often to wonder when exactly William Webber finally left Tunbridge Wells and what happened to him and his family. Then at the beginning of April 1997 a neighbour living in Frog Lane appeared at my window saying there was a young couple from New Zealand in the lane and they wanted to ask a question. So I popped out of the back gate and there they were. 'My name's Webber', said the young man. 'Oh yes,' I said, joking, 'and I suppose you're connected with the Webber riots.' 'Yes,' came the response, 'He was my great-great-grandfather.' So, after a chat in the study, I was able to walk them down the hill and show them no.7 Mount Sion where great-great-grandfather Dr William Webber and his family had faced the wrath of the Tunbridge Wells mob that famous day in 1864. And what could he tell us about the doctor's subsequent fate? Well, he was living in London in 1869 and he died in 1875, probably in Brighton; but the interesting point is that he had a larger family than has appeared so far. There were the three daughters who were all at home in 1861 but, as well as young Henry, who was away from home on the fateful evening, there were four more sons, three of whom emigrated to the Antipodes, one becoming Bishop of Brisbane and another an auctioneer and land speculator in Tasmania. The youngest of the emigrants had qualified as a surgeon in 1863, while giving his address as Tunbridge Wells, and sailed to New Zealand the same year where he died in tragic and curious circumstances five years later at the age of 27 – not, however, before he had married in New Zealand and fathered one child, a son .... without whom, of course, it would scarcely have been possible for our visitor to be strolling up Frog Lane that sunny April day. The single son in New Zealand himself fathered 14 children and his son seven, of whom our visitor, Warren, born in 1953 and a veterinary surgeon, was one. Henry stayed in England and became a stockbroker and JP and, as a lieutenant in the South Lancashire Regiment, was killed in action in the Great War at the age of 68. Eliza Jane, the eldest girl, also favoured the Antipodes. In December 1869 she left for New Zealand with her new husband, the newly consecrated Bishop of Auckland – and her husband's journal records that in September 1869 she went to London to her father's house to pack before setting sail. Whatever we may think of Webber of the Riots, as a progenitor he was quite a success.

One of the joys of delving into Tunbridge Wells history over the last twenty or so years has been the practice, usually more fortuitous than intentional, of what I have christened reverse genealogy. The usual practice is to start with parents and grandparents and work backwards in time for as many generations as you can manage. In reverse genealogy you start by identifying a character or family in the past and try to find a living descendant. I have had a few successes including, through no effort of my own, that of the Webber descendant, but one conspicuous failure has been with the man who dominated the first chapters of this story – John Brett. This trail disappeared into the sand in Norfolk but I still live in hope that one day a Brett descendant may surface unexpectedly and claim possession of a long-lost family story. Calling all Bretts out there! Including those in the female line whose names have changed!

Farewell then to the Mount Sion story! The more I delve, the more I realise there is to discover; but I daresay there are those who will say enough is too much already. Nevertheless, I am conscious of enormous gaps. All those visitors, the very reason for the existence of the place, where are they? Lady Jerningham and her ailing dancing husband, John Braham the tenor, the Princess Anne possibly possibly … is this all we can find? And what about the labouring poor, the house of office emptiers, the maidservants, the waiters, the grooms – we catch a glimpse of them in Little Mount Sion but if they have no property they are non-existent. For with a few exceptions this is a story of property. John Brett's machinations, the George Anne Bellamy saga, Katharine Ashenhurst's fraternal squabble, Thomas Bayes and probability, the Delves dynasty, Aretas Akers and Potter's ghost, the attempted abduction of Ann Jeffery and her happy ever after, the Girls' School at Fairlawn and of course the Webber Riots, these may distract and divert but it is basically about things for which records survive: births, marriages and deaths, wills and the transfer of houses and land. Nevertheless, a picture emerges of a middling sort of people living and loving and very often marrying within the community, falling ill and dying, working and struggling in a closed, local society somehow removed from the floating world of visitors who were their bread and butter. Mount Sion originated as adjunct to a health spa and tourist resort and the reason for its existence was to house the visitors and their horses and carriages and to cater for their needs and entertain them. In this it was no different from a seaside resort or tourist centre and its history was essentially that of the permanent population not of those who came and went. On Mount Sion, however, the balance between permanent and transient changed gradually during the 19th century. Nevertheless, a sufficient number of built monuments remain to remind us of its original purposes and their number will not, I hope, be permitted to fall below present proportions. The basic geography and the shape of the roads are, I think, safe enough – whether or not the roads still belong after three hundred years to the Trustees of the Grove.

Commentary and References

Books
Books will be referred to by the surname of the author, with initials or forename if duplicated and numbered if more than one work is involved. See Bibliography pp.469ff for details.

Old and New Style dates
For a discussion see p.33 comment below.

Abbreviations

BL	British Library
CKS	Centre for Kentish Studies, Maidstone
DNB	*Dictionary of National Biography*
ESRO	East Sussex Record Office, Lewes
IGI	International Genealogical Index
MJ	*Maidstone Journal*
N & R	Notes and References to RTW below
Pr	proved (of wills)
PRO	Public Record Office, Kew
RTW	my *Royal Tunbridge Wells – A Pictorial History*
SAE	*Sussex Agricultural Express*

The Reference Library means the Tunbridge Wells Reference Library
The Museum means the Tunbridge Wells Museum and Art Gallery

Page 1 This is all well travelled ground. Details of 1684 documents will be given later. A discussion of Frances Walsingham and South Frith Manor is to be found in N & R p.26. The introduction to RTW has more on the extent of South Frith Manor with comments in N & R p.14.
Savidge (p.39) and Hembry (p.83), both give 1684 as the date of Purbeck's death, Savidge saying circumstantially but without quoting his source that he died abroad in a duel. Morris (p.137 note) (see p.267 comment below) says Purbeck was killed in a duel in 1684. Woodgate has (p.39): '... having wasted his fortune and involved himself in debt, he went abroad as his father did to avoid his creditors, and at Liège was killed in a duel by Col. Lutterell in 1686 in the twenty-ninth year of his age'. Hasted to whom Woodgate refers (2nd, ed. 1799, vol.5, p.235) gives no date or details concerning Purbeck's death. Since the first leases are dated November 1684 it is rather crucial to know whether Purbeck died in '84 or '86. If 1684 the leases are almost certainly the work of the widow but if '86 much depends on when Purbeck went abroad.
The print of Ulick de Burgh is in the National Portrait Gallery archives.

Page 2 For Henrietta's visit see N & R, p.3. For a sample from the British Library see RTW, plate 7 and for more on royal visits N & R, p.4 *et seq*.
For the Princess of Babylon story see Grammont, pp.90 *et seq*. and also Barton pp.132 *et seq*.
For the history of the Chapel and his theory of community meeting place see Fuller.

'Fresh-faced country girls' – quoted from Grammont, p.209, 'Here young, fair, fresh-faced country girls, with clean linen, small straw hats and neat shoes and stockings, sell game, vegetables, flowers and fruit'. For the general story see RTW, Introduction. For the history of Rusthall Manor see Farthing (2), pp.29, *et seq.*

Page 3 The Chancery case reference is PRO C6/100/7 – quote comes from first page of 'The Several Answers of Thomas Weller gent ...' – see p.9 comment below and chapter 4.
The list of leases is in CKS U38 T1 – for more on this see chapter 2.
I can find no consensus in estimates of 18th- and 19th-century money values; if anything, suggested multipliers seem to me on the low side. See also pp.34 and 112 comments below.

Page 4 The first leases are the subject of chapter 2.
For a detail from Symondson's map see RTW, Plate 1.
John Seller's map – there is a copy in the Reference Library

Page 5 Bowra's Plan is one of three parts of his 'Survey of Tunbridge Wells'. A detail of his general map can be found in RTW, Plate 47 together with the complete Plans of Tunbridge Wells Walks and Mount Sion Hill at Plates 48 and 49. Originals are held at the Tunbridge Wells Museum and the British Library.

Page 6 The lease dates come from CKS U38 T1 – see p.3 above.
Statements about lease strips will be justified in relevant chapters.

Page 7 Colonel Waring – see Waring, p.9.
Lease of manor to Constable – CKS U749 E25.
The Pantiles shop rent is recorded in a rental dated 1699, CKS U38 E1. Other Allen family details are in the deeds of Richmond Villa (owner's possession) in particular the will of Ann Luck dated 28 Apr 1767.
Thomas Scoones – see Blatcher.

Page 9 For the 'exception' see chapters 13-15 – the alignment of Little Mount Sion. The Chancery case (discovered by Christopher Chalklin and reported in his thesis) is at PRO C6/100/7. The document is not wholly legible (by me!) owing to tears, creases and stains but I have a fairly complete, rough transcription in my notebooks and on my computer.

Page 10 The description of Sir Thomas Meeres is in a reference to a 1682 deed in CKS U38 T1, which also contains the list of leases started in 1684 in a schedule to a conveyance from John Earl of Buckingham, Sir Thomas Meeres and Mr Hatcher to Thomas Lake, Thomas and George Weller dated 26 Nov 1702.
For the year when the Viscountess was widowed see p.1 comment above.
Later documentation: the acreage listed in the Chancery case 1708 amounts to about 105 acres but no calculation can be precise owing to sharing, possible duplication and the use of rods and perches; and anyway only those leases having a bearing on the Chancery case would have been documented.

Page 11 South Frith Manor – see p.1 comment above.
William Baynes brewer – of Tonbridge is named as purchaser in a conveyance by Lease and Release dated 18/19 May 1719, one of the deeds of Sion House, of which I have details although the originals have been lost. The Tonbridge Reference Library has a bundle of documents reference TU1 T58 in two of which dated 28 Sep 1720 and 27 Mar 1722 Thomas Banes Tonbridge Brewer is a party. In the same bundle are documents

concerning a lease of 10 Dec 1689 and a conveyance of 27 Nov 1702 to William Ba(y)nes Tonbridge carpenter; but a related Deed Poll of 19 Nov 1731 mentions that William King now has the house where Banes used to dwell.
The large house is 'Ashton Lodge' 69 London Road. For the Jeffery connection with Mount Sion see chapters 14 and 24.
Calverley – PRO Fleet Marriages 9 Nov 1714. There are references to Calverley land transactions in the Bristol Estate papers at Bury St Edmunds – see N & R, p.18.

Page 15 Thomas Neale – see DNB (which gives death in 1699) and Pepys. For an image see RTW Plate 22 or Rowlands, ed., p.31.
The 'obscure' descriptions run as follows: 'And also one other piece or parcel of land adjoining on the east side of the same wheat gratten containing likewise by estimation four acres which said last mentioned pieces or parcels of land do bound upon other part of the said lands called Inghams formerly demised unto William Fullman (?) towards the west (??) to a common called Bishops Down and to a parcel of ground demised to Richard Waghorne towards the north to a parcel of the said lands called Inghams called Waghornes Forest and late in his occupation where is now laid out a way and (?) used (??) towards the east to a parcel of Wood called Inhams Bush and to a small slip of ground now likewise used for a way of the breadth of two rodd towards the south Except so much of the said two pieces of land as is of the breadth of three rodd straight cross the same two pieces as the same is now used for a way from Southborough to Tunbridge Wells And also one other piece or parcel of rough ground being likewise part of the said land called Inhams containing by estimation twelve acres and bounding to other part thereof demised to Richard Constable towards the west to land of John Wyburne Esquire towards the south to other part of the said land called Inhams and to a hedge (?) and bank there towards the east to another bank there towards the north'. This describes part of the land leased to Thomas Neale on 10 Feb 1685/6. There seem to be two firm anchorage points here: Inhams Bush which is the Grove; and the way from Southborough to Tunbridge Wells which is the High Street. Two pieces of land are intercepted 'straight across' by the road which is 3 rods (16 ½ yards wide) and one piece abuts the Grove. The reader may judge the strength of this evidence to identify the site of the Grove Houses.

Page 16 Brooke/Constable Partition – I am indebted to Dr Christopher Chalklin for drawing this invaluable piece of evidence to my attention. It is to be found in the Kent Archaeological Society Library at Maidstone (Ward Collection, Tonbridge File). The full text runs as follows:

20.9.1686
1. Robert Brooke of Maidstone, ironmonger
2. Richard Constable of Speldhurst, Mercer

Reciting that Rt. Hon. Margaret Viscountess Purbeck & Sir Thomas Meres knt. By indenture of 4.11.1684 leased to '1' and '2'

Part of a certain Heath called Inhams containing in breadth eleven rodds and in length on the east side 23 rodds and on the west side against a way there to be made 27 rodds & also one parcel of the same heath in breadth 13 rods and in length 20 rods part whereof is now fenced in for a bowling green lying on the south side of the former mentioned piece; both of which pieces do bound to other part of the said heath called Inhams appointed for a way towards the N., W., and S., and to other part of the same heath demised or intended to be demised to Edward Martin towards the E., and contain 3 acres 1 roode in Tonbridge: and another part of the same heath containing eight acres bounding as the same is marked out to other part of the same heath and to a ditch and bank there towards the north and to the forest of Waterdowne towards the west and to an intended way and to land demised to Edw. Martin E., and S. 'as the same is new measured marked and dowled out'; also another piece of same heath 3 rods in breadth and 16 in length bounding to Byshopps Downe N., and to part of the heath intended for a way south; and also a reasonable way for carts, &c, out of and from the common called Byshopps Downe for 50 years at £7 per annum.

This deed is a partition best shown by map attached but fully described in the deed.

Sg. Robert Brooke
Wtnessed – John Humforey
Geo: Weller
Endorsed – Brookes Deuison

Page 17 The description of land sold to Winefrith Brooke is in PRO C6/100/7 (see p.9 comment above) – The Joynt and Severall Answers of Thomas Lake Esquire George Weller Gent and Daniel Tilden Gent Defendants to the Bill of Complaint of John Villars Earl of Buckingham Viscount Purbeck Henry Marsh and James Scott complainants.

Page 19 For more on Nicholas Wood see chapters 10-12.
Benge Burr's footnote is to p.103 and is subscribed 'Mr. W.S.' – whoever he may be; and the Sprange footnote, reproduced, is on p.6 of the Second Part, with no subscript.

Page 20 Pantiles shops – see Chalklin (1).
For Burlington House and the *Blue Anchor* see chapter 12; for the Widow Fry's house chapter 22; for nos.19-25 Mount Sion chapters 17 and 18.

Page 21 The petition to the House of Lords can be found in the 7th report of the Historical Manuscripts Commission and in the Lords Journal Volume 11 – both at the BL. In the Lords Journal the name is spelled WYBORNE with an O.

Page 22 My record of the Chancery case covers the following sources – there may be others:
PRO C6/100/7; CKS U38 T2, U38 T22 and U2737 Box 1 – see p.36 comment below. The references to John Wyborne are scattered here and there. For more on U2737 see p.186 comment below.

Page 23 C6/100/7 The Severall Answers of Thomas Weller gent one of the Defendants to the Bill of Complaint of John Villars Earl of Buckingham Viscount Purbeck Henry Marsh and James Scott Complainants – near the beginning.
Thomas Neale lease – see List of Leases CKS U38 T1.

Page 24 The map is taken from the 1/500 scale Ordnance Survey map of the Mount Sion area held by the Reference Library. It is inscribed as published in 1887 but surveyed in 1866 and 1873. Since many significant changes took place between 1866 and 1887 it would be misleading and confusing to refer to these maps by the date of publication and I have therefore captioned this and further examples 'Ordnance Survey 1866' (omitting the second year of survey for the sake of brevity). See also p.139 comment below.

Page 25 The Barrow map, one of the vital sources for Tunbridge Wells history, is at the BL, the Reference Library etc – T.T. Barrow, 'A Plan of Tunbridge Wells ... showing the situation of all the Lodging Houses' etc 1808. It is reproduced in RTW,

Plate 64.
The 1710 document, an Indenture Tripartite dated 30 Nov 1710, is at CKS, U38 T22.

Page 26 Abergavenny land – the Abergavenny estate included property between Cumberland Walk and Nevill Street – see the Tithe map (Abergavenny Lodge can just be seen at the extreme left of the map on p.24).
The photograph of Chapel Place comes from Mauldon and no doubt the Reference Library Collection.

Page 29 Sale of Manor – see Rowlands ed., p.30.
John Brett – will pr PCC 16 Nov 1719.
Col Johannes Brett – will pr PCC 28 Mar 1672.
Dr Hugh Chamberlen senior – The Chamberlens were sufficiently famous to feature in the DNB and that is how I found out that Peter Chamberlen's eldest son, Hugh, married on 28 May 1663, at St Paul's, Covent Garden, Dorothy, daughter of Colonel John Brett. It also told me who John Brett's father was – something I did not know before – and how to find his will which revealed that John Brett had two brothers, Thomas and Nathaniel, as well as the sister who married the doctor – but it did not tell me anything about the Colonel. For the story of the Chamberlen midwifery forceps see Aveling.
Fuller – p.94 – see bibliography.
For an explanation of the Poor Rate records see chapter 8; for the full Angel sequence chapter 26.

Page 30 The photograph is scanned from a photocopy provided by Keith Hetherington, source unknown. For more on the landlords see chapter 26.

Page 32 I have not yet found a primary source for the death of the lady.
Beau Feilding – see DNB.
Villiers, John (1677?-1723) is DNB entry for 'Earl of Buckingham'. Danvers, Robert in the DNB is probably the grandfather, the illegitimate Robert Wright who assumed the name Manvers, his son Robert reverting to Villiers and marrying Lady Muskerry. See Woodgate pp.38-9 and Savidge p.39.
Page 33 Will of Richard Constable at CKS dated 20 Oct? 1702, pr 1 Nov 1703.
Winefrith Brooke was certainly a widow by the time of the conveyance.
Chapel Trust Deed – a complication is that the deed puts this in the second year of the reign of Queen Anne. The exact wording goes: '... the fifteenth day of February in the second year of the reign of our sovereign lady Anne defender of the faith etc ... Anno Domini 1703'. Anne succeeded according to the DNB on 8 March 1702 (New Style presumably) and therefore the second year of her reign ran from 8 March 1703 to 7 March 1704 (both New Style) and must include the 15 February 1704 (New Style) – which I write 1703/4. The days from 1 January to 24 March used of course to be included in the 'previous' year (Old Style) until 1752 when the New Style was introduced.

Page 34 £100,000 – see comments on pp.3 above and 112 below.
Rusthall Manor – see comment on p.2 above.

Page 36 The illustration is a scan of a corner of the opening page of the Chancery Case, PRO C6/100/7, from a photograph provided by the PRO. Only a small portion of each line is shown, the parchment document being far too wide to show a whole line at a readable size. There is not therefore much point in trying to provide a transcript; but those interested may find 'Honoble Lord Cowper' on the top line, 'Your Orator John Villars Earl of Buckingham' on the next line followed by [St A]'lbans (decd)' (concluding the titles of John's mother) 'and Henry Marsh of the Parish of St Paul' on

the third line; and on the bottom two lines 'Thomas Weller of Tonbridge in the County of Kent Gent' and 'the said Sir Thomas Meeres of the Second part' – all proving I hope that there is some reality behind my story. The full text, covering the same number of lines runs as follows:
'26th January 1707 To the Rt Hon William Lord Cowper Baron of Wingham High Chancellor of Great Brittaine
Complaining (?) show unto your Lord[ship?] your orator John Villars Earl of Buckingham Viscount Purbeck son and heir of Margaret Viscountess Dowager Purbeck (decd) who was formerly wife of Charles Lord Viscount Muskerry (decd) and daughter and heir of Ulick late Marquess of Clanricard and Earl of St Albans (decd) and Henry Marsh of the parish of Saint Paul Covent Garden ... Mdx laceman and James Scott of the City of London grocer
That by Indenture Tripartite bearing date the 17th day of March 1684 {1664?} made or mentioned to be made between the said Charles Lord Viscount Muskerry and the said Lady Margaret then his wife of the first part the Right Noble George Duke of Albemarle and Sir Peter Killigrew (?) the Elder of Westminster Knight (both since decd) of the second part Richard Belling then of the Strand ... Mdx Esq afterwards Sir Richard Belling Knight and Dansell Arthur of London merchant of the third part And Indentures Quinquapartite bearing date the 20th March 1682 made or mentioned to be made between the Rt Hon Robert Lord Viscount Purbeck and the said Lady Margaret Viscountess Purbeck then his wife of the first part the said Richard Belling and Dansell Arthur of the second part Sir James Butler Knight and Francis Bourke Merchant of the third part Maurice Fitzgerald Esq of the fourth part and Sir Thomas Meeres of London Knight Thomas Hatcher Esq and Thomas Cox Esq of the fifth part And Indenture Quinquapartite bearing date the 16th May 1701 made ... between your Orator John Earl of Buckingham of the first part the Rt Hon Honora Lady Dowager Bergavenny Widdow Relict of George late Lord Bergavenny (Decd) Benedict Richards ... parish ... St Giles in the Fields Mdx Esq and William Guise of Grays Inn Mdx Esq (which said Benedict Richards and William Guise are executors of the last will and testament of the said late Lord Bergavenny) Sir John Webb of Odstock (?) Wilts Baronet and Barbara his wife Thomas Stonor ... Oxon Esq and Isabella his wife (the said Lady Honora Bergavenny Barbara Webb and Isabella Stonor being three of the daughters and coheirs of the Rt Hon John Lord Bellasise (?) of Worlaby (?) (decd) of the second part John Talbot of Salwary (?)Worcester Knight surviving executor of the last will and testament of the said John Lord Bellasise of the third part Thomas Lord Fauconbridge eldest son and heir of the Hon Sir Rowland Bellasise Knight of the Hon Order of the Bath (decd) John Bellasise Esq and Rowland Bellasise Esq brothers of the said Thomas Lord Viscount Fauconbridge (which said Thomas Lord ... John Bellasise and Rowland Bellasise are nephews and heires in Gavelkind according to the custom of the county of Kent) of the Rt Hon Thomas late Earl of Fauconbridge (decd) of the fourth part and Thomas Lake of the Middle Temple London Esq Thomas Weller of Tonbridge ... Kent Gent and George Weller of Tonbridge ... Gent of the fifth part And Indenture Quinquapartite bearing date the 20th November 1702 and made ... between your Orator ... of the first part the said Sir Thomas Meeres of the second part the said Thomas ... '

The main document in the case, C6/100/7, is lengthy but can be sub-divided into (1) the complaint of the Earl of Buckingham and others (5 A4 pages on my computer); (2) the several answers of Thomas Weller (11 A4 pages); (3) the joint and several answers of Thomas Lake, George Weller and Daniel Tilden (3 A4 pages). Relevant also are (4) the several answers of Henry Weller CKS U38 T2; (5) the judgement of 30 Nov 1710 CKS U38 T22; and (6) the final conveyance by Lease and Release dated 12/13 Aug 1715 consisting of two documents both at CKS U2737 (see p.38 comment below). The documents are long and repetitious and pin-pointing of quotations is difficult but I

have tried to indicate from which of the above categories my quotations come. CKS U38 T2, (4) above, is a copy or draft written on paper in a very difficult and untidy hand. It is bundled for no apparent reason with a number of documents dealing with the site of the Chapel of King Charles. However it seems to be more or less a repetition of what Henry's brother Thomas Weller said in his defence and obviously did not affect the outcome. It is initialled by the Commissioner as taken on 22 Oct 1708. For CKS U38 T22, (5) above, see p.38 comment below.
Date of hearing, 1 May, comes from the release of 13 Aug 1715 – see p.39 below.

Page 38 The outcome of the case came to light only because of the chance discovery of a document among the Weller papers at CKS, not the PRO. The reference is CKS U38 T22. It is the release part of a conveyance dated 29 and 30 Nov 1710, attested copies of both parts of which are also in CKS U2737 Box 2.

Page 39 Heneage – this name and the fact that she was his mistress comes from Woodgate p.39. The DNB says he married *c*.1700.
Foreclosure – All this final information is in the Release of 13 Aug 1715 which together with the Lease of 12 Aug forms the conveyance of all the mortgaged property by the Earl of Buckingham to John Brett for what was owing plus £50. These documents are part of the uncatalogued collection CKS U2737. Copies examined with the original by J. Brett and Thos Wakeham of both the Lease and Release dated 12/13 Aug 1715 are in Box 1. I have a photocopy of the Lease and a transcription of the Release.
Brett and Pickering – see next chapter.

Page 40 John Brett – dates of will 22 June and of death 13 Nov – source is Decree in Chancery 12 Aug 1747 CKS U2737 Box 14.
Marriage of Dorothy – see p.29 above.

Page 41 Essex Street – see Chamberlen Hugh the Elder MD in DNB (1908, vol.IV)

Page 42 The 'bond' reference is CKS U2737 Box 14.
Details of income and expenditure on this and following pages come from schedules to a 'Report in Chancery by H. Montague dated 24 July 1752 – CKS U2737, Box 14.

Page 43 I was fortunate that a search at *www.familysearch.org* revealed a marriage between Margaret Brett and Robert Pickering in the IGI. Confirmation came from the register of marriages of the parish of St Clement Eastcheap (Guildhall Library Ms 4783): 'Robert Pickering of Cowley in the County of Canerbury widower and Margaret Brett of Tonbridge Wells in Said County widow by Lic[ence] 14th November 1724'. There can be no doubt that this is the right marriage despite some anomalies – there are three Cowleys in England but the most likely is in the London area near Uxbridge and cannot be in the 'County of Canterbury' which must refer to Kent, the correct county for Tunbridge Wells. Putting Cowley in the 'County of Canterbury' I take to be a clerical error. Robert was therefore a Londoner – one possible reason for the marrage having taken place in London.

Page 45 Events from 1727 to 1744 are recorded in 'Decree in Chancery – Brett and Others v Mallory and Others' – 12 Aug 1747 – CKS, U2737, Box 14.

Page 47 Lanthorn House – there are a number of documents in CKS, U2737, Box 3 – one dated 19 July 1787 describes 'All that messuage commonly called the Lanthorn House wherein John Brett deceased father of the said John Brett party hereto did in his lifetime inhabit and dwell but now standing empty and untenanted'. See RTW,

Plate 78 for a plan.
John Brett senior – a copy of the will pr 11 Sep 1784 is in CKS, U2737, Box 3.
Vergil's Eclogue and career of John Brett – see Hart (Tonbridge School Register), p.171 at Tonbridge Reference Library.
The Marriage Settlement dated 8 Nov 1777 and Conveyance by Lease and Release of 3 Grove Houses and 12 acres dated 5/6 Dec 1786 are in CKS, U2737, Box 1.
Grimston living – verbal communication from Vicar of Grimston.

Page 48 The Abergavenny collection copy reference is ESRO, ABE 21U. An original is held by the Tunbridge Wells Borough Council (telephone confirmation by Ann Cackett). Other copies must exist, although I cannot find one at CKS. An accessible full transcription is to be found in *Sprange's Guide* 1786.

Page 49 The Fairlawn House conveyance 27/28 Nov 1702 is in CKS, U2737, Box 14.
Neale – see p.14 comment above.

Page 50 A copy of the Tunbridge Wells Improvement Act 1890 can be seen at the Reference Library. Part XIII deals with the Grove and the Agreement of 27 Mar 1890 is at Schedule III.

Page 51 Birdcage Walk archway – see p.60 comment below.

Page 53 Kip's engraving is so well known it hardly needs comment. It is an engraving of a drawing made by Badeslade for Harris's *History of Kent*, 1719. This is a small detail only, of course. Many more will follow. Considerable credibility can I think he given to the authenticity of the information contained in the drawing. Where confirmation can be found it is usually in agreement and where there is doubt who is to say that I am right and the drawing wrong?
The engraving is in the Museum collection.

Page 54 Marriage Settlement – see p.47 above. Note that the houses on the north side of the Grove according to the Grove Trust Deed are on the west in the conveyance – illustrating the 'points of the compass problem'!

Page 55 For some of these arboreal facts see Pope: 'A Word about the 'Grove' addressed by the Rev. W.L. Pope, MA, Curator and Conservator, to Conservatives and Liberals 'For they are all honourable men' and will not grudge Three-pence towards the Repair of the Constitution of the Grove NB – The proceeds of the Sale will be applied for labour in the Grove' Tunbridge Wells W. Nash and R. Pelton, Parade, and St John Colbran, High Street (William Brackett, Machine Printer, High Street, Tunbridge Wells), 1868. For Brackett Printer see p.256 above.
The *Maidstone Journal* (MJ) started publication in January 1786 and I have perused it for Tunbridge Wells news from that date until 1837 when the *Sussex Agricultural Express* was more conveniently available in Tunbridge Wells but my examination of that newspaper did not unfortunately take in more than a few years more. Both papers are available to the public on microfilm, the MJ at Tonbridge Reference Library (and Maidstone Library) and the *Sussex Agricultural Express* (SAE) at Tunbridge Wells Reference Library; those so inclined may check my quotations at these places or at the BL Colindale site.
Sand in eyes – I am afraid I cannot trace the reference in the MJ.

Page 56 The North/Cumberland anecdote is to be found in Cumberland (Supplement) pp.33-4.
Sussex Hotel – see MJ, 22 Jan 1793.

Pantiles re-paving – there is in the Museum a fascinating poster detailing the income and expenditure on this project, giving the names and subscriptions of all donors and listing the stages in bringing the stone by sea to the Medway then upriver to Wateringbury and onwards.

Page 57 John Fry will – the PRO microfilm does not show the last page of a codicil and therefore the date of probate is not available from this source. The main will is dated 30 Sep 1801.

Page 58 The time capsule was not found during the recent building work.
Christ Church History – see bibliography (Banner).

Page 59 Rev J. Banner – letter dated 8 Aug 2000.

Page 60 Meadow Hill – see Tithe map and Award for this information.
Cottenham – see 1881 census.
Grecian Villa site – in CKS U2737 Box 13 there is a Mortgage Deed dated 18 Oct 1821 whereby Joseph Delves lends £500 to William Lushington on security of a field called Slaughter House and of the 'Grove Field' which abutted the Grove on the west or north-west, on land of William Lushington on the north or north-east, on lands of the widow Friend on the east or south-east and on the high road from Mount Sion to Woodsgate and Pembury on the south or south-west. On the outside of this deed is a memorandum that the deed is covenanted to be produced by Miss Charlotte Lushington to Dr Thomas Mayo. From this evidence, and the fact of Dr Mayo's later ownership of the house, it must surely follow that the Grecian Villa site was bought by William Lushington, inherited by his daughter and sold by her to the doctor (or perhaps to John Ward who then sold to the doctor).
The archway, sometimes called the Birdcage Walk Arch, is a listed building Grade II; but the listing, apart from a Mid C19 dating, gives no historical information only an architectural description.
Grove School – date of foundation – 1845 was claimed in an advertisement in the *Tunbridge Wells Gazette*, 6 Jan 1882 – certainly it was going strong in 1851 as shown by the census. The whole of this paragraph is based on the censuses, the directories of the period available at the Reference Library and the Ordnance Survey Map of 1866 (see p.24 comment).

Page 61 The Rev James Fry – see 1874 *Directory* – address on will proved 18 Jan (June?) 1886 was South Lawn, Teignmouth, Devon – age 79.
I was given a photocopy of Spiers' history by Rev Banner – see bibliography.

Page 62 John Mercer will pr 21 Nov 1833 but there are two copies in a deposit by Walker, Templer and Thomson ref CKS U746 T206/156 of which one looks contemporary but the other is later (*c*.1800?) and has interesting annotations.

Page 64 Robert Mercer will – pr PCC 22 Nov 1759 – there is a copy in the deeds of the *Compasses*.

Page 67 Whitbread deeds – I shall continue to use the name Whitbread in frequent references to these documents which were held by Whitbread archives in Maidstone but are now, as far as I can establish, in the hands of the solicitors to new pub owners Enterprise Inns of Solihull.

Page 68 Sprange finances – the suggestion is made in fact by the nephew of John Goulden of the late Goulden and Curry which itself took over from Colbran's printing

and library business in the High Street. Richard Goulden has just completed a bibliography of Kent Town Guides and also written an article in a British Library publication on Edmund Baker and Jasper Sprange – and I must acknowledge my debt to his work.
Compasses – most of this information comes from an 'Abstract of Title of Messrs John Newnham Edmund Kelsey and Henry Kelsey to a Public House called *The Compasses* situate at Mount Sion Tunbridge Wells Kent', one of the Whitbread deeds.
For Ann Friend see chapters 10-12 – her will pr 9 Apr 1832 is at the PRO.

Page 69 For Thomas Fry see chapter 15.

Page 70 Miles Garage deeds – in private possession – see chapter 12.

Page 72 Probate Inventory of Thomas Mathews is at CKS, DRa Pi 1/3A,B.

Page 73 Licensees recognizances 1718 are at CKS, Q RLv 1/56.

Page 74 Ann Bodle's will pr 6 Mar 1754 is at CKS DRb PW58
Richard Newnham's will pr 16 Apr 1748 is at CKS DRb/PW57.
The full version of the Sprange poster will be used in chapter 22.
The double entry for Mr Penney in the Poor rate is because for the years 1702 to 1704 the entry 'Mr (Thomas) Penny or tenant for a new house' is followed immediately by 'Mr Penny for a Barne and Coachhouse' suggesting that the barn entry merges with the 'new house' entry in the subsequent years. The whole topic is problematic. Spasmodic records of Licensees' Recognisances do exist including complete ones for 1715 and 1718. The curious thing is that the *Compasses* appears in neither; and yet Thomas Mathews 'of the Compasses Mount Sion' is certainly in the burial register in October 1718 and the recognizances are dated 21 Aug 1718. On the other hand Thomas Mathews appears as the victualler at the *Carpenters Arms* in 1718 and also in 1715. In 1718 Robert Petitt and Francis [Dudy?] stood surety for him as did the more familiar names of Robert Friend and William Mercer in 1715 – in fact the Mercer connection might be significant. Did the inn on Mount Sion change its name from the *Carpenters Arms* between August and October 1718? Or did Thomas Mathews move – but if he did, why was the *Compasses* not listed already? Or did the *Compasses* only start business in September? This is where the Poor Rate record would have come in useful if it had not been for the gap between 1714 and 1728. Widow Mathews appears in 1728 and thereafter there is a good sequence until 1797 but the link back to 1714 is tentative. It is based on position on the collector's route. Widow Mathews is listed between 'Mr Bland for Riders' and the brewhouse occupied by William Baines (Philip Seale's inventory assistant) and later by Thomas Baines and William King. On the 1714 side of the gap exactly the same position is occupied by 'Mr (Thomas) Penny or tenant for a new house'. This listing continues back to 1702 and then stops. Some confirmation is provided by the fact that Thomas Penny paid 6 shillings in 1714 and Anne Mathews exactly twice that in 1728.
Sprange posters are at the Museum.

Page 75 *Old Pubs* co-author is Keith Hetherington – my thanks to him. His information on pub landlords, here and elsewhere, comes from newspapers, including in particular reports of the regular 'brewster sessions' of Magistrate's Courts. The photograph comes from *Old Pubs*.

Page 76 Tonbridge Parish Overseers' Accounts are at CKS, P371/12/1-6 – Vol.4 covers 1730.

The Southborough Court Book with record of Court Leet held 4 Nov 1796 is at CKS, U249 M2.

Pages 78-85 References are to be found within the text itself. The six volumes of the Poor Rate at CKS, P371 12/ 1-6 cover the years as follows: Vol.1 – 1670-1688; Vol.2 – 1689-1704; Vol.3 – 1708-1714 and part of 1715; Vol.4 – 1728-1761; Vol.5 – 1762-1784; Vol.6 – 1785-1806 but details of properties cease in 1797.

Page 86 The quotation begins the 'Whereas' recital of a 4-part indenture dated 13 July 1701 ref CKS, U749 T8 (one of the first documents I examined at the Kent Archives Office – old name for Centre for Kentish Studies).
Edward Martin – see earlier discussion in chapter 1 and elsewhere including the text of the 1686 Partition Plan (p.16 comment above). For his trade see the subscription boards inside the Chapel or Waring p.9.
1684 lease see p.10 comment above.

Page 87 The shading gives a good general idea of the strip. Bowra's scale of perches (rods) can be used to check the width.
John Waghorne – see Waring, p.9 also.

Page 88 Nicholas Wood will – proved 15 Mar 1725 ref CKS, DRb/PW 51.
Edward Martin will – pr 16 Aug 1708 ref CKS, DRb/PW 46.

Page 89 Mary Latter will – pr 30 Nov 1716 ref CKS DRb/PW 49.
1765 turnpike – see Carley.

Page 90 Edmund Wood deeds are at CKS, U214 T397.

Page 91 The Abstract of Title is at CKS, U55 T527.

Page 93 It is interesting (and might even be of practical value) to see that water can be obtained at a depth of 38 or 39 feet. See p.250 and page comment below.
Mr Montier is known as a Tunbridge Wells architect; Mr J. White of Brighton was presumably James White one of the vendors – see next page.
Bethlehem Chapel – this was the only reference in my *Encyclopaedia Britannica* DVD – if anyone knows more please get in touch.
The deeds of 37 Little Mount Sion are with the present owners – my thanks to them.

Page 94 There are two Committee Books: CKS, P371E 25/1 contains the Trust Deed extract; 25/2 contains copies of conveyances – see p.221 comment below.
The 'Female National School' is shown on the map in *Clifford's Guide*, 6th edition, probable date 1834 – but note that not all copies have the map.
1859 plan and conveyance – 37 Little Mount Sion deeds.

Page 95 Constant visitor – *Tunbridge Wells Gazette*, 17 Dec 1858.

Page 96 Warwick House – the property is described in the sale document of 15 Dec 1875 as – 'All that messuage tenement or dwelling house then formerly called Martins Upper House afterwards called Doyles Lower House and then called Warwick House situated … foot of Mount Sion … occupation of … Edmund Wood deceased afterwards Francis Doyle since of Henry Goldstone then of Richard Delves afterwards of Charles John Cook or his tenants then since of the said AR Sydall and then late of the said F Duly deceased And also all those two other messuages or tenements situated … at

the back of the aforesaid messuage ... late ... occupation ... ________ Clifford and __________ Cook ... Which two last mentioned messuages ... were erected on garden ground belonging ... first mentioned messuage ...' So there were two houses built in the back garden of Warwick House.
1889 – see *Kelly's Directory*.

Page 97 59-61 High Street – the deeds were then in the keeping of solicitors Thomson, Snell and Passmore They include posters concerning the Auction Sale to be held under the will of John Colbran on Friday 31 Oct 1890 by Brackett & Son at the Royal Sussex Assembly Rooms of : nos 59-63 High Street comprising the *Tunbridge Wells Gazette* Office with Dwelling House and Printing Works adjoining, the Royal Library with Show Room and Dwelling House over and a Capital Corner Shop; and 13 Dwelling Houses and a Shop, nos 1, 3, 11, 13, 15, 17 19, 21, 23, 25, 27, 29 & 31 Little Mount Sion.

Page 98 The Robert Stapley Estate papers are at CKS, U746 T101.
The Stage Coaches notice is on pp.338-9 of *Sprange's Guide*, 1808.
The information about the building and sale of these cottages comes from the Goulden deeds –Abstract of Title to Lot 1.

Page 99 Edward Dunkley – this information comes from notes made by John Goulden's father now in his son's possession – photocopy with me.
The Lewis Place printing works can be seen on the map published with *Colbran's Guide*, 1840.

Page 100 Scholes – *Colbran's Guide* 1840 has the information about Jabez Scholes being clerk to the Chapel and Mrs Stapley treasurer of the British School.

Page 103 1850 purchases – the Conditions of Sale (see p.97 comment above) specify that the title to Lot 6 commenced with a conveyance dated 23 April 1850 between Benjamin Slight and John Colbran and that to Lot 7 a conveyance dated 1 April 1850 between Edward Sole, John Jeffery Sole and William Charles Sole (whose role in the sale I can only guess), Thomas Stapley and John Colbran.
Stapley sell-off – see p.98 (CKS, U746 T101).
Butcher bankrupt – see MJ, 26 February and 30 April 1813.

Page 104 Woods and brothers – see Wilson, pp.160 *et seq.*
Nicholas Wood will – see p.88 comment above.

Page 105 Whitbread deeds (see p.67 comment) – the document among the Grove Tavern deeds is the Lease part dated 30 Jan 1833 of 'Release in fee and Covenant to produce deeds with Lease for a Year annexed' Mr Thomas Fry and Mr William Jewhurst to Mrs Sarah Bonham dated 30/31 Jan 1833.

Page 106 The Pantiles information and quotation come from Chalklin (1) and (2).

Page 107 For Ashenhurst and his sister, see Chancery Court proceedings PRO, 5/222/22.

Page 109 Will of Thomas Ashenhurst, written 5 Feb 1713, pr 15 Oct 1714, is at PRO, PROB11/542 f121.
For the Income and Expenditure accounts see the reference for p 107 above.
For the Dashwoods see Dashwood; and Farthing (2) for Rusthall Manor.

Page 110 Most of the commonplace biographical information comes from the DNB.

Page 112 Hertfordshire Quarter Sessions – see Munby p.23. The Economic History's online calculator at *www.eh.net/hmit* says that £63 9s. 1d. in 1707 was worth £7,284.70 in 2001 but they do not give the basis for their calculation and I do not agree for the reasons stated.

Page 113 Conveyance of Berkeley Place by Philip Benge – on 23/24 Oct 1781 – this information is in the Schedule to the 1833 Release etc referred to at p 105 above. For more on the Wood family including a family tree see chapter 12.
Deaths of the Wood sisters – attested by Miles Garage deeds in owners' possession – opening recitals in 'Abstract of Title of the Devisees in Trust for Sale under the Will of the late Mrs Mary Ann Hodgson deceased to a Dwelling house and premises known as No.33 Mount Sion Road in Tunbridge Wells' say that Sarah Wood died in April 1811 intestate and unmarried and Mary Wood junior died in August 1818 also intestate and unmarried.

Page 114 Tunbridge Wells, 1951– see *Tunbridge Wells Advertiser*.

Page 115 John Brown application – Tunbridge Wells Borough Council Planning Department archives Envelope 853.

Page 116 The photograph of the Agricultural Show committee came, with a caption, courtesy of Keith Hetherington. His source was the ' Tunbridge Wells and South Eastern Counties Show 1862-1962, July Centenary Show Souvenir' published by the *Kent and Sussex Courier*.

Page 117 Will of Edmund Wood, pr 5 Feb 1774, is at CKS, DRb/PW60.

Page 123 The second deed is a Whitbread document (see p.67 comment): 'Release in Fee with Lease for a Year' James Richardson and J.B. Stapley to Mrs Bonham widow dated 30/31 July 1834.

Page 124 Details of ownership all come from Whitbread's *Grove Tavern* deeds (see p.67 comment).

Page 126 Pub landlords – see p.75 comment above.

Page 127 Will of John Bonham pr PCC 29 Oct 1825 is recited in the deed named in p.123 comment above.

Page 129 The sale notice of 1882 is in the Reference Library collection.

Page 130 The Johnson albums are in the Museum.

Page 131 Pub landlords – see p.75 comment above.
Wilful damage – see *Kent & Sussex Courier*, 28 Jan 1898.

Page 133 Fanny Burney – see p.202 comment below.

Page 138 The sketches of the house and of the bedroom on the next page come from the *Belle Vue Magazine* papers at CKS, U1157 – for more see chapter 23.

Page 139 Ordnance Survey – by the time the 1/500 map was published in 1887

Burlington House had in fact been demolished, showing beyond a doubt that it is the date of survey that provides the evidence in these maps – see p.24 comment above.
Burlington House Sale Particulars – see Brackett's Catalogues at the Reference Library.
For more on Nicholas Wood's will see p.88 comment above.

Page 140 Death of Jane Akers – this is noted in the Belle Vue papers CKS, U1157 F3 (vol.III p.453) : ' ... Mon 2 May 1842 at Tunbridge Wells after a few hours illness, aged 69, widow of Aretas Akers, formerly of St Christopher West Indies, and daughter of Rev James Ramsey'.

Page 141 Fellmongery – I have some records of correspondence with the named institutions – for more see chapter 22.
Richard Fry of Mitchells, the old name for the estate which is now Holmewood House School.

Page 142 The Poor Rate record runs as follows:

1689 (May)-1714	Nicholas Wood (Nicholas died 1724 or 5)
1728-1739	Mr William Wood
1740-1776	Thos Wood Jun for Mr Wm Woods
1777-1790	Wood Thos for late Thos Woods
1791-1796	Thos Wood for Widow Woods
1791-1797	Thos Wood for late Wid Woods

Pages 142-143 There is a short recital of William Wood's will in the lengthy Abstract of Title to Goldstone's or the Great House Field – see p.91 comment above. It gives the date of the will as 28 Aug 1755 and the date of PCC probate as 19 Sep 1755. The will of Thomas Wood Senior (CKS, DRb/PW 58) dated 8 Oct 1755 refers to his lately deceased brother William – the will of Thomas Wood junior is at CKS, Dra/PW15 – the will of Thomas Wood III I have not found but it is recited (naming him as a goldsmith) with some details in Abstract of Title of the Devisees in Trust for Sale under the Will of the late Mrs Mary Ann Hodgson deceased to a Dwelling house and premises known as No.33 Mount Sion Road in Tunbridge Wells (Miles Garage deeds in owners' possession – but I have a full transcript) This document also contains a full recital of the sale of Burlington House by Ann Friend to Isaac Hodgson 1827 – a transaction also referred to in the Sale Particulars for the Burlington House estate (Conditions of Sale – title to Lots 1, 2 and 3 – Lease and Release dated 22/23 January 1827 between Ann Friend, Isaac Hodgson and John Stone) – see p.139 comment above.
Aretas Akers letter book CKS, U1157 E1.

Page 144 For the reference to Mrs Allen's Ladies School see *Tunbridge Wells Gazette*, 6 Jan 1860 and 16 May 1861 for the Thompsons.
Mary Ann Hodgson's will – made on 13 Sep 1843 and pr PCC on 30 Apr 1873. The information on daughter Clara comes from the Miles Garage deeds (in Miles family hands), specifically an Indenture dated 6 July 1844 between (1) George Cowie (Clara's husband) and Henry Thomas Harrison and (2) Mary Ann Hodgson, Thomas Delves and Thomas Beeching.

Page 145 C.E. Ansell – Tunbridge Wells Borough Council Planning Department archives – Envelope 1555. For Robert Brown see Envelopes 229 and 131.

Page 146 For Johnson's photograph and comments look in the Museum collection. Johnson lived at 59 Mount Sion – see photograph at end of chapter 19.

Page 147 The exact date of the *Courier* article quoted in a 13 July 1982 letter from the Borough Reference Librarian to Mrs Puxty of Rusthall is 27 Oct 1933.
Reminder – Nicholas Wood will is at CKS, DRb/PW51.

Page 148 See p.142 comment above for the main Poor Rate sequence.
Licensees' Recognizances are at CKS, Q/RLv/1.
Page 149 For turnpikes see Carley.
The long document is the main part of the Miles Garage deeds – see p.143 comment above.

Page 150 Tunbridge Ware – see Austen p.148; and for the Fenner's Turnery quote p.145.

Page 151 For 1827 and Isaac Hodgson see p.143 comment above (Miles Garage deeds).

Page 152 Among the posters preserved at the Museum is one announcing a benefit performance at the theatre on Friday 25 September 1840 for Mr John Battman the 'veteran whip' who had 'driven a Stage Coach between this Place & London for a period of 40 years' but was 'now incapacitated by age and infirmity'. I wonder if he could be related to, or even the late husband of, Mary Battman the schoolmistress!
Family history – see Strange, Charles Hilbert (2) p.9 – copy at Reference Library.
Robin Montier Freeman, a great-grandson of the 'Remembrances' authoress (see p.308 and comment thereon), has recently been in touch and provided a second edition of the family history, dated Aug 1994. See also p.246 comment below.

Page 154 For the origins of this photograph see p.200.
Brooke and Constable – see list of leases – p.10 comment above.

Page 155 There are two documents both held by the Tonbridge Reference Library under the reference TU1 T57: the Deed of Assignment dated 6 Aug 1700 and the Deed of Purchase from the Earl of Buckingham's trustees dated 28 Nov 1702. The two together provide much of the information examined in the next few pages, including the fact of Thomas Moyce's sub-lease from Brooke and Constable at £3 per annum.
Philip had to borrow on mortgage – I assume this is what he did because the deed of 1700 talks of paying off encumbrances on his property.
Vestry books ref CKS, P371E 8/2.
Death of wife and remarriage – for a discussion of the family tree see p.185 comment below.
Page 156 Seale family – see p.185 comment below.
Richard Constable's will (see p.165 comment below) says Francis Combridge is his brother-in-law.

Page 158 The reference of the 1701 deed (see p.86 comment above) is CKS, U749 T8.
Square rods – a rod, pole or perch is 5 ½ yards in length and we all know that four of them make one chain or cricketpitch length; but almost as well known is the fact that farm fields for example are measured for accuracy not just in acres but also in rods, poles or perches. A rood on the other hand is a quarter of an acre and contains 40 rods. The Grove is assessed in the 1890 Improvement Act at 4 acres, 2 roods and 7 perches. I think my 16 (square) rods is a defensible interpretation.

Page 160 For a reference to Rosebury Place see p.101.

Page 161 The printed sermon is in the Tunbridge Wells Reference Library.
Strange, Charles Hilbert (1) pp.15 & 17.

Thomas Jordan appears as a Poor Rate payer for Jordans House from 1728 to 1738 but efforts to find out more have failed. There seems to be no will at the PRO for a start.

Page 162 Colbran 1840 (footnote to p.85 where it is said to come from the 'Dramatic Mirror', vol.2, p.644). It does.
Below the greatest – see DNB.
Bellamy, George Anne 'An Apology ...' and see also 'Memoirs of George Anne Bellamy, by a Gentleman of Covent Garden Theatre, 1785'.
For a print of Bellamy and Garrick on stage see RTW, Plate 41.
Mrs Godfrey was formerly Arabella Churchill, sister of the Duke of Marlborough and one time mistress of James, Duke of York. For a portrait see RTW, plate 39.
By 'the people at Maidstone' I mean the Kent Archives Office now CKS. I had some correspondence with them and with Dr Felix Hull in 1988. The information about William Seale in 1698 comes in a letter from Kent Archives dated 2 June 1988 signed Donald Gibson – I failed to find a will at the PRO. I have been unable to find the source for the information on the Seales of Yalding although this most probably came also from the Kent Archives Office. Dr Hull (21 Sep 1988) said that there was some evidence for a Quaker Meeting at Maidstone in the late 17th century but the group quickly died out and he could not remember any reference to the name Seale. I thought it was he who told me that Kent Quaker registers had been lost but Mr Christopher Stacey of Mount Sion confirms.

Page 163 See *Kent & Sussex Courier*, 21 March 1913.

Page 164 For Queen Anne's visits see N & R, pp.32-5.
For Seale genealogy see p.185 comment below.
The reference to John Seale and the farm comes from a South Frith Court Roll at CKS, U1109 M1.
Tonbridge Reference Library A18 has a number of Seale documents including Mary Seale's will pr 31 Dec 1763, the Marriage Settlement of Thomas Seale and Priscilla Wagon 1721 and others.

Page 165 For Seale genealogy see p.185 comment below.
Tonbridge Parish Overseers' accounts – the Philip Seale entry is at CKS, P371 12/2.
Richard Constable – date of burial at Speldhurst was provided by a trustworthy source but I have not checked it myself. The source is a descendant of Richard Constable who is researching him – Mrs B. Bush of Boughton Monchelsea. There is a copy of his will at CKS, DRb/PW 43 and possibly also at Tonbridge Reference Library – it was dated 20 Oct 1702 and proved 1 Nov 1703.
See the opening paragraphs of chapter 22 for the marriage of William Fry and Mary Seale.

Page 166 Marriage Settlement – see p.164 comment above.
For the Prince of Wales see Elwig p.6.

Page 168 *Presbyterian History* – see Vol.2 of the Journal.
The print which appears in Strange, Charles Hilbert (1) is in the Museum collection.
For an up-to-date survey of the field see Dale (Prof Andrew Dale of the School of Mathematical and Statistical Sciences, University of Natal, Durban).

Page 169 Bayes' will is at PRO Prob 865, pr 30 Apr 1761.

Page 170 The photograph, taken by Johnson in 1915, is in the Reference Library collection.

IMS Bulletin – *Institute of Mathematical Statistics Bulletin* – Vol.19, No.3, 1990.

Page 171 Information on William Johnston comes from Dr Williams's Library, London Photograph - she also brought one of the Chapel itself which is reproduced in RTW (Plate 42).

Page 172 The Wesley quotation is taken from Strange, Charles Hilbert (1), p.19.
Dilapidation – see Pearce, Luke (1), p.69 (Bailey p.16 says the 'walls and roof alone' remained).
Colbran's Guide, 1840, p.78.
'Beautiful structure' and 'Friends' – see Pearce, Luke (2), p.16.

Page 173 The Charity Commission has a file (23790) on the sale of the Chapel.

Page 174 The Sale Notice is in the Reference Library.

Page 175 The Johnson photograph is in the Museum collection.

Page 176 Planning – see Tunbridge Wells Borough Council Planning Department archives – Envelope 540.

Page 178 Martha Harrison's will is at CKS, DRa PW5.
Marriage – see IGI – George Fry's death is recorded in CKS, U2737 Box 9 (Indenture dated 31 Jan 1821) – see also the Fry pedigree in Chapter Six.

Page 180 Death of Michael Stapley – this is a deduction from the Goulden deeds.
Phippen – private research – see Ludlam. There is an illustration of the inscribed rock at Plate 91 in RTW.
The South Eastern Railway (SER) deposited plan is at CKS, Q/Rum 254. The plan (but not its Book of Reference) is illustrated in RTW plate 97 on a necessarily small scale. Cripps Nursery is numbered 357 and the area at an enlarged scale is partially shown in the bottom left-hand corner of the illustration. For more on the deposited plans of 1844 and also 1852 see chapter 23, pp.342 *et seq.* and commentary thereon.

Page 182 Jane Smith – *Tunbridge Wells Gazette*, 2 Nov 1860; Alfred Caffyn day unknown Aug 1864.
Trade in 1913 – Hetherington and Griffiths p.23.

Page 183 Philip Seale's will is at CKS, DRb/PW55.
For the field exchange see CKS, U2737 Box 13.

Page 184 Thomas Seale's will is at CKS, Dra/PW8
Priscilla Seale/Edward Mercer marriage settlement is at CKS, U746 T182.

Page 185 The settlement of 1765 is at Tonbridge Reference Library TU1 T57.
The will of Edward Mercer, pr 19 June 1790, is recited in the Great House Field Abstract U55 T527 – see p.91 comment above.
The Seale family tree is a mixture of sourced facts and conjecture; but in general it can be relied on. The Tonbridge parish registers record the christenings of Philip son of Philip Seal (1689), Elizabeth daughter of Philip and Elizabeth Seal (1691), Mary daughter of Philip Glazier of the Wells (1697), Thomas son of Philip and Mary Seale of the Wells (1702), Thomas son of Thomas and Priscilla Seale at the Wells (1722) and Priscilla daughter of Thomas and Priscilla at the Wells 1725. The existence of a son William, cordwainer of East Greenwich, is attested by Philip's will. The

Kent IGI for Seal(e) records these christenings: Philip, son of Philip, 23 Oct 1689; Elizabeth, daughter of Philip & Elizabeth, 13 Nov 1691; Richard, son of Philip & Elizabeth, 9 Dec 1693; Mary, daughter of Philip, 28 Mar 1697; Sarah, daughter of Philip & Mary, 12 Mar 1699; Ann, daughter of Philip & Mary, 25 Apr 1700; Thomas, son of Philip & Mary, 10 Nov 1702; Thomas, son of Thomas & Priscilla, 4 Sep 1722; Mary, daughter of Thomas & Priscilla, 13 Mar 1723; Priscilla, daughter of Thomas & Priscilla, 5 June 1725. I have no record of the death of Philip's first wife nor of his second marriage which presumably took place in another parish and is not recorded at Tonbridge but I assume, because of the name, that Mary of 1697 was the first child, besides which the Deed of Assignment of 1700 shows that the marriage was by then concluded. That Mary was born Combridge is evidenced by a pedigree which forms part of a bundle of documents in CKS, U2737 Box 13 (see page 184 comment above) which also included a copy of Philip's will. The pedigree is headed 'Philip Seale = Mary Combridge' and records the burials in Tonbridge of daughter-in-law Priscilla (1773) and daughter Mary (1764) and granddaughters Mary (1746) and Priscilla (1775). A trustee of the settlement under the Deed of Assignment of 1700 was surnamed Combridge and I have no doubt he was Mary's father, the Francis Combridge named as brother-in-law and executor in the 1702 will of Richard Constable. The Tonbridge register records the marriage of Mary Seale and William Frey [Fry?] in 1699. For the argument that Mary was Philip Seale's sister see pp.321/22 of chapter 22. Finally the Tonbridge register records the sad successive deaths in September and October 1735 of the two Thomases, father and son; as well as those of Philip himself and his wife shortly before him.

Page 186 Ward Papers – this refers to the documents of John Ward which form the main part of CKS, U2737 deposited by the then Buss, Stone, solicitors, in about 1986. This collection has not yet been catalogued and the closest reference possible is to the number of the box holding assorted documents.
Rev. John Elton – CKS, U2737 Box 13 – see p.183 comment above.

Page 188 Thomas Fry's poem can be found in the *Tunbridge Wells Gazette*, 24 Feb 1860.

Page 189 Mr Fry's School advertisement – MJ, 30 Dec 1806.

Page 190 Edward Mercer will – see p.185 comment above.
Ann Okill legacy – see legatees' receipts in CKS, U2737 Box 13.
Crowborough School – see King Charles Vestry Minutes 7 March 1744, CKS, P371E 8/2 and Farthing (3) Spring 1995.
The list of lodging houses is in the Sprange poster collection at the Museum.

Page 191 The Great House Field Abstract – see p.185 comment above – gives the date of making Jane Baker's will, 30 June 1791 but not the date of probate which is given with an extract from the will in a bundle of documents dealing with the exchange of a field in U2737 Box 13 – see comments on pp.183 and 186 above.
The Southborough Manor Court Books are at CKS, U249 M1 and M2.
Toc H kindly provided an Abstract of Title copy to which a number of references will be made.
Holy Trinity burials are at CKS, P371L 1/17.

Page 194 The picture comes from a postcard but is based on a painting by Sidney Baker, a landscape painter who exhibited 1881-1883 – it was featured in Lady Elizabeth Hope.

Page 195 The deed is at CKS, U746 T186 – but see chapter 21.
Sale of Brunswick House – see chapter 21.

Page 197 Block Plan submitted to the Borough in June 1889 (Tunbridge Wells Borough Council Planning Department archives – Envelope 933).

Page 198 Ordnance Survey map – see p.24 comment above.
William Arnold's death and will – the date of his death and details of his will, pr PCC 29 June 1898, are recited in the Toc H Abstract of Title.
The deeds of 26/28 Little Mount Sion are in owner's possession.

Page 200 The newspaper concerned is the *Kent & Sussex Courier*.
Photograph by H.H. Camburn, 21 Grove Hill Road.

Page 201 For the Manor of Rusthall history see p.2 comment above.
For the Cadena Café meeting see report on the 21st birthday of the Toc H branch in the *Tunbridge Wells Advertiser* of 11 Feb 1944 which coincidentally carries a report on the death on 20 Nov 1943 of Miss Ada Carr of Broadwater Down and her bequest of £100 to the Toc H branch.
Toc H hall – see Cobb, p.36.
1938 and 1947 applications – Tunbridge Wells Borough Council Planning Department archives.

Page 202 Fanny Burney – see Burney, entry for Oct 1779 (pp.38-45 in the Everyman edition).
Partition Plan – see comment on p.16 above.
Land sold to Winefrith Brooke - the quotation is from near the beginning of 'The Joynt and Severall Answers of Thomas Lake Esquire George Weller Gent and Daniel Tilden Gent Defendants to the Bill of Complaint of John Villars Earl of Buckingham Viscount Purbeck Henry Marsh and James Scott complainants' (PRO, C6/100/7).

Page 204 The photograph is in the Museum collection. It appeared in the *Town Guide*, 1955 under the heading 'Old-World part of the Town'; and is reproduced as Plate 150 in RTW.

Page 205 For the dust nuisance see Chapel Vestry Minutes CKS, P371E 8/2. There are entries in 1726 ('Mr Newnhams Bill, being employed to lay the Dust ye backside of the Walks etc £4 14s. 6d.'), 1727 and 1729 ('I Richard Newnham of Speldhurst do hereby covenant and agree to Water the road leading from Isaac Luckhursts to the *Angel Inn* near Mount Sion and from the house of the said Isaac Luckhurst to the *Gloucester Tavern* in such manner that the Dust shall not be troublesome to the Gentry upon Tunbridge Walks the Season for the sum of £10 10s. 0d. As Witness my hand the 5 day of July 1729.') The entries do not continue but I imagine the operation did not cease.
York House – own photograph.
Auction notices – see MJ, 14 June and 27 Dec 1831.

Page 207 Gilbert's cart shed – Tunbridge Wells Borough Council Planning Depertment archives – Envelope 53.

Page 208 The Johnson photographs are at the Museum. 'The Twitten' is Plate 149 in RTW.

Page 209 The deeds of 4 Frog Lane are with the solicitors of the present owner.

Page 210 Ordnance Survey map – see p.24 comment above.

Page 211 Deeds of Frog Cottage are with the owner.

Page 212 Anne Ashdowne – for will see CKS, Dra/PW5, for Probate Inventory CKS, DRb/Pi 28/2.

Page 213 Ward papers – see John Brett Marriage Settlement 8 Nov 1777 in CKS, U2737 Box 2 and the earlier mortgage dated 18 June 1764 in Box 1.

Page 214 Union Hall – for the full design which is in the Museum, see Plate 65 in RTW.
1797 – see Sprange poster collection – at Museum.
Vestry Minutes – see p.190 comment above.
Gen Murray – see Sieveking; and Philipport (copies at the PRO).
Muster Roll – the reference given on my photocopy is PRO, AIR 27/887 115033.
Gen Murray's will is at the PRO, pr 16 July 1816 and 10 0ct 1817.

Page 215 Information on the baronetcy comes from Burke.
The Johnson photograph is at the Museum.

Page 217 The two marriages and information on the grooms are recorded incidentally under the years 1833 and 1838 in the deeds of Caxton House which came into the hands of the Museum recently – the IGI for Kent records the marriage of Charlotte Susanna on 29 Oct 1833.
The Rev. Pope – The following pen-picture, from Pitt-Byrne, vol.IV, p.274, is worth recording: '... an old man, but not so venerable as Mr Benson. He had a round, rubicond face set on a very short neck, giving him a soupçon of resemblance to a pouter pigeon, the rather that he was also stout, and fussy, and important. He was not the ideal of of a country parson, but was popular for all that. He had a smile – perhaps a little too patronising – for everyone, and a pleasant word for us children, who used to meet him about everywhere, find him a standing dish at all small parties, whether our own or those of friends, and to hear of him at all the card parties of the quieter sort, fancy bazaars, flower shows, and assembly-room concerts. Even at the races and at the little theatre when stars came down from London, "the Pope of Tunbridge Wells" was sure to put in an appearance'.

Page 218 The Committee Books are at CKS, P371E 25/1 and 25/2 – see also p.94 comment above.
For Diggens and Cumberland Villa see Richmond Villa deeds – owners' possession.

Page 219 Girls' dinner – *Tunbridge Wells Gazette*, 3 Feb 1860.
Car park – own photograph – about 1970.

Page 220 Schools' sale – see Charity Commission Files 405430 and 405431.
I do not have a record of the date of demolition nor does the Town Hall Planning Department. Patrick Harbour thinks 1967 but is not absolutely sure. I have a Land Registry map photocopy (Title No.K307835) dated 10/68 which shows the whole Murray House site empty.
The photograph is in the Reference Library collection (No.328). The wording above the door says: 'W Crossland Fly Proprietor Little Mount Sion'. The annotation by Johnson is written on the back of the cardboard mount.

Page 221 I have a photocopy of the affidavit. Where an official copy might be deposited

I do not know.

Page 222 My notes on the deeds at CKS read as follows: Conveyance dated 27 Mar 1874 by Rev WL Pope to Walter Sprott and William Nash of the west end of Murray House.
Reciting the conveyance dated 20 Dec 1858 by James White and Thomas Jenks and others to W.L. Pope for £850 of All that messuage ... on the west side of the Bowling Green ... known by the name of Murray House ... and also all that 3 stall stable ... lying in the lane at the back of the Great Bow Window House of Joseph Delves ... together with the coach house thereunto adjoining ... and also all that piece ... of ground about 32 feet in width by a varying depth of about 78 feet formerly described as having formed a yard and the site of a coach house and 2 stables built at the rear or lower part of the same yard ... all which said ... premises .. were then better known as all that messuage ... called Murray House ... late in the occupation of ... ______ Beane ... and whereas the premises were conveyed to WL Pope as a convenience and not to trustees and DJ Robertson died in 1859 and by deed poll or deed of conveyance dated 25 June 1859 the east end of Murray House together with the yard gardens and premises adjoining (edged blue on plan) was conveyed by W.L. Pope to T. Mayo and W Sprott for a school for labouring manufacturing and other poorer classes of Tunbridge Wells only and T. Mayo died in 1871 and W. Nash was appointed in his place and whereas part of the premises conveyed to W.L. Pope in 1858 are still vested in him Now W.L. Pope conveys to W. Sprott and W. Nash the west end of Murray House and the said stable and coach house and premises occupied by ____ Powell in the rear of the said messuage (all which are edged in red).
Sketch of Frog Lane – said to have been copied from an old painting.

Page 224 Winefrith Brooke – see p.17 comment above.

Page 225 I hope one day to prepare a package on the Sion House deeds for CKS but for the moment all the evidence (notes and photocopies) rests with me.

Page 227 For Kip's engraving see p.53 comment above.

Page 229 The details on Margaret Pickering's heiress come from a schedule to the main document in the deeds of Walmer Cottage – in owners' possession but I have a full transcription of this document.

Page 230 Great Fire – see *Tunbridge Wells Gazette* 20 Mar 1857. I am indebted to this report for much of the next two pages.
Mr Corke – the *Gazette* report names Henry Corke, draper and clothier, as the shopkeeper and no doubt he is the same man who was there in 1841 (see p.229), although the Tithe Award names Richard Corke as owner.

Page 231 Mr Dadsford – I think I have read somewhere of a mobile photographic studio and I suppose that this is what Mr Dadsford had but I have never heard of him before. More information would be welcome.
Field the watchmaker was I suppose near the entrance to Chapel Place. It is curious that the Tithe map and Award shows a house here called Sion Cottage – see p.397. Were there then two Sion Cottages within fifty yards of each other or did the name transfer between 1840 and 1857? Edwards the butcher was in Russell Place on the other side of the High Street. I thought his shop faced the London Road because that is where the drain of Webber riot fame was located but maybe the shop faced two ways?

Page 232 The photograph is in the Johnson collection at the Museum.

Page 233 The photograph is in the archives of the Girls' Public Day School Trust at their Wimbledon school.

Page 234 There are a number of documents concerning Eleanor Reed and the Calverley Hotel building in CKS, U2737 Box 15 including a solicitor's A3 diagram showing the tortuous path by which Eleanor Reed became heiress to this estate.
The document is dated 29 Sep 1813 and is a six part indenture between 1) Nicholas Stone, Mayfield, surgeon 2) John Stone, Speldhurst, gentleman 3) Elizabeth Paige, Mayfield, widow 4) Thomas Taylor, Speldhurst, plumber 5) John Habens, Tunbridge Wells, cordwainer and 6) Thomas Delves, Tunbridge Wells, gentleman.

Page 235 Water supply – see Savidge, p.122 – he names Thomas Taylor, plumber, as laying on the supply to the Walks/Mount Sion area in 1814.

Page 236 Report of the Town Commissioners meeting – see *Tunbridge Wells Gazette*, 3 Aug 1860.
The picture is at the Museum, a tinted print, inscribed 'No 1 and 2 Blenheim Place and Fountain Cottage Mount Sion Tunbridge Wells – From nature and lith H Harris – Printed by Graf & Soret – *c*.1830'

Page 237 Evidence that Jeffrey and Riplingham were bakers is in the (lost) Sion House deeds – see Jeffery et ux to Riplingham 7 Mar 1719/20 (No 7 in my notes) where John Jeffery of Tonbridge is named as a baker as is also John Riplingham of Speldhurst.
The document 40 years later is one of the Sion House deeds – 'Mr John Mercer by Direction of Mrs Ann Mercer and Mr Thomas Mercer and at the Nomination of Mr Thomas Wood to Mr Elias Hurrion – Assignment of a Term to Attend the Fee' dated 5 Jan 1758 (No 29 in my notes).

Page 238 Own photograph, taken 1997.

Page 239 This is a photocopy of one of the lost Sion House deeds.

Page 241 1757 Conveyance – another Sion House deeds photocopy.
Southborough Manor Court Book – CKS, U249 M2.
Death of Edward Strange – see Strange (2), the family history (p.152 comment above).

Page 242 Ann Friend's will – see p.69 comment above.
Sale of Crescent Lodge – see deeds of the house in owner's possession.
The photograph is by D.J. Johnson at the Museum.
Thomas Wood will – see p.143 comment above.

Page 243 Sion House in 1998 – own photograph.
The Rev. Johnson – I suppose this is the Rev. William Johnston whom we met at Belgrove House in chapter 14 – perhaps he lived in Thomas Wood's cottage before going to Belgrove House?
Frog Lane in 1998 – own photograph; in 1934 by Johnson at Museum.

Page 244 Thomas Wood's will (CKS, DRb/PW 58) pr 1758 – but I have no specific date of death.
Chimney sweeps – see Strange, K.H.

Page 245 Family facts and tree - see p.152 comment above.

Page 246 Strange Family History – see p.152 and p.308 comments.

Page 247 Death of Thomas Wood III – the only information I have is in the Miles Garage deeds (see p.143 comment above) which say among the opening recitals that he died about July 1807 which surely means that the year 1807 is certain but the month less so.
The dates on the family tree come from scattered sources most of which will, I hope, have been noticed in their places.

Page 249 Johnson's comments are mostly written on the backs of his photographs.

Page 250 This information comes mainly from the deeds of Sion House and Crescent Lodge.
Discovery of well – I was told about this by telephone in March 2003.

Page 251 The Caxton House deeds were praiseworthily brought into the Museum within the last two years by a previous owner who came across them among his possessions and did the right thing. Let this be an example to others!
For a sketch of the brewery in 1824 see RTW, Plate 76.

Page 252 The will of Richard Newnham the elder dated 16 Nov 1747 and proved 16 April 1748 is at CKS, DRb/PW57 – from this I guess 1748 is the year of death.
The indenture at CKS (dated 19 May 1770) is between Newnham and Foley – U746 T182.
There are two sets of deeds: 1. those brought into the Museum and 2. those in the possession of the owner, Mrs Heatley, in 1985 and which are presumably held by the present owners. The first set is the earlier and runs from the marriage of Mary Fry and Samuel Parman in 1778 to the purchase by Henry Edwards in 1860. The second set is smaller and continues the story from 1861 to 1964. From the second set I have two photocopied pages numbered 6 and 7 which appear to be part of the document of sale to Huxtable and which contain the following passage: 'All that piece or parcel of land situate in Tunbridge Wells in the county of Kent having a frontage of 68 feet to Mount Sion there and also a frontage to a Lane there called Frog Lane of 59 feet with a return frontage to a side passage leading from the said Mount Sion to Little Mount Sion. Together with the two messuages or dwellinghouses workshop coachhouses buildings and premises erected thereon or on some part thereof and called or known as 'Caxton House' and 'Montague House' otherwise Nos 19 and 21 Mount Sion Tunbridge Wells aforesaid as the same premises were then in the occupation of the purchaser and were formerly known by the description following (that is to say) 'All that messuage or tenement then and for several years past converted into and used as two dwellings respectively Numbered 1 and 2 and called or known by the name of Montague Place being the site or part of the site on which a messuage or tenement was formerly erected and built by Richard Parman and which was some years afterwards known by the name of Parmans Lower House Together with the outhouses buildings yards gardens and ground thereunto belonging or therewith respectively held used occupied or enjoyed situate lying and being on Mount Sion at or near Tunbridge Wells in the Parish of Tonbridge in the County of Kent abutting to the Queen's highway leading from Tunbridge Wells aforesaid to the Bowling Green on Mount Sion aforesaid towards the south west to other premises late of Richard Delves since of Edward Colsill Edlin towards south east and to the premises next thereinafter described towards the north east and to a certain passage or way running between the said messuage or tenement thereby conveyed and certain messuages or tenement formerly of Elizabeth Wood afterwards of Ann Friend Widow and late of _____ known by the name of Crescent Passage towards the north west And also all that piece or parcel of ground situate next a lane or bye way called Frog Lane with the buildings thereon consisting of two stables

with lofts respectively over the same and a double coach house and which said piece or parcel of ground adjoins to and lays behind the messuage or tenement and other the premises thereinbefore described one of which said dwellings with the coach house and stable in the rear is now in the tenure or occupation of Richard Turner his executors or administrators under an agreement and the other of which said dwellings is in the occupation of __________ and the coach house and stable in the rear thereof were then in the occupation of the said H. Edwards'. Delves and Edlin owned Bricklands and Wood and Friend Sion House and Crescent Lodge, What I cannot explain is the name Richard Parman. I know of no Parman of that first name and anyway I am sure it was Richard Newnham who built the house – as stated in the marriage settlement. I therefore conclude that Parman is a mistake and should read Newnham.
The year of acquisition of Bricklands is derived from the Poor Rate – see p.258.

Page 253 The will of Sam Parman is at PRO, Prob 11/1222 pr 18 Aug 1792.
The will of Richard Delves is at the PRO, pr 2 Aug 1804.
Land Tax Commissioners – I must have noted this reference but regret I cannot now trace it.
Information on the sale to Richard Delves comes from the first (Museum) set of deeds.

Page 254 Elizabeth Montagu (1720-1800) and Stone House – see Savidge, p.76.
Tunbridge Wells Visitor, Sat 5 Oct 1833 announced the auction to be held on 11 Oct.

Page 255 The 1831 plan is in the first set of deeds.
For Richard Turner see p.406 comment below.

Page 256 A.W. Brackett – see Brackett (3).
Mrs Simmonds – for more see p.401.

Page 259 *Tunbridge Wells Visitor* – see Vol.2 p.72.
The Sale Notice of 15 Sep 1859 is in the Reference Library.

Page 260 Lady Repton – see *Tunbridge Wells Gazette*, 1 Jan 1864.
Richard the Spirited – see the Family Tree on p.291.
The Sale Notice of 28 Jan 1874 is in the Reference Library.
William Henry Delves – *Courier*, 3 Apr 1874 records Mr and Mrs W.H. Delves at Forest Prospect.
Royton House – private communication from Messrs Weekes.

Page 262 For the Partition Plan see p.16 comment above.

Page 263 For John Waghorne and the Chapel see Waring p.9.
Will of Richard Constable – CKS, DRb/PW43.

Page 264 For the Chancery Court decree 1752 see Chapter 20, p.284.
For the Brett marriage settlement see p.213 comment above.
The photograph is in the Museum collection.
The will of Joseph Delves senior is at the PRO, pr 15 May 1827 – the original will, before codicils were added, was signed on 6 Apr 1825 which means that either Dr Mayo had not yet moved into Grecian Villa or the will was out of date in this particular.

Page 265 Deeds of Mansfield House in owners' possession.
All the information about the American Chattertons comes from the late Arthur Chatterton, with appreciation.

The mortgage of 1872 and the sales of 1876 and 1896 are recorded in the Mansfield House deeds, as is the Weekes presence later.

Page 266 Lord Mansfield – Barton p.320 – Evans p.145 – Savidge p.89 – MJ, 5 Sep 1786 and 8 July 1788.
For the building of St Mark's Church see *Tunbridge Wells Gazette* 21 Oct 1864 'Laying of Foundation Stone' – architect Robert Roumieu – builders Messrs Mansfield & Sons. The Holy Trinity burial register (CKS, P371L 1/17) records the burial of Elias Walker Durnford 19 Mar 1850 (age 75) but Lydekker whose article contains comprehensive information on all the Sapper Durnfords and on the death of Col A.W. Durnford says he died 8 Oct 1849. See also Mary Durnford who mentions an ancient connection by marriage temp Henry VIII between Durnford and Edgecombe of Mount Edgecombe – is there some Tunbridge Wells story hidden here?
Dr Durnford – *Colbran's Guide*, 1884, p.152.

Page 267 The glass negative is one of the Johnson relics held by Mr and Mrs Ted Mepham known to me.

Page 268 Macaulay – vol.1, p.169.
Sun Insurance register at the Guildhall Library – in the reference which I was given the year cannot be specified more precisely than 'probably 1727/8'.

Page 269 Celia Fiennes – see Fiennes, pp.109-11 and Morris pp.132-5.
Bowling green turf – see Grammont, p.209 (and p.2 comment above).
Macaulay is quoted in Martin and Row, p.11.
For the move to the Pantiles see Savidge, p.63.

Page 270 The quote is from Barton, p.303.
Cumberland House – see Cumberland (Supplement), pp.442-3.
The second Cumberland quotation is to be found, with more, in Melville, p.114.

Page 271 The Pitt Byrne quotation which I found in Melville, p.112 is on p.251 of Vol.IV of the 1899 edition of her 'Gossip of the Century' – see Bibliography. It appears that the author was Julia Carla, daughter of Hans Busk the elder, that she was born in 1819, married William Pitt Byrne in 1842 and died in 1894. She lived as a child at her father's house 'Culverdens' which adjoined Chancellor House on Mount Ephraim, then the property of John Becher. See DNB.
AW Brackett (1) p 26.

Page 272 Ordnance Survey map – see p.139 comment above.
Burlington House Sale particulars – see p.139 comment above.
Melville, p.112 – Barton, p.319.

Page 273 Barton, p.314 records the 'Mamma' story.
Cricket – Openshaw, pp.11-15.
Theatre history – see Hodgson.

Page 274 Savidge, p.85 says son not son-in-law.
Barton, p.311.
Temple of the Muses - MJ, 21 April 1801.

Page 275 Date of Cumberland's death – see Foster, p.178.
1752 – see Chapter 20, p.284.
John Fry's will – see p.56 comment above.

Vestry Minutes – see p.190 comment above.
Mrs Wogan – see *Sprange*, 1786, p.84, 1796, p.84 and 1797, p.107.

Page 276 6 Jan 1860 – *Tunbridge Wells Gazette Residents' List*.
James Deane – the funeral is reported in the *Tunbridge Wells Gazette*, 17 Mar 1865; other events (1833 Local Act Committee, Victoria School foundation stone, dines with Duchess of Kent, loyal address) in the *Tunbridge Wells Visitor*, 1833/34.
Jane Smith – see p.182 comment above.
James Deane will – pr 11 April 1865.

Page 277 Brackett Sale Catalogues are in the Reference Library.
Planning application of 17 Aug 1877 – see Tunbridge Wells Borough Council Planning Depertment archives Envelope 1411.
William Barnsley Hughes – see an article by Vera Coomber in Royal Tunbridge Wells Civic Society Newsletters Spring and Summer 1994.

Pages 279-281 The information on Mrs Murrell, the Mission Hall and the Quakers is derived from the 1884 planning application (Tunbridge Wells Borough Council Planning Department archives Envelope 379); a Brackett Sale Notice at the Reference Library dated 16 Feb 1894; a private communication from Christopher Stacey of the Friends; and an article in the *Courier* of 16 Oct 1987 by Margaret Askew.

Page 282 Davis, Terence, p.27.

Page 283 Thomas Hills and Thomas Tilden – the wills are at CKS, pr 22 June 1717 and 4 July 1704.

Page 284 Chancery documents 1752 – I have in my possession photocopies made at CKS of copies made on 14 May 1825 by two clerks to Messrs William and John Scoones from the originals of 5 and 10/11 August 1752. The copies are in CKS, U2737 Box 2.

Page 285 Ward papers – see p.186 comment above.
The Pembury register at CKS contains the entry Richard Delves and Dorothea Mercer of Tonbridge were married by Licence 16 Oct 1752.

Page 286 Eden House photograph (taken 28 Aug 1968) – source is English Heritage National Monuments Record – Plate 103 in RTW.

Page 287 The Delves family papers are held by Claude Delves of Richmond, grandson of William Henry the Mayor. When I first contacted him after some tracing difficulty he kindly (and rashly perhaps) sent them all to me in the post. I have notes and shall have occasion to refer to them from time to time. For the marriage see comment on previous page.
Butchers' prices – see Burr, p.278.

Page 288 The aerial photograph comes from Aerofilms Limited (now Simmons Aerofilms) – see the whole photograph at RTW, Plate 163.

Page 289 See MJ, 11 Nov 1788 for the melancholy circumstance.
Will of Richard Delves dated 5 Dec 1798, pr PCC 2 Aug 1804.
The Delves family tree has been extensively researched by the late Arthur Chatterton of Indiana, by Jeffery Delves of Suffolk, by the late Richard Delves of Tunbridge Wells, and to a lesser extent by myself. Nearly all genealogical facts stated can be

justified by church register entries. If there is doubt I will try to explain.
The marriage of Thomas Delves and Mary Ann Mills at Shoreditch is recorded in the Delves Family Papers but a chart drawn up by Arthur Chatterton from information supplied by Jeffery Delves gives a precise date – 6 Sep 1799 – and another for the baptism of Sarah at Shoreditch – 29 Dec 1796 – and the next child at Tunbridge Wells – 22 Feb 1800.
The Woodgates of Summerhill (copy at the Tonbridge Reference Library) – see Woodgate.

Page 290 For Southborough Manor see p.191 comment above.
A copy of the Deed of Partition by Fine dated 17 Sep 1804 is in CKS U2737 Box 14.

Page 291 Will of George Weller dated 5 Aug 1785, pr PCC 3 June 1786.

Page 293 The Widows' Flats – see Cobb, p.65.
Print of Marlborough House – I found this in a second-hand shop in the Monson Road some years ago – the lettering on it reads as far as I can tell 'F SEARS & CO' on the left and 'STANLEY Nr L'POOL' on the right. A game of cricket seems to be in progress in the garden, so it probably dates from the house's time as a school.
The Cecil Court deeds are held by the solicitors to Haig Homes in Horsham who have been very helpful, as were the previous solicitors to the Officers' Families Association and of course the principals themselves. I have a photocopy of the lengthy Abstract of Title of Mr Wm Hy Corke to a messuage and premises known as Marlborough House Tunbridge Wells Kent dated 31 Dec 1877.

Page 295 Philip Seale will – see p.183 comment above.

Page 296 Map dated 1828 – see Britton.
The framed map is now stored in the basement. It is inscribed 'Map of Tunbridge Wells in the county of Kent showing the situation of the new Church and the contiguous proposed improvements on the Calverley Estate as designed by Decimus Burton 1828 Engraved by John & Josh Neele 352 Strand'.

Page 297 Knipe – see bibliography.
MJ, 14 Nov 1820 and 23 Oct 1827.

Page 298 Eleanor Reed – see p.234 comment above.
The *Kent & Sussex Courier* published a letter from me on 7 Mar 1986 appealing for information from local people about this precious print – but of course with no result.
Wills – Joseph Delves senior, see p.264 comment above; Richard Delves, p.253 comment above.

Page 301 For the marriage see MJ, 18 Nov 1828 and the birth 24 Nov 1829.
For the creditors' meeting see MJ, 23 Nov 1830.

Page 302 Richard Delves – see MJ, 29 Dec 1835: 'On Monday, the adjourned general meeting of the commissioners was held at the *Clarence Tavern* ... to take into consideration the complaints which had been made by several parties relative to the supposed inequalities of the rate. Mr Richard Delves, on behalf of some of his friends, objected strongly to the rate, inasmuch as it was in his estimation very unfair and unjust ...'
Pelham House 1841 – see census.
The picture is at the Museum and is Plate 84 in RTW.
Steward to Lord Abergavenny – The fact seems to be generally acknowledged but I can put my finger on just one piece of evidence confirming this position – in the Cecil

Court deeds a list of the parties to the conveyance dated 31 Dec 1877 includes 'William Delves of Hargate Lodge Broadwater Down of Tunbridge Wells Sussex Steward'. In the 1861 census his occupation is given as 'Land Agent'.
See will of Henry Delves – at PRO, pr 10 Feb 1869.
Tunbridge Wells Visitor, 28 June 1834.

Page 303 1840 facts – see Tithe map and Award.
Will of Thomas Delves – PRO - pr 26 Dec 1846.

Page 304 Baptisms – see p.289 comment above.
Second marriage of Thomas – the fact that Elizabeth Nye was daughter of James Nye the Tonbridge ware manufacturer is attested by a note connected with the ownership of the Tuttys estate in CKS, U840 T[5]27. The marriage is recorded at Speldhurst by the Rev. William Gordon on 10 Sep 1817 and the subsequent baptisms are a bit puzzling. On 4 Dec 1817 'Henry Fenner Delves son of Thomas and Elizabeth' was christened at the Tunbridge Wells Chapel but on 2 May 1818 Henry Fenner Delves was buried at Frant aged four months. On 7 Mar 1819 twin sons of Thomas and Elizabeth were baptised in Tunbridge Wells and named Henry Fenner and Benjamin. Fenner and Nye were of course partners in the Tunbridge Ware business at about this time. Anyway Thomas and Elizabeth went on to have another seven children together.

Page 305 Will of Joseph Delves son of Thomas – pr PCC 31 Mar 1871.
For the Eden connection see Dickinson.
Incomplete documentation – deeds in possession of the owners of Eden Villa.

Page 306 Sale Particulars 1879 – see copy in Reference Library for 11 July 1879.
1874 was the big sell-off of Delves property – see particulars at Reference Library of sale scheduled for 16 Apr 1874.
Horticultural Shows – see MJ, 6 May 1834 and 28 June 1836.

Page 307 The descent of the Tuttys Estate from 1732 to 1846 is recorded in CKS, U840 T[5]27.
Grecian Villa – I wrote to the Royal Archives Windsor on 23 Apr 1996 but was told on 14 May that they had no information on the change of plan.
Tunbridge Ware quotation – see Pinto, p.42.
Obituary of William Henry Delves – see *Courier*, 7 April 1922.
The visit of the Queen and Prince Albert on 23 June is reported in the SAE 30 June 1849.

Page 308 The Duchess of Kent's visit is reported in the same newspaper from 21 July to 13 Oct 1849 (Grecian Villa 21 July; Eden House 4 Aug; arrival 11 Aug; departure 13 Oct).
'Remembrances' by Mary Agnes Montier who married Edward Hilder Strange in 1855 – see the 'Family of Strange' on p.245 and pp.152 and 246 comments above.
The 1878 and 1879 Sale Notices are at the Tunbridge Wells Reference Library.

Page 309 'Acropolis' – information from the present owners.
Sir Frank Benson – the Reference Library has a *Courier* cutting of May 1966 saying he was born at Eden House in 1858 and a librarian's note adds 14 December. Savidge, p.163, says simply December 1858. The *Tunbridge Wells Gazette* 6 Jan 1860 records Mr and Mrs Benson as visitors at Eden House – no mention of little Frank. For a picture see RTW, plate 132.
Mount Edgecombes – see *Tunbridge Wells Gazette*, 25 Sep 1862.

Page 310 Tunbridge Wells High School – see Chapter 24 for sources.
The demolition photograph is one of a series of slides kindly provided by Devon Twells who took the photographs.
Death of Joseph the surgeon – the Cecil Court Abstract of Title (see p.293 comment above) recites that Joseph died on or about the 10th day of February 1862 without having been married – no details of course why, where or how he died at only 38. The information on Charles and William Percy is also in the Cecil Court deeds.
Trinity Arts – formerly Holy Trinity Church – see tombstone in the grounds.

Page 312 The 'Australian' Family Tree is based on information acquired in the course of the discoveries outlined here.
I have a loaned signed copy of the family history which I have promised to return when an opportunity arises but I have photocopied all the pages. For details see the bibliography. The book contains photographs of *inter alia* 'Yerangle' and Roy Johnston and his father.

Page 313 Photograph of Charles Perry and Miriam Kate Hobson and baby was sent by Lyn who says: ' The original photograph, now with Diana Lindeman, is 2 3/8 inches wide x 3 5/8 inches long and on the back has Royal Photographic Studio, a crest with a Lion and a Unicorn supporting something with a crown on top and under that Mr. Jabez Hughes, Photographer to The Queen and H.R.H.The Prince of Wales Arcade, Ryde, Isle of Wight.' Diana Lindeman is one of the 6 siblings of Lyn's mother about whom Lyn supplies the following additional information: Mary m Dudley Hayes (parents of Dawn Delves Hanley); Claire m Laurie Hurle; Diana Delves m Gordon Lindeman (parents of Pamela Delves Thomson); Patrick m Josephine; John m Joan; Mick (Edward) m Barbara – see the Family Tree on p.312. Note the survival of the Delves name in Australia!

Page 314 Christ's Hospital Horsham – I wrote to the Guildhall Library but a search of the school records from 1854 to 1872 failed to find Charles Perry Hobson (their reply 30 Jan 2002).
The old photographs are with Lyn Bowman in Canberra.
Court Guide – Maidstone, Canterbury, Dover and Tunbridge Wells Directory and Court Guide 1865-66. Edward was brother of the better-known Thomas Sims.

Page 315 Death of Elizabeth Jane – at Tunbridge Wells '22 ult' reported in MJ, 2 June 1835.
Christ's Hospital records are at the Guildhall Library.
Steward – see p.302 comment above.

Page 316 The Notice of Sale (in the Reference Library) cites the Chancery reference Delves v Delves 1872 D.190 and says the sale is pursuant to an order in the above cause, and with the approbation of the Vice Chancellor, Sir Richard Malins. The following, from the description of Marlborough Villa, is worth noting: 'On the south and east sides of the house are Kitchen and Pleasure Gardens, with a Summer-house, two Vineries, and a Potting Shed therein, and adjoining the gardens a valuable Paddock, with a piece of Ornamental Water' – see the plan on p.306.
Names of purchasers – Thomas Guilford – the deeds of Eden Villa (in owners' possession) contain a copy of the conveyance on 29 Dec 1875 to Thomas Guilford of 'All that messe tenement or dwelling house known as Marlborough Villa situate on Mount Sion Tunbridge Wells afsd with the stables outbuildings hothouses vineries gardens paddock or piece of Meadow or pasture land and piece of land covered with water thereto adjoining'.
Alfred Tulk – see Kelly 1882 and Pelton 1886 and 1892; the Trustees of the will of

Alfred Tulk MRCS sold Forest Prospect on 19 Jan 1894 (Brackett Sale Catalogues at the Reference Library) saying that he had been in occupation for some years and had spent considerable sums of money on it.
The Rev. Peile – see *Pelton* and *Kelly* directories 1895/7.
WH Corke from the Cecil Court deeds and directories (see next page).
Corke school – see directories – Kelly 1878 and 1882 (Corke William Henry, classical and commercial school); Pelton 1886 (Corke William H. boys' school, Marlborough House).
Furniture auction – see *Kent & Sussex Courier*, 5 June 1874.
The Bedford Place sale took place actually in 1869 – details in chapter 26.
Aunt Lily's album was kindly lent to me by Claude Delves and I took more or less satisfactory photographic copies.
William Henry – information comes mostly from the *Courier* obituary – see p.307 comment above.

Page 318 Proclamation photograph, Plate 135 in RTW, is in the Reference Library collection.

Page 319 Will of Sarah Langley – dated 19 June 1790 – see *Brackett Sale Catalogues* at the Reference Library – Conditions of Sale 28 Oct 1873 'By Order of the Trustees of the late Mr EW Gilbert'.
The 1852 conveyance by Edward Willett is at CKS, U746 T186.
A stray record in Box 2 of U2737 certifies that Mary Willett widow was buried on 4 Sep 1786.
Statutory Declaration – this forms part of the deeds of Richmond Villa in owners' possession – see chapter 25 for more.
In CKS, U2737 Box 4, is an extract from the will of Edward Willett which confirms some of my suppositions: he leaves all to his wife Mary for life and then to his daughters Mary and Sarah and if they die to his nieces Sarah, Mary and Ann Wood daughters of his sister Mary Wood.

Page 320 The deed of 1787 is referred to in the Schedule of Copies of Deeds relating to the Sale of 'Two Spring Meadow' to John Ward by William Marsdin in CKS, U2737 Box 3.
Sources for residents of Brunswick house: 1817 – *Sprange Guide*; 1827-32 – *Pigot's Directory*; 1840 – Tithe map and Award; 1847 – *Bagshaw's Directory*.
Planning Application dated 29 Jan 1875 – Tunbridge Wells Borough Council Planning Department archives – Envelope 1093.

Page 321 Will of William Fry is at CKS dated 18 Mar 1728 pr 23 May 1729.
Frey/Seale marriage – see Tonbridge register 28 Nov 1699.

Page 322 The mortgage deed dated 13 Mar 1782 is at CKS, U746 T182.

Page 323 List of original leases – see p.3 comment above.

Page 324 Ward papers – U2737 Box 13.
John Fry will – see p.56 comment above.
MJ – 26 June 1786 – Mr and Mrs Cumberland, Miss Cumberland, Mr C. Cumberland and Mr W. Cumberland are all listed amongst 'families already arrived for the season' – 28 Aug 1787 – report of Capt Cumberland's horse racing victory – 12 Mar 1805 – Charles Cumberland removing to town – 23 July 1805 – estate of John Fry deceased.
Charles Cumberland – married 23 Oct 1799 – see Foster p.182.

Page 325 Poor Rate 1831 and 1834 – see page 85 in the Poor Rate chapter (8) for more on Poor Rate entries post 1797 – here are examples where these have proved useful.
Knocklofty, Upper Cumberland Walk – This house was built in the 1930s by SS Weekes and I assume was named Knocklofty in memory of the Weekes family's former association with the Sion Lodge area – see later in the chapter.
Burlington House Sale Particulars – see p.139 comment above.
The Climbing Boys see Strange, KH, also p.244 comment above.

Page 326 For Ann Friend's will – see p.69 comment above.
Fellmongers – see Campbell.

Page 327 Some of my information on fellmongery comes from correspondence with these institutions.
For a chronology of rail progress see N & R p.21 (introduction 6th page) and Marshall, C.F.D.
For the Misses Dawkins see the *Tunbridge Wells Gazette Residents' List*, 6 Jan 1860.
Delves auction – see p.306 comment above.
School Committee minutes – see p.94 comment above.
Cumberland House – see Kelly 1870.
1860 Residents' list – in *Tunbridge Wells Gazette.*

Page 328 Louis Beale – the reference to the drawings is CKS, U1761.
There is also a 'Revised Plan of Madeira Park' in Tunbridge Wells Borough Council Planning Department archives – Envelope 1436.

Page 329 Madeira Park – see *Kelly's Directories* 1895-6, 1896-7 and 1898-9.
For a comprehensive study of the Warwick Park development see Cunningham.
Johnson photograph – in Museum collection.

Page 330 Fellmonger Cottages – own photograph.
1873 Sale and Ann Friend – see pp.325-6 comments above.

Page 332 Edmund Wood – for document references see pp.90-1 comments above.

Page 334 1877 – Planning – see Tunbridge Wells Borough Council Planning Department archives – Envelope 1404.
House numbers – see the Reference Library's Kelly and Pelton Directories for the relevant years.
John Lloyd's death and the contents sale are reported in MJ 22 Aug 1826 and 6 Mar 1827.

Page 335 The Akers letter books and the *Belle Vue Magazine* are at CKS, U1157.
Baptismal register of King Charles the Martyr 1813-1845 – CKS, P371E 1/11.
Some details of the life of Aretas Akers by IC Bradley (with some help from a great-grandson) are to be found in 'Tonbridge School Historical Sketches' 1968 – at Tonbridge Reference Library.
The portrait is in the *Belle Vue* magazine.

Page 336 *Tunbridge Wells Visitor* 12 Oct 1833 (gas lighting) and 9 Aug 1834 (loyal address).
The quotation is from the article by Bradley.
The story is in the *Belle Vue* magazine, Volume 1, pp.313-27, Aug 1840.

Page 338 The picture comes from the *Belle Vue* magazine.

Page 342 Tithe map – the references are CKS, CTR 371 D for Tonbridge Parish and 371 E for Tunbridge Wells at the larger scale.
Railway Deposited Plans – the comment on p.180 above also refers. There are two relevant plans, of 1844 for the Hastings line and of 1852 for the loop line to the old West Station. Each has a Book of Reference listing the descriptions of numbered properties, their owners, lessees and occupiers. Their CKS references are Q/RUm 254 (1844) and Q/RUm 344B (1852). A large part of the 1844 plan is reproduced in RTW Plate 97. I have a photograph of part of the 1852 plan but it has not been reproduced. I have notes on the Books of Reference. There is also at Tonbridge Reference Library a copy of the Act 8 and 9 Victoria Cap clxvii which has a schedule of properties, owners and occupiers.

Page 343 To find the allotment gardens on Plate 97 look between the right-hand end of the tunnel under the Grove and the number 347, just between the marked road which is Knocklofty Lane and the centre line of the projected railway. The gardens are not numbered on the main map but the numbers are shown on a larger scale detail of which the relevant part is missing in the reproduction – see the bottom left corner of Plate 97 marked 'Cripps Nursery'. The allotment garden numbers are 332 (James Denton) on the left to 338 (James Standing) on the right.

Page 344 Apsley Ranger – see CKS, Q/RUm 254.

Page 345 1854 – see Tonbridge School Historical Studies, p.335 comment above.
I had a letter from the great-great-granddaughter of Henry Buttress confirming that he worked for the SER and saying that he died suddenly on 6 Jan 1852 while living at 4 Bedford Terrace – perhaps he moved there because Belle Vue House was to be demolished.
Planning application – see Tunbridge Wells Borough Council Planning Department archives – Envelope 1441.

Page 346 Delves v Cripps – PRO, C33/1173-1382.
Deeds of 65 Claremont Road – in owners' possession.
Sale Particulars 1877 – in Reference Library.

Page 347 Johnson's photograph is in the Museum. The date (19 Sep 1934) is significant because the Eye & Ear Hospital had just moved to the new Kent and Sussex Hospital – see RTW, Plate 151.
Adams, yeoman of Speldhurst – will pr 6 Nov 1728, CKS, DRa/PW7.

Page 348 1702 conveyance – see CKS, U2737 Box 14.
Will of Thomas Scoones senior – pr 27 Nov 1705 – CKS, DRb/PW44.

Page 349 Information on the children is to be found in the Ward Papers, particularly the Family Arrangement of 1726 (see p.350 below); and in the wills of Henry and Mary Scoones who died within a month of each other – pr 5 June and 26 July 1754, CKS, DRb/PW58.
Thomson, Snell and Passmore – There is a strong, if not perfect, case for assuming the link with the solicitors. Thomas Scoones junior is described in the Family Arrangement as a 'salesman' and the same description is used in the will of the father of the first lawyer Scoones, a framed copy of which is proudly displayed in the Reception Room of the firm's Tonbridge offices. The will was proved on 28 Feb 1760 and is to be found at the PRO. There is nothing in it inconsistent with the hypothesis that the testator was

the son of Thomas Scoones of Mount Sion; his wife's name Mary, for instance, fits. On the other hand there is no mention of brothers or sisters or of Mount Sion property, which might have provided an incontrovertible link. There is however a property linkage in the 1799 Marriage Settlement. One of the items is a messuage called Lyons in Tonbridge Town formerly occupied by Henry Scoones, then Richard, then Sarah Jeffery; and Lyons is the present Tonbridge office of the law firm. The deeds of this property held at Lyons however commence only in 1875. For further details (and how the salesman 'cut his son off' with 5s.) see the history of the firm by Blatcher (copy available at the Tonbridge Reference Library). It has since been republished but the earlier version is more informative.
Thomas Wilson – see Wilson, pp.160 and 166.

Page 350 Knight's – there is a Poor Rate sequence Knight/John Knight/Widow Knight from 1689 to the gap at 1714 but its linkage after the gap is very uncertain and there is no clue to its location. However Wilson's 'front of Mount Sion' is probably a mistake for Foot of Mount Sion meaning it was somewhere on the High Street.
The 'Family Arrangement' is an Indenture Quadripartite dated 23 June 1726 in the Ward papers (CKS, U2737 Box 14).
Will of Sarah Scoones – pr 9 Dec 1730 – CKS, Dra/PW7.
The Funeral Sermon is in a bound volume of sermons in Dr Williams's Library, 14, Gordon Square, London.

Page 351 Will of Richard Jeffery junior – pr PCC 14 Feb 1789 – copy in CKS, U642 T10.
Many other details in this family story are to be found in the Ward Papers CKS, U2737 Box 14: in particular the Marriage Settlement dated 15 Jan 1799; the Conveyance dated 2/3 Dec 1805; and copies of burial certificates.
Details about the Rev. Savage and his wife Hannah and the Chancery suits of 1789/90 are at the PRO, C12 1546 43 & 62.

Page 353 Abduction – see Sparrow and contemporary reports in British Library 515 L2 (195).
Case of Clementina Clarke – see British Library 6495 aaa 17.
I do not think that John Jeffery would have taken on the position of 'next friend' if he had not been related; but I have been unable so far to pin-point the relationship.

Page 354 Bankruptcy of John Jeffery and position of the Rev. Stephens as Assignee: see CKS, U2737 Ward Papers Box 14, Bargain and Sale dated 7 Dec 1816, enrolled in Chancery 21 Jan 1817; and other documents.
I do not have a precise date for the wedding.
Some information on Thomas Stephens is in Alumni Oxonienses (1715-1886) as follows: 'Stephens, Thomas, s, William, of Spittal, co Pembroke, gent. Magdalen Hall, matric 14 July 1790 aged 32 BCL, 1807 DCL 1807'. To what extent Stephens was a Welshman and spoke like one is speculation! The age given here (32) does not quite tally with the MJ's report of death in the 79th year in 1832.
Doctor of Law degree – see MJ, 29 Dec 1807.
Great Lodge, Pembury came with the Wilkin inheritance.
Country gentleman – see MJ, 4 Sep 1792 (Game Certificate); 23 Dec 1828 (farm bailiff).
Tonbridge historians – this story first came to my attention in Margaret Blatcher's 'First Four Hundred' – see above p.349; she based it on the court case at which William Scoones was clerk but could not remember (personal communication) her source. It later transpired that it apparently originated with the two Tonbridge historians. The books of King and Neve are at the Tonbridge Reference Library. The story may be read on pp.32-5 of Neve's revised edition 1934 but it evidently originated in King's

earlier work – see the entry dated 1789. Either way the coincidences with the Mount Sion story are remarkable: the year 1789, the time of year (November in Neve, September on Mount Sion), the age of the girl and her heiress status, the post-chaise and, above all, the name of the man she eventually married – the Rev. Dr Stevens. 'This lady was afterwards married to the Revd Dr Stevens' says King but I suggest that he did not check too carefully that it was the same lady!

Page 355 Furniture Sale – see MJ, 11 Jan 1791.
Henry Fry – probably son of John of the *Sussex Tavern* – see p.56.
The conveyance of the house is in the Ward papers CKS, U2737 Box 14 dated 2/3 Dec 1805.
Five Guineas reward – see MJ, 18 May 1802.

Page 356 Fairlawn – see map in *Pelton's Directory*, 1908.

Page 357 The 'pigeon pair' is deduced from later events. The son's date of birth can be deduced from his entry in Alumni Oxonienses: 'Stephens, William Wilkin, s, Thomas, of Tunbridge Wells, Kent, doctor. Exeter Coll. matric 23 Jan 1810 aged 18. BA from St Mary Hall 1822 MA 1823.'
Doctor of Law degree – see p.354 comment above.
Magdalen Hall – private communication from Magdalen College.
Death of Mrs Jeffery – see MJ, 14 Feb 1815 (Mrs Jeffery died 'a few days since … ')
Marriage at Speldhurst – see MJ, 22 Jan 1822 - the absence of any reference to the Rev. Thomas Stephens in Rivington's *Clerical Guide or Ecclesiastical Directory* of 1817 suggests that his clerical performances were rare.
Accident – see MJ, 10 Oct 1826.
Royal Academy exhibition (No 1089) – see MJ, 26 May 1829.

Page 358 For more on Great Lodge/Colebrook Park see (a) Tithe map and Award; (b) Greenwood p 125; and (c) correspondence Tunbridge Wells Reference Library/ Newman (1967) & Smith (1975).
Home farm – I assume that it was the 'Home Farm' that was referred to in the Marriage Settlement of 1799, after the Mansion House, as the 'Farm house near Great Lodge formerly occupied by Thomas Chambers and about 26 acres formerly occupied by Edward Mercer and then Thomas Chambers … '
Southfield Park – see Greenwood, *op. cit.*; and correspondence John Wheeler/late Lord Southborough in Tunbridge Wells Reference Library.
See MJ as follows: 19 Aug 1823 (Race Ball); 11 Jan 1831 (marriage); 4 Oct 1831 (birth); 28 Aug 1832 (death).
Will of Dr Stephens – pr PCC 1 Sep 1832.

Page 359 See the Wheeler/Lord Southborough correspondence (previous page comment) for the W.W. Stephens story.
Will of W.W. Stephens – Somerset House pr 4 Feb 1869 and related documents.

Page 360 The picture of Nancy Storace comes from the front cover of the book by Leonard Chick (see bibliography) published by the former Tradescant Trust in aid of the Museum of Garden History at St Mary at Lambeth, Lambeth Palace Road, where a memorial to Nancy may be seen; but several enquiries have failed to locate the original miniature.
Pringle – see MJ, 6 Aug 1827 & 21 July 1829.

Page 361 Braham – see MJ, 8 July 1828 and a long entry in the *Dictionary of National Biography*.
For hops see MJ, 2 Sep 1828 and for the furniture sale 2 Nov 1830.

Joseph Delves: Frant Burial Register 30 Mar 1827; will pr PCC 15 May 1827.
For the Delves family generally see chapters 20 and 21 *passim*.

Page 362 See MJ, 30 July 1833 (Octavia Boys); 3 May 1836 (Johnstone arrival); 13 Sep 1836 (Johnstone birth).
Queen's visit – see comment on p.307 above.
'Jack Woods' was the name of the first Tunbridge Wells Railway Staton before the tunnel to the Central Station was built. It later became the Goods Station. For more on 'Jack Woods' see pp.41 and 290 – also N & R caption 98.
See *Tunbridge Wells Gazette*: 1 Jan 1860 (Fletcher); 27 July 1860 (Furniture Sale).
Seeley – see 1861 census.

Page 363 Misses Gibbons – see *Tunbridge Wells Gazette* 6 Jan 1882.
Hodges' Yard – when the yard was offered for sale by the executors of John Hodges on 16 May 1884, purchasers were promised an Abstract of Title commencing with Indentures of Lease and Release dated 29/30 Sep 1830 made between Harriet Beale, Robert Foreman and William Hodges (see the Sale Notice in the Tunbridge Wells Reference Library and Illustration B). This fits neatly with Large's departure from Fairlawn House and surely pin-points the start of Hodges' interest; but the vendor was not Joseph or any other Delves but two successive owners of Jerningham House. I can only guess that the 'yard' had been added to the adjoining Jerningham House property at some earlier date; but I am sure that William Large continued to be the occupier until 1830.
The Bay Ponies advertisement was in the MJ of 7 April 1835.

Page 364 William Hodges will – pr PCC 24 Feb 1855.
Auctioneer's comments – see Sale Notice.
John Hodges will – pr London 26 May 1870; his death from pneumonia, private communication from a descendant.
JF Bates – see Chapter 18, p.256.
Workshop – a foundation stone on a wall was laid by J.T. Clarke AMIME on 4 July 1920.
Stidolph, Land Surveyor – see *Tunbridge Wells Visitor*, 1834, p.173.
Waterworks – 'A Map of Tunbridge Wells showing the line of the Water Works belonging to the Rt Hon the Earl of Abergavenny' by T. Stidolph Surveyor etc Cumberland Terrace Tunbridge Wells 1838 is in the Abergavenny Archives at the East Sussex Record Office, Lewes.

Page 365 Girls' High School – the main source of information is the half-centenary issue (1883-1933) of the school magazine, *The Record*, of which there is a copy in the Tunbridge Wells Reference Library together with some copies of annual magazines. One of these reports the decision to close the school.
Purchase or Lease? An old ledger in the Girls' Public Day School Trust archives at their Wimbledon School suggests just a lease e.g. – 1882 Dec 13 To one years rent to Dec 25 per FW Stone £38
1899 June 14 To lessors solicitors charges …
1900 April 4 Dilapidations per Stone Simpson & Ss £342 …
William Delves, died 6 Aug, buried at Frant 10 Aug, will pr (Somerset House) 13 Sep 1886.
William Henry Delves, will pr London 12 May 1922; information on Lilian Jane comes mainly from family sources.

Page 366 Iron Room – application dated 13 Aug 1887 and plan are in Tunbridge Wells Borough Council Planning Department archives – Envelope 719; other details from 'The Record'.

Page 367 Eye and Ear Hospital: previous history, see Savidge, p.156 and Kent and Sussex Hospital (Sixty Years of Service). The plan in the centre of Butler, Farthing and Hetherington (The Pantiles Guide) shows the precise location in 1896.

Page 368 Proposed new wing – see *Courier*, 27 April 1900.
Deeds – private correspondence with the three firms.
1917 and 1921: see *Kelly's Directory* for these years.
Miss Swindale – see Cobb pp.116-8 in paperback edition.

Page 369 Miss Moberley (daughter of a master at Rugby School) left to become head of the Girls' Public Day School Company's school at Newcastle-on-Tyne. Miss Julian became Principal of the Avery Hill Training College in 1908 – see issues of *The Record* in the Reference Library.
Transfer of patients etc.: see Kent and Sussex Hospital, *op. cit.*
Details of office uses are taken from the relevant *Kelly's Directories*.

Page 370 Lower Walk – see Bowra's plan of the Pantiles and Butler, Farthing and Hetherington.
Cumberland Walk – the Tithe map clearly shows Abergavenny land on the Kent side of the brook.
List of leases (in CKS, U38 T1) – see p.3 comment above and elsewhere.
The deeds of Richmond Villa (in owners' possession) contain the will of Ann Luck (dated 28 Apr 1767, pr PCC 24 Jan 1769) and an Abstract of Title of 1880 which includes earlier information.

Page 371 The 'new house' – this is a matter of interpreting the Poor Rate entries with help from the reference in Ann Luck's will (p.370).

Page 372 Memorial to Ann and John Luck – own photograph 1998.
Sale to William Beale – Richmond Villa deeds.

Page 373 Jerningham House – own photograph 1998.
The Jerningham story – general information comes from Castle (The Jerningham Letters); but in particular I was kindly supplied with photocopies of all 26 letters written from Tunbridge Wells by the University of Birmingham which holds all the material. A couple of these letters were printed by Melville (pp.227 and 229) but I was able to reveal others for the first time in connection with Tunbridge Wells history in a lecture to the Tunbridge Wells Civic Society on 10 Sep 1998 and in a three-part article in the Civic Society Newsletters of Spring and Autumn 1999 and Spring 2000.

Page 375 The illustration is scanned from one of the Birmingham photocopies – just to give an impression of the look of the originals.

Page 376 Mrs Eden – for a possible connection with Eden House see p.305.

Page 377 The drawing is my very rough drawing of the sketch made, presumably by a solicitor, in the margin of one of the documents in the Richmond Villa deeds – a conveyance dated 9/10 Feb 1826 of 'Mrs Beale's Plat' to Stephen Sawyer.

Page 378 Howard Lodge – own photograph 1998.

Page 379 Marine House and Cottage – own photograph 1998.
Marine House as vicarage – see Waring, p.46.

Page 380 The *Tunbridge Wells Visitor* may be seen at the Tunbridge Wells Reference Library.

Page 381 Gillray cartoon – source is 'The Stanhopes of Chevening' by Aubrey Newman Macmillan, 1967 (Copyright British Museum).
Major Stanhope Taylor – see Savidge, p.127.
There is a memorial to Stanhope in Rusthall churchyard – No.583 – with a column in memory of Ensign Stanhope Taylor killed at Jhansi, Central India, by the mutineers of his regiment, the 12th. Bengal Native Infantry, on 5 June 1857, aged 20 years.

Page 382 Conveyances in 1856 and 1857 – information comes from the Schedule to the 1934 conveyance – see next page comment.
'A Suspicion Cleared Up' – see *Tunbridge Wells Gazette*, 10 June 1864.

Page 383 Mrs Read's school – see *Kent and Sussex Courier*. Payne-Jenkins closed his studio in 1972.
Changes in owners/occupiers – information on the sale to Miss Mottram in 1934 comes from the deeds of Jerningham House (in owners' possession); other facts from *Pelton* and *Kelly Directories*.
For a report on the rubbish pit by the budding archaeologist Anthony Streeten see Tunbridge Wells Museum and Art Gallery reference 74/22 (1). Interestingly some bottle fragments were stained by deposits of iron, suggesting they may have contained the Chalybeate water.

Page 384 For more on John Wybourne see chapter 3, p.23 in particular. I have found no direct proof of his claim on the Chapel Place block but there is no doubt he was there. Mr John Wybarne (note the spelling) appears in the Poor Rate record (without any location specified of course) from 1670 through to 1689 and then in 1690 comes the entry 'Mr Brett for John Wibarnes'.
For the construction of the *Angel Inn* see chapter 3, p.28, *et seq*.

Page 385 Deaths of Robert and Margaret Pickering – see chapter 5, p.45.

Page 386 Thomas Turner – see Jennings, Appendix, p.80.
The tiny print of 'Bedford Place', undated, is in the Museum.
The season – see MJ, 31 July 1787.
Bedford Place – a remote possibility is that Bedford Place was the name used at the time for what we now call Chapel Place, in which case the building might have been called Sion House at the same time, throwing the dating of the print into doubt; but I know of no evidence that Chapel Place was ever called anything else and the building was certainly called Bedford Place subsequently.

Page 387 Cabinetmaker – Fry's Cabinet Warehouse is shown on the Barrow map at this location and the legend at Foot of Mount Sion says: '2 – Mr J Fry – Manufacturer etc'.
Henry Delves will – proved PCC 10 Feb 1869.
1897 Sale Plan – in Reference Library.

Page 388 Lease and option – see will of Henry Delves (previous page comment).
Mortgages etc – the details are in the deeds of 10 Bedford Terrace in owner's possession.
Chapel Place photograph – from an original in Hall's Bookshop – my thanks to Sabrina

Izzard.
Dr Trustram – obituaries in *Medical Times and Gazette*, 6 July 1872 and *The Lancet*, 20 July 1872; information from the Royal College of Surgeons of England and the *Tunbridge Wells Journal* where his death is reported on 27 June 1872 and the funeral on 4 July with a short obituary. On 18 July it is reported that his practice has been purchased by Dr James Bisshopp from London and furthermore that GH Lawrence of the Mount Sion School of Photography has a 'faithful' carte de visite portrait of Dr Trustram – where oh where is it now?! The photographic premises were of course just on the other side of the road from the doctor's residence.

Page 389 Dr Manser – 1874 see *Kent & Sussex Courier*, 3 Apr 1874; also the 1881 census.
Trustee of will – see, p.304 comment above for will of Thomas Delves.
The photograph by Johnson is in the Museum collection.

Page 390 The original photograph was taken by a local resident and copied by me. A lot of this gossip is within living memory and hardly calls for specific sourcing. For a long time the side wall of the fancy gabled building was adorned with the sign 'To the Baths' and local residents remember having seen them or the remains of them but I am still unsure what sort of baths they were: medicinal or just for cleaning the body. A resident of the Sherwood Estate told me the story of the tailor who shot himself upstairs while his boss was downstairs, and someone else had a story of a throat cut in the basement, whether murder or suicide I am not sure. Don Roberts was certainly not a myth as the present Little Mount Sion barber worked for Don and Don worked on my wife's hair. The other names are to be found in *Kelly's Directories* including the School of Dancing which I can vouch for personally.
Royal Tunbridge Wells Civic Society report for the year 1972-73 – see Reference Library archives.

Page 391 The report by Dr Anthony Streeten, with drawings and photographs, is in the Museum.

Page 392 Photograph – as for page 390 above.

Page 393 Apologies if all the little numbers are confusing – the full key, legend or reference can be found on Plate 64 of RTW.

Page 395 Industrial School – the *Tunbridge Wells Gazette*, 5 Oct 1860 carried an advertisement for the sale of all the equipment of the 'Girls' Industrial School Little Grove House' including 26 beds.
Veterinary surgeons – see Directories.
1764 and 1777 – see page 213 comment above.

Page 396 *Tunbridge Wells Visitor* – 9 Nov 1833.
Walter Sprott and the Rev. Pope – for the story see Waring, pp.42-3.
Rehoboth Chapel – this building proclaims its date of erection on its façade.
Strange, C.H., p.9 also refers (see p.172 comment above).
George Stevens, *Directory of Tunbridge Wells*, Tonbridge and neighbourhood, 1886.
Sussex View, – Cobb, p.28, *et seq*.

Page 397 John Holyer – could he be of the same Holyer family who were butchers at no 9 the Pantiles in the 19th century? – see Butler, Farthing and Hetherington p.17.
Quintin Hair – see for example *Tunbridge Wells Gazette*, 2 Nov 1860 ('Mr Quintin Hair

The Established Dentist at Tunbridge Wells during the last 24 years Patronised by HRH the Duchess of Kent etc etc').
Angel Inn – see Chapter 3 pp 28 *et seq.*

Page 398 Riplingham was a co-commissioner with John Brett in the 1708 Chancery case. The print is in the Museum collection – 'Tunbridge Wells Published 1 May 1804 by Richard Phillips 72 St Paul's Church Yard'. Draughtsman and engraver indecipherable.

Page 399 E.H. Strange death – the following notice appeared in the MJ on 17 June 1823: 'Jane Strange respectfully returns thanks to the Nobility and Gentry, Visitants of Tunbridge Wells, and to her Friends in general, for the favours conferred on her late Husband; and begs to state, that it is her intention to continue the Business of the HOTEL and POSTING as heretofore; trusting, that by assiduity and attention, she shall be found deserving of their patronage and support.'
Angel – Savidge, p.105.
1826 print – see next page comment.
Landlords – private communication from Keith Hetherington.
Hetherington – *Old Pubs* – p.32.

Page 400 1826 print – there is a brilliant colour copy of this print in the BL Print Room and a copy hangs in the Museum corridor inscribed: 'View of Tunbridge Wells Baths Chapel – Dedicated by permission to the Duchess of Kent by Her Royal Highness's obedient and very humble Servant H. Jones – Published Septr 1st 1826 Tunbridge Wells – Printed by W. Day 59 Gt Queen St'.

Page 401 The photograph comes from the Museum collection but nothing is known about it. It is reproduced as Plate 129 in RTW.
Greengrocer's – there is an annotated photograph of the greengrocer's shop in the Reference Library's extra-illustrated edition of *Pelton's Guide* 1893 (facing page 98).
Shops – I am indebted to Sabrina Izzard of Hall's Bookshop for information on the dates and locations of Simmonds and Hall's.
Frank Simmonds, aged eight, and three younger brothers along with father Thomas (37) and mother Sarah (40) are enumerated at the Draper's in Chapel Place in 1861.

Page 402 Waring – p.17.
Cripps Harries Hall have since moved from their old office in Calverley Road to Mount Pleasant Road but I assume they took the two tin trunks with them.

Pages 404 *et seq.* Details concerning Dr Webber and the Webber Riots come almost entirely from relevant issues of the *Tunbridge Wells Gazette* which will be noticed in their places below. There may be other sources for the riots but I have not looked. In particular I regret not having investigated the Town Hall archives which may well contain information on this and other subjects.

Page 404 Webber – see his entry in Plarr's 'Lives of the Fellows of the Royal College of Surgeons'. Born in 1800, he qualified in 1822 and practised first in Norwich (hence the birthplaces in Norfolk, Suffolk, Yarmouth etc recorded in the 1861 census against his wife, daughters and two servants) and moved to London in the 1850s. 'Webber was continually in the midst of controversy always a "man with a grievance".' His publications include *An Essay on the Cattle Murrain and Pole Axe Murders* (London 1865) and *Vaccination as it was and as it is* (London 1871).
Princess Victoria – the sketch, by an unknown artist, is held by the Royal Archives, Windsor. It is reproduced in RTW as Plate 85 but in the caption I have made a silly mistake. The sketch is dated 24 August 1834 as can be seen but the comment on the

Rev. Pope's sermon refers to Sunday 23 August 1835 as is shown by the Queen's journal (see Victoria, Queen, p.128).

Page 405 Hon & Lady Knox – *Tunbridge Wells Gazette Residents' List*, 6 Jan 1860. Sir Charles Grey – 1861 census & *Tunbridge Wells Gazette Residents' List*, 16 May 1862.
Eden House – *Tunbridge Wells Gazette Arrivals and Departures*: 17 July 1862 Lady DalKeith; 24 July Marchioness of Abercorn; 27 September Mount Edgecombes.
Benson – there is a photograph of Frank Benson in costume at Plate 132 in RTW. Mr and Mrs W. Benson are recorded at Eden House in the *Tunbridge Wells Gazette*, 6 Jan 1860 – see N & R, caption 132.

Page 406 Four Ladies' Schools – for Mrs Read see p.383 and for all four the 1861 census.
Mansfield House School – see *Tunbridge Wells Gazette*, 27 July 1860 and p 265.
Girls' Industrial School – see *Tunbridge Wells Gazette*, 6 July and 5 Oct 1860 and p.394.
Richard Turner, surgeon – obituary in *Tunbridge Wells Gazette*, 26 Oct 1860 – see also p.255 and, for Howard Lodge, p.382.
Robert Gream – see census 1861 and *Residents' List Tunbridge Wells Gazette*, 6 Jan 1860.
Mrs Gilbert – see *Tunbridge Wells Gazette*, 6 Jan 1860.
New Commissioners Meeting – see *Tunbridge Wells Gazette*, 5 Oct 1860.

Page 407 William Delves Steward – see p.302 comment above.
Mr Haines – see *Tunbridge Wells Gazette*, 30 March 1860.
The Delves brothers, Simmonds and Kinlan are to be found in the 1861 census while Kinlan and William Fox (Chapel Place – established 1828) advertise in the *Tunbridge Wells Gazette* on 6 Jan and 24 March 1865 respectively. Kinlan's loss is reported as part of the cross-summons Kinlan v Webber in the *Tunbridge Wells Gazette*, 29 July 1864.
Quintin Hair – see p.397 comment above.
Crime figures – see *Tunbridge Wells Gazette*, 12 Oct 1860.

Page 408 Webber is reported as a resident on 8 June 1860, but not on 1 June in the *Tunbridge Wells Gazette*.
Webber was born in 1800 according to his entry in Plarr's *Lives of the Fellows of of the Royal College of Surgeons of England*.
3 Sion Terrace – see *Tunbridge Wells Gazette*, 27 July 1860.
Tunbridge Wells School of Photography Mount Sion proprietor G.H. Lawrence is advertised in the *Tunbridge Wells Gazette*, 17 June 1864 and see p.232 'First studio occupied by Lawrence 1860'. See also report 19 Aug 1864 of bankruptcy proceedings involving Lawrence who had 'rented the roofs of his own and another house for photographic purposes'.
Webber's visit to Buxton and details of the libel case are reported in the *Tunbridge Wells Gazette*, 14 Feb 1862. His letter to the *Gazette* is in the 16 May issue.

Page 409 Royal Marriage – the later editorial was that of the *Gazette*, 22 July 1864.
Kentish Royal Hotel Company – *Tunbridge Wells Gazette*, 29 Jan 1864.
Local director – *Tunbridge Wells Gazette*, 12 Feb 1864.
Tunbridge Wells Hotel Company – *Tunbridge Wells Gazette*, 4 March 1864.

Page 410 Local Government Act meeting – *Tunbridge Wells Gazette*, 4 March 1864.
Joseph Delves – the Residents' List of 1 April shows Joseph now at Heath Villa.

Letter from Webber – Tunbridge Wells Gazette, 29 April 1864.

Page 411 Cartoon – the caption to Plate 109 RTW tells all that is known: 'This uncaptioned cartoon, from the papers of the late Mr Pratley of Hall's Bookshop, shows the hotel entrance, a notice 'Site for New Hotel', Dr Webber in a donkey cart and (shouldering tools) possibly the Town Surveyor'. The identification with Dr Webber is mine alone but there can be no doubt. No one has challenged it since publication anyway.
The Hotel that 'Web' Built – *Tunbridge Wells Gazette*, 17 June 1864.

Page 412 I hope I am right in my interpretation of 'Erin-go-brach'.
Kinlan and Branigan – see census 1861.
The drain – all these details come from a leading article in the *Tunbridge Wells Gazette* of 1 July 1864 entitled 'Mr Webber's Charge against the Town Commission'. It has to be said that the *Gazette*'s reporting reflected the prevalent anti-Webber feeling in the town and my account, based solely on the *Gazette*, might be unfair to the doctor – but I do not think so. Webber certainly thought there was a 'Crusade' against him – see his letter to the 'indignation' meeting (p.423).

Page 413 *et seq.* The *Tunbridge Wells Gazette* appeared weekly on a Friday. All issues in July 1864 from the 1st to the 29th and those of 5th and 12th August carry contributions to the unfolding story: reports of Court and Town Hall proceedings, letters and editorials.

Page 414 The 1861 census shows three daughters Eliza (25), Emily (17) and Ellen (15) as well as Henry (11). The occupants of the house on the night of the riot were detailed by the prosecuting barrister at the trial of the 'Tunbridge Wells Four' reported in the *Gazette* on 29 July.

Page 415 Sion Terrace 1997 – own photograph.

Page 417 *Camden Hotel* and old Town Hall – the photograph is in the Museum collection. It is reproduced as Plate 161 in RTW. I know of no other image of this hotel which was the scene of the celebratory dinner of 1864. The shored-up building to the right was the Town Hall and I suppose contained the courtroom since the *Camden Hotel* was described as 'nearby'.
Wells v Webber – if anyone has a copy of this publication I should be grateful for a sight.

Page 418 Seven-barrelled – I merely repeat the words of the *Gazette* article. A revolver normally has six chambers – I suppose this is what is meant by 'barrels' but seven seems an odd number to design. However *Encyclopaedia Britannica* says: 'in early revolvers, sheaves or bundles of tubes serving as barrels were revolved by hand to allow more than one shot without reloading'. Perhaps this accounts for Webber's seven-barrelled revolver.
It is a pity that not more of the cartoons have survived which must have been circulating at the time. If anyone knows of one, or suspects that one he knows may be connected, please get in touch.

Page 419 The photograph comes from English Heritage National Monuments Record and is reproduced in RTW at Plate 110. See N&R Caption 111 (a mistake for 110!) for more. A copy in the Reference Library is dated *c.*1880. The landlord's name 'late Stuckey' (see p.399) however puts the date at (shortly?) after 1870. The reason for the coach when rail travel must have been quicker and more comfortable seems to be that it was a touch of old times for tourists in the summer!

Page 421 Great Fire in Tunbridge Wells – reported at length in the *Tunbridge Wells Gazette*, 26 Aug 1864.

Page 422 Public Meeting for the relief of Sufferers – see *Tunbridge Wells Gazette*, 2 Sep 1864.
Riot Prosecution Fund – see *Tunbridge Wells Gazette*, 9 Sep 1864 for the Commissioners' Meeting and 30 Sep and 7 Oct for the Mansfield correspondence.

Page 423 For Dr Hunter's report see *Tunbridge Wells Gazette*, 7 Oct 1864.
New drain – the *Sussex Agricultural Express*, 17 Mar 1838 reports the acceptance of a tender for building a main drain – see N&R Sixth Page comments. Dr Trustram said in the course of the discussion on the report that the new drain was put down in 1835.
For the 'indignation meeting' see *Tunbridge Wells Gazette*, 21 Oct 1864.

Page 424 Farce in Seven Acts – see *Tunbridge Wells Gazette*, 28 Oct 1864.
Mansfield v Webber – *Tunbridge Wells Gazette*, 18 Nov 1864.
Nisi Prius Court Maidstone – see *Tunbridge Wells Journal*, 22 Mar 1866.
Court of Bankruptcy 11 Oct – see *Tunbridge Wells Journal*, 18 Oct 1866.

Page 425 Order for release – see *Tunbridge Wells Journal*, 15 Nov 1866.
Court of Common Pleas – see *Tunbridge Wells Gazette*, 31 May 1867.
Dr Webber's death in 1875 is attested by his entry in Plarr's *Lives of the Fellows of the Royal College of Surgeons of England.*
Details of the doctor's family come from private communications with descendants in New Zealand and from a New Zealand lady who is writing a book about Eliza Jane, Dr Webber's eldest daughter, the wife of Bishop Cowie. Webber's wife was born Eliza Preston, daughter of baronet Sir [Thomas?] Preston of Beeston Park, Norfolk and her will refers to a marriage settlement dated 9 Dec 1834 which was no doubt the source of her invaluable private income. Her will, made on 18 Dec 1876 and describing her as a widow of Brighton, is the evidence for Dr Webber's move to Brighton. The journal of Bishop Cowie however tells of a visit by Eliza Jane to her father's house in Isleworth, London to pack on 1 Sep 1869. Dr Webber's eldest son William (future Bishop of Brisbane) was at this time working as a vicar at Red Lion Square in central London and his house may also have served as a family base.

Page 426 Trustees and Roads – see p.50 for this story.

Bibliography

ALMACK, Richard ed., *Papers relating to proceedings in the County of Kent AD 1642–1646.*

AMSINCK, Paul, *Tunbridge Wells and its neighbourhood*, Miller and Lloyd, 1810.

ARCHER, John, *A sermon preached at the opening of the New Chappel at Tunbridge Wells*, August 1st, 1720, Richard Ford, 1720.

ASHWORTH, Phyllis G., *Johnston Family Tree*, first published in Australia, 1980, ISBN 0 9594818 0 X.

AUSTEN, Brian, *Tunbridge Ware and Related European Decorative Woodwares*, W. Foulsham & Co. Ltd, 1989.

AVELING, J.H., MD, FSA, *The Chamberlens and the Midwifery Forceps*, London, 1882.

BAILEY, Lorna, 'A history of non-conformity in Tunbridge Wells, Tonbridge and Southborough', Typescript, *c.*1970.

BANNER, Rev J., *Christ Church History – Parish of Holy Trinity with Christ Church – A Modern Miracle*, 1997.

BARTON, Margaret, *Tunbridge Wells*, Faber, 1937.

BEAVIS, I.C., See ROWLANDS and BEAVIS.

BELLAMY, George Anne, *An apology for the life of George Anne Bellamy late of Covent Garden Theatre*, 4th edition, London, 1786.

BLATCHER, Margaret, *1570-1970. The First Four Hundred. A History of the Firm of Thomson, Snell & Passmore*, Private publication, 1970.

BOASE, Frederic, *Modern English Biography*, Frank Cass & Co Ltd, 1965.

BRACKETT, Arthur W. (1) *Tunbridge Wells through the Centuries*, not dated.

— (2) *Spa Hotel and Tunbridge Wells through the Centuries*, not dated.

— (3) *Centenary and Three generations, with a short history of Tunbridge Wells*, Brackett & Co, 1928.

BRETHERTON, F.F., 'John Wesley's Visits to Tunbridge Wells' in Proceedings of the *Wesley Historical Society*, Vol.X, December 1916.

BRITTON, John, *Descriptive Sketches of Tunbridge Wells*, London, 1832.

BURKE, John, *Dictionary of the Peerage and Baronetage of the British Empire*, London, 1842.

BURNEY, Fanny, *Diary and Letters of Madame D'Arblay (1778-1847)* as edited by her niece with preface and notes by Austin Dobson MacMillan, 1904.

BURR, Thomas Benge, *The history of Tunbridge Wells*, 1766.

BUTLER, Geoff, FARTHING, Roger and HETHERINGTON, Keith, *The Pantiles – A Guide*, Private publication, 1999.

BYRNE, *Mrs Pitt Gossip of the Century*, in four volumes, London, Downey & Co. Limited, Covent Garden, 1899.

CAMPBELL, R., *The London Tradesman*, 1747.

CARLEY, James, *The Turnpike Roads of Kent*, Kent County Library, not dated.

CASTLE, Egerton ed., *The Jerningham Letters (1780-1843)* being excerpts from the correspondence and diaries of the Honourable Lady Jerningham and of her daughter Lady Bedingfeld – edited with notes by Egerton Castle MA FSA with Portraits in two volumes, London, Richard Bentley and Son, 1869.

CHALKLIN, C.W. (1) 'The Rise of an English Town, Tunbridge Wells, 1680-1840', unpublished article.

—(2) 'A Kentish Wealden Parish [Tonbridge], 1550-1750', Oxford B.Litt. thesis, 1960, (typescript at Tonbridge Reference Library and at CKS).

—(3) 'Estate Development and the Beginnings of Modern Tunbridge Wells 1800-40' in *Archaeologia Cantiana*, Vol.C, 1984.

CHAPMAN, Frank, *David Peacock's Tunbridge Wells Sketchbook*, Perspective Press, Tonbridge, 1978.

CHICK, Leonard H., *Nancy Storace – Mozart's First Susanna*, The Tradescant Trust, London, 1987 (in aid of the Museum of Garden History at St Mary at Lambeth, Lambeth Palace Road).

CLIFFORD, John (1) *The Tunbridge Wells Guide*. Various editions from 1817-43.

—(2) *Visitor's Guide to Tunbridge Wells and its Environs*, 1817-1843.

COBB, Richard, *Still Life*, Hogarth Press, London, 1983.

COLBRAN, John, *Colbran's New Guide/New Guide abridged/Handbook and Directory*, Tunbridge Wells ed James Phippen, in various editions, 1839-1871.

COLBRAN, St John, *St John Colbran's guide and visitor's handbook to Tunbridge Wells and neighbourhood*, 1880, 1881, 1884.

COOMBER, Vera, 'William Barnsley Hughes' in *Royal Tunbridge Wells Civic Society Newsletter*, Spring and Summer, 1994.

COPUS, Geoffrey, *A Miscellany* (including 'The Calverley Stone Quarry'), private publication, 1987.

COPUS, Geoffrey and Brenda, *Royal Tunbridge Wells Civic Society Walks – No 5 – Boyne Park*, 1976 and *No.8, The South-east*, 1988.

CUMBERLAND, Richard, *Memoirs of Richard Cumberland* written by himself, 1806, with a Supplement and Index, 1807, London Lackington, Allen & Co., Temple of the Muses, Finsbury Square.

CUNNINGHAM, John, 'The Origins of Warwick Park', typescript, 1999.

DALE, Andrew, *Most Honourable Remembrance: The Life and Work of Thomas Bayes*, Springer-Verlag, New York, 2003.

DASHWOOD, Francis, *The Dashwoods of West Wycombe*, London, Aurum, 1987.

DAVIS, Terence, *Tunbridge Wells: The Gentle Aspect*, Phillimore, 1976.

DICKINSON, Violet, ed., *Miss Eden's Letters edited by her Great-niece*, London, 1919.

DURNFORD, Mary, *Family Recollections of Lt Gen Elias Walker Durnford*, 1863.

ELERS, F. Wadham, *The Tunbridge Wells General Hospital: a diary from its foundation in 1828 to the present time*, Pelton, 1910.

ELWIG, Henry, *A Biographical Dictionary of Notable People at Tunbridge Wells*, 17th-20th centuries. Also a list of local place-names, 1941.

EUROPEAN MAGAZINE AND LONDON REVIEW, 'Memoir of Mr. William Dowton', Feb 1813.

EVANS, John, LL.D., *An excursion to Brighton, with … a visit to Tunbridge Wells*, 2nd edition, Chiswick, 1823.

FARTHING, Roger, (1)—*Royal Tunbridge Wells – A Pictorial History*, Phillimore, 1990. Notes and References are available in typescript at Tunbridge Wells Reference Library and CKS and on Kent Family History Society Microfiche no.1754.

—(2) 'History of the Manor of Rusthall' – in ROWLANDS ed.

—(3) *Royal Tunbridge Wells Civic Society Newsletters*, Spring 1993, Spring and Autumn 1994, Spring 1995, Spring and Autumn 1999 and Spring 2000.

—(4) See also BUTLER.

FIENNES, Celia, *Through England on a Side Saddle in the Time of William and Mary being the Diary of Celia Fiennes with an Introduction By the Hon Mrs Griffiths*, London, 1888. See also MORRIS.

FOSTER, Joseph, *Our Noble and Gentle Families of Royal Descent*, Hatchards, Piccadilly, 1885.

FULLER, John, *The Church of King Charles the Martyr, Tunbridge Wells – A New History*, The Friends of the Parish Church, Tunbridge Wells, 2000.

GIRLS' HIGH SCHOOL, Girls' Public Day School Trust – *Tunbridge Wells High School Jubilee Record 1883-1933*.

GOULDEN, R.J., *Kent Town Guides 1763-1900*, British Library, 1995.

GRAMMONT, Comte de, *Memoirs of the Court of Charles II* (by Anthony Hamilton, ed. Sir Walter Scott), London, George Bell & Sons, 1891.

GREENWOOD, G., *An Epitome of County History*, Vol.1, County of Kent, London, 1838.

GRIFFITHS, Alun, See HETHERINGTON.

HAMILTON, Anthony, See GRAMMONT.

HARRIS, John, *The History of Kent in Five Parts*, London, 1719.

HART, Walter Gray, ed., *The Register of Tonbridge School ... 1553 to 1820*, London, Rivingtons, 1935.

HASTED, Edward, *The History and Topographical Survey of the County of Kent*, Canterbury Vol.V, 1798.

HEMBRY, Phyllis, *The English Spa 1560-1815 – A Social History*, London, The Athlone Press, 1990.

HETHERINGTON, Keith, 'John Brown: Victorian Dairyman and Baker of Tunbridge Wells' in *Bygone Kent*, Vol.8, No.12, Dec 1987.

—See also BUTLER

—with GRIFITHS, Alun, *Old Pubs of Tunbridge Wells & District*, Meresborough Books, 1986.

—with TUCKER, Peter, *Yesterday's Bottles*, Kent and Sussex Bottle Club, 1981.

HODGSON, Norma, *Studies in English Theatre History*, 1952.

HOLLAND, J.D., 'The Reverend Thomas Bayes, F.R.S. (1702-61)' in the *Journal of the Royal Statistical Society*, 1962.

HOPE, Lady Elizabeth Reid, *Tunbridge Wells and its neighbourhood*, Sevenoaks Salmon, 1909.

JENNINGS, G.H., ed., *Thomas Turner – The Diary of a Georgian Shopkeeper*, Oxford University Press, 1979.

JOHNSTON, William, *Funeral Sermon for Mrs Sarah Jeffery*, London, 1771 (in Dr Williams's Library).

JOURNAL OF THE PRESBYTERIAN HISTORICAL SOCIETY OF ENGLAND, 'Early Presbyterianism at Tunbridge Wells', By a member of the editorial team, Vol.2 (2), May 1923.

KENT AND SUSSEX HOSPITAL, *Sixty years of service 1928-1988, the story of the Kent and Sussex Hospital, Tunbridge Wells Health Authority*, 1988.

KING, John, *Chronology of Events in and about Tonbridge*, 1739-1840.

KNIPE, Henry, R., *Tunbridge Wells and neighbourhood ... 1608 to 1915*, edited by H.R. Knipe, *Tunbridge Wells*, Pelton, 1916.

LINNELL, C.L.S, see WILSON.

LUDLAM, Frank, 'Preliminary Research relating to James Phippen', three typed sheets, 6 May 1983, 35 Walnut Tree Avenue, Wilmington, Kent DA1 1IJ.

LYDEKKER, J.W., 'A Soldier Family' in the *Royal Engineers Journal*, Sep 1933.

MACAULAY, Lord, *The History of England from the Accession of James the Second*, 2 vols, London, Longmans, Green, Reeder and Dyer, 1883.

MARSHALL, C.F.D., *A History of the Southern Railway*, revised R.W. Kidner, London, Ian Allan, 1963.

MARTIN, W. Stanley and ROW, B. Prescott, *Tunbridge Wells of Today*, not dated.

MAULDON, Jean, *Tunbridge Wells As It Was*, Hendon Publishing Co. Ltd., Lancashire, 1977.

MCMILLAN, Aubrey Newman, *The Stanhopes of Chevening*, 1967.

MELVILLE, Lewis, *Society at Royal Tunbridge Wells in the Eighteenth Century – and After*, Eveleigh Nash, London, 1912.

MORRIS, Christopher, ed., *The Journeys of Celia Fiennes*, London, The Cresset Press, 1947. See also FIENNES.

MUNBY, Lionel, *How much is that worth?* (The Local Historian at Work 4), British Association for Local History, 1989.

NEVE, Arthur Henry, *The Tonbridge of Yesterday*, Tonbridge Free Press, 1933 revised 1934.

ONELY, Rev. Richard, *A General Account of Tunbridge Wells and its Environs: Historical and Descriptive*, London, 1771.

OPENSHAW, Carl, *History of the Tunbridge Wells Cricket Club Bi-Centenary 1782-1982*. Published by the club.

PEACOCK, David, *Tunbridge Wells Sketchbook*. See CHAPMAN, Frank.

PEARCE, Luke,—(1) *Historical associations of the free churches of Tunbridge Wells: 1642-1904*, Tunbridge Wells, Pearce, 1904.

—(2) *Historical associations of Royal Tunbridge Wells from 1606 to 1909*, Tunbridge Wells, Pearce, 1912.

PELTON, Richard, *Pelton's illustrated guide to Tunbridge Wells*, R. Pelton, editions 1871 to 1905.

PEPYS, *Samuel, Diary and Correspondence of Samuel Pepys*, in 4 vols, George Bell and Sons, 1894.

PHILIPPORT, J, *The Royal Military Calendar*

PHIPPEN, James,—(1) Editor early Colbran Guides.

—(2) *An Account of the Planting of the Royal Victoria Grove at Tunbridge Wells on the 12th day of February 1835*, Brighton, Levy Emanuel Cohen, 1835.

PINTO, Edward H. and E.R., *Tunbridge and Scottish Souvenir Woodware*, 1970.

POPE, Rev. W.L., A Word about the 'Grove' addressed by the Rev. W.L. Pope, MA, Curator and Conservator, to Conservatives and Liberals Tunbridge Wells W. Nash and R. Pelton, Parade and St John Colbran, High Street, 1868.

ROW, B. Prescott, See MARTIN, W. Stanley.

ROWLANDS, M.L.J., ed., *Tunbridge Wells and Rusthall Commons – A History and Natural History*, Tunbridge Wells Museum and Art Gallery, 2001.

—with BEAVIS, I.C., *Royal Tunbridge Wells in Old Photographs*, Alan Sutton, 1991, and '*A Second Selection*', 1994.

ROYAL ENGINEERS JOURNAL See LYDEKKER.

SAVIDGE, Alan, —(1) *Royal Tunbridge Wells*, Midas Books, 1975.

(2) *History of the Church of King Charles the Martyr*, Tunbridge Wells, 1969. With postscript by the Rev. Simpson, 1989.

SIEVEKING, Paul, ed., *British Biographical Archives.*

SPARROW, Gerald, *The Great Abductors*, London, 1964.

SPIERS, R.E.A., *A History of Christ Church Tunbridge Wells 1835-1946.*

SPRANGE, Jasper, *Tunbridge Wells Guide*, 1780, 1786, 1797, 1801, 1808, 1811 and 1817, Tunbridge Wells, J. Sprange.

STRANGE, Charles Hilbert (1)—*Non-conformity in Tunbridge Wells*, Courier Printing Co., 1949.

—(2) *The Family of Strange*, Private publication, Nov 1920, 2nd edition, Aug 1994.

STRANGE, K.H., *The Climbing Boys,* Alison and Busby, London, 1982.

THOMSON, Rev. John Radford, ed., *Pelton Guides* from 1871.

TONBRIDGE SCHOOL HISTORICAL SKETCHES, Aretas Akers, 1968.
TUCKER, Peter, see HETHERINGTON.
TUNBRIDGE WELLS ADVERTISER, *Tunbridge Wells 1951: A Pictorial Record of Tunbridge Wells to mark the Festival of Britain*, 1951, *The Tunb. Wells Advertiser*, 1951.
TURNER, Thomas, see JENNINGS.
VICTORIA, Queen, *The Girlhood of Queen Victoria: A Selection from the Diaries 1832-1840*, ed., Viscount Esher, 2 vols, London, 1912.
WARING, Col. L.H., *The Story of the Church of King Charles the Martyr*, Hepworth, 1936.
WILSON, Thomas, *The Diaries of Thomas Wilson D.D., 1731-37 and 1750*, ed. C.L.S. Linnell, S.P.C.K., 1964.
WOODGATE, Rev. Gordon and Giles M.G., *A History of the Woodgates of Stonewall Park and of Summerhill in Kent and their Connections*, printed for private circulation, 1910.

Index

Page numbers in **bold** refer to illustrations